LINCOLN

AND THE POWER OF THE PRESS

DISCARDED

Lincoln at Cooper Union: The Speech That Made Abraham Lincoln President
Lincoln President-Elect: Abraham Lincoln and the Great Secession Winter, 1860–1861

THE WAR

for PUBLIC

OPINION

LINCOLN

AND THE POWER OF THE PRESS

———————— ◆ ————————

HAROLD HOLZER

SIMON & SCHUSTER
New York London Toronto Sydney New Delhi

Simon & Schuster
1230 Avenue of the Americas
New York, NY 10020

Interior design by Joy O'Meara
Jacket design by Tom McKeveny
Jacket art: Portrait of Lincoln © John Hay Library, Brown University via Abraham
    Lincoln Book Shop, Inc.

Manufactured in the United States of America

10   9   8   7   6   5   4   3   2   1

Library of Congress Cataloging-in-Publication Data

Holzer, Harold.
    Lincoln and the power of the press : the war for public opinion / Harold Holzer.
— First Simon & Schuster hardcover edition.
       pages   cm
    Includes index.
    1. Lincoln, Abraham, 1809–1865—Relations with journalists.   2. United
States—History—Civil War, 1861–1865—Journalists.   3. United States—
History—Civil War, 1861–1865—Press coverage.   4. Press and politics—
United States—History—19th century.   5. United States—Politics and
government—1861–1865.   I. Title.
    E457.2.H77   2014
    973.7'1—dc23   2014021392

ISBN 978-1-4391-9271-9
ISBN 978-1-4391-9274-0 (ebook)

For Edith

CONTENTS

A More Efficient Service

---

*"He who moulds public sentiment, goes deeper than he who enacts
statutes or pronounces decisions."*

—Abraham Lincoln, August 21, 1858

To many of his thriving neighbors, Abraham Lincoln's hometown of Springfield, Illinois, seemed by the 1850s nothing less than a "paradise in miniature."
Abundant with "stores, taverns, and shops," and illuminated by modern, gas-
fed lights, even the unpaved, mud-mired streets could not inhibit what Lincoln called "a great deal of flourishing about in carriages."[1]

Behind its serenely bustling facade, however, the frontier capital also ranked
as one of the most contentiously riven political hotbeds in the country—a
seething two-party battleground where election campaigns took on the mili-
tant urgency of outright war, and combatants deployed newspapers as their
most powerful weapons. Such was never more the case than in 1859—the
eve of the most potentially divisive presidential election in American history.

As a state capital boasting some nine thousand permanent residents—and
far greater than that number whenever politicians and lobbyists jammed into
town for annual legislative sessions—Springfield served as a year-round stage
for partisan speeches, rallies, parades, picnics, barbecues, illuminations, conventions, and outright street brawls over both issues and candidates. Even

with its population in perpetual flux owing to the almost daily arrival and departure of new residents, its voting-age men stood equally (some said hopelessly) divided between Democrats and Republicans. Whether the legislature was in or out of session, Springfield's citizens remained passionate about their politics year-round, ever ready to argue the issues of the day, both in person and in print.[2]

Fueling this combustible mix were Springfield's two major newspapers. Both covered neighborhood news with anodyne charm, but when it came to local, state, and national politics, both stoked the ferment with an overtly partisan style that combined advocacy with almost libelous criticism. One paper was dependably pro-Democratic, the other unfailingly pro-Republican, and each was steadfastly, often maliciously, opposed to the other. Rather than merely reprint what one editor termed the city's constant "flood of eloquence"[3] from politicians on both sides, these irreconcilable journals could be depended on to laud allies and eviscerate opponents. When they were not dishing out equal doses of praise and rage in their regular editions, they engaged their presses to print party pamphlets and political orations. If they were fortunate and well connected, they received rewards for their loyalty in the form of government printing jobs. The mutual interdependence that grew up between the press and politics made for a toxic brew. No politician was above it, no editor beyond it, and no reader immune to it.

Now, with the next national election only a year away, with the contest already being widely touted as the most crucial of the century, and with the issue of slavery roiling the country, local interest in national issues and personalities approached a fever pitch in Springfield, in part for a reason unique to this otherwise typically divided Western city. For by 1859, its residents could boast that their town had incubated two immensely gifted potential aspirants for the White House: United States senator Stephen A. Douglas, and former congressman Abraham Lincoln.

Douglas, the "Little Giant," led the pack among his fellow Democrats. And while "Long Abraham" was perhaps not yet widely known enough nationally to rank as a top-tier contender for the Republicans, he remained an intriguing dark-horse possibility for their ticket—perhaps, as some ardent supporters began whispering, for vice president. No one knows precisely when Lincoln began aiming still higher, but to bring the presidency within his sights he certainly knew where he needed first to burnish his political profile: in the Republican Party press, and not just among the usual loyalists who

read the newspapers in his hometown. Lincoln had been assiduously courting editors in nearby villages and cities for years. Describing his ambition as
"a little engine that knew no rest," his law partner and political confidant,
William H. Herndon, testified that Lincoln "never overlooked a newspaper
man who had it in his power to say a good or bad thing of him."[4] For now,
however, Lincoln still lacked both real political power and routine attention
in the press beyond Springfield. And he still thirsted for both.

That May, Lincoln made a remarkable move to recalibrate this frustrating
political equilibrium. The lifelong and voracious newspaper reader decided
to become a newspaper *owner* as well—by acquiring a weekly journal complete with its own printing press and a politically compatible editor ready to
churn out enthusiastic editorials lauding him. It did not seem to matter that
he would never be able to read the product himself. For the paper would be
printed in German, a language he had only briefly studied but never mas-
tered. Moreover, it would be composed in Gothic-style Fraktur typeface, an
elaborate black-letter script no more decipherable to him than Sanskrit.[5]

To comprehend what motivated this indelibly American politician to
purchase a foreign language newspaper he could never hope to comprehend
requires a quantum leap of historical imagination—back to an era when the
press and politics were profoundly interconnected, and newspapers themselves became more overtly partisan, more narrowly targeted, yet more deeply
influential than at any time before or since.

Abraham Lincoln's emergence as a newspaper publisher constituted but
one example of the pervasive and sometimes incestuous relationships that
grew up between politicians and journalists in the fierce battles for public
opinion and government power in the decades leading up to the Civil War—
and beyond. That such affiliations, however common at the time, were still
considered vaguely unsavory by some, seems evident in how assiduously Lincoln kept his own newspaper investment quiet. Except for his private banker,
his law partner, and but one fellow Illinois Republican politician, he seems to
have told no one about the purchase at the time, or, indeed, for the rest of his
life. For four score years, his involvement remained largely unknown even to
biographers.[6] Yet the truth is, the arrangement would likely have surprised,
much less scandalized, few of his contemporaries.

Lincoln was neither the first nor the last politician of his era to dabble
in the newspaper business—ethnic or otherwise, covertly or not. Countless
prominent officials of the mid-nineteenth century did so with confident aban-

don, making partisan journalism an integral cog in their political machines. This vanished tradition informs the neglected story explored in this book: how in the age of Lincoln the press and politics often functioned in tandem as a single, tightly organized entity in the furious competition to win power and to promote—or, alternatively, resist—political and social change. The financial and popular success that many newspapers enjoyed in pursuit of political goals enabled them to influence both leaders and events, and emboldened them to report on politics with a biased fury unimaginable in previous or subsequent generations. Not until the Civil War would precedent-shattering conflicts arise between government and the press, forcing these traditions into dramatic (and perhaps overdue) change.

To explore these complex relationships, and calculate their profound impact on history, this book proposes to reexamine Lincoln's political life through prominent period newspapers and their editors—focusing not just on how newspapers reported on and influenced his ascent, but how his own struggle for power, and that of most of his political contemporaries, unfolded within a concurrent competition for preeminence among newspapermen to influence politics and politicians. Newspapers of the day occasionally manufactured politicians, just as politicians often manufactured newspapers—but in the end they were of, by, and for the same environment. They became mutually dependent and totally inseparable—weapons in the same arsenal. In some cases, they synchronized their efforts so closely that it was impossible to determine where one organization ended its work and the other began it. Lincoln embraced and thrived in this milieu, yet the story has escaped full scrutiny since.

The emergence of a party press had begun in earnest the century before. In the mid-1790s, the explosive growth of political enthusiasm and the slow but sure development of improved printing technologies coincided to make newspapers more widely available as well as more openly partisan, and served to connect politicians to both editors and their subscribers. In time, readers came to align themselves with party newspapers as routinely as they began aligning themselves with political organizations: both loyalties helped define their identities. In this atmosphere, political parties commenced openly funding and promoting sympathetic newspapers, while newspapers began overtly shilling for party organizations. Newspapers not only brought people together, Alexis de Tocqueville observed, but remained "necessary to keep them together"—and, as it often turned out in a vast and increasingly sectionalized nation, to keep them apart.[7]

George Washington's second administration was the first to endure this seismic shift in the relationship between politics and publishing. An increasingly robust anti-Washington press surprised and dismayed the father of his country, who was accustomed to universal approbation, and its growth may have helped dissuade him from seeking a third term. The long, subsequent conflict between John Adams's Federalists and Thomas Jefferson's Democratic-Republicans further hardened newspaper loyalties, inspiring press attacks on political leaders that occasionally bordered on the scurrilous. Benjamin Franklin's grandson, Benjamin Bache, founded the *American Aurora* specifically to advance the Jeffersonian worldview and eviscerate Adams's affection for the British.[8] Adams infamously reacted by signing a sedition law that imposed fines and imprisonment on editors who dared to "print, utter or publish . . . scandalous and malicious writing or writings against the government of the United States." No less convinced that newspapers presented "only the caricatures of disaffected minds," Jefferson variously courted and suppressed the press, too. Late in life, he claimed that he read only the *Richmond Enquirer*, "and in that chiefly the advertisements," as he caustically remarked, "for they contain the only truths to be relied on in a newspaper."[9]

Yet there was no ignoring the press's growing ubiquity and influence. New York state alone boasted thirty-one hand-printed newspapers by the beginning of the new century.[10] Within ten years, the country at large could count 376 papers selling more than 22 million copies annually—even though fully half the American population was then sixteen years old or younger, a fifth were slaves barred from reading altogether, and most literate subscribers commonly shared their papers with as many as twenty friends and relatives each. As Noah Webster marveled: "In no other country on earth, not even in Great Britain, are Newspapers so generally circulated among the body of the people, as in America."[11]

To speed government news to this scattered population, leading politicians and journalists hatched the transformational idea in around 1800 of designating one particular Washington-based newspaper as an official political "organ." For generations thereafter, whenever one party or another took over the White House, an anointed journal assumed the privilege of breaking administration news in the capital, and introducing debate points that papers in outlying cities could readily adopt for their own readers.

By this time, only the absence of faster printing presses and more reliable transportation systems stood in the way of spreading political information more rapidly throughout the news-hungry young nation. Even editors privy to exclusive stories could not yet rush them to readers dwelling in isolated rural outposts. Communications remained so sluggish that press reports of the European peace treaty ending the War of 1812 failed to reach either General Andrew Jackson or his British foes at New Orleans in time to prevent them from fighting a fierce battle there. Jackson proceeded to lead his troops to a victory that won him glory—and perhaps the presidency—but in retrospect proved unnecessary. As an occupier, he promptly limited freedom of the press in the city, in one case arresting a citizen for publishing a critical letter to the editor (a case Lincoln would later cite in defending his own wartime restrictions on freedom of the press). Jackson firmly held that newspapers often villainously misled the public "through ignorance but more frequently from dishonest design." [12]

"Old Hickory" apparently learned from such experiences. For one thing, he named Amos Kendall, editor of the pro-Democratic *Argus of Western America*, as postmaster general. [13] Expanding on the tradition of rewarding loyal newspapers once he became president, he saw to the creation of an entirely new, official administration organ called the *United States Telegraph*. Its editor, a Missouri-born former Indian fighter named Duff Green, who remained professionally active into the Civil War era, composed his editorial "batteries" with "such vigor and clamor" that he quickly earned the nickname "Rough Green." [14] Green innovatively used his position as the president's official journalist to establish a large personal following and a wide network of pro-Jackson publications nationwide—essentially the first newspaper "chain," one in this case linked by shared political beliefs.

To broaden circulation of the *Telegraph*, Green initiated a more dubious tradition by seeing to it that Democratic congressmen assumed the cost of distributing his paper in their home districts, a practice that not surprisingly invited abuse. One representative was soon discovered to be using his free postal privileges to send more than sixteen hundred papers to constituents in Kentucky. [15] Unthinkable today, such crossover relationships became commonplace in the early nineteenth century, when newspapers were expected to remain faithful to their political patrons, and vice versa. In this linked political culture, there was no room for dissent. When the hot-tempered Jackson later lost patience with the increasingly independent Duff Green, the president scuttled their relationship and helped establish the *Washington Globe* as the party's replacement mouthpiece.[16] Jackson's enemies even whispered that he edited the new paper himself. Although untrue, Old Hickory's rumored personal involvement seemed fully credible at the time. For his part, Duff Green joined the opposition Whigs.

It is little wonder that one nineteenth-century author soon came to regard the term "party organ" as a "misnomer" for the nation's newspapers, "or rather, only a half name." As L. D. Ingersoll argued: "They should have been called 'hand-organs,' for the palpable reason that hand-organs can only grind out those particular tunes which the machines are manufactured to play."[17] But Jackson was hardly the sole organ grinder. Criticizing the *Telegraph* as "scurrilous and abusive," his Whig political enemy John Quincy Adams saw to the establishment of the Washington *Daily Intelligencer* in time to advance his run for president against Old Hickory in 1824. The *Intelligencer* soon boasted its own web of well-financed satellite papers across the country, and eventually counted leading politicians like Daniel Webster among its contributors.[18]

By the late 1830s, with printing processes now modernizing rapidly, many cities and towns across the country boasted successful newspapers of their own. The growing hunger for information—coupled with a rising literacy rate along with a soaring passion for politics—increasingly spawned not one but two rival publications in even the smallest villages. Soon, if a municipality bred one particular journal targeted to local Democrats, it invariably hosted another dedicated to (or run by) the Whig opposition. These papers alternatively endorsed or assailed the official White House line, and applied rigid partisan judgments to regional, along with national, issues and candidates. Within this increasingly connected partisan world, publishers began entering electoral politics themselves, just as politicians—like Jackson and, later, Lincoln—occasionally backed newspapers to expand their influence and reach.

By the time both Lincoln and his future rival, Douglas, came of age politically in the American West in the 1840s, newspaper publishers were routinely and overtly participating in grassroots politics and vice versa. Elected officials and aspiring candidates labored in tandem to plan campaign strategy, draft speeches, circulate propaganda, and attend conventions not only as correspondents but as official delegates. Working together, they drafted party resolutions and platforms, printed circulars and special "extra" editions during election campaigns, offered printing services and copyediting for orators, and openly advised candidates and officeholders. American newspapers, as historian Mark E. Neely acutely observed, became a virtual "branch of politics," and in parallel fashion, politicians became full partners in newspaper publishing.[19] In the words of early nineteenth-century New York congressman Jabez Delno Hammond, newspapers became "to political parties in this country what working tools are to the operative mechanic."[20]

Such alliances were often inspired by motives other than a shared philosophy of government. To maintain loyalty among friendly journalists, those holding political office routinely doled out such incentives as paid advertising, lucrative printing orders, and publicly financed subscriptions, not to mention well-paid nourishment from the patronage trough and choice seats at the tables of power. Publishers in turn provided the officials whom they favored with unlimited news space and unbridled political support. The inviolable line that today separates politics from the print press—at least as an ideal— had yet to be drawn. Rather, the worlds of politics and the press functioned in tandem, within a system of widely accepted mutual interdependence in which each fueled the success of the other, sought the destruction of the opposition, and often encouraged practitioners to occupy both professional spheres at once.

Functioning as more than merchants of information, journalists became part of well-lubricated political operations that disseminated opinion-laced government and campaign news and organized the party apparatus to pull voters to the polls on Election Day. In the process, the newspaper business, once a mere trade, blossomed into a major American industry, although, importantly, never a truly national one.[21] As one early historian of the press put it, the notion of a "[news]paper despotism"—the rule of a "[London] Times Jupiter in America"—remained inconceivable in a nation of disparate state and regional interests and locally managed political organizations.[22]

It comes as no surprise that on one of his visits to America, British writer Anthony Trollope found himself appalled by what he read in this country's newspapers. They were not only "ill-written, ill-printed, ill-arranged, and in fact . . . unreadable," he lamented, but also unreliable. "Justice and right judgment, are out of the question with them. A political party end is always in view, and political party warfare in America admits of any weapons."[23] A

German visitor named Ludwig Gall experienced a similar shock when he sought an understanding of the raging debate over Governor DeWitt Clinton's proposed Erie Canal. One evening, he overheard New Yorkers arguing about the project, and left the debate hoping that the next day's press would provide clarity. At a "municipal bourse" the following morning, Gall eagerly "paged the New York newspapers," but to no avail. "To my amazement," he confessed, "I found *for* Clinton in the *New-York Columbian* and *against* Clinton in the *National Advocate*," and in "the same language my dinner companions had used." Gall remained perplexed until he ran into a French acquaintance who cautioned him: "Believe nothing a newspaper . . . says that in any way might support a party or a person."[24]

These English, German, and French visitors were on to something important: American politicians and publishers had by then settled on a journalistic dynamic that stressed opinion over news, and party over public interest. The antique values of political independence and journalistic impartiality, if they ever really existed, vanished with the rise of political parties and the development of steam-driven Napier printing presses fast enough to produce some five thousand printed pages every hour. Nothing comparable to this rapid, rancid brand of journalism would ever be seen again—until the era of undisguised television advocacy as exemplified in the twenty-first century by Fox News and MSNBC (which despite their own blaring partisanship inspire no more than 50 percent turnouts in presidential elections and an ever-decreasing number of voters willing to align with the Democrats or Republicans—the opposite of the stimulating effect the press exerted on voters and voting a century and a half ago).

By the 1850s, the era that welcomed so-called Lightning Presses capable of four times the hourly production of the Napier machines, almost no independent voters were left in America, only Democrats and Whigs (most of whom later became Republicans), and nearly all of them avid readers of newspapers. Kept in a perpetual state of political arousal by journalism, and further stimulated by election cycles that drew voters to the polls several times each year, not just on the first Tuesdays of November, the overwhelming majority regarded politics with a fervor that approached religious awakening, evoking interest characteristic of modern sports or entertainment. With only a few notable exceptions, few unaligned newspapers prospered.

Nor were their readers' increasingly rigid political affiliations hard to decipher. There was no such thing as a true secret ballot during this period of our history. Until 1849, for example, voters in Lincoln's Illinois chose their candidates by voice votes fully audible to their neighbors. Later, adult white men—by and large the only citizens eligible to participate in elections (women remained disenfranchised and black voting rights, rare and impermanent)—made their Election Day choices by openly depositing preprinted, often gaudily colored, paper ballots, clearly labeled for one party or another, into transparent glass bowls. Another important mark of political belief was visibly conveyed by the newspaper one took by mail, or toted through the streets. If, say, a New York reader of the 1860s carried the *Tribune* around town, he was clearly a progressive Republican. If he bundled the *Daily News* in his arms, he was a conservative Democrat. In Chicago, a subscription to that city's *Tribune* similarly identified one as a Republican; taking the *Times* meant you favored the Democrats. Voters embraced their newspapers to tout their convictions in much the same way they wore campaign ferrotypes and medals on their coats—or today affix bumper stickers to their vehicles. As historian Elizabeth R. Varon has put it: "The function of antebellum newspapers, which were organs of political parties, was to make partisanship seem essential" to men's lives and identities.[25]

To the modern reader, the notion of Abraham Lincoln as publisher of a foreign language weekly that he was unable to read fluently has a slightly absurd ring to it, more in line with his legendary sense of humor than with his seldom acknowledged aspiration to control the press. In fact, much as he yearned to communicate with crucially important foreign-born voters, Lincoln was no linguist. In one hapless effort to boost his appeal to the most important voting bloc in his region, he actually enrolled briefly in a German course in Springfield. But according to a dentist who attended class with him, "Lincoln told so many stories that we laughed at them instead of studying the lessons."[26]

German instruction may have been a laughing matter to Lincoln, but German voting power, and the ability of the German language press to reach this crucial and expanding electorate, was deadly serious business. By 1860, Lincoln's new publishing partner, Theodore Canisius, estimated that sixty-seven daily and weekly German language newspapers already existed in the Northwest.[27] Their cultivation was but one aspect of the broader goal of befriending politically compatible publishers in outposts across the nation, wherever voters could be converted and coaxed to the polls by an editorial call to arms or, conversely, inspired to angry retribution by a scathing attack on the opposition. In this atmosphere, traditional salesmanship and manipulation—what today we call public relations or marketing—was but one weapon in a smart politician's arsenal.

As noted, the business deal that turned politician Lincoln into publisher Lincoln was far from unique, however assiduously he shielded it from public view. Some of his contemporaries boasted equally strong, and far more visible, connections to individual newspapers. Some, like former congressman Caleb Blood Smith of Indiana and Senator Simon Cameron of Pennsylvania, both of whom later became members of Lincoln's presidential cabinet, had served as influential editors years before they held public office. (Cameron actually won his U.S. Senate seat by defeating another newspaperman destined to work closely with President Lincoln: John Wein Forney.) Maryland leader Montgomery Blair, Lincoln's future postmaster general, could trace his political roots to a journalist father who operated the pro-Jackson *Washington Globe.* Wartime minister to Russia Cassius Marcellus Clay served early in his career as both a Kentucky state legislator and as publisher of a local antislavery newspaper called the *True American*—more than once enduring mob attacks for daring to advocate freedom in a slave state. And Lincoln's first vice president, Hannibal Hamlin, commenced his professional life as a compositor for a newspaper in Maine.[28] While Lincoln became known as "The Rail Splitter" for his early labors with an ax, Hamlin earned a title of his own that proudly reflected his youthful origins in publishing: "The Type Sticker."

Unlike Smith, Cameron, and Hamlin, all of whom quit journalism for politics, as well as Lincoln, who concealed his own late involvement in publishing, a number of publishers who craved elective or appointed office never entirely abandoned their newspaper careers merely because they held down government jobs. Instead, they played the roles of publisher and politician concurrently, to little surprise, much less outrage, from a public that largely perceived no conflict in such arrangements. The powerful New York Republican chairman Thurlow Weed, for one, controlled Empire State politics for years while—or as some said, *by*—running an influential Albany daily. Horace Greeley sought or served in elective office several times while publishing his *New York Tribune*—even though he later unctuously termed it "impossible for a journalist to reconcile independence in his profession with office-holding."[29] Greeley's journalistic competitor, Henry J. Raymond of the *New York Times*, functioned as both an elected and a party leader without ever relinquishing editorial duties at his newspaper. Then there was the tangled case of Fernando Wood, the Democratic mayor of New York at the outbreak of the Civil War, who responded to the secession crisis by proposing that his city quit the Union, too, the better to preserve its profitable trade with the South. Wood owned no newspaper of his own to ballyhoo his treacherous proposals—at least not technically. Formal title to the daily that most vigorously cheered his call for municipal independence, the anti-Lincoln *New York Daily News,** resided officially with Benjamin Wood—the mayor's brother, who later sought and won election as a congressman (as did Fernando as well, after losing his bid for another term in the mayoralty). However corrupt such combinations may seem by modern standards, the system seldom aroused questions, much less challenges, in the Lincoln era—except, of course, from the opposition press.

As these crossover relationships demonstrate, politicians of the nineteenth century did far more than court the press, and the press in turn did more than merely report on politics and politicians. The development of America's two-party system brought with it the birth of the *one*-party newspaper. Their intertwined, mutually enriching, potentially conflicted relationships dominated, indeed defined, both politics and the press for more than a century. That the system also encouraged crucial debate on freedom and slavery, nationalism and state rights, and ultimately spawned breathtaking reforms in American life, remains one of the marvels of nineteenth-century history. For in many ways, the absence of an independent, national American press—or even a monolithic regional press—also increased sectionalism and hastened disunion, war, and ultimately, a new nationalism predicated on a new definition of freedom.

By the time of the secession crisis, the institutions of politics and the press had become almost indistinguishable—having joined forces in open and impassioned collaboration. It took no less existential an event than the Civil War itself to unravel this incestuous partnership. Secession and rebellion upended tradition, but not before unleashing convulsive repercussions—including a widespread appetite for censorship and repression—that threatened the future of the free press itself. In one perhaps inevitable result of this longtime collusion, once the war of words exploded into a war of bullets, newspapers, once employed as weapons, instead became targets.

---

* Not to be confused with the modern-day tabloid newspaper of the same name.

• • •

What this book proposes to explore is how the leading characters of the most divisive era in American history, political and journalistic alike, used (and in turn were used by) the increasingly popular and influential press to define and occasionally distort political debate, to make and break political careers, and ultimately to revolutionize American society. It aims to show how the leading figures in the intractably linked worlds of politics and the press waged a vigorous, often vicious, competition to determine which political belief system would emerge with more popular support and thus shape the national future.

In a sense, the saga is too big to be told in a single volume, for at its most robust the industry involved thousands of editors and politicians nationwide, hundreds of thousands of readers, and millions of pages of newsprint. This is decidedly not another book about the so-called Bohemian Brigade—the band of battlefield correspondents who fanned out to cover the battles and leaders of the Civil War, a worthy subject amply covered by other authors.[30] Nor is it a book only about how newspapers treated Abraham Lincoln. Instead, this work seeks to explore the broader story of nineteenth-century political journalism through a much more focused lens: by tracking the chief political and journalistic personalities of the day to weave together two specific, ongoing, and historically vital competitions. The first percolated for more than a generation between a pair of rival politicians of the era, and the second raged for decades among three extraordinary journalists who covered them—and of course attempted variously to cheer, vilify, and influence them (and each other) as well.

The political focus will fall on the twenty-year-long political battle between fellow Illinoisans Abraham Lincoln and Stephen Douglas. The Whig-turned-Republican Lincoln and the lifelong Democrat Douglas emerged as the two most prominent leaders in the most contentious era in American history, opposed each other at crucial moments for major offices, filled the press with their oratory, and earned both praise and criticism in newspaper accounts published not only in their home state, but from New York all the way to the national capital.

A concentration on Lincoln and Douglas is justifiable not only historically—they ended up running against each other for the U.S. Senate in 1858 and for the presidency in 1860—but also statistically. A research survey conducted for this book in the comprehensive newspaper holdings of the American Antiquarian Society more than vindicates this emphasis. Year after year, beginning in the 1850s, Lincoln and Douglas ranked among the most widely covered leaders of their age. From the time they first attracted notice, through their battles for the Senate and presidency, and on through Douglas's sudden death in 1861, the names of these longtime opponents appeared in print more often than any of their political contemporaries: 6,500 stories for Lincoln, and an equally impressive six thousand for Douglas. And these statistics come from an archive that is representative, but in no way complete.[31]

While placing Lincoln and Douglas at the core of the *political* story from the 1830s through the 1860s, the book will construct the parallel *press* story around three of the most successful and influential newspaper publishers of the Lincoln-Douglas era: the aforementioned Horace Greeley and Henry Raymond, fellow Whigs who eventually turned Republican, but starkly different around the edges of their basic principles, personalities, loyalties, and methods of operation; and alongside them, their flamboyant and ruthless competitor James Gordon Bennett, owner of the sensationalistic, deeply conservative *New York Herald*, which nearly always tilted Democratic. Unlike the *Tribune* and the *Times*, indeed most of the leading politically aligned papers of the day, the *Herald* made a virtue of its supposed political independence—although Bennett never disguised his deep suspicion of the antislavery movement or his rancid hatred of black people, Jews, and Catholics—even as he revolutionized journalistic taste, news-gathering techniques, printing technologies, and advertising, in the process attracting the largest readership of any American newspaper. The unpredictable Bennett flirted with but ultimately opposed the Whigs and, later, the Republicans (including Lincoln) often enough to make political comparisons with Greeley and Raymond endlessly fascinating. One thing is certain: the three became and remained the most widely read and most famous journalists of their age, national celebrities in their own right who invented their newspapers and made them bold reflections of their own oversized personalities.[32]

To be sure, many of the colorful contemporaries of these three newspaper titans, and the politically motivated exploits of their publications, will also make appearances on these pages. In addition to acknowledging other leading editors in New York, the book will explore parallel journalistic rivalries in Springfield, Chicago, and, of course, Washington, in all of which Lincoln and Douglas competed for newspaper space as their own political aspirations expanded beyond Illinois. The thriving weekly press will be addressed along with the daily, as will the abolitionist and black press (and the overtly white supremacist papers as well). The editors of pro-secession and Confederate journals will appear, as will the creators of the new pictorial weeklies. As Lincoln's years as a "German publisher" demonstrate, the foreign press played an important part in this history as well. But the focus will remain fixed on the trio of extraordinary New Yorkers and their profound influence on the American press and politics.

The rationale is simple: perhaps New York was never representative of the entire country, either culturally or politically, but no editors anywhere amassed or deployed more truly national editorial power from the 1840s through the 1860s than Greeley, Raymond, and Bennett. None maintained their influence longer—cast it wider—or proved more essential to the crusades to preserve the Union and destroy slavery, either in support or in significant opposition, and sometimes a bit of both—than did these three flawed giants. From a purely dramatic point of view, no competitors spent so much time conducting warfare of the most personal kind, in the words of one contemporary, "constantly hammering away at each other," as if their own rivalry supplanted those of the leaders whom they covered.[33]

The three were also remarkable individuals. They loved their profession as passionately as they loathed each other, and each believed, in his own way, that he was all but ordained to chart the course for the future of civilization. As surely as did the principal political advocates of the day, the *Times, Tribune,* and *Herald* vigorously defined and debated public issues. As overtly as candidates, they sought and corralled votes. As aggressively as armies in the field, they fought battles. Although they differed enormously in personality— Bennett was an audacious showman, sly and given to the grandiose; Greeley a self-righteous reformer, passionate but easily dismayed, diverted, and bruised; and Raymond a civic-minded moderate, progressive but sometimes maddeningly practical—each believed without question that he best understood the pulse of the country, and offered the only worthwhile advice to keep it beating.

No one in their own time doubted the preeminence of the New York editors—not even their counterparts in other cities. One contemporary, editor John Russell Young, put it simply: "When the war came, journalism in the East was governed by Horace Greeley, James Gordon Bennett, and Henry J. Raymond."[34] And journalism in the East in turn seeded, influenced, and dominated journalism throughout the nation. When improved rail service began linking cities more closely, the *Philadelphia Inquirer* admitted that trains carried "New York over every railway, sets it down at every station, and extends it everywhere."[35] Describing New York's dailies as the nation's only "true newspapers," a onetime *Herald* correspondent agreed that its widely circulated papers "penetrate everywhere." But it was "very rare that a daily paper, published East, South, or West, is sold in New York. . . . A curious law is observed . . . all papers go from east to west, with the sun, and scarcely ever in the opposite direction."[36]

According to another period observer, the New York papers reached "the controlling minds of the country . . . in all reading-rooms, exchanges, bank parlors, insurance offices, counting-rooms, hotels, and wherever else the ruling men of the country congregate." But above all, the "grand reason why the New York papers" enjoyed unparalleled "national importance" came through "the scissors": for out-of-town journalists routinely clipped and reprinted what the New York editors originated. Bennett, Greeley, and Raymond effectively created "daily copies for all editors to follow."[37] Of at least equal importance, the *Tribune*, *Times*, and *Herald* also circulated nationally in their own extraordinarily popular weekly editions—the equivalent of *Time* and *Newsweek* magazines a century later.

For all these reasons, no three editors became more famous, feared, controversial, or assiduously courted than "The Old Philosopher" Greeley, "The Little Villain" Raymond, and "His Satanic Majesty" Bennett—derogatory sobriquets that haunted them for much of their careers. None better represented the confluence of press and politics. None aspired to more power. None more exhaustively covered the battles, leaders, and politics of the antebellum and Civil War periods, or sought more audaciously to direct the war's outcome and either guide or impede its leaders, Lincoln included. And none was surpassed as source material for the political and military events of that bloody struggle. Greeley, Raymond, and Bennett became national celebrities by inventing different styles of partisan journalism—templates that endure to this day—and despite their endless squabbling, they brought newspapers to the summit of their power over American life. Among them, for better or for worse, they invented modern journalism.

Along the way, the *Times*, *Tribune*, and *Herald* did nothing less than produce what is often, and justifiably, called the first draft of nineteenth-century American history. Certainly, historians still scour their pages for reliable contemporary information about slavery, secession, and the rebellion. This data their archives undoubtedly contain—though a reader examining each of the three for accounts of specific wartime events may still come away with entirely different impressions and opinions. As this book hopes to demonstrate, the products of nineteenth-century journalism—and their leading producers—cry out for a reappraisal that takes into account the filter through which their landmark work was originally accomplished: that of unbridled political partisanship, and a desire to influence, and in some cases, participate in government. Hopefully, this study will provide a fresh way to reexamine that first draft of history in light of the undisguised philosophies and raw politics that inspired so much of what not only informed, but also divided, those who read and lived through it.

"Public sentiment is everything," Abraham Lincoln declared during his 1858 senatorial debates with Stephen Douglas. "With public sentiment, nothing can fail; without it, nothing can succeed. Consequently," he added in a remarkably frank admission, "he who moulds public sentiment, goes deeper than he who enacts statutes or pronounces decisions."[38] It is time we took Lincoln at his word and examined his extraordinary focus on—and mastery of—political journalism as a means to earn and sustain voter support.

For the most part, history has always focused on "statutes" and "decisions." Yet in their own time and for several generations, Lincoln and his political contemporaries devoted a remarkable portion of their energies to mould public sentiment through the press: not just by appealing to journalists but in influencing the press directly and in some cases managing the press themselves. A fresh exploration of these alloyed historical currents, with the press not merely reporting the momentous events, but functioning as an integral part of the forces that shaped them, may hopefully shift, or at least balance, the historical emphasis. It will shed new light on a crucial but neglected aspect of Lincoln's leadership.

What follows is the story of an epic partnership involving politicians who rose and fell on the currents of American journalism and newspapermen who labored to abet, or impede, their political aspirations. It is a story of both unexpected alliances and brutal wars—uncivil wars.

Nineteenth-century newspapers often burdened themselves with long, formal names that reflected not only their cities of origin and publishing frequency, but also their political orientations. This last-named method of identification grew muddled when the Federalist Party passed into oblivion, and especially after the National Republicans morphed into either Democrats (who endured) or Whigs (who subsequently faded away, too). So it happened that some newspapers later affiliated with Lincoln-era Republicanism continued to call themselves "Democrat" as in the old days, while others who remained committed to the Democrats, slavery, and secession still bore the Jeffersonian-era name "Republican." Whenever such incongruities arise, they are noted for clarity in the text or in the source notes.

For this book, newspaper names are abbreviated and modernized to save space and stave off ennui. Thus, Springfield's pro-Republican *Illinois Daily State Journal* is identified only as the *Illinois State Journal*, while its rival paper, the Democratic *Daily Illinois State Register* (no one knows why the word "Daily" appeared in different places on the mastheads of each paper) is redacted to the *Illinois State Register*. Similarly, the *Chicago Daily Times* is called the *Chicago Times*, and the *Chicago Daily Press and Tribune*, the *Press and Tribune*—that is, until its owners dropped the word "Press" and it became the *Chicago Tribune*. Similarly, the *New-York Daily Times* is referred to here as the *New York Times*, the *New-York Daily Tribune* as the *New York Tribune*—the names they adopted years later, sans their endearing but obsolete hyphens (no disrespect intended to the durable New-York Historical Society).

It is hoped that these simplified titles will make the text less cumbersome and more coherent.

Abraham Lincoln holds a newspaper to the camera in an 1854 photograph by
Polycarpus von Schneidau taken in Chicago. Although he clutched a different newspaper
in the original photo, the *Chicago Press and Tribune* later added its own masthead.

PART ONE
DRUMBEAT OF THE NATION

CHAPTER ONE

The Types Are in Our Glory

————————————◆————————————

The two odd-looking young men who ventured off from their respective family homes, half a continent apart, in that same summer of 1831—each determined to find success on his own, and each fated to loom large in the other's struggles for fame and power—were as yet totally unknown to one another.

Nothing but coincidence dictated that they launch their adult lives at nearly the identical moment in time, with so few prospects, and in such remarkably coincident circumstances. Yet there were astonishing similarities to their journeys. For one thing, when both boys took leave of their parents, they had accumulated so little in the way of possessions that each was able to squeeze his meager belongings into a single kerchief borne over his shoulder on a stick. Both began their long voyages on foot.

On the surface, they looked as different as any two pioneers on the continent. To be sure, both were unconventional in appearance. One, however, was almost absurdly tall, deeply bronzed, lean but well muscled, with a face creased and "gnarled" well beyond his years; the other, slight in stature, was moon-faced, spectrally pallid, and "angelically cherubic," far more youthful in appearance than in age.[1] Intellectually and emotionally they were unalike as well, one laconic and shy, the other ebullient and confident. Both of them gifted and curious, the taller one was blessed with a rare power of concentration, the smaller barely able to focus his attention on one subject before lurching to embrace another. Had any of their later admirers somehow managed to encounter both of these wanderers that year they would surely have predicted that the two opposites could never become friends. And in a sense, such observers would have been correct. Yet eventually, Abraham Lincoln and Horace Greeley came not only to know each other well, but to figure crucially in each other's future.

More than fifteen years would pass before Lincoln and Greeley finally met in the whirlwind of mid-century politics. Not for a quarter of a century would they come to affect each other's lives as well as the destiny of their country—with an enormity that neither could have imagined at the time they began their adult journeys in 1831. These two men would never come fully to know or understand the other. Yet one would become the century's greatest subject, and the other its most influential observer.

In a sense, these two contrasting strangers on the move that summer had much more in common than anyone who met them later might have realized. Even in 1831, when no one but friends and relatives knew that these boys existed, much less mattered, the similarities between them would have been marked as extraordinary. Each had been dwelling with his family in a crowded, primitive log cabin. Each had worked the land, but had stolen precious time whenever possible to feed an insatiable hunger for reading. And each was poor—nearly destitute. As one of their contemporaries observed: "Both sprang from obscurity; both were cradled in poverty; both worked their way up by sheer brain work; both were excessively simple, democratic, and homespun in their manners and dress; both were awkward in gait; both abounded in quaint dry humour." [2]

Both Lincoln and Greeley came of age on hardscrabble farms, yearning for education but lacking access to formal schooling. Lincoln long regretted learning only "by littles" from itinerant instructors who knew no more than "'*readin, writin, and cipherin*' to the Rule of Three." Greeley, as a friend recalled, "seldom had a teacher that could teach him anything"—perhaps as much a testament to the future editor's sometimes galling self-assurance as to the scarcity of competent instructors in the hinterlands. [3]

Each boy had nearly died as a result of a childhood accident: Lincoln kicked in the head by a horse and "apparantly [*sic*] killed for a time," as he quaintly put it; Greeley "half drowned" after bravely plunging into a river in an attempt to rescue his brother from drowning.[4] Most distinctly of all, both boys seemed from the outset oddly different from their friends—more serious, more studious, more distracted—and both painfully awkward with the opposite sex. Of young Lincoln, his stepmother frankly admitted: "He was not very fond of girls." A New Hampshire acquaintance similarly recalled that where young Greeley was concerned, "For girls, *as* girls, he never manifested any preference."[5] (As it happened, Greeley married Mary Cheney when he was twenty-five; not until he was thirty-three did Lincoln wed *his* Mary.)

Not that either youth shrank from the grueling physical work farm boys of the day were expected to perform. Both grew accustomed to physical labor, specializing in felling trees and cutting logs, though neither grew to love such work, and only Lincoln emerged from the experience with a physique worthy of his labors. Unknown to each other they may have been, but the two boys shared another attribute destined to define their lives: their unquenchable thirst for the printed word. From an early age, each had turned to reading whenever and wherever afforded the luxuries of leisure and light. And each sought intellectual nourishment in both the permanent and ephemeral publications that so many among even the poorest American families strove to keep in their homes: first and foremost the Bible, of course—but also newspapers.

With his horizons vastly broadened by what he discovered in his omnivorous reading, Lincoln ultimately decided to enter political life. Greeley determined early that his destiny was to report it. Each would come to believe his respective profession offered not only the best means to improve his own condition, but the best way to wield the power to shape national destiny. From the beginning of their slow rise to national fame, they likely understood that the worlds of politicians and journalists were inextricably bound together.

Lincoln, at twenty-two the older, and certainly the more robust of the two, had for years devoured as much reading material as he could lay his hands on, especially after the teenager's family migrated from Kentucky to Indiana, where periodicals were readily available. "I think newspapers were had in Indiana as early as 1824," his stepmother later recalled. "Abe was a constant reader of them—I am sure of this for the years of 1827-28-29-30. The name of the Louisville Journal seems to sound like one."[6] The boy often read them "very late at night" after he completed his chores, testified a cousin, who remembered Abe habitually turning a chair upside down near the hearth, then placing a pillow on the underside of the seat to support his head while he unfolded his newspaper. He would "lie there for hours," she remembered, "and read" these papers, sometimes out loud.[7] Young Lincoln was mad for them. The more political their content the better. As his future law partner once asserted: "Mr. Lincoln's education was almost entirely a newspaper one."[8] And he pursued it with little encouragement from a stern father who preferred that his son stick exclusively to his responsibilities on the farm.

Inspiration came from both his empathetic stepmother and from appreciative strangers. At one point, the curious teenager began borrowing a pro-temperance paper to which a neighbor named William Wood subscribed. Lincoln, at most nineteen years old, soon composed an essay of his own on the evils of drink, and proudly shared it with Wood, who found to his astonishment that "the piece excelled for sound sense anything that my paper contained." Impressed, Wood showed the article to a local preacher, who in turn sent it on to a paper in Ohio, which published it. Once it was in print, Wood read the article "with pleasure over and over again."

When Lincoln followed this small triumph by composing yet another essay, this time on political issues, Wood handed it over to a local attorney, who saw this latest treatise into print as well. In it, the young man argued that education "should be fostered all over the Country" in order to nourish "the best form of Government in the world." As Wood saw it, Lincoln's eagerness to see such views broadly cast at such a young age showed unusual maturity. Although still not twenty and virtually untaught, Abe had already published two newspaper articles, exploring themes to which he would return many times in years to come: sobriety, education, and American exceptionalism. But from the start, writing for Lincoln was a means, not an end. He wrote about policy issues not only to influence others, but to gain influence for its own sake—for himself. Even when he saw his first newspaper printing press at Vincennes, Indiana, he left no comment about the mechanics of making news.[9]

After his solitary 1831 journey from his parents' cabin, Lincoln moved to a tiny Illinois mill town called New Salem, where his new neighbors noticed at once that his nose was always pointed toward a printed page. "History and poetry & the newspapers constituted the most of his reading," testified one. A local shoemaker similarly observed that Lincoln read "all kinds of newspapers," sitting up, lying down, or walking in the streets. Yet a third concurred. "More than he did books," he said of Lincoln, "he read papers."[10] Always eager to perform, if he found something particularly amusing or instructive on their pages, he would read the item aloud to anyone within earshot. Though the distinctive new arrival "rapidly made acquaintances and friends," as he proudly put it, he yet considered himself without real direction in life, trying, then abandoning, a succession of jobs: as a blacksmith, surveyor, and storekeeper, in the last of which he ended up owing creditors so much money that he began referring to his crushing obligations as the "national debt." Although he never considered giving up and returning to his parents' fold, young Lincoln remained, he lamented, "a piece of floating driftwood." [11]

At least, part-time work as the New Salem village postmaster enabled him to read his neighbors' newspapers as soon as they arrived, before recipients could claim their subscriptions for themselves. His neighbor, Dr. John Allen, joked that he "Never saw a man better pleased" with a job. As postmaster, Lincoln had "access to all the News papers—never yet being able to get the half that he wanted before." [12] Without complaint, perhaps even sensing with pride that their well-liked, yarn-spinning postmaster was destined for greater things, residents of New Salem patiently grew accustomed to receiving their papers late, badly wrinkled, and carelessly refolded. [13]

Horace Greeley, the other young man who began his initial adult journey in 1831 but at age twenty, a year shy of his legal majority, not only commenced his career at a younger age, but with a keener sense of his destiny.

What he called his "unromantic life" began in a log home near Amherst, New Hampshire, like Lincoln on a cold February day. He entered the world struggling for breath so laboriously that few in his family expected him to live more than a day. [14] The infant surprised his parents by surviving, but grew up so pale of complexion that acquaintances nicknamed the "feeble, sickly child" the "Ghost." Treated almost like "a guest or a pet" in his own home, the boy nonetheless performed his share of work. From age six to fifteen, he did his best to cut down small trees, drive oxen, and help till the "rocky" New England ground. He was certainly less proficient at such work than Lincoln. But like Lincoln, whenever he could steal time, young Greeley read voraciously—read, some later claimed, even before he could speak. He could "read very thoroughly at 4 years of age," he boasted, and "quite passably with the book upside down." Spelling, he remembered, "was my favorite, as is natural for a child of tenacious memory and no judgment." From the beginning, it was the Holy Book, and eventually "the newspaper he was given to play with"— an Amherst weekly to which his father subscribed. The Bible and newspapers: for both Lincoln and Greeley they represented equally compelling gospel.[15]

From an early age, Horace knew what he wanted to do with his life. "Having loved and devoured newspapers—indeed, every form of periodical—from childhood," he remembered, "I early resolved to be a printer if I could."[16] Responding, appropriately enough, to a newspaper advertisement, Greeley's father apprenticed the young man in 1826 to the publisher of a modest journal called *The Northern Spectator* in East Poultney, Vermont, twelve miles from their home. Horace was only fifteen.

For the next five years he worked industriously at the struggling paper, learning every aspect of the trade, from typesetting to writing. In return, he received six months' free board and a forty-dollar annual stipend for clothing. Before long, he recalled, "my hands were blistered and my back lamed by working off the very considerable edition of the paper on an old-fashioned two-pull, wooden Ramage press—a task beyond my boyish strength."[17] If it seemed to young Horace like a form of slavery, he never specifically said so. He not only gained no physical strength from his labors; he lost his good eyesight. At a young age, the owlish-looking Greeley already took to wearing wire-rimmed spectacles to correct his vision. Like Lincoln, he remembered making "many valued friends" in his new surroundings. Yet when *The Northern Spectator* folded in 1830, Greeley made no effort to linger in Vermont. Instead, with nowhere else to go, he retreated to his family at its new homestead in the wilds of northwestern Pennsylvania.[18]

He was reduced to "chopping wood" again, and by his own admission neither "efficiently nor satisfactorily." By spring, Greeley concluded that "the life of a pioneer was one to which I was poorly adapted." Determining to make "one more effort to resume my chosen calling," he scoured the region for a newspaper position, finally securing one at the nearby *Erie Gazette* for the salary of fifteen dollars a month.[19]

Young Greeley held this job only until summer, when he turned down an opportunity to put his money where his ambition lay and become a junior partner at the struggling *Gazette*. It seemed to him the wrong enterprise at the wrong time. To his professed horror, its proprietor, Joseph M. Sterrett, seemed to love politics more than journalism. The publisher actually aspired to a seat in the Pennsylvania State Senate, and Greeley admitted that at the time he heartily disapproved of such inclinations. The young man even seemed shocked that local readers suffered from a similar "intense addiction to partisan strife." As he remembered of his own naïveté: "I was fairly appalled by the assiduity and vehemence wherewith political controversy was prosecuted by nearly every man and boy I met in Erie." For now, the kind of political activism in which Greeley would come enthusiastically to specialize seemed repellent, antithetical to journalism itself—though he later admitted that he, too, became "an ardent politician when not yet half old enough to vote."[20] He instead applied for an editor's job at distant Wilkes-Barre, but lacking sufficient experience was rejected.

With only ten dollars in his pocket, few realistic prospects in his adopted state, and, as he took note, with a surfeit of equally ambitious printers beginning to head west in search of opportunity, Greeley made a bold, if unexpected choice. In an ironic reversal on the advice for which he would later become famous, the young man decided to go east. Unlike Lincoln, who elected to begin his career in a tiny village, Greeley headed to the fastest-growing city in the nation.

Horace Greeley reached New York City on August 17, 1831, still not quite twenty-one years old, dressed in "scanty and seedy clothes," and with but "ten dollars in my pocket and not an acquaintance within two hundred miles"—another piece of "floating driftwood," but at least in a bigger pond, and more certain than ever about his professional goals.

Here, Greeley would have encountered a breathtaking skyline crowned by church steeples almost as far as the human eye could see, all surrounded by a harbor choked with ships, large and small, lurching upriver and down, and from shore to shore, in all directions at once. Here were horse-drawn carriages and overstuffed sidewalk bins vying with pedestrians for precious space along newly paved streets and sidewalks; and brick and wooden structures sitting cheek to cheek along streets that faded at their eastern and western extremes toward the mysterious uncertainties of the docks. Greeley arrived in town in the middle of the hottest month of the summer, a time when, as another visitor of the day complained, even when dressed "in the thinnest clothing, the perspiration streams from every pore, trickles from every hair of the head, and falls in a shower to the floor." Residents had no choice but to drink profusions of the "fresh" water that, according to warning signs adorning every public pump, might well cause death from cholera. To Greeley, it was a paradise.[21]

By his own description "slender, pale, and plain," he remained so rustic-looking he feared no one would take him seriously. In fact, the editor of the prestigious *New York Journal of Commerce* refused him a place, telling him that he resembled "a runaway apprentice from some country office." Only later would Greeley learn proudly to emphasize his singular appearance—until his country hats, long coats, and, later, chin whiskers, became not impediments but instantly recognizable trademarks.[22]

The very morning after his arrival, August 18, the aspiring journalist landed his first New York job at a Chatham Street printing establishment run by one John T. West. The youngster's unenviable assignment—which he quickly concluded he had secured because no one else in town would take it—had little to do with newspaper work. It required him painstakingly to set a tiny Bible in such minuscule type he could barely see it. Worse, when Greeley finished the arduous project, he found himself unemployed again: West had no further work for him. Horace moved on to a monthly publication, which reneged on his meager salary, and then slunk back to West's to typeset a new edition of the Book of Genesis. The only mark of upward mobility he could afford was a "second-hand suit of clothes" purchased from a "Hebrew" who "shaved me villainously for them."[23]

Greeley was beginning to feel as if he might spend the rest of his life bent over type racks fourteen hours a day. He considered looking for work in Washington, but "could not pay my way" to the capital. On New Year's Day 1832, Greeley at last secured a promising new post as a compositor at the *Spirit of the Times*, a thrice-weekly sporting journal that two of the young printers from West's had recently launched on nearby Wall Street. Initially "their paper did not pay," Greeley lamented, adding: "I know that it was difficult to make it pay *me*."[24] But Greeley might have been willing to pay his new employers for the priceless experience he began acquiring. Eventually the salary came trickling in. And exactly a year later, on January 1, 1833, Greeley felt he had enough experience and, more miraculously, enough funds, to launch a newspaper of his own. Readers evidently disagreed. Greeley's new *Morning Post* survived a total of twenty-one days. Its editor, Greeley admitted of himself, "had neither money nor brains."[25]

In New Salem, which boasted no papers of its own, Abraham Lincoln meanwhile openly embraced the interlocking worlds of partisan politics and journalism that Greeley still eschewed. Out-of-town newspapers provided for him both a source of political news from afar and a means of expanding the reach of his political voice at home. In the same year Greeley went to work at the *Spirit of the Times*, 1832, Lincoln not only began reading law, but though not yet an attorney, parlayed his growing neighborhood popularity into his first run for public office. He launched his bid for a seat in the State Assembly by doing precisely what his experience as a teenage freelancer in Indiana had taught him: publishing his views in the nearest paper. In this case, it was the newly established *Sangamo Journal.* He would remain its close and loyal friend, and sometimes more, for the better part of the next three decades.

Just the previous November, a husky, determined, Connecticut-born, thirty-five-year-old publisher named Simeon Francis had established the *Journal* with his brother Josiah in the nearby town of Springfield. Situated about twenty-two miles southeast of New Salem, Springfield was still a backwater—except perhaps in comparison to the primitive outpost Lincoln still called home. Not yet the capital of Illinois, it boasted a few multistory wooden buildings and a good deal of boglike mud occupied principally by roaming pigs. As for Francis, he had an unpromising track record in the journalism business: he had already launched and lost two previous papers, one in New London, the other in Buffalo, the latter put out of business when sacked by an anti-Masonic mob—a violent fate to which "radical" presses of the day were occasionally subjected. Turning dejectedly for a time to farming, Francis yearned to resume his press career. After a brief stint in St. Louis, where the palpable existence of slavery made him uneasy, Francis decided to gamble on establishing his new paper in Illinois.

No one is quite certain why. With no more than eight hundred inhabitants, most of them recent arrivals who yet lacked a sense of community and had little cash money to spare for subscriptions, Springfield seemed an inhospitable place for the news business. The town had already seen three earlier papers come to life—and promptly die for lack of readers. Nor would its many conservative, Southern-born residents look kindly on the newly arrived Yankee publisher or his politics, which emphasized free labor and government-funded improvements to roads and canals. But Springfield was also a town increasingly populated by equally ambitious newcomers similarly attracted to its possibilities, and determined to grow along with it. Illinois, Simeon Francis earnestly believed, was "the country for poor men—rich in soil, healthy, and pleasant." [26]

Urged on enthusiastically by Josiah, who rosily insisted that the town was the perfect spot for their new enterprise, the Francis brothers launched their weekly paper with just fifteen subscribers in hand at an advance price of $2.50 a year. By 1832, Josiah would boast, "we are now publishing upwards of 600."[27] But the economics of the business remained a challenge. Advertising was scarce. That first year, the weekly took in just $4.50 for six insertions of a paid notice seeking the return of "a prisoner who broke jail." Four weeks' worth of legal notices for a writ of attachment brought in only $3.75. Seven repetitions of an advertisement for a local school yielded but $2.75.[28]

Nor was editorial copy easy to come by. For its earliest editions, with scant local news to report, the Francis brothers filled their four-page sheet with reprints from established journals like the *Albany Argus* and the *Liverpool Mercury*. This was standard procedure at the time for isolated rural papers. Because copyright laws of the day were either lax or unenforceable, small, remote journals were emboldened to purloin articles from the big-city papers that arrived by mail. The earliest editions of the *Journal* featured maudlin fictional stories lifted from out-of-town literary journals, standard how-to pieces (like a primer on breastfeeding captured from Washington's *National Intelligencer*), and polemics that included an article on women's domestic obligations (emphasizing obedience to their breadwinning husbands) "contributed" by (more likely stolen without permission from) no less than Catherine Beecher. Most of the *Journal*'s advertisements came from out-of-town papers, too, and were likely unpaid. Its earliest local news items more often than not carried no addresses, for the simple reason that few of Springfield's streets had yet been given names.[29]

Initially the paper made a show of appearing multi-partisan, vowing to print any article that was "decorously written." To refuse to carry contrary viewpoints, it trumpeted in February 1832, would abridge "the freedom of the press—'the palladium of our liberties.'"[30] Even in these formative days, however, readers would have little doubt about the *Journal*'s philosophy—and as the custom of the day already dictated, newspapers were usually founded around specific political principles and party organizations, and with few exceptions remained loyal to both. The earliest issues of the *Journal* championed improvements to roads and canals, endorsed high protective tariffs for foreign imports, and assailed President Andrew Jackson as a tyrant—standard doctrine for any anti-Democratic publication worth its subscription price.

The *Journal*'s undisguised antagonism toward a powerful president whom many foes regarded as a despot was reflected in its gasconading motto: "Not the glory of Caesar but the Welfare of Rome!" The *Journal*'s founding prospectus reiterated this crusading inclination in more plainspoken language: "In a word, whatever will tend to advance the prosperity of this highly favored state, develop its resources and exhibit its advantages to the immigrating inhabitants of all other States, will receive deserved attention." [31] Developing "resources" was a code phrase for "internal improvements," crucial to Henry Clay's proposed "American System," which emphasized community building projects. The *Sangamo Journal* would quickly evolve into a party organ, and as such a natural home for Abraham Lincoln's political views and potential voters. By the time Lincoln contributed his campaign appeal to the paper a few weeks later, the *Journal* had established a toehold among the community's anti-Jacksonians. As a whole, Illinois remained largely Democratic, and the opposition still fragmented, but like the *Sangamo Journal*, Lincoln "sided with [Daniel] Webster against [John C.] Calhoun, and with [Henry] Clay against anybody." [32] In the *Journal*, Lincoln found not only sympathetic editorial coverage, but a lifetime ally.

In his open letter to "the People of Sangamo County," published March 15, 1832, the young candidate not surprisingly echoed the paper's founding principles, coming out strongly for "the opening of good roads . . . the clearing of navigable streams," and "the construction of a rail road." The proposals were specific, the style compact and unornamented, if stiff and rather formal, and the tone modest. Lincoln pledged that while "it is better to be only sometimes right, than at all times wrong, so soon as I discover my opinions to be erroneous, I shall be ready to renounce them." [33]

The letter is famous now only because it was a future president's maiden political message, but here in print was nothing less than the birth of an original political voice. "I am young and unknown to many of you," Lincoln concluded his editorial with self-effacing charm. "I was born and have ever remained in the most humble walks of life." He had no ambition "so great as being truly esteemed of my fellow men." If victorious, he promised to be "unremitting in my labors. . . . But if the good people in their wisdom shall see fit to keep me in

With regard to existing laws, some alterations are thought to be necessary. Many respectable men have suggested that our estray laws—the law respecting the issuing of executions, the road law, and some others, are deficient in their present form, and require alterations. But considering the great probability that the framers of those laws were wiser than myself, I should prefer meddling with them, unless they were first attacked by others, in which case I should feel it both a privilege and a duty to take that stand, which in my view, might tend most to the advancement of justice.

But, Fellow-Citizens, I shall conclude.— Considering the great degree of modesty which should always attend youth, it is probable I have already been more presuming than becomes me. However, upon the subjects of which I have treated, I have spoken as I thought. I may be wrong in regard to any or all of them ; but holding it a sound maxim, that it is better to be only sometimes right, than at all times wrong, so soon as I discover my opinions to be erroneous, I shall be ready to renounce them.

Every man is said to have his peculiar ambition. Whether it be true or not, I can say for one that I have no other so great as that of being truly esteemed of my fellow men, by rendering myself worthy of their esteem. How far I shall succeed in gratifying this ambition, is yet to be developed. I am young and unknown to many of you. I was born and have ever remained in the most humble walks of life. I have no wealthy or popular relations to recommend me. My case is thrown exclusively upon the independent voters of this county, and if elected they will have conferred a favor upon me, for which I shall be unremitting in my labors to compensate. But if the good people in their wisdom shall see fit to keep me in the background, I have been too familiar with disappointments to be very much chagrined.

Your friend and fellow-citizen,
A. LINCOLN.
New Salem, March 9, 1832.

Sangamo Journal, March 1832: Lincoln's first signed newspaper article, proposing himself for the Illinois state legislature.

the background," he concluded fatalistically, "I have been too familiar with disappointments to be very much chagrined."[34] Chagrined Lincoln may well have been when Francis buried his manifesto on page two of the *Sangamo Journal*—along with other routine local news. The editor's quest for readership and revenue trumped even party fealty. Advertising, not news, appeared on the cover.

Then Lincoln, too, found a higher calling than his campaign for the legislature. On April 21, just a few weeks after publishing his message, he temporarily abandoned his political battles to enlist in an altogether different kind of war. An Indian chief named Black Hawk had violated a recent treaty and reentered the state with a small army of warriors. Along with many of his New Salem friends, Lincoln joined up for military service after the governor called for volunteers to repel the invasion. Never in real danger, Lincoln thoroughly enjoyed his military experience, relished his election as company captain, and happily reenlisted twice, remaining on duty, and off the political hustings, for nearly two months.

Unable to work the district for votes while he remained in the service, Lincoln's unremarkable military record—characterized at its most hazardous, he later admitted, by his "struggles with the musquetoes [*sic*]"—proved far too lackluster to impress his constituents at home.[35] Worse, when the *Journal* printed the names of the local men who had served in the recent war, Francis inadvertently left Lincoln off the list. Lincoln protested and a correction appeared, but the damage had been done.[36] Shortly after his demobilization, and with but a few days left to make up for lost time, Lincoln made a last-minute quest for support. It proved too little, too late. He lost the August 6 election for the State Assembly. Though New Salem residents, who knew him best, gave him a heartening 277 of their three hundred votes, he ran badly in the district-wide race, finishing eighth in a field of thirteen. He had reprinted his *Sangamo Journal* letter as a handbill, but it did scant good.[37] Lincoln was still learning how newspapers and politicians might best collaborate to achieve common goals.

One way to prod public opinion, he discovered, was to write newspaper copy himself, and electoral defeat notwithstanding, Lincoln now became a regular, if anonymous, contributor of partisan, occasionally intemperate articles to the *Sangamo Journal.* As editor Francis published all such screeds unsigned, or over a pseudonym, there is no way to know for certain how many of these uncredited pieces Lincoln submitted over the years.[38] But as New

Salem post office clerk James Matheny remembered, "Lincoln used to write Editorials as far back as 1834 or 5 for Francis." Matheny claimed he personally "took hundreds of such Editorials from Lincoln to the Journal office." [39]

On occasion, eager to see his views in print, "Honest Abe" may even have abused his privileges during his days as a postal employee in order to speed his editorials through the mail at no cost. As village postmaster, Lincoln enjoyed the franking privilege—merely signing his name atop a folded letter that formed a self-envelope was enough to secure its free delivery—but technically he was entitled to use it only for official material, a category into which his essays decidedly did not fit. Otherwise *recipients* of mail, not *senders*, paid for postage. With the price set by law at a forbidding six cents per sheet, the impoverished Lincoln may have concluded that if his editorial contributions arrived postage due, the newspaper might decline them unopened.

By whatever means they were dispatched, these hortatory and sometimes defamatory articles by authors identified only as "A Looker-On," "Sampson's Ghost," and "Kentucky Volunteer" were likely all the work of Abraham Lincoln, partisan journalist. The unattributed columns inspired one Democratic editor to fume that he had nothing but contempt for "anonymous scribblers . . . who, without the courage to appear unmasked, vindictively and falsely assail the characters and actions of public men." [40] Later, the local Democratic paper was more specific, alleging: "The writers of the Journal have had a *late acquisition*—a chap rather famous not only for throwing filth, but for *swallowing it afterwards*," leaving no doubt that its charge referred specifically to the "jester and mountebank" Lincoln. [41] One of Lincoln's ripostes, as neighbor Caleb Carman remembered, was so truculent that even Simeon Francis would not print it. Determined to see it published somewhere, the rejected editorial writer instead sent it to the nearby *Beardstown Chronicle*. [42] Broadening his reach was also a sign of Lincoln's growth. He now regularly read not only the Springfield paper but also the *Louisville Journal* and *Missouri Democrat*. By 1834, however, Lincoln assumed a new title reflecting his ongoing, primary connection to the newspaper that remained crucial to his future political success: he became New Salem's official local agent for the *Sangamo Journal*. [43]

Half a continent away, the eleven daily newspapers serving New York City devoted only cursory coverage to the Black Hawk War in distant Illinois, and of course none at all to the obscure races there for its state legislature. Far more urgent and compelling stories vied for their attention and ink. An epidemic of plague in 1831 took the lives of more than 3,500 New Yorkers. The metropolis continued its struggle to recover from a sustained national financial downturn. Most intoxicating of all, the 1832 presidential election was fast approaching, and when Jackson won nomination in May for a second term, with Clay his opponent running as a National Republican, the anti-Democratic papers unleashed renewed warnings of dictatorship. The national political contest may not have engaged specialty publications like Greeley's *Spirit of the Times*, but here in the nation's commercial hub, it elicited regular coverage on the pages of the leading dailies.

As of 1832, the city's major newspapers were oversized six-cent broadsheets. By tradition, copies were hawked on the streets by newspaper carriers employed directly by the publishers, or sold to customers who came calling at the newspapers' home offices in lower Manhattan's overcrowded financial district. The remainder went off to subscribers by mail (though many recipients did not pay). The most widely read publications included James Watson Webb's pro-Whig *Courier* and David Hale and Gerard Hallock's elite and pro-Democratic *Journal of Commerce*, along with papers bearing such forbidding names as the *Mercantile Advertiser*, the *Journal and Advertiser*, the *Mechanics' Advertiser*, and the *Gazette and General Advertiser*. As their titles accurately suggested, these publications were designed primarily for men who engaged in trade and supposedly thought of little else. Yet ironically the narrow editorial focus of these so-called gentlemen's papers served to limit the trade in newspapers themselves.[44] In a city whose population was approaching 250,000, only 45,000 were said to read one daily paper or another, and most frustrated publishers believed the rapidly growing market remained largely untapped. The average daily circulation of these cumbersome "blanket sheets" was stuck at around 1,700.[45]

Another crucial factor contributed to these modest numbers in New York and elsewhere. On the one hand, newspapers of the day enjoyed "privileged" status from the U.S. postal system, which meant they were not only cheap to send, but also earned priority treatment for delivery. While this policy helped broaden their reach, it worked to limit their profitability, because subscribers very often shared them. The mails sped papers to distant subscribers in as few as seven days, making the news each delivery brought breathtakingly "fresh"—that is, only a week old. But when readers were done examining them, many forwarded the papers by post to friends and relatives at the same favorable mailing rates. By the 1830s, Americans had learned to communicate as frequently through the exchange of used newspapers as through personal letters. That was because until 1845, the cost of sending a one-page letter by mail was many times higher than that of mailing an entire newspaper. Struggling families separated by hundreds of miles but determined to maintain contact with their distant kin found it more economical to repurpose their local papers than to post original notes. Sometimes correspondents added family news by scribbling personal messages in the margins alongside the printed columns.

Sensing it was losing vast amounts of postal revenue because of these "transient" papers, Congress ultimately banned handwritten messages from reposted journals. Clever correspondents evaded the new regulations by hiding personal greetings in hard-to-spot places, or ingeniously connecting words, or blacking out, circling, and highlighting letters of the alphabet within news articles to form coded messages. In 1830 alone, some sixteen million newspapers arrived through the U.S. Post. In just one three-month period in the 1840s, as historian David Henkin discovered, a single small Alabama town received 6,829 newspapers in the mail—seven for each of its residents.[46] Yet within New York City, local readership still lagged behind population growth. As late as the 1830s, the best-selling morning newspaper in town counted only 4,500 readers, the most popular evening journal but three thousand.[47] The secret of how successfully to circulate newspapers on its crowded streets remained elusive.

The immediacy, reach, and breathtaking power of the daily press in New York—a commercial metropolis emerging even then as the publishing center of the nation—grew exponentially in 1833, not long after Andrew Jackson began his second term. Early that September, a twenty-three-year-old former *Journal and Advertiser* compositor named Benjamin H. Day, now proprietor of his own modest printing establishment, decided to launch a new paper. A "man made of granite," according to his admiring grandson, Clarence—who earned quite a literary reputation of his own decades later—Ben Day was, unlike most of his newspaper contemporaries, no political crusader.[48] He had a surpassingly practical reason for launching his enterprise: he wanted to keep his otherwise idle presses fully engaged. Day called his new daily the

Sun and designed it to be much smaller than the broadsheets—a precursor of the twentieth-century tabloids. Pledging "to lay before the public, at a price within the means of every one, ALL THE NEWS OF THE DAY" (perhaps a coy play on his name), the publisher priced his paper at only a penny, a fraction of the cost of the established six-cent dailies.[49]

The enterprise was out to create a new paradigm for publishing success. Ever since the establishment of the first major American daily, the *Pennsylvania Packet*, back in 1784, most newspapers, not only New York's, had catered to business-minded readers by offering them information they needed to make money, and relying for income on advertisements, not paid circulation.

Ben Day, founder of the *New York Sun* and inventor of the "penny press."

Day upended this model, first by feeding a public starving for reports of exciting events, however obscure or titillating. "Give us one of your real Moscow fires, or your Waterloo battlefields," the paper declared, "let a Napoleon be dashing with his legions throughout the world, overturning the thrones of a thousand years and deluging the world with blood and tears; and then we of the types are in our glory."[50] The *Sun* emphasized sensational crime news, theater reviews, municipal gossip, and human interest stories on subjects ranging from pets to drunks to duelists—which it termed "useful knowledge among the operative classes of society." Before long, it boasted three thousand daily readers, principally among "those who cannot well afford to incur the expense of subscribing to a 'blanket sheet' and paying ten dollars per annum."[51] This was a paper for the literate poor.

In yet another innovation, copies were not merely mailed or sold at the publication office. At first Day hired the usual squad of eager newsboys, many homeless, to peddle the *Sun* on Manhattan's busy streets, paying them two dollars a week and requiring each to work until every one of his papers was sold.[52] Soon enough, Day improved on that model. Adopting a distribution system pioneered in London, he began selling bulk copies to profit-minded news dealers at two-thirds the cover price—67 cents for bundles of a hundred—giving these middlemen the financial incentive to broaden circulation by having their newsboys hawk them on the streets at the full retail price. Such innovations helped the *Sun* reach eight thousand New Yorkers a day by 1834. Within another year, it initiated a further industry revolution by replacing its one-cylinder flatbed printing machine with a rapid-acting cylinder press, which made it possible to print more papers, more quickly, than ever. Daily circulation of the *Sun* soon approached an astounding twenty thousand.[53]

Inevitably, imitators soon flooded the market with penny papers of their own. One called itself *The True Sun* in a blatant effort to lure readers away from Day's original. It failed. Another pretender, the *Morning Star*, appeared around the same time—founded by a compositor at the *Courier* about whom nothing else is known except his name: Lincoln. Like his namesake in the West, this Lincoln, it was reported, "could write paragraphs with some ability."[54] Unlike the other Lincoln, of whose existence New York publishers still remained entirely ignorant, he soon vanished from history.

Within this hotly competitive atmosphere, even the most high-minded papers soon began replicating Day's business plan—and mimicking some of his emotionalism as well. No blanket sheet of the period, for example, reached more readers than the progressive *New York Evening Post*—founded by Alexander Hamilton in 1801, and by the early 1830s dominating the afternoon market with a daily run of three thousand copies. Certainly no editor in the nation seemed more distinguished than the *Post's* William Cullen Bryant, famous since 1817 for beloved poems like "Thanatopsis." At first he had been reluctant to take on the kind of full-time newspaper job that was increasingly a realm occupied by professional printers, not writers. Twisting the knife, broadsheet rival James Watson Webb sneered that Bryant "had embarked in a pursuit not suited to his genius." Literary critics sadly concurred, one complaining in 1831 that "what he is [now] writing, is as little like poetry, as Gen. Jackson is like Apollo."[55]

Bryant surprised the doubters by throwing himself into political journalism, and coming quickly to speak eloquently for the city's progressives. Ultimately, however, even a poet could become infected with the competitive virus gripping New York journalism. One day, in full view of startled spectators outside City Hall, Bryant took a cowhide whip to the editor of the *Commercial Advertiser*, William Leete Stone. Flabbergasted onlookers struggled to separate the enraged combatants on the street. Even the most staid of publications seemed to be rising—or sinking—to a new level of fierce rivalry whose potential for inciting outright violence lurked just beneath the surface.

Bryant himself sheepishly admitted to the bad reputation increasingly attached to professional newspapermen, himself perhaps included: "Contempt is too harsh a word for it, perhaps, but it is far below respect."[56] Other New Yorkers had already become so accustomed to street brawls between journalists that when the blasé man-about-town Philip Hone spied the Bryant-Stone squabble from his window as it unfolded, the incident did not seem unusual enough to interrupt his shaving.[57] It was not that Hone lacked for strong views of his own when it came to New York's daily press—it was just that these opinions were universally negative. Suspicious of friends who claimed they never read the scandalous penny papers, Hone suggested in his diary that "every man who blames his neighbor for setting so bad an example occasionally puts one in his pocket to carry home to his family for their and his own edification."[58]

Most readers of the penny press were uninhibited about revealing their affinity for one penny daily or another. "These papers are to be found in every street, lane, and alley, in every counting-house, shop, etc.," a Philadelphia journal reported after a visit to New York. "Almost every porter and dray-man, while not engaged in his occupation, may be seen with a paper in his hands." [59] And yet some aspiring publishers believed there were not enough choices yet.

The most widely read, most financially successful—and, some later com-plained, most outrageous and disreputable—New York newspaper of them all would now make its sensational debut. Tucked away in one of the *Sun's* editions from 1834—between reports of a man accused of stealing a ham, and another noting the tragic death of a girl tempted to "drink a pint of rum on a wager"—was the following seemingly routine item: "James G. Bennett has become sole proprietor and editor of the Philadelphia *Courier.*" [60] As it turned out, the report was incorrect. James Gordon Bennett was destined for a far larger field.

That summer, after several failures and false starts, this foreign-born, thirty-nine-year-old veteran journalist instead traveled to New York and sought a job interview with none other than Ben Day. Overflowing with self-assurance, Bennett arrived armed with new ideas for further hiking the *Sun's* already robust circulation. Day was intrigued, but his business partner took one look at Bennett and concluded he would be too costly and untamable an employee to add to the staff. The *Sun* would pay dearly for this rebuke.

By 1837, financial panic sharply reduced circulation among the *Sun's* principal audience: the city's poorest residents who suddenly had no dispos-able pennies to squander on mere newspapers. The following year, Day would sell his interest in the struggling enterprise and vanish prematurely from the New York publishing scene he had done so much to transform. The genre he introduced, however, thrived and expanded—thanks to the indefatigable promoter he so ill-advisedly turned away. On May 6, 1835, James Gordon Bennett opened a paper of his own in the dank basement of a small building on Wall Street. He called it the *New York Herald*.

Born in Banffshire, Scotland, in 1795, and growing up with what he ros-ily described as "a taste for poetry," Jamie Bennett had studied for a time at seminary but felt no calling for the priesthood. [61] Instead he left home, just as Greeley would, at age twenty. He then spent four fruitless years in search of career opportunities in Glasgow and Aberdeen before sailing to Halifax, Nova Scotia, in 1819. There, and later in Maine, he briefly and discontentedly taught school. His next job, however, was as a proofreader in Boston, and though he disliked the tedious work, he was taken with what he called "the charms of a printing and publishing house." [62] By 1822, Bennett was dwelling in South Carolina, employed at the *Charleston Courier*, where he specialized in translating the South American news from the Spanish language newspapers that arrived each morning by ship. [63] He was learning the newspaper business, such as it was, from the bottom up.

Increasingly restless and ambitious as he neared age thirty, Bennett remained frustratingly unfulfilled. Then he moved for the first time to New York. Judging the press there to be "wretched," he decided to quit journalism for good and open some sort of commercial school. [64] Unable to attract investors, however, Bennett soon abandoned this scheme. Instead, he began writing articles for the *Sunday Courier* on a freelance basis and briefly considered buying the paper himself until he concluded it would never earn a profit. Perhaps put off by his irritating Scottish burr and his saturnine appearance—Philip Hone described him as a "serpent" and an "ill-looking, squinting man"—the proprietors of other papers in town, including the *Commercial Advertiser* and the *American*, turned Bennett away when he applied for staff jobs. [65] But Bennett had "studied" the town's leading editors and "gathered from their conduct . . . the true temper of the men he aspired to rival and excel." [66] He was hardly ready to admit inadequacy, much less failure.

Showcasing his versatility, a tireless Bennett began contributing economic analyses to the *Mercantile Advertiser* and exposés of financial fraud to the *National Advocate*—sometimes simultaneously. In 1827, still a freelancer, he reinvented himself as a humorist for the pro-Jackson *New York Morning Enquirer*, a paper edited by a colorful Jewish playwright, diplomat, and early Zionist named Mordecai Manuel Noah. [67] The contrast between these two flamboyant characters must have approached the theatrical: one a Sephardic Jew from Philadelphia, the other a Scot who spoke with a pronounced burr. But both were talented professionals who needed each other, and Bennett's contributions for the *Morning Enquirer* made it a livelier paper. One of his earliest essays for Noah tweaked "our national propensity to *shake hands*," offering example after rib-tickling example of different salutations as practiced around the world. This and subsequent comic turns caused a minor sensation around town and increased the *Enquirer's* circulation, though critics accused editor Noah of lowering his standards to publish "froth." [68] The notoriety was enough to earn Bennett a promotion to a full-time job as associate editor, though Noah never quite took to the ambitious Scotsman, perhaps sensing his deep and incurable anti-Semitism. When the paper's Washington correspondent lost his life in a duel, the editor dispatched Bennett to the national capital as a replacement, in all likelihood happy to see him leave the New York office.

In Washington, Bennett finally made a real mark. Beginning in January 1828, he regularly transmitted richly detailed "letters" in the style of English author Horace Walpole's celebrated *Correspondence*. Bennett's encyclopedic columns colorfully described scenes ranging from Andrew Jackson's clamorous White House receptions to spirited floor debates in Congress that the journalist observed from the press galleries. "These letters were lively, they abounded in personal allusions, and they described freely, not only Senators, but the wives and daughters of Senators," marveled the young journalist Benjamin Perley Poore, "and they established Mr. Bennett's reputation as a light lance among the hosts of writers" covering the capital. Poore marked Bennett as "naturally witty" and "sarcastic"—but also "sensible"—a combination of gifts he regarded as rare and marketable.

At the time, Democratic Party dogma was dispensed in Washington by the official administration organ, the *United States Telegraph*, edited by Duff Green, but allegedly financed by Old Hickory himself. Equally privy to official policy was the *Washington Globe*, the pro-Jackson paper edited by Francis Preston Blair, Sr., whom yet another Democratic editor described as "thoroughly familiar with the great chieftain" in the White House.[69] Indeed, Blair, who lived in a town house situated just across Pennsylvania Avenue from the executive mansion, served simultaneously as a personal advisor to the president, a member of the coterie of confidants known as the "Kitchen Cabinet." Though young Bennett never disguised his own Democratic bias—he was a "rampant Jackson blockhead," he admitted—he boasted no such close ties with the president, covering the political scene with what he called "all the ease which a sense of freedom inspires."[70]

A year later, Mordecai Manuel Noah's *Enquirer* merged with James Watson Webb's *Courier*, and the new ownership under Webb summoned Bennett home to reassume the post of associate editor. Webb's editorial policies, however, quickly made its star writer uneasy: he wholeheartedly supported the controversial Second Bank of the United States, against which Bennett and fellow Jacksonians had consistently railed. Frustrated, Bennett "abandoned" the *Courier and Enquirer* "in consequence of its abandonment of General

Jackson."[71] In 1832 he again tried establishing his own paper, but it survived barely two months. His application to Blair for a job at the *Globe* went nowhere. Growing desperate, Bennett briefly relocated to Philadelphia to edit a Democratic campaign organ called *The Pennsylvanian*.

Like most loyal party journalists of the time, Bennett believed his ultimate salvation should arrive in the form of appointment to a well-paying patronage post from the administration on which he had lavished so much praise. After all, similar rewards regularly came to other editors friendly to the party in power. In Washington, the last Congress had awarded the leading Democratic paper $353,000 in printing business.[72] But party leaders, Vice President Martin Van Buren included, harbored doubts about Bennett's reliability. However gifted his prose or ardent his support, he was hard to discipline. His strange demeanor, grating accent, and permanent squint continued to make people uneasy; he still seemed uncomfortably alien. The job to which Bennett aspired—the consulship at Bremen—went to someone else. Suspicion ran so deep that the party would not even advance Bennett money to launch a brand-new Democratic paper in the manner of Duff Green—another increasingly common practice political organizations employed to reward (and control) press allies. "They treated me very badly," Bennett fumed. He sounded rather more disconsolate than embittered when he confided to his diary: "I have endeavored to secure a high position in parties, and to settle myself in life. I have always failed—why so?"[73]

In 1835, Bennett answered his own question. Perhaps success had eluded him in New York, Washington, and Philadelphia alike because he had remained independent and irascible, but within the strict, unforgiving party-press culture. What he needed was to establish his own rules—to work for himself. Somehow he managed to scrape together enough money to strike out on his own—after young Horace Greeley declined to become his partner in a decision that surely changed journalistic, and conceivably American, history. Instead Bennett elected to follow Ben Day's example, but to tweak it ever so brilliantly, and to labor as hard and as publicly as it took to make it a success.

Opening shop in cramped offices, with desks made of wooden planks thrown atop crates, Bennett proved tireless. During the infancy of his newly minted *Herald,* he served as the sole reporter of local news—and more. He bought and read all the rival papers so he could "adapt" their state, national, and foreign reports for his own pages. He wrote literary reviews and founded a trenchant "Money Market" column to report on financial events in language ordinary New Yorkers could understand (accompanied, for the first time, by close-of-trading stock prices). He sold advertisements himself. He personally tended to the bills and accounts. Meanwhile he took to boasting in print that he was leading a life of leisure, claiming his daily routine allowed him to dine "moderately and temperately" at 4 P.M., then "read our proofs—take in cash and advertisements, which are increasing like smoke—and close the day by going to bed always by ten o'clock, seldom later. That's the way to conduct a paper with spirit and success." [74] But energy and braggadocio alone did not make him successful.

Shrewdly, Bennett aimed his sights from the start at a slightly more sophisticated audience than that of the penny press pioneers. He targeted a more middle-class readership whose demand for news would not fluctuate with the economic climate, and who would likely patronize a daily newspaper that combined a passion for politics with the irreverent spice of the penny press. At ten-by-fourteen inches in size, the *Herald* was smaller than the blanket sheets, but larger than the *Sun.* Unafraid of either form of competition, Bennett vowed in his premiere issue that the *Herald* would work to become the "equal of any of the high priced papers for intelligence, good taste, sagacity, and industry, [until] there is not a person in the city, male or female, that may not be able to say—'well, I have got a paper of my own which will tell me all about what's doing in the world—I'm busy now—but I'll put it in my pocket and read it at my leisure.'" Here was bombast with a common touch, composed in the edgy tone that became Bennett's trademark. The declaration went on:

> Our only guide shall be good, sound, practical common sense, applicable to the business and bosoms of men engaged in every day life. *We shall support no party—be the organ of no faction or COTERIE, and care nothing for election or candidate from president down to constable.* We shall endeavor to record facts, on every public and proper subject, stripped of verbiage and coloring, with comments when suitable, just, independent, fearless, and good tempered. It is equally intended for the great masses of the community—the merchant, mechanic, working people—the private family as well as the public hotel—the journeyman and his employer—the clerk and his principal. [75]

Of course, Bennett well knew he would never attract legions of readers by being "sound" and "good tempered." He had no intention of being either.

His target was the vast audience bored by the blanket sheets and mortified by the *Sun*. "There are in this city at least 150,000 persons who glance over one or more newspapers every day," he calculated. "Only 42,000 sheets are issued daily to supply them. We have plenty of room, therefore, without jostling neighbors, rivals or friends, to pick up at least *twenty or thirty thousand* for the HERALD."[76] In this goal, he actually proved too modest. More in keeping with his overabundant confidence was a promise he made only privately: "That I *can* surpass every paper in New York, every paper will acknowledge— that I *will* do so, I am resolved, determined." In print he showcased his gift for acerbic humor, and his willingness to take on the pompous and powerful.

He boasted that by eschewing "dry detail—uninteresting facts—political nonsense—personal squabbles—obsolete news," he had "infused life, glowing eloquence, philosophy, taste, sentiment, wit and humor into the daily newspaper." Bennett was not modest. "Shakespeare is the great genius of the drama—Scott of the novel—Milton and Byron of the poem—and I mean to be the genius of the daily newspaper press."[77] Other examples of his uninhibited bombast included likening himself to Napoleon, Confucius, Charlemagne, and Alexander the Great.[78] Not since Benjamin Franklin did an editor become such a successful promoter of himself.

Bennett managed to live up to his own publicity. And he did so, uniquely, while remaining unpredictable in, but not aloof from, politics. Partisan papers attracted readers by attacking their political foes. Bennett attracted readers by attacking *all* politicians, typically labeling them, regardless of party, as "tricksters," "loafers," "parasites," and "vagabonds," among other epithets.[79] His paper appealed to readers who cared more for news than for party affiliation. Yet Bennett maintained political influence by never abandoning his appetite for the political arena itself. For example, he took on rival editors during the municipal campaigns of 1837, backing the Tammany Hall Democratic machine, though it went on to suffer a pummeling at the polls. One New York print publisher responded with a cartoon gleefully depicting editors, including Webb, shooting an arrow into the heart of a defeated Indian (representing Tammany), while trampling on Bennett, who can be seen cringing on the ground shouting: "Murder! . . . Save me! I'm the Ladies' Favorite! . . . Squint Eye! Oh!!"[80] Bennett and the *Herald* became staples in anti-Democratic caricature—another mark of the editor's growing power and celebrity.

Though he remained aligned with Democratic principles, Bennett punished the national Democratic establishment for its previous neglect of him.

He abandoned Van Buren and the Democrats during the 1840 presidential contest and threw his support behind Whig challenger William Henry Harrison. Eventually Bennett did return more reliably to the Democratic fold, too conservative on issues like race to flirt with Whig politics permanently. But his 1840 defection made it clear he was not to be taken for granted.

Certainly he was no progressive. In print, as in life, Bennett staunchly opposed abolition and ridiculed the notion of equality for African Americans. Otherwise his targets had little in common except that they had somehow aroused his enmity. He mercilessly demonized the Art-Union—a new organization formed merely to link painters with potential patrons—as a secret antislavery society. Although born Roman Catholic, he branded the pope "a decrepit, licentious, stupid, Italian blockhead" and later picked a protracted fight with the bishop of the New York diocese.[81] He feuded with theatrical impresarios, ward heelers, newspaper competitors, and perceived idlers. His pen was both prolific and toxic. Bennett labeled the rival *Sun* as a "dirty, sneaking, driveling contemporary nigger paper" and endorsed slavery as the "natural position of the Southern colored races." Jews he declared to be "without a single redeeming feature, except the beauty, excellence, black eyes, small feet, and fine forms of their women."[82] A lapsed advertiser who took his business elsewhere was labeled a bamboozler. Politicians who irked him, fellow journalists who questioned him, and celebrities who merely seemed ripe for humiliation inspired venom more poisonous than anything a metropolitan newspaper had ever printed. Bennett reveled in the chaos he created, and unlike his peers never seemed to take his feuds too seriously.

On one hand Bennett introduced the public-spirited tradition of reprinting important political orations promptly, and in full, and invented the tradition of investigative journalism. On the other, he recklessly targeted revered institutions and unexpectedly savaged innocent organizations. He also zestfully raked the muck when it came to reporting violent crime, prostitution, theatrical feuds, and scandals among both the high-born and the low. He seemed to relish being ornery and unpredictable, basked in his reputation for contentiousness, enjoyed being feared, and cherished his growing reputation for putting "a penny-worth of scandal on every man's breakfast table."[83]

The dynamic editor made no pretense to lofty idealism, nor did he overestimate his audience. He confidently believed New Yorkers "were more ready to seek six columns of the details of a brutal murder, or of testimony in a divorce case, or the trial of a divine for improprieties of conduct, than the same amount of words poured forth by the genius of the noblest author of the times." His own "picture of the world," he conceded, took him "wherever human nature and real life best display their freaks and vagaries." [84] Unashamedly, he admitted that "there was more journalistic money to be made in recording gossip that interested bar-rooms, work-shops, race courses and tenement houses, than in consulting the tastes of drawing rooms and libraries." [85] Yet even his most billious screeds had to be well crafted. Bennett was a strong and persuasive writer, and he maintained a lively, accessible, sardonic literary style that appealed to all classes, even those who were ashamed to tell their friends they read the *Herald*.

While Bennett taunted his competitors with the self-assurance of an Old World potentate and the bravado of a circus ringmaster (becoming something of a Barnum well before Barnum took on that role himself), he ran the business side of his enterprise with the acuity of a modern technocrat. Like Benjamin Day at the *Sun*, Bennett priced his lively paper at a penny, and organized its distribution according to the London Plan, selling copies at reduced rates to newsdealers. Once established, Bennett's resiliency proved remarkable, his ability to triumph over tragedy uncanny. When fire—a constant danger in poorly ventilated buildings where employees smoked freely while setting hot type—destroyed his equipment and headquarters in August 1835, he simply secured a new office on Broadway. In the meantime, Bennett grandiosely humbled himself by advertising the *Herald*'s

James Gordon Bennett of the *New York Herald*, ca. 1840s.

imminent revival on the pages of the yet more popular *Sun*.[86] After a hiatus of only nineteen days, he bombastically relaunched a "larger, livelier, better, prettier, saucier, and more independent" paper than ever.[87]

Pledging that his resuscitated publication would become "the earliest of the early," Bennett invested in the fastest new steam-driven printing presses, and threw himself into the task of gathering news more rapidly than his rivals.[88] To acquire foreign news, most competitors were still content to dispatch employees to wait at the city's wharves, there to meet ships carrying European newspapers whose already outdated reports could be purloined at no cost. Bennett instead hired "news boats" to intercept the papers while the ships were still at sea.

Bennett also began exploiting the rapidly expanding railroad system to speed his papers to readers in Boston, Philadelphia, and Albany, making his the first truly regional daily. He became one of the first to embrace the telegraph as a means of receiving news faster than ever. He introduced maps and line illustrations on his front pages. He pioneered in foreign correspondence and introduced the interview to journalism. And he eventually created a national weekly edition to expand the *Herald*'s reach well beyond New York, including an edition translated into French.[89] Meanwhile, he famously demanded cash in advance for advertising. The *Herald* accepted notices not only from legitimate businessmen, but also from patent medicine salesman, medical charlatans, spiritualists, and even professional "escorts," as long as they paid up front. Before long, the paper became the first to boast a classified section larger than its news space.

To create what he called "a commercial paper for the millions," Bennett endeavored to be "serious in my aims, but full of frolic in my means." Not everyone was amused. The *Courier and Enquirer* labeled him "a beggarly outcast, who daily sends forth a dirty sheet," and the *Journal of Commerce* added that "if he got his desserts," Bennett "would be horsewhipped every day." In response, the *Herald* defiantly reprinted and mocked the criticism.[90] Bennett's audacious tone, irreverent voice, and most of all his growing success, irritated his envious rivals almost to distraction.

The competition eventually became too much for one of them in particular: his onetime employer, *Courier and Enquirer* editor James Watson Webb. Already a veteran of several public brawls, Webb confronted Bennett in the business district one day in 1836 and shoved him down the front steps of a brokerage house in full view of astonished traders and speculators. Then for good measure Webb struck him with his walking stick. Recovering quickly, no worse for the scrape, Bennett took to print to taunt his old boss for losing both his temper and the spat he had initiated. "My damage is a scratch . . . and three buttons torn on my coat, which my tailor will reinstate for a sixpence," the *Herald* editor gloated after the fracas. "His loss is a rent from top to bottom of a very beautiful black coat, which cost the ruffian $40, and a blow in the face, which may have knocked down his throat some of his infernal teeth for anything I know." Perhaps, he gleefully added, Webb had aimed his cane at Bennett's head in an attempt "to let out the never-failing supply of good humor and wit, which has created such a reputation for the Herald, and appropriate the contents to supply the emptiness of his own thick skull." Bennett assured his readers that "My ideas, in a few days, will flow as freely as ever, and he will find it so, to his cost." [91]

Soon enough, such public scrapes practically became part of the *Herald* editor's daily routine. Outraged readers, along with those insulted by his coverage, periodically attacked him on the streets as well. When Peter Townsend of the *Evening Star* struck him in the face one day on Wall Street—"a decent chastisement for his impudence," crowed the *Sun*'s Ben Day—Bennett challenged his assailant to a duel. The two

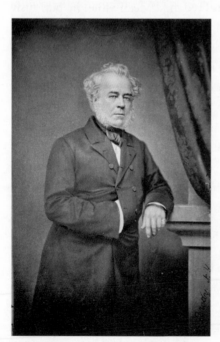

newspapermen then met across the river at Hoboken, where Bennett fired the first shot but missed; fortunately for the *Herald* editor, his opponent's aim was no better. On yet another occasion, Bennett escaped serious injury from a letter bomb only because black powder leaking from the otherwise innocent-looking parcel aroused suspicion before it was opened. Rather than shrink from danger, the editor proudly reported every dustup in the *Herald*, invariably noting after each fight that he had given more than he got. The ensuing publicity made Bennett more prominent still, and his paper ever more popular with readers.

James Watson Webb, duel-happy editor of the New York *Courier and Enquirer*.

Frustrated competitors ultimately took to inventing less violent schemes to destroy him. In 1844, they launched a so-called moral war against the *Herald*, charging in print that Bennett was "notorious for daily habits of blasphemy, obscenity and falsehood." Particularly eager for revenge, James Watson Webb took to the effort enthusiastically, labeling Bennett a "disgusting obscenity" and a "moral pestilence." Charging, with a touch of the obscene, that common prostitutes viewed the *Herald* as their "special organ," Webb urged decent New Yorkers: "*purchase* not, *read* not, *touch* not."[92]

Initially, Bennett replied by suggesting in print that "Field Marshal Webb"—the *Courier and Enquirer* editor often called himself "Colonel"—should take holy orders. But when the *Herald*'s circulation began to erode under the onslaught from the *Courier and Enquirer*, Bennett devised the most ingenious counterattack yet. Although Webb had earlier suggested that a man would as soon choose a bride from a brothel as wed a woman who read the vile *Herald*, Bennett brazenly appealed for public sympathy by doing just that: taking a bride himself. He further shocked his enemies (and even some of his admirers) by announcing the event in his own paper under the brazen headline: "Declaration of Love—Caught at Last—Going to Be Married." In his usual bemused tone, he boasted: "I must fulfill the awful destiny which the Almighty Father has written in broad letters of my life against the wall of Heaven. I must give the world a pattern of happy wedded life."[93] Exasperated rivals resorted to lobbying Congress to enact a law banning the shipment of newspapers in bulk, a system that advantaged the efficiently bundled *Herald*. The proposal failed. Bennett celebrated its defeat by making the paper even bigger, and installing a new steam-driven press capable of printing five thousand copies an hour.

Rivals simply loathed him. Webb called him the "lowest species of humanity," and even his ex-employer Noah referred to him as a "polluter of the press." Typical of the criticism that found its way into print was this description from an 1842 edition of the short-lived *New York Aurora*: "A reptile marking his path with slime wherever he goes, and breathing mildew at everything fresh or fragrant; a midnight ghoul, preying on rottenness and repulsive filth; a creature, hated by his nearest intimates, and bearing the consciousness thereof upon his distorted features, and upon his despicable soul; one whom good men avoid as a blot to his nature—whom all despise, and whom, no one blesses—*all this* is James Gordon Bennett." The author of the piece was a young writer named Walt Whitman. "It would be incorrect to call him a liar," another of Bennett's enemies later railed, "because he is wanting in that sense of truth by which a man makes himself a liar. . . . That region of the kind where conviction, the sense of truth and honor, public spirit, and patriotism have their sphere, is in this man mere vacancy." Yet raging against Bennett only frustrated his enemies, since the editor relished each and every attack. "He has been horse-whipped, kicked, trodden under foot, spat upon, and degraded in every possible way; but all this he courts, because it brings money," lamented British-born writer Frederick Marryatt. "Horse-whip him, and he will bend his back to the lash and thank you; for every blow is worth so many dollars. Kick him, and he will remove his coat-tails, that you may have a better mark. Spit upon him, and he prizes it as precious ointment."[94]

In desperation, Bennett's enemies sunk to secretly backing publication of an anonymous, sixty-four-page-long 1844 pamphlet, *The Life and Writings of James Gordon Bennett*, complete with an engraved caricature depicting the editor as a scrawny, hawk-nosed, cross-eyed blackmailer in tasteless check-patterned pants, standing on the sidewalk in front of the *Herald* offices playing a bagpipe—a mocking reference to his heritage. Describing Bennett as "exceedingly violent and profane in his language, to those in his employ, treating them habitually with the most vulgar abuse," the booklet added: "As would naturally be expected, he is soft, servile, and cringing in his manners to those whose wealth or position place them beyond his power."[95] Ordinarily, such charges might have soured the community on Bennett, but the authors made the fatal mistake of padding their publication with "choice extracts" from the *Herald*'s most sordid stories in an effort to horrify readers with reminders of its founder's wickedness. These had precisely the opposite of their intended effect. Readers clamored for copies of the pamphlet, apparently delighted to have their favorite *Herald* articles collected in a new format.

In the end, nothing could dent the paper's wild popularity. Bennett's abiding secret was simple: unscrupulous, unpredictable, and unlovable he may have been as a man, but as an editor he understood precisely what people yearned to know. As one of his later competitors ruefully admitted: "It would be worth my while . . . to give a million dollars, if the Devil would come and tell me every evening, as he does Bennett, what the people of New York would like to read about next morning." The admirer's name was Henry Jarvis Raymond, and in due time he would launch a New York newspaper of his own, but like Greeley, with the goal of reforming government, not belittling it.

James Gordon Bennett's flair for self aggrandizement, charisma, and infuriatingly sarcastic style—combined with an undeniable genius for business and promotion—earned him a fortune and made him prominent, but ironically limited his influence in American political life. By choosing not to make the *New York Herald* a party newspaper, he may have maintained his political independence, but he also reduced his ability to influence official policy and promote friends, much less himself, for appointive office.

Though he grew into an inescapable presence and an authentic celebrity, he remained very much an outsider: volatile, belligerent, sensationalistic, sacrilegious, suspiciously foreign, irritatingly flippant, and so immensely successful he provoked not only envy but also outrage—not to mention ridicule and occasional violence.[96] Bennett became and remained rich and powerful primarily because his readership and advertising base grew gargantuan—and kept expanding. Not even his jealous competitors could deny that Bennett's vigorous prose earned him something more valuable than admirers: customers. For better or worse, he became the father of modern tabloid journalism. In politics, however, James Gordon Bennett was courted and feared, but never quite respected—or even respectable.

CHAPTER TWO

Not Like Any Other Thunder

———◆———

Throughout the 1830s, serious, reform-minded journalism aroused far more admiration than the scandalous penny press or the hotly divisive political organs. But the reformers also provoked a deadly animus of their own. This was particularly so when the reforms they advocated included the abolition of slavery, still an appallingly radical notion to most white Americans, even in the North.

To express their hostility, the opponents of abolition did more than cancel subscriptions. In an all too typical response that occurred on July 30, 1836, an enraged mob broke into the headquarters of the *Philanthropist*, an abolition journal in Cincinnati, "scattered the type into the streets, tore down the presses, and completely dismantled the office." Then the rioters triumphantly dragged the damaged press toward the riverbank, shattered it to pieces, and threw them into the river before launching an indiscriminate attack on "the residence of some blacks." [1]

A similarly motivated outbreak of vigilantism in Lincoln's own home state ignited an even more violent outcome the following year. The victim, Elijah Parish Lovejoy, a Maine-born antislavery minister and previously the editor of the anti-Jackson *St. Louis Observer*, was no stranger to such attacks. After criticizing a Missouri judge for failing to indict white men suspected of lynching a free black, a mob had seized and destroyed Lovejoy's printing press. Refusing to be silenced, the editor defiantly set up a new abolitionist paper, the *Alton Observer*, across the Mississippi River in the free state of Illinois, funded by the state's Presbyterian synod. But the townspeople of Alton, many of whom had migrated from the South, proved no less sympathetic to slavery, and no more welcoming to an abolitionist newspaper, than the residents of St. Louis. They stoned Lovejoy's office and sacked three of his printing presses.

On November 2, 1837, Lovejoy dismissed the escalating resentment in an impassioned but provocative speech. Denying he was insensitive to local sensibilities, he contended he had "published sentiments contrary to those generally held in this community . . . because I fear God." Lovejoy admitted he was likely to be tarred and feathered, but vowed he would not be driven out again. "If I leave here and go elsewhere, violence may overtake me in my retreat," he declared. But "if I am not safe at Alton, I shall not be safe any where." [2]

Five days later, after Lovejoy narrowly escaped an attack on his home, another angry mob descended on the riverfront warehouse where he had secured his newest printing press, demanding that he surrender it. When he

THE PRO-SLAVERY RIOT OF NOVEMBER 7, 1837.   DEATH OF REV. E. P. LOVEJOY.

The 1837 attack on the Alton, Illinois, structure housing
abolitionist editor Elijah Lovejoy's printing press.

refused, his assailants began pelting the building with rocks. From inside, the besieged editor and his supporters next took, and then returned, a volley of gunfire, leaving one of the attackers dead in the street. The mob's fury grew. Shouting "Burn them out," attackers threw ladders against the warehouse walls and tried climbing to the top armed with torches, meaning to set fire to the roof. When Lovejoy bravely threw open the front door in order to shove one ladder away, a shotgun blast from somewhere in the crowd ripped into his chest, abdomen, and legs. Minutes later, the editor lay dead.[3]

Not yet satisfied, the mob stormed past Lovejoy's lifeless body and into the warehouse, hurled his printing press out the window onto the riverbank below, and in a frenzy smashed what remained of it and hurled the fragments into the Mississippi. No one was ever prosecuted for the crimes.[4] But in death, Lovejoy became a symbol for abolitionists and free press advocates in many parts of the North. Decrying mob violence as "an enemy to freedom," Horace Greeley hailed Lovejoy as "a martyr to public liberty."[5] Even though the opposition to Jacksonian Democracy had by then coalesced into a formidable new Whig Party, most Whig newspapers in Illinois remained strangely silent, perhaps fearful of inciting further violence and certainly not yet prepared to commit against slavery itself. Unlike many of his moderate Whig contemporaries, however, Abraham Lincoln decided to speak out.

Although he became almost chronically reluctant to address contentious issues quickly, only three months after the Alton atrocity Lincoln took on the Lovejoy issue in an oration at a Springfield church. This was not the same Lincoln who had failed in his amateurish maiden race for public office just a few years before.

In 1834, he had made a second try for the State Assembly, and this time won. Two years later, in 1836, he declared his candidacy for reelection with another lively letter to the *Sangamo Journal.* "In your paper of last Saturday," it began, "I see a communication over the signature of 'Many Voters,' in which the candidates who are announced in the Journal, are called upon to show their hands.' Agreed. Here's mine!" His platform was simple: "I go for all sharing the privileges of the government, who assist in bearing its burthens. Consequently I go for admitting all whites to the right of suffrage, who pay taxes or bear arms, (by no means excluding females.)" His nimble appeal ended as wittily as it began—with a declaration of Whig loyalty couched in Lincolnian modesty: "If alive on the first Monday in November, I shall vote for Hugh L. White for President."[6] As a politician and writer, Lincoln's growth was apparent. Springfield had grown, too—larger and, like Lincoln, more prominent. By 1837 it had become the state capital, as well as the young legislator's permanent new home.

Now accepting an invitation to address the town's Young Men's Lyceum, Lincoln responded on January 27, 1838, with a long speech best remembered for its advocacy of "cold, calculating reason" in the face of extremist emotionalism. It was Lincoln's first major public address outside the legislature, and while his style was not yet as lean—as "Lincolnesque"—as in his later, more famous orations, the issue of press violence had clearly inspired in him an almost uncharacteristic display of passion, even if its principal message was the rejection of passion. Lincoln never once mentioned Lovejoy by name—it would be "tedious, as well as useless," he asserted, to recount specific "horrors." But the editor's death was surely on his mind—and those of his listeners—when he assailed what he called "the increasing disregard for law which pervades the country; the growing disposition to substitute the wild and furious passions, in lieu of the sober judgment of courts; and the worse than savage mobs, for the executive ministers of justice."[7]

"Whenever this effect shall be produced among us," Lincoln warned, "whenever the vicious portion of population shall be permitted to gather in bands of hundreds and thousands, and burn churches, ravage and rob provision stores, *throw printing presses into rivers, shoot editors* [emphasis added], and hang and burn obnoxious persons at pleasure, and with impunity; depend on it, this Government cannot last." Insisting that there could be "no grievance that is a fit object of redress by mob law," Lincoln urged that "reverence for the laws" become "the *political religion* of the nation."[8]

The speech, which was dutifully printed in full by the *Sangamo Journal* a week later—no doubt at Lincoln's instruction—did little to inhibit the assaults that increasingly targeted progressive editors and their presses. But it did serve to elevate Lincoln's local reputation for political moderation, moral character, and oratorical talent. It also marked his first official acknowledgment that freedom of the press—and the security of its editors—was crucial to preserving democracy itself. Not for another twenty-five years would Lincoln come to question that belief.

• • •

Springfield was anything but unanimous in applauding its increasingly influential Whig politician. A new pro-Democratic newspaper had begun appearing in central Illinois, with a rapidly rising new political personality as its chief object of attention and affection. In 1836, a Delaware-born, Washington-based professional printer named William Walters had launched the *State Register* in the then state capital of Vandalia.

There was never a doubt about the editor's political loyalties. Democratic Party leaders themselves had recruited him for the task. Walters had been working as a newsroom foreman at Washington's influential *Daily Intelligencer*, but unlike its Whig proprietors, tended personally toward Jacksonian Democracy. At one point he impressed the Illinois Democrats then serving in Congress by taking on influential Washington editor Duff Green in a typographers' labor dispute. One of these congressmen, former governor John Reynolds, who longed to see a thriving pro-Jackson organ operating in his home state, concluded that Walters was just the man to create such a

William Walters, founding editor of the
pro-Democratic *Illinois State Register*.

paper. Eager for a challenge, Walters agreed to head west to Illinois. Once in Vandalia, he bought a used press and type and issued the first edition of the new *Illinois Register and Vandalia Republican* on February 12, 1836— ironically enough, the twenty-seventh birthday of the man whom the paper would spend the next quarter century relentlessly excoriating: Abraham Lincoln. By June, Walters's endeavor had attracted a thousand subscribers, more readers than the entire population of Illinois's tiny capital city.[9]

The new enterprise received an early boost when Democrats in the state legislature voted Walters the lucrative job of official state printer for the 1836–1837 session, a reward that political majorities routinely and unashamedly earmarked for their newspaper supporters to ensure further loyalty. This guaranteed that Walters would receive enough well-paid orders for legal notices and printed legislative proceedings to subsidize his fledgling weekly. Two years later, in 1839, Walters relocated the *Register*[10] to the new state capital, where the Francis brothers' *Journal* quickly greeted their new rival by editorializing that its debut issue "contained such a tissue of fabrications and misrepresentations that many of the patrons of the paper complained of it. Indeed, we doubt if any of the Loco Focos*, who had not been dipped in brimstone, would undertake to justify its publication."[11] By this time, Walters's teenage brother-in-law was working alongside him at the paper, learning the trade from the bottom up. The young man's name was Charles Henry Lanphier— Charlie to his friends.[12]

Born in 1820 in Alexandria, Virginia, and reared in downtown Washington opposite a boardinghouse typically crowded with newsworthy politicians, Charlie enjoyed life in the national capital. But he happily agreed to migrate to Springfield for a job as a printer's devil with his brother-in-law when Walters returned briefly to Washington in 1836 to gather his family and take them west. Lanphier's father usefully advised him that "to become an Editor you must acquaint yourself" with the enterprise, work on bookkeeping and penmanship skills, and "read when ever y[ou]r business admits (not novels and trash) usefull [*sic*] books and publications."[13]

Young Lanphier followed his father's sensible advice: he made himself increasingly "useful" and the *Register* continued to grow in circulation and

---

*Loco-Foco was the sobriquet given to the radical, New York–born wing of the Democratic Party committed to hard money. The name came from the newly introduced matchsticks these insurgents had held aloft when Tammany Hall regulars turned out the lights in an attempt to shut down a political meeting before the opposition could be heard.

influence. By 1837, William Walters was able to report that he had "prospered beyond all my expectations," adding of his young second-in-command: "Charles is everything I wish him and if he continues to act as he has, which I believe he will, he must rise also when he comes to be a man, and shall, if my influence can make him." [14]

The paper's strongest champion—who in turn became the principal beneficiary of its increasingly powerful advocacy—was the physically small but charismatic young Democratic politician Stephen Arnold Douglas. "Douglass," as he was first known (he dropped the second "s" years later, some said, so as not to be confused with one of the objects of his white supremacist disdain: Frederick Douglass) had been born in Brandon, Vermont, in 1813. His father died young, and the impoverished family had resettled on an uncle's farm a few miles away, where young Stephen, like so many of his struggling contemporaries, performed grueling field labor to earn his keep. More rewardingly, he spent a third of each year at school. Later, he attended a full-time academy in Canandaigua, New York. Until 1833, this soon-to-be-famous Westerner admitted that he had never "beheld a Prairie." [15]

That fall, Douglas left home to make his own way in the world, settling at first in one of Illinois's up-and-coming villages, Jacksonville, where fruitful employment eluded him. Too poor to stay long without work, he moved on to nearby Winchester to teach school for three dollars per student. "Here I am, as Jack Douning [sic] would say," he cheerfully wrote to his brother-in-law that December. "I have become a *Western* man, have imbibed Western feelings principles and interests and have selected Illinois as the favorite place of my adoption." In these words Douglas revealed himself as an already faithful reader of the press, for "Major Jack Downing" was a fictional character, created by Maine journalist Seba Smith, whose humorous adventures appeared in many papers across the country (often "adapted" by other writers, and increasingly tending toward political satire).

Though still a schoolteacher, not a politician, Douglas was already immersed in the press. And very soon he would cross paths with Abraham Lincoln, who regularly read Jack Downing's letters, too, though Lincoln had little else in common with the new arrival, either physically or politically. [16]

• • •

From the start of their own intense rivalry, the two young newspapers in the state of Douglas's "adoption" advocated Western principles of entirely opposite kinds.

The pro-Whig *Sangamo Journal* trumpeted the restoration of the Bank of the United States, a steep protective tariff on imported goods, and community-improving government investments in roads and canals. The Whig Party had initially attracted the country's financial elite, but was now winning converts among ambitious people of more modest means. One of them was Lincoln, who equated the right to upward mobility with the central promise of the American founding. Conversely insisting that the Whigs remained the party of privilege, Democrats and their party organs rejected the idea of an all-controlling national financial system and opposed import duties they argued would inflate the price of goods at home. Warning against debt-inducing public works projects that would invariably cause tax hikes, they appealed primarily to workingmen and the poor. Neither of these mainstream parties as yet expended much energy on the slavery issue, though ultraliberal Northeastern Whigs were among the first to call for restricting, even abolishing the institution. Not for another decade and a half, however, would slavery come to dominate American political and press discourse.[17]

Reveling in their incompatible philosophies, the *Journal* and the *Register* went at each other tooth and nail from the first. They covered the same public meetings, lyceum speeches, political rallies, and legislative sessions. Yet a stranger arriving in town and innocently comparing their reports line by line would be hard pressed to understand how journalists reporting identical events could describe them so differently. In this regard, however, Springfield was no different than any other city. James Silk Buckingham, an Englishman who visited the United States in 1838, recognized the growing tendency toward partisan journalism everywhere in America, pronouncing himself appalled by what he called the "exaggerated pictures drawn by the writers on each side." As he observed:

> Everything is distorted to serve party views. If the largest meeting is got up on one side, the opposite party declares it to be a mere handful in numbers. If the parties are ever so wealthy and respectable, they are pronounced to be a set of needy vagabonds. If the talent of the speeches should be of the highest kind, they would call them mere drivellings; and if the order was disturbed for a single moment, they would describe it as a beer garden. . . . When a writer of the Whig

party has to describe a meeting of their own side, however, he can find no terms sufficiently swelling and lofty in which to express himself. . . . Their "thunder" is not like any other thunder that was ever heard before, and the very globe seems to be shaken to its centre by their gigantic powers.[18]

Buckingham made these perceptive comments about a particular, unnamed Whig newspaper, but his observations applied to Democratic ones as well, and by extension to both of the party publications in Springfield. In fact, the *Journal* and *Register* were equally prone to exaggeration—and, occasionally, outright deceit—to advance their respective causes and candidates. And politicians were expected to reciprocate with tangible demonstrations of gratitude when they could. The Democratic legislative majority, as noted, subsidized Walters's *Register*. By contrast out of power and financially strapped, Lincoln at least made sure his law firm regularly placed legal notices in the *Sangamo Journal* throughout 1842, 1843, and 1844. Simeon Francis's surviving advertising records show that each of these multiple insertions brought the struggling paper—and cost Lincoln—the significant sum of five dollars, not much less than what the attorney might be expected to receive at the time for pleading a case for a poor client and enough to help keep a friendly journal in print.[19]

In this fiercely competitive atmosphere, the naturally pugnacious Stephen Douglas rose swiftly within Illinois's Democratic political hierarchy, first as state's attorney, then as a legislator, register of the federal land office, Illinois secretary of state, judge of the State Supreme Court, and later as a congressman. As he advanced through the ranks, Douglas came increasingly to expect (and often revel in) unsparing criticism from Simeon Francis's pro-Whig *Journal*, and lavish praise from William Walters's pro-Democratic *Register*. These newspapers were more than reporters, even advocates. They became integral cogs in their party's organizational machinery, operating as journalists from inside their party structures looking out, not outside the organizations looking in. This proved especially the case during the bitterly contested presidential campaign of 1840, when editors and politicians virtually organized themselves into opposing armies in the battle for the White House. In an era in which presidential candidates did no public campaigning of their own—tradition forbade it, and the country was yet too vast and unconnected to permit it—the printed word became the chief weapon in battles for the presidency.

That year, incumbent Martin Van Buren faced a serious challenge from Whig war hero William Henry Harrison. Having learned valuable lessons from Clay's recent defeats, Harrison forces wisely downplayed potentially divisive issues. In the country's first "log cabin and hard cider" campaign, the Whigs instead focused on the general's inspiring personal résumé, particularly his humble origins. Democrats in turn strove to transform Van Buren's reputation for craftiness into a political virtue. Lincoln actively electioneered for Harrison, Douglas for Van Buren—both often emphasizing superficial and emotional subjects that might sway undecided voters. For their parts, Douglas and Lincoln bridged the gap completely, while nationally many politicians with strong ties to local newspapers of their own did likewise. It was hard for a time to know which profession—politics or journalism—was originating party dogma, and which was merely advocating it.

Lincoln and Douglas did both. In addition to campaigning, they worked directly for newly launched campaign newspapers—"extras," as they were known at the time. When, that year, a new, temporary Democratic newspaper called *Old Hickory* in Jackson's honor began rolling off the presses at Springfield, Douglas saw no conflict in playing the concurrent roles of editor, letter writer, advocate, and, of course, political leader.

In February 1840, the *Old Hickory* published an article charging that Harrison had earned the Whig presidential nod only because timid supporters feared that perennial favorite Henry Clay would again prove unelectable. Knowing this claim was sure to irk longtime Clay admirer Lincoln, who in fact felt understandable guilt over switching his allegiance to Harrison, Douglas and other members of the Democratic State Committee made a show of calling personally at the hostile *Journal* office with screed in hand, proposing that the entire text now be republished in Simeon Francis's Whig paper.

While Francis refused the demand, to no one's surprise the pro-Douglas *Register* printed the piece in full just a few days later. Omitted from Douglas's ostensibly forthright request to the *Journal*, however (the text of which editor Walters featured along with the reprint), were the full details of the elaborate alliance that had inspired creation of the new Democratic extra in the first place. Readers of the time knew that Douglas was a prominent Van Buren man, but most probably did not know he was also one of the leading but unnamed "Democratic Citizens" responsible for founding and editing the *Old Hickory*, whose birth as a campaign organ had been promoted in—of course—the *Register*.[20]

Not that Lincoln was above embracing such overtly partisan press ventures. At the time, he was not only a member of the state's Whig State Central Committee, but also one of the principal backers of his party's own campaign extra: the *Old Soldier*. Named in tribute to Harrison, the paper openly aimed to energize the party faithful "into 'battle array'" for the approaching election. At first, Whigs hoped to keep publication plans secret for as long as possible in order to spring the new paper on a complacent opposition. The *Register*, however, got hold of a confidential circular detailing their plan, and gleefully reprinted it on January 31. Openly promising that its new publication would "be devoted exclusively to the *great cause* in which we are engaged," the notice urged that "every Whig in the State MUST take it," adding: "YOU MUST RAISE A FUND AND FORWARD US FOR EXTRA COPIES—every county ought to send FIFTY OR ONE HUNDRED DOLLARS,—and the copies will be forwarded to you for distribution among our POLITICAL OPPONENTS." Unmasked earlier than they hoped, the Whigs went forward with their effort anyway and launched the paper on February 1, at least getting a two-week jump on the opposition *Old Hickory*. Now the real press war began. By March 1, a delighted Lincoln could report: "Subscriptions to the 'Old Soldier' pour in without abatement. This morning I took from the post-office a letter from [state representative Jesse K.] Dubois inclosing the names of sixty subscribers; and carrying it to Francis, I found he had received one hundred and forty more from other quarters by the same day's mail. This is but an average specimen of every day's receipts." [21]

Openly identifying himself as one of the editors of the *Old Soldier* (he oddly likened his role to that of a "superintendent"), Lincoln provided a direct appeal on its pages, exhorting prospective readers "to aid us in filling its columns with such 'burning truths' and 'confounding arguments' as may sear the eye-balls, and stun the ears of the Old hero's thousand-tongued calumniators." This may have seemed tough language from the man who only a few years earlier had preached civility at the Young Men's Lyceum. In virtually the same breath, the paper vowed to publish no "*vile falsehood*" in the *Old Soldier*. Nothing would "appear in its columns, *as facts*, which we do not, on the fullest investigation in our power to make, believe to be true." [22] Its assaults against Van Buren (and Douglas) proliferated anyway. Lincoln later alluded to "the infernal Extra Register" to indicate that the opposition campaign sheet did no less in return. [23] In the era long before political action committees could buy time to air negative advertisements, these campaign extras served the very same purpose: providing a forum for merciless and often irresponsible attacks on the opposition.

The inevitable reprisals were not always limited to the printed page. They sometimes turned physical. The corpulent but feisty Simeon Francis was certainly no stranger to outright violence. A few years earlier the rotund editor had been "rudely assaulted in the street" by one Jacob M. Early, a hot-tempered local doctor-turned-preacher known in the community as the "fighting parson" because of his penchant for brawling, often in defense of the Democratic Party.[24] On the last day of February 1840, Douglas himself grew so agitated over Francis's recent articles—one of which likened the politician to a horse thief—that he launched a physical attack of his own against the much larger Whig editor on a busy Springfield street. The contest ended quickly and inconclusively, with little permanent damage to either combatant and much amusement for eyewitnesses. Lincoln found the episode droll enough to report to a friend the following morning: "Yesterday Douglas, having chosen to consider himself insulted by something in the 'Journal,' undertook to cane Francis in the street. Francis caught him, by the hair and jammed him back against a market-cart, where the matter ended by Francis being pulled away

from him. The whole affair was so ludicrous that Francis and everybody else (Douglas excepted) have been laughing about it ever since."

Douglas supporters resumed their own laughter soon enough. Declaring the overweight six-footer Francis as a "compound of *goose fat* and *sheep's wool*," the *Old Hickory* boasted that Douglas could never be "injured by the croaking of all the *Old Grannies* about the Journal office." Francis promptly retorted that he had actually escaped harm because the Little Giant's "stick was too heavy for him to wield, our head too high for him to hit,

Stephen A. Douglas—darling of Walters and the *Register*—his earliest known portrait, a painting by Charles Loring Elliott, ca. 1840.

or . . . he adopted a retreat too soon for his success." According to the *Journal*, Douglas "came, he saw, he got mad . . . he got a stick bigger than himself . . . his mighty hand raised the stick, and we received the blow upon an unoffending apple." [25] Their physical confrontation may have been over, but both men gleefully returned to exchanging vitriol on the pages of their party extras.

Although historian Mark Neely aptly labeled such campaign specials "the quintessence of early American journalistic art," the role they really played had little to do with the original art of journalism. [26] They were designed specifically to energize faithful voters to the polls, organize geographically scattered supporters around unifying themes, and raise funds to do more of both. They contained no advertising, only editorials and items related to the campaign. Not even the party-affiliated town papers could so brazenly devote *all* their space to politics. The campaign extras did so freely. But the parent papers still maintained involvement of their own. Just as the *Old Hickory* enjoyed promotion from the *Register,* the *Old Soldier* remained connected to the *Sangamo Journal*: the Whig extra was in fact printed on the very presses Simeon Francis owned and operated to print his Springfield weekly, and more than likely the *Old Hickory* shared printing facilities with the *Register*.

The additional business put much needed cash in the publisher's pocket at a time when the economy was so bad it was said that the *Journal* stayed above water only because of the income it collected by printing bankruptcy notices. As Simeon Francis confided to one of his brothers that September, he felt compelled to "toil at my profession until money is more plenty." Aside from Whig patronage, Springfield seemed to him "dull," with "nothing doing in the way of business." [27] Fighting the "cursed" Van Buren administration by assigning his presses to pro-Whig campaign extras generated money and not a little excitement. It suited Simeon's politics, too. Still filled with "enthusiasm" for the Whigs, Francis yearned for the day "Martin leaves the cage at Washington, which he has so long besmirched and dishonored. It will take some time for old Tip to rig and fix the ropes of the ship of state as they were before Jackson and Van took the helm—but I can see in the distance a brighter day for our country." [28]

For Francis, brighter days for the nation arrived sooner than he expected, although his impact on the race proved indecisive. Always dependent on busy election campaigns to get him past the lean years, by the end of 1840 his *Old Soldier* was reaching more Illinois readers than the *Journal* itself: eight thousand statewide. [29] "We have the numbers," Lincoln boasted, "and if properly organized and exerted, with the gallant HARRISON at our head, we shall meet our foes, and conquer them in all parts of the Union." [30]

In this prediction Lincoln proved incorrect. The war of words among the rival campaign extras, not to mention the openly partisan Springfield dailies, ended triumphantly for the Democrats, not the Whigs—at least statewide. A narrow 51–49 percent majority gave Van Buren Illinois's five electoral votes. But Harrison prevailed nationally, and headed to Washington to assume the presidency the following March. Barely a month after his inauguration, however, he disproved the famous adage that old soldiers never die. After braving the March wind to deliver his record-long inaugural address without benefit of a topcoat or hat, William Henry Harrison succumbed to bilious pleurisy, the first president to perish while in office, on April 4, 1841. Harrison's successor, Vice President John Tyler, was a former states' rights Democrat with weak ties to the Whig organization. If Tyler was a man without a party, the official Whig newspapers now regarded themselves as a party without a man.

Two years later, however, *Journal* editor Simeon Francis demonstrated that Tyler's unexpected ascendancy had sapped none of his (or his readers') enthusiasm for the vehicle of the campaign extra as a means of restoring party supremacy. For a mere off-year congressional election in the spring of 1843, Francis introduced yet another new, four-page *Extra Journal*, offering subscriptions at thirty-seven and a half cents apiece.[31] Along with endless reports of alleged violence directed against Whig papers upstate, its pages featured attacks not only on the Democrats, but on the rival *Register*, which it accused of "*Falsehood and Ignorance*," comparing its editors, William Walters and Charles Lanphier, to "sellers of 'ready-made clothing.'"[32] Here was another political press project that Lincoln, by then a regular visitor to the *Journal* office near Capitol Square, not to mention a frequent, uncredited contributor to its pages, surely knew about and endorsed.

Lincoln had never quite relinquished his concealed role as a contributor of rancorous editorial copy to the *Journal*. Of course, many neighbors and political allies knew of his second "career" as an anonymous editorial writer. In William Herndon's words, "Whatever he wrote, or had written, went into the editorial page without question."[33] In public he could remain the "good" Lincoln—advocating reverence for the laws. In print, without attribution, he could assume the role of "bad" Lincoln, excoriating Democrats in his recognizable sarcastic writing style. In one such instance, Lincoln came perilously close to the kind of violence he had mocked when Stephen Douglas was a protagonist a few years earlier. This time the dangerous episode involved not only Lincoln but his fiancée, Mary Todd, and, inevitably, editor Simeon Francis. Historians long searching for credible explanations of what brought the seemingly mismatched Abraham and Mary together have overlooked one obvious answer: the press. Aside from evident physical attraction, newspapers played a significant role in their love affair: the couple enjoyed not only reading them, but contributing to them as well—almost always anonymously and sometimes recklessly. They both seemed to relish the danger.

Still, their relationship proved rocky. For reasons still unknown, the lovers broke off their engagement on or just before January 1, 1841, sending each into a prolonged depression. In more ways than one, it was the local Whig paper that ultimately brought them back together. For one thing, editor Francis and his wife facilitated a reconciliation by making their comfortable Springfield home available for courting when the two began seeing each other again the following year. There, Abraham and Mary probably hatched the plan to compose what came to be known as the "Rebecca" letters, a series of heavy-handed satires aimed at Illinois's Democratic state auditor James W. Shields, and all published, of course, in Francis's *Journal*.[34] The Irish-born Shields had recently infuriated Whigs with a ruling that devalued state banknotes, even for citizens hoping to use them at face value to pay their taxes. Lincoln's response came in the form of at least one of the barbed critiques, all crafted as mock letters from an outraged pioneer widow named "Rebecca," and all mercilessly lambasting Shields not only as a deceiver of the poor but as a malodorous popinjay. "Shields is a fool as well as a liar," the August 27 "letter" charged. "With him truth is out of the question, and as for getting a good bright passable lie out of him, you might as well try to strike fire from a cake of tallow."[35]

The personal attacks infuriated the thin-skinned Shields, and his anger only intensified when this latest "Rebecca" letter was followed into the pages of the *Journal* by a lacerating, unsigned poem admittedly composed by Mary and one of her lady friends, asserting, with no shortage of anti-Irish contempt, that the fictional old "Rebecca" had fallen for Shields: "Ye jews-harps awake! The A[uditor]'s won— / Rebecca, the widow, has gained Erin's son. / The pride of the north from the emerald isle / Has been woo'd and won by a woman's sweet smile"—"*very* silly lines" she carried off to "the daily paper."[36]

For Shields, this proved the limit. The auditor stormed into the *Journal* headquarters to demand that Simeon Francis identify the author of all the calumnies he had so recklessly published. After waiting a few days for things to cool down—they did not—the editor summoned Lincoln to his office and asked him how best to respond. As Mary proudly remembered, her future husband "felt, he could do, no less, than be my champion." Gallantly, Lincoln instructed Francis to give his name away as the sole author. He alone "would be responsible"—for the poem and letters alike.[37] On September 17, the aggrieved Shields responded to this revelation by sending Lincoln a letter of his own, entirely lacking in the comic, demanding "a full, positive and absolute retraction of all offensive allusions" inflicted by the victim of what Shields called "your secret hostility." That same day, Lincoln wrote a maddeningly legalistic reply complaining that "without stopping to enquire whether I really am the author, or to point out what is offensive . . . you demand an unqualified retraction. . . . Now, sir, there is in this so much assumption of facts, and so much of menace as to consequences, that I cannot submit to answer that note any farther than I have."[38]

Understandably dissatisfied, Shields responded with typical frontier bravado and challenged Lincoln to a duel. Days later, the two men actually headed off to "Bloody Island," a strip of land in the Mississippi River, technically part of the state of Missouri where dueling was legal. There they came shockingly close to facing off in deadly combat—and all over newspaper articles. Lincoln saved the day—and, perhaps, his life as well—by exercising a challenged party's right to choose weapons and proposing outsized broadswords that would have put the much shorter Shields at a disadvantage. Their seconds then arranged a truce and the duel never occurred, but the episode may at last have dissuaded Lincoln from further forays into published satire. It also bound the two lovers together, perhaps closer than ever. Just a few weeks after the incident, Abraham and Mary Lincoln were wed—a marriage in a real sense forged in partisan journalism.

By one account, wedlock and the passage of time soon emboldened Lincoln to believe he might have won the fight with Shields after all. "I could have split him from the crown of his head to the end of his backbone," the bridegroom allegedly boasted to his law partner about the aborted duel.[39] In a somewhat less nostalgic frame of mind, Mary recalled years later that her husband "thought, he had some right, to assume to be *my* champion, even on frivolous occasions." She added that she and her husband were "always so ashamed" of the "foolish and uncalled for *rencontre*" that "Mr L & myself mutually agreed, never to refer to it & except in an occasional light manner, between us, it was never mentioned" again.[40]

During the Civil War, a Union general appeared one day at a White House reception and, in Mary's words, "said, playfully, to my husband 'Mr. President, is it true, as I have heard that you, once went out, to fight a duel & all for the sake, of the lady by your side.' Mr. Lincoln, with a flushed face, replied, 'I do not deny it, but if you desire my friendship, you will never mention it again.'" When, on another occasion, one of the actual "participants of the affair" turned up in Washington and similarly attempted to get Lincoln to "rehearse the particulars" of the episode, a "sore" president again demurred, complaining: "That man is trying to revive his memory of a matter that I am trying to forget." As Mary put it: "This affair, always annoyed my husband's peaceful nerves."[41]

At the time it happened, the "matter," or "affair," certainly demonstrated to the future bridegroom that there were better, and safer, ways for a busy politician to use newspapers to his advantage. Not that Lincoln or the Whig press ever lost their zeal for energetically attacking Democrats in print—and vice versa.

Horace Greeley had meanwhile been busy in the newspaper world as well—but not yet profitably. He had tried establishing a printing business in New York in partnership with one Francis V. Story, press foreman at the successful sport and entertainment weekly *Spirit of the Times*. But their joint enterprise died not long after Story drowned in the East River. Still the ambitious Greeley would not give up. In 1834, after failing with his quickly aborted *Morning Post*, the thrifty, abstemious twenty-three-year-old dreamer, still as cherubic-looking as the day he left his father's farm, but now thinner than at any time in his life, somehow cobbled together $1,500, found a new partner in Jonas Winchester, and launched an ambitious sixteen-page weekly of his own. He called it the *New-Yorker*.[42]

Headquartered on bustling Nassau Street in the heart of Manhattan's publishing center, the paper proposed to offer "general literature" without the "humbug."[43] This promise the *New-Yorker* kept—publishing fiction by Charles Dickens and Edgar Allan Poe as well as essays on science, government, and other "questions of absorbing national interest." Auburn-based bookseller James Cephas (J.C.) Derby, who became its upstate distribution agent, noted appreciatively that the *New-Yorker* "seemed to fill a void for . . . readers who were inclined to well-written, original articles."[44] In one year its circulation rose from fifty to 4,500. Greeley hardly became rich, but felt himself successful enough, at least, to resist an 1835 invitation from James Gordon Bennett that they join in partnership to found a new penny daily. Bennett, after all, was not only irascible; he had spent just enough time covering news in South Carolina, Greeley sensed, to regard slavery with the smug satisfaction of a plantation master.[45]

At first striving to be nonpartisan, the *New-Yorker* editor could not resist politics for long. Greeley found himself increasingly attracted to Whig philosophy, especially once financial reverses threatened the survival of his unaffiliated paper. To Greeley, Whig economics promised the best path toward not only national—but personal—recovery. And Whig fealty offered access to political inner circles where Greeley felt ever more comfortable. Fortuitously, one of the party's most prominent leaders had caught wind of Greeley's growing Whig leanings: the shrewd political wire-puller Thurlow Weed, who ran the influential *Albany Evening Journal* while managing upstate New York's Whig Party machine.[46] Although a onetime publisher's apprentice himself who insisted he was but a "poor printer . . . on the same footing with Mr. Greeley," Weed was by then successful and powerful. A former New York state assemblyman, the party boss had already helped engineer the election of a handpicked state senator—his protégé William H. Seward—and now planned to promote Seward for governor of New York by establishing a temporary State Committee campaign newspaper. To run it, he wanted someone with both "principles" and "talents"—the very words he used to describe Horace Greeley, whom he had yet to meet. And Greeley, who admitted he had "struggled on in the face of imminent bankruptcy" for years, desperately needed a well-financed patron to rescue his own paper from ruin.[47]

One November day in 1837, Weed strode unannounced into the *New-Yorker*'s attic office in search of the idealist he sensed might now make an ideal party editor. There at the type racks, setting up the next issue for printing, one letter at a time, he encountered for the first time a "young man with light hair and blond complexion, with coat off and sleeves rolled up," as Weed described him. "This youth was Horace Greeley."[48] Weed fervently made his pitch. It succeeded. In part to save his own struggling publication, Greeley accepted the part-time Albany job Weed offered that day, which came with a much needed annual stipend of $1,000. "Weed took in Greeley when the rascal had not two pair of breeches to his legs," rival James Gordon Bennett scoffed, "and gave him a clean shirt, a good dinner, and a new pair of boots."[49] The *New-Yorker* proprietor may indeed have accepted Weed's "clean shirt" out of desperation to save his own enterprise, but the move marked a turning point in Greeley's career for another reason: the formerly independent journalist became, in a sense, owned and operated by the Whig Party, devoted now to shaping and supporting the organization's future. On that day, Greeley embraced the inevitable alliance between politics and the press—and their dependence on each other for survival and influence.

Editing two newspapers, in two different cities, one of them a party-run operation, may not have afflicted Greeley's conscience, but it severely tested his stamina. Every Saturday, he steamed up the Hudson aboard a riverboat, labored in Albany to put the Weed paper to bed by Tuesday night, then took a night boat back to Manhattan and went immediately to work to get the *New-Yorker* out by Friday. As soon as he prepared copy for his latest edition, Greeley packed his "valise for Albany again."[50] Yet in the rigorous grind of putting out a party newspaper, Greeley became a better journalist.

Though the new campaign paper, the *Jeffersonian*, soon achieved a circulation of some fifteen thousand readers, Greeley came to believe that his ponderous early articles wearied or offended most of them. "There is nothing that bores people like instruction," he confided to a friend. "It implies that they do not know everything already, which is very humiliating." Perhaps with an eye on Jamie Bennett's successful self-promotion, he admitted: "I have not done enough for effect." But Weed heartily approved of his new editor: "He was unselfish, conscientious, public spirited, and patriotic. He had no habits or tastes but for work, steady, indomitable work."[51] When the *Jeffersonian* folded as scheduled in early 1839, with Seward now governor, Greeley returned to the *New-Yorker* full-time. Widened visibility and capital infusion notwithstanding, however, profits still eluded him.

Again Weed came to the rescue, this time inviting Greeley to take charge of a newer, bigger version of the *Jeffersonian*: the *Log Cabin,* a Harrison-for-president campaign extra to be published by the Whig State Committee for the 1840 presidential race and distributed throughout the Northeast. Again Greeley accepted, and went back to work as a party editor—the equivalent of today's campaign strategists and spokesmen. Having learned much from his previous experience with the *Jeffersonian*, Greeley made sure the new venture emphasized the rousing hullabaloo spirit of the Harrison effort. Readers—who eventually numbered an unprecedented eighty thousand—were treated to song lyrics and stories about parades, rallies, and the ceremonial construction of log cabins. Greeley illustrated the paper with woodcuts depicting Harrison's battle triumphs, and filled it to overflowing with exuberant if dubious reports of steady Whig gains in keenly contested states. It was even rumored that Greeley invented the unforgettable motto, "Tippecanoe and Tyler, too!" Passing harsh judgment on the endeavor, Philadelphia journalist John Wein Forney thought the paper something of an embarrassment to its editor. Forney called the *Log Cabin* "a model and guide to those who desire to make merry at the Philosopher's expense," employing the competition's latest nickname for the intellectual Greeley. But Weed lauded the product as both "zealous" and "spirited." It certainly helped Harrison carry New York against Van Buren, the state's onetime governor.[52]

It also emboldened Greeley to aspire for the first time to political reward outside journalism. Earlier in his career, he had criticized editors who expected patronage jobs in exchange for party fealty. But when opportunity presented itself in the afterglow of the Harrison victory, Greeley emphatically expressed his belief that "not many had done more effective work on the canvass than I had."[53] At least briefly he considered making a formal request for an appointment. In an absurd burst of overconfidence, he aimed as high as the president's cabinet. "Two or three papers have named me for *Postmaster General*," he crowed to one intimate, though in the same breath he insisted he wanted "none of their dirty spoils." To Governor Seward, however, he bitterly complained when he was not immediately "counted in," and soon enough he was blaming Thurlow Weed for ignoring him, too. Weed, who claimed he initially believed Greeley "indifferent to the temptations of money and office," later scoffed that "had Governor Seward known . . . that Mr. Greeley coveted an inspectorship, he certainly would have received it." Though Greeley would remain politically aligned with Seward and Weed for years to come, the editor's revenge, as had been the case with the spurned Bennett before him, came now through the creation of a bigger, better, and more independent Whig newspaper that would eventually surpass Weed's own.[54] In short, Greeley determined to become a political power himself. He decided to found yet another newspaper.

"I had been incited to this enterprise by several Whig friends," Greeley wrote of the new venture, "who deemed a cheap daily, addressed more especially to the laboring class, eminently needed in our city, where the only two cheap journals then . . . existing—the *Sun* and the *Herald*—were in decided though unavowed, and therefore more effective sympathy and affiliation with the Democratic Party."[55] In April 1841, boasting only five hundred advance subscribers (mostly "warm personal and political friends," he admitted), a staff of ten whose salaries he could not afford, a rented printing press, and a modest new office on Ann Street—and burdened with staggering new debts from the loan he procured to pay for it all—Horace Greeley published the first issue of the *New York Tribune.* His "folding and mailing," he later joked, "must have staggered me but for the circumstance that I had few papers to mail, and not many to fold." At age thirty, its editor was "in full health and vigor" and by his own unselfconscious description already "favorably known to many thousands."[56]

What Greeley lacked most—cash—he quickly attracted to the enterprise. Within months, he took on a new partner, a successful book distributor and party loyalist named Thomas McElrath, to handle the business side. He openly called the move essential to "strengthen the *Tribune* in the confidence and affections of the Whigs of New York." For his part, Greeley's savvy new partner saw a commercial opportunity. Convinced that the *Sun* and *Herald,* while popular among "business men and clerks," had not "very often penetrated into the parlors or sitting rooms of the uptown residents." Acknowledging the importance of "the patronage of a political party," McElrath also believed that "a circulation in the cultivated and influential families of the city was quite as important"—and here the investor saw a niche for the new *Tribune.*[57] McElrath's crucial $2,000 financial infusion freed Greeley from pecuniary worries, except, he admitted, when he imprudently lent money to bounders.[58] Under McElrath's management, the publication offered neither subscriptions nor advertisements on credit, requiring every reader "to pay for whatever he chose to order." The *Tribune,* Greeley proudly recalled, required no further investment, "except through the liberality of its patrons."[59]

From the very start, the new, one-cent paper's earnest though occasionally indiscriminate public spiritedness struck readers as fresh and appealing—somewhat like medicine, occasionally distasteful but usually good for them. Its prospectus boldly described the *Tribune* as nothing less than "a New Morning Journal of Politics, Literature, and General Intelligence" that would "advance the interests of the people, and . . . promote their Moral, Political and Social well-being." Along with Whig Party interests, it advocated workers' rights, improved status for women, temperance, and utopian social improvement. With a bold swipe at the *Herald,* Greeley pledged that "the immoral and degrading Police Reports, Advertisements, and other matter which have been allowed to disgrace the columns of our leading Penny Papers, will be carefully excluded." The *Tribune* would be "a welcome visitant at the family fireside."[60]

The editor's "leading idea," he declared, "was the establishment of a journal removed alike from servile partisanship on the one hand and from gagged, mincing neutrality on the other. Party spirit is so fierce and intolerant in this country that the editor of a non-partisan sheet is restrained from saying what he thinks and feels on the most vital, imminent topics." Democratic and Whig journals alike, Greeley knew, were "generally expected to praise or blame, like or dislike, eulogize or condemn, in precise accordance with the views and interest of its party. I believed there was a happy medium between these extremes." The editor pledged to remain loyal to his party's "guiding convictions," but also "ready to expose and condemn unworthy conduct or incidental error." Hewing to this credo for the rest of his career, Greeley would come to be seen as an unpredictable, undependable gadfly by governors and presidents, but as an incorruptibly honest and freedom-loving wise man to his devoted readers.[61]

Yet Greeley nearly went out of business on that very first day. Eight years earlier, the maiden issue of his *Morning Post* had reached city streets just as the boulevards all but vanished beneath a swirling New Year's Day snowstorm. Now a surprise April blizzard once again blanketed the city, as a result of which most of the *Tribune's* initial run of five thousand copies went unsold. No doubt feeling himself cursed, Greeley bravely soldiered on. One of his chief assets, he believed, was his talented staff of young writers, especially the eager twenty-year-old from the *New-Yorker* he began training as his right-hand man. This particular novice, Henry J. Raymond, future editor of the *New York Times*, would serve at the *Tribune* for some thirty-six months.

Rapidly, the *New York Tribune* found both its voice and its audience. Smaller in size than the blanket sheets and attractively priced as well, its crusading spirit moreover captured a growing mood for reform. Most subscribers forgave the fact that Greeley was irresistibly drawn to fringe movements like Fourierism, named for a French socialist who advocated the creation of classless "Harmony" communes. Skeptics had a field day tormenting Greeley as "Horatius the Fourierite."[62] Such criticism did not inhibit Greeley from advocating his "new and original" plan for social reorder. Eschewing what he dismissed as "piece-meal reform," Greeley also embraced a broad socialist program he called "Association, or Principles of a True Organization of Society." It would, he vowed in a front-page column in 1842, "correct the

Frauds, Extortions, Monopolies, and Adulterations of Commerce," not to mention "the Tricks and Injustice of the Law" that political parties were unwilling to address. Greeley's concept of "Attractive Industry and Association," promised to do away with "vice, crime, drunkenness and brutality" through education, and eliminate the "Drudgery and Degradation of Labor" by "uniting Labor and Capital in the same hands." Quick to grasp the commercial threat posed by Greeley's upstart venture, Moses Beach's *New York Sun* resolved to "crush" the new paper by bribing—and when that failed, publicly whipping—newsboys to discourage them from hawking the *Tribune* on the city's streets. When the circulation war escalated, the usually peaceful Greeley dispatched thugs of his own to retaliate violently. At one point Beach himself was seen on the streets trading blows with the "emissaries" hired by the new competition. Somehow the *Tribune* weathered the attempts to destroy it. Readers flocked to buy copies because they immediately sensed that Greeley's paper offered twice the news for the same price.[63]

Greeley's sudden emergence as a journalistic rival prompted a resentful James Gordon Bennett to commence an acrimonious feud with his new competitor—a battle that would last for a quarter of a century. When, for example, the *Tribune* began preaching social change in the early 1840s, the *Herald* proudly defended America as it was, boasting that its unmatched circulation and advertising numbers showed that patriotic New Yorkers agreed that major upheaval was unnecessary. In 1844, Bennett published a supplement offering his "regular and respectable subscribers" (as opposed to the *Tribune*'s "street buyers and loafer purchasers") an unprecedented package of rare Western news. He could not resist accompanying the bonus with a notice that managed to include both a self-congratulatory reminder of the *Herald*'s popularity and a subtle swipe at Greeley's slavish party loyalty and his frequent dissatisfaction with the status quo. "We are enabled to go to the expense of doing so," ran the *Herald* announcement,

> from the extraordinary patronage and popularity which the American people, through this wide Republic generously bestow on a fearless, honest, independent and truthtelling newspaper, bound to no party, but above all parties. At this moment our circulation is equal, if not greater, than *two-thirds of the whole daily newspaper press of New York*. This great fact, alone, indicates the mighty intellectual and moral revolution now going on in the public mind of this most wonderful nation;—a nation—a people now in the first throes of civilization,

higher and holier—wider and deeper—more massive and mightier than the old world ever imagined or knew.[64]

Only an editor with Bennett's craft and brass could manage to praise and insult his readers at the same time.

The Bennett-Greeley feud exploded into open warfare during the bitter 1844 Henry Clay–James K. Polk presidential campaign. The *Tribune* supported Whig Clay and the *Herald* endorsed Democrat Polk, with each publisher not only editorializing, but appearing at campaign events to stump for the candidate of his choice. "Poor Horace!" chortled Bennett a few weeks after Polk won the White House. "His whig friends wont listen to the voice of the charmer, and as they refuse to be comforted, coolly turn round upon him and aver that his sad miscalculations of the strength and prospects of the whigs blinded them to their danger, and had no small influence in producing their defeat."[65] The *Herald* added injury to insult by publishing a gloatingly satirical poem, "The Last Procession," which described in dirgelike meter a "sullen" funeral march for Clay's dead campaign whose mourners included the grieving *Tribune* editor: "And as along the dusky way / its darkening course it kept, / Beside it with his Clay 'Tribune,' / Poor Greeley walked and wept."[66]

The attacks did not abate after Polk's victory. Dismissing Greeley as an addled and dangerously indiscriminate do-gooder, Bennett assigned the *Tribune* editor such disrespectful monikers as "our amiable contemporary philosopher" or "the man in the white coat," a reference to his fondness for light-colored dusters.[67] Whenever Greeley responded in kind, the *Herald* dropped the coy name-calling and unleashed furious salvos of invective. After Greeley published a rueful commentary on the late presidential election, charging the *Herald* with "misrepresentation of every whig principle and measure," Bennett denounced Greeley for exhibiting a "total depravity" typical of the party press and "promulgating . . . miserable subterfuge . . . gross fabrications . . . forgeries, and frauds of all kinds."[68] Greeley in turn charged that Bennett had joked during a Pennsylvania campaign swing that he "had no care" about leaving his New York office to give speeches because "it had been hired for the campaign by the locofocos." Outraged, but keenly aware that readers found such squabbles irresistible, Bennett replied in print that Greeley was guilty of nothing less than "licentiousness," and demanded that the editor produce an eyewitness or admit he lacked "reputation" and "character."[69]

Not to be outdone, when Bennett commenced his long and ugly new feud with John Hughes, the Catholic bishop of New York, Greeley republished Hughes's long, angry letter identifying Bennett as "the first and persevering chief" of his "assailants" and "calumniators."[70] This did nothing to inhibit Bennett from charging in turn that Greeley was growing increasingly "bewildered." He "twists and turns like a fish thrown ashore by a chance wave," chortled the *Herald,* "with its belly up, tossing and tumbling on the sandy beach." Although the *Herald* dutifully reported one of Greeley's well-received campaign speeches at a Whig rally at City Hall, it gloated that he had been barely audible to the rowdy crowd. "Alas! Poor Yorick!" Bennett further gloated after the *Tribune* inadvertently misidentified a U.S. senator in one of its reports on congressional debates. "Greeley had better devote the remainder of his days to the culture of vegetables and Fourierism."[71]

Above all, Bennett loved taunting Greeley whenever the *Tribune* founder launched an esoteric new crusade for the betterment of mankind. When Greeley began consoling himself after Clay's loss by advancing another experimental new idea, Bennett crowed: "Horace in this dilemma has taken himself to philosophy, and has engaged one of the most distinguished Swedenborgians in the country to enlighten the readers of the *Tribune,* while he himself pays some attention to Fourrierism [*sic*], which has latterly been in rather a declining state, whilst the chief apostle was engaged in saving the country."[72] After the *Herald* discovered in late 1844 that the *Tribune* editor had endorsed "water cures," it promptly reported "the newest favorite idea of Philosopher Greeley" under the headline: "HORACE GREELEY'S LATEST ENTHUSIASM."

When Greeley embraced a bran-heavy diet as the ultimate path to a purer immortality, Bennett sarcastically warned that even cleansed by bran into nothing more than an "aroma," dead Whigs might one day return in "their original elements of rowdyism and brandy-smashers."[73] "The world is an excellent world," the *Herald* editorialized in early 1845. "It is a happy world. It is clothed with beauty." By criticizing all of society, rather than those who violated its laws, Greeley was attempting to reorder God's plan. In Bennett's view, his rival's "new philosophies" promised "a system founded on gloomy, distorted, and morbid views of human nature." Greeley and his "ilk," charged Bennett, "act like the wicked men in the scripture who, when asked for bread, give the starving applicant a stone."[74]

Greeley's passion for pet social theories, all routinely plumped in the *Tri-*

bune, did not prevent him from participating with gusto in the city's rowdy newspaper wars. In print, he continued to give as good as he got. The *Herald*, he declared in one such outburst, was best suited to "houses of depravity." Bennett returned this particular volley by calling the "unmitigated blockhead" Greeley a "miserable dried vegetable" no more capable to edit a paper than "a large New England squash."[75] Jumping into the fray, the *New York Sun* declared its new competitor guilty of writing "dirty, malignant, and wholesale" falsehoods, and suggested that Greeley "go to school and learn a little decency."[76]

Mere mockery never inhibited Greeley from taking up faddish causes. He advocated trust-busting, profit sharing, gender equality, Sabbatarianism (the rigorous observance of the day of rest), utopian socialism, and the liberal Transcendentalist movement (placing one of its strongest early voices, Margaret Fuller, on his staff as a book critic, and later giving her local and foreign assignments, making her one of the first females in New York given a chance to write on nondomestic matters).[77] Greeley even embraced the then radical idea of labor unions.

Ever the optimist, he stressed his incurable belief in "the essential Harmony of Interests,"[78] and flaunted his personal commitment to spiritual and physical well-being—"temperance in all things," as he put it—by preaching the sanctity of marriage and (like Lincoln) disdaining liquor and tobacco (occasionally reminding readers of his own nightmares about a repellent chore from his boyhood: lighting his mother's foul pipe for her evening smoke). For a time, he eschewed red meat and took up residence in a Grahamite rooming house (named for dietary innovator Sylvester Graham) where hard drink, constrictive clothing, and sexual urges were all discouraged. Greeley also embraced the growing rage for spiritualism—widely derided by nonbelievers as paganistic fakery.[79] His onetime employer Thurlow Weed could not help chortling over such *Tribune* obsessions as "'table-rappings,' 'Brook farms,' and various 'isms' by which Mr. Greeley was from time to time misled." Greeley shrugged off such scorn by grandly contending: "The tombs of dead prophets are built only of the stones hurled at them while living."[80]

Besides, not all of Greeley's proposals proved irrelevant or impractical. When, for example, the editor pressed city fathers to create a "House of Industry" to teach useful job skills to indigent young people, philanthropists soon took up the cause as well. A privately funded school bearing just that name soon opened in New York's most horrific slum, the notorious "Five

Points." [81] Greeley's unrelenting commitment to civic improvement won him many famous admirers, most of whom applauded his energy even while acknowledging his impatience. And his sincere opposition to slavery earned appreciation from the abolitionist movement. In 1846, when Greeley reprinted a letter from Ireland that abolitionist Frederick Douglass had published in the antislavery movement's principal press organ, the *Liberator,* during his recent European speaking tour, the African-American leader wrote to thank the *Tribune* editor "for the deep and lively interest you have been pleased to take in the cause of my long neglected race." Douglass was sorry to hear that Greeley's "immediate neighbors are very much displeased with you, for this act of kindness to myself, and the cause of which I am an humble advocate." But he felt certain—overoptimistically, as it turned out—that Greeley's enthusiasm was one of those "indications on the part of the press—which, happily are multiplying through all the land—that kindle up within me an ardent hope that the curse of slavery will not much longer be permitted to make its iron foot-prints in the lacerated hearts of my sable brethren." [82]

When Ralph Waldo Emerson came to New York for a lecture swing of his own, he accepted an invitation to dinner—vegetarian, of course—at Greeley's dwelling, and then wrote to Margaret Fuller to share his conflicting impressions. "Greeley is a young man with white soft hair from New Hampshire, mother of men," Emerson wrote, "of sanguine temper & liberal mind, no scholar but such a one as journals & newspapers make, who listens after all new thoughts & things, but with the indispensable New York condition that they can be made available. . . . He declares himself a Transcendentalist, is a Unitarian, a defender of miracles, &c[.] I saw my fate in a moment & that I should never content him." [83] Rather envious of his growing influence over growing numbers of Americans, Emerson complained that Greeley "does all their thinking and theory for them, for two dollars a year." [84]

Whatever his quirky facade, Greeley was not only capable and self-assured, but determined to do nothing less than reinvent daily journalism (and the American way of life in the bargain). The *Tribune* could not yet compete against the penny dailies' profitable stranglehold on advertising (some whispered that the *Herald* and *Sun* extorted paid notices from their seamier advertisers by threatening to expose them to the police). So Greeley focused on amassing paid subscribers, and offering them promptly and reliably reported government news, abetted by scoops provided by friends in Governor Seward's administration, together with treatises on social and moral improvement.

To some, the overzealous Greeley seemed a humbug. But behind the mask of the lofty ideologue he was a shrewd newspaper professional who worked endless hours to ensure success. "I am not now . . . Editorial Manager of the Tribune office," he protested years later. "I am a writer of Editorials."[85] But at the beginning, Greeley was a true managerial innovator. To get news first from Boston, Greeley used a flock of carrier pigeons. To make sure stories from the state capital of Albany could be reported quickly, he arranged for compositors to ride the Hudson River steamers heading south to Manhattan, ordering them to typeset political speeches while still on board so they could be rushed into print as soon as the boats docked.[86] He began collaborating with the blanket sheets to forge a network of pony express, steamboat, and railroad to deliver pooled news more quickly.

Greeley also hired superb journalists and gave them room to express themselves and learn the business. At one point, his glittering staff of writers and associate editors included not only Raymond and Fuller, but literary critics George Ripley and Herbert Bayard Taylor, music critic William Henry Fry, and correspondent Charles A. Dana, who eventually became managing editor. Greeley even convinced Henry David Thoreau to write for him, and though the submission disappointingly proved "not in the Reformist vein," the editor proudly told a friend that at least it was "full of Poetry and Nature."[87] Wary of the fact that Greeley had "no education at all, except what he had acquired himself," fellow Transcendentalist (and Fourierite) Dana, who had attended Harvard, held that the "worst education that a man can be sent to, and the worst of all for a man of genius, is what is called a self education." Yet to Dana's amazement, the publisher's "wit and his humor flowed out in idiomatic forms of expression that were surprising and delightful."[88]

When, like Bennett before him, Greeley was forced from his maiden headquarters by fire (which in this case nearly spread to the *Sun*), he brushed off the disaster as a mere nuisance and despite $8,000 in uninsured losses soon moved the *Tribune* into expanded space on nearby Nassau Street.[89] Again like Bennett, he used the relocation to promote the paper's durability. But it was his earnest editorial writing that set Greeley—and the *Tribune*—apart. Dedicated to providing his readers more than "a dry summary" of "the most interesting occurrences of the day," Greeley aimed at creating "a newspaper, in the higher sense of the term." As he explained it: "We need to know, not only what is done, but what is purposed and said, by those who sway the destinies of states and realms."[90]

The brilliant staff of the *New York Tribune* in the 1840s: from left to right, financial correspondent George Snow; music writer William H. Fry; literary critic Herbert Bayard Taylor; managing editor Charles A. Dana; editor Horace Greeley; assistant editor Henry J. Raymond (who had already left the paper); and literary editor George Ripley.

Perhaps most effectively of all, Greeley transformed himself into a genuinely original New York character: an eccentric humanitarian dreamer who conveniently looked the part, topping his ghostly pale, prematurely balding head with dented top hats and ambling through town in scuffed boots and ink-stained white dusters whose pockets overflowed with scraps of paper. He earned renown as a "great wit," one upstate newspaperman fondly remembered, who "said cute things because he could not help it." [91] His public appearances often sold out, but even an admirer like fellow temperance advocate Theodore Cuyler conceded that Greeley's weak voice and "quaint queer way" usually elicited a "titter" from audiences before his earnest logic lured them into rapt attentiveness "tight as in a vice." [92]

When not working at the paper or making speeches to spread its gospel and fame—along with his own—the myopic daydreamer might be spotted wandering Manhattan's boulevards aimlessly, it seemed, his clothes disheveled and his posture stooped, apparently lost in abstract thoughts. One of his most persistent enemies, James Fenimore Cooper, the celebrated novelist who sued him more than once for libel (winning $200 in one such judgment), joked that Greeley was "so rocking in gait that he walks down both sides of the street at once." [93]

Whether the image of homespun philosopher was carefully calculated or the product of authentic idiosyncrasy, it certainly helped Greeley to promote himself and his newspaper, and to arouse the jealousy of his competitors. Accusing him of dangerous "tomfooleries," his broadsheet rival James Watson Webb once fumed of Greeley: "He lays claim to greatness by wandering through the streets with a hat double the size of his head, a coat after the fashion of Jacob's of old, with one leg of his pantaloons inside and the other outside of his boot, and with boots all bespattered with mud, or, possibly, a shoe on one foot and a boot on the other, and glorying in an unwashed and unshaven person." [94]

But Greeley was much more than a caricature—as often as he began appearing as such in period cartoons that typically depicted him as a windmill-tilter. In one sense the editor exuded a carefully crafted humility, once urging people to come early to one of his lectures at Cooper Union so they could obtain seats close enough to hear his all but inaudible voice. Yet his modest affect masked a burning faith in his abilities and opinions. He may have portrayed himself as a careless-looking farmer's son eager to experiment with panaceas for the betterment of mankind, but his seeming guilelessness masked the reality of a tirelessly ambitious and self-assured, some said self-centered, professional. As a later employee put it, Greeley "knew no language but his own, but of that he possessed the most extraordinary mastery." [95] Whoever the real Greeley was—crusader, crank, or both—he emerged by the late 1840s as one of the ablest and most outspoken young newspapermen not only in New York, but also in the country. At decade's end, the *New York Tribune* came close to equaling the robust circulation of the *New York Herald*: an astounding thirty thousand a day. Beginning in September 1842, Greeley, like Bennett before him, also began publishing a weekly synopsis edition available for a dollar a year to readers across the country—later to include among its 200,000 subscribers a rising politician in distant Illinois named Abraham Lincoln.

In a sense, both these editors—the outrageous, shoot-from-the-hip Bennett and the earnest, do-good gadfly Greeley—triumphed in mid-century New York journalism because they had more in common professionally than either would have admitted. They were both brilliant writers, willing not only to cover but create the news. And they were high-strung, unrepentant individualists, both set somewhat apart from conventional society: Bennett the cunning, foreign-born, mercenary rogue and Greeley the airy, experimental do-gooder. Though they differed dramatically in personality, detested each other with a vengeance, and shared nothing but their passion for journalism, in their fierce pride in their outsider status and in their power to influence the masses while thumbing their noses at the rich and powerful, they were frighteningly alike. It was no accident that their talent made each rich and powerful himself.

Professional illustrators of the day, whose work could uncannily capture, and sometimes influence, public attitudes, were quick to catch on to the two editors' potential as contrasting artistic prototypes—one representing the more sinister aspect of the newspaper business, the other its crusading side. A representative cartoon of the day—conceivably the first ever to depict rivals Greeley and Bennett together—showed the *Herald* proprietor outdistancing his younger competitor in the race for a lucrative Post Office printing contract (a reminder that newspapers of the day did furious battle over outside

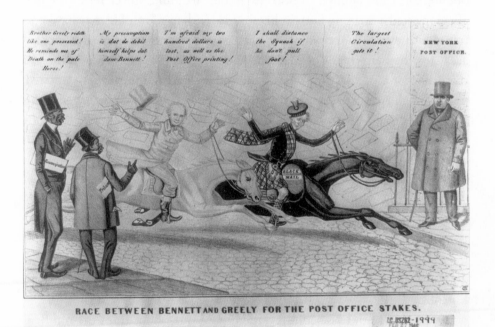

Greeley (left) and Bennett race for the "Post Office Stakes," in an 1843 cartoon mocking the rival editors' unseemly competition for a lucrative printing contract.

publishing jobs as well as politics). The circa 1843 lithograph presented the *Tribune* editor as a translucent ghost astride a reformer's symbolic white steed, a battered hat falling away to reveal a prematurely receding hairline. ("He reminds me of Death on the Pale Horse," comments a well-dressed African-American bystander in the foreground, a none too subtle suggestion that Greeley's readership was composed of dangerous abolitionists and overprivi-leged free blacks; his less elegant companion agrees—in dialect—"My pre-sumption is dat de debil himself helps dat dam Bennett!"). An extravagantly cross-eyed and hook-nosed Bennett, by contrast, is portrayed riding a black charger, and, to remind viewers of his alien status, wearing a kilt, plaid tartan sash, and Scottish tam o'shanter, boasting he has outraced "The Squash" in the race toward the New York Post Office. "The largest circulation gets it!" comments an indifferent postmaster. The saddlebag on Bennett's horse tells a different story about the competition. In a blistering indictment of Bennett's ethics, it is labeled: "Black Mail." [96]

Throughout their long competition for readership and influence, Greeley remained much more the faithful party man than Bennett, though neither editor was ever reluctant to admit disappointment when he felt his orga-nization had chosen an inferior political nominee. During the presidential election of 1844, Bennett's *Herald* endorsed Democrat James Polk, but not before charging that "a more ridiculous, contemptible, and forlorn candidate was never put forth by any party." [97] That year, the *Tribune* editor threw "heart and soul" into the doomed campaign for Henry Clay (a politician whom Greeley, like Lincoln, "profoundly loved"). [98] Polk triumphed in New York state as well as nationally, but soon enough the new president handed Greeley an issue with which to launch yet another crusade: a controversial war with Mexico in which victory almost guaranteed the expansion of American slave territory.

For the next two years, Greeley railed against Polk and his divisive Mexican adventure, while Bennett cheered both. By the end of 1847, more powerful than ever, Greeley had helped set the stage for a new session of congressional debate over Mexico, for a national referendum on Polk's policies in the next presidential election, and for an even more prosperous era for the increas-ingly influential newspaper he owned. In this arena, freshman congressman Abraham Lincoln and first-term senator Stephen A. Douglas were destined to meet in Washington in a renewal of the fierce political combat for which they would continue to rely on the party press for both fuel and fire.

• • •

Back in Lincoln's Springfield, almost as if inflamed by his own pro-war edi-torials, *Register* founder William Walters determined he must do what fellow pro-war editors like Bennett never considered: fight in Mexico himself—with bullets instead of mere words. Entrusting the paper to his young assistant, Charles Lanphier, Walters enlisted and left town in 1846, determined to see battle action. He never did. Nor did he ever return home. Before reaching the front, Walters died in St. Louis of "congestion of the brain"—brought on, his critics whispered, by years of heavy drinking. When morticians submerged his body in an alcohol preservative before shipping his lead coffin back to Springfield, even his closest hometown friends winked that Walters would have been as "content in that environment" as he had been for so many years in the toxic brew of newspaper competition in Illinois.[99]

CHAPTER THREE

That Attractive Rainbow

Though certain to be hotly contentious, the 1848 presidential election was still almost a year away when Abraham Lincoln and Stephen A. Douglas made their way to Washington to represent Illinois in Congress.

The war with Mexico, however controversial, was winding down with what loomed as a triumph for the United States. In ordinary times, the approaching holiday season might have signaled a period of calm and unity in America. But in December 1847, with the House and Senate heading back into session, politicians and editors eager for advantage were not about to let the volatility or bitterness of the past few months evaporate. After all, healing threatened to translate into voter apathy and with it, diminished readership of newspapers. The war itself was nearly over, American victory was assured, but the fight over the conflict's meaning was just getting under way. The partisan press, now endowed with better technology for both receiving and printing news and making it available to readers faster and cheaper, was more emboldened than ever not merely to report, but to inflame, the waning drama.

Early in the month, the two rising political stars from Illinois arrived in Washington to take their seats in the 30th Congress: Democrat Douglas and Whig Lincoln, not only physical opposites but already political foes, if not quite yet outright rivals. The same August 1846 election that saw Lin-

Congressman-elect Abraham Lincoln,
age thirty-seven, in his first photograph, taken by
Nicholas H. Shepherd in Springfield around 1846.

coln elected to the House of Representatives with a record-high Whig vote in his district also produced a sufficient Democratic majority statewide to assure the selection of a Democrat to the United States Senate.[1] To no one's surprise, when state legislators met in Springfield that December to choose the next senator, they elevated Douglas. So it happened that these future political opponents made their way to Washington around the same time to assume the highest posts to which either had ever ascended.

Actually, one of the two had already done previous service in Congress, while the other probably could have. Douglas, by then a veteran of three terms in the House, had briefly occupied his new Senate seat nine months earlier. Then he married the wealthy Martha Martin, returned to Illinois once the session ended, and relocated his residence to the rapidly growing lakefront city of Chicago. Not long after his own victory in the race for Congress in and around Sangamon County, Lincoln found himself pressed by local Whigs to run in a special January 1847 election for a neighboring House seat made vacant when the incumbent resigned to fight in Mexico. Success, which seemed likely, would have entitled Lincoln to proceed to Washington immediately instead of waiting an exasperating thirteen months to take office on his own, as the rules of the day required.

Further signaling the increasingly open alliance between politicians and editors, Whig leaders hatched the plan to hasten Lincoln to Washington at meetings in the offices of the party organ, the *Sangamo Journal*. This clearly meant the idea had the full backing of editor Simeon Francis, who more than ever expected to influence, not merely cover, politics. By then the local

Whig cabal that crafted political strategy at the newspaper had acquired a new name: the "Journal Junta." The title suggested that the paper, even more than the politicians, represented the group's unifying principles. Among its leading members was Lincoln. But in a rare display of resistance to the *Journal*'s aspirations for him, he declined to undertake another exhausting campaign so soon. Thus, for entirely different reasons, it was not until the first week of December 1847 that the two manifestly talented Illinois adversaries converged in the nation's capital.

For politicians so far apart in terms of fame and fortune, not to mention their differences on the leading issues of the day, they enjoyed curiously similar excursions en route to the capital. Douglas barreled into town fresh from a visit to his new bride's eight-hundred-acre family plantation in North Carolina. Lincoln and his brood journeyed across the country from Springfield, but not before stopping for three relaxing weeks at his own in-laws' home in Lexington, Kentucky. Though Lincoln's antislavery credentials already outdistanced Douglas's, his itinerary created an irony that testified to the complexity of the slavery issue: like Douglas, Lincoln, too, had vacationed before entering Congress at a luxurious Southern home attended by slaves.

By June, however, the Douglas family ascended to an even loftier plateau: they became slave masters themselves when Martha Martin Douglas's father died and bequeathed her a 2,500-acre Mississippi plantation complete with some 150 slaves. Sensitive to how such a dubious legacy might be regarded back home, the senator made certain that the bequest bypassed him in favor of his wife (though it did make him something of an out-of-town overseer). Title would eventually pass to the newlyweds' future children. Douglas accepted the inheritance, but embarrassed, or worried, carefully instructed the editor of the Democratic paper back in Springfield: "I do not wish it to come before the public." [2]

The Douglases' Illinois counterparts were, by comparison, impoverished. Newly arrived in Washington, the Lincolns—Abraham, Mary, and their sons, four-year-old Robert and Edward, not quite two—registered temporarily at Brown's Indian Queen Hotel, a handsome building along Pennsylvania Avenue, midway between the Capitol and the White House. Centrally located near the city's bustling market, Brown's was renowned for its lavish facade and "elegantly furnished" rooms.[3] But the establishment may have proved a bit too elegant—and certainly too expensive—for the financially strapped Lincoln family. Soon enough the Lincolns took up permanent residence at Mrs. Ann Sprigg's boardinghouse on Carroll Row, a block of connected homes that stood just across the plaza from the Capitol.[4] Here, in a crowded, noisy establishment favored by so many compatible politicians that it became known as "The Whig House," the new congressman, his wife, and their two young boys could be politically, if not always physically, comfortable in their snug, one-room chamber. At least access to the inn's library and other common rooms was included with rent. So were meals. One boarder remembered appreciatively that Mrs. Sprigg served mush "twice a day," washed down with "*very good*" milk.[5]

As the Lincolns probably knew, or at least came soon to realize, the Sprigg establishment was in fact owned by a member of their own extended family, who happened also to be one of the most prominent Whig journalists in all Washington—none other than the onetime Jacksonian editor Duff Green— who had purchased the entire block of buildings in the 1830s to provide investment income. Green was also a relative of Mary Lincoln's by marriage— the brother-in-law of her sister's husband, Ninian Wirt Edwards. By the time the Lincolns moved in with Mrs. Sprigg, the area was known as "Duff Green's Row," and the influential Green himself boarded in a nearby house.[6] Lincoln no doubt saw him often.

Excited as they may have been to see and live in the national capital for the first time, however, Lincoln and Mary, like many visitors, likely recoiled at the city's shocking imperfections. Washington was at best unfinished, at worst primitive. A swampy nightmare of a town whose streets turned to boggy mud (rivaling Springfield's) in wet weather and swirled with dust and debris when the weather turned dry, Washington was hugged to the south by fetid waterways and pocked throughout town by the incongruous sight of wooden shacks nestling alongside grand public buildings. Just a few years earlier, a visiting English novelist had observed "spacious avenues that begin in nothing, and lead nowhere," and worst of all, populated with slaves horrifically "linked to each other by iron fetters."

In the grip of winter, added the writer, the "unhealthy" city seemed "freezing cold," made still more unbearable by the "occasional tornado of wind and dust." The English visitor could not help noticing, too, that Congress, its ornate chambers notwithstanding, appeared to be "the meanest perversion of virtuous Political Machinery that the worst tools ever wrought." Sessions were characterized by "cowardly attacks upon opponents, with scurrilous newspapers for shields, and hired pens for daggers."[7] The observer's name was Charles Dickens. And not much had changed since his recent visit.

While Lincoln and Douglas established themselves in different circles—despite occasional exceptions to the unwritten custom, most legislators at the time socialized exclusively with men of their own party—the two made for quite a contrast whenever their paths crossed in Washington. A virtual anecdote machine, the gangly giant Lincoln moved with an awkward gait, often seemed lost in thought, and invariably appeared too long in the limbs for his country-made broadcloth suits. The hard-driving Little Giant, by contrast, made up for his diminutive stature by drinking and smoking to excess and boiling over with an aggressive energy that one contemporary sniffed revealed "a touch of the rowdy." [8] The elderly Whig congressman John Quincy Adams, for his part, was repelled by the sight of Douglas hurling "abusive invectives" during one of his typical congressional orations. As Adams noted in his diary: "His face was convulsed, his gesticulation frantic, and he lashed himself into such a heat that if his body had been made out of combustible matter it would have burnt out. In the midst of his roaring, to save himself from choking, he stripped off and cast away his cravat, unbuttoned his waistcoat, and had the air and the aspect of a half-naked pugilist." [9]

Legend would later hold that, back in Springfield, earlier in the decade, Lincoln and Douglas had both courted the vivacious Mary Todd. Neither swain was much to look at even then: the thickset, short-legged Douglas was hardly more pleasing to the eye than the tall, angular Lincoln, whose spiky hair had a way, he joked, of "getting up in the world," and whose acne-pitted skin, a reporter later noted, looked "indented, as though it had been scarred by vitriol." [10] Perhaps Mary ultimately found Lincoln the more appealing of the two because he was less forward with women; his rival, squat physique notwithstanding, ostentatiously considered himself a ladies' man. Mary herself would only admit, many years later, that both "choice spirits" had indeed once been "habitués of our drawing room," but proudly maintained that Lincoln was "always a 'World above them all.'" In a cutting reference to Douglas's nickname, she pointedly added that he was "a very little, *little* giant by the side of my tall Kentuckian." [11] Douglas went out of his way to remain polite to Mary for the rest of his life, but may have regarded his failed pursuit of her as a loss worth avenging on his political nemesis.

Physically, Lincoln may have stood taller, but professionally, there was no doubt about which of the two had risen higher. Politically, "Long Abraham" was dwarfed in the much larger shadow of the "Little Giant." Douglas ascended to the Senate before his thirty-fourth birthday. Lincoln, though four years his senior, had never before even set foot in Washington, much less served there. As fellow freshmen, to be sure, the roles both men could play in their respective chambers would remain for a time somewhat limited by the fusty traditions of Congress. Yet both men arrived in the capital in December 1847 aspiring to notice. And once seated, they resumed waging a war there that uniformed armies had all but ceased fighting. Imminent military victory notwithstanding, the press, along with politicians like Abraham Lincoln and Stephen Douglas, clung to the Mexican conflict in an effort to maintain readership and voter enthusiasm.

The violence that had triggered the war between Mexico and the United States had erupted in April 1846 on Texas land that Lincoln described poetically as the "stupendous desert" between the Rio Grande and Nueces Rivers—territory claimed by both countries.[12] Without waiting for the border issue to be resolved, President Polk charged that Mexico had "passed the boundary of the United States" and spilled American blood on indisputably American territory.[13] Congress declared war two days later and Polk promptly dispatched an invasion force.

By early 1847, superior American armies had overrun Mexican defenders at Buena Vista, Veracruz, and Cerro Gordo, and by September occupied Mexico City. Now Polk, a Democrat committed to the policy of coast-to-coast expansion known as Manifest Destiny, sought ratification of a peace treaty that promised to vastly enlarge American territory in the Southwest at Mexico's expense. Under its terms, the United States would "purchase" at a bargain price of $15 million (and assumption of Mexico's debts to American claimants) some 500,000 square miles of land in what are now California, Nevada, Utah, Wyoming, Colorado, New Mexico, and Arizona, not to mention previously annexed Texas, where the war had flamed to life the year before.

More than during any previous war, Americans readers at home came to consider themselves participants in the saga. Their hunger for information was nourished by new technologies that made it possible for publishers to rush firsthand coverage to readers more speedily than ever before. Transported via steamboat, railroad, Pony Express, and, when possible, the newly introduced telegraph, dispatches from the front occasionally reached Washington in advance even of official military reports transmitted via the U.S. mails. It was said that Polk himself first learned of the American victory at Veracruz from forty-year-old *Baltimore Sun* publisher Arunah Shepherdson Abell.[14] A

Rhode Island–born, New York–trained penny press pioneer, Abell championed the innovative uses of Pony Express, carrier pigeon, and ultimately telegraphic transmission of news, and also introduced the novelty of establishing a Washington bureau to cover government affairs firsthand. Now he beat the army itself in announcing an important victory.

One of the newspapers on which Abell had modeled his Baltimore daily, the increasingly popular *New York Sun*, further expanded the role of the press in wartime. Its new publisher, Ben Day's successor, Moses Yale Beach, agreed at one point to carry a secret, unofficial peace feeler from the White House to the Mexican capital. But the *New Orleans Picayune* violated the secrecy of the mission and announced the editor's arrival. Suspected of entering the country to stir antiwar sentiment, Beach barely evaded capture by Antonio López de Santa Anna, the feared general who had conquered the Alamo.[15] Ignoring such risks, Beach's star reporter, a fortyish woman journalist named Jane McManus Storm, continued churning out war dispatches for the *Sun* under the pen name "Montgomery."[16]

Displaying what Senator Thomas Hart Benton admiringly called a "masculine stomach for war and politics," history's first female war correspondent later boasted, with some credibility: "I can and do control over half of the entire daily circulation [of the *Sun*] and from my position thus hold the balance of opinion on any man or measure." Fiercely committed to territorial expansion, she wrote from the front to demand that all of Mexico "be transferred" to American rule. Not everyone accepted her as a professional. When she tried to pass vital information to commanding general Winfield Scott, "Old Fuss and Feathers" huffily told her editor that he was opposed to receiving intelligence from "a plenipotentiary in petticoats."[17]

Her sex made "Montgomery" unique, but she was but one of many such influential opinion makers stationed with the troops at or near the Mexican front. For the first time, battlefield correspondents embedded themselves within war zones and dispatched eyewitness reports while news was still reasonably fresh. The papers closest to the action naturally enough provided the timeliest coverage. Taking advantage of its geographic proximity to Mexico, for example, the *New Orleans Picayune* generated dispatches with unheard-of speed. Editor-publisher George Wilkins Kendall made himself his own star reporter, producing reports that found their way into papers nationwide.[18]

Although their editors continued to battle over the justification for the Mexico adventure, to their credit, their battlefield correspondents kept the

American public more informed, more promptly, about this war than about any conflict in the country's young history. To keep up with demand, newspaper owners replaced their steam-powered cylinder presses with improved, double-cylinder models capable of printing double the number of editions within the same time. The reward for pouring money into modernization was a vastly increased readership and with it, vastly increased revenues.

More than any other innovation, it was the telegraph that entirely revolutionized the newspaper business. Although inventor Samuel F. B. Morse had made the words "What hath God wrought?" his first message over the new system, he quickly followed it with another equally important question: "Have you any news?" Realizing the advantage he could earn over his competitors with promptly transmitted dispatches from the front, James Gordon Bennett paid for the installation of telegraph wires at the *New York Herald*, and offered bonuses for scoops. During the war, Manhattan streets teemed with newsboys from the various dailies loudly hawking extra editions that came fresh from busy presses, day or night, whenever a major story broke.

When it came to introducing expensive technological advances, many newspapers chose to begin working in tandem, political divisions notwithstanding. Earlier in 1847, despite its loathing for Henry Clay, Bennett's *Herald* triumphantly arranged for a Clay speech in Lexington to be telegraphed to New York, sharing the text—and the cost of assembling and transmitting it—with other journals in both New York and Philadelphia. The idea of a national wire service was being born. By May of the election year, 1848, Bennett's managing editor, Frederic Hudson, together with future newspaper titan Henry Raymond, then working for the *Courier and Enquirer*, organized a coalition of six New York papers to secure cheaper telegraph rates. And in January 1849, six of the big city's largest newspapers would band together to form the New York Harbor News Association, pooling resources for the first time to end the historic rivalry for shipping news.[19] (Ironically, the cost of receiving telegraphed news put an added burden on small village newspapers like Springfield's rival sheets, the *Journal* and the *Register*, although both had little choice but to respond by converting from weekly to twice weekly, and eventually daily publication around this time.)

With such extraordinary new technology at their disposal, it is not difficult to understand why, when the fighting in Mexico ceased, Whig newspapers proved disinclined to rejoice, and Democratic ones seemed unwilling to call for unity. There was far more profit to be made by continuing to stir up the public. The new technologies only encouraged the frequency and volume of their provocative salvos. By the end of the war, most of the larger papers had replaced their double-cylinder presses with even faster revolving presses capable of printing a breathtaking twelve thousand copies an hour.[20] Such technological advances made the bitter debate over Mexico more ubiquitous than ever, just as the growing conflict over slavery expansion was making it more acrimonious.

So Lincoln discovered—to his pleasure, for he, too, sensed political opportunity in extending the Mexican quarrel—when he first arrived in Washington. Lincoln, of course, was accustomed to operating in the overlapping milieu inhabited by both rowdy politicians and rival papers. Here in the national capital, however, their roles were greatly magnified. For one thing, Washington was where truly important news originated: the District's Whig and Democratic journals generated the very stories routinely reprinted by isolated rural presses like those back home in Springfield. More importantly, Washington editors served often and openly as advisors to government leaders, or as politicians themselves, obscuring the firewall that would only much later separate journalists from elected officials to preserve objectivity.

When the opening sessions of Congress gaveled into order, pro-war Democrats squared off against antiwar Whigs, with newspapers editorializing on the dispute on an almost daily basis. Their readers included senators and representatives now debating armistice terms, among them both of the Illinois freshmen learning the rules and traditions of their respective houses. In the upper chamber, Douglas took to the Senate routine with obvious relish, confidently savoring his opportunities to engage senior colleagues in public debate. Lincoln, quickly bored by the routine tasks required of mere congressmen—such as shepherding constituent requests to federal bureaus—found it more congenial to exchange political gossip by the fireside at the cramped House post office, where he emerged as a favorite.

Correspondent Benjamin Perley Poore remembered that Lincoln became the "champion story teller" among the "jovial *raconteurs* who met almost every morning in the Capitol hideaway to exchange witticisms.[21] Yet Lincoln also attended formal sessions diligently, often arriving before the noon call to order and sometimes remaining at work throughout sessions that lasted until nine or ten at night, attending to correspondence and writing speeches from

First photograph of the U.S. Capitol with its original dome, as it looked when Lincoln arrived to begin his term in Congress in 1847. The House of Representatives met in the wing at left.

his backbench desk, for congressmen of that era had neither separate office quarters nor staff.[22]

In the opening days of the session, as legislators and journalists commenced debating Polk's proposed pact to end the war with Mexico, they continued as well to quarrel over how the conflict had begun. Fearing that the proposed territorial acquisitions would swell the nation's slave territory, thus perpetuating the longtime dominance of Southern pro-slavery interests in Congress, "Conscience" Whigs like Lincoln vehemently protested both the treaty and the war that preceded it. Although the *Sangamo Journal* had reported back in July 1846 that all members of the party had at first "united in support of the war with all their power and influence"—pointing out that even Lincoln attended one patriotic Springfield rally that summer—Whig enthusiasm for the adventure rapidly eroded, with the slavery issue driving the wedge. Within six months, the *Quincy Whig* assailed Douglas for a willingness to "gratify the south in their cherished desire of forming more Slave States in the south west."[23]

One Washington newspaper that amplified the Mexico debate with particular vehemence was the long-influential, pro-Whig *National Intelligencer*. Brothers-in-law Joseph Gales, Jr., and William Winston Seaton had turned the sleepy paper into a daily back in 1812, in the throes of a much earlier and, they argued, more justifiable foreign war. For years thereafter, the *Intelligencer* supplied readers—and posterity—with the only gavel-to-gavel newspaper transcripts of House and Senate debates, its reporters occupying seats in each chamber between the presiding officer and "the snuff-box," and evolving into the *Congressional Record* of the early nineteenth century.[24] Published from a sprawling, barnlike building at Seventh and D Streets, near which the publisher's huge mastiff dog could often be seen carrying a basket of mail in his mouth bound for the post office,[25] the *Intelligencer* opposed the Mexican War from the start. Now it warned that the war's territorial conquests would seed vast slavery expansion.

Co-owner Seaton wielded two kinds of influence about town. The man whom one contemporary described as "my *beau-ideal* of a true Virginia gentleman," functioned primarily as a newspaperman, but like many editors of his generation, doubled as a working politician as well.[26] At age sixty-two, he ran not only the *Intelligencer*, but the city as well, as the elected mayor of Washington. A "model magistrate" who earned acclaim for expanding the District's school system, Seaton was said to operate "in the society of choice spirits and Christian moderation," enough so to attract Dickens himself to his social circle during the author's well-documented Washington visit.[27] The editor's "quaint humor" was reported to be so irresistible that he could make even the fierce Daniel Webster dissolve into "contagious laughter." This was hyperbole, perhaps; but in 1848 politicians still beat a path to Seaton's door, questing not only for press coverage and social recognition, but also for official favors.[28]

The press lords of Washington, D.C., during Lincoln's congressional career. Left to right: Joseph Gales, Jr., and William Winston Seaton of the pro-Whig *National Intelligencer*, and Thomas Ritchie of the pro-Democratic *National Daily Union*.

On the opposite side of the war issue—as well as the furious rivalry for both readers and influence—was Seaton's long-ago colleague at the old *Richmond Enquirer*, Thomas Ritchie, newly installed as the editor of Washington's rival, pro-Democratic *Daily Union*. Though Ritchie consoled himself that he harbored "no mistrust on the score of age" when President Polk arranged for him to run the new administration mouthpiece in the capital—replacing Blair's *Globe*—he was now past seventy.[29] A quaintly anachronistic character partial to plantation garb—"nankeen [yellow cotton] trousers, high shirt-collars, and broad-brimmed straw hats" long out of fashion—Ritchie seemed to the rising young journalist John Wein Forney little more than a "genteel old fogy." He was "the Grandfather Whitehead of the politicians, the Jesse Rural of the diplomats," Forney chortled, his "efforts at making peace between contending rivals generally ending in the renewal of strife and his paragraphs in defence of the Administration awakening new storms of ridicule."[30] But old Ritchie still had clout at the White House, where he continued to enjoy the president's ear. He and Seaton had long ago become journalistic competitors and political opponents, but Seaton's daughter maintained that their "early personal relationship" survived "forty years of wide divergence in political sentiment."[31] Friends they may have remained, but Seaton's paper repeatedly assailed the Polk administration, while Ritchie's zealously defended it, cheered the American victory over Mexico, and applauded the proposed peace pact. In return, the *Daily Union* maintained the privilege of publishing administration news first.

To the victor the spoils still belonged—in journalism as well as politics. John C. Rives of the pro-Democratic *Washington Globe* spoke for most of his newspaper rivals (especially those currently enjoying the rewards that came in return for fealty to the reigning political majority) when he employed a set of novel arguments to defend the practice of congressional grants for the district's newspapers. "I recommend it," Rives declared, "because it keeps up two daily papers here, advocating the principles and interests . . . of the two great parties into which the Union is happily . . . divided; each of them giving full and fair reports of the debates in Congress, which . . . is worth more to the government, or the people, for each and every year, than the printing of both houses of Congress costs in ten years." Rives, for one, was convinced that press patronage actually made newspapers more independent by guaranteeing them the subvention necessary to keep them in business. His peculiar logic extended to worrying that if the government instead awarded its printing projects to the lowest bidder, the public would "repose little confidence" in the results. It came as no surprise to most observers that the promise of such rewards only further hardened traditional editorial biases.[32]

On December 6, 1847, the very day Lincoln first squeezed his immense frame into his new desk before a large window in the rear of the House chamber, the anti-Administration *Intelligencer* denounced President Polk as a "bully" who had "scooped out with thumb a prostrate adversary's eye." To Gales and Seaton, the president was "the savage of the court-yard"—a description that insatiable newspaper reader Lincoln almost certainly perused before making his exhilarating debut on the House floor the following month. He likely noted as well that the very next morning, the pro-administration *Union* responded in kind by declaring the late war "just," "gloriously" waged, and well worth pursuing "till its great ends of peace and justice are obtained." Moreover, predicted the paper, American voters would surely "crush and grind to powder" any politician who rebuked the glory wrought by military victory.[33] If the warning resonated with Lincoln (as perhaps it should have), he showed no fear at the time.

Lincoln never publicly subscribed to the conspiracy theory which held that Polk had waged war expressly "for the purpose of extending slave territory," a charge frequently repeated in the Whig press. He preferred to view the Mexico adventure as a "war of conquest brought into existence to catch votes."[34] At least, that is how he cast his position when reflecting on it from a distance of twelve years. While serving in Congress, however, he had no compunctions about forging alliances with abolitionist New England Whigs who believed that just such pro-slavery plotting had indeed inflamed Democratic war fever.

Together, this Whig coalition constituted a formidable bloc, though never powerful enough to derail administration policy. Lincoln would vote aye "at least forty times," by his own proud, though exaggerated, reckoning, for the Wilmot Proviso—a rider introduced by Whig congressman David Wilmot to bar slavery from all territory acquired from Mexico. The measure regularly failed in the Senate.[35] In reality, Lincoln never voted for the original Proviso, which was introduced before he ever entered Congress. But supporters did subsequently resubmit amendments echoing its sentiments, and Lincoln reliably supported them all because, as he put it, they reflected "my opposition to the extension of slavery into territories now free."[36] He may have shied away subsequently from identifying himself with those who viewed the Mexican

War as a ploy to expand the institution, but his actions at the time spoke louder than his words would later.

Eager to "distinguish" himself in the House, Lincoln caused a genuine stir just two weeks into his term by offering resolutions demanding that the president inform the House of the precise "spot" in Texas where Mexican forces had first spilled American blood the previous year—the act that had provoked Polk's response.[37] Hostilities were winding down, but Lincoln and his fellow Whigs intended to harp on the notion that no evidence existed to support the claim that the original confrontation had occurred on indisputably American soil.

Then, on January 12, Lincoln rose to deliver his first major address: a forty-five-minute-long attack on the Polk administration couched within a spirited defense of those "Spot" resolutions. His only previous "speech-making" from the floor had come on a minor "post-office question of no general interest . . . by way of getting the hang of the House," as he reported home, adding: "I was about as badly scared, and no worse, as I am when I speak in court."[38]

"Scared" or not, Lincoln put his mesmerizing talents on full display that afternoon, offering a grandiloquent oration oozing with vitriol, couched as a closely argued and devastating critique of Polk's recent pro-war message to Congress. "As to the mode of terminating the war, and securing the peace," he charged, "the President is . . . a bewildered, confounded, and miserably perplexed man." His assault growing more impassioned as it progressed, Lincoln climaxed his speech with the kind of hyperbole that would later vanish from his political vocabulary. No doubt hungry for press coverage, he turned to a newspaper for inspiration for its most orotund flourishes. A year earlier, Horace Greeley's *New York Tribune* (in an article faithful reader Lincoln undoubtedly noticed) charged that America had launched a war "in which Heaven must take part against us." As Greeley saw it, "The laws of Heaven are suspended and those of Hell established in their stead. It means that the Commandments are to be read and obeyed by our people, thus—Thou *shalt* kill Mexicans; Thou *shalt* steal from them, hate them, burn their houses, ravage their fields, and fire red-hot cannon balls into towns swarming with wives and children."[39]

Now Lincoln summoned God in unmistakably similar terms to demand answers of his own from the president. There seems little doubt that he had modeled his remarks at least in part on Greeley's impassioned editorial. Lincoln expressed it this way in his most famous congressional speech:

As a nation *should* not, and the Almighty *will* not, be evaded, so let him attempt no envasion—no equivocation. And if, so answering, he can show that the soil was ours, where the first blood of the war was shed—that it was not within an inhabited country, or, if within such, that the inhabitants had submitted themselves to the civil authority of Texas, or of the United States . . . then I am with him for his justification. . . . But if he *can* not, or *will* not do this—if on any pretence, or no pretence, he shall refuse or omit it, then I shall be fully convinced, of what I more than suspect already, that he is deeply conscious of being in the wrong—that he feels the blood of this war, like the blood of Abel, is *crying to Heaven against him* [emphasis added]; that he ordered General Taylor into the midst of a peaceful Mexican settlement, purposely to bring on a war; that originally having some strong motive—what, I will not stop now to give any opinion concerning—to involve the two countries in a war, and trusting to escape scrutiny, by fixing the public gaze upon the exceeding brightness of military glory—that attractive rainbow, that rises in showers of blood—that serpent's eye, that charms to destroy. . . .[40]

The one-two punch provided by his lawyerly "Spot" resolutions and his impassioned antiwar floor oration helped establish Lincoln's Whig bona fides in Washington. His "military glory" oration in particular earned the congressman his first trickle of press attention in regions outside the West. One particular item by an observant Washington correspondent soon found its way into print in small Whig newspapers in New Jersey, Virginia, and New York state's Hudson Valley. It was far from blanket national coverage. But it was a start:

ABRAHAM LINCOLN, the only Whig Member of Congress from Illinois, being the successor of Col. Hardin, is described as a tall, raw-boned, thin, and dark-complexioned man, six feet four inches high. He made his debut in the House last week, in a speech on the War and the President and displayed the rapidity of utterance, abundance of gesture, and striking figurative language which are common to Western men. Speaking of the President being led away by military glory, he said: "Military glory is a rainbow which rises in the heavens and dazzles with its luster, but it comes forth from the CLOUDS OF DESOLATED CITIES AND SHOWERS OF HUMAN BLOOD."[41]

The report mischaracterized his speaking style, and in the bargain misquoted his address, but at least recognized his unique appearance and identified him as a freshman worthy of future attention. The coverage also earned Lincoln a rather ignominious nickname back home: "Spotty Lincoln." Springfield's Democratic *State Register* labeled him the "Benedict Arnold of our District," predicting he would thereafter be "known here only as the Ranchero Spotty of one term."[42] To all Democrats there, and perhaps even a few local Whig hawks ambivalent about slavery, he suddenly seemed a gadfly whose antiwar obsession might betray a lack of patriotism.

Sensing an opportunity to diminish him, the *Register*'s Charles Lanphier personally urged a Democratic member of the Illinois House delegation to show Lincoln no mercy. "Our long-legged friend from the 7th dist. has very properly damned himself 'by resolution,'" Lanphier wrote John A. McClernand.* ". . . He may well exclaim 'Out damned *spot!*' for Cain's mark is on him. Give him hell." (Lanphier may have already known that Lincoln's favorite Shakespeare play was *Macbeth*, and had surely read his recent remarks in Congress comparing wartime casualties to the "blood of Abel.")[43] Critics, many of whom knew better, whispered that Lincoln was unwilling even to support funding to supply American troops—a misrepresentation he was compelled to deny for years.

Undaunted, Congressman Lincoln proudly sent off the text of his House speech to Springfield for hometown publication. The *Journal* duly carried the remarks in full on February 10 and for wider circulation reissued it as a pamphlet that Lincoln could mail free to his constituents using his congressional franking privileges. Editor Simeon Francis sought additional attention for Lincoln—and himself—by daring the opposition *Register* to print the oration as well, charging that Lanphier's rival Democratic paper "fear[ed] to have it go to his readers." Unwilling to succumb to a dare that might result in widening the reach of Lincoln's words, the *Register* surprised no one when it refused to carry what it characterized as Lincoln's "imbecile" remarks.[44]

The city's two opposing party organs were not in business to publicize opposition arguments, but its editors likely sensed that a good political feud might boost the circulation of both. So when, soon thereafter, Douglas took the floor of the Senate to deliver a ringing defense of the war, the *Register* not only published the entire text, but challenged the *Journal* to run the senator's oration, too, belatedly offering to reprint the Lincoln address after all if it did.

---

*As president, needing Democrats to defend the Union cause, Lincoln would one day name McClernand a general in the federal army.

Neither paper took the bait. As a result, Democratic readers alone learned that Douglas had asked, as if in direct response to Lincoln: "Whose heart did not swell and pulsate with patriotic pride as he heard the shout of the glorious victories achieved by our countrymen . . . striking terror to the hearts of all enemies of republican institutions, and demonstrating that ours is the first military, as well as civil power, upon the globe?"[45] Lincoln supporters, however, never read these words because the *Journal* declined to print them. Whig and Democratic newspaper subscribers enjoyed access only to party doctrine since they read the party newspaper of their choice—and unless they were professional politicians who routinely scoured the opposition journals for mention of their names, *only* the party newspaper of their choice.

However routine, the publication of Lincoln's House oration in the hometown Whig paper nonetheless alarmed some of his closest friends and supporters. Mere rumors of his antiwar stance were enough to inspire his adoring but self-important law partner, William Herndon, to dash off an anxious letter expressing concern that Lincoln's position would ruin him with local voters, particularly if he indeed opposed funding to feed and clothe the troops, as rumored. Lincoln assured Herndon that while he considered Polk's war policies "unjust," he would continue to "vote supplies," though "perhaps not in the precise form recommended by the President."

Then Lincoln urged his partner to read his "pamphlet speech" even if he became "scared anew by it," confidently adding: "After you get over your scare, read it over again, sentence by sentence, and tell me honestly what you think of it."[46] Before Herndon could reply, Lincoln shot off yet another justification, this time questioning whether Polk or any president could ever make himself "the *sole* judge" of when and whether to invade another country. Raising doubts about the very powers he would years later seize for himself, Lincoln warned against granting a chief executive the right "to make war at pleasure."[47] One can only imagine Lincoln laboring away at this self-justifying correspondence amid the unceasing din of the House floor, where even whispers famously bounced off the chamber walls and into enemies' ears; or perhaps composing it at his equally bustling quarters at Sprigg's boardinghouse—made particularly boisterous by his temperamental wife's occasional outbursts and his children's more than occasional misbehavior. Like other congressmen of the day, even senior members, Lincoln had no government-funded office in which to attend to his paperwork, or see visiting constituents. All such labor was conducted in the noisy House chamber.

If the freshman's debut Mexico speech was meant, in part, to impress his older House colleagues, its impact proved tragically short-lived, particularly for the most eminent Whig among them. Just a month later, on February 21, the frail John Quincy Adams suddenly collapsed at his desk in the chamber just after voting "no" on a resolution to decorate the military heroes of the Mexican War, the victim of a stroke. He expired two days later in the speaker's room adjacent to the House floor. "Old Man Eloquent" was eighty years old. The death of the antislavery icon, as revered a congressman as he had been a reviled president, ironically deflated what was left of Capitol Hill resistance to peace on Polk's terms. It also relegated Lincoln's maiden antiwar speech to the status of a footnote (however dutifully it was later recalled in the future president's canon of early oratory). Lincoln's only "spot" now was his position on the thirty-member House committee assigned to accompany Adams's body to its temporary resting place at the Congressional Burial Ground.[48]

Whig objections notwithstanding—and despite complaints by expansionist Democrats like Stephen Douglas who thought that America should have demanded even *more* land from vanquished Mexico—the Senate ratified the Treaty of Guadalupe Hidalgo by a wide margin in March 1848. The Mexican Senate followed suit as expected in June. The war was finally, officially over. But so, in a sense, was Lincoln's career in Congress. Aside from reprints of his occasional speeches, the sole notice he had elicited in the all-important *National Intelligencer* since his arrival in Washington seven months earlier was the briefest of acknowledgments that he and Mary had joined a crowd attending a January performance of the "Ethiopian Singers" at Carusi's Saloon. The "saloon" was more than its name implied; the elegant hall had hosted presidential inaugurals for a generation. But not even the sobriquet "Ethiopian" could conceal the fact that the performers that night were blackface minstrels.[49] However hostile toward slavery, Lincoln never quite lost his taste for "darky" entertainments.

Not long after the Senate ratified the peace treaty with Mexico, Whigs back in Illinois substituted another candidate to stand for Congress in Lincoln's district in 1848. Lincoln was but midway through his term in office. Among historians, it has been a matter of dispute over the generations as to whether the party's decision to retire him resulted from growing hometown anger over his antiwar stance. William Herndon, who later wrote a highly influential

Lincoln biography, nourished that interpretation in part because it made his own earlier warnings about Lincoln's risky position seem more prescient. In Herndon's blunt assessment, opposition to the Mexican War "sealed Lincoln's doom as a Congressman;" his friend and senior partner had done nothing less than commit "political suicide" in Washington.[50] For a long time Herndon's self-serving view earned wide acceptance. Only later did historians point out that Lincoln's short-lived House career terminated for more prosaic reasons, and that early biographers like Herndon invented the myth of his political downfall to make his subsequent phoenix-like rebirth seem all the more extraordinary.[51]

In fact, neither the Whig Party as a whole, nor its various newspaper organs, ever truly retreated from their steadfast opposition to the Mexican War. Even after peace was restored, Horace Greeley's *Tribune* perpetuated Whig disgust over the adventure. Greeley maintained a vigil over what he continued to call "the great question—which our vast acquisitions from Mexico had suddenly invested with the gravest importance—of excluding Slavery from the yet unattained Federal Territories."[52] By contrast, Bennett's *Herald* had not only supported the contest, but broke the news of the peace treaty before the government was ready to release it—inspiring angry senators to summon the paper's Washington correspondent to Capitol Hill for questioning in an unsuccessful effort to discover his source.

As if oblivious to the larger controversy still raging in Washington, Greeley—one of whose early biographers reported that he now believed himself nothing less than the new "target-General to the Press, Pulpit, and Stump of the United States"—accepted a challenge from Bennett to compare their newspapers' respective daily circulation figures, proposing that an independent committee count the numbers. The loser, it was agreed, would give $300 to one of New York's orphanages. As it turned out, the *Herald* won the contest, though just barely, 28,946 to 28,195. Greeley made the requisite donation to charity, grumbling that Bennett had achieved the superior number by counting one of his campaign extras (in fact, the daily circulation figures alone did show the *Herald* with a slight lead).[53]

Unwilling to drop the story, Greeley went on to accuse his competitor in print of "bullying" the *Tribune* into the competition, but more importantly of a "studied pandering to depraved tastes and vicious inclinations," and a "careful avoidance of giving offence to any popular vice or profitable corruption." In typically fearless fashion, the *Herald* republished the *Tribune*'s unsportsmanlike diatribe, pleased to find an excuse of its own to prolong the circulation debate and claiming the last word by charging: "It is certainly very amusing in the philosophers of the *Tribune*, to compare their morality, their regard for religion, or any thing touching on public or private virtue, by way of injurious comparisons to the *Herald* or its conductor. . . . We have never advocated socialism, the next stop to infidelity, folly, demoralization, and licentiousness of the worst kind. We have never advocated anti-rentism, that atrocious system of legalized plunder, depriving a man of his property by popular agitation and popular outbreak."

When Greeley responded by renewing the charge that the *Herald*'s advertising columns alone revealed its depravity, Bennett shot back that the *Tribune*'s own paid notices so often abounded with "quack advertisements . . . about 'dyspepsia,' and the 'piles,' 'syrup of Naphtha, the only cure for consumption,' 'liverwort and tar,' 'compound syrup for nervous debility,' calomel, and all sorts of medicines and disorders, scattered through its columns," that "the man who can talk about ours, has a degree of impudence harder than brass, yea, even than steel itself." [54]

Bennett was on to something. Whatever his fondness for arcane philosophies, Greeley never lacked for brass and steel, whatever ridicule he inspired. However spirited his arguments with Bennett, nothing aroused the *Tribune* editor more passionately than issues involving war and politics. And he never permitted his paper to abandon its incurable hostility to American involvement in Mexico. On the very day after Lincoln's "Spot" resolution speech on the House floor—which the *Tribune* failed to cover—the paper's Washington correspondent, filing a report under his usual pseudonym, "Richelieu," did note: "This is the anniversary of the day on which James K. Polk unnecessarily and unconstitutionally commenced the war with Mexico." [55] The *Tribune*'s opposition to the Mexican adventure remained strong, and Greeley's image in period cartoons became ubiquitous. He emerged as something more than a celebrity. He was a symbol.

To his Whig base, Lincoln hardly appeared isolated or extreme on the Mexican War issue. His peace position neither compromised his standing among party and press leaders (if the press recognized it at all), nor imperiled his renomination, however belittling the attacks it increasingly provoked from Illinois's Democratic newspapers—criticism that in one sense served to elevate, not reduce, Lincoln's stature. [56] Though it flew in the face of the early belief that Congressman Lincoln had been important enough to denounce and defeat, the true explanation for his retirement was far less dramatic: the

ONE OF THE YOUNG BO-HOYS IN ECSTACIES BEFORE THE COONS OF 1844

PATENT BALANCING BY AN AMATEUR.

Greeley—an immediate mainstay in political caricature—dances to the tune of radical "coons" during the 1846 New York gubernatorial campaign; and as a tightrope walker wavering between Free Soil candidate Martin Van Buren and Whig nominee Zachary Taylor during the 1848 presidential race.

nomination for the congressional seat was, by previous agreement, irrevocably scheduled to rotate among other ambitious Whigs back home. Lincoln had himself secured the nod in 1846 (similarly succeeding sitting congressman Edward D. Baker) with the understanding that he, too, would serve but a single term and then yield the seat to another. Salving political egos at home clearly remained a higher priority for local Whigs than building influence for the district through congressional seniority.

Although Lincoln did confide to friends that he would have liked to scuttle the arrangement and take his record back to the voters, it was remembered that when Baker plotted a similar maneuver to win renomination two years earlier, Lincoln had insisted to a Whig editor: "Turn about is fair play."[57] Baker was a family friend—Abraham and Mary had named their younger son, Eddy, in his honor—but Lincoln had shown no reluctance to pressure him to yield. Now, Lincoln's "word and honor" forbade an outright fight for his own renomination. "Turn about" was still "fair play."[58]

In a version of the succession saga later drafted by Lincoln himself—eager to quash the idea that he had lost his seat over policy issues that hurt his popularity—he described the prearranged transition as fully "in accordance with an understanding among leading Whigs of the district, and by which Col. John J. Hardin and Col. E. D. Baker had each previously served a single term from the same district."[59] At the time, however, he left the door to renomination ajar, telling Herndon up to the last minute that "if it should so happen that nobody else wishes to be elected, I could not refuse the people the right of sending me again."[60] "The people," however, never demanded his return.

A fresh look at the succession question suggests that the full story is perhaps more complex than the revisionist scenario has suggested, with Lincoln perhaps deserving more responsibility for the ultimate political result that year in Sangamon County than modern scholars have been willing to assign him. After all, on Election Day, the unbroken string of recent Whig successes in his congressional district did come to an end. A once safe Whig seat turned over to the Democrats; the "enemy" did prevail. And Lincoln's widely publicized antiwar stance surely played some role, even if his name did not appear on the ballot.

To be sure, the Whig nominee to succeed him, saddled with the burden of defending Lincoln's record in Washington, notably lacked the incumbent's nimble debating style and extraordinary magnetism on the hustings.[61] But most voters also knew that the 1848 candidate, Stephen Trigg Logan, was not only Mary Lincoln's cousin, but years earlier had shared a law office with none other than her husband. Their once intimate professional and personal association likely did Logan more harm than good. Lincoln may have consoled himself in the belief that Logan lost the state's only Whig congressional seat only because he was a lackluster campaigner with a prickly personality to boot. But at the time, the Democratic press openly promoted the Democratic nominee, Major Thomas Harris, as a hero of the war that Lincoln had supposedly disgraced by opposing it.

Candidate Harris pushed hard for the pro-Democratic *Register* to "*light up* the district in a blaze" during the campaign, urging the paper to "severely" criticize not only Logan, but also Lincoln and the pro-Whig press, until the resulting "thunder and lightning" made voters "exclaim with Lady Macbeth 'out damned spot.'" Harris was sure the district's "young men," specifically those Mexican War veterans arriving home in time to cast their votes, would vote to reclaim the seat for the Democrats. Delighted to oblige, the *Register* proclaimed that it was now up to each voter to choose between "the side of his country," or "with *Illinois Journals* and A. Lincoln."[62]

Voters chose "country"—albeit barely. Logan lost the August election by only 106 votes out of some 14,500, with a third-party "Liberty" candidate siphoning off enough support to defeat him—or, reading the results another way, reflecting additional anti-Whig sentiment. Returning veterans, disenfranchised in 1846 (guaranteed absentee voting for soldiers did not yet exist), probably made an additional difference in Harris's favor.[63] In the end, however, it is difficult to reach any other conclusion but that the 15 percent voter swing back to the Democrats was at least in part a rebuke of the Whig incumbent, even if Lincoln himself was not a candidate.[64] He certainly lost renomination through no fault of his own, and hardly committed political suicide by denouncing the war; but had he secured the Whig nod and stood for a second term, what Herndon accurately labeled "defections from the party ranks" might well have doomed his own candidacy, too. In any case, the Democratic newspapers in the district helped ensure Whig defeat by using Lincoln as their punching bag.[65]

For a time, Lincoln tried ignoring the result, telling one friend merely "that he would rather not be put upon explaining how Logan was defeated in my district."[66] But he and his supporters surely smarted over the defeat. In Springfield, the Whig loss so unnerved Lincoln's principal press advocate, Simeon Francis, that the editor published a wild charge alleging that the Democratic victor was no war hero at all, but a coward guilty of "skulking" at the battle of Cerro Gordo. Infuriated, Congressman-elect Harris armed himself with a walking stick and stormed into the *Sangamo Journal* office to avenge his honor by confronting the huge man he derisively referred to as "*Fatty.*"

Finding the editor at his desk in his second-floor office, Harris barked: "Mr. Francis, I wish you to stop the publication of the low personal lies against me, with which your paper is of late filled." Desist, he warned, "or I shall force you to do so with this big cane." Francis—as sedentary as Harris was virile—daringly retorted: "Suppose, Major, you try it now." Harris then turned to leave, but the editor rushed at him and tried to seize him by his coat. The congressman-elect flicked him away with his cane, whereupon Francis grabbed a nearby mallet and lunged back at Harris.

The ensuing brief scuffle proved more comical than dangerous. Harris departed uninjured, and later joked: "I was more fortunate than even at Cerro Gordo—for there I admit my breeches were torn by the chaparral, while here, neither skin nor knuckles were injured." Authorities took the dustup more seriously, slapping Francis with a $21 fine.[67]

However ludicrous, this latest incident demonstrated how volatile the intersection of press and politics remained, and how close to the surface real violence lurked, especially once incendiary news began reaching readers by telegraph while it was still "hot." Unfortunately for Lincoln, the press's growing ability to report news rapidly began to increase just as his ability to generate it began to diminish.

As for the war between Horace Greeley and James Gordon Bennett—and anyone else who questioned their politics—it continued to rage long after the American army withdrew from Mexico.

It was expected that the big-personality editors of the day devote editorial space to their pet causes and peeves, and for all his insistence that he cared only for the poor and voiceless, Greeley rarely ignored an opportunity to focus attention on himself. Thus, although he lost the widely publicized circulation competition to Bennett's *Herald*, Greeley seemed to take almost perverse comfort when another bitter enemy, the *Courier and Enquirer*'s James Watson Webb, was tried and convicted for participating in yet another duel, and sentenced to two years in Sing Sing. (Not surprisingly pardoned by his friend and fellow Whig Governor Seward, Webb never served a day in prison, and in gratitude even named his next son "William Seward Webb," a consecration of the marriage of politics and the press if ever there was one.)

When Webb responded to Greeley's lack of sympathy by launching one of his periodic and highly personal editorial assaults on the *Tribune* editor, Greeley replied with a lengthy third-person plea for understanding—and advantage: try as he might to play the misunderstood philosopher, Greeley as usual gave as good as he got.

> It is true that the editor of the Tribune chooses mainly (not entirely) vegetable food; but he never troubles his readers on the subject; it does not worry them; why should it concern the Colonel [Webb]? . . . It is hard for *Philosophy* that so humble a man shall be made to stand as its exemplar. . . .
>
> As to our personal appearance, it does seem time that we should say something, to stay the flood of nonsense with which the town just by this time be nauseated. Some donkey a while ago, apparently anxious to assail or annoy the editor of this paper . . . originated the story of his carelessness of personal appearance; and since then every blockhead of the same disposition and distressed by a similar lack of ideas, has repeated and exaggerated the foolery; until from its origin in the Albany *Microscope* it has sunk down at last to the columns of the *Courier and Enquirer*, growing more absurd at every landing.[68]

War had come and gone without demonstrably propelling Abraham Lincoln's political ascent, certainly not with any permanence. But war—between nations and between newspapers—had brought Horace Greeley as close as he had ever come to nationwide fame, and as far as he ever stood from bankruptcy. The "philosopher" was very nearly king.

By 1850, newspapers had emerged as the most important galvanizing force in communities as small as Springfield and as mighty as New York—bringing rapidly reported news, useful commercial advertising, provocative commentary, and reliable party doctrine to tens of thousands of homes, businesses, and street corners.[69] It was this new capacity for what passed at mid-century for instant mass communication that gave newspapers their power. The editor of the *Home Journal*, Nathaniel Parker Willis, grew positively giddy when he contemplated the impact of the typical daily paper, "opened at the same moment, by thousands, and . . . filling them all, on the instant, with the self-same thought."[70] And by now, whatever his foibles, no newspaperman influenced public thought more than Horace Greeley.

Even a decade before the outbreak of the Civil War, the streets of Manhattan abounded with a printed-word assault on the senses: signs on nearly every window, billboards pasted to wooden fences, and huge whitewashed messages competing for attention along building walls. Added to this spectacle of words was the sight and sound of newsboys hawking papers along the busy outdoor thoroughfares and newsstands piled high with daily and weekly journals and crowded with eager customers reaching for their favorite paper, or, intrigued by an unexpected headline, grabbing for a new one. "As the human tide descends," observed *Tribune* reporter Junius Henri Browne in his guide, *The Great Metropolis,* "the heaps of papers rapidly diminish. There is no conversation between buyer and seller. The money is laid down, the journal, taken up, and the change given, without a word."[71] It was as if what needed most to be expressed was to be found only within the pages of the New York papers.

Such rituals may have lacked for words—for not every newspaper buyer wanted friends, strangers, or tradesmen to know which paper he purchased on the street (a sure indication by then of a purchaser's political orientation)—but taken together and repeated six days every week, they loudly amplified the collective voice of the city's principal editors.

Every time Bennett or Greeley spoke out in print, tens of thousands heard. And many obeyed.

CHAPTER FOUR

A Position We Cannot Maintain

————◆————

Abraham Lincoln's lame-duck congressional career limped along without attracting much national press attention for another inglorious year. Not that it had brought him widespread acclaim before his district chose a Democrat to succeed him.

Early biographers tended to exaggerate Lincoln's centrality in the Washington debate over Mexico as surely as they overemphasized the premature reports of his political suicide in Illinois.[1] This was the inevitable result of viewing these events through the prism of the proto-Lincoln's extraordinary future development. Such Lincoln-centric scrutiny fails to acknowledge the preeminence in the House of Representatives, and certainly in the press, of more senior opinion leaders whose words carried far more weight in the late 1840s. Lincoln may deservedly be the leading character in his own posthumous biographies, but he was hardly a major figure on Capitol Hill while he served there, certainly not as reported by the major newspapers in the commercial and political capitals of the country: New York and Washington. Such attention remained fixed on his elders. And it also shone brightly on the remarkable young Senate freshman Stephen Douglas, whose own ascent, by comparison to Lincoln's, seemed meteoric.

With breathtaking speed, Douglas secured the chairmanship of the powerful Senate Committee on Territories, in whose hands rested responsibility for the future of slavery in the Mexican cession and other Western lands. The assignment ensured that Douglas was destined to play a major role in deciding whether America's most controversial institution, slavery, would expand beyond the states where it had long existed—and into territory where it had long been banned under terms of the Missouri Compromise. As his political influence expanded, Douglas's views increasingly earned broader press coverage. His speeches began to draw large and admiring crowds to the Senate galleries. A pro-Democratic editor doubling as a campaign biographer did not exaggerate when he observed that Douglas was no longer "compelled to address empty benches or an inattentive audience." The senator was enjoying "an increased popularity . . . adding greatly to his rising fame as an orator and debater."[2]

Further evidence of the Illinois rivals' divergent trajectories could be inferred from their contrasting relationships with the most famous Capitol Hill veteran of all. Lincoln was flattered merely to be invited to the occasional Saturday breakfast with Whig Senate lion Daniel Webster (whom he had first met when the orator visited Springfield back in 1840). At these meals, Lincoln at least shone by telling amusing stories that gave "great delight to 'the solid men of Boston' assembled around the festive board," as one journalist allowed at the table recalled.[3] Douglas, on the other hand, was unafraid to confront Webster directly on the Senate floor—as a peer. "In a constitutional argument," marveled James Gordon Bennett's increasingly pro-Democratic *New York Herald*, Douglas "has completely worsted some of those—among them Webster . . . who have heretofore been considered as preeminent authorities."[4]

By contrast, politically speaking, Lincoln became something of a dead man walking, and with fully half his term still before him. (According to the rules of the day, his successor would not take his seat until December 1849.) But this particular lame duck had no intention of serving out the session in obscurity if he could help it. Instead, he summoned the enthusiasm to entertain the House with yet another stinging attack on Democratic policies, this time of the domestic variety. In a June 20, 1848 speech, Lincoln railed against both James K. Polk, who had decided not to seek a second term, and Lewis Cass, the 1848 Democratic choice to succeed the president. Returning to a longtime passion, Lincoln denounced Democratic opposition to internal improvements. Polk had long insisted that government support for public works was unconstitutional. From a practical perspective, added the president, such investments invariably favored one state over another, and if applied equally would bankrupt the Treasury.

The Democrats' recently adopted national platform reiterated this position, defending Polk's veto of an earlier internal improvements bill, an action Gales and Seaton's pro-Whig *Intelligencer* had labeled "proof" that the Democratic administration was "fast degenerating into a mere quadrennial elective despotism" (Whigs also believed presidents should not casually exert their veto power).[5] In his latest speech, Lincoln ignored the veto issue altogether to offer standard, pro-improvements Whig doctrine, but in a syllogistic style more recognizable today as Lincolnian: "The just conclusion from all of this is, that if the nation refuse to make improvements, of the more general kind, because their benefits may be somewhat local, a state may, for the same reason, refuse to make an improvement of a local kind, because it's [*sic*] benefits may be somewhat general."

Lincoln ended the oration with a flourish, urging the nation to "take hold of the larger works, and the states the smaller ones," thereby taking full advantage of "the intelligence and enterprize of it's [*sic*] people."[6] Reporting that Lincoln "well understood the subject," Greeley's *Tribune* offered him a rare tidbit of praise, calling his oration a "very sensible speech."[7] And in an item appearing on the same crowded front page that boasted a story on "The Death of a Clam"—but not as prominently—Gales and Seaton's *National Intelligencer* at least reported in passing that Lincoln had "delivered a speech on the subject of internal improvements."[8]

Apparently not satisfied with this unusual little burst of newspaper attention, Lincoln dashed off a grouchy letter to Herndon the very day the New York item appeared, describing himself as "a little impatient" for more pro-Whig press coverage back home. "I, at the beginning of the session made arrangements to have one copy of the [Congressional] Globe and Appendix regularly sent to each whig paper of our district," he complained. "And yet, with the exception of my own little speech, which was published in two only of the then five, now four whig papers, I do not remember having seen a single speech, or even an extract from one, in any single one of those papers. With equal and full means on both sides, I will venture that the [Democratic] State Register has thrown before it's [*sic*] readers more of Locofoco speeches in a month, than all the whig papers of the district, have done of whig speeches during the session."[9] Try as he might to focus his concern on the scant coverage that party journals were giving fellow Whigs, Lincoln could barely conceal, between the lines of his truculent letter, the neglect he felt he was enduring himself.

Clearly hungering for more coverage, the increasingly press-savvy Lincoln looked not to the future, but to the past. Like many Whigs who believed that, peace notwithstanding, the smoldering war issue still presented the most fertile ground for political and press harvests, Lincoln remained reluctant to move entirely past the Mexico controversy. And he remained a stickler for facts on the issue, even among friendly journalists. This was particularly so if his meticulous reading of the press might earn acknowledgment from the journalistic elite. A case in point occurred as Congress neared its 1848 summer recess. Lincoln spied a minor error regarding Mexico in the columns of the *New York Tribune*, a paper he now followed religiously. Somewhat like a precocious child determined to prove his father wrong, Lincoln seized the opportunity to pen a correction to editor Horace Greeley, whom he had seen briefly for the first and—so far—only time the previous July in Chicago. There they had both served, along with five thousand fellow delegates, at a "rowdyish" convention—billed as the largest mass meeting ever held in America—promoting river and harbor improvements.[10] During the thronged sessions the busy newspaperman managed to take notice of "Hon. Abraham Lincoln, a tall specimen of an Illinoisan, just elected to Congress from the only Whig district in the State," who "spoke briefly and happily" at the convention.[11] According to another eyewitness, the elongated and careworn Lincoln in fact looked so woebegone at Chicago, dressed in a "short-waisted, thin swallow-tail coat, a short vest of some material, thin pantaloons, scarcely coming down to his ankles, [and] a straw hat and a pair of brogans with woolen socks," that a visiting orator anointed him then and there with a nickname that stuck: "Old Abe."[12]

Now, a year later, "Old Abe" wrote familiarly to "Friend Greeley" to point out that his "little editorial" of July 26, 1848, had mistakenly contended that Whigs and Democrats alike concurred that Mexico's boundary with Texas "stopped at the Nueces" River. "Now this is a mistake which I dislike to see go uncorrected in a leading Whig paper," Lincoln lectured. "Since I have been here, I know a large majority of such Whigs of the House of Representatives as have spoken on the question have not taken that position. Their position, and in my opinion the true position, is that the boundary of Texas extended just so far as American settlements taking part in her revolution extended; and that as a matter of fact those settlements did extend, at one or two points, beyond the Nueces, but not anywhere near the Rio Grande at any point."

In retrospect, this rather high-handed example of nitpicking seemed a ploy to attract notice from an influential newspaperman. But by "putting us in the position of insisting on the line of the Nueces," Lincoln insisted at the time, "you put us in a position which, in any opinion, we cannot maintain, and which therefore gives the Democrats an advantage of us." Barely disguising his attempt to impress America's leading Whig journalist, the congressman enclosed a copy of his own speech on the subject for Greeley's elucidation.[13] Lincoln no doubt was referring to both his letter *and* his speech when the congressman added in an almost pleading tone: "Will you look at this?" Doubtless to Lincoln's pleasure, the *Tribune* at least published his complaint in full a few days later under the headline, "The Boundary of Texas—Letter from the Hon. Abraham Lincoln of Illinois."[14] But Greeley ignored Lincoln's strong hint and did not publish his long oration.

Consistent press attention beyond Illinois's borders still eluded the Springfield Whig. More dispiriting still, just a few weeks after communicating with Greeley, a disappointed Lincoln received a letter from his law partner, William Herndon, enclosing a batch of "newspaper slips"—the term of the day for press clippings—whose contents Lincoln found "exceedingly painful to me."[15] Herndon's letter and enclosures have long since disappeared—Lincoln was a notoriously poor record keeper—but one can reasonably speculate from the congressman's disheartened reaction that the package bulged with negative home state coverage of his stubborn opposition to the late war, as collected by the young acolyte who had warned of just such a calamitous response. To add insult to injury, one of these clips, by Herndon's own admission, featured a published report on his own recent rant against "the old fossils in the party."[16] It was no wonder Lincoln found the communication from his junior partner "painful."

With no real way to increase his influence in Congress during his brief remaining time in Washington, Lincoln wisely turned his attentions primarily to the approaching contest for the White House. Its potential for press coverage certainly played a role. A presidential campaign offered countless opportunities for Whig surrogates to speak out for the ticket, and to coax their stump orations into print in the party press. Political calculations factored into Lincoln's new emphasis as well. After all, if a Whig won the White House in the fall, there would be plenty of federal jobs to go around. An outgoing one-term congressman with limited electoral prospects at home might still enjoy a political soft landing via a prestigious federal appointment. Taking no chances, Lincoln had earlier dropped his longtime support for his political "beau ideal," perennial candidate Henry Clay, the loser to Polk four years earlier who yearned for yet one more chance at the White House.[17] Instead, the outgoing Illinois congressman declared himself early and "decidedly" for the more electable Zachary Taylor—conveniently ignoring the fact that General Taylor was one of the signal heroes of Mexico, and that Lincoln had come close to denouncing him as a Polk puppet in his first speech on the war only months earlier.

Other Whigs proved more reluctant to abandon the "Great Compromiser," particularly the influential Greeley, who hastened to Washington in late April in an effort to head off defections from the Clay camp. The *New York Herald* chortled that the desperate Greeley had told fellow Whigs that "if he can't get Clay, he will take [Ohio senator] Tom Corwin—if he can't get Tom Corwin, he will take Mr. [John] McLean [Associate Justice of the Supreme Court]—if he can't get Mr. McLean he will take General Scott."[18] For Greeley, it was anyone but Taylor. None of Greeley's dark-horse alternatives gained traction, but it is not difficult to understand why the crusading editor had such difficulty embracing "Old Rough and Ready." Ready Taylor may have been in 1848, but for four decades, he had not even bothered to vote, and worse, as progressives complained, he unapologetically owned slaves.

Such details proved inconsequential once the popular general made himself available to a party thirsting for a return to power. A meeting of Whig power brokers at the *Tribune* offices may have inspired nine cheers "for Harry Clay," and as many groans for General Taylor."[19] But with formerly dependable admirers like Lincoln defecting, the seventy-year-old career politician proved no match for the hero of Buena Vista when balloting got under way June 7 at the Whig National Convention at Philadelphia. Taylor won the nomination on the fourth ballot, and Millard Fillmore of New York emerged as the choice for vice president. Both Lincoln and a disgruntled Horace Greeley were on hand for the proceedings. Unable to accept the result with grace, Greeley stormed out, threatening to abandon the ticket altogether. The *Tribune* editor thereupon turned up at the offices of the Philadelphia *North American*, "carpet bag in hand," and eager to share his discontent. Encountering a roomful of Taylor supporters, he "scowled upon them, turned around, and started for the door."

"Where are you going, Mr. Greeley?" asked the socially prominent and gentlemanly *North American* editor, Morton McMichael.

"I'm going home," came the snarling reply.

"But there's no train to-night," McMichael pointed out.

"I don't want any train," snapped Greeley. "I'm going across New Jersey, afoot and alone." And out he stormed, vowing to air his disappointment on the pages of the *Tribune*.[20] Besides, he had walked part of the way to New York to begin his career years earlier. Such a trek would make even better copy now.

James Gordon Bennett, never one to shy away from sharing his pleasure over his rivals' misfortunes, exceeded even his own reputation for self-aggrandizement when he reminded his readers that if "Taylor is to be elected President," it would be because he "was first named in connection with the Presidency, after his first battle on the Rio Grande, in the columns of the *New York Herald*."[21]

Not until autumn did Greeley reluctantly throw his weight behind the Whig choice, taking one last opportunity to extol Clay, but conceding "the impossibility of defeating" Democratic nominee Cass "otherwise than by supporting Gen. Taylor." Admitting that both men had once been "wrong" on the "atrocious" Mexican War, Greeley now offered that Taylor at least had a better excuse for his enthusiasm, having been "reared under slaveholding influences." Most important of all, he argued, a Taylor victory would at least "expel from power the advocates and instate instead the opponents of Slavery Extension."[22]

Late in July, Lincoln took to the House floor to deliver a stirring Taylor endorsement of his own. But the oration was principally notable because it featured a withering attack on Democrat Cass's supposed heroics during the War of 1812, a record that of course paled before the widely reported exploits of Old Rough and Ready in Mexico. Returning to the vitriol of his "Rebecca" letters period, this time in full view of fellow congressmen and reporters, Lincoln made short and hilarious work of Cass's claim to glory. He "*in*vaded Canada without resistance," Lincoln taunted, "and he *out*vaded it without pursuit."[23] Colleagues howled with laughter. As if in anticipation of such attacks, Bennett's *Herald* had warned back in March that Cass was "not the imbecile man that some of the journals represent him," predicting: "If the whigs . . . think to carry their objects by underrating his popularity, his acquirements, his talents, or his position, they will make a fatal mistake." [24] Lincoln paid no heed; he decided the Cass record was ripe for mockery.

As witnesses to his House performance attested, Lincoln's public speaking style differed markedly from fellow Illinoisan Douglas's, even if it yet attracted sparser crowds in the visitors' section. Rather than plant himself behind his desk, there to peel off successive layers of clothing in heated fury—the Little Giant's signature oratorical technique—Lincoln preferred to stroll casually up and down the aisles as he spoke, "gesticulating" as he snaked his way among his colleagues, pausing occasionally to return to his back-row desk to check his notes or sip some water while keeping fellow congressmen "in a continuous roar of merriment." [25] Douglas's oratory was designed for the galleries; Lincoln's for his peers, and for newspaper subscribers, too, for whom humor and straightforward language often proved more readable than grandiloquence. Perhaps uncertain that his latest effort would earn the attention it merited, Lincoln arranged for this oration, too, to appear in pamphlet form for hometown consumption in Springfield and environs. Pamphlets never substituted for press coverage, but they usefully expanded the reach of both politicians and party newspapers, which were often called on not only to reprint such orations but also to handle their sale and distribution.

Later that election season, Lincoln demonstrated further appreciation for the political power of the press by supporting yet another Whig campaign newspaper, this one launched by Washington's national party headquarters. Entitled *The Battery*, it made no pretense at offering anything but party-line propaganda. Loyalists were expected to promote it. In a letter to a fellow Whig back in Illinois, attorney Stephen A. Hurlbut—probably not the only such appeal he wrote, but the sole surviving example—Lincoln dutifully inserted Hurlbut's name onto a pre-printed subscription sheet and strongly urged him to support the new paper and enlist others to do likewise. The flyer made no secret of its object. The newspaper's mission was to *"promote the election of Gen. ZACHARY TAYLOR to the Presidency."* And in sending it, Lincoln made no secret of his own enthusiasm for the venture:

> *I respectfully request you to obtain subscribers for the paper in your immediate vicinage. Please send a list of names, and the amount that will be due according to the terms proposed, and I will see that the subscribers get their papers through the mail. As a general dissemination of this paper will, it is believed, be of high importance to the success of the Whig cause, permit me to solicit an immediate attention to the subject.*

Enclosing a handwritten cover note, Lincoln added a personal endorsement, advising Hurlbut, as if he were doing him a favor: "I could think of no better way of fitting you out, than by sending you the Battery." Showing no loss of enthusiasm for the tried-and-true vehicle of the party extra, the congressman urged his friend to "get as many subscribers as you can" for the new Taylor sheet, adding a money-back promise worthy of a professional salesman: "I have put you down for one copy, the subscription for which I will pay myself, if you are not satisfied with it." [26] No record of a reply is known, but Hurlbut almost certainly did as he was asked.*

Lincoln proved indefatigable that season in his support for the Whig presidential choice. After attending House sessions in the broiling summer heat through adjournment in August, he embarked on a long and undoubtedly tiring Eastern campaign swing in Taylor's behalf. The tour took him through Maryland and then up to Massachusetts. The usually indifferent *National Intelligencer* took brief but welcome notice of his appearance at Rockville, Maryland, acknowledging "a most interesting speech" before the county's "Rough and Ready" club by "Hon. Mr. Lincoln of Illinois." On his return to Washington to deliver another address "in laudation of General Taylor and in opposition to the Democracy," Lincoln earned another notice, this time in the *Baltimore Clipper*.[27]

Press coverage only intensified when Lincoln reached New England. The *Boston Daily Atlas* hailed the congressman's September 19 speech at Chelsea, Massachusetts, noting that, "for aptness of illustration, solidity of argument, and genuine eloquence [it] is hard to beat." When Lincoln spoke the next day at Cambridge, the *Atlas* correspondent admiringly described the visitor as not only a "popular and convincing speaker," but "a capital specimen of a 'Sucker Whig,' six feet at least in his stockings, and every way worthy to represent the Spartan band of the only Whig district in poor benighted Illinois." [28]

Lincoln went on to deliver a well-received ninety-minute oration at a meeting of the Boston Whig Club, "which, for sound reasoning, cogent argument and keen satire," raved the *Atlas*, "we have seldom heard equaled." The paper reported that "the audience gave three cheers for Taylor and Fillmore, and three more for Mr. Lincoln, the Lone Star of Illinois." [29] Here in Boston, Lincoln also for the first time met Horace Greeley's sometime ally, the New York Whig star William Seward, eight years Lincoln's senior and on the verge

---

*Years later, Lincoln would repay Hurlbut's loyalty not only by commissioning him a major general, but by sidetracking investigations into persistent charges of corruption.

of a significant career in the U.S. Senate. The two men shared the same stage at a Whig rally at the Tremont Temple on September 22. Seward was of course the main attraction, but after Lincoln exhibited his customary "humorous strain of Western eloquence" to the distinguished Eastern audience, this event, too, concluded with "three hearty cheers for 'Old Zack,' three more for Governor Seward, [and] three more for Mr. Lincoln." [30]

Legend holds that at this, their first face-to-face meeting, Lincoln warned Seward of inevitable future national conflict over what the congressman allegedly called "this slavery question"—at least so Seward later remembered. [31] But Seward's further recollection—that "the following night we passed together in Worcester, occupying the same lodging room at the hotel"—is open to challenge (Seward poured it on, adding the self-congratulatory memory that Lincoln later told him "that I was right in my anti-slavery position and principles"). As Seward's most recent biographer, Walter Stahr, has convincingly shown, the two men did not even pass that night in the same city, calling the entire account into question. But the future president and his future secretary of state did at least share a speaker's platform to promote Whig principles, and there began an acquaintance, and competition, that would be dramatically rekindled during another presidential campaign twelve years later. [32]

Crowded for space after reprinting Seward's address, the *Boston Atlas* found no room to print Lincoln's full remarks. But the *Boston Daily Advertiser* reported approvingly that Lincoln had spoken "in a clear, and cool, and very eloquent manner, for an hour and a half, carrying the audience with him in his able arguments and brilliant illustrations,—only interrupted by warm and frequent applause." Not only was the speech "masterly and convincing," the *Advertiser* reported; the "very tall and thin figure, with an intellectual face" had shown "a searching mind, and a cool judgment." [33] On September 25, providing an "answer to the many applications which we daily receive from different parts of the State for this gentleman to speak," the *Daily Atlas* felt compelled to report that "Hon. Abraham Lincoln" had "left Boston on Saturday morning, on his way home to Illinois." [34]

In his entire career, Lincoln had never earned more enthusiastic out-of-town reviews, or more gratifying acknowledgment at home. Predictably, Democratic journals in Illinois mocked the peripatetic congressman for spending so much time campaigning in safe Whig territory like Massachusetts. "We are pleased to observe that his arduous duties since the adjournment of Congress in franking and loading down the mails with whig electioneering documents, have not impaired his health," taunted the *State Register* when Lincoln returned to Springfield, almost grudgingly adding: "He looks remarkably well."[35] On Election Day, both of the Eastern states where he had campaigned went handily for Taylor, and doubtless would have so voted without his help. The general won the national contest by a healthy margin, but to Lincoln's disappointment, Cass prevailed in Illinois, fatally hurt by a third-party campaign by former Democratic president Martin Van Buren, running as an antislavery Free Soiler—pledged (like Lincoln and most Northern Whigs) to keeping slavery out of the West in order to safeguard opportunity for white labor.[36] Lincoln had done his best to deliver his home state to the Whigs— giving speeches in Peoria, Beardstown, Jacksonville, Petersburg, Metamora, Magnolia, Lacon, and other towns—to little avail. The final outcome in Illinois may not have startled the Taylor camp, but it hardly boosted Lincoln's chances for a significant, post-congressional presidential appointment.

The national Whig victory notwithstanding, when Lincoln and Douglas resumed their seats in December 1848 for the second session of the 30th Congress, it was Democrat Douglas whose career seemed to be on the ascendant. By contrast, Representative Lincoln's political prospects appeared bleak, his options limited, and his relationship with the national press, such as it was, stalled.

One thing in Washington did change, and dramatically, when the House reconvened in December: none other than Horace Greeley arrived in Washington, too, not as a correspondent for the *Tribune*, but as a congressman himself. Whig leaders had installed Greeley as a compromise choice to occupy a disputed New York seat for the final three months of the session.[37] Greeley, who had briefly flirted with the idea of supporting Van Buren over Taylor for the presidency, had finally endorsed the general in October. Perhaps grateful for the last-minute support, New York's Whig political boss, Thurlow Weed, offered him the interim seat as a reward, and Greeley, who for years had yearned for public office, seized the opportunity, however brief.[38]

Once again the intersection of politics and the press was destined to blur the line between reporting and making news. Even with *Philadelphia Daily Sun* editor Lewis C. Levin in his second term in the House, few in Washington could remember so prominent a working journalist ever taking a seat in Congress. The crusading Greeley of course saw nothing inappropriate about continuing to manage the *Tribune* from Washington while serving there himself. Greeley used his new status and enhanced access to ferret out Capitol Hill scoops and pen highly critical "insider" commentary. The editor marked Christmas 1848, for example, by publishing a column entitled "Waste of Time in Congress." He branded the lethargy there as "so chronic and in my judgment so pernicious—operating at once as a serious detriment to public interests and a cruel wrong to individuals who have just claims against the government," that he vowed to continue exposing conditions there until the House began accelerating its work schedule.[39]

Greeley proceeded to make himself further obnoxious to his new colleagues by fearlessly challenging House traditions and introducing impossibly idealistic bills, which he publicized lavishly in his own paper even though they were all doomed to defeat. That he had become an irritant was evident when he tried in January 1849 to stall a routine allocation to fund the salaries of naval officers, arguing that the service was burdened with more commissioned officers than it needed and had too little money to pay ordinary seamen. But the weak-voiced Greeley was no Lincoln when it came to oratory. Once the editor concluded his appeal on the House floor, Georgia congressman Thomas Butler King rose in his seat to jeer that "not a word that he had said could be heard" in his part of the House. Greeley's whispered amendment was rejected.[40]

Greeley's presence in the Whig congressional caucus nonetheless presented a major opportunity for Lincoln to impress his important new colleague. It did not happen. However alike their early life struggles, however compatible some of their progressive views, they simply failed to connect with each other on either a personal or political level. Lincoln was too practical for Greeley's taste. And Greeley was too idealistic to suit Lincoln. Whether or not they ever got the opportunity to trade memories of their eerily similar migrations into adult life in the summer of 1831, we just do not know.

Overall, Greeley paid Lincoln only casual notice in Congress, and barely acknowledged their association years later in an autobiography published at a time when it would have been unthinkable to ignore a man so recently elevated to national sainthood (even if he had made little impression a generation earlier). Infused with antislavery zeal, Greeley recalled Lincoln as typical of "the very mildest type of Wilmot Proviso Whigs from the free States." The editor unenthusiastically recalled his colleague as "a quiet, good-natured man" who "did not aspire to leadership and seldom claimed the floor. I think he made but one set speech during that session, and this speech was by no means a long one." Greeley did acknowledge Lincoln's "unhesitating, uncalculating, self-sacrificing devotion to the principles and aims of his party"—but his assessment remained unpublished until 1891, nearly five decades after the fact.[41] Merely a temporary congressman, and an unelected one at that, Greeley nonetheless considered Lincoln, not himself, a "new member," conceding only that he was "personally a favorite on our side."[42] If he remembered Lincoln's recent "correction" on the Texas boundary editorial, he never afterward bothered to say so.

Tellingly, Greeley later admitted that while he regarded Lincoln as a "buoyant, cheerful spirit," the editor never once heard the celebrated yarn-spinner tell "an anecdote or story,"[43] a sure sign that their acquaintance only went so far. Lincoln was already renowned for amusing fellow congressmen with a bottomless trove of well-aimed humor. Even the crusty House sergeant-at-arms, himself an old newspaperman who had earned his post years earlier in return for favorable coverage of the party, remembered Lincoln as "ever ready to match another's story by one of his own."[44] Greeley's obliviousness suggests that he and Lincoln kept their distance. It was a lost opportunity—for both ambitious men. Easily enough, they might have found early common ground on such nonpolitical subjects as child-rearing. Greeley worried that his young son had a "terrible propensity for mischief,"[45] and few in the vicinity of Sprigg's boardinghouse who remembered the fractious Lincoln boys before their father sent his wife and children packing for her father's home in Kentucky would have thought otherwise of the irascible Bob and Eddy.

Greeley was not always easy to like, but Lincoln lost a valuable chance at forging a lasting alliance by not more aggressively courting the editor as a friend. In turn, Greeley forfeited the chance to exert more influence on a future statesman by failing to recognize Lincoln's promise. Their paths would cross many times in the future, but as historian Harlan Hoyt Horner pointed out in a joint biography of the two men, they remained functionally irreconcilable: Greeley the incurable idealist, and Lincoln the hard-nosed realist. Their personal incompatibility could never really be bridged. For the rest of their lives, the two men remained trapped in an uneasy and occasionally volatile relationship.[46]

Lincoln remained largely ignored not just by Greeley but by most of the influential Whig journalists in the capital. His first known direct written communication with the editors of his party's most important Washington paper came in an innocuous note to "Messrs. Gales & Seaton" of the *Intelligencer* in January 1849. The letter had nothing to do with policy matters. It merely sought collection of $1,500 due on drafts drawn by an unknown character named Thomas French—an episode whose details are lost to history. "Let me hear from you on the subject," Lincoln concluded his brief appeal to the editors. No record of a reply survives.[47] The issue at hand likely involved an outstanding debt incurred for writing or jobbing out some forgotten campaign publishing project. It would have logically fallen to an outgoing freshman like Lincoln to close the books on such an arrangement. Editors Gales and Seaton themselves operated at a far loftier level.

So did the opposition press, which functioned not only as reporters of the outgoing Polk administration, but also as counselors. When Congress neared passage of milestone legislation to organize the newly acquired Oregon Territory with slavery banned, Polk summoned close advisors to the White House in his final weeks in office to discuss whether to approve it. Among them was none other than septuagenarian Thomas Ritchie, editor of the *Union,* who strongly urged a presidential veto. Polk ultimately rejected his advice and signed the bill into law, but typically, old Ritchie had participated in the story not only as a journalist, but as a would-be policymaker, too.[48]

Lincoln's finest hour in Congress came in January 1849 when, with Congressman Greeley no doubt in attendance, he offered a resolution to ban slavery in the District of Columbia. No one knows exactly what inspired Lincoln to take so liberal a stand on this stormy issue at this specific moment. By his own description always "naturally anti-slavery," he had nonetheless long been inclined, as he later put it, to "bite my lip and keep quiet."[49] But the horrors he routinely observed in the slave city of Washington may have aroused the latent abolitionist in him. One particularly nauseating incident at Sprigg's boardinghouse a year earlier no doubt contributed to this awakening. There, an African-American waiter named Henry Wilson had been violently cornered, shackled, and dragged from the residence bound for a slave pen, in full view of horrified boarders. The servant's sole "offense" was coming but $60 short in an ongoing effort to buy his own freedom for $300. Although Wilson was still making payments, his owner had tired of waiting for his money and decided to sell him south. Apparently taking offense that such a tussle had erupted in the home he leased to Mrs. Sprigg, Duff Green himself went to court to seek Wilson's release. "By the well-timed efforts, we learn, of Mr. Green," reported the local abolitionist journal, the *National Era*, "Henry was brought back to the city." Antislavery Ohio congressman Joshua Giddings, another boarder at Sprigg's, quickly raised the balance of Wilson's debt from colleagues on the House floor, and the waiter was legally manumitted.[50]

As if this was not enough motivation to stir antislavery feeling even among the nonabolitionists, from some windows of the Capitol itself, Whig members of Congress at the time could easily see what Lincoln described with disgust as a nearby "negro-livery stable, where droves of negroes were collected, temporarily kept, and finally taken to Southern markets, precisely like droves of horses."[51] Lincoln, for one, had seen enough.

Illinois Free Soil man Isaac N. Arnold, a political intimate and biographer, would later describe Lincoln's 1849 legislative initiative in glowing terms, recalling: "The future great leader of emancipation introduced a bill to emancipate slaves in the District of Columbia."[52] Written in hindsight after Lincoln's martyrdom, Arnold's gilded assessment is a bit overblown, viewed from the post-emancipation era backward, instead of the other way around. In fact, though a brave effort on Lincoln's part, it was also a typically cautious one, proposing to liberate only the children of slaves born after 1850, and requiring them thereafter to serve apprenticeships. Moreover, Lincoln proposed that emancipation take effect only if a majority of Washington's white residents voted to approve it. For some it was not enough. Focused at the time on an alternative bill of his own that would have instead outlawed the District's odious slave trade, Horace Greeley sarcastically likened Lincoln's plan for a slave owners' referendum on slavery to "submitting to the inmates of a penitentiary a proposition to double the length of their respective terms of imprisonment."[53] It was the first time the two men actually opposed each other on a major congressional initiative. That the disagreement portended years of struggle over the issue neither man could have suspected.

Still, Lincoln's legislation seemed radical enough at the time to send many fellow Whigs running timidly for political cover. Disheartened, he complained that most of the "former backers" on whose support he relied "abandoned" him at the crucial moment, ensuring the bill's failure.[54] But the event marked significant moral growth in a man who, only two years earlier, while already a congressman-elect, had agreed to take on the legal case of a slave owner seeking to recover his runaways.[55]

The unsettling experience did bring Lincoln closer at last to *National Intelligencer* editor William Seaton. "I visited Mayor Seaton," he recollected, ". . . to ascertain if a bill such as I proposed would be endorsed by them." There he no doubt found the legendary Whig editor in his customary place behind his cluttered desk at the paper's "smoke-stained" headquarters, his hands interlocked, reclining in his chair, and regarding Lincoln with his customary "native politeness." Informed by the mayor and his co-publisher, Joseph Gales, that his emancipation initiative "would meet with their hearty approbation," Lincoln attested: "I gave notice in congress that I should introduce a Bill." Later he declared from the House floor that no fewer than fifteen of Washington's leaders supported his measure, but when challenged by Democrats with shouts of, "Who are they? Give us their names!" he refused to identify anyone; his new acquaintance with Mayor Seaton went unreported.[56] And of course his bill died. At least the *New York Tribune* later took notice of the effort, praising Lincoln as "conspicuous in the last Congress—especially during the last session, when he attempted to frame and put through a bill for the gradual Abolition of Slavery in the District of Columbia," adding, in a backhanded compliment: "He is a strong but judicious enemy to Slavery, and his efforts are usually very practical, if not always successful."[57]

Antislavery forces were long accustomed to failure. Far more prominent freedom spokesmen than Lincoln hungered in vain for positive coverage in the newspapers. Denied respectful attention in the mainstream press—subjected, rather, to frequent and merciless attack—they thrived largely on the pages of their own abolitionist journals. Back on New Year's Day 1831, William Lloyd Garrison had founded one of the most famous of them, the *Liberator*, with an editorial pledge to be "harsh as truth and uncompromising as justice." Garrison accompanied this declaration with a famously contemptuous attack on the U.S. Constitution as "a covenant with death"—a condemnation right out of the Book of Isaiah.[58] Garrison nearly paid for his daring with his life. In 1835, a mob cornered the editor backstage at Boston's Faneuil Hall, placed a noose around his neck, and marched him outside as if to lynch him; police came to his rescue just before his assailants could do him real harm.[59] Fearlessly and unapologetically, Garrison's paper continued for years to rail against slavery each and every week, operating out of an attic loft at Merchant's Hall in Boston. There the crusading abolitionist lived and worked amid "dingy walls . . . small windows, bespattered with printer's ink; the press standing in one corner; the composing stands opposite; the long editorial and mailing table, covered with newspapers; the bed of the editor and publisher on the floor." [60]

In his very first edition, Garrison and his partner had vowed to "print the paper as long as they can subsist upon bread and water, or their hands obtain employment. The friends of the cause may therefore take courage; its enemies may surrender at [their] discretion." With the approach of the 1850s, Garrison neared

William Lloyd Garrison, abolitionist editor of *The Liberator*.

his twentieth anniversary of continuous publication by declaring that he had been so long "looked upon with contempt" that the "outrageous abuse" had all but lost its meaning. Not that the paper was ever truly read widely. For years, as an example, the only place where residents of Pennsylvania's state capital could buy *The Liberator* was at a local, black-owned oyster restaurant. (The owner's son later became a Civil War battlefield correspondent, one of the few African Americans to cover the war.) [61]

The late 1830s had seen the launch of a promising new African-American-owned and operated newspaper as well. But New York City's *Colored American*, founded in 1837, lasted only until late 1841. Subsequent titles rose and fell, struggling for advertising and influence even though most had scant hopes of reaching beyond small audiences of free blacks and like-minded abolitionists. The future editor of one such paper remembered that his earliest experience as a "young, ardent, and hopeful" free man in 1841—just three years out of bondage at the time—had come working to sign up subscribers for the *The Liberator* as an agent for the Massachusetts Anti-Slavery Society. The escaped slave's name was Frederick Douglass, a self-described "graduate from the peculiar institution, with my diploma *written on my back*." [62]

Rapidly making a mark as a mesmerizing lecturer and orator, Douglass briefly took the abolitionist gospel to Europe. After returning to America in 1847, he decided to devote himself to "wielding my pen as well as my voice in the great work of renovating the public mind, and building up a public sentiment, which should send slavery to the grave." In short, he proposed establishing a newspaper of his own, devoted to restoring "liberty and the pursuit of happiness" to "the people with whom I have suffered." Friends warned Douglass that another new antislavery paper "was not needed" and "could not succeed." Further, they cautioned, the very idea of a "wood-sawyer"—the period term for effervescent public speakers whose gestures resembled sawing wood—"offering himself to the public as an editor" was "absurd." Undeterred, Douglass relocated to Rochester, New York, and there established the most famous black-owned newspaper of them all: *The North Star*—later renamed *Frederick Douglass' Paper*, and ultimately *Douglass' Monthly*. "Now," he proudly recalled, "I had an audience to speak to every week." [63]

Douglass went on to do battle not only against slavery, but against the reigning suspicion "that both my editorials and my speeches were written by white persons." So low was the "estimate of Negro possibilities," he noticed, that Southerners visiting nearby Niagara Falls frequently detoured to Rochester to see for themselves whether "an uneducated fugitive slave could write the articles attributed to me." [64]

Frederick Douglass, editor of *Frederick Douglass' Paper*, later *Douglass' Monthly*.

Not that the novice editor abandoned the lecture circuit entirely—even if his appearances invariably elicited brutally racist coverage in the conservative dailies. Typically, when Douglass spoke at the American Anti-Slavery Society in May 1847, he provoked nothing but condemnation in the *New York Sun*. In what the orator described as "a weak, puerile, and characteristic attack upon me," the *Sun* protested against "the unmitigated abuse heaped upon our country by the colored man Douglass." Tongue-in-cheek, Douglass considered it something of a victory to be labeled a "colored man" and not "a *monkey*" in the mainstream press.[65]

In Washington, similarly, the long-established, party-affiliated *Intelligencer* and *Daily Union* of course exerted far more influence than the capital's new, official paper of that same Anti-Slavery Society, the *National Era*, which was edited by a courageous New Jersey–born physician named Gamaliel Bailey, Jr. Even though his would later be celebrated as the first paper to serialize Harriet Beecher Stowe's *Uncle Tom's Cabin*, Dr. Bailey endured constant condemnation along with outright threats of violence. During Lincoln's first months in Congress, Bailey's office and home both came under direct attack from anti-abolition mobs.[66]

Although he left no comment about the hotly discussed Bailey incident, the event must have reminded Lincoln painfully of the atrocities committed by the mob that had killed Elijah Lovejoy back in Illinois in 1837. This latest attack, which occurred after seventy-two slaves were caught trying to flee the capital on a ship moored in the Potomac, unnerved all of Capitol Hill. Slave catchers detected and dragged the escapees back to their bondage soon enough, but after trying without success to lynch the ship captain, a mob turned their rage onto the *National Era*.[67] Bailey and his paper barely escaped their fury. When, around the same time, John P. Hale, an antislavery senator from New Hampshire, offered a bill that would impose federal oversight on all private property in the District, newspapers included, an outraged Southern colleague invited him to visit Mississippi and "grace one of the tallest trees in the forest, with a rope around his neck." It took an increasingly influential, compromise-minded Stephen Douglas to step in and calm the dispute, burnishing his own reputation in the process.[68]

The brief and indecisive 1849 congressional debate over slavery in the District of Columbia occurred at the precise time the *Tribune*'s reform-minded antislavery editor was himself serving in the House. But even Horace Greeley could exert little impact on the chamber in the scant three months he served there. While his staff back home later claimed, "No member was ever more faithful to his duties, and no one ever received smaller reward,"[69] Greeley himself conceded that "much" was said but "little was achieved" during "that short session." He explained: "As those were the last sands of an Administration already superseded, the old heads of either party were indisposed to have much done beside passing the necessary Appropriation bills."[70]

In fact, showing little understanding that editorializing was a different art than legislating, the editor-congressman bombarded various House committees with proposals, parliamentary objections, and floor amendments that had almost no chance for serious consideration, much less passage. Greeley's quirky initiatives included a measure to provide homesteads on public lands (a cause Lincoln would not embrace for another generation), another to cut funding for the recruitment of soldiers (his argument was that merely "planting the flag" would attract volunteers), yet another to deduct the cost of publicly funded book purchases from congressmen's salaries, and one particularly bizarre proposal to change the name of the United States to "Columbia" in order to dampen states' rights and promote nationalism. While the editor steadfastly maintained that his windmill-tilting "did some good," Greeley's bills, including his slave trade prohibition, routinely went down to defeat.[71]

These failures did not entirely demoralize Greeley, who at least got the opportunity to rail against what he believed to be Congress's hidebound indifference to progress—on both the House floor and in his own paper. He particularly relished one dubious highlight of his brief congressional career. It was a fight he picked over a routine proposal that the House as usual "pay from its contingent fund seven dollars and a half per column inch each to The Union and the National Intelligencer respectively for reporting and printing our debates." This was standard end-of-session fare: a payout to both Democratic and Whig papers for their months of gavel-to-gavel coverage. But ever the zealous reformer, Greeley took issue with the tradition. And he proved stubborn in his opposition.

Even when the bill's sponsor barked at him, "I believe you have been a member of this House some four or five days, and you seem to begin early to decide what measures can and what cannot pass," Greeley dug in his heels. "No matter," he defiantly retorted, "you can't pass that measure here." Embarrassed, the majority temporarily tabled the motion, which proved a pyrrhic triumph for Greeley. He had made powerful new enemies. "Up to this period," he admitted, "I had been favorably regarded and kindly treated by Messrs. Gales and Seaton, the excellent but unthrifty editors of The National Intelligencer; but they wasted no more civilities nor smiles on me so long as they lived." Indeed, from that day forward, Gales and Seaton believed that

Greeley had opposed their bonus payment out of either "personal hostility or general malignity."[72] For years to come, the rivals would joust for national attention—and later, for Lincoln's favor as well. Sometimes the warfare *between* Whig papers could prove more acrimonious than that between Whig and Democratic ones.

So could conflicts among Whig politicians. Greeley's most ill-fated, but perhaps best-remembered, legislative initiative came when he sought to expose, and curtail, the padded eight-dollar-per-twenty-mile travel expense allowances routinely claimed by congressmen journeying between Washington and their home districts. Though loosely required to submit reimbursement requests based on standard but outdated "postal routes," many members unsurprisingly preferred charting meandering itineraries that enabled them to visit appealing tourist attractions, or perhaps deliver political speeches along the way to and from the capital. Greeley firmly believed that while new steamboat routes were indeed "much more swiftly and cheaply traversed," they were also less direct than the older stagecoach roads, and thus both lengthier and costlier for the government to reimburse.

At first, the actual travel records proved so hard to obtain that Greeley hired "a reporter" just to search through the appropriate files and transcribe the relevant information.[73] As Greeley suspected, the elusive archives proved damning. And the *Tribune's* research showed that among the guilty congressional wanderers was none other than Abraham Lincoln. His most recent journey home had detoured significantly to include his Taylor-for-president speaking tour, followed by a westward sojourn along a circuitous route that enabled him, with his wife, to see Niagara Falls. The natural wonder had set an awestruck Lincoln to pondering the days "when Moses led Israel through the Red Sea."[74] But given his zeal for House rules, Greeley probably would have censured Moses himself for wandering too slowly toward the Promised Land. At least Lincoln again got his name prominently mentioned in the *New York Tribune*, though this time it was for allegedly pumping up his expense account. Shortly before Christmas 1848, the paper published what Greeley called "an elucidated exposé of the iniquities of Congressional mileage," including a chart that indicated that fellow Whig Lincoln had added more than eight hundred miles to the "actual no. of miles by postal route," resulting in an excess allowance of a hefty $676.80.[75]

In January, after the holiday recess, Greeley brought his official complaints about travel abuse to the House floor, attempting to affix a mileage reform amendment to a military appropriations bill. His effort prompted an outcry from colleagues like Thomas J. Turner of Illinois, who accused Greeley of altering the records, misunderstanding travel needs, and displaying an unwillingness to speak "the truth"—prompting Greeley to reply that "gentlemen" did not use "such language . . . in my section of the country." After one particularly heated exchange on the issue, an equally offended Representative Robert C. Schenck of Ohio demanded of Greeley: "Do I understand the gentleman's reply to be that he did not intend a sneer upon members of Congress?" To which Greeley replied, to derisive laughter, "No I didn't say that." [76] On January 25, Greeley hit back at Turner for calling him "a malignant and wanton defamer," but in the end watched helplessly as his amendment went down to defeat by a voice vote. Angry colleagues would not even permit a roll call. Reporting his defeat with pride in an article grandly headlined, "The Funeral of Mileage Reform," the "Correspondent of the Tribune"—Greeley himself—lamented: "Thus endeth the last chance to affix a Mileage Reform proviso to any bill which must pass." [77]

"Members did not relish the exposure of their dishonesty," Greeley's junior editors later understated, "but their talking did not in the least disturb Mr. Greeley's equanimity." [78] The editor may have been a bit more unnerved when James Gordon Bennett summarized his brief congressional career by commenting:

> We have not, probably, in the last thirty years, been blessed with such a perfect specimen of a little, mean, pettifogging demagogue in Congress, as Hon. Mr. Greeley has furnished in his own career during the past few months. His extreme affectation of morality, his ultra professions of humanity, the claims he puts forth for political purity, have been amply and fully illustrated in his miserable . . . equivocating, shuffling, sniveling course on the Mileage of Members, and on the Book Expenditures of the House. . . . We are glad that the noise and clap-traps of Master Greeley to catch the little applause of ignorance and envy, have been thrown overboard, as they deserved to be.[79]

Inevitably, Greeley's campaign against fellow Whigs also delighted opposition Democrats in the House. One of them—a congressman who had earned the nickname "Sausage" Sawyer for demanding the expulsion of a reporter for eating a bologna sausage sandwich behind the speaker's chair—admitted that Lincoln's orations on the floor were often "pretty good." But unable to resist a comment on his wandering style—and the recent travel dustup—Sawyer wickedly added: "I hope he won't charge mileage on his travels while delivering it." [80]

To no one's surprise, the House of Representatives never took formal action against Lincoln or his equally peripatetic colleagues on the matter of travel expenses. Instead, they mounted an effort to expel Greeley from Congress—until a Democratic representative from Illinois, "Long" John Wentworth (himself a newspaperman), blurted out to his colleagues: "Why, you blessed fools! Do you want to make him President?" Escaping ouster, the crusading editor remembered appreciatively that since Lincoln did not support "the active cabal against me, though *his* mileage figured conspicuously in that exposé, I parted with him at the close of the Congress with none but grateful recollections." Not all of his congressional colleagues were equally forgiving, specially the pro-slavery Democrats on the other side of the aisle. "I am confident," Greeley admitted after one session marked by particularly violent outbursts, "I could not have passed quietly through that side of the House between ten and two o'clock of that night without being assaulted; and, had I resisted, beaten within an inch of my life, if not killed outright." [81]

The *Tribune* lamented the apparent conclusion of Lincoln's own national political career by praising him, along with other outgoing Whigs, in a story signed by "X," but likely composed by the editor himself:

> Hon. ABRAHAM LINCOLN of Ill. also goes out, having declined a reelection. He is an universal favorite here—an entirely self-made man, and of singular and striking personal appearance. It is said that his District will send him back here at the next election, *nolens volens* [willingly or unwillingly]. [82]

Years later, Greeley insisted that while Lincoln was indeed "liked and esteemed" in his congressional days, ". . . there were men accounted abler on our side of the House." In Greeley's estimate, "had each of us been required to name the man among us who would first attain the presidency, I doubt whether five of us would have designated Abraham Lincoln." [83] "Five" may actually have constituted an exaggeration. Lincoln's brief exposure to Washington officials and journalists alike, ending in early 1849, had made him a wiser, but not yet a more conspicuously promising, politician. As for Greeley, he ended his own brief congressional career "not likely," he admitted, ever to hold office again. Yet he valued the experience, acknowledging: "I saw things from a novel point of view; and if I came away from the Capitol no wiser than I went thither, the fault was entirely my own." [84]

Greeley maintained in one of his last and longest House addresses on February 26, 1849, that he had come to Congress "to act, not to talk," proclaiming: "I do not think my constituents want any speechmaking from me." Indeed, during his brief but eventful three-month term, whenever he did orate he spoke so softly that clerks and colleagues had trouble hearing him. But with only five days left in his term, the editor rose one more time to note that too much energy had recently been expended debating slavery, as a result of which too much business had been "left undone." Not even Greeley, however, whether as a powerful editor or a powerless temporary congressman, could hope to hold back the national tide on the slavery issue. He was never more wrong than when he told his colleagues that day: "It strikes me that *that* topic is well nigh exhausted." [85]

Greeley remained in Washington until March so he could attend Zachary Taylor's inauguration, and then returned quietly to New York to resume full-time work on the *Tribune*. "With no applauding shouts was Horace Greeley welcomed on his return from the Seat of Corruption," lamented one of the editor's earliest biographers. ". . . Do the people, then, generally feel that an Honest Man is out of place in the Congress of the United States?" [86] Greeley himself provided what he hoped would serve as an answer on the pages of his newspaper: "Calling me a hypocrite or demagogue cannot make a charge of $1,664 for coming to Congress from Illinois and going back an honest one." [87] It sounded almost as if Greeley was departing Washington with a slap against Illinois's Abraham Lincoln.

Lincoln's own most prominent political target also "came away" from Washington in March 1849, no doubt delighted that he would never again have to endure attacks by Lincoln, Greeley, and their more powerful Whig allies over his record as chief executive. After the inaugural, a relieved James Polk left the capital to make way for his successor, Zachary Taylor. Just three months into his retirement, however, the exhausted fifty-three-year-old ex-president died at his home in Nashville, inspiring press eulogies that ranged from respectful to worshipful. Democratic journals like the *Union* extolled the late chief executive as a demigod, while the Whig press—even the long-hostile *Intelligencer*—paid muted tribute. Not every Whig organ concurred. In New

York, William Cullen Bryant's antislavery *Evening Post* reminded readers that Polk had demonstrated a "low tone of character" throughout his battles with the Whigs over issues of war and national expansion. Back in Washington an outraged Thomas Ritchie denounced the *Post* as "unable even under such circumstances, to control its savage temper," adding: "Surely, the viper should be shaken from the skirts of democracy." [88]

In fact, the "viper" of press warfare outlived the Polk and Taylor administrations alike, the Mexican War and its acrid aftermath, and the earliest rumblings of renewed political agitation over slavery. The war of words over sectional issues was just beginning to percolate. At full boil, abetted by further improvements in transportation, as well as new printing and news-gathering technologies that all worked to make newspapers yet more affordable and available to readers more quickly than ever, the press stepped up attacks not only on opposition politicians but, with increasing furor, on each other as well. Once the realm of ink-stained country printers, newspapers had become a major American industry.

For a time, Lincoln postponed his own departure from Washington. Although surely yearning for a reunion with his wife and children, he, too, remained in the crowded and reenergized national capital for Taylor's inauguration but unlike Greeley lingered a few weeks more to lobby the new administration for a job. Not until March 20 did he retreat toward Springfield, only to return to Washington in June to campaign further in his own behalf—and not without enduring some mocking press coverage for his efforts, with the pro-Douglas hometown *Register* deriding his quest for patronage as a "steeple chase" in the "federal capital." [89] More portentously, an incident occurred along the way that the superstitious and self-deprecating Lincoln loved to recount ever after. Somewhere between Springfield and Washington, a fellow stagecoach passenger offered the office seeker tobacco, which he politely refused, then liquor, which the abstemious Lincoln rejected as well. This prompted the traveler to observe: "See here, stranger . . . my experience has taught me that a man who has no vices has d—d few virtues." [90]

In the competition for political reward, Lincoln's virtues proved insufficient to earn him an advantage. He fared no better in securing the kind of post he expected than had the perennially frustrated aspirant Horace Greeley. Among the similarly disappointed and dispossessed were Gales and Seaton of the *Intelligencer*, who paid the ultimate price for their earlier criticism of Taylor's nomination. At the new president's insistence, the Whig Party stripped them of their longtime role as official administration organ and terminated their contracts for official government printing. The *Intelligencer*'s days of Whig Party influence were over.[91]

Lincoln's new goal was securing a presidential appointment to the post of commissioner of the General Land Office, a major federal agency that oversaw the surveying and selling of publicly owned acreage nationwide. Here was a patronage job in turn rich with considerable patronage power of its own. Back in Springfield, Whig editor Simeon Francis could barely contain his enthusiasm. His appetite for influence over so vast a trough thoroughly aroused, the editor joined a group of Whig leaders urging Lincoln to fight hard for a position they judged "important enough to the interests of Illinois" to require "one of our own" installed in the post. Six days later, a Whig leader from neighboring Jacksonville similarly urged Lincoln into the fray, asking him to forward copies of Francis's newspaper, no doubt so he could keep abreast of the "official" party-wide campaign for the Land Office.[92]

But the editorials published in his behalf by Whig papers in Illinois fell on deaf ears in Washington; the ex-congressman ultimately lost out to another patronage aspirant from Illinois. Disappointed as he was, Lincoln still hoped to secure an equally prestigious appointment that might enable him to avoid returning to live and work in rustic Springfield, which he surely felt he had outgrown. Yet, when the Taylor administration instead came through with another viable offer, Lincoln regarded the proposed outpost—the governorship of Oregon Territory—as too *far* from his hometown. Taking his acceptance for granted, Greeley's *Tribune* prematurely announced his appointment on September 22, 1849, belatedly acknowledging that he had been "conspicuous in the last Congress." Only now, when it was too late, did the paper heap somewhat discounted praise on Lincoln, describing him as "a man of sound judgment, good though not brilliant mind, and capable, mentally and physically, of great endurance,—qualities very essential to the position he is about to assume."[93] Assume the position he did not; Lincoln declined the consolation prize in the Far West.

For a time, however, Lincoln tried to get the administration to consider another local candidate for the office: none other than editor Simeon Francis. In an impassioned letter to the new secretary of state, John M. Clayton, Lincoln acknowledged that by declining it himself, he had forfeited the "right to claim the disposal of the office." But he hastened to add that "under all the circumstances"—no doubt an allusion to his tireless campaigning and disappointment in losing the more prestigious Land Office—Francis "ought to receive the appointment" in Oregon. As Lincoln calculated his qualifications: "If a long course of uniform and efficient action as a whig editor; if an honesty unimpeached, and qualifications undisputed; if the fact that he has advanced to the meridian of life without ever before asking for an office, be considerations of importance with the Administration, I can not but feel that the appointment, while it will do him justice, will also do honor to the Administration." [94] Once again, however, the White House ignored Lincoln's appeal. Francis did not get the job—although his longing to migrate to Oregon only intensified. Nor was Lincoln more successful in securing an appointment for one of Simeon's brothers and co-publishers, Allen Francis, who implored him to "personally present my case to Old Zack," adding: "Secure it for me and I will be grateful to you forever—and my wife will pray that no cloud may ever darken the sunshine of your prosperity." [95]

Encountering the frustrated office seeker and would-be patronage dispenser not long thereafter, a surprised friend greeted Lincoln by exclaiming: "I supposed you were going to Oregon as governor." Typically this reminded Lincoln of a funny story. "Two men were playing cards, and one said to the other, 'Go to Hell!' The one addressed said: 'I will go to hell when I am obliged to, and not one minute before.'" [96]

Now home, he believed, to stay, the disappointed ex-congressman was forty years old, and denied the political reward and influence he felt was his due. He had good reason to believe that his best days were behind him. Reduced in his first few weeks in Springfield to refereeing local squabbles for other, lesser federal offices, peppering the State and Navy departments, and even the new president, with recommendations for other patronage seekers, he found the state capital as divided as the national capital had been over America's Mexico experience, and just as unwilling to forget it. [97] Nor had the conflict been experienced in Springfield solely through reports of the debates in distant Washington. After all, the two local Whigs who had preceded Lincoln in the House had both served gloriously in the war: John J. Hardin, killed in action at Buena Vista, and Edward Baker, who led a regiment at Cerro Gordo. And Stephen Douglas's own devoted friend and press ally William Walters was dead as well, even if he had never reached Mexico.

Walters's young successor at the helm of the paper, his onetime apprentice and brother-in-law Charles Lanphier, brought scant managerial experience to his new post, but much knowledge from his years under Walters, along with unbounded enthusiasm for Democratic politics. As early as 1839, he had served as a Democratic Party poll watcher.[98] Six years later, in 1845, Stephen Douglas reached out to Lanphier to flatter him into his political orbit, writing: "I believe you . . . possess talents that would be very serviceable to the Democratic cause."[99] Requiring no further encouragement, Lanphier enlisted fully in the cause. The same state legislature that chose Douglas for the Senate back in December 1846 rewarded the editor with the post of Public Printer—still a coveted prize for local publishers.[100] Buoyed by his new official role, and benefiting from further support from a new investor in the perennially struggling paper—attorney George Walker—Lanphier, like his late brother-in-law before him, became one of Douglas's most reliable, ardent, and effective supporters, and one of Lincoln's most unrelenting enemies, in the press.

Meanwhile, although disappointed by his failure to secure a federal post from the Taylor administration, Simeon Francis sought to take his Whig paper to a new level, too. In 1847 the weekly *Sangamo Journal* became the *Illinois Daily State Journal*, better to reflect not only its increased publishing frequency but also its widening influence, or at least to imagine and boast about it.

The Mexican War had spiked reader interest in both of the town's rival newspapers, the *Register* and the *Journal* alike, each of which had provided accounts and analyses of the fighting. Occasionally both had offered welcome, if outdated, news from the home front for the consumption of local troops stationed far away, but fortunate enough to receive cuttings from their loved ones by mail. One thing was certain: more people were now reading the two papers than ever. Perhaps thousands saw the *Register*'s story marking Abraham Lincoln's homecoming by labeling the returning ex-congressman a "moral traitor."[101] It proved but the opening salvo in a new war of words.

As for Douglas, even with the Whigs now in power in Washington, he continued steadfastly maintaining that the conflict with Mexico had been "a war of self-defence, forced upon us by our enemy, and prosecuted on our part in vindication of our honor, and the integrity of our territory." The senator's argument certainly resonated with widely read big-city papers like James Gordon Bennett's *New York Herald*, and by the time Lincoln resumed his residence in Springfield, it was clear that a majority of voters at home endorsed this position, too. For as long as Douglas could score political points by regurgitating Lincoln's antiwar record in Washington, he never let his once and future rival forget his opposition to the Mexican-American conflict.

Most significant of all, it was Douglas alone who took a seat in Washington for the next session of Congress, enlarging his career in the Senate and further expanding his stature and influence. Lincoln, denied the federal appointment he coveted, resumed his professional life as a private citizen in Springfield. He was again a lawyer, not a lawmaker. Once more he was a reader, not a maker, of news.

With a touch of self-pity, Lincoln summarized his diminished status by lamenting his exit from—but not his incurable love of—politics. "I will go home and resume my practice, at which I can make a living," he wistfully told an acquaintance, "—and perhaps some day the people may have use for me." [102]

CHAPTER FIVE

A Mean Between Two Extremes

————◆————

"**A**bler and stronger men I may have met," Horace Greeley conceded after his professional association with the younger journalist Henry J. Raymond ended acrimoniously in the 1840s, but "a cleverer, readier, more generally efficient journalist I never saw." Finally admitting that he had unwisely paid his protégé a smaller salary than he was worth, the veteran editor acknowledged that Raymond's "services were more valuable in proportion to their cost than those of any one else who ever aided me on the *Tribune*." Almost wistfully, Greeley concluded: "I never found another person, barely of age and just from his studies, who evinced so signal and such versatile ability in journalism as he did."[1]

Greeley may have come close to choking on these generous words. For he used them to describe one of the few journalists in his orbit who refused to remain permanently under his yoke. Henry Raymond not only quit the *Tribune* to work for a rival Whig daily, he went on to establish a newspaper of his own that grew into the only major competition the *Tribune* ever faced for readership and influence in Whig and, later, Republican and antislavery circles: the *New York Times*.

The only perceived sins Greeley held against the talented, tireless Henry Raymond were his departure—and his success. Raymond, however, went from admiration to outright contempt for Greeley's frequent departures from party ideology and discipline. "The Whig party is one of order and stability eschewing radicalism in every form," Raymond once lectured him in print, "and the better way for 'The Tribune' would be to admit that it is Whig only on the subject of the tariff and then devote itself to the advocacy of anti-rent, Fourierist, vote-yourself-a-farm doctrine"—enumerating some of Greeley's more far-flung passions and "isms." [2] Although he came of age professionally under Greeley's tutelage, Raymond's career—and the distinct brand of journalism he introduced—would follow a different course from his mentor's scattershot idealism. For Raymond, as progressive as he remained at his core, reason, order, and caution trumped zealotry every time. He was a genuine moderate. In this way, he was far more like Abraham Lincoln than Greeley ever was.

Henry Jarvis Raymond was born on a farm in the rural village of Lima, in western New York state, on January 24, 1820 (a "poor boy from the country," one of his obituaries would emphasize). [3] Contemporary admirers claimed that he could read fluently by the age of three, and speak in public at five. His parents sent their prodigy to study classics at the newly established Genesee Wesleyan Seminary, and after graduation, the boy clerked in a country store for $1.50 a week, then turned briefly to teaching school before demonstrating literary flair by composing a patriotic ode for Lima's 1836 Fourth of July festivities. Later that year, Raymond set off for the University of Vermont in Burlington—the first of the "big three" editors to matriculate at college—where a schoolmate remembered him as "a young, delicate, intellectual-looking student."

The experience opened new doors. When Henry Clay came to Burlington in the summer of 1839 to attend the college's annual Junior Exhibition, Raymond dazzled the audience with a startlingly mature student oration. "That young man," the Great Compromiser was heard to comment, "will make his mark. Depend upon it, you will hear from him hereafter." [4] Instead, it was tiny Lima that heard from Raymond again, and within the year. With no clear career path before him, Raymond returned home in the fall of 1840 after graduating with honors. For a time, he occupied himself by delivering rousing "Tippecanoe and Tyler Too" campaign speeches in neighboring communities, even though he was himself still too young to cast a vote of his own.

Raymond had been devouring Horace Greeley's work ever since strolling into the Lima post office at age fifteen and asking, "what was the best news-paper to subscribe for?" As the young man remembered of the moment that changed his destiny: "The postmaster threw me half a dozen which had been sent to him by the publishers as specimen numbers; and after due deliberation I selected the *New-Yorker* as the one which promised to be the most interest-ing and instructive. I sent my three dollars' subscription," and became a faith-ful reader.[5] While still a teenager, he journeyed to Albany to meet Greeley in person, and corresponded with him throughout his college years. The older and younger man shared a passion for Whig politics. At age twenty, Raymond summoned the presumption to propose migrating to the big city to start at the top: by taking over Greeley's newspaper.

"I have never had any experience . . . in the business of publishing or printing," he gamely wrote Greeley in June 1840. "If I could obtain a place in the New Yorker under the shadow of your wing, I should be exceedingly well suited."[6] Gently, Greeley replied: "You are a good writer on your own ground; and I think would make an interesting paper." But "time, talents, and unwea-ried industry are necessary." Without a financial investment to buy his way into the business, the *New-Yorker* had no room for a novice. Greeley ended his rejection letter with a remarkable assessment: "A newspaper ought to have some hobby, and some clique influence, some *esprit de corps* enlisted in its support," he wrote. "I believe I have erred in making my tastes too catholic." Sounding regretful that his paper had been so moderate, Greeley admitted that the "affectation of impartiality and independence" was not enough to guarantee success in journalism. "If I had embraced and zealously advanced Millerism, Mormonism or Survival Magnetism years ago, I should have been *independent* in the better sense now. Remember this; and if you ever become an Editor, attach yourself to some distinct interest, not noisily, but in such a manner as to secure its support."[7] Raymond would never embrace this advice, though Greeley would make it his future business model.

Undeterred, Raymond began submitting freelance contributions to Gree-ley's weekly, and then in December 1840 headed downstate and waltzed into the *New-Yorker* office, where despite the previous lack of encouragement he again requested a paying job. Small of stature, dark-complexioned, square-jawed, and intense, with piercing eyes, short black pomaded hair, broad shoulders, and a slight paunch, Raymond made for a striking contrast to the ghostly-pale, underfed Greeley. The youngster again impressed the *Tribune* proprietor with his energy and gravitas, but Greeley had just hired another young editorial associate. He could offer Raymond nothing more than an open invitation to visit his establishment whenever he chose, and to pitch in and help the staff as he saw fit—but strictly on a voluntary basis, without compensation.

Even after turning to law studies, Raymond could not get the newsroom out of his blood. He spent his off-hours at the cramped *New-Yorker* headquarters happily absorbing the rituals and rigors of the business. "I added up election returns," he remembered, "read the exchanges for news, and discovered a good deal which others had overlooked; made brief notices of new books, read proof, and made myself generally useful." Once Raymond even composed a "fancy advertisement" for vegetable pills.[8] Weeks later, however, strapped for cash, young Henry received a more permanent offer he felt he must accept. In response to a paid notice he had placed in the *National Intelligencer*, a community in North Carolina had offered him a classroom job at its local school. Hearing this, Greeley invited Raymond to stroll with him to the post office, and along the way asked how much the new job would pay. Replied Raymond, "four hundred dollars a year."

"Oh," Greeley shot back with typical impulsiveness, "stay here—I'll give you that."

"And this," Raymond recalled, "was my first engagement on the Press, and decided the whole course of my life."[9]

Not that this paltry salary alone could support him in New York. For a time, Raymond augmented his small income by contributing freelance articles to out-of-town newspapers like the *Cincinnati Chronicle*, the *Buffalo Advertiser*, and the *Bangor Whig*, noting proudly that "none of these journals paid me less than five dollars a week, and one or two of them gave me six."[10] Facing constant deadlines while pursuing his studies of Latin and the law kept his "leisure reasonably well employed." But when, a year later, Greeley opened the *New York Tribune*, Raymond abandoned all his outside activities and devoted his full energies to the new venture as deputy editor and correspondent.

"He remained with me eight years," Greeley recollected, ". . . and is the only assistant with whom I ever felt required to remonstrate for doing more work than any human brain and frame could be expected long to endure." In truth, young Raymond served Greeley for only half that time, but perhaps performed so much labor that it seemed like double to his appreciative employer.[11] "I was with him less than four years, instead of eight," Raymond corrected Greeley's version of the story, "and, though I did work, I believe, quite as hard during that time upon the *Tribune* as he now gives me credit for having done, I think I have worked still harder for a good many years since." The fact was, Raymond coolly admitted, "I did it from no special sense of duty,—still less with any special aim or ambitious purpose. I liked it; I knew no greater pleasure." [12] In appreciation, Greeley expanded Raymond's beat to include political meetings, crime, courtroom trials, book reviews, and financial news.

For the most part the work was drudgery, but everywhere he looked in New York, Raymond could see the promise of future comfort, fame, and influence. Walking down Broadway one day, he found himself striding alongside "a tall, handsome, silently dressed young man" adorned in white kid gloves and diamond studs. The struggling journalist fancied the stranger "one of the nabobs of the town," and "could not help contrasting my own position with his . . . dazzling splendor." The next day, Greeley sent Raymond to the Barclay Street offices of *Porter's Spirit of the Times,* a popular weekly specializing in horseracing and other sports and leisure news, to pick up the latest copy of the paper. To his astonishment, while waiting at the front desk, in strode "my magnificent friend of the day before, all accoutered as he was. . . . He walked into the back part of the office, took off, folded and put away his white gloves, hung up his hat and coat, put on an ink-stained linen jacket, and set himself to work *writing wrappers* [news summaries]. I felt decidedly encouraged as to the prospects of New York life!" [13]

What he still lacked in comparable glamour Raymond supplied in hard labor. When he took ill after one particularly grueling assignment and missed several days of work, Greeley visited Raymond at his room on the top floor of a Church Street boardinghouse. After climbing the steep stairs, the editor sat down solicitously at his deputy's bedside, but then instead of inquiring about his health, made the mistake of impatiently asking exactly when Henry planned to return to the office. Perhaps emboldened by fever, Raymond retorted: "Never, on the salary you paid me," pointedly using the past tense. Startled, the editor asked how much the young man required to stay on. Raymond demanded a staggering raise—from eight to twenty dollars a week. Bolting for the door, Greeley vowed he would never pay so high a salary to so inexperienced an employee.[14] Eventually he yielded. But even the increased compensation was not enough to sustain the Greeley-Raymond relationship for very long. Politics—the shared belief system that had brought them together in the first place—was now beginning to drive them apart.

Raymond feared Greeley was becoming too radical, and Greeley in turn complained that Raymond was growing too stodgily conservative—"too infernally Tory in your leanings, both in Church and State," the editor lectured him—and increasingly unsympathetic to "true democracy," the brand of reform populism the *Tribune* increasingly espoused.[15] Their bond was fraying. The Greeley whom Raymond had first admired in the days of the *New-Yorker*—the man who offered a "fair examination of both sides of the political topics which divided the country . . . unbiased by party feeling"— had, Raymond believed, abandoned the "calm, dispassionate character" of his early writing. Raymond, too, believed in political journalism, but maintained it required more subtlety and calm than Greeley was willing to inject. In 1843, when crusty newspaper veteran James Watson Webb offered Raymond a better-paid position at his *Courier and Enquirer*, both Raymond and Greeley were ready for a professional divorce. Greeley refused to match the five-dollar increase that came with Webb's new job. Raymond departed and, according to his earliest biographer, "turned his back forever upon Mr. Greeley and the *Tribune*."[16]

Raymond's subsequent attempt to revive the *Courier and Enquirer* proved challenging. Editor Webb, still handsome at age forty-one, and blessed with a military bearing forged in genuine combat experience, considered himself the "Apollo of the Press," and was also demanding, ill-tempered (a "burly, honest kind of savage," in James Gordon Bennett's estimation), and locked into a fading form of journalism.[17] The old broadsheet still retained political influence as well as a faithful if dwindling readership, but in the new era dominated by the racier penny press and the high-minded *Tribune*, its glory days were behind it. Raymond did introduce a number of reforms that at least brought the paper up to date, reorganizing its news page under more distinct categories, ordering darker ink to make its columns easier to read, and for the first time publishing both humor pieces and transcriptions of political speeches. "That little Raymond" complained the paper's "phlegmatic" old business manager, Thomas Snowden, "will not rest contented till he has turned *The Courier and Enquirer* into a two-cent paper."[18]

In a far more aggressive move to hike circulation, the combative Webb unleashed a brutal attack on Greeley in early 1844, accusing his rival of "unbearable . . . affectation and impudence" and questioning everything from his weakness for radical causes to his mode of dress and personal hygiene. "The editor of the *Tribune* is an Abolitionist; we precisely the reverse," the attack concluded. "He is a philosopher; we are Christian. . . . He seeks for notoriety by pretending to great eccentricity of character and habits, and by the strangeness of his theories and practices; we on the contrary, are content with following in the beaten path, and accomplishing the good we can, in the old-fashioned way." [19]

Always primed for a fight if challenged, Greeley wasted no time in responding in the modest third person, but with a venomous swipe of his own on his assailant's recent pardon from Governor William Seward, who had spared Webb the prison sentence some New Yorkers thought he deserved: "The object of this silly raillery has doubtless worn better clothes than two-thirds of those who . . . assailed him,—better than any of them could honestly wear, if they paid their debts otherwise than by bankruptcy; while if they are indeed more cleanly than he, they must bathe very thoroughly not less than twice each day. . . . That he ever affected eccentricity is most untrue; and certainly no costume he ever appeared in, would create such a sensation in Broadway, as that James Watson Webb would have worn but for the clemency of Gov. Seward." [20]

The *Tribune* had the last word in this particular exchange, but the initial attack permanently soured Greeley on Raymond (he began referring to him as "The Little Villain"—a nickname that stuck).[21] No doubt the published assault had originated with Webb, not Raymond, but Greeley believed that his disgruntled onetime employee had at the least told his new editor inside, personal stories, and done too little to prevent Webb from lashing out.

Soon enough Greeley and Raymond came into direct and protracted conflict in a series of printed exchanges on a far more existential topic. This time, the argument ostensibly involved Fourierism, the brand of communal socialism that had all but hypnotized the editor of the *Tribune* and inspired him to help establish the Sylvania Colony in Pennsylvania (a "stupendous humbug," declared the *Courier and Enquirer*). For eight long months beginning in August 1846, Raymond and his former boss conducted an engrossing, if repetitive, debate that eventually embraced such subjects as human character, labor rights, education, and the institution of marriage. As if confronting each other at a series of political rallies, Greeley would issue a statement, Raymond would respond a few days later, and then Greeley would offer a rebuttal, establishing a pattern that persisted for more than half a year.

Deftly, Raymond used the series to stake out major differences with Greeley, not only on the subject of socialism, but also on the very nature—and limits—of progressive reform. Always unable to resist an argument, Greeley's willingness to participate in these battles with so junior a journalist served not only to expose his pet causes to repeated criticism, and occasional ridicule, but also to elevate Raymond's reputation in the bargain. Raymond was no longer just Greeley's onetime protégé; their debate transformed him into Greeley's peer. In the process, their protracted argument served to catalogue their sincerely different approaches to both journalism and politics.

"Throughout this discussion," Raymond concluded in his final installment, "the *Tribune* has charged us with being hostile to all reform, and especially to every attempt to meliorate the hard lot of the degraded poor. The charge is as unfounded as it is ungenerous. We labor willingly and zealously, as our columns will testify, within our sphere, in aid of everything which seems to us TRUE REFORM,—founded upon just principles, seeking worthy ends by worthy means, and promising actual and good results"—an obvious slap at Greeley's weakness for lost causes. In his own final appeal, Greeley shot back that without an unwavering commitment to the "spiritual, life-giving, heart-redeeming principles" of Christianity, the world would remain "without HOPE." [22]

More than mere concluding arguments, here were statements that not only laid bare the dichotomies within American society at large, but revealed these two combatants as they really were: Greeley the self-appointed representative of God and men, and Raymond the pragmatic problem solver. Politically, the exchanges also exposed major fissures between conservative Whig stalwarts like Raymond and Webb, and impatient liberals like Greeley. Raymond, for one, made it clear he opposed making faddish "isms" into statutes. "When as the editor of a popular Whig Journal," Raymond lashed out, "he [Greeley] ventures to urge his idle theories upon the Corporation of our city for their adoption, it is our duty gravely to rebuke his fanaticism, and to protest against his folly and monomania being made to attach to the Whig party." Greeley himself admitted that while the "series of controversial letters" made "a few zealous converts" to "new ideas," they "aroused . . . more vehement adversaries." [23]

To be sure, the debates hardly left Greeley a beaten man. They may have helped seal the doom of Fourierism in New York, but they failed to dethrone its champion as the city's reigning apostle of social justice. That he was anything but embarrassed by the exchanges was evident when Greeley agreed to "co-author" with Raymond a pamphlet version of their debates, which appeared in 1847 and ran to more than eighty pages of text. But Greeley never again regarded Raymond as an ally. Though his occasional letters to his onetime employee over the years invariably began with the salutation "Friend R," Greeley reached out to him with increasing rarity. Even when compelled to write to him on mutually important banking issues six years later, the *Tribune* editor was quick to caution: "I see no necessity for any correspondence between us. I answer your letter because it contains a request that I do so. . . . Understand that I ask no favor from you—none whatever."[24] Their professional competition and personal animus would endure for a quarter of a century.

As for Raymond, six years after joining Webb, the increasingly restless journalist decided he needed further outlets for his own ambition and talent. Not even an unforgettable recognition that came one day from Mrs. Daniel Webster—in Raymond's presence she had told her husband, "You needn't give yourself any trouble, Daniel, about your speeches, as long as Mr. R. reports them"—the young editor wanted to do more than reprint oratory.[25] An effective orator himself—much more so than Greeley—his job at the *Courier and Enquirer* provided him a print platform to advance Whig doctrine, but offered no real political outlet outside journalism. So, like many other newspapermen of his day, Raymond turned to politics. In 1849, the same year Greeley began his brief congressional service in Washington, Raymond sought elected office for the first time in New York, running for the State Assembly (as the candidate of a Wall Street clique, James Gordon Bennett sniffed, suddenly anxious about the young man's ascent). Raymond later claimed he decided to be of "service" to the party only when it became clear that Webb would not be sent overseas with a diplomatic appointment he craved.[26] Whatever his principal motivation for running, Raymond went on to launch his new career without abandoning his primary job as a newspaper editor.

Heading up to Albany as a freshman legislator, he quickly found himself repelled by the city's pervasive culture of corruption: on his second day in office, following a drawing to select desks, he witnessed several colleagues offering up to twenty dollars (a significant sum at the time) for the choicest seats so they could "readily command the Speaker's attention & thus secure the floor." When not shocking, the Albany routine proved boring, although it left him plenty of "leisure" time to fulfill his duties as a journalist. On a typical working day in January, Raymond dutifully studied his copy of the governor's latest annual message, then wrote an editorial on slavery for the *Courier and Enquirer*.[27] During a recess, an Assembly colleague visited him at his newspaper office, where the two examined applications for a lucrative political plum, the collectorship of New York.[28] Somehow, Raymond made his twin careers work. "Mr. Raymond, it is true, occupied, by his own choice, in a certain degree, a sort of dual role before the public," the *New York World* conceded in tortured acknowledgment of his success. He never "absolutely abdicated his real and invisible authority as a writer when he assumed the insignia of a more palpable but less genuine influence as a politician."[29]

Raymond ultimately found legislative work less fulfilling than he had expected. When he returned to Manhattan after the session ended, he considered abandoning his flirtation with government service and instead taking on a greater role at the *Courier and Enquirer*. Webb had departed for a long sojourn in Europe, leaving the office under Raymond's full control, and what was more had sold his young assistant editor a financial stake in the paper. Even so, Raymond proved unable to resist politics. As fellow editor John Russell Young perceptively said of Raymond: "He was a journalist in everything but his ambitions, and these tended to public life."[30] Changing his mind again, Raymond sought and won reelection to the Assembly in 1850, and the following January the Whig majority elevated him to the exalted post of speaker—a huge honor for a thirty-year-old legislative sophomore, and a testament to his growing influence within the party organization.

Inevitably, Raymond's dual careers led to occasional, awkward conflict. When the state legislature set about its lawful task of choosing a new United States senator from New York, another journalist on the prowl for political power—none other than his boss, James Watson Webb—made clear that he desired the seat for himself. Like so many party editors who expected tangible rewards for their loyalty, Webb had

Henry Jarvis Raymond as he looked when working for James Watson Webb at the *Courier and Enquirer* in the late 1840s.

yearned for office ever since switching his affiliation decades earlier from Andrew Jackson's Democrats to the new party whose name he was said to have coined himself: the Whigs. That early defection cost Webb a valuable contract to handle State Department printing, and Raymond remembered his editor returning from Washington "terribly enraged and resolved to . . . abandon the Administration." His junior associate talked him out of taking revenge in print.[31] More recently, the Senate had refused to confirm him as minister to Austria. This most recent blow no doubt made Webb crankier than ever, if his growing penchant for street brawls and editorial feuds was any indication.[32] Now, with a Senate vacancy in prospect, he concluded that if Raymond could serve in elective office, so should he. The Whig majority in Albany, however, had other ideas—Webb never became a serious contender—and Raymond was compelled to bluntly inform his intemperate employer that he would not advocate in his behalf. The seat went instead to the state's Whig governor, Hamilton Fish. Now Webb joined Greeley in imagining himself a spurned mentor whom Raymond had wronged.

The remainder of that year's legislative calendar proved equally frustrating for the young speaker. The session ended after unresolved fights over internal improvements and increasingly fractious squabbles about slavery. (In his first term, Raymond left a strong clue to his future attitude on the volatile issue by "insisting on the propriety of taking ground with caution.")[33] At least Raymond got the chance to showcase his considerable oratorical skills by stepping down from the speaker's chair from time to time to engage his colleagues in floor debate. But once the Assembly adjourned, an exhausted Raymond decided to vacation in Europe himself. Still seething over his recent political disappointment, Webb, who disapproved of Raymond's growing antislavery sentiments anyway, told him that his departure would be interpreted as a resignation from the paper. Defiantly, the speaker left for Europe anyway. The break proved final. "You will probably have seen that I am no longer in the Courier and Enquirer," Raymond casually informed his brother from London in June 1850. "Two gentlemen in Albany propose to start a new paper in New York in September and I shall probably edit it."[34]

Although Raymond never identified the two Albany "gentlemen" who first suggested a new downstate daily, one was probably Seward's political angel (and supposed Greeley ally), Thurlow Weed, who had come to know Raymond even before the assemblyman began serving in the legislature. Just as he had plucked Greeley from relative obscurity a few years earlier, this shrewd judge of talent recognized Raymond's potential earlier than most. As early as 1848, the Albany boss reputedly offered to sell Raymond his *Albany Evening Journal*, perhaps in anticipation of a major political appointment of his own from the incoming Taylor administration—which never came. Raymond might have pursued that flattering opportunity had not one of Weed's partners balked at relinquishing his own shares in the paper. During the failed negotiations, however, Raymond renewed his friendship with an Albany banker whom Weed had employed to broker the aborted *Evening Journal* deal: George Jones, onetime business manager of the *Tribune*, in whose offices the two men had met years earlier. By 1849, they began exploring the alternative notion of establishing a new Whig daily in New York City. For a time, however, their discussions led nowhere.[35]

Jones rekindled Raymond's interest early the next year by shrewdly confiding that the *Tribune* had just reported a staggering annual profit of $60,000. The news set Raymond's competitive juices aboil. Surely there was ample room in the marketplace for another Whig journal after all, and now was as good a time as any to launch one. Earlier, Raymond had been reluctant to cross an ethical line by promoting his employer for the Senate. Now he used his legislative clout to aid the entire banking industry—and perhaps in the bargain shake loose much needed funding for his newspaper enterprise—by opposing a bill in Albany to regulate financial institutions. As it transpired, the regulatory law passed anyway. But Raymond's stance may have helped lure investors to the business-friendly speaker's newspaper venture. Within months, the newly established firm of Raymond & Jones attracted additional backers from Albany, Auburn, and Manhattan, who handsomely capitalized the new enterprise to the tune of $100,000—some fifty times the modest amount with which Greeley had launched the *Tribune* just a decade earlier. On September 18, 1851, the new firm of Raymond & Jones published the maiden edition of the paper they called, in homage to the great London powerhouse, the *New-York Daily Times*.*

In a prospectus issued to announce the paper, Raymond promised that his new, one-penny broadsheet would offer the "news of the day, in all departments and from all quarters, special attention being given to reports of

---

* "Daily" vanished from its iconic logo in 1857; the hyphen in "New-York" disappeared in 1896.

legal, criminal, commercial, and financial transactions in the city of New York, to political and personal movements in all parts of the United States, and to the early publication of reliable intelligence from both continents." In addition, the paper would feature foreign correspondence "written expressly for the *Times*," plus literary reviews, drama and music criticism, and "tales, poetry, biography . . . editorial articles upon everything of interest or importance that may occur in any department,—political, social, religious, literary, scientific, or personal, written with all the ability, care, and knowledge which the abundant means at the disposal of the subscribers will enable them to command." [36] The paper would appear in both morning and evening issues six times a week—every day but Sunday. Subscribers could sign on for four dollars per year. A weekly national edition, featuring "interesting and valuable" summaries, would be "mailed to subscribers in any part of the country" for two dollars per annum.

From the outset, Raymond pledged himself to a journalism that emphasized restraint over sensation, orthodoxy over tub-thumping. His prospectus promised that the *Times* would not commit itself to "the advancement of any party, sect, or person." It would subject "the character and pretensions of public men," "governments," and "administrations" to equal scrutiny. Notwithstanding its vow to shun promoting "any party," the circular left little doubt as to where the newspaper—and its editor—would tilt politically: "It will be under the editorial control and management of HENRY J. RAYMOND; and while it will maintain firmly and zealously those principles which he may deem essential to the public good, and which are held by the great Whig party of the United States, its columns will be free from bigoted devotion to narrow interests, and will be open, within necessary limitations, to communications upon every subject of public importance." Its governing principles would be defined by "Christianity and Republicanism . . . devotion to the Union and the Constitution, obedience to Law, and a jealous love of that Personal and civil Liberty which constitutions and laws are made to preserve."

Overtly reaching out to woo disgruntled *Tribune* readers, Raymond pledged almost oxymoronically that the *Times* would be "CONSERVATIVE, in such a way as shall best promote needful REFORM." Distancing itself from Greeley's quixotic windmill-tilting, the new paper pledged to "avoid rash innovation, and to defeat all schemes for destroying established and beneficent institutions." Raymond added a final principle that would in fact guide the *Times* for generations: it would be "a family newspaper" committed to "allay, rather than excite, agitation."

Front page of the first issue of the *New-York Daily Times*, September 18, 1851, introducing the logotype that remains virtually unchanged to this day.

From a purely entrepreneurial perspective, Raymond was convinced he could carve out a profitable niche in New York's congested newspaper arena. The city's population was growing rapidly, and even the fastest new printing presses could barely keep up with rising demand. Circulation was booming. Led by Bennett's *Herald*, about to achieve a milestone of fifty thousand daily paid copies, readership of all the city papers had exploded from one for every sixteen residents in 1830, to one for every 4.5 by 1850.[37] Newspapers had become big business. The *Herald* alone now boasted thirteen staff reporters and editors, twenty compositors, and sixteen pressmen. Within a few years, Greeley would employ a staff of a hundred. Proliferation of the telegraph and the expansion of news associations had sped the transmission and receipt of news. The nation's rapidly growing railroad system was dramatically reducing delivery time. And postal rate reform would soon make newspapers more cheaply available by mail.[38]

Even so, Raymond's success was by no means guaranteed, and during its first days in business the *Times* endured the kind of bad luck and minor catastrophe that seemed to plague fledgling newspapers. As a headquarters, the editor secured a handsome building still under construction on Nassau Street not far from City Hall, and promptly ordered office furnishings for the upper floors, along with a $20,000 Hoe-brand Lightning Press to be installed under the sidewalk in the basement. But as publication day neared, the structure was not yet ready for full occupancy, and for weeks an embarrassed Raymond, who always favored lavish professional surroundings, was forced to operate from a cramped temporary location around the corner. The *Times*'s opening days in print were similarly compromised. One early humiliation occurred when the paper publicly doubted the authenticity of a widely reported major fire. Not only did the fire story prove accurate; to Raymond's embarrassment, while the *Times* ignored the catastrophe, the *Tribune* and *Herald* both wrote it up in irresistibly gruesome detail. Worst of all, Raymond's new but untested cylinder press, capable as it was of printing hundreds of newspapers each minute, at first produced illegibly overinked impressions, compelling the *Times* to apologize for its initially smudgy appearance.[39] Eventually, reporters and machines began functioning more reliably.

For his part, no doubt feeling jilted, Greeley did everything in his power to sabotage the upstart competition. Where social issues were concerned, "Uncle Horace" may have emphasized his avuncular image as a bleeding heart, but in business he was as cutthroat as they came. And he regarded the birth of the *Times* as both an unforgivable personal affront and a genuine professional threat. The *Tribune* greeted its debut by warning each local newsdealer that he would "forfeit his right of property in the *Tribune* route" if he dared to carry the new daily. The dealers defied him. During the ugly circulation war that ensued, each editor accused the other of constituting a danger to both New York City and the Whig Party. Greeley branded Raymond a radical abolitionist and a party hack. The *Times* founder struck back by dangling the offer of higher pay to poach a compositor and a pressman from the *Tribune*.[40]

"We have not entered upon the task of establishing a new daily paper in this city, without due consideration of its difficulties as well as its encouragements," Raymond admitted. "We understand perfectly that great capital, great industry, great patience are indispensable to its success, and that even with all these, failure is not impossible. But we also know that within the last five years the reading population of this city has nearly doubled, while the number of daily newspapers is no greater now than it was then; that many of those now published are . . . made up for particular classes of readers; that others are objectionable upon grounds of morality; and that no newspaper, which is really *fit* to live, ever yet expired for lack of readers." In a "malicious desire to prejudice the public mind," Raymond charged, unscrupulous competitors had falsely warned that the *Times* would be a radical journal. But he insisted he would make the paper "acceptable to the great mass of our people, and shall spare no effort to do so." With another slap at Greeley, he added: "we shall *make it a point to get into a passion as rarely as possible*."[41]

Raymond proved no less savvy a marketer than Greeley. By the time its fourth issue hit the streets, the *Times* had placed nine-by-six-inch circulars under the doors of thousands of Manhattan residences, offering trial home subscriptions at only "sixpence" a week, guaranteeing "an immense amount of reading matter for that price." Generations before the introduction of recycling, the handbill added an offer to remove used papers from each doorstep daily.[42] As always, Raymond's writing style proved crisp and accessible, devoid of complicated phrasing and allusions to arcane philosophies, even if his relentless capitalization of pet words like "Law" and "Liberty" sometimes bordered on the fatuous. Few of the *Times*'s initial readers would have doubted its bold opening prediction that it would remain a force "for an indefinite number of years to come."[43]

At the end of his first year in business, Raymond could report to his readers that neither early miscues nor the hostility of his rivals had inhibited the *Times*'s rapid growth. "It has been immeasurably more successful," he trumpeted, "than any new paper of a similar character ever before published in the United States. . . . After one year's experience, encouraged by the abundant support of the public we have received, we are resolved to go forward."[44] Go forward he did, his goal still to avoid the "white heat" of typical American editorial writing and replace it with the "sober elaborate essay embracing none but mature results of reflection."[45]

Greeley bristled at Raymond's success, and not only because it came, he believed, at the expense of the *Tribune*'s constituency. For Greeley, it also created a humiliating competition for political influence on, and once exclusive access to, Whig political leaders. Only recently, Greeley had cheered former governor Seward's 1849 selection as U.S. senator by editorializing that "no man ever yet appeared for the first time in Congress so widely known and warmly appreciated."[46] Now, to the veteran editor's irritation, Seward's speeches began turning up in print in the *Times* before the texts ever reached the *Tribune*. This gave "the impression," Greeley complained bitterly to the senator, "that the Times is your special organ and its filibustering editorials and general negation of principle especially agreeable to you."[47] Seward and Weed, however, could no longer afford to allow the unpredictable Greeley exclusive advance access to Whig news. Their longtime political and journalistic alliance—a triumvirate often dubbed the "firm" of Seward, Weed, and Greeley—came under unprecedented strain. And Raymond, now sporting side-whiskers and a mustache as if to punctuate his growing influence, became a force to be reckoned with.

As for the ever-boastful James Gordon Bennett, though typically unprepared to sit on the sidelines while two competitors squabbled—there was no circulation advantage in remaining above such a fray—he astonished even his admirers by giving himself credit for Raymond's success. When it came to self-promotion, no one did it better than Bennett, especially in offering suspect compliments to competitors. Now he perversely claimed that the *Times* had found an audience only because the "machinery and facilities of the *Herald*" could not keep up with the huge public demand for his own paper. "The surplus of readers unsupplied offered a fair margin for a new journal," Bennett rationalized, and Raymond's "experience had taught him to abandon the . . . old stage-coach and sailing-ship epoch of the *Courier and Enquirer*, and to fall in with the new school of the *Herald*." Had Bennett's new, modern Lightning Press been operating in 1851, the penny press pioneer congratulated himself, "there would have been no opening for the *Times*."[48] Greeley thereupon reinserted himself into the feud by telling a parliamentary committee during a visit to London that year that the *Herald* was "a very bad paper."[49]

Raymond's onetime *Tribune* colleague, Charles A. Dana, came closest to the truth in explaining the *Times*'s success: it attracted a loyal reader base because it filled a void. Raymond triumphed, Dana maintained, because he "aimed at a middle line between the mental eccentricity of the *Tribune* and the moral eccentricity of the *Herald*, at the time of those great newspapers' greatest greatness, marking out for the *Times* a mean between the two extremes." As the pioneer of journalistic history, Frederic Hudson, put it, the *Times* thrived because of its "respectability of tone and matter:" it stood for the "*juste milieu*"—the middle ground.[50]

In politics, the two "extremes" in Illinois never seemed more so when the second half of the nineteenth century began—fighting with increasing ferocity over taxes, tariffs, and public improvements even as Democrats and Whigs struggled in Washington to find common ground to bottle up the increasingly explosive issue of slavery. Temporarily retired from electoral politics and reengaged in the practice of law, Abraham Lincoln passed the years from 1850 to 1854 largely out of the public spotlight. But those who suggest that he totally abandoned interest in national affairs need only consider his growing addiction to out-of-town political news during this period. Lincoln's stepped-up newspaper reading hardly suggested indifference. He continued to take the weekly *New York Tribune* and the *Illinois State Journal*, and soon began subscribing as well to a new Republican Party daily from Chicago. He and law partner Herndon also sent away for abolitionist papers like the *Anti-Slavery Standard*, the *Emancipator*, and the *National Era*, and to keep track of Southern public opinion, the *Richmond Enquirer* and the increasingly strident *Charleston Mercury.*[51]

His supporters continued in vain to urge Lincoln back into politics, often planting press items designed to prod him back into the game. In the spring of 1850, the *Tazewell* (Illinois) *Mirror* predicted the ex-congressman would make a new effort to regain his old House seat. To put a halt to such speculation, Lincoln insisted that Simeon Francis publish a letter in the *Journal* "to say that I neither seek, expect, or desire a nomination for a seat in the next Congress." Not yet ready for a comeback, Lincoln insisted that "the whigs of the district have several other men, any one of whom they *can* elect . . . quite as easily as they could elect me." The district could "be made *right side up*," he argued, without interrupting his semiretirement.[52]

Yet Lincoln's voice was never entirely stilled during these fallow years. In July 1850, when President Taylor died suddenly after eating tainted fruit on a hot Washington day, Lincoln journeyed to Chicago to offer a fulsome eulogy to the leader who had so stingingly rejected his quest for a federal job. Two local newspapers reprinted the oration, even though the tribute did not come across as particularly earnest: the eulogist made several factual errors in relating the late president's biography, and seemed comfortable only when quoting six maudlin stanzas of one of his own favorite poems. At one point Lincoln tellingly reminded his listeners that Taylor's greatest virtue had been "a sober and steady judgment, coupled with a dogged incapacity to understand that defeat was possible"—attributes to which, many admirers knew, he aspired himself.[53]

Lincoln sounded no more convincing when he confided to a similarly disappointed office seeker a few weeks later: "I have felt, and do feel, entirely independent of the government."[54] Yet Taylor was barely in his grave before Lincoln began recommending patronage applicants to the late president's White House successor, Millard Fillmore. Otherwise Lincoln did concentrate primarily on legal business and family affairs. For one thing, the law offered him his only source of income. And tragedy at home required his attention as well. The Lincolns' son Eddy died at the age of three in 1850 and although Mary bore a third son, Willie, later that year, and yet another boy, Thomas (Tad), in 1853, the couple never fully recovered from that devastating loss.

Abraham and Mary may have found solace in the anonymous poem "Little Eddie," which appeared in the *Illinois Journal* just five days after their son's burial. Once mistakenly attributed to the grieving parents themselves—whose mutual love for poetry and close relationship with the paper long suggested them as likely authors—it turns out that the poem was actually the work of a St. Louis verse writer named Ethel Grey. Its appearance in Lincoln's hometown newspaper, however, was surely not coincidental. To friends and neighbors, and perhaps editor Simeon Francis himself, the rhyme no doubt seemed the perfect vessel through which to express sympathy to the Lincolns. At the very least, its publication showed that condolences through the press had become an accepted expression of grief—to be shared widely in print as uninhibitedly as campaign speeches:

> *Angel boy—fare thee well, farewell,*
> *Sweet Eddie, we bid thee adieu!*
> *Affection's wail cannot reach thee now,*
> *Deep though it be and true.*
> *Bright is the home to him now given,*
> *For such is the kingdom of heaven.*[55]

Eulogies of all sorts, especially of the prose kind, routinely found their way into newspapers large as well as small, and they often reflected more evidence of political sympathy than of personal grief. When Lincoln's onetime hero Henry Clay died two years later in 1852, Lincoln again took to the public stage to mourn, this time one of many to do so. The editor of the *New York Tribune* also produced a lengthy and heartfelt oration. Lincoln delivered his notable Clay tribute in the Illinois State Capitol, and again earned local publicity. Greeley's appraisal of the hero he familiarly called "Harry Clay" reached thousands more readers, of course, through the pages of the popular *New York Tribune*.[56] Coincidentally or not, both eulogies tellingly stressed Clay's devotion to human equality, and reminded their audiences that the unresolved slavery issue was becoming increasingly threatening to the nation. As yet, Lincoln's own expressions on the subject of slavery remained muted—and largely unnoticed outside his home state.

The depth of Lincoln's frustrating political isolation became further apparent in 1852. That January, he drafted an enthusiastic resolution of local support for Hungarian revolutionary (and former journalist) Louis Kossuth, then conducting a goodwill tour through America. Support for European reformers was strong among Whigs, but if Lincoln hoped his commentary would earn coverage in sympathetic out-of-state newspapers, he was in for yet another disappointment. Lincoln's effort went unreported in the East. Just a few weeks earlier, editor and Assembly Speaker Henry Raymond personally took center stage as New York welcomed the Hungarian hero to town. Raymond spoke for the entire municipal press establishment in offering the first toast and the principal oration in Kossuth's honor.[57] (Bennett, for his part, questioned Kossuth's appeal, while James Watson Webb expressed unvarnished hostility.) It remained extremely difficult for isolated Western politicians like Lincoln to compete for coverage against Eastern political powerhouses who also happened to own their own newspapers.

Kossuth himself understood these circumstances as well as Lincoln did. When crowd noise made it impossible for him to offer his first prepared address to New Yorkers, he simply gave up and handed his text to reporters so it could be reprinted. Even had he been able to deliver his oration, the Hungarian leader believed that "whenever and wherever I publicly speak, it is always chiefly spoken to the Press." The newspaper, he argued, was "that great controller of every word spoken by a public man."[58]

The Little Giant knew this as well as anyone. In sharp contrast to Lincoln, Stephen Douglas basked in the attention the press lavished on him both in Washington and at home during the first years of the decade. Few—even his enemies—doubted he had earned it. In 1850, the young senator helped revive a crucial slavery compromise after Henry Clay's omnibus bill died in the Senate. Thereupon, the much less experienced Douglas seized management responsibilities for the legislation, ingeniously broke it into separate pieces, and steered their passage through Congress, one element at a time—including the heinous Fugitive Slave Act, which required Northerners to return escapees. The Compromise of 1850 also called for admission of California to the Union as a free state, and the abolition of the domestic slave trade in Washington (while guaranteeing that slavery itself would remain protected in the nation's capital). The agreement required enough concessions from both Northern and Southern legislators to arouse bitter complaints about the result from both. But Bennett, who had compared Senator Douglas favorably to Webster and Calhoun, poured on the praise. The slavery genie was back in the bottle—for a few years, anyway.

Even Greeley's antislavery *New York Tribune* now grudgingly acknowledged the senator's mastery of "the practical business of legislation."[59] An especially remarkable legislator because he was still a "bantling"—a mere child—in the admiring view of Bennett's *Herald*, Douglas further lived up to the description by emerging as the quintessential representative of the Young America movement, an inchoate but alluring crusade to replace the "old fogies" in power with a new generation of energetic spirits.

Before long, supporters began openly mentioning Douglas as a serious contender for the 1852 nomination for president. He was still not forty years old.[60] "In regard to the Presidency," Douglas confided to Charles Lanphier of the *Register* just before the new year, ". . . Things loom well & the prospect is brightening every day. . . . Perhaps you & our friends at Springfield may be able to exert some influence upon the subject." When the *Washington Union* instead endorsed Sam Houston for president, Douglas, his eye increasingly fixed on publicity, responded with an anonymous editorial extolling his own virtues. He ended by quoting a recent Senate address famous for his impossible promise: "I have determined never to make another speech upon the slavery question."[61]

Though not officially a candidate, Douglas advanced his White House interests by making efforts to tighten his control over press coverage in his home state. He had stuck close to Washington for many months, unavoidably neglecting politics at home, and in his absence the *Quincy Whig* acted to deflate his growing reputation by reminding readers about the senator's potentially damaging personal connection to slavery: his wife's plantation inheritance. Now Douglas turned to the *Register*'s Lanphier to argue: "It is true that my wife does own about 150 negroes in Miss. & cotton plantation. My father-in-law in his lifetime offered them to me & I refused to accept them." Of course, Douglas neglected to point out that under Illinois law, his wife's property was considered his own. "It is our intention," he instead vowed, ". . . to remove all our property to Illinois as soon as possible."[62] He did no such thing, but for months labored to change the conversation by bombarding Lanphier with letters, most meant for publication, vigorously defending his record in Congress. Douglas's focus was well placed. By then, the *Register* counted subscribers throughout Illinois and in nearby out-of-state cities like St. Louis.

Douglas could always rely on Lanphier, but even with its broadened circulation the *Register*'s reach remained limited. The senator still counted no dependable organ in upstate Chicago, whose voting and reading populations were rapidly expanding. Thus when John Wentworth's *Chicago Democrat* opposed the Compromise of 1850, Douglas decided it was time to encourage competition. First, Douglas urged the *Washington Union*'s recently departed associate editor Edmund Burke to establish a new Democratic paper in Chicago. When that overture fell on deaf ears, Douglas asked Abraham Lincoln's Springfield neighbor Isaac Diller to consider relocating there for the same purpose. This effort failed as well. A sympathetic journalist named Ebenezer Peck ultimately did establish a Democratic sheet in Chicago, but Douglas continued to feel neglected there. Powerful national politicians like the Little Giant expected to fully control the party press at home—not worry about its absolute loyalty while serving the state's interests in distant Washington.

For a time, Douglas was compelled to depend on Charles Lanphier to fill that crucial role. At least additional praise could be expected from the *Quincy Herald*, but it literally came at a cost. Douglas had sent financial contributions to sustain that paper, and now expected—and received—support in return.[63] Not until the summer of 1854 would the senator finally persuade Washington journalist James Washington Sheahan to launch another Democratic daily in Chicago. Douglas not only provided financial backing for the start-up venture, he personally saw to the distribution of a circular promoting the new *Chicago Daily Times* as "the only true and reliable Democratic Paper published in this City." For the rest of the decade, the *Times* would serve as the senator's principal press organ outside Springfield, its reach and influence limited only by what editor Sheahan insisted was its undercapitalization. Douglas had been generous. But not generous enough.[64]

None of these manipulations

Charles Lanphier, anti-Lincoln editor of the *Illinois State Register* throughout the 1850s, as he looked in later life.

worked to Douglas's benefit in time for the 1852 presidential race. New Hampshire's Franklin Pierce, not the Little Giant, won the Democratic nomination that year after forty-nine exhausting convention ballots. Though keenly disappointed, Douglas turned his attentions to winning reelection to the Senate (which he easily accomplished) and campaigning loyally for the party's White House choice against his Whig opponent, Mexican War hero Winfield Scott.[65]

Two milestone events that year—the death of Clay and the birth of Scott as a presidential candidate—brought Lincoln closer to resuming an active political life. Within two years, he again sought and won election to the state legislature. He also found himself "debating" Douglas for the first time in years over the presidential contest, albeit in separate Illinois towns and on different days.[66] Their rivalry was heating up again.

So were the New York City newspaper wars, ignited to a fever pitch, as usual, by the quadrennial contest for the nation's highest office. Only reluctantly did Greeley throw his support behind Scott. "He is a Know-Nothing, body and soul," the editor privately lamented (a reference to the Nativists who opposed immigration—particularly by Catholics—but professed to "know nothing" of the rapidly expanding antiforeigner movement). To Greeley, the war hero was "an aristocrat, and anything else but wise and winning."[67] Worse for Greeley was the fact that the general was a Virginian by birth, and as with Taylor, Greeley doubted that any Southern-born Whig would reliably oppose the expansion of slavery. Trying to advance the antislavery cause, the editor publicly questioned the late Henry Clay's longtime advocacy for the colonization of African Americans, suggesting that he was now willing to encourage free black settlement in America. He only inspired Frederick Douglass to reply sarcastically: "We are glad that the *Tribune* is '*willing*' that the blacks should colonize in this country. . . . Be patient, Mr. Greeley, a nation may not be born in a day, without a miracle."[68]

In response to Greeley's misgivings about Scott, the ever-loyal organization man Raymond—who personally covered (and became a last-minute replacement delegate to) the Baltimore convention that nominated Scott—tried to read Greeley out of the Whig Party entirely. Greeley huffed that he would not be kept "silent about slavery" even to elect another military hero. Meanwhile, the pugnacious James Watson Webb, who also harbored doubts about

Old Fuss and Feathers, picked an ill-fated fight of his own with Raymond—verbal, for once—at the Baltimore convention. But it was the *Times* editor who emerged as the more important leader, with Webb's influence further reduced. Thurlow Weed later recalled that Raymond "bore himself with becoming calmness and dignity" at the convention, offering his "clarion voice" to herald the "death-knell of slavery." [69] As for James Gordon Bennett, he lived up to expectations by dredging up long-discredited charges against Scott and attempting to eviscerate the war hero's hard-earned reputation.

When Democrat Pierce prevailed with outright popular majorities in both Illinois and the nation that November, Stephen Douglas commenced to call in political debts to make sure his supporters were amply rewarded. "Do you want anything besides the Patronage for your Paper? and if so what?" Douglas wrote Charles Lanphier in December. ". . . Answer me directly & frankly on all these points. Your answer will be *confidential.*" Meanwhile, Douglas asked Pierce to name John Moncure Daniel, editor of the *Richmond Enquirer* and "a man of . . . sound political faith," as minister resident to Belgium "or some one of the other European powers." No one, Douglas bluntly argued, "on account of partizan service, has stronger claims upon the favor & support of

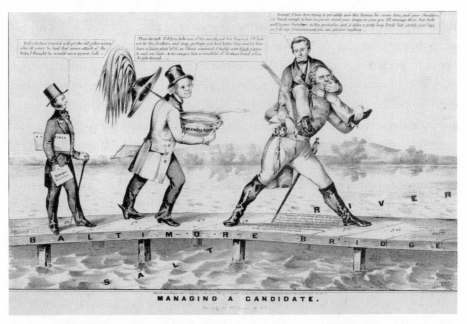

Greeley carries General Winfield Scott's oversized, plumed military hat in a cartoon mocking the war hero's 1852 Whig presidential campaign. Henry Raymond trails behind the procession, holding a copy of the *Times*.

a Democratic Administration." The White House obligingly named Daniel as minister to Sardinia, a post he held for the next eight years—until Lincoln himself assumed presidential patronage power and replaced him.[70]

Lanphier, however, had no interest in a political job from the Pierce administration. He preferred to remain at the helm of Springfield's *Register*, and by late 1853 Douglas was again reminding him of his abiding loyalty to the newspaper—yet, as usual, fretting that he felt somewhat out of touch with Illinois affairs. "Why don't you send me the Register?" he flattered the editor on November 11. "I have not seen a copy for more than six months. I am certainly a subscriber to it, altho I may never have paid my subscription. Send me the Register that I may see what you are doing & saying. I know all is right & that the paper takes the right course, yet I want to read it so much the more on that account." And then, perhaps in a sly effort to stimulate another presidential boom in his own behalf, Douglas counseled the editor to make no efforts at all to promote him for the 1856 nomination—yet. "I see many of the newspapers are holding me up as a candidate for the next Presidency," he reported. "I do not wish to occupy that position. . . . Let us leave the Presidency out of view"—tellingly adding, "for at least two years to come."[71]

Both politics and newspaper technology were changing rapidly, each in a sense because of the other. Politicians now routinely subjected their opponents to ever-more-rapid responses in the hope of attracting daily coverage; the press obligingly reported their increasingly heated debates within days, even hours. In New York, the Harbor News Association hired its own boat, appropriately rechristened the *Newsboy*, to meet approaching ships, secure overseas reports, and speed them to shore even before the dispatch-bearing transatlantic vessels docked. When a well-publicized need for repairs exposed the steamer's perilous financial condition, Henry Raymond led a collaborative effort to rescue it from default.[72]

On a larger scale, a newly formed news-gathering consortium calling itself the Associated Press was now routinely distributing the latest copy from all these sources by wire, including reprints from New York papers, an innovation that served to increase their reach and influence exponentially. The AP had been founded by five of the principal New York dailies back in 1846— the *Sun, Herald, Courier and Enquirer, Journal of Commerce,* and *Express*—in an effort to pool news-gathering operations and, more importantly, share the high cost of transmitting and receiving telegraphed reports from Mexico during the war. Greeley's *Tribune* joined the AP three years later, followed in short order by Raymond's *Times*. One of the earliest books on the growing power of telegraphic transmission boasted at the time that if the governor of New York delivered a five-thousand-word speech in Albany, it could be type-set and dispatched for publication in downstate newspapers within only two hours. An upstate New York paper called the AP "the most potent engine for affecting public opinion the world ever saw."[73]

Even though he had helped launch all of these remarkable advances, James Gordon Bennett loved to boast that he had not altered his own time-tested daily routine in more than a decade. He was not about to change it now. Instead, Bennett directed his energies to initiating a new and newsworthy feud with impresario P. T. Barnum and to promoting the handsome, pro-slavery Tammany Hall Democrat Fernando Wood for mayor of New York. And since he believed that all of his readers—and his jealous competitors, too—desperately wanted to know the full details of his personal schedule, he made sure it was fully reported in print.[74]

Though he was now nearing sixty, Bennett informed his followers that he still unfailingly arrived at his brick-and-limestone headquarters shortly after 7 A.M. each day, ascended to his upstairs office, and for an hour pored over the day's letters to the editor, diligently separating those he deemed worthy of publication from those destined for the trash bin. By eight o'clock he com-menced reading the city's rival dailies over a modest meal of tea and toast, and an hour later summoned an office boy to rapidly dictate editorial copy, "making his points with effect . . . sometimes smiling as he raps one of his dear political friends over the knuckles," and invariably ending each outpour-ing of prose with the phrase, "that will do." At midday the publisher conferred with his associates on news placement, reviewed copy, and sent stories to his staff of compositors. By 2 P.M. he personally had proofread galleys, then ap-peared in his pressroom to make "pithy speeches" meant to boost employee morale. He checked the arts reviews with particular attention (claiming he never liked to authorize a bad notice), and headed off by eight to take in a play or concert himself.[75]

Late each night, Bennett returned to his seat of power for one last glance at late-breaking dispatches, earmarking some for last-minute publication, and composing fresh copy himself—in a reportedly fine hand, of course. (Horace Greeley's scrawl, by contrast, was widely ridiculed as so indecipherable that it often provoked "strong language" from frustrated typesetters.)[76] Bennett claimed he concluded each of his busy workdays by listening attentively for the reassuring vibrations that sent gentle tremors through his building whenever the huge presses began rumbling to life in its basement. By 1849 the editor could even claim to be performing twice the work on Monday evenings, for starting that year the *Herald* began publishing eight-page double-sheet editions every Tuesday.

Bennett's rivals enjoyed no more sleep or performed any less labor than the titan at the penny press. But only Bennett made his sacrifices and toil matters of public interest and civic virtue. In his self-congratulatory official view of himself, which he promoted with deadpan earnestness, there was no time for feuds, fistfights, or the amassing of money—all of which he managed to pursue inexhaustibly as well. "My ambition is to make the newspaper Press the great organ and pivot of government, society, commerce, finance, religion, and all human civilization," he insisted. "I go for hard work, just principles, an independent mind, a name that will last for ages after death, and a place in the glorious hereafter."[77] Although many contemporaries believed that the celestial jury was still at best deliberating on the matter of Bennett's eternal rest, the earthly newspaper business boasted no more famous a name in the 1850s than this vainglorious innovator.

Sir John E. E. D. Acton—the English journalist and intellectual best remembered for coining the phrase "Power tends to corrupt and absolute power corrupts absolutely"—may not have had New York newspaper editors in mind when he invented that aphorism, but surely found nothing to contradict it when he visited the city in June 1853. He found the *Tribune* to be "ultra-democratic in every question," but had harsher things to say about its proprietor. "Greeley," observed Lord Acton, "has taken up a number of hobbies, such as temperance, which he pushes to extravagance. He defends his topics through thick and thin. He is sincere, though much suspected, for there is so much method in his madness as to make it seem likely." The English visitor was no more impressed by the *Tribune*'s competitors. "The N.Y. *Herald*," he wrote, "corresponds, on a somewhat inferior scale, to the *Times*. It discovers which way public opinion will turn, and by bending its course accordingly appears to direct where it really only follows." Not surprisingly, Lord Acton reserved his harshest observations for James Gordon Bennett—dismissing him as "a Scottish adventurer, who began by editing a low paper, which he made himself notorious, and wrote his way up." Yet Lord Acton was surprised to discover that the *Herald* "is not a venal paper," adding: "I am curious to know whether that can be said of the rest of the press."[78] If he ever discovered the answer to that question, Lord Acton kept it to himself.

Abolitionist newspapers and their editors, by contrast, continued their struggle merely to survive—financially as well as in peace and safety within their communities. In particularly hostile Washington, Gamaliel Bailey's *National Era*, a paper that years earlier had come perilously close to destruction by mobbing, found new life beginning in June 1851 by serializing a new novel about life in the slaveholding South. For the next forty weeks, *Life Among the Lowly* by Harriet Beecher Stowe created a sensation. When the book version appeared in 1852, few doubted that it would prove equally popular. Within three years, however, newly retitled *Uncle Tom's Cabin*, it sold a staggering 300,000 copies in the United States, and a million more in Europe. The total number reached two million by the end of the decade, by which time the indelible characters introduced in an abolitionist newspaper—Uncle Tom, Little Eva, and Simon Legree—had become staples of American folklore, and rallying cries for the growing antislavery movement.[79]

In June 1853, a full two years after the tale initially appeared in the abolitionist press, the *New York Times* acknowledged the immense impact and growing influence of the most widely read and noticed book "ever issued in this country." As the *Times* pointed out: "Such a book was scarcely needed to demonstrate to the people of the North the odiousness of many of the features of Southern slavery." Optimistically, the paper predicted, "it cannot fail to do good in the South."[80]

Though he increasingly admired Stephen Douglas and lavished considerable praise on him in print, James Gordon Bennett withheld approval when in May 1854 the senator masterminded passage of yet another congressional initiative designed to calm the roiling slavery issue. Much as Bennett hated abolition and feared Negro equality, he opposed expanding slavery into the West. Douglas's most important piece of legislation ever, the new Kansas-Nebraska Act, threatened to do precisely that.

The bill passed after five months of acrimonious debate in the House and Senate, leaving neither Southerners nor Northerners satisfied that their interests had prevailed, and sending sectional tensions percolating to a fever pitch. To the horror of antislavery forces, the legislation effectively repealed the long-standing Missouri Compromise, which for thirty-four years had outlawed slavery above latitude 36°30'. Under the terms of its most hotly disputed provision, the bill granted white settlers in new Western territories the right to vote for themselves on whether to permit slavery within their boundaries. Eager to organize these territories so they could accommodate a transcontinental railroad, Douglas sincerely believed that the bill would calm the emotional slavery issue altogether. He actually imagined that Popular Sovereignty, his name for this new system of voter choice, would quiet the simmering debate over slavery. Instead, it blew the lid off the slavery cauldron altogether and inspired a wave of violence in disputed Kansas Territory.

In some ways, Bennett viewed passage of the Douglas legislation not only as a welcome blow to abolitionism, but as a sign of the "decay" infecting abolitionist newspapers. The *Herald* crowed about the "curtailment of the anti-slavery journals of this city," reserving special gloating for Greeley and Raymond, whose readership Bennett contended had declined because of their sympathy for abolition. "In the matter of circulation," Bennett bragged, "the *Tribune* led the way, in a marked reduction of its size, and in the substitution of a cheap and inferior quality of paper in place of a comparatively expensive article. Next, our junior Seward organ,—the *Times*, adopted the same expedient of 'making both ends meet.'"[81] In truth, neither rival paper showed any sign of "decay" following passage of Kansas-Nebraska. In fact, the controversy they began fanning in response to the legislation made them greater forces than ever. Each editor sought to distance himself from the crumbling remains of the Whig Party and launch a new national political organization more strongly opposed than ever to slavery expansion in the West.

Greeley had long made manifest his own staunch opposition to slavery expansion. On January 5, 1854, the *Tribune* called on Northerners to unite in battle against what he called a blatant effort by the South—and Douglas— "to make the West pastureland for slavery." Calling for "resistance to the last," Greeley confidently predicted: "The passage of the Nebraska bill will *arouse* [emphasis added] and consolidate the most gigantic, determined and overwhelming party for freedom that the world has ever known." As Greeley vowed, *"The United States will extinguish slavery before slavery can extinguish the United States."* George William Curtis of the popular new illustrated periodical *Harper's Weekly* saluted the reinvigorated Greeley for pounding out what he called the "drumbeat of the nation."[82]

Despite its growing influence, the *New York Tribune* had yet to turn a consistent profit, or so managing editor Charles Dana later maintained. At one point, Greeley managed to persuade his archenemy Raymond to hike the street price of both their papers to three cents in order to raise additional revenue from circulation. But Jamie Bennett, awash in revenue and eager to squeeze his competitors, was said to have "scotched" the deal (ethnic slur surely intended) by refusing to go along. Dana thought he had a solution for the *Tribune*'s woes. "The Whigs," he suggested in 1854, "have got to nominate Greeley for Governor."[83] Politics remained a journalist's refuge of final resort. New York Whigs, however, now far closer to Raymond and the *Times*, would have none of it.

"Nebraska," as Northerners later began calling the landmark 1854 legislation, brought Abraham Lincoln roaring back into the political arena, reinvigorating the rivalry with Douglas that had been dormant since Lincoln's exit from Washington five years earlier. As Lincoln admitted, "I was losing interest in politics, when the repeal of the Missouri Compromise aroused me again"—once more, as he had done while serving in Congress, deploying a word he may have consciously borrowed from the weekly *New York Tribune* that he read so religiously. Confirming this epiphany in a later autobiographical sketch, Lincoln resorted to the third person, but used that same bold word yet again—"arouse"—to describe his impassioned reaction to Douglas's initiative: "the repeal of the Missouri compromise aroused him as he had never been before."[84] Greeley was still no particular friend, but evidently remained an inspiration.

At first, Lincoln chose to fight back using an old weapon of choice—the anonymous editorial. His initial criticism of Kansas-Nebraska appeared in a column for Springfield's renamed *Illinois State Journal* on September 11, 1854. In it, Lincoln likened supporters of the legislation to knaves

Horace Greeley, around the time of the 1852 presidential election, wears a woolen shawl to accentuate his image as a common man.

and fools who "pulled down the fence for the purpose of opening the meadow for his cattle" (tellingly employing much the same "pastureland" metaphor Greeley had used in print eight months earlier).[85] Lincoln was likely responsible as well for a series of additional editorials that followed onto the pages of the *Journal*. Soon enough, however, he returned to another familiar platform: the political stage.

After delivering a brief anti-Nebraska speech at Bloomington on September 12, Lincoln headed back to Springfield in time for the annual state fair. With the city overflowing with excited visitors, he appeared at the State Capitol on October 4 to offer a three-hour-long reply to an impassioned defense of the bill by Douglas. Describing him as "the Goliath of the anti-Nebraska black Republicans," even Lanphier's *Register* conceded that Lincoln "made what some of his hearers seemed to consider good hits, and called forth the cheers of his friends." But the Democratic paper hastened to add: "It might as well be expected to crush the Rocky Mountains with a snow flake as to put down the principle of popular sovereignty, sustained and advocated by such a man as Stephen A. Douglas."[86]

As for Douglas, he returned to the State Capitol to hear Lincoln's October 4 reply for himself, and according to eyewitnesses interrupted it repeatedly, frontier style, inspiring the *Journal* to comment wickedly: "We venture to say that Judge Douglas never in the Senate chamber or before the people, listened to just such a powerful analysis of his Nebraska sophisms, or saw such a remorseless tearing of his flimsy arguments and scattering them, to the winds, as he endured yesterday from Mr. Lincoln." As usual, the opposition press saw things quite differently. The *Register* insisted it was Douglas who "went over every one of Mr. Lincoln's points, and when he concluded there was nothing left of his arguments . . . he seemed not content to butcher his antagonist with tomahawk and scalping knife, but he pounded him to pumice with his terrible war club of retort and argument."[87]

Then, on October 16, Lincoln delivered his most powerful and influential political address to date, a long oration at Peoria in response to yet another stem-winder by Douglas. The Kansas-Nebraska Act was "wrong," Lincoln thundered, "wrong in its direct effect, letting slavery into Kansas and Nebraska—and wrong in its prospective principle, allowing it to spread to every other part of the wide world, where men can be found inclined to take it." Though he maintained that he harbored "no prejudice against the Southern people"—that, indeed, they were "just what we would be in their

situation"—Lincoln made no secret of his moral indignation at the retrograde notion of owning other human beings:

> This *declared* indifference, but as I must think, covert *real* zeal for the spread of
> slavery, I can not but hate. I hate it because of the monstrous injustice of slavery
> itself. I hate it because it deprives our republican example of its just influence in
> the world—enables the enemies of free institutions, with plausibility, to taunt
> us as hypocrites—causes the real friends of freedom to doubt our sincerity, and
> especially because it forces so many really good men amongst ourselves into an
> open war with the very fundamental principles of civil liberty—criticising the
> Declaration of Independence, and insisting that there is no right principle of
> action but *self-interest*.[88]

Western Whig papers applauded vigorously. The *Chicago Daily Journal*
called the performance "as thorough an exposition of the Nebraska iniquity
as has ever been made," noting that Lincoln's "eloquence greatly impressed
all his hearers." In the equally enthusiastic judgment of the *Quincy Whig,*
Lincoln established himself at Peoria as "one of the 'truly great men' in Illinois."[89] The hometown *Sangamo Journal* echoed these sentiments, publishing
the opus in its entirety after first printing the text in advance for Lincoln to
use as his reading copy. The newspaper had now become so closely identified
with Lincoln that it had all but commenced serving as his personal typesetter.

For the *Journal*'s newspaper version, William Herndon himself supplied
the accompanying editorial encomium (the editors gave to "Lincoln and to me
the utmost liberty in that direction," he blithely admitted). Herndon's commentary extolled the "anti-Nebraska speech of Mr. Lincoln" as "the profound-
est in our opinion that he had made in his whole life. He felt upon his soul
the truths burn which he uttered, and all present felt that he was true to his
own soul."[90] Still, as yet New York's leading dailies remained uninterested in—
and Eastern readers generally unaware of—Lincoln's political reemergence.

As one political rivalry was gathering renewed steam in the West, a mighty
political fraternity began crumbling in the East. On November 11, 1854,
just one month after Lincoln galvanized antislavery forces with his speech in
Springfield, Horace Greeley unleashed a salvo of his own meant to scuttle
his longtime political alliance with Senator William Seward and editor-boss

Thurlow Weed in New York—although, dying along with the Whig Party itself, their coalition had all but ceased to exist anyway.

Deeply frustrated by years of perceived neglect when it came to political reward, Greeley had decided he must make a dramatic break with his oldest and closest allies. In a long, overheated letter to Seward, the *Tribune* editor terminated their political relationship—or, as Greeley grandiosely put it, announced "the dissolution of the political firm of Seward, Weed, & Greeley, by the withdrawal of the junior partner" effective February 1, 1855. Over the years, Greeley had disagreed with his two colleagues over such subsidiary issues as monetary policy and voting rights for new citizens. But there was no concealing Greeley's primary gripe: above all, the editor felt the two upstate politicians had repeatedly failed to give him the respect and reward he deserved.

Greeley's extraordinary litany of slights began with the complaint that Weed and Seward had boycotted a recent Anti-Nebraska "or Republican" state convention at Saratoga Springs. (Henry Raymond, for one, had attended as a delegate from his old Manhattan assembly district.) But what aggravated Greeley the most occurred a few weeks later, when the regular Whig convention nominated Raymond for New York lieutenant governor. That was the final straw. It was not just that both the senator and the political boss continued clinging to "a shadow" political organization. It was that Greeley had himself yearned to be governor, or as a fallback, lieutenant governor. Weed had cunningly dissuaded him from both races, and now Raymond had earned not one but three nominations for the latter post—from the Whigs, Free Soilers, and Temperance Party—winning election to the state's second-highest office with a plurality of nearly thirty thousand votes.[91]

In a precise and self-pitying account of what he considered a decade and a half of mistreatment, Greeley poured forth his resentments. He charged that Weed had already read him "out of the Whig Party," claiming he was "no longer either useful or ornamental in the concern." Long before that, Greeley bristled, he had been passed over for patronage after repeatedly doing service to the organization. Greeley had "loved" editing Weed's old campaign extra, and "did it well," he recalled. But "when it was done," he charged of Seward, "you were Governor, dispensing offices worth $3,000 to $20,000 per year to your friends and compatriots, and I returned to my garret and my crust, and my desperate battle with pecuniary obligations heaped upon me by bad partners in business and the disastrous events of [the Panic of] 1837. I believe it did not then occur to me that one of these abundant places might have been offered to me without injustice; I now think it should have occurred to *you*."

Continuing his enumeration of all the perceived slights to which Seward and Weed had subjected him, Greeley reminded the senator that after the election of 1840, he "ought to have asked that I be postmaster of New York"; that Whig investors should have provided far more generous financial backing when he founded the *Tribune* the following year; that Seward had further wronged him in his response to an 1848 libel case; and of course that Weed had "humiliated" him by cruelly informing him that the party would not support him for governor in the recent 1854 contest. Had Seward insisted, Greeley hastened to add, it would have been enough to elect him "to any post, without injuring myself or endangering your reelection." Worst of all, much as he might have loathed the largely ceremonial job of lieutenant governor, "I should have gloried in running for the post." Instead, in the unkindest slight of all, the nomination had gone to his enemy Raymond, and "the fight left to me"—in return for which support he had since been "rebuked" by "the Lieutenant-Governor's paper."

"I trust I shall never be found in opposition to you," the aggrieved Greeley concluded in his undoubtedly cathartic letter. Vowing to take a sabbatical from journalism, he declared: "I have no further wish than to glide out of the newspaper world as quietly and as speedily as possible."[92] True to his word, the editor soon went off to join his family on a European vacation, and then commenced a national lecture tour. For a time, Greeley seemed to be following the historic advice he had once given young Josiah Grinnell: "Go West, young man, go West. There is health in the country, and room away from our crowds of idlers and imbeciles."[93]

Not all his journalistic colleagues were impressed by Greeley's dramatic break with his Whig allies. The *Brooklyn Eagle* later condemned the entire "resignation" episode as only a sad "exemplification of the uses to which politicians expect and endeavor to turn journalists," who were expected "to be self-sustaining advocates of a party and its leaders, content to exhaust every energy of brain and muscle in behalf of the cause." In a more forgiving tone, Ohio diplomat Donn Piatt, one of those politicians who later turned to journalism, summed up the schism this way: "Horace Greeley, who to the ignorance and trusting simplicity of a child added a strange power of persuasion with his pen, could not understand that he was disqualified for office because he knew too much, and could not be controlled by the two for whose information on any subject he had a profound contempt."[94]

As it transpired, Greeley's self-imposed exile proved even briefer than Lincoln's. Before long, the editor was back in New York at the helm of the

Tribune, as fractious and determined as ever, but animated now by a single, inspiring new cause: the eradication of slavery. Although his diatribe to Seward remained unpublished for six years, Greeley began searching for new political partners—and a new political party.

Raymond, meanwhile, continued his own quest to coalesce press and political power. Although his earliest biographer argued that "the record of his life would have had no deep shadows" had he "remained a journalist, untouched by the corrupting influences of party chicanery," Raymond clearly found the political spotlight too alluring—not to mention too good for his newspaper business—to resist. Returning to Albany in January 1855, the new lieutenant governor told the State Senate: "I am profoundly sensible of the dignity and responsibility of the position I am called to fill." At around the same time, as if to echo Raymond's rising status in politics, the *New York Times* moved to a larger headquarters on the corner of Nassau and Beekman Streets.[95] In fact, the "Big Three" were all prospering. The "*Herald, Times*, and *Tribune*," admitted a contemporary critic, "occupy a prominent position in the ranks of journalism." But their preeminence, maintained journalist-poet Lambert A. Wilmer, was attributable to one regrettable trait: their "swaggering impudence."[96]

Early in 1855, a somewhat demoralized group of loyal Whigs joined anti-Nebraska Democratic legislators and their increasingly powerful pro-Douglas brethren for a convocation inside Springfield's capitol, the scene of so much recent ringing oratory. Now their job was to choose a new junior United States senator from Illinois, a task still constitutionally assigned to legislatures, not the direct votes of the people. By anyone's reckoning, Abraham Lincoln entered the contest the prohibitive favorite. But Douglas, who had been keeping the *Register*'s Charles Lanphier fully updated on reaction in Washington to the Kansas-Nebraska debate, wanted nothing more than to sabotage any effort to bring Lincoln back to the national capital as his colleague in the U.S. Senate.

Douglas predicted, as he anxiously told Lanphier, that "the Whigs will stick to Lincoln to the bitter end" even if the legislature was forced to adjourn before selecting a winner—an indecisive outcome the Little Giant thought "better than the election of Lincoln or any other man spoken of." Writing to both Lanphier and James W. Sheahan, the journalist only recently installed as editor of the *Chicago Times*, Douglas urged support for Democratic incumbent James Shields, the very politician Lincoln had come close to dueling years earlier. Now, the calculating Douglas provocatively advised the Irish-American Sheahan that if Shields should fall short of a majority, the press should "throw the responsibility on the Whigs of beating him because he was born in Ireland. . . . Let this be made the issue in the Newspapers & the Legislature & everywhere."[97]

In the end, however, it was Bloody Island all over again—much bluster but no fight. There would be no Lincoln-Shields duel for the U.S. Senate after all. Shields fell out of the running quickly. As for his former tormentor, after leading in all the early counts, Lincoln dropped out after nine ballots, fearful that if he remained in contention Douglas forces would rally support for a pro-Nebraska Democrat. This was too dangerous, and Lincoln responded by directing supporters to a compromise candidate. On the tenth ballot the legislature chose anti-Nebraska Democrat Lyman Trumbull as the new junior senator from Illinois.

"The agony is over at last," a distraught Lincoln wrote to a friend.[98] Eastern press reaction—or, more accurately, the lack of it—indicated that his pain was not shared by the major opinion makers. Failing to acknowledge that Lincoln had even contended for the seat, Greeley's *Tribune* celebrated Trumbull's victory as "a fitting finale to the repeal of the Missouri Compromise by Douglas & Co."[99]

Douglas may have won the battle to keep Lincoln out of Washington, but he still faced a larger and more dangerous political war. The next Senate seat up for a vote was his own—and the post would be contested in just three years. Between now and then, no one in government or the press believed that Lincoln would again retreat from politics or restrain the journalists yearning to advocate in his behalf.

CHAPTER SIX

The Prairies Are on Fire

———————⋯◈⋯———————

One autumn afternoon in Chicago—just hours after delivering his latest antislavery stem-winder—the tall, unmistakable figure of Abraham Lincoln could be seen strolling the city's streets alongside his friends Isaac Arnold and George Schneider. Typical Chicagoans—meaning they hailed from elsewhere—New York–born politician Arnold was a Free Soil ex-Democrat; Schneider, an abolitionist German immigrant editor who had switched from the Democrats to the Republicans earlier that year. It was Schneider who had invited Lincoln to speak in town this day, October 27, 1854.[1]

The editor's latest venture was the German-language antislavery daily, the *Illinois Staats-Zeitung*. Since purchasing the paper three years earlier, Schneider, as a contemporary noted appreciatively, had been "attacking everywhere it seemed necessary and useful" to the cause of freedom.[2]

The three men soon found themselves standing next door to the *Staats-Zeitung* offices on Lake Street, before a photo gallery run by Schneider's friend, a Swede of Austrian descent boasting the elaborate name of Johan Carl Fredrik Polycarpus von Schneidau who had learned his trade as an apprentice to Mathew Brady.[3] Schneider managed to importune Lincoln upstairs to the studio, and there persuaded him to pose for a daguerreotype, his first in eight years. Examining the primitive but hypnotic result, it is difficult to choose the most striking among its startling details.

Lincoln looks almost sleepy in the portrait—as he well might have felt after delivering such a long oration and then sitting through dinner with his Chicago friends. Adding to his otherworldly appearance, he wears an absurd-looking Prince Albert topcoat adorned with velvet-trimmed lapels, over which tumbles an oversized bow tie that appears so light in hue it may well have been yellow. Most astonishing of all, Lincoln grasps in his hands—its front page held to the camera as if in a gesture of endorsement—what appears in some surviving copies to be an edition of Schneider's newspaper.

Other, divergent claims have been made about the photograph since—each of them intriguingly supported by retouched prints based on the long-lost original daguerreotype. The suggestion has been made that Lincoln actually posed that day holding the *Chicago Daily Democrat*. In one ambrotype copy that probably dates to 1858, Lincoln seems to be clutching the *Chicago Press and Tribune* (which did not even become a Republican daily until 1855, the year *after* von Schneidau took the original). A definitive identification of the prop remains elusive. But it is perhaps less important to know precisely which newspaper Lincoln displayed for the camera that day than to acknowledge how credible each explanation seemed, both then and now.[4] Before this, as far as we know, Lincoln had sat for only one stiffly posed photograph. Yet now, in an era of so-called occupational portraits that showed fireman gripping hatchets and blacksmiths standing proudly before anvils, here was Lincoln immortalizing himself in the year of his political comeback by posing with the principal tool of his own trade: a newspaper.

Once the *Chicago Press and Tribune* emerged as "Lincoln's paper" in the fastest-growing city in his state, what could be more plausible than for its proprietors to order any trace of Schneider's more radical journal retouched out of the photograph and replaced with the most important new Republican daily in the West? That it could be done so successfully is as remarkable as the fact that Lincoln's Chicago supporters concluded it was worth doing.

The reinvigorated *Chicago Tribune* was in part the brainchild of Canadian-born Joseph Medill, thirty-two years old when he took over the troubled paper. Trained as an attorney, Medill found himself irresistibly drawn to journalists and journalism. At first content just to sell subscriptions to Greeley's *Weekly Tribune*, Medill admitted that "the law lingered a little while to reclaim the recusant, but he had tasted the delights of Franklin's nectar, and he never returned."[5]

While courting his future wife, whose father owned Ohio's *Tuscarawas Advocate*, Medill learned typesetting, printing, and editorial writing, and in

1849 purchased a paper of his own, the neighboring *Coshocton* (Ohio) *Whig*. He changed its name to the *Republican*, and initially it did well enough to encourage him to pursue publishing full time. His path to success, however, was neither straight nor swift. By 1851 Medill wrote to Horace Greeley asking whether the famous editor might help him find a purchaser for his struggling paper. "My office, the 'Coshocton Republic[an]," he sadly reported, "is for sale cheap." Medill paid two dollars for a *Tribune* advertisement offering his entire enterprise for $3,200.[6]

But journalism was in his blood. After selling, he moved on to Cleveland, where he founded a new daily, later merging it with a local Free Soil paper to form the formidable *Cleveland Morning Leader*. Impressed with his editorials, Greeley made Medill his official Cleveland correspondent. Around this time, or so Medill claimed, he first suggested the name "Republican" for the emerging new national antislavery party. He even contended he received a written blessing from Greeley himself—the hard evidence was apparently later destroyed in the Chicago Fire—who allegedly assured him: "If you can get the name Republican started in the West it will grow in the East. I fully agree to the new name and the new christening."[7] Late in life, Medill jokingly offered to share credit with Democrat Stephen Douglas for "pulling down the bars and letting the South into the free territory. The North," he explained, "united under the name of the National Republicans to drive them out of it."[8]

In 1854, the same year that Lincoln posed for von Schneidau, the conservative, anti-immigrant co-owner of the struggling *Chicago Daily Tribune* visited Medill in Ohio and urged him to move to town and become its managing editor. By then happily married and fond of Cleveland, Medill at first resisted. Eventually, though, he heeded Horace Greeley's advice that he, too, go west (Medill actually insisted the famous instruction was originally directed at him!). Medill decided not to work for the Chicago paper, but to buy it. He forged a partnership with Dr. Charles H. Ray, who had left his medical practice to devote himself to the ardently antislavery Galena, Illinois, *Jeffersonian*. Medill would own a larger share and manage the reorganized enterprise; Ray would serve as managing editor.

Working quickly, the new publishers replaced the paper's worn-out type with a fresh set boasting durable copper facing. They bought a modern Hoe-brand steam press, capable of churning our nine thousand sheets an hour, to replace the *Tribune*'s ancient Adams printer, which allegedly obtained its "power" by means of a blind horse walking slowly around a rotating shaft.[9]

Within months, by increasing efficiency and affiliating strongly with the Republicans, the paper hiked its readership and gained new influence in town. Medill would make the *Tribune* the cornerstone of a journalistic dynasty, building it on antislavery convictions and a growing support for the increasingly dynamic political force from the state capital: Abraham Lincoln.

The two first met the following spring. Medill heard heavy footsteps outside his office and turned to find a strange-looking visitor slouching at the door. "He was a very tall, remarkably thin man," the senior partner recalled. "His legs were absurdly long and slender, and he had enormous hands and feet."

"Please tell me whom I have the pleasure of addressing," Medill inquired.

"Well, down on the Sangamon River they used to call me Abraham Lincoln," came the reply. "Now they generally call me Old Abe, though I ain't so very old, either. . . . I'm in a hurry, but I ran up to subscribe for your paper." And then, Medill insisted, "he pulled from the cavernous pockets of his jeans a pocketbook, untied the strap and counted out four dollars."

"I like your paper," Lincoln volunteered as he paid for a six-month subscription. "I didn't before you boys took hold of it; it was too much of a Know-Nothing sheet."

Medill's quaint recollections, published posthumously forty-five years later, lack the ring of authenticity. It defies belief that the already distinguished lawyer and politician would wear denim on a visit to Chicago in 1855, or that he might volunteer a nickname that he despised. But one thing is certain: Lincoln soon made the *Tribune* office his unofficial Chicago headquarters, and grew intimate enough with Medill and Ray that the senior partner could berate him one

Joseph Medill, who devoted the *Chicago Tribune* to Republican office-seekers in general and Abraham Lincoln in particular.

day: "Get your damn feet off my desk, Abe." [10] Even if he remained irritatingly informal, Lincoln more than made up for his lax manners in private when speaking publicly for Republican principles. At times, Medill recalled, "Lincoln seemed to reach up into the clouds and take out the thunderbolts." [11] Charles Ray found inspiration through more prosaic rewards. In 1856, in return for editorial support for Republican presidential candidate John C. Frémont, Ray earned the influential political post of commissioner of the Illinois and Michigan Canal.

In Lincoln's Springfield, meanwhile, the aging, longtime pro-Whig editor Simeon Francis experienced far more difficulty finding a comfortable new political orientation for his onetime party mouthpiece, the suddenly unaffiliated *Sangamo Journal*. The Whigs were dead, but Francis was courageously disinclined to ally himself with the antiforeigner Know-Nothings. Yet he maintained incurable antipathy toward abolitionism.

Unable to gain his bearings as nimbly as ex-Whigs like Greeley, Raymond, and Medill, who were quick to embrace the Republican Party, Francis at age sixty-three was moreover physically exhausted from nearly a quarter century running a financially challenged family-owned newspaper. After learning that another journalist planned to establish a pro-Republican daily in Springfield, he decided to surrender rather than compete. In 1855, the Francis clan sold the *Journal*. As consolation for surrendering the enterprise, Simeon and his brothers received $8,000, twenty times what they had invested to launch the paper.

The purchasers were two ambitious young progressives from conservative downstate Illinois: William H. Bailhache and Edward L. Baker. The thirty-year-old Bailhache had all but grown up in the newspaper business; his father long edited the pro-Whig *Alton Telegraph*. Four years Bailhache's junior, Baker was a recently licensed lawyer who soon married into local royalty by choosing one of Mary Lincoln's nieces as a bride. The new owners immediately declared their aspiration to widen their paper's horizons—and readership—by renaming it the *Illinois State Journal* and vowing in their opening editorial to "do battle fearlessly and independently for the right." [12] For the rest of their tenure, those battles, like those embraced by Medill and Ray in Chicago, would be waged in behalf of Abraham Lincoln.

Baker and Bailhache quickly established their antislavery credentials, too,

enthusiastically promoting the 1856 Deca-
tur convention credited with officially establishing the Republican Party in Illinois. Like
every other journalist who attended a subsequent event in Bloomington, however, they
became so mesmerized there by what became
known as Lincoln's "Lost Speech" that they
put down their pencils in awe and failed to
record a word of it. Baker and Bailhache
went on to publish texts and flattering commentary on Lincoln's increasingly frequent
political speeches, and encouraged him to
submit unsigned editorial copy whenever he
chose. In 1856, the paper ardently supported
John C. Frémont, the new party's first presidential candidate.

Edward L. Baker, who co-published
Springfield's *Illinois State Journal* and
devoted it to Lincoln's political future.

The Frémont campaign may have faced long odds, but the *New York
Times*'s Henry Raymond managed to deliver an electrifying speech at a February 1856 Pittsburgh convention, credited with rallying the faithful to organize the national Republican Party. Declaring fealty to both the Constitution
and the Union, the editor charged that slavery interests had for too long
waged an aggressive campaign to dominate the federal government, vowing
"to secure the repeal of all laws which allow the introduction of slavery in to
territories once consecrated to freedom." [13]

During the fall campaign, Raymond worked energetically for Frémont,
notably engaging in a well-attended, two-part public debate with Tennessee
Democrat Lucien Bonaparte Chase. The encounters commenced at a Brooklyn museum and climaxed at the Broadway Tabernacle in Manhattan. In his
final oration, Raymond charged that the South was conspiring "to acquire
an absolute ascendancy in the Congress of the United States . . . vindicating
slavery upon principle . . . demand[ing] its extension into the territories." [14]
Lincoln could not have expressed it better himself.

Greeley's *Tribune* advocated for the doomed Frémont campaign that year
as well, but as usual no editor came closer to gauging—and perhaps influencing—the shifting public mood than James Gordon Bennett. The *New York
Herald* began the 1856 campaign season by endorsing Frémont. But then
Bennett did a complete about-face and became an ardent defender of Demo-

THE "MUSTANG" TEAM

In an 1856 Nathaniel Currier cartoon, Republican candidate John C. Frémont finds a tollgate blocking his way to the presidency—on a wagon piloted by (from left) Greeley, Raymond, and Bennett (with James Watson Webb clinging to the carriage from behind).

cratic candidate James Buchanan. In November Buchanan lost New York but won the presidency.

Once again, despite support from his own press allies, Stephen Douglas not only failed that year to mobilize enough delegate strength to win the Democratic nomination for president, but then to his irritation found his new Chicago press organ threatened by significant inner turmoil. As Douglas followed the crisis from Washington, editor James Sheahan engaged in an acrimonious squabble with his partner at the *Daily Times*, Isaac Cook. Typical of Chicago feuds, the fight involved charges of political corruption. When Douglas failed to step in promptly to reprimand Cook, Sheahan accused his co-publisher of intercepting the senator's letters. This particular charge seemed credible at least based on the element of opportunity, for like so many newspapermen, Cook served in political office as well: as Chicago's postmaster.

It was time for the senator to take personal control of the situation, and he did. Agreeing that Cook was "the most obstinate man I ever saw," Douglas intervened on the side of Sheahan. "You must retain the Times," he instructed him, "and if you should be deprived of it by law, you must start another paper and I shall stand by you in so doing." [15] Armed with Douglas's support, Sheahan prevailed, and political punishment followed. Shortly after Buchanan became president, Douglas wielded his still formidable patronage power to exact his—and his loyal editor's—revenge on Sheahan's erstwhile partner: Isaac Cook found he was no longer Chicago city postmaster.

Settled or not, the *Times* contretemps continued to worry Douglas, who needed Illinois Democrats to remain united in support of Kansas-Nebraska and himself. As he warned Sheahan: "No party, no matter how patriotic its men, and how fine its principles can survive such a suicidal course." [16] Chicago was not yet like New York—not yet big or diverse enough to sustain journalists who agreed with each other politically but battled over style. Certainly no one doubted Douglas's political gifts. In New York, even Horace Greeley conceded the Little Giant's intelligence. But he added a caveat. "Douglas has brains," he editorialized in 1856. "So did Judas." [17]

Such harsh language did nothing to lower the temperature of the overheating sectional debate over slavery, or to temper the violence it increasingly inspired against journalists and politicians alike. That same year, as astonished onlookers watched helplessly, pro-slavery Arkansas congressman Albert Rust (later a Confederate general) used his fists to pummel Greeley outside the U.S. Capitol. When the stunned editor wobbled to his feet and bravely pursued his assailant to the nearby National Hotel, Rust struck him again in the arm, this time with his cane. The incident marked the first—and as it turned out, the last—time the *Tribune* editor ever endured a physical assault. Undaunted, the frail but feisty Greeley boasted to his public that he would continue to "unmask hypocrisy, defeat treachery, and rebuke meanness." While promising to avoid future "brawls," he pledged, when necessary, to "defend myself." [18] Although Greeley declined to press charges against Rust, Joseph Medill took up Greeley's cause in Chicago, berating the congressman: "He had been accustomed to lashing male, and knocking down female slaves, in the State from whence he came. . . . Fresh from women-whipping, those cotton lordlings import their plantation airs and manners to the federal city." [19]

Just four months later, armed with his own rock-hard cane of gutta-percha, South Carolina representative Preston Brooks launched a far more ferocious attack on outspoken Massachusetts abolitionist Charles Sumner—right on the Senate floor. Forced to abandon his duties for more than a year while he recovered from the near-fatal beating, Sumner became a living martyr to antislavery. Speaking for many outraged Northern journalists, Raymond's

New York Times condemned the "ruffianly assault" as "another example of the arrogance and overbearing insolence by means of which a portion of the champions of the slave power seek to crush out all liberty of speech or of the Press wherever that privilege is exercised in behalf of Freedom." [20]

Events now moved swiftly, propelled by political and economic currents that no politician, and no editor, had the power to predict, much less arrest. First a severe financial panic threatened all but the most established papers, including the revived *Chicago Tribune.* "The whole pathway of newspaperdom is strewn on either side," the paper fretted in March 1857, "with the bleaching bones of defunct concerns." [21] Somehow Medill kept his young concern above water—fending off creditors because he believed the issues of the day too important to permit the mere specter of bankruptcy to still his voice.

That same month, the U.S. Supreme Court took the slavery debate to a provocative new level when it issued its eagerly awaited ruling in the landmark case of *Dred Scott v. Sandford.* In a majority opinion written by eighty-year-old Chief Justice Roger B. Taney, the court found that the enslaved Scott had failed to gain his liberty by domiciling temporarily in a free state. In a broader conclusion that outraged much of the North, the majority declared the Missouri Compromise unconstitutional and held that blacks could never be citizens and enjoyed "no rights which the white man was bound to respect." In one ironic sense, the decision burst Stephen Douglas's dream of Popular Sovereignty as a remedy for slavery agitation—for Taney's opinion implied that slaves could now be dragged into unpaid service anywhere in the country, North or South. Even supporters of Popular Sovereignty had no legal excuse to bar slavery.

The ruling aroused the New York press into a frenzy. Denouncing Taney's ruling as "wicked" and "atrocious," Horace Greeley spent the better part of a week hurling volleys at the "cunning chief" for his "collation of false statements and shallow sophistries" and his "mean and skulking cowardice." Slavery was now *"National,"* warned the editor. "At this moment, indeed, any wealthy New York jobber connected with the Southern trade can put in his next orders: 'Send me a negro cook, at the lowest market value! Buy me a waiter! Balance my accounts with two chambermaids and a truckman!' " [22]

"Slavery is no longer a local institution," echoed Raymond's *New York*

Times. ". . . It is incorporated into the Constitution of the United States. . . . It is not too much to say that this decision revolutionizes the Federal Government, and changes entirely the relation which Slavery has hitherto held towards it." Sounding at long last like a radical, Raymond further charged that Taney had "laid the only solid foundation which has ever existed for an Abolition party," predicting: "it will do more to stimulate the growth, to build up the power and consolidate the action of such a party than has been done by any other event since the Declaration of Independence." [23]

To no one's surprise, James Gordon Bennett vehemently disagreed with these sentiments, expressing entire satisfaction with the *Dred Scott* decision. In one sense, Bennett was speaking for many New Yorkers who were eager to see the slave system protected in order to safeguard the city's profitable trade with the South. But he also viewed the court ruling as a political watershed he predicted would destroy the new Republican organization before it gained national power. The *Herald* expressed the hope that the court "at a single blow, shivers the anti-slavery platform of the late great Northern Republican party into atoms." Bennett's reasoning came disconcertingly close to the arguments advanced in celebratory editorials published in response to *Dred Scott* throughout the South. In a typical example, the *Richmond Enquirer*

Roger B. Taney (left), long-serving chief justice of the United States, and Dred Scott (right), the subject of his most infamous Supreme Court decision, which ruled blacks ineligible for citizenship.

hailed the Supreme Court justices "as learned, impartial, and unprejudiced as perhaps the world has ever seen," insisting: "The *nation* has achieved a triumph, *sectionalism* has been rebuked, and *abolitionism* has been staggered and stunned." To the *New York Herald* as well, the Taney ruling constituted "supreme law" as "expounded by the supreme authority"—meaning that "disobedience is rebellion, treason, and revolution." [24]

Lincoln, for one, was inclined to do precisely what the *Herald* cautioned against—directly challenge the Supreme Court decision—though typically he took his time to do so. Ultimately seizing the issue as a club against his political nemesis, Lincoln responded to *Dred Scott* with an impassioned speech in Springfield on June 26, in which he assailed Taney and Douglas alike. Heretofore, Lincoln thundered, "our Declaration of Independence was held sacred by all, and thought to include all; but now, to aid in making the bondage of the negro universal and eternal, it is assailed, and sneered at, and construed, and hawked at, and torn, till, if its framers could rise from their graves they could not at all recognize it." In an emotional conclusion, he asked: "Are you really willing that the Declaration shall be thus frittered away?—thus left no more at most, than an interesting memorial of a dead past? Thus shorn of its vitality, and practical value; and left without the *germ* or even the *suggestion* of the individual rights of man in it?" Medill's *Chicago Press and Tribune* seemed particularly impressed by the speech's "force and power." In the East, few yet paid attention. [25]

At least Lincoln was working assiduously to keep the local press in his corner. In recent years, Lincoln had markedly stepped up his efforts to court the press—aiming not only to reach more voters through the newspapers, but also to curry long-term support among Republican editors and increase the circulation and distribution of their journals in every part of the state. Sometimes his efforts proved less than subtle.

On one occasion he sent ten dollars to the editor of the Paris, Illinois, *Prairie Beacon*, apologizing that he had read the paper for "three or four years, and have paid you nothing for it." He quickly added that he now expected the paper to endorse two judicial candidates he favored, sweetening the gesture by promising to pay a "reasonable charge" to have the *Beacon* print up electoral ballots. A few months later, he submitted a provocative anonymous editorial to several Galena newspapers warning local Germans that Democrats were "anxious to deprive foreigners of their votes." And soon thereafter he asked a Chicago editor to send "a hundred german papers . . . in one bundle" to a

Bloomington supporter, and fifty more to another in Mount Pulaski, with the clear object of widening circulation. Added Lincoln, with undisguised urgency: "Pray do not let either be neglected." Then in 1857, Lincoln joined six political allies donating a total of $500 "to be used in giving circulation in Southern and Middle Illinois" to the pro-Republican *Missouri Democrat*. He was now looking for support from as far away as St. Louis.[26]

By late 1857, Illinois Republicans seemed nearly united in the conviction that Abraham Lincoln should be the next leader to occupy the United States Senate seat that Stephen Douglas had held for nearly twelve years. But Lincoln had been down this tempting path before. Two years earlier, he had entered a legislative session called to fill another Senate seat as the overwhelming favorite, only to be left at the altar by his supporters. Understandably, Lincoln hesitated to risk another humiliation, making clear that he would stand for the Senate again only if the party united behind him at the outset of the 1858 canvass.

Preparing to launch his own campaign for a third term, Douglas pugnaciously reminded Springfield editors Lanphier and Walker: "The Battle will soon begin. We will nail our colors to the mast and defend the right of the people to govern themselves against all assaults from all quarters. . . . *Send me your paper.*"[27] Douglas's bravado (and curiosity about what the Springfield press was writing) was understandable. In New York, Horace Greeley, of all people, had begun hinting at the unthinkable: that he might throw his support not to his former congressional colleague, Lincoln, but to the Democratic incumbent, Douglas. Half a continent removed from the maelstrom of Illinois politics, Greeley had come to believe that Douglas at least represented the more progressive wing of the opposition and might actually align himself with antislavery forces in the future.

To Greeley's satisfaction, Douglas had recently broken with President Buchanan to oppose a bitterly disputed pro-slavery constitution in violence-plagued Kansas. The senator's principled position on the obviously bogus Lecompton Constitution, Greeley believed, showed that Douglas sincerely meant to exclude slavery wherever white citizens opposed it. Ironically, a stand that was irreparably splitting Democrats now came close to earning the Little Giant Republican support. The *Tribune* soon invited its subscribers "to read and say whether Mr. Douglas does not speak the words of common sense as well as patriotism."[28] Greeley was not alone in this flirtation. In Chicago, even Joseph Medill began imagining that Douglas might "gradually drift toward our side and finally be compelled to act with us in 1860," the year of the next presidential election.[29]

Insisting he was "not complaining" about these unsettling developments, Lincoln nevertheless assumed an uncharacteristically angry tone when he wrote, just after Christmas 1857, to the man who had defeated him in the previous Senate contest: Lyman Trumbull. His point was that the Republican press had no business endorsing Democrats, ever: "What does the New-York Tribune mean by it's [sic] constant eulogising, and admiring, and magnifying Douglas?" he railed. "Does it, in this, speak the sentiments of the republicans at Washington? Have they concluded that the republican cause, generally, can be best promoted by sacrificing us here in Illinois? If so we would like to know it soon; it will save us a great deal of labor to surrender at once." Acknowledging Greeley's powerful influence in the West through the ubiquity of his national edition, Lincoln warned that "if the Tribune continues to din his [Douglas's] praises into the ears of it's [sic] five or ten thousand readers in Illinois, it is more than can be hoped that all will stand firm."[30] James Gordon Bennett seized the opportunity to impugn "Massa Greeley" as the "deposit banker of the Washington lobby."[31]

Complicating matters further, Chicago's two top opposing editors met on their own in March 1858 to plot another way out of the looming competition between Lincoln and Douglas. Fresh from a visit to Washington, James Sheahan of the Democratic *Times* informed the Republican *Tribune*'s Charles Ray that Douglas might actually be willing to surrender his Senate seat without a fight and "go into private life for a brief period"—or alternatively run for the House of Representatives from Chicago, providing Republicans agreed not to field an opponent—so determined was the Little Giant to "break the back of Buchanan in every county in Illinois." Lincoln was aghast when he heard this latest news. Repudiating the idea of forming any "strange and new combinations," he lectured: "My judgment is that we must never sell old friends to buy old enemies."[32]

Around the same time, Lincoln's surrogate William Herndon decided (no doubt with Lincoln's encouragement) to undertake his own trip to the national capital—the first of his life—in hopes of discovering exactly where matters stood. Arriving there, he consulted a number of antislavery politicians, learning little he did not already know. Though Douglas was ill, the senator, too, agreed to see Herndon, concluding a "pleasant and interesting interview" by suggesting that the young attorney return to Springfield and tell Lincoln, "I have crossed the river and burned my boat," the precise meaning of which seemed maddeningly indistinct. En route home, Herndon stopped in New York to take Greeley's political pulse as well, and there discovered that the editor was indeed on the verge of making official his shocking political defection. Writing home when he reached Boston, Herndon alerted his law partner: "He evidently wants Douglas sustained and sent back to the Senate. He did not say so in so many words, yet his *feelings* are with Douglas." Indeed, Greeley had advised Herndon: "Douglas is a brave man. Forget the past and sustain the *righteous*. . . . The Republican standard is too high; we want something practical." At least Herndon discovered that Greeley was "not at all hostile to Lincoln."[33]

Not surprisingly, the message did not sit well with the victim of all this elaborate scheming. With "mingled sadness and earnestness," Lincoln dejectedly told Herndon on his return: "I think Greeley is not doing me right. His conduct, I believe, savors a little of injustice. I am a true Republican and have been tried already in the hottest part of the anti-slavery fight, and yet I find him taking up with Douglas, a veritable dodger,—once a tool of the South, now its enemy,—and pushing him to the front. He forgets that when he does that he pulls me down as well."[34] Lincoln was by then accustomed to total loyalty from party editors. He would remember Greeley's threatened defection for the rest of his life.

In late May, just weeks after Douglas secured the Democratic nomination for reelection, Lincoln buttonholed a few allies in Springfield's State Capitol library and grimly confided that it appeared that the New York editor "would be rather pleased to see Douglas re-elected over me or any other republican. It is because he thinks Douglas' superior position, reputation, experience, and *ability*, if you please, would more than compensate for his lack of a pure republican position, and therefore his re-election do the general cause of republicanism, more good than would the election of any one of our better undistinguished pure republicans."

Making an attempt to kill the unorthodox editor with kindness, Lincoln added a remarkably generous coda conceding Greeley's pure motives. "I do not know how *you* estimate Greeley," he told supporter Charles L. Wilson, "but *I* consider him incapable of corruption, or falsehood. He denies that he directly is taking part in favor of Douglas, and I believe him. Still, his *feeling* constantly manifests itself in his paper, which, being so extensively read in Illinois, is, and will continue to be, a drag upon us."[35] This was a new Lincoln. The old version might have tried to eviscerate foes by taunting them on the stump or mocking them in unsigned editorials. Where fellow Republicans were concerned, the politically seasoned Lincoln now preferred malice toward none, the better to corral their support later. And Lincoln by this time probably sensed that, if his luck held, he would remain politically entangled with Greeley forever after.

Lincoln did not allow himself to dwell on Greeley's lack of enthusiasm. Instead he and his supporters worked hard behind the scenes to convince state Republicans to endorse his Senate candidacy, in part to counter the official Douglas designation by the Democrats, and in part to neutralize Greeley's flirtation with the opposition. Just as he hoped, on June 16 the party convention resolved that "Hon. Abraham Lincoln is our first and only choice for United States Senator."[36]

That very evening, Lincoln mounted the platform in a familiar venue, the assembly chamber of Springfield's State Capitol, to formally accept the unprecedented "nomination." What followed was his most important oration to date: the speech that became known as the "House Divided" address. Few of Lincoln's supporters believed he should deliver it, certainly not after he read it aloud to a select group in advance. One of those in attendance colorfully advised Lincoln that it was a "d——d fool utterance." In its biblical insistence that "A house divided against itself cannot stand," Lincoln seemed to be charting a radical course that allowed for no future compromise on the slavery issue. But as Lincoln calmly insisted after his rehearsal: "The time has come when these sentiments should be uttered and if it is decreed that I should go down because of this speech, then . . . let me die in the advocacy of what is just and right."[37]

In one sense, Lincoln nearly did "die" that evening, but because of his script, not his sentiments. When he rose to speak on June 16, he carried with him a freshly printed version of his speech, obligingly typeset from his own manuscript at the offices of the *Illinois State Journal* (the easier to rush it into print afterward). What Lincoln did not know—perhaps never realized until he began reading aloud from the actual sheets that publishers Baker and Bailhache provided him—was that their compositors had inadvertently transposed some of the initial paragraphs, garbling his opening thoughts.[38] Such was the danger of relinquishing original, handwritten texts, even to the friendliest of newspapers.

A lesser orator might have lost his balance. Somehow, Lincoln made his way through his address without mishap, and to a roaring ovation. But tellingly, when later he assembled a definitive scrapbook of all his 1858 campaign speeches and debates, he chose a June 19 *Chicago Tribune* reprint of the "House Divided" address based in part on a transcript made on the scene, rather than the mangled version imperfectly typeset from his manuscript and printed in the June 18 *State Journal*. (Lincoln's priceless, handwritten original has never been found.)

In whatever form it appeared, Lincoln's speech aroused attention and, not surprisingly, some concern, from the country's Republican editors. When John L. Scripps of the *Chicago Daily Democratic Press* (a pro-Lincoln paper despite its name) wrote to compliment the address—with reservations—Lincoln assured him that while "much flattered by the estimate you place on my late speech . . . yet I am much mortified that any part of it should be construed so differently from any thing intended by me." He had never meant to imply that he favored interfering with slavery "in the States where it exists," he told Scripps, only preventing its spread westward. In a letter he did "not intend for publication," Lincoln tried to assure Scripps that the speech was less radical than the editor feared. Speaking in a way meant to convince all moderate journalists alarmed by the oration's do-or-die catchphrase, Lincoln insisted: "I have declared a thousand times, and now repeat that, in my opinion, neither the General Government, nor any other power outside of the slave states, can constitutionally or rightfully interfere with slaves or slavery where it already exists. I believe that whenever the effort to spread slavery into the new teritories [*sic*], by whatever means, and into the free states themselves, by Supreme court decisions, shall be fairly headed off, the institution will then be in the course of ultimate extinction; and by the language used I meant only this." (Three weeks later, Scripps merged his paper with Medill and Ray's to form the new and stronger *Chicago Press and Tribune*.)[39] Like Scripps, Horace Greeley, too, ultimately acknowledged the "House Divided" address as "memorable" and "in the right key." But as late as July, Greeley still stubbornly believed Douglas should have been "conciliated."[40]

One thing was certain: as far as candidate Lincoln was concerned, the Republican press represented one maddeningly divided "house" whose divisions he would no longer tolerate. He made this clear by firing off a barrage of both public and private post-nomination letters to Illinois editors. In rapid order, he defended a close ally against charges that he had undermined a fellow Republican over a House seat, corrected the record with regard to his old congressional votes on Mexico (*against* the war but *for* supplying the troops), and blasted another Republican for getting too cozy with a Democrat in neighboring Indiana—all in the space of two weeks, during which Lincoln strongly demonstrated that he now expected to harness the party press.

These latest volleys commenced on June 8, after the *Chicago Tribune* reprinted rumors of Judge David Davis's opposition to Illinois congressional candidate Owen Lovejoy, brother of the martyred Alton editor Elijah. In response, Lincoln not only defended his longtime personal and professional ally Davis, but also demanded unity around "the vitalizing principle of Republicanism."

Next, on the 25th, in the wake of new press charges that he had opposed House appropriations to support American troops in Mexico, Lincoln assured Medill, "you may safely deny that I ever gave any vote for withholding any supplies whatever, from officers or soldiers of the Mexican War." The *Chicago Times's* insistence otherwise, bristled the candidate, was based only on "its' [*sic*] blind rage to assail me." Just two days later, Lincoln flew into another rage at Medill's partner, Charles Ray. The *Press and Tribune* had reprinted a recent article urging that Republicans support the reelection of Democratic congressman John G. Davis of Indiana because, like Stephen Douglas, he had bravely opposed the pro-slavery Lecompton Constitution for Kansas.

A few weeks earlier, David Davis, increasingly angry at Medill and Ray over the earlier slight, had advised Lincoln that "The Editor of a newspaper, who knowingly permits such things to be done—is to say the least a bad leader—& ought to be rebuked." Now Lincoln took that advice to heart. "How in God's name do you let such paragraphs into the Tribune," Lincoln exploded in his letter to Ray. ". . . Does Sheahan write them? How can you have failed to perceive that in this short paragraph you have completely answered all; your own well put complaints of Greely [sic] . . . ? And what possible argument can be made why all Republicans shall stand out of Hon. John G. Davis's way in his district in Indiana that can not be made why all Republicans in Illinois shall stand out of Hon. S. A. Douglas's way? The part in larger type is plainly editorial, and your editorial at that, as you do not credit it to any other paper. I confess it astonishes me."[41] Through authoritative communications like these, Lincoln had by July strong-armed the Republican press into full conformity and allegiance, at least in Illinois. Independent-minded, out-of-state renegades like Greeley, primarily eager to injure the Buchanan administration by encouraging dissident Democrats like

Douglas, proved harder to tame. Their unpredictable behavior convinced stalwart David Davis that the Republican Party remained merely "confederated," not "consolidated," and unless brought into line would be powerless to battle "the infernal South, that prolific monster of ruin, *niggers*, and disunion."[42] Bring the statewide party and press into line Lincoln did. Now it was time to take the Senate battle to the people.

The "hullabaloo," public aspect of the Senate campaign got under way quickly. Better-known and far better-financed, Douglas returned to Illinois from Washington and commenced traveling the state in an ornately decorated private railroad car, drawing large crowds almost everywhere he went. The underfunded Lincoln had little option but to trail Douglas into town after town, asking audiences to reassemble to hear him rebut the senator's latest orations. It did not take the Democratic press long to taunt that since there were already "two very good circuses and menageries traveling through the state," it might be appropriate to "include a speech from Lincoln in their performances" as well. "In this way Lincoln could attract respectable audiences and his friends be relieved from the mortification they all feel at his present humiliating position."[43]

On July 22, the *Chicago Press and Tribune* came up with a far better idea: "Let Mr. Douglas and Mr. Lincoln agree to canvass the State together, in the old western style." By chance or design, a newspaper had proposed what would evolve into the most canonical political debates in American history. Days later, Lincoln formally challenged Douglas "to divide time, and address the same audiences." When Douglas initially demurred, the *Tribune* accused him of cowardice, editorializing that he "would rather go about the country like a strolling mountebank, with his cannon, to[a]dies and puffers, to shout, cheer, and blow him, than to stand up to the world with a full grown man to confront." Cornered, the incumbent had no choice but to accept.[44]

"Two men presenting wider contrasts could hardly be found as the representatives of the two great parties," William Cullen Bryant's antislavery *New York Evening Post* commented in August when the two combatants launched their joint meetings. Not surprisingly, the *Post* sneeringly described Democrat Douglas as a "short, thick-set, burly man, with a large, round head, heavy hair, dark complexion, and fierce bull-dog bark"—a Vermont native who had clearly forgotten "the ancestral hatred of slavery to which he was the heir." Lincoln, portrayed by contrast as "very tall, slender, and angular, awkward even, in gait and attitude," was admittedly not very "comely" in repose. "But stir him up," marveled the *Post*, and "the fire of his genius plays on every feature. . . . The Republicans of Illinois have chosen a champion worthy of their heartiest support, and fully equipped for the conflict." Within a month, the *Post* took the temperature of the growing political excitement in Illinois and declared: "The prairies are on fire."[45]

Contrary to their golden historical reputation, the Lincoln-Douglas debates did not actually bring out the best in either candidate. With progressive northern Illinois tilting to the Republicans, and the conservative southern part of the state firmly behind the Democrats, the candidates focused their fierce battle on the middle ground—both geographically and politically. This required Douglas to appear less retrograde, and Lincoln less liberal. In debate after debate, Lincoln repeated his warnings that Douglas intended to "plant slavery over all the states." Douglas returned the salvos by accusing Lincoln of harboring secret plans to endow blacks with equal rights, a radical aspiration embraced at the time by only a tiny enlightened minority, few among them Illinois voters. Lincoln gave as good as he got. Even before the skirmishes commenced, however, a *Tribune* correspondent assigned to cover the campaign noted that Douglas had "an opponent who is fully his equal in nature, talent, and whose bold, candid and straightforward manners, when placed in contrast with the sophistry which is apparent in all of Judge Douglas's campaign speeches, give the people more confidence in his living up to his professions, and a stronger faith in his honesty."[46]

At the first debate at Ottawa, Illinois, on August 21, Lincoln felt compelled to defend himself against Douglas's charges that he favored racial amalgamation by pointing out: "I have no purpose to introduce political and social equality between the white and black races. There is a physical difference between the two, which in my judgment will probably forever forbid their living together upon the footing of perfect equality, and inasmuch as it becomes a necessity that there must be a difference, I, as well as Judge Douglas, am in favor of the race to which I belong, having the superior position." Lincoln may have still considered African Americans inferior, but there was "no reason in the world," he insisted, "why the negro is not entitled to all the natural rights enumerated in the Declaration of Independence, the right to life, liberty and the pursuit of happiness. I hold that he is as much entitled to these as the white man."[47] Even that sentiment was sufficiently radical at the time to carry political risk.

The debates proved gigantically popular as spectacles. The public flocked to them, turning the encounters into day-long political festivals whose audiences toted handmade signs and banners, cheered themselves hoarse, shouted back at the speakers, and ate and drank with a delirious enthusiasm usually reserved for weddings and county fairs. The rhetoric the crowds heard was more often ugly than elevated, but it hardly dampened public enthusiasm. Ultimately, the Lincoln-Douglas debates achieved mythic status not because of what the debaters said, but because of what the press made of their words.

While the debaters toured the state, in Springfield tempers frayed. When onetime Shawneetown newspaperman John McClernand—an ardent Douglas supporter and former congressman now running for the House again— took exception to a charge published in the *State Journal*, he demanded that its editors retract it. They refused, and McClernand went looking for Edward Baker on the street to demand an apology in person. When Baker feistily insisted that he regretted nothing, McClernand attacked him with his cane— clearly the weapon of choice in the recent spate of duels. Neighbors had to pull the combatants apart.[48]

From the outset, dueling press "puffers" like Baker and his Democratic counterpart played active roles in the campaign that went far beyond mere coverage. They doubled as outright propagandists—what today we would call press secretaries or communication directors. Early on, for example, the *Register*'s Charles Lanphier provided Douglas with an 1856 clipping about Lincoln's congressional voting record that the senator read aloud to great effect at the first debate at Ottawa. "I see that your quotation from our old file has made an uproar," Lanphier proudly wrote Douglas five days later. With a sly wink at Lincoln's old "Spot" resolutions, Lanphier gloated, "the point you made is not affected by their denial of the 'spot.' "[49] Joseph Medill and Charles Ray, who worried about the "mischief" such war talk might engender, tried to get Lincoln to provide them with an autobiographical sketch they could print in the *Press and Tribune*. "*You* are the only man who can furnish the facts," Ray implored him on June 29. ". . . We do not care for a narrative—only a record of dates, place of nativity, parentage, early occupations, trials, disadvantages, &c &c—all of which will make, if we are rightly informed, a telling story."[50]

Ray was on to something; he was one of the first journalists to comprehend that emphasizing Lincoln's inspiring rise from obscurity would attract far more support than debate points on divisive issues like slavery and race. For now, however, the editor would be compelled to tell Lincoln's life story without the benefit of the candidate's personal help; Lincoln was not yet prepared, or perhaps was simply too busy, to provide the details, even when Ray pointed out that he "need not shrink from the declaration of an origin ever so humble."[51] Ray's overall fears were confirmed when he concluded that Lincoln had put in a lackluster performance at the initial debate. "For God's sake," he urged his friend, Illinois congressman Elihu Washburne, after the August 21 encounter at Ottawa, ". . . tell him to 'Charge, Chester! Charge!'"—a famous line from Walter Scott's poem "Marmion."[52] Ray went so far as to draft a response Lincoln might use should Douglas again accuse him of "radical" notions on slavery.[53]

As close as Horace Greeley had earlier come to endorsing Douglas, the *New York Tribune* nonetheless commended Lincoln's debate performances with enthusiasm. The Ottawa encounter was not just "a passage at arms between two eminent masters of the art of intellectual attack and defense," the paper commented. Lincoln had accomplished nothing less than to transform an Illinois Senate race into "a contest for the Kingdom of Heaven or the Kingdom of Satan—a contest for advance or retrograde in civilization."[54] Greeley ordered the debate reprinted word for word in the *New York Tribune*, editorializing that "Mr. Lincoln has decidedly the advantage" in doctrine and demeanor, if only because Douglas "reminds us more of the wild and unscrupulous athlete of his earlier days than of the noble displays of last Winter, when he stood forth in the Senate Chamber as the champion of popular rights against Executive usurpation."[55] Old fixations died hard for Greeley, but the transcript of the Lincoln-Douglas debate at Ottawa clearly diminished his sympathy for Stephen Douglas.

The New York paper's revolutionary "full report of the speeches on both sides" became possible because the Lincoln-Douglas debates inspired the first sustained, so-called phonographic reporting in politics—that is, complete, gavel-to-gavel transcriptions specifically designed for reprinting in newspapers. Over a two-month period, through all seven joint meetings and twenty-one hours of oratory, stenographers worked in both blazing sun and biting gales to record every word the protagonists uttered (or at least their own versions of these remarks). Within days of each encounter, leading party newspapers in Chicago and Springfield published what they promoted as faithful complete records. Out-of-town papers like the *New York Tribune* often followed up with reprints, summaries, and commentary. Tens of thousands of Illinoisans may have attended the debates in the towns of Ottawa, Freeport, Jonesboro, Charleston, Galesburg, Quincy, and Alton. But hundreds of thousands more read the speeches when they appeared, soon after each encounter, on the pages of the press.

Providing exact transcriptions proved an elusive goal, however, and there is no real way to measure how faithful the results actually were. The debaters themselves used no written scripts; for the most part, they spoke extemporaneously, except when quoting themselves or each other. For occasional reference, Lincoln carried with him a small scrapbook in which he had glued newspaper clippings of his earlier speeches. The first time he took the book from his coat pocket at Ottawa. As he slowly leafed through its small print in search of a citation, a wag in the crowd shouted out: "Put on your specs." Lincoln complied, looked out at the audience, and replied to much laughter: "Yes, sir, I am obliged to do so. I am no longer a young man."[56]

The debaters delivered their speeches without benefit of amplification. Stenographers invariably sat behind, not in front of, them on the temporary wooden platforms erected for each encounter, and if the breeze was at the speakers' backs, the candidates' words proved difficult to hear, much less transcribe accurately. As a result, the texts that appeared in the newspapers suffered from unexplained gaps and occasional garbling. But they clearly differed in other ways, too, depending on which politically affiliated journal published them. Somewhere along the trail leading from stenography, transcription, and editing, to typesetting and publication, other variances inevitably crept into the texts. And many contemporaries attributed these inconsistencies to naked politics. Not even supposedly verbatim transcripts were immune from the unrelenting politicization of mid-nineteenth-century journalism.[57]

The flaws originated with the stenographers, who harbored undisguised political loyalties of their own. Initially, the *Chicago Press and Tribune* placed overall coverage of the meetings in the hands of a young newspaper veteran named Horace White. "I did not expect much of him," White admitted of Lincoln before he first heard him speak four years earlier. Afterward, he exulted: "Lincoln is a mammoth. He has this day delivered a speech, the greatest ever listened to in the state of Illinois, unless himself had made a greater."[58] Now a true believer, White discovered to his distress that the Douglas camp had imported two shorthand experts to transcribe the debates word for word. Recognizing "the necessity of counteracting or matching that force," White

Painting of the Lincoln-Douglas debate at Charleston showing newspaper stenographers—Robert Hitt of the *Chicago Press and Tribune* and Henry Binmore of the *Chicago Times*—on either side of Lincoln transcribing as the Republican candidate orates.

urged Medill and Ray to hire young Robert Roberts Hitt, "the pioneer" of this "new feature in journalism in Chicago," to join him on the debate trail and produce transcripts of his own.[59] Lincoln quickly came to regard the pro-Republican stenographer as indispensable. At the second debate, he tried delaying the start of his opening speech until the tardy transcriber reached the platform. To the amusement of those within earshot, Lincoln was overheard asking: "Ain't Hitt here? Where is he?"[60]

Performing "phonographic" work for the Democrats was Henry Binmore, a twenty-five-year-old Englishman who had worked earlier for the *St. Louis Republican*—a Democratic organ despite its name (appropriately enough, the *Missouri Democrat* tilted Republican). Binmore's flattering early coverage of Douglas's pre-debate stump speeches attracted the attention of the *Chicago Times*. Aiding Binmore was James B. Sheridan, who had been employed at the *Philadelphia Press*, one of Douglas's strongest press advocates in the East.

These experts all ranked as reliable professionals gamely struggling to record everything they heard, but as a result of their own idiosyncratic methods, their political biases, and their partisan publishers' penchant for generous editing, the debate reprints featured in their respective newspapers differed markedly. Republican papers recast Lincoln's sometimes meandering impromptu style into cogent paragraphs and did little to burnish Douglas's often overheated prose. Democratic journals softened Douglas's occasional racist tirades, altering his persistent use of the word "nigger," for example, to "negro," while claiming they left Lincoln's incoherent speeches alone. Each stenographer invariably imagined cheers and applause apparently inaudible to his counterpart. Although few Democrats read the Republican papers, and few Republicans saw the Democratic journals, the stark differences in the results soon triggered a campaign debate of its own. Both sides furiously accused the other of intentional inaccuracy, triggering a controversy nearly as entertaining as the joint meetings themselves.

When, for instance, Republican editors complained that Lincoln's remarks seemed incomprehensible as printed in the Democratic *Chicago Times*, the paper shot back that the *Tribune* was guilty of publishing cogent "paragraphs of which Lincoln's tongue was innocent." Republicans, the *Times* alleged, "were ashamed of his poor abilities and wanted to divert attention from them, under the cry of mutilation and fraud." In his defense, stenographer Hitt steadfastly denied that "Mr. Lincoln's speeches were doctored and almost re-written before they were printed . . . as was often charged at that time in the fury of partisan warfare." [61]

For its part, the *Chicago Times* similarly insisted that its transcripts were not only faithful, but that there was "no orator in America more correct in rhetoric, more clear in ideas, more direct in purpose, in all his public addresses, than Stephen A. Douglas." If Republicans objected to the paper's version of Lincoln's performance at the first debate, it was only because "they dare not allow Lincoln to go into print in his own dress, and abuse us, the TIMES, for reporting him literally." Anyone who "has ever heard Lincoln speak," the paper concluded its scathing analysis, ". . . must know that he cannot speak five grammatical sentences in a row." [62]

Rising to the challenge, Chicago's Republican *Press and Tribune* condemned the rival *Times* for undertaking a libelous campaign "to blunt the keen edge of Mr. Lincoln's wit, to mar the beauty of his most eloquent passages, and to make him look like a booby, a half-witted numbskull." Democrats, the *Tribune* charged, had specifically instructed stenographer Sheridan "to garble the speeches of Mr. Lincoln and amend and elaborate those of Mr. Douglas." Sheridan's malicious transcriptions left Lincoln's words "so shamefully and outrageously . . . emasculated" that if doctoring prose became a crime, "the scamp whom Douglas hires to report Lincoln's speeches would be a ripe subject for the Penitentiary." [63] *Tribune* headlines announced throughout the campaign: "Mutilation of Lincoln's Speech," "Mr. Lincoln—the Times' Slanders," and "Garbling Lincoln's Speeches."[64] Meanwhile its own stenographers, the *Tribune* maintained, were neither "hired puffers nor paid libelers." Three days before the opponents met for their final debate at Alton, the *Times* attempted to have the last word by accusing the *Tribune* not only of mauling Douglas's stirring speeches, but "rewriting and polishing the speeches of . . . poor Lincoln," who "requires some such advantage."[65]

Neither Lincoln nor Douglas themselves ever admitted to countenancing, much less ordering, either the enhancement of their debate performances or the mutilation of their opponent's. In fact, Lincoln later insisted rather piously that he had never revised his own remarks, while Douglas "had two hired reporters traveling with him, and probably revised their manuscripts before they went to press; while I had no reporter of my own, but depended on a very excellent one sent by the Press & Tribune; but who never waited to show me his notes or manuscripts; so that the first I saw of my speeches, after delivering them, was in the Press & Tribune."[66] For his part, all Douglas would ever concede was that the debates had been conducted "in the open air to immense crowds of people, and in some instances, in stormy and boisterous weather, when it was impossible for the reporters to hear distinctly and report literally."[67] Of course, both papers, and all the stenographers, were in a sense equally guilty as charged.

Many decades later, when an old man, reporter Horace White confessed that in preparing Hitt's transcripts for publication in the *Press and Tribune* he had perhaps yielded to "the temptation to *italicise* a few passages in Mr. Lincoln's speeches, where his manner of delivery had been especially emphatic." What was more, in those "few cases where confusion on the platform, or the blowing of the wind, had caused some slight hiatus or evident mistake in catching the speaker's words," White had authorized occasional improvisations. But he never admitted to either the wholesale rewriting of Lincoln's performances, or the intentional desecration of Douglas's. White conceded only that the *Times* simply "took more care with Mr. Douglas's speeches," just as the *Tribune* did with Lincoln's. Errors and gaps had been "straightened out" by friendly reporters on both sides.[68]

Friendly press, however, proved insufficient to propel Lincoln to the Senate. On Election Day, the popular vote split, with a slight edge going to the Republicans. But in the all-important battles for local legislative seats, Douglas's party emerged with more than enough support to reelect the senator to a third term. Lincoln would not go back to Washington after all. Even before the state legislature met to make Douglas's reelection official, Greeley's *Tribune* conceded "the triumph" to the incumbent.[69]

Lincoln's attorney friend Henry Clay Whitney maintained that "nobody except Lincoln, supposed the speeches would even be preserved, but that they would suffer the fate of all newspaper literature." But before the legislature convened in January to crown Douglas with his third term, Lincoln hatched a plan to make brilliant new use of the record of his defeat, flawed or not. Not long after recommending a loyal young German-born Republican journalist named John G. Nicolay to Horace Greeley—"He wishes an arrangement to correspond for your paper," Lincoln wrote, "and, so far as I am capable of judging, [is] altogether competent for such a situation"[70]—Lincoln informed Charles Ray that he desired "to preserve a Set of the late debates (if they may be called so) between Douglas and myself." The unsuccessful candidate asked Ray to ship him two copies of each of the seven issues that featured debate transcripts—*three* separate whenever the reprints had been published back-to-back. Lincoln explained that he intended to keep one full set of newspapers intact, while cutting articles from the others to assemble a "Scrap-book" of the encounters. If Ray was still depressed over the outcome of the election, as widely reported, Lincoln offered this encouragement: "Quit that. You will soon feel better. Another 'blow-up' is coming."[71] Ray would have found it hard to imagine that the next "blow-up" would be stimulated in part by his own back issues.

By December 1858, Lincoln had collected the necessary old newspapers, including copies of the *Chicago Times* reports of Douglas's speeches. Showing them one day to an old friend "with great satisfaction," he reported that "he had got a book binder to paste the speeches, in consecutive order, in a blank book, very neatly." On Christmas Day, Lincoln would update Henry Clay Whitney: "There is some probability that my Scrap-book will be reprinted."[72] By the following March a number of publishers were expressing interest in the project. And in the fall of 1859, Lincoln engaged the Columbus, Ohio, firm of Follett, Foster & Co. to bring out a book edition of the complete debates and sent Nicolay to carry his scrapbook to the publisher. It proved nothing less than the most brilliant publishing venture Lincoln ever initiated. Although the contest for the White House was still a year away, Ohio's Republican chairman recognized from the outset that the new volume promised to become "essential . . . to the cause."[73] Even the *Richmond Enquirer* had characterized the debates as "the great battle of the Presidential election."[74]

In masterminding their republication, Lincoln emerged from the project—and from his failed quest for the Senate—as a national leader willing to be judged by his words, even in what had turned out to be a losing cause. It was an inspired strategic move, showcasing Lincoln's genius for both politics and public relations. "Our government rests in public opinion," Lincoln had declared a few years earlier. "Whoever can change public opinion can change the government."[75] He had said much the same thing during the first debate at Ottawa: "In this and like communities, public sentiment is everything. With public sentiment, nothing can fail; without it, nothing can succeed. Consequently he who molds public sentiment goes deeper than he who enacts statutes or pronounces decisions."[76] Lincoln was finally on his way to doing both.

The book version of the Lincoln-Douglas debates succeeded beyond even Lincoln's wildest imaginings. Eventually, the volume became a best-seller, boasting more than thirty thousand copies in print by the presidential election year of 1860. Since proper presidential candidates of the day were expected to remain publicly silent during campaigns, the book became for Lincoln a vehicle to convey his political views without speaking anew. Countless visitors who made their way to Springfield in the summer and fall of 1860 to visit the Republican candidate for the White House came away with a gift from Lincoln's own hands—a copy of the *Political Debates Between Hon., Abraham Lincoln and Hon., Stephen A. Douglas in the Celebrated Campaign of 1858, in Illinois*—often autographed by the man who appeared, after ingeniously shepherding newspaper transcriptions into book reprints, almost to have won by losing that "celebrated campaign."

But lose Lincoln did. "Glory to God and the Sucker Democracy," the *Register*'s Charles Lanphier exulted to the senator in reporting the official legislative vote in early January 1859. "Douglas 54 Lincoln 46. . . . Town wild with excitement." Replied the vindicated senator when he heard the news: "Let the voice of the people rule."[77] In New York, Bennett's *Herald*, which had earlier demonized Douglas for breaking with President Buchanan over Kansas, wickedly expressed the hope that the senator's close call would prove a "wet blanket" to his national ambitions and "restore him again into full communion in the democratic church." But as Bennett predicted: "From all the indications of the day he will do no such thing; and the elusive victory which he has just achieved will only mislead him and his followers to destruction."[78]

Eager to reinvigorate his rivalry with the *Tribune*, Bennett charged that Greeley had wanted his "friend" Douglas to win all along to embarrass Buchanan, whom the *Herald* supported. "Hon. Massa Greeley went for him, old white coat and all," he editorialized, "because he was supposed to be 'a little of color' on the nigger question, and a little is better than nothing for the *Tribune* philosophers."[79]

Publicly, Greeley interpreted the result otherwise—a defeat for Lincoln, to be sure, but a good showing for the party. He was still not quite sold on the Illinois Republican. "Mr. Lincoln's speeches were doubtless more attractive to their hearers, far more readable by others, than they would have been had he devoted them mainly to the demolition of Mr. Douglas's castle," he editorialized. ". . . While we think no man could have upborne the Republican standard more gallantly than Mr. Lincoln has done, it seems to us possible to have done so more skillfully—therefore more effectively. If this criticism seems unkind, we shall regret the misapprehension, not the frankness which impelled it." By the same token, Greeley admitted that while "Republicans of Illinois" had "fought their late battle under serious disadvantages . . . the popular verdict, the popular intelligence, are clearly on their side. The Future is theirs."[80] Greeley was not yet ready to concede—or remained so blind he could not see—that the future of Lincoln and the party were now intertwined.

Writing a decade later, Greeley refused to apologize for his lack of enthusiasm for Lincoln in 1858. "It seemed to me," he insisted, "that not only magnanimity, but policy, dictated to the Republicans of Illinois that they should promptly and heartily render their support to Mr. Douglas." Acknowledging that the hearts of Illinois Republicans "were set on . . . their own special favorite and champion, Abraham Lincoln, who, though the country at large scarcely knew him," Greeley admitted that Western Republicans "did not, for a while, incline to forgive me for the suggestion that it would have been wiser and better not to have opposed Mr. Douglas's return." But he hastened to add: "I still abide in that conviction."[81]

Disappointed as he was, Lincoln had no choice but to look ahead. "The fight must go on," he advised one supporter. "The cause of civil liberty must not be surrendered at the end of *one*, or even a *hundred* defeats."[82]

In 1858, the *Illinois State Journal* congratulated itself on twenty-seven years of continuous publication by issuing a prospectus inviting new subscribers to sample its daily, tri-weekly, and weekly editions, and offering anyone who brought in ten subscribers or fifteen dollars in advertising "an extra copy for his trouble." Although the leaflet maintained rather unconvincingly that the *Journal* had been an "impartial newspaper"—"never sacrificing the interests of one class of its readers for the benefit of any other class"—publishers Bailhache and Baker left no doubt where its political loyalty still resided. "It will continue faithfully to support the principles of the Republican party," the *Journal* boasted. "Against the slavery-extension policy of the mis-named Democratic party, the JOURNAL will make increasing and unrelenting warfare."[83]

The following May, Lincoln introduced a new weapon into the ongoing press wars with his decision to become a publisher himself: he bought into the new German-language Springfield weekly. His partner in the venture was a thirty-three-year-old, Westphalia-born physician-turned-journalist named Heinrich Theodor Canisius—later Americanized into "Theodore." Like many so-called Forty-Eighters—Germans who migrated to the United States after the failed European revolutions of 1848—Canisius became a liberal anti-slavery man, and joined the Republicans. At the time Lincoln invested in his newspaper, the doctor had been an American citizen for just four years.

An ardent Lincoln supporter during the recent Senate race, Canisius impressed the candidate by working to ensure that none of his fellow émigrés would be, as Lincoln put it, "cheated in their ballots"—denied the right to vote by having their citizenship questioned. This trick Lincoln believed Democrats "sometimes practiced on the German" to inhibit reliably Republican turnout.[84] Casting his eyes on the future, Lincoln sensed that the growing German vote in the West would assume added significance. Perhaps with proper cultivation it might even tip the balance to the Republicans in several key swing states.

Working toward the same goal, Canisius had undertaken an effort of his own to increase Republican influence among local Germans. Early in 1858, just in time to support Lincoln's ill-fated campaign against Douglas, Canisius bravely established a paper called the *Freie Presse* in overwhelmingly Democratic Alton at the southern end of the state—a town where, two decades earlier, progressive-style journalism had aroused mob violence and murder. It was a doomed initiative from the start. The paper attracted few readers in the pro-slavery bastion. After just a few months of struggle, Canisius abandoned it, turning over the publication to a fellow German who somehow kept it limping along for another year.[85]

In March 1859, the doctor resurfaced farther north—in Lincoln's hometown of Springfield. There he determined to launch a new German paper in Illinois's more hospitable state capital.[86] Some historians have claimed that Canisius commenced publishing by May, but there is no evidence that such was the case. That month, more likely, he was still trolling for investors.

Meanwhile, Canisius made a foray into political organizing. He rallied local German Americans in denouncing a proposed new anti-immigration initiative in Massachusetts. The amendment sought to deny the vote to all foreign-born residents until two years after their naturalization.[87] From New York, Horace Greeley warned that its adoption "would work enormous mischief, especially throughout the Free West," and might even "defeat the election of a Republican President in 1860" by reducing German voting strength in bellwether states.[88] German-language papers in Iowa and Indiana took up the fight and sounded similar alarms. As another German-born newspaperman, Henry Villard, explained: "There was not an intelligent politician in the Northwest that was ignorant of the importance of his 'German friends.'" German journalists, in turn, "worked with the peculiar zeal, earnestness, and indefatigableness with which the German mind is wont to make propaganda for its convictions."[89]

Under Canisius's leadership, Springfield Republicans assembled for a public meeting on May 14 to decry the "Two Year" threat. The press attended the event, but Lincoln himself did not. Unwilling to risk offending local Nativists, whose support he also coveted, he avoided the gathering though he did send his usual surrogate—William Herndon—who delivered a full-throated warning against "despotism," which his senior colleague undoubtedly reviewed beforehand.[90] Unable to maintain his own silence for long, Lincoln provided Canisius with a personal statement on the issue just three days later on May 17—as usual, delayed but effective.

Conceding that the Bay State was "sovereign and independent," and that he lacked the "privilege . . . to scold her for what she does," Lincoln offered a strong generic defense of immigration. As he ingeniously explained, in a manner designed to remind progressive readers of his record on another key issue, slavery: "Understanding the spirit of our institutions to aim at the *elevation* of men, I am opposed to whatever tends to *degrade* them. I have some little notoriety for commiserating the oppressed condition of the negro; and I should be strangely inconsistent if I could favor any project for curtailing the existing rights of *white men*, even though born in different lands, and speaking different languages from myself."[91]

The declaration appeared the next day in the *Illinois State Journal*, complete with guest commentary by Canisius lauding Lincoln as "one of the gallant champions of our State." The doctor hailed Lincoln's message as fully "in accordance with the views of the whole German population, supporting the Republican party, and also with the views of the entire German Republican press."[92] With Canisius's help, translations enjoyed further circulation in several German-language papers.[93] For Lincoln, the episode marked another successful test of his political skills, public relations acumen, and moral commitments. For Canisius, it represented a professional triumph that surely increased his influence in town. The two men were soon to collaborate to advance each other's interests further.

But first things went terribly wrong for the editor. With few readers and even less advertising, his successor at Alton had shuttered the *Freie Presse* only weeks earlier, and the doctor apparently ordered its idle presses and metal type shipped north to the state capital. Within days, however, no doubt drowning in debt from his Alton fiasco, he seems to have surrendered the precious publishing equipment to a Springfield creditor. To his rescue came Lincoln—who likely saw in Canisius's desperation an opportunity not only to reward the editor for his political loyalty, but also to increase his own control of both the medium and the message among German readers whose support he would need for future success.

Negotiations for a bailout seem to have commenced even as Lincoln was considering his immigration statement, and might even have been discussed in tandem. At first, Lincoln hoped the Republican State Central Committee would provide the necessary cash infusion to help Canisius open a paper. But its chairman, his close friend and ally Norman Judd, proved cool to the idea. "I cannot presume to act in that matter of the newspaper without direction of the Committee," Judd bluntly advised Lincoln on May 13, hinting that the proposed rescue was somewhat unsavory besides and might be closely scrutinized: "I am watched more than in other times and must be guarded about taking responsibility as this world is awfully jealous and given to slander and detraction."

Judd had further reason to object to the rescue plan: he neither liked nor trusted Dr. Canisius, who had apparently asked for and received underwriting before. "I can only say in confidence," he warned Lincoln darkly, ". . . that Canisius is a leech. He sucked more blood from you at Springfield and from the Com[mittee]. than the whole establishment was worth. You can get no guarantee that if you make the first expenditure there will not be afterwards continued calls." But the committee had apparently granted Lincoln some kind of unrestricted monetary "assessment" to allocate as he wished, and Judd was unable to persuade his friend to, as he put it, avoid the editor's "premises." [94] Whether or not the needy doctor was a "leech," Lincoln appreciated his political potential and determined to help him establish the new paper, even though he, too, was financially strapped at the time. He may have earmarked his precious "assessment" to Canisius. On the other hand, William Herndon hinted later that Lincoln simply appropriated a recent $500 legal fee and handed most of it to the doctor even though he customarily split such income with his partner. In "the coolest way," Lincoln joked: "Herndon, I gave the Germans $250 of yours the other day." [95]

Frustratingly, not a single issue of the newspaper Lincoln and Canisius cofounded survives. [96] Their original contracts, however, for which, traditional admonitions notwithstanding, Lincoln served as both client and his own lawyer, endure intact. Under its terms, Lincoln agreed to rescue Canisius's printing press and "german types" from the doctor's Springfield creditor. Astonishingly, the funds would in a sense be laundered to disguise their origins. As Lincoln noted on his copy of the contract, dated May 30, 1859, Jacob Bunn—his personal banker—"bought the press, types, &c. . . . for me, and with my money." [97] Lincoln promised that after the 1860 presidential election, he would then hand the precious supplies back to "Canissius" without compensation.

The deal specified that the doctor would solely manage the new paper, assume all the costs of running it, and retain "all incomes and profits" that the enterprise generated. Lincoln tacked on some boilerplate requirements: the paper would publish at least weekly, and remain headquartered in Springfield. It was to appear "chiefly in the german language," but could be supplemented by "occasional translations into English" at the editor's "option." [98] (A savvy politician like Lincoln well knew that newspaper presses could be put to other uses, between editions, churning out political pamphlets, broadsides, preprinted election ballots, and other useful propaganda.)

Lincoln hardly expected Canisius to "cheat" like a Democrat, but the heavily invested silent partner did impose one ironclad clause stipulating the consequence of political disloyalty. Lincoln did not much care whether the paper earned or lost money, or even maintained a minimum circulation level. He did not even know how to spell his new partner's family name—

Final page of the 1859 contract between Lincoln and Theodor Canisius (this is Canisius's copy) for their secret partnership to publish a German-language Republican weekly in Springfield.

always adding one "s" too many. All he demanded was that "in political sentiment," Canisius pledge "not to depart from the Philadelphia and Illinois Republican platforms"—that is, the most recent national and statewide declarations of party principle.[99]

To make certain the editor remained faithful to Republican ideology, Lincoln crafted what today would be called a "drop-dead clause." Should Canisius ever manifest in print any "material departure" from Republican dogma, or publish "any thing opposed to, or designed to injure the Republican party," Lincoln could "at his option, at once take possession of said press, types &c, and deal with them as his own." Plainly stated, if the weekly ever came out "against the Republican party," Lincoln could essentially shut the operation down.[100] On the other hand, if the new paper remained "conformable" until after the presidential election of 1860—a due date that suggests Lincoln's already blossoming ambitions for the White House a full year before the nominating convention—then the enterprise would become Canisius's sole property. Where Lincoln hoped he was going after 1860, he would have little use for a Springfield weekly in any language.

By July 1859 at the latest, the *Illinois Staats-Anzeiger*—German for "State Advertiser"—began appearing in Springfield every Saturday under its concealed new ownership, with individual copies priced at a hefty seventy-five cents.[101] His penchant for secrecy notwithstanding, Lincoln quickly developed such pride in the product that he was unable to resist the temptation to promote it. He commenced sending what he called "specimen" copies "of the new german paper started here" to leading German-American Republicans in nearby Illinois towns, urging them to order copies and to get friends to do likewise. "I think you could not do a more efficient service," he cajoled one prospect, "than to get it a few subscribers, if possible."[102] Never in these sales pitches did he reveal that the *Staats-Anzeiger* actually belonged to him.[103] Lincoln's efforts were not calculated to help him recoup his financial investment. He expected his reward solely in political capital: loyal editorial support and reliable Election Day votes from Illinois Germans.

Once they signed their contract, Lincoln never again had to remind "his" editor about the political obligations it required. Less than a year after they struck their deal, Canisius would travel to Chicago to boost Lincoln's candidacy for president at the Republican National Convention. In a city teeming with would-be kingmakers, Canisius labored hard to sway fellow Germans who initially resisted backing the Springfield dark horse. Soon enough, German-born delegates abandoned their early favorite and defected to Lincoln, who won the prize on the third ballot.

During the ensuing presidential campaign, the paper would remain unfailingly pro-Republican and lavish in its praise of the party's nominee—who also happened to be its owner. Though copies of the *Staats-Anzeiger* have disappeared, in a surviving advertisement in Springfield's English-language daily that June, Canisius unapologetically described the weekly as completely "devoted to the advancement of the Republican Party and its standard-bearer, Abraham Lincoln."[104] We can surmise that in the months to come, it lived up to this boast, since the publication survived the election and beyond; Lincoln never had a reason to close it down for political nonconformity, as the contract allowed. Although, true to tradition of the day, the candidate made not a single campaign speech that summer or fall, he faithfully kept the *Staats-Anzeiger* in print through Election Day—and beyond. Shortly after Lincoln's triumph, the *Illinois State Journal* would acknowledge Canisius's contribution to the result by declaring: "The Republicans of Sangamon [County] are greatly indebted for their victory to the gallantry of the service of the Anzeiger, the German Republican organ of this city." [105]

Late in the presidential race, with Republican victory in the air and local supporters already jockeying for political rewards, Lincoln himself acknowledged his gratitude to Canisius with a potentially useful testimonial to his good character. He had yet to learn how to spell his partner's name, but he no longer harbored any reservations about his fealty. As Lincoln put it: "The bearer of this, Dr. Theodore Canissius, is the editor and proprietor of the Republican newspaper, published in German here; and is a true and worthy man. Any kindness and attention shown him will be appreciated by me." Still no mention was made of their business relationship. [106]

None ever was. A month after he won the election, however, Lincoln would live up to his side of the bargain he had so meticulously crafted the previous year. On December 6, 1860, the president-elect scribbled a brief addendum to Canisius's copy of their original contract: "Dr. Theodore Canissius having faithfully published a newspaper according to the within, I now relinquish to him the press, types, &c. . . . without any further claim of ownership on my part." [107] Thus was their unsung deal finally and fully satisfied. Having served its purpose, the *Staats-Anzeiger* limped along for only a few months more, then ceased publication and vanished into history.

Lincoln's "kindness and attention" to its editor, however, were only beginning—although the incoming chief executive initially seemed reluctant to lavish further recognition on him. Once he gained control of federal patronage, Lincoln conspicuously began handing *other* German Republicans coveted diplomatic posts abroad—they were among an ambitious group Henry Villard nicknamed the "Teutonic expectants" [108]—but to the annoyance of some of his closest allies, Lincoln at first neglected Canisius. When the president-elect named German-born editor Frederick Hassaurek of Ohio as minister to Ecuador, and St. Louis–based journalist Charles L. Bernays as consul to Zurich, one of the most prominent Illinois Germans of all, former lieutenant governor Gustave Koerner, could stand no more. After all, both Hassaurek and Bernays had originally supported Missourian Edward Bates, not Lincoln, for the nomination. Describing Canisius as "an original Republican" who ". . . has worked hard in the cause," Koerner pointedly reminded the president-elect that he had "been honestly at work for your success" while others "whom Doctor Canisius had to fight to the very death at Chicago, when they used every effort to defeat you," had already received "high and distinguished offices." Concluded Koerner: "Now this does seem strange, and it ought to be remedied. . . . May I not hope that Dr. Canisius will succeed?"[109]

Ultimately, Lincoln gave in and obliged—naming Canisius to a plum post after all: American consul to Vienna. "The place is but $1,000 [annual salary] and not much sought," the president explained to Secretary of State William Seward in ordering the appointment in June 1861, "and I must relieve myself of the Dr. Illinoisan, tho, he be."[110]

This bit of shorthand was perhaps intended to obfuscate the transaction, but it is decipherable to the historian. Evidently, the diplomatic corps was already bulging with an abundance of appointees hailing from the president's home state of Illinois. Political operative Norman Judd, for example, who had so adamantly opposed Lincoln's purchase of a German-language paper, had in a supreme irony won the job of U.S. minister to Berlin. Secretive about his newspaper experience to the end, Lincoln neglected to tell Seward in writing about his past involvement with Canisius's publishing venture, or that the editor's new post actually paid a third more than the president was willing to admit: a handsome $1,500.

With this final and substantial recompense, Abraham Lincoln's brief, largely ignored career as a newspaper entrepreneur concluded with a lucrative political bonus that, however surprising to the modern reader, would have surprised few of "Honest Abe's" contemporaries. In the age of Lincoln, the blatant exchange of editorial support for political reward was routine, traditional, broadly accepted, and unlike his quietly transacted arrangement with Canisius, practiced with almost defiant transparency. In what represented the final footnote in this chapter of Lincoln's brief life as a press führer, the Republican-dominated Illinois state legislature that gaveled into session in Springfield in the early weeks of 1861 found it perfectly appropriate to reward one particularly loyal editor as a way of expressing solidarity with its neighbor on the eve of his departure for Washington and the presidency: it voted to subscribe en masse to Theodore Canisius's German-language newspaper.

Perhaps Lincoln's recently dissolved ownership interest with the *Staats-Anzeiger* had finally come to light. Possibly Lincoln or his intermediaries had directly requested an additional prize for its loyal editor. For whatever reason, between January 7 and February 22, 1861, the Illinois State Senate and General Assembly purchased more than five hundred copies of the weekly newspaper the president-elect had owned until just a few weeks earlier. For these "official" subscriptions, the once bankrupt Theodore Canisius collected more than $504 from the state treasury—surpassing by four dollars Lincoln's original investment in the publication the year before. Precisely what English-speaking legislators were to do with the foreign-language weeklies was never explained, though they may have been expected to mail the editions to their own German constituents. At the same time, Republican and Democratic legislators voted funds to create bound copies of the *Journal* and *Register*—evidently as souvenir keepsakes from the 1860 campaign year. One thing was clear: the new infusion of funds from the legislature would surely help finance Canisius's relocation to Vienna.[111]

Earlier, one of Lincoln's oldest and most steadfast press supporters had decided to relocate as well. Not even Lincoln had been able to protect Simeon Francis and his successors at the *Illinois State Journal* from new local competition—not Canisius's German weekly but an upstart daily called the *Springfield Republican.*

Loyal to the *Journal,* Lincoln had viewed the establishment of yet another party organ in Springfield as "unfortunate," but was careful "to throw no obstacle in its way." His wife demonstrated far less sympathy for the "obstacle" that its arrival soon created on her front porch. When the maiden issue landed on her doorstep, an annoyed Mary reprimanded Lincoln: "Now are you going to take another worthless little paper?" Lincoln replied to her "evasively," as he later admitted to the new paper's editor, John E. Rosette, saying only that he told his wife: "I have not directed the paper to be left." Next time it was delivered, Lincoln was away, and Mary apparently used sharp language to shoo the news carrier away. The dustup inspired an embarrassing "little paragraph" in the new *Springfield Republican*, compelling Lincoln to excuse the whole incident as a "mistake." William Herndon, who loathed Mary, interpreted his law partner's defensive letter to editor Rosette "as a specimen of the perplexities" that frequently beset him "when his wife came in contact with others."[112] But it also shows that, despite his longtime loyalty to the *Journal,* Lincoln was more than willing to see friendly new Republican journals prosper in Springfield. They could only, he reasoned, widen his appeal.

For his part, Simeon Francis forever after believed that Lincoln should have done more to protect his former paper (and its new owners) from such competition, but Lincoln, in turn, thought Francis had made a mistake in selling the *Journal* to William Bailhache and Edward Baker. "You say this was an error," the former editor wrote morosely. "It may be so—it probably was so. . . . My life has probably been an error. I have thought too much of others—little for myself." [113]

For a time, the onetime crusader who had brawled in the muddy streets of old Springfield with Stephen Douglas tried his hand at operating a local grocery store, but suffered extreme "pecuniary distress" in the financial Panic of 1857. Two years later, he emigrated to the Northwest, where he soon became editor of the *Oregon Farmer*. "I have always been your friend," Francis assured Lincoln when he arrived in his new home. Though he reported that he loved "the mountains—the rivers,—the peaks . . . covered with the eternal snows" in Oregon, Francis found the "virulence of political parties" there much like Illinois in the 1830s.[114] Before he departed, Francis submitted a guest editorial to the *Journal* proposing Lincoln as a presidential candidate for 1860—"the best man for the times," as he put it in a letter to his old friend. "I have talked with Messrs. B[aker]. And B[ailhache].," he added, "and they seem to be of my opinion. Indeed they asked me to write an article on the subject." [115] For his part, Lincoln would not forget Francis's long friendship or recent support. In 1861, he made him an army quartermaster at Fort Vancouver in Washington Territory.

Simeon Francis's departure from Springfield held symbolic importance for Lincoln, and very likely Lincoln both understood and accepted it. For nearly twenty years, he had relied on the portly founding editor, and his young successors, to bring his message to voters and to cheer his accomplishments on the pages of the hometown *Journal*. He remained a "frequent visitor," often bringing his "two small

Simeon Francis, Lincoln's first newspaper ally—founding editor of the *Sangamo* (later *Illinois State*) *Journal*—as he looked after selling the paper and moving to Oregon. Francis wears the uniform of an army quartermaster, a post with which Lincoln rewarded him at the start of the Civil War.

boys" to the *Journal* office. There, Willie and Tad repeatedly sneaked off to the workrooms, where they no doubt began playing with the type and ink. Lincoln would repeatedly "find that the boys had gone," and "go and find them, leading them back by the hands; this would occur two and three times at each visit." But when not distracted by his sons' antics, Lincoln would occupy his time talking intensely with new editor Edward Baker "and reading the *New York Tribune* and other eastern papers."[116] But the Canisius and Francis appointments were still in the future—as was the 1860 presidential election.

As he waited for the campaign to begin, Lincoln had ample time to ponder the impact that the press had made on the nation since he began his political career and he immediately sensed what historians later proved. The United States now boasted more than four thousand newspapers and periodicals, and 80 percent of them could be classified as political. Perhaps it was no coincidence that voter turnout in presidential elections now regularly approached that same 80 percent. Yet in a lecture on discoveries and inventions that he delivered several times from 1858 to 1860, Lincoln took pains to describe the communications revolution through a nonpartisan lens. "*Writing,*" he told his audiences, "—the art of communicating thoughts to the mind, through the eye," was nothing less than "the great invention of the world." But the world remained mired in "the dark ages" until writing could be mass-produced. "At length," Lincoln declared, "printing came. It gave ten thousand copies of any written matter, quite as cheaply as ten were given before; and consequently a thousand minds were brought into the field where there was but one before. This was great *gain*; and history shows a great *change* corresponding to it." Lincoln's tone may have been uncharacteristically ponderous—these lectures were usually failures—but the lecturer surely understood that his own political ascent had taken flight on the wings of that "great change."[117]

Lincoln's sights were now aimed nationally, not locally, practically, not philosophically. For future success, he needed support not just from Springfield, but from Chicago and New York.

He would now have to enlist those most stubbornly indifferent of potential champions: Henry Raymond and Horace Greeley. The latter would pose a challenge. As the *Chicago Tribune*'s Horace White bluntly put it, Lincoln still had a "score . . . to settle" with Greeley.[118]

CHAPTER SEVEN

The Perilous Position of the Union

A s the tempestuous 1850s drew to a close, the rift between North and South—and their increasingly rabid newspapers—widened further over the smoldering issue of slavery. Within the quintessentially Northern metropolis of New York, the dailies intensified their own rivalry, hardly surprising since political fissures within the city itself had expanded as well. More than ever, Gotham seemed, both in print and on the streets, to be living up to its growing reputation as a city of stark, irreconcilable contrasts—of "clouds and sunshine, corpse lights and bridal lamps, joy-anthems and funeral-dirges," in the words of one observer. On New York's thronged streets, the rich rubbed elbows with the poor, the honest with the "rough," bohemians with "deadbeats," and seldom harmoniously.[1]

The white population, no matter how impoverished, enjoyed far broader rights than the black. Many free African Americans could achieve no higher social status than that of the beggars who crowded trash bins outside the best hotels waiting to rummage through the day's garbage heaps for scraps of food. Appalled by the treatment of blacks there, the English journalist Edward Dicey described New York's African Americans as "a race apart, never walking in company with white persons, except as servants."[2] Facing such restrictions, it was little wonder that the city's black population had stopped expanding—

though its community newspapers continued to attract readers; New York still offered scant opportunities to people of color, and countless restrictions. Confronting these inequities, an elite white philanthropic antislavery minority tried agitating for reform, often clashing with commercial-minded forces determined to preserve the lucrative trade with the South, even if doing so required tacit approval of slavery—for slave labor harvested most of the crops and goods profitably imported from Dixie into New York docks.

Unconstrained urban sprawl in 1850s Manhattan butted up incongruously against picturesque, but ever-scarcer green space, although the plan for a vast new uptown "Central Park" promised future relief. One of the oldest of these precious oases was the cherished little City Hall Park, its enduring "freshness and beauty," however, growing ever more dissipated by overcrowding and neglect. At the northern end of this modest plot of grass and trees stood the jewel-like, marble-fronted City Hall, already an unofficial historic landmark, having served as the seat of municipal government since 1812. To the south, perpendicular to the cobblestoned crosstown boulevard known as Park Row, ran the narrow, north-south thoroughfares now crowded with undistinguished two- and three-story brick buildings lately occupied by printing presses, editors, artists, engravers, lithographers, and reporters—the merchants and employees of the city's rapidly growing publishing industry. This was their neighborhood, too. By the end of the decade the area served as home to all but a handful of the skyrocketing population of city newspapers: 174 dailies, weeklies, monthlies, and foreign language journals (there were now four thousand newspapers and periodicals nationwide—more than three thousand of them political in nature).[3] The latest entries in Manhattan included the wildly popular new picture press: *Frank Leslie's Illustrated Newspaper*, founded in 1852; the *New York Illustrated News*, which first appeared in 1859; and the behemoth of the fledgling industry, *Harper's Weekly*, launched in 1857, abounding with superb woodcut portraits and cartoons, inflected by such steadfastly moderate politics at first that some Northern critics scoffingly dubbed it "Harper's Weakly," but nevertheless avidly read by 200,000 subscribers.[4]

Beginning to edge slightly northward, ever closer to the park, were the newly expanded headquarters of New York's major dailies. After a few years of occupancy at a succession of inadequate buildings along nearby Nassau Street, Henry Raymond in 1858 hired an architect to build a Romanesque, five-story *New York Times* tower, the most lavish newspaper headquarters ever built, on the site of the Old Brick Church on Park Row between Nassau and Beekman Streets. Raymond drew much criticism for buying and tearing down the "mouldering," ninety-year-old house of worship, but the controversy did the *Times* little permanent harm. Once constructed, his ornately colonnaded new headquarters quickly became a tourist attraction.[5] Punctuating his arrival uptown, Raymond's large "Daily Times" sign, surmounted on the roof by flagpoles flying the national colors, could be seen for blocks, staking the paper's claim to both neighborhood and industry dominance.

Until then, as Raymond biographer Augustus Maverick recalled in 1870, "New York journals had always been housed in dilapidated headquarters" near Wall Street, where windows "remained unwashed till the grime of years formed cakes and diligent spiders spun dense and endless cobwebs in uncleansed corners." In stark contrast, the *Times*'s gleaming new tower drew praise as "the wonder of its day."[6] Notwithstanding the latest national economic panic, the *Tribune* and *Herald* began making plans to follow Raymond into the neighborhood.

The formidable new structures that rose around what soon came to be known as "Newspaper Row" pointedly faced City Hall, as if to turn their backs on the financial district to the south that had spawned the town's first

Printing House Square in New York, an undated lithograph by Endicott & Co., showing the new headquarters of the *New York Times* and, at left, the *Tribune* building.

commercial broadsheets. Now they looked northward as if to announce that politics, not trade, had become their principal beat. Theirs were New York's first skyscrapers, and the structures literally looked down on municipal government. Whatever else transpired on the street and green, the dailies' close proximity to City Hall hinted to the mayor, the Common Council, and the courts that the press was watching over them.

From its own warren of offices farther downtown (not for another few years would James Gordon Bennett abandon them for Newspaper Row), the *New York Herald* achieved no less notice. According to one visitor, the *Herald*'s "very crooked and extremely dark" headquarters "consisted of half a dozen houses, taken up one by one, as the business of the paper had grown." As he remembered the intimidating warren of rooms, "You had to go up or down two or three steps as you passed from building to building, the floors being on a different level, and there were any number of quaint nooks and corners" to navigate—behind any one of which lurked the possibility of running unexpectedly into the ferocious Bennett himself.[7]

Writing in 1859, veteran journalist Lambert A. Wilmer acknowledged that, however outmoded his headquarters and vituperative his prose, Bennett's "power and influence" were now "universally acknowledged"—and as often copied as condemned. As Wilmer put it: "Although the *Herald* is denounced from one end of the country to the other as the most corrupt and profligate in existence, its opinions on almost every subject are often quoted as indisputable authority, and hundreds of other newspapers adopt its views and republish its statements without the least reservation." Wilmer had nothing good to say about Greeley, James Watson Webb, or Duff Green, either, but he reserved his bitterest venom for Bennett. To Wilmer, he was "the arch-contriver of our present newspaper system, with all its ambitious, unscrupulous and diabolical peculiarities," a schemer so perverse that he relished every duel and brawl he had survived. "He has been horse-whipped, kicked, trodden under foot, spat upon, and degraded in every possible way," Wilmer reminded readers, "but all this he courts, because it brings money. Horse-whip him, and he will bend his back to the lash and say thank you. . . . Kick him, and he will remove his coat-tails, that you may have a better mark. Spit upon him, and he prizes it as precious ointment." It particularly galled Wilmer that Bennett was a foreigner. Not that Bennett enjoyed any personal popularity overseas, either. When a British author included Bennett and Greeley in an encyclopedia devoted to *Famous Boys, and How They Became*

Great Men, the *London Spectator* took exception, arguing that neither man, "Bennett especially . . . should be held up as a model to show English youths how to accomplish the end of earnest living." [8]

They may have been locked in mortal combat, fighting over which of the two had more influence, but by the end of the decade both Greeley and Bennett had become wealthy men. Though they continued to battle over preeminence in teeming lower Manhattan, Bennett now lived in a splendid estate at the northern tip of the island in Washington Heights, while Greeley spent considerable time at his farm at Chappaqua in Westchester County.

Experienced newspapermen were not the only observers appalled by the *Herald*'s power—and popularity. Samuel Bowles III, the young editor of the *Springfield* (Massachusetts) *Republican*—which Greeley thought "the best and ablest country journal published on the continent"—was similarly horrified "to see the greed with which the *Herald* is snatched up and devoured on its earliest arrival here in the evening, and what is worse, to see the simplicity of these Southern fellows who seem, to pin their whole faith upon it." In Bowles's opinion, "While Northerners look at it only for amusement, as they look at *Punch* or *Frank Leslie*, Southern men swallow it gravely with a sigh and a knowing shake of the head." [9]

Many contemporaries fretted that the balance of power in American life had tipped too radically toward journalism. "The Newspaper Press," carped one disapproving observer near decade's end, "controls the state and the church; it directs the family, the legislator, the magistrate, and the minister. None rises above its influence, none sink below its authority." [10] And most of that authority concentrated in New York. One envious Philadelphia editor complained that the city's news transportation network "literally carries New York over every railway, sets it down at every station, and extends it everywhere." Even the quintessentially Southern *Charleston Mercury* was forced to admit: "We have to go to New York papers for news of our own affairs." [11] Critics wary of the surging influence of the New York press proved powerless to reverse this trend, or unwilling to sacrifice the support of their own affiliated political supporters by contesting it.

Like most leading politicians, Abraham Lincoln respected (and utilized) his favorite newspapers without expressing similar crises of conscience. His reputation for enthusiastic support of friendly journals grew so widespread that a supporter from the tiny village of Lexington, Illinois, took the liberty of writing him in February 1860 to report, "we have a Paper Published in our Town that has been neutral in Politicks and I think there is a chance to enlist it for the Republican Party." If Lincoln would endorse the scheme, the writer was willing to take his letter of support to fellow Republicans and "Get Them To Take hold of the Paper and sustain it during the campaign."[12] Though his reply has never been found, there is no reason to believe that Lincoln did not subscribe to the effort to establish an additional Republican journal in Illinois, even in a hamlet of twelve hundred people. Indeed, Lincoln made sure to visit the offices of local pro-Republican papers whenever his law practice or speaking schedule brought him to new vicinities, always endeavoring to convert journalists into supporters.

On April 27, 1859, for example, Lincoln strolled unannounced into the office of the *Central Illinois Gazette* in the hamlet of West Urbana and asked to see its young editor, William Osborn Stoddard, who was busy setting type at the time. "Stoddard!" the paper's owner called upstairs to him. "Old Abe is here and he wants to see you!" Annoyed to be interrupted while he was busy working, the editor murmured that he would "go down" and "wash my hands but I would not roll down my sleeves," adding of Lincoln: "I did not believe he would care much about a little ink and light clothing." Indeed, the gigantic visitor barely noticed. He offered Stoddard his hand and "plunged at once into the causes" that interested him, pausing only to ask about voting trends in specific local precincts—"almost," Stoddard admitted with astonishment, "as if he had lived among them." From that moment on, the young editor counted himself a Lincoln admirer. A few days later, the paper so noted in print: "We had the pleasure of introducing to the hospitalities of our sanctum a few days since the Hon. Abraham Lincoln. Few men can make an hour pass away more agreeably."[13]

In town after Illinois town, Lincoln repeated this courtesy, calling on editors, putting his feet up on their desks, setting them at ease with his droll stories, dazzling them with his local political knowledge, imparting his ideas, and leaving each premises having converted a stranger into a new, fast friend. Once, when his steamboat ran aground en route home from an 1859 speaking appearance in Iowa, stranding him in Missouri, Lincoln used the time to visit the office of the *St. Joseph Journal* and charm its editor, too. "In personal appearance," the paper cheerfully reported on August 19, "he looks like any other 'six-foot' Kentuckian, and is very affable in manners."[14]

Lincoln spent the most time, of course, at the offices of his hometown paper. The *Journal*'s editorial rooms fronted the same public square as the Lincoln-Herndon law office, and between cases the firm's senior partner could often be found reading out-of-town papers from the journal's "Exchange List," or playing "Fives"—a form of handball—against the building's outside wall. Preston Bailhache, brother of the paper's co-publisher, remembered that "'Old Abe' was always champion" of the matches outside the *Journal*, "for his long arms and long legs served a good purpose in reaching and returning the ball from any angle." [15] Lincoln hosted many a political conference at the *Journal* office, too, but as Senator Lyman Trumbull once admitted to Chicago reporter Horace White, "communicated no more of his own thoughts and purposes than he thought would subserve the ends he had in view." [16]

Lincoln had not only grown close enough to Republican editors to dominate conversations around the stove, borrow incoming papers at will, and suggest editorials; he was now powerful enough to kill stories, too. In April 1859, for example, Thomas J. Pickett, editor of the *Rock Island* (Illinois) *Register*, invited Lincoln to come to town to deliver a lecture on "[Discoveries and] Inventions," a talk that the politician had already offered publicly without generating much enthusiasm at other venues. Pickett frankly hoped to use the visit for other purposes. "I would like to have a 'talk' with you on political matters," he wrote Lincoln, "—as to the policy of announcing your name for the Presidency—while you are in our city. My partner . . . and myself are about addressing the Republican editors of the State on the subject of your name for the Presidency." [17]

Pickett was no ordinary small-town printer. A two-term state senator, Pickett was also president of the Illinois Editorial Association. Nonetheless, Lincoln was not yet ready to visit Rock Island "to deliver a lecture, or for any other object," as he put it in his carefully worded reply. It was too early to encourage a presidential boomlet. "I must, in candor, say I do not think myself fit for the Presidency," he took pains to add. "I certainly am flattered, and gratified, that some partial friends think of me in that connection; but I really think it best for our cause that no concerted effort, such as you suggest, should be made." [18] At least not yet. But Lincoln would warmly remember Pickett's early support, and reward him as soon as he was able.

Two months later, Lincoln renewed his subscription to Joseph Medill and Charles Ray's *Chicago Press and Tribune*, taking pains to accompany his check with a self-effacing but wholehearted endorsement: "Herewith is a little draft to pay for your Daily another year from today. I suppose I shall take the Press & Tribune so long as it, and I both live, unless I become unable to pay for it. In it's [sic] devotion to our cause always, and to me personally last year I owe it a debt of gratitude, which I fear I shall never be able to pay."[19] Like Thomas Pickett, Medill and Ray no doubt were already looking to the day when their favorite politician ascended to a position that made it possible for him fully to repay them for their loyal support.

Notwithstanding his assertions of modesty, Lincoln now began actively, if quietly, planning a strategy for winning the 1860 Republican presidential nomination, a plan that hinged on securing support from the newspapers he had been so assiduously courting. Above all, he needed to obtain the crucial *Chicago Tribune*'s enthusiastic, if initially covert acquiescence. Then Lincoln would proceed to secure a succession of other Illinois endorsements, culminating in the formal backing of Medill's *Tribune*. In the meantime, the candidate would work to give no offense to the supporters of other states' favorite sons, instead making himself implicitly, but prominently, available as everyone's second choice. Medill would lobby Republican leaders in Lincoln's behalf and advocate—successfully and, as it turned out, crucially—to bring the forthcoming national convention to Lincoln-friendly Chicago. Medill later credibly claimed that the entire campaign blueprint was hatched in his newspaper's own office.[20]

In September, Medill went a step further, encouraging Lincoln to undertake a speaking tour through Ohio ostensibly to rebut recent pro–Popular Sovereignty speeches by Stephen Douglas, but principally to expose his impressive oratorical skills to a wider public. The one-time Ohioan Medill confidently predicted that Lincoln would "draw big crowds and be well received" in his native state. But the editor did more than act as a cheerleader; he had specific instructions for "his" unannounced candidate. "Do not consider me presumptuous for offering a suggestion or two," he wrote. "As you are not a candidate you can talk out as boldly as you please. . . . Dont act on the defensive, but pitch hot shot into the back log doughface and pro slavery democracy. Rake down the swindling pretension of Douglas that his Kansas Nebraska Bill guarantees or permits popular sovignty [sic]. We have made a leading article on that subject in our today's paper. . . . Do not fail to get off some of your 'anecdotes & hits.'. . . Go in boldly, strike straight from the shoulder,—hit *below* the belt as well as above, and kick like thunder."[21]

• • •

Certainly no newspaper kicked back at slavery more thunderously than the nearly twenty-year-old enterprise founded and still dominated by the irrepressible Horace Greeley. And no paper of the day reported more often on its own crusading editor. One of his earliest biographers maintained that the attention the *Tribune* lavished on its founder was entirely appropriate, since no journalist ever did "more to make editing of a newspaper the noblest work that any of us ever set to do."[22]

Yet for all the publicity he generated for himself, public opinion remained divided on the subject of Horace Greeley, even as the editor grew just as famous, and nearly as influential, as the leading politicians in the country— thanks at least in part to his relentless self-promotion. "Meek as he looks," no less a literary celebrity than Harriet Beecher Stowe wrote admiringly, "no man living is readier with a strong sharp answer. Non-resistant as he is physically, there is not a more uncompromising opponent, and intense combatant, in the United States."[23]

Greeley himself admitted: "I have been accused of all possible offenses against good morals, good taste, and the common weal; I have been branded as an *aristocrat*, a *communist*, an *intellectual*, a *hypocrite*, a *demagogue*, a *disunionist*, a *traitor*, a *corruptionist*." Yet he seemed to relish each charge, even as his enemies stepped up their attacks in proportion to the editor's expanding influence. Texas politician Sam Houston denounced him as "the *whitest* man in the world," explaining: "He wears a white hat and a white coat; and . . . his liver is of the same color." Even admirers conceded he often acted the distracted innocent, one observer maintaining, "if he goes to a restaurant to dine, he puts down a bill to pay for his meal and never looks at the change . . . he is often cheated with counterfeit notes by persons who know his carelessness and unconcern in such matters."[24]

His absentmindedness may have grown to legendary proportions, but Greeley's selfless earnestness struck a chord among sympathetic readers and respectful fellow professionals alike. Praising him as "unselfishly devoted to the public good, especially to the lowly and oppressed," Pennsylvania newspaper editor A. K. McClure spoke for many journalists of the period when he said of Greeley: "He did not thirst for power, for he had little regard for the usually empty honors of office, but I never knew a man who more earnestly yearned for the approval of his countrymen." McClure believed that Greeley "taught through the Tribune with more power than that of the President."[25] Expanding his reach even further, Greeley augmented his newspaper work by publishing a book about his recent trip to Europe, and issuing a collection of his speeches and writings.[26]

Of course, Bennett fumed over his fellow editor's rising reputation and growing success. What particularly irked the owner of the *New York Herald* was that much of Greeley's political power came from the *Tribune's* well-read national edition, the best-selling synopsis of the age. This weekly spread Greeley's editorial opinions throughout the country. Its circulation quadrupled to nearly 200,000 by decade's end. For his part, Greeley reveled in its popularity. In an unusually daring slap at Bennett, whose own New York edition still outsold the *Tribune* locally but whose national compendium lagged behind it in circulation, Greeley went so far as to place a provocative paid notice for his national paper on the pages of the rival *Herald*. The heavy-handed, tongue-in-cheek pitch cautioned potential advertisers *not* to place such notices in the *Weekly Tribune*. Buying space would prove "dangerous to your quiet," warned the advertisement, citing the experience of a tobacco seed importer who had unsuspectingly advertised his product with Greeley. "I did not anticipate so many applications, and consequently I was quite unprepared for it," testified St. Louis merchant Oliver Tarbell Bragg. ". . . Your paper must certainly have an enormous circulation, judging from the many applications for seed which I have had."[27] Bennett, who had often been called upon to defend the *Herald's* policy of publishing any advertisement paid for with cash in advance, no matter how objectionable or tasteless, had little choice but to print Greeley's taunt.

Their latest squabble, however, ended almost before it began. It was superseded by the seismic cultural and political shock waves that swept the country when news of a sensational event sped its way north from Virginia to New York. As never before, the incident and its aftermath set North and South, and their respective newspapers, at each other's throats over the slavery issue. In October 1859, just one month after Greeley planted his playful advertisement in the *Herald*, "Osawatomie" John Brown of Bleeding Kansas repute stealthily marched a band of armed abolitionists—including five African Americans—into Harpers Ferry, Virginia, the riverfront site of a well-stocked federal arsenal and armory. His plan was as simple as it was fantastic: to seize the installation by surprise, inspire local slaves to flee their plantations and join his force, and then to deploy his growing army and newly acquired weapons to launch a widespread slave revolt across Virginia.

The plot failed in a miasma of bloodshed. On October 18, Colonel Robert E. Lee, dispatched to lead a force to quell the revolt, cornered Brown's vastly outnumbered band inside a firehouse on the arsenal grounds and then stormed the structure. Ramming their way inside, Lee's troops killed ten of the raiders on the spot and captured seven more—among them John Brown himself. Though wounded in the brief but pitched battle, Brown faced a quick trial for both treason and inciting a slave revolt. To the surprise of few, Brown was convicted and condemned to hang. He died on the gallows on December 2.

In a single, daring, and violent gesture against an inherently violent institution, John Brown ratcheted up the slavery debate to an electric new intensity. Realistically or not, abolitionists took solace from the episode, convinced that Brown had gravely wounded the slave power simply by piercing the Mason-Dixon line, thereby raising a glimmer of hope that a massive slave insurrection might yet be possible in the future. With equal, almost paranoid fervor, slaveholding interests, fearful of bloody midnight massacres at the hands of their long-suppressed slaves, reacted by condemning abolitionists and abolitionism with unprecedented vitriol. The *Times* and *Herald* both reported breathlessly on the complicity of the so-called Secret Six— New England men of some standing who had bankrolled Brown. That discovery made the raid not just the act of a sole madman, but a widespread plot by perfidious abolitionists.

Slavery, many Southerners now insisted, must not only be protected but made national. The slave power demanded that all future federal officeholders denounce illegal acts like Brown's and endorse the perpetuation, indeed the

Abolitionist John Brown, whose 1859 raid on Harpers Ferry inflamed the sectional crisis and divided editors nationwide.

widening, of slavery. If Northern officials failed to renounce abolitionism, newspapers in the Deep South began openly threatening, then slave states were ready to consider abandoning the Union. For their part, Republicans expressed renewed determination to resist threats by the South's unbreakable power, recognizing that any additional new slave territory would only generate new and increased Democratic, slave state representation in the U.S. House and Senate, not to mention the Electoral College. The odious result would be "Slave Power" domination of all branches of the government—for Senate consent was required to name new federal judges—in perpetuity.

Caught in the middle of this enormous row, moderates like Abraham Lincoln wanted nothing more than to ignore the John Brown episode or characterize it as an aberration, hoping its roiling impact would quickly fade away. As the *Chicago Tribune*'s Charles Ray confided frankly to Lincoln just a few days after Brown's capture: "We are damnably exercised about the effect of Old John Brown's wretched *fiasco* in Virginia upon the moral health of the Republican party! The old idiot—the quicker they hang and get him out of, The way, The better." Then Ray tantalizingly added what sounded like an offer of support—in return for caution: "Do you know that you are strongly talked of for the Presidency—for the Vice Presidency at least." [28]

In truth, Lincoln needed no such alluring reminders that he would be wise to hold his tongue (Ray admitted that Lincoln was by nature "close-mouthed and cautious").[29] Displaying his usual facility for prudence, Lincoln for months said as little as possible on the contentious subject of John Brown's raid, save for an unrecorded speech in the small Illinois village of Mechanicsburg, where, according to a brief summary for the *Illinois State Journal*, he placed blame for "agitation," "sectionalism," and "wrangling on the slavery question" not on John Brown, but on Democrats in general and Stephen Douglas in particular.[30]

Inconveniently, Lincoln soon found himself on a previously scheduled out-of-state political speaking tour in Kansas, the scene of Brown's earlier antislavery attacks. Now, and particularly here, the toxic subject of John Brown was impossible to avoid. Yet in a speech in the sleepy town of Elwood, on December 1, 1859, Lincoln still only "adverted briefly to the Harper's Ferry Affair," according to an account in the local paper. "He believed the attack of Brown wrong for two reasons," the report continued. "It was a violation of law and it was, as all such attacks must be, futile as far as any effect it might have on the extinction of a great evil." Yet Brown had "shown great courage," Lincoln added—deftly citing Virginia governor Henry A. Wise, who had earlier said much the same thing. "But no man, North or South," Lincoln hastened to add, "can approve of violence or crime."[31]

Lincoln's most extensive comments on the Harpers Ferry raid came forty-eight hours later on December 3 at Leavenworth, just one day after Brown died on the rope. Now there was no way to avoid confronting the subject. "Old John Brown has just been executed for treason against a state," Lincoln acknowledged almost nonchalantly at the end of his long antislavery address. "We cannot object, even though he agreed with us in thinking slavery wrong. That cannot excuse violence, bloodshed, and treason. It could avail him nothing that he might think himself right." Turning the tables, Lincoln ended with a frank warning to Southerners threatening to quit the Union should a Republican win the White House the following year: secession would be no less treasonable than insurrection. In Lincoln's view, "if constitutionally we elect a President, and therefore you undertake to destroy the Union, it will be our duty to deal with you as Old John Brown has been dealt with."[32]

For entirely different reasons, the usually outspoken Stephen Douglas had comparatively little to say about John Brown, either, and what he did express ultimately proved less than helpful to his own political ambitions. Complicating the matter for him was the fact that he was stuck in Washington, not only to attend the latest session of Congress; he had placed himself in virtual exile at his residence there to nurse his wife through a grave illness. In mid-November, his Illinois mouthpieces, the *Chicago Times* and Springfield *State Register*, did publish a Douglas manifesto on the subject in which he predictably placed primary blame for slavery agitation on an increasingly radicalized Republican opposition. To his credit, Douglas acknowledged how "sensitive large numbers of professedly respectable citizens at the north" had become "on this subject of slavery." Southerners, he suggested, would be well advised to abandon their "wild and absurd" calls for the nationalization of slavery and "meet the northern democracy [his own wing of the Democratic Party] on a middle tenable ground"—as well as end their "unreasonable hostility" to his own efforts to achieve both compromise and national office.[33] It was not a message calculated to satisfy Southern Democrats who felt themselves increasingly threatened by violent uprisings allegedly inspired by Republican zealotry.

Still, as far as Douglas was concerned, this was hardly a moment for Northern and Southern Democrats to risk widening their already substantial differences—not with their own next presidential nominating convention scheduled for April 1860, and set to take place in a hotbed of pro-slavery militancy: Charleston, South Carolina. To cement his status as front-runner and Illinois favorite son, Douglas quickly enlisted the *Register*'s Charles Lanphier to make certain that friendly local delegates, rather than Buchanan men, would be chosen for the upcoming convention. Using a politician's prerogative to make suggestions about the newspaper business, the senator asked, too, if Lanphier was in the habit of exchanging political articles with Alabama's moderate *Mobile Register*. "If not you ought to do so," he advised. "It is making a glorious fight on the right line." The Little Giant very much wanted middle-of-the-road papers in the South to exchange friendly editorials with his supporters in the North.

One of the costs of holding a federal office was geographic isolation in the national capital. Douglas was feeling increasingly remote from his home base. "Write me in full," he implored Lanphier, "*and send me the Register. I do not get. Be sure to send it regularly to Washington.*" Concurrently, the senator strove to build his reputation for statesmanship, already recognized by Horace Greeley, to Lincoln's dismay, by reaching out to New York's other prominent Republican editor. Douglas flattered the *Times*'s Henry Raymond (in the act of trying to get him to publish one of his speeches) by acknowledging "the courtesy and kindness which it alone of all the New York journals, has shown me." [34]

For the most part, the journalists themselves evinced none of Lincoln's or Douglas's restraint in their commentaries on the John Brown affair. Coverage was ubiquitous and often incendiary. In articles that paralleled, and no doubt further fueled, the rage on the political hustings, editors accused each other variously of fomenting race war or encouraging destruction of the republic. Unlike the moderate politicians boxed into safe silence by Brown's violent gesture, even the more temperate newspapers could not afford to let their inhibitions stand in the way of securing, featuring, and commenting breathlessly on news of the volatile topic. It was simply too big a story to ignore. As much as some Republicans wished that interest would fade, John Brown's raid, trial, and execution dominated the New York press for months to come.

Predictably, Raymond's *Times* took the most measured approach. At the outset, it declared the Harpers Ferry raid a "Negro Insurrection" and a "desperate" act by a "notorious" man long associated with "scenes of violence."

But with his eyes open to the public's insatiable appetite for news from the scene of John Brown's ill-fated adventure, Raymond also dispatched a special correspondent to the adjacent village of Charles Town to provide detailed coverage of Brown's trial and hanging. The *Times* journalist soon reported melodramatically—and with a hint of sympathy—on Brown's final hours, which included an emotional last meeting with his distraught wife.[35] Raymond's paper never quite decided whether John Brown was a terrorist or a martyr.

Careful to remind readers that "the way to Universal Emancipation lies not through insurrection, civil war and bloodshed, but through discussion . . . humanity and justice," the *New York Tribune* condemned the outbreak, too, speculating that it was "the work of a madman," yet significantly withholding outright condemnation of the raiders. "They dared and died for what they felt to be the right," Greeley editorialized, "though in a manner which seems to us fatally wrong. Let their epitaphs remain unwritten until the not distant day when no slave shall clank his chains in the shades of Monticello or by the graves of Mount Vernon."[36]

Greeley's mixed message, combining mild rebuke with florid eulogy, incensed editors in the South as well as Democratic journals in the North eager to lump the *Tribune* and Brown's raiders together as part of a broader conspiracy to encourage violence. "The Tribune considers the act of Brown as the act of a patriot, which future ages will admire and extol," fumed the *Charleston Mercury.* "To become a hero and a martyr, in the Tribune's estimation, is to go to the South and excite the slaves to rise and cut the throats of their white masters." Claiming it had canvassed the more restrained Southern papers, the *Mercury* further reported that the alleged outrages by both Brown and Greeley had ignited secession fever even in the conservative Old Dominion: "The boast of her presses that 'there are no disunionists in Virginia,' if true six months ago, we trust is now a thing of history," reported the fire-eating Charleston daily, "never again to be asserted, until the South is safe and free in the Union, or independent out of it."[37] Indeed, the *Richmond Enquirer* reported near Christmas Day that the "Harper's Ferry *invasion* . . . has revived, with ten fold strength, the desire of a Southern confederacy."[38]

Southern papers were not alone in condemning both Brown and Greeley, or using the episode as a means to hike circulation and damage Republicans. The Democratic *Cincinnati Enquirer,* for one, offered its opinion that the raid revealed the "danger of having a Republican-Abolition President" in the future.[39] Typically, the ever-provocative Bennett had it both ways. A year earlier, he had openly boasted that his was "about the only National journal that has unfailingly vindicated the Constitutional rights of the South." Now, while bitterly denouncing Brown, he too simultaneously sent correspondents down to Harpers Ferry to file breathless daily reports on Brown's trial and execution. Bennett calmly dispatched another of his first-rate writers to the residence of the wealthy upstate New York abolitionist Gerrit Smith, one of the Secret Six who had unapologetically helped finance the raid. The resulting story, uniquely conversational in tone, proved not only a sensational exclusive, it marked what most historians of journalism acknowledge as the birth of the "interview," yet another milestone coup for the *Herald.* In October, the paper exclusively published the transcript of an interrogation of Brown by Virginia senator James M. Mason, in which Brown maintained (no doubt to Bennett's disappointment): "No man sent me here, it was my own prompting, or that of the Devil, whichever you please to ascribe it to."[40]

Bennett was never prone to let a torrid story go cold, or to miss a chance to use raging controversies to smear rival editors. Seizing on the additional, irresistible opportunity the John Brown affair offered to isolate Greeley and his defenders as dangerous radicals, Bennett accompanied his news reports with editorials damning his antislavery press rivals, adorning these rebukes with invective rare even by *Herald* standards. "This misguided fanatic," declared the *Herald* of John Brown, "so dangerous to the peace of society, has passed off the stage of existence by the ignominious death due to his crimes. But his sympathizers are not willing to let his memory die. On the contrary, they are determined to 'keep it green in their souls,' and to make political capital out of his execution on the gallows, and thus to render him more formidable in death than he was in life . . . a saint, a martyr, a hero, a demi-god." Chiefly complicit, Bennett implied, was Greeley himself. "So depraved, so lost to public virtue have the republican journals become, that they glory in their shame, and endorse revolution and bloodshed, and the dismemberment of this great republic." At least, Bennett concluded his diatribe, John Brown himself could be given credit for "pluck," and "in that respect he deserves admiration as compared with the sneaking cowards who have hounded him on to his doom, and now make political capital out of an exploit for which they had not sufficient courage themselves."[41] Still pouring on his angry commentary two weeks after Brown's martyrdom—or his richly deserved execution, depending on one's point of view—Bennett labeled the "insurgent and traitor" the direct product of "the Republican party" and the *Tribune* "the leading organ of the revolutionists." [42]

When Greeley's onetime Whig colleague, James Watson Webb of the *New York Courier and Enquirer*, tried shifting the conversation by branding the *Herald*, not the *Tribune*, as the "chief agitator" of sectional discord, and excoriating its editor as "a reckless and unprincipled foreigner, who has nothing in common with our people and our country," Bennett eagerly returned the salvo by savaging the "invincible military chieftain, the Chevalier Webb" with even more brutality than he had heaped on Greeley. After all, Webb had once horsewhipped Bennett on the streets, and it was never too late for revenge. Even in the process of naming Webb " 'the chief' of slavery and disunion agitators," however, Bennett made certain to take another swipe at the more powerful *Tribune* and its vaster readership: "We charge that all hands concerned in this conspiracy, endorsers and subscribers, are guilty of moral treason, and are among the most dangerous disorganizers of these critical times. The Chevalier Webb would doubtless have figured with his republican collaborators, Weed and Greeley. . . . We know that 'birds of a feather flock together,' and we know that when a general conspiracy is projected against the South . . . we are doing the work of patriotism in exposing the perilous position of the Union." Greeley would surely be "subpoenaed in due time," Bennett crowed on December 29. "This is as it ought to be." [43]

Greeley never did face prosecution over the John Brown affair. The evidence of his complicity simply did not exist. But Bennett had it indisputably right on one account: the Union was now in a more perilous position than ever. And newspapermen were no longer immune to questions not just about their politics, but about their patriotism. Before the new year, the inexhaustible *Herald* was calling on a newly organized U.S. Senate investigative committee to look into William Seward's and Frederick Douglass's alleged roles in covertly supporting John Brown. Bennett interpreted their absence from the country at the time of the raid as dispositive proof of their foreknowledge of the "invasion."

Actually, Seward was then in the midst of a kind of proactive valedictory: an ill-timed world tour designed to burnish his international reputation preparatory to what he and his supporters felt confident would be a coronation as the 1860 Republican presidential nominee. Douglass had far more reason to worry about such threats to his liberty. Although friends had raised the funds to purchase his freedom, he had indeed known, befriended, and encouraged Brown's militancy in the past, though in fact he had strongly advised him not to undertake the attack on Harpers Ferry, believing it was doomed to failure. Nonetheless, encouraged by Bennett's *Herald*—which called for Douglass's scalp with headlines such as "Fred Douglass and Other Abolitionists and Republicans Implicated"—the state of Virginia issued a warrant for the Rochester editor's arrest for "the crime of murder." Douglass had no other option but to leave the country.

"The black Douglass having some experience in his early life of the pleasures of Southern society had no desire to trust himself again even on the borders of the Potomac," Bennett sneered in a particularly ugly update.[44] Douglass traveled first to Canada, then on to Great Britain, returning only when word reached him of the death of his daughter. But not before he published one more powerful editorial in *Douglass' Monthly*, defending Brown for striking "a blow" that might "prove to be worth its mighty cost." Besides, as Douglass pointed out: "Slavery is a system of brute force. It shields itself behind *might*, rather than *right*. It must be met with its own weapons."[45]

It is impossible to know whether Abraham Lincoln read this particular turn of phrase, or indeed, ever saw any issue of Douglass's abolitionist paper. To admit so in 1859 would have been, as far as most mainstream voters of the day were concerned, tantamount to confessing to reading pornography. But in just three months, Lincoln would make an unforgettable "right" and "might" statement of his own in New York City. It may very well be that he got the idea for the phrase he went on to make famous at Cooper Union from the self-exiled and, like him, self-educated Frederick Douglass.

Abraham Lincoln agreed to deliver his maiden speech in the nation's largest commercial city at the invitation of a group of young New York Republicans opposed to their own senator's presidential ambitions. In mid-1859, this anti-Seward coalition, which included a number of prominent local journalists, determined on a plan to showcase alternative Westerners in a series of well-promoted local lectures. It was not just that the group disliked and distrusted Seward, which they did. Its members also sincerely believed that any Eastern presidential candidate, particularly one, like Seward, who had recently warned provocatively of an "irrepressible conflict" with the South, faced the likely prospect of voter rejection in the conservative Western states, and would thus lose the White House just as Frémont had done in 1856. On the other hand, they reasoned, a Western candidate would have little trouble winning the dependably Republican bastions of New England and New York, and would put up a much stronger fight in Illinois, Indiana, and Ohio. The Young Men's Central Republican Union boasted its share of youthful members hooked on politics, but tellingly its senior advisors included powerful Republican editors Horace Greeley and William Cullen Bryant, and the meeting at which their organization agreed to pay Lincoln an irresistible honorarium to lure him to town took place at the offices of Bryant's *Evening Post.* Greeley was by this time privately, if not publicly, committed to scuttling Seward's White House dreams by whatever means required.

The group's original October 1859 invitation summoned Lincoln to speak not at Cooper Union, but at Brooklyn's iconic Plymouth Church. Its presiding minister, Lincoln well knew, was Henry Ward Beecher, not only the nation's most celebrated preacher, but also a brother of the author of *Uncle Tom's Cabin* and a contributing editor to the antislavery *New York Independent.* As a political opportunity, this was not a venture—or a venue—to be taken lightly. What was more, the hosts offered a fee of $200 plus expenses. Fortunately for him, as it turned out, Lincoln successfully contrived to delay his trip until late February 1860, perhaps determined to become the final speaker in the church series or, more likely, uncertain at first about precisely what to say on a stage as important as Beecher's pulpit.

Inspiration struck after Lincoln's archrival, Stephen Douglas, caused a national stir with an audacious article in the otherwise reliably progressive *Harper's New Monthly Magazine.* The senator's nineteen-page piece, entitled "The Dividing Line Between Federal and Local Authority: Popular Sovereignty in the Territories," took direct aim at Lincoln's all-free or all-slave "House Divided" philosophy. There could be "no truce in the sectional strife," Douglas warned, until antislavery Republicans like Lincoln accepted the Union as the founders made it: "divided into free and slave States, with the right on the part of each to retain slavery so long as it chooses, and to abolish it whenever it pleases." In defense of "the great principle of self-government in the Territories," Douglas cited extensive but somewhat specious research— conducted in part with the help of the distinguished historian George Bancroft, an admirer—to argue that the founding fathers had expected individual states to decide for themselves whether slavery would be permitted within their borders in the future, precisely as he had legislated in the controversial 1854 Kansas-Nebraska Act.[46] Douglas was so pleased with the resulting article that he ordered twenty-five hundred pamphlet reprints. He proudly called the finished product "the finest specimen of the Printing art that I have ever seen."[47]

Publication of the Douglas tract spurred Lincoln to conduct a laborious research project of his own (which he conducted with no help at all), aimed at showing that the founders—by his convenient definition the signers of the Constitution—had demonstrated through subsequent votes, speeches, and writings that they in fact fully embraced the idea of using federal authority in the future to regulate slavery in the territories. Lincoln's paradigm was no more authoritative than Douglas's: he might as easily have investigated the signers of the earlier Declaration of Independence, in which case his tabulations would have yielded far less satisfying results. Instead he chose a methodology that would most easily prove his own thesis, and even so he may have exaggerated his conclusions. Among his most reliable primary sources were the back issues of the *New York Tribune*'s national edition stacked in Springfield's state library.

Lincoln worked tirelessly to make his upcoming lecture a success, despite many distractions, including criticism from *Chicago Times* editor James Sheahan over the pending publication of the 1858 Lincoln-Douglas debates, which Sheahan and other Democrats worried had been edited to improve Lincoln's speeches at the expense of Douglas.[48] In another brilliant stroke, to make certain that he would arrive in the East as the principal Republican voice of the West—or at least of Illinois—Lincoln meanwhile deftly conducted significant behind-the-scenes wire-pulling aimed at earning himself the crucial pre-journey endorsement he most craved. Writing to his political ally Norman Judd two weeks before his scheduled departure for New York, Lincoln confided: "I am not in a position where it would hurt much for me to not be nominated on the national ticket," he wrote, "but I am where it would hurt some for me not to get the Illinois delegates. . . . Can you not help me a little in this matter, in your end of the vineyard?"[49]

Judd knew precisely what Lincoln's almost tortured flurry of double negatives meant: he desired the blessing of the Republican press—at once. Just one week later, the *Chicago Tribune* obliged with an editorial calling for "the nomination of Lincoln for the first place on the National Republican ticket." Heading into a make-or-break journey to the newspaper capital of the nation, the former one-term congressman from Springfield was now his state's favorite son Republican candidate for president of the United States. Judd proudly fired off a letter to ask the newly anointed man: "You saw what the Tribune said about you. Was it satisfactory?" Perhaps Judd, like Lincoln, already knew the answer to that question.[50] What Chicago's *Tribune* wrote, New York's *Tribune* was sure to read.

What the *New York Tribune* reported next, however, both surprised and further challenged Abraham Lincoln. Arriving in New York after an exhausting cross-country rail journey, he found notices of his upcoming address gratifyingly printed in Greeley's paper. But as the report made clear, his speech was not to take place at Beecher's Brooklyn church after all, but rather at entrepreneur Peter Cooper's newly opened co-educational college in Manhattan. To add to the pressure, the *Tribune* urged "earnest Republicans to induce their friends and neighbors of adverse views to accompany them, to this lecture."[51]

Suddenly aware that he would be speaking before a secular, not a church, audience, Lincoln was forced to spend considerable time during his first two days in New York recasting his lengthy oration to suit its new venue. Though he made an all but obligatory appearance for Sunday worship services at Plymouth Church on February 26, Lincoln politely declined a luncheon invitation from Henry Bowen, editor of the *Independent*, a paper to which he subscribed back home, so he could return to his hotel room, lock the door, and further rework his text. The influential Bowen was already anxious about this odd-looking Westerner's New York debut. The day before, Lincoln had turned up unexpectedly at the *Independent*'s Ann Street headquarters to introduce himself to Bowen and ask if he might be briefed on the details of the Monday speaking engagement. When the editor agreed to oblige, Lincoln flopped his huge frame onto the office couch to listen. Studying his gargantuan star speaker as he sprawled on his sofa, Bowen remembered feeling so "sick at heart" at the sight of his "travel-stained" clothes and "woe-begone" appearance that "there came to me the disheartening and appalling thought of the great throng which I had been so instrumental in inducing to come and hear Lincoln." Bowen's publisher, Joseph H. Richards, who had put up the money to fund Lincoln's appearance, was equally horrified. Richards later admitted that "when I saw the awkward manner, long legs and arms of this man I could not help having serious forebodings concerning the financial outcome of the venture."[52]

Bowen and Richards need not have worried. By February 27, fully aware of the stakes, Lincoln was more than ready. And although the crowd that night did not quite fill Cooper Union's capacious Great Hall, the throng still approached fifteen hundred, and included a healthy smattering of recognizable Republican leaders. The press certainly turned out in full force. As one of the official hosts, Bowen was of course in the house, along with co-organizer and *Independent* writer Theodore Tilton. Both Horace Greeley and Samuel Sinclair of the *New York Tribune* appeared, at last showing interest in the politician the paper had so long ignored or slighted. Prominent for his absence was Henry Raymond of the *New York Times*. A year earlier, the *Times* had conceded that "some of 'Old Abe's' friends look still higher for him." [53] But more recently, Raymond had left his readers little doubt that no Western orator could convince his paper to advocate for anyone for the presidency but his ally William Seward.

The task of introducing Lincoln at Cooper Union fell to none other than the extravagantly bearded elder statesman among the city's antislavery editors, the *Evening Post's* William Cullen Bryant (Lincoln confided that it was "worth a visit from Springfield, Illinois, to New York to make the acquaintance of such a man").[54] Bryant took the stage and hailed the speaker of the evening as "a gallant soldier of the political campaign of 1858" and a "great champion" of the Republican cause in Illinois." [55]

William Cullen Bryant, antislavery poet and longtime editor of the *New York Evening Post* who introduced Lincoln at Cooper Union. They had never met before.

Lincoln more than lived up to the old poet's warm introduction, firing off a ringing, two-hour-long disquisition that alternately impressed, amused, and ultimately roused the "large and brilliant" audience.[56] Opening with a precisely argued rebuttal to Douglas's *Harper's* article, in which he identified Republicans with George Washington and Thomas Jefferson, Lincoln shifted gears mid-speech to address Southern concerns over supposed Republican extremism, assuring slaveholders that he and the party posed no threat to the institution where it already existed, and distancing Republicans from radical abolitionism. "John Brown was no Republican," he insisted, "and you have failed to implicate a single Republican in his Harper's Ferry enterprise." In words that must have warmed Greeley's heart, he thundered: "You need not be told that persisting in a charge which one does not know to be true, is simply malicious slander." [57]

Then shifting tone yet again, Lincoln devoted the third, final, and most earnest section of his address to arguing the righteousness of the antislavery cause and advocating fearless and tireless support for freedom. "Never let us be slandered from our duty by false accusations against us, nor frightened from it by menaces of destruction to the Government nor of dungeons to ourselves," he concluded, ending by consciously or unknowingly paraphrasing Frederick Douglass—but using all-capital letters perhaps to remind himself to shout: "LET US HAVE FAITH THAT RIGHT MAKES MIGHT, AND IN THAT FAITH, LET US DARE TO DO OUR DUTY AS WE UNDERSTAND IT." [58]

Lincoln's triumph at Cooper Union owed something to modest advance expectations and of course a great deal to his stellar performance onstage, a situation neatly bookmarked in press that preceded and followed his career-altering journey. On the day he left Springfield to head east, his hometown nemesis, the pro-Douglas *State Register*, bade him a caustic and deflating adieu by noting: "The Honorable Abraham Lincoln departs for Brooklyn under an engagement to deliver a lecture before the Young Men's Association of that city, in Beecher's Church. Subject, not known. Consideration, $200 and expenses. Object, presidential capital. Effect, disappointment." Now, just five days later, the once unenthusiastic *New York Tribune* declared, as if in direct response: "No man ever before made such an impression on his first appeal to a New-York audience." Greeley judged Lincoln's "unsurpassed" performance "the very best political address to which I ever listened—and I have heard some of Webster's best." At long last, the *Tribune* editor had seen and appreciated the mature Lincoln in action—not the awkward, joke-slinging freshman congressman he had first encountered in Washington more than a decade earlier, and not the frontier debater he had doubted and then praised, but never personally observed, during the 1858 Illinois Senate race. Now Lincoln suddenly seemed "one of Nature's orators, using his rare powers . . . to elucidate and to convince, though their inevitable effect is to delight and electrify as well." [59]

Few of Lincoln's speeches ever won such widespread praise so quickly, but the press had as much to do with building and burnishing its reputation as did the orator. The transformational reputation of the Cooper Union address owed a major debt to the New York newspapers that reported and praised it—Greeley's in particular, for the *Tribune* not only promoted and covered the event, but gave Lincoln the opportunity to edit his remarks before they went into print, then offered fulsome praise for the results. Lincoln helped his own cause by bringing down the house at Cooper Union. But fully aware that many times the number of people filling its Great Hall on February 27 might read his speech in newspaper reprints on February 28, Lincoln not only crafted an oration that enthralled his hearing audience on the evening of its de-

Just hours before making his New York City oratorical debut at Cooper Union on February 27, 1860, Abraham Lincoln poses for photographer Mathew Brady.

livery, but made certain that the text was faithfully reproduced for the vastly wider reading public the following day.

After a celebratory supper in his honor at a nearby private club, the undoubtedly exhausted Lincoln nonetheless limped to the offices of the *New York Tribune*—his brand-new boots pinched his aching feet—where he personally proofread the newly typeset version of his Cooper Union address not once but twice before clearing it to appear in the paper. Printing the final sentence in all capital letters was probably Lincoln's own idea, meant to reflect the passion and volume with which he delivered it.

This fact-checking expedition had almost certainly been arranged in advance with the *Tribune*, although there is no evidence that Greeley was on hand in his newsroom for what must have seemed to him a commonplace occurrence. As for Lincoln, still smarting from his missed opportunity to check his "House Divided" address before it was mangled in his hometown paper two years earlier, he undoubtedly asked this time for the personal opportunity to shepherd the most important speech of his career into flawless permanence for New York readers. Clearly, some sort of pool arrangement prevailed that evening as well, for the transcripts that appeared in four major dailies the following day—the morning *Tribune, Times,* and *Herald,* as well as the *Post* that afternoon—were precisely alike, with Bennett's *Herald* as usual adding its own flourishes by providing a valuable record of audience interruptions for laughter, applause, and cheering where they occurred.

Unfortunately, Lincoln departed the *Tribune* newsroom that night without his original handwritten manuscript, and it has never come to light since. Presumably he left it behind to be swept away with the other handwritten material set in type for the February 28 edition—for such was the tradition at busy newspapers nationwide. Besides, Lincoln never cared much about archival records for their own sake, and had yet to begin gauging the potential monetary or historic value of his writings—that knowledge would come only during the Civil War, when charitable organizations commenced clamoring for autograph documents that could be sold to raise funds for the benefit of wounded soldiers. His primary mission on the night of February 27, 1860, was to speed a correct version of his painstakingly prepared speech to as many readers as possible, as accurately as his own concentration could guarantee, and as promptly as technology would allow. Lincoln's exhausting attention to detail produced not only the kind of press attention that would later be termed "blanket" coverage, but also a meticulously perfect transcription. Within days, newspapers in Chicago, Washington, Detroit, and other major cities reprinted the speech for their own readers.

Greeley was not the only major New York editor to heap adulation on the oration. Bryant's *Post* hailed Lincoln's "certain mastery of clear and impressive statement." Even Raymond's pro-Seward *Times* conceded that the address had inspired "three rousing cheers . . . for the orator and the sentiments to which he had given utterance." But the *Tribune* proved the most effusive of all in its praise for the man they had so long resisted. In Greeley's estimation, "The Speech of ABRAHAM LINCOLN at the Cooper Institute last evening was one of the happiest and most convincing political arguments ever made in this City." [60]

Not unexpectedly, the address attracted its share of detractors as well, from political and press opponents who had never before taken Lincoln seriously enough to assail him. The new, pro-Democratic *New York Daily News,* for example, owned and operated by the brother of the city's pro-Southern mayor, bristled that Lincoln and his fellow Republicans "have no weight nor influence against the simple fact that the Constitution does not give the [slavery prohibition] power to the Congress." And the *Herald* weighed in predictably by railing against Lincoln's attempt to recruit the nation's founders as antislavery allies. "It is idle to quote the fathers of the Republic, including Washington and Jefferson in favor of the present Republican crusade against slavery," Bennett bristled two days after Lincoln's speech. "It is true that Jefferson for a time became tainted with the French revolutionary leveling notions about negro slavery, and other things; but he afterwards changed these opinions."[61]

In point of fact, such condemnation exerted far less influence than the praise. At the time of the speech, the only significant political battle under way was the struggle for the Republican presidential nomination scheduled to be decided only three months hence, and this fight would be waged exclusively among Republican editors and their readers. Snide remarks by Bennett and other Democratic-leaning newspapermen would have little impact until the general election campaign in autumn. And after Cooper Union, as far as Joseph Medill and Charles Ray's *Chicago Tribune* viewed their candidate's prospects: "If the States of the Northwest shall unite upon him, and present his name to the Chicago convention, there is a strong probability that he will receive the nomination, and as certain as he is nominated he will be president."[62]

Aiding his own cause, Lincoln hastened north on February 28 for a well-covered speaking tour in neighboring New England. In stop after stop, he largely reiterated his Cooper Union message, struggling to freshen it enough at each location to sustain the interest of audiences who had already read the original in papers like the *Tribune*. "I have been unable to escape this toil," the fatigued orator complained to his wife from his son Robert's boarding school at Exeter, New Hampshire. ". . . The speech at New-York, being within my calculation before I started, went off passably well, and gave me no trouble whatever. The difficulty was to make nine others, before reading audiences, who have already seen all my ideas in print."[63] The prospect of delivering a tenth speech, however, proved one too many. When his original Cooper Union hosts asked him to deliver yet another oration, Lincoln drew the line. Refusing the additional invitation, Lincoln suggested a worthy substitute: "Mr. Greeley."[64]

Within a week, Greeley contributed further to Lincoln's Cooper Union momentum by publishing a *Tribune Tract* booklet edition of the February 27 speech, offering it for sale at the paper's headquarters at four cents a copy, and by mail at ten dollars per thousand to feed bulk demands from Republican clubs.[65] More reprints quickly rolled off presses in other cities. "Pamphlet copies of my late speech at Cooper Institute, N.Y., can be had at the office of the N.Y. Tribune; at the Republican Club Room at Washington, and at the office of the Illinois State Journal at this place," a clearly well-informed Lincoln wrote a friend from back in Springfield in early April. "At which place they are the cheapest, I do not certainly know."[66]

In its initial analysis, the *Tribune* conceded that even "a very full and ac-curate report" could never evoke "the tones, the gestures, the kindling eye and the mirth-provoking look" that Lincoln had evinced at Cooper Union. These defied "the reporter's skill." But such personal quirks, however captivating, did not much matter in the speech's aftermath. Lincoln's New York success was assured and extended not in person but in print, not through gestures and glances, but through republication and mass distribution.

Even before leaving for New York, Lincoln accomplished something else of significance designed to ensure his continued, strong presence in the medium of print. Two years earlier, he had resisted the repeated invitations from the *Chicago Tribune* to provide an autobiographical sketch focusing on his per-sonal story. But now Lincoln penned just such a text, perhaps briefer than expected, after his friend, former and future newspaperman Jesse W. Fell, secretary of the Illinois Republican State Committee, requested one that might be used to introduce the presidential aspirant to Eastern readers, most of whom still knew almost nothing about him. "There is not much of it," Lincoln jocularly wrote Fell of the enclosed two-and-a-half-page document, completed around December 1859, "for the reason, I suppose, that there is not much of me." He had no objection if others wanted to use it, but sensitive to potential criticism over self-promotion, he cautioned, "it must not appear to have been written by myself."[67]

Fell forwarded the result to a rather obscure Pennsylvania reporter named Joseph J. Lewis, who then used it as the basis for a highly flattering profile that first appeared on the front page of the *Chester County Times* on February 11, 1860. As Lincoln and Fell hoped, the modest biography quickly inspired reprints in Republican journals around the country. Here, based on Lincoln's own descriptions, appeared for the first time in print some of the key ele-ments of what evolved into a mythic life story: his antecedents had been "undistinguished." His grandfather had been "killed by indians." He had grown up in "a wild region, with many bears and other wild animals still in the woods." Education had been scarce, with "no qualification . . . ever required of a teacher, beyond 'readin, writin, and cipherin,' to the Rule of Three." As to his growing fame, Lincoln modestly reported only that he had been "losing interest in politics, when the repeal of the Missouri Compromise aroused me again. What I have done since then is pretty well known."[68]

In the end, what Lincoln had "done since"—even at Cooper Union—proved insufficient as far as Horace Greeley was concerned. Although increasingly convinced that the Republicans had a strong chance to win the White House in 1860, he still did not believe Lincoln was the man to lead the effort—or the country. Animated principally by his hatred for Seward, the editor determined "to fix on the proper candidate for President," as if the task of anointing the winner belonged to him alone. Greeley's ultimate choice shocked almost everyone: former congressman Edward Bates of the slave-holding state of Missouri. The venerable onetime jurist was a Westerner, all right, but also a former anti-immigrant Know-Nothing who had little sympathy for Greeley's political agenda. Bates had not even bothered to announce his opposition to the extension of slavery into the West, the central rallying cry of the Republican organization. The most conservative of all of the Republicans spoken of for the presidency, he alone had yet to join the party. And at age sixty-six, he was the oldest contender in the field, the only one born in the eighteenth century. Aside from fulfilling Greeley's convoluted sense of political expediency, Bates's only possible claim to the editor's favor was the memory of the Missourian's brief service thirteen years earlier as chairman of the 1847 Chicago River and Harbor Convention, which the editor (and Lincoln) had attended.

Nonetheless, Greeley convinced himself, and attempted to convince his readers, that Bates alone was capable of stopping Seward at the convention. Years later Greeley insisted that he had sincerely believed Bates was also best positioned to win a multi-sectional victory for the party. "If not the only Republican whose election would not suffice as a pretext for civil war," he insisted, "he seemed to me that one most likely to repress the threatened insurrection, or, at the worst, to crush it. I did not hesitate to avow my preference, though I may have withheld some of my reasons for it."[69] Incredulous, Frederick Douglass wrote that "Mr. Greeley has the greatest passion for making political nominations from the ranks of his enemies of any man in

America." But not even the unpredictable Greeley, Douglass lamented, had ever summoned such a "frog" out of the "pro-slavery mud."[70] Connecticut editor Isaac Hill Bromley, who went on to cover the May 1860 Republican convention in Chicago, came to believe that the *New York Tribune* editor was "inopportune," even "ill-balanced," concluding that Greeley had no excuse for supporting Bates save for bitterness over his own, thwarted "political ambition," for which he stubbornly held Seward responsible.[71]

Greeley hastened to the Chicago convention, too, and quickly became an official voting delegate, filling a vacancy that arose from, of all places, Oregon. Among the other influential editors who poured into town was Seward's chief backer, Thurlow Weed, the publisher who two decades earlier had given Greeley his start in political journalism and now probably regretted it. A few months earlier, an old Ohio friend had warned Weed about "Mr. Bryant, Mr. Greeley, and others," who were all said to be "hard at work" accumulating alternative candidates to undermine Seward. Though long aware of Greeley's hostility, Weed bravely insisted: "I think there is no danger of that." As Weed rosily viewed the convention landscape, "something more than their opposition will be required to accomplish the defeat of a man upon whom the people have set their hearts." Not long afterward, that same prescient Ohio politician encountered Greeley himself in a public corridor of New York's swank Astor House hotel, and listened as the editor hissed at him: "We shan't nominate Seward, we'll take some more conservative man." When the Ohioan hastened upstairs to warn Seward, who happened to be staying at the hotel, the senator calmly replied that Weed had only just brought Greeley to his room to see him personally. The Ohioan was unnecessarily worried, Seward chirped. Greeley was "all right." No, the visitor insisted, "Greeley is cheating you. He will go to Chicago and work against you." And so Greeley did.[72]

Making an appearance in Chicago as well was Henry Raymond, undisputed star of the first Republican National Convention four years earlier, and now fresh from a rejuvenating trip to Europe and equally confident of Seward's imminent success. Duel-happy James Watson Webb journeyed west to represent the *Courier and Enquirer.* Young Murat Halstead, who also covered the Democratic convention at Charleston for the *Cincinnati Commercial,* now arrived in Chicago to report on the opposition, as did the enterprising German immigrant Henry Villard, whose articles appeared in the *New York Herald.* Joining them was George William Curtis, who had launched his career on Greeley's *Tribune* before striking out on his own as editor of *Putnam's*

Magazine. And Francis Preston Blair, Jr., scion of a powerful political dynasty and editor of the pro-Republican *Missouri Democrat*, arrived in town to place the name of favorite son Edward Bates in nomination.[73]

Chicagoan Charles Ray was of course on the scene here in his hometown to cover the event for the *Tribune*, performing double duty as both a correspondent and a political operative on the team of Lincoln floor managers operating out of the Tremont House hotel. Ray arranged things so each and every delegate was welcomed to town by a long and enthusiastic convention-eve *Tribune* editorial headlined "Abraham Lincoln, the Winning Man." The piece ended with this ringing endorsement: "We present our candidate, then, not as the rival of this man or that, not because the West has claims which she must urge; not because of a distinctive policy which she would see enforced; not because he is the first choice of a majority; but because he is that honest man, that representative Republican, that people's candidate, whose life, position, record, are so many guarantys of success—because he is that patriot in whose hands the interests of the government may be safely confided."[74]

For the next two days, Medill and Ray busied themselves with both journalism and politicking, issuing a convention extra newspaper while concurrently counting heads on behalf of their candidate and, as some later whispered, promiscuously offering future cabinet posts to state delegations whose votes might be available to Lincoln after the first ballot. In the heat of the battle to persuade wavering delegates, Ray allegedly confirmed to Medill that he promised to buy Pennsylvania's support by offering the Treasury Department to the state's favorite son Simon Cameron. An exasperated Medill responded, "What will be left?" To which Ray supposedly shot back: "Oh, what is the difference? We are after a bigger thing than that; we want the Presidency and the Treasury is not a great stake to pay for it." Or so Medill recalled years later. It was Medill, in turn, sitting with his old friends in the Ohio delegation, who reportedly whispered that the Treasury Department might instead go to the Buckeye State's first choice, Salmon P. Chase, if their votes, too, shifted in Lincoln's direction on subsequent ballots.[75]

Deeply concerned when he heard the rumors of such unauthorized deals, Lincoln urgently sent his most trusted press ally, Edward Baker of the *Illinois State Journal*, rushing from Springfield to Chicago to clarify the candidate's positions—both political and philosophical—for the benefit of floor managers and curious delegates alike. First, Lincoln offered his views about front-runner Seward's most controversial positions: for the record, he agreed with the New York senator's "Irrepressible Conflict" warnings. (How could he not? He had said much the same thing in his own "House Divided" address.) But, as Lincoln added, "I do not endorse his 'Higher Law' doctrine"—citing and implicitly criticizing Seward's onetime declaration that the Constitution could be superseded by moral opposition to slavery. As his backers shared the contents with wavering delegates, Lincoln's message had the bombshell impact of a convention speech.

Lincoln accompanied his statement with a private postscript meant to inhibit his brazen operatives as they trolled the various delegations offering to trade cabinet jobs for convention support: *Make no contracts that will bind me.*" Perhaps because he preferred that no official record of the communication survive, Lincoln did not commit these crucial, last-minute instructions to a formal letter. Rather, he communicated them in much the same way ordinary Americans had shared their most important thoughts a generation earlier when, unable to afford general postage, they had scrawled personal messages on recycled newspapers. Lincoln scribbled his final pre-convention instructions onto a copy of the pro-Republican newspaper anachronistically called the *Missouri Democrat*.[76]

From their separate Chicago hotels, the major New York Republican editors tirelessly cajoled, negotiated, filed dispatches and commentary, and generally created as much commotion as the candidates themselves might have stirred had tradition of the day encouraged them to attend the convention personally. In their absence—Seward remained in Auburn, New York, Lincoln in Springfield, Illinois, waiting anxiously for news by telegraph—delegates pursued the celebrated Greeley, Weed, and Raymond for comments, advice, and clues about the pending vote.

Weed—who promptly acquired the new nicknames "Lord Thurlow" and "the general" in tribute to his formidable arm-twisting at the convention— labored strenuously behind the scenes to keep pledged Seward delegates in line. In marked contrast, wearing his trademark ankle-length white duster, Greeley automatically attracted admiring crowds wherever he turned up— and, as several delegates noted, he seemed to turn up everywhere. If Raymond had been the darling of the first Republican convention in 1856, Greeley emerged as the principal eminence of the second convention in 1860. "The way Greeley is stared at as he shuffles about, looking as innocent as ever,"

Albany editor and state political boss Thurlow Weed (left) and his preferred candidate for the Republican presidential nomination in 1860, U.S. senator William H. Seward (right) of New York.

Murat Halstead reported, "is itself a sight. Whenever he appears there is a crowd gaping at him, and if he stops to talk a minute with someone who wishes to consult him as the oracle, the crowd becomes dense as possible, and there is the most eager desire to hear the words of wisdom that are supposed to fall on such occasions."[77]

"On one memorable occasion," Connecticut editor Isaac Hill Bromley recalled with relish, "some mischievous fellow pinned a Seward badge on his coattail; it amused the crowd for a moment without giving him the slightest disturbance."[78] Taking note of the very same incident, the *Times* reported that "for several hours" Greeley "unconsciously carried the irrepressible badge with him," arousing laughter from everyone familiar with the editor's hatred for his home-state U.S. senator. Greeley and his New York rival Henry Raymond occupied opposite political camps that week but, to his credit, the *Times* editor generously acknowledged that it was Greeley who "made a great sensation" in Chicago, noting: "He is surrounded by a crowd wherever he goes, who besiege him for a speech, and failing in that seduce him into conversation, which inevitably becomes a speech." Greeley made his mark on the convention floor as well, introducing a resolution holding "liberty to be the natural birthright of every human being," and declaring "that slavery can only exist where it has been previously established." The *Cincinnati Commercial*'s Halstead admitted that when the chairman called the roll on the motion, Greeley's name elicited "the greatest ovation" of all the delegates, adding a bit snidely that "those who know him well know that nobody is more fond of the breath of popular favor than the philosophic Horace."[79]

Greeley's dogged opposition to Seward, however, infuriated his fellow New Yorkers. When the Empire State delegation—all of whom remained firmly committed to the senator—hosted a dinner the night before the scheduled balloting for president, speaker after speaker rose not only to praise the senator, but to denounce Greeley, who did not attend. But in his own remarks, Raymond "defended Mr. G. from the imputation of selfishness, and vindicated his right to act as the best interests of the Republican Party seem to require."[80] For his part, Greeley wired his paper from Chicago on the eve of the balloting: "My conclusion, from all that I can gather tonight, is that the opposition to Gov. Seward can not concentrate on any candidate, and that he will be nominated."[81] Once again, Horace Greeley had not only chosen the wrong horse, but taken the wrong measure of his colleagues.

Charles Ray came far closer than Greeley to assessing the mood of the convention when he wired Lincoln: "Your friends are at work for you hard, and with great success. Your show on the first ballot will not be confined to Illinois, and after that it will be strongly developed. . . . A pledge or two may be necessary when the pinch comes. Don't be too sanguine. Matters now look well and as things stand to-day I had rather have your chances than those of any other man. But don't get excited."[82]

The Republican National Convention gaveled to order on May 16 inside a massive temporary wooden structure near the lakefront dubbed the Wigwam. Three thousand spectators, many gaining entry with counterfeit tickets sup-

Dr. Charles H. Ray of the *Chicago Tribune*, who doubled as a floor manager for Lincoln's surprise victory at the 1860 Republican National Convention.

posedly issued by the Lincoln campaign, filled its galleries to overflowing. After passing an antislavery-expansion platform as expected, delegates began casting their votes for president on May 18, but not before the *Chicago Tribune* issued what Murat Halstead called "a last appeal to the Convention not to nominate Seward." [83] Even so, going into the first ballot, Halstead, for one, agreed with Greeley that the New Yorker's nomination was a foregone conclusion. Their certainty notwithstanding, Seward came up short on the first ballot, but to the astonishment of many, it was not Chase of Ohio, Cameron of Pennsylvania, or Bates of Missouri who came in second, but Lincoln of Illinois. From that point on, the Seward nomination was doomed.

After two more rounds of noisy balloting in which Lincoln's strength steadily increased as Seward's first stalled, then ebbed, Lincoln won the nomination. The galleries, thick with partisan Illinoisans, erupted in an ear-shattering roar that Halstead likened to "the rush of a great wind in the van of a storm." As the city went "wild with delight," Medill and Ray ordered the offices of the *Chicago Tribune* illuminated with bright lights and decorated with Lincoln memorabilia. "On each side of the counting room door," the paper proudly reported, "stood a *rail*—out of the three thousand split by 'honest Old Abe' thirty years ago on the Sangamon River bottoms." [84] Heading home to Cincinnati hours later, Halstead could still hear from his train window "the thundering jar of cannon, the clamor of drums . . . and the wild whooping of the boys, who were delighted with the idea of a candidate for the Presidency who thirty years ago had split rails . . . and whose neighbors name him 'honest.'" [85]

Lincoln received word of his triumph in the secure, convivial setting to which he had retreated so often during the past decade to strategize, submit editorial copy, or simply exchange gossip with his closest friends and advisors in politics and the press: the rustically furnished editorial rooms of Bailhache and Baker's *Illinois State Journal*. There, a breathless runner arrived from the town's nearby telegraph office clutching the decisive wire, screaming at the top of his voice as he rushed up the stairs, "Mr. Lincoln, Mr. Lincoln, you are nominated!" Hearing the shouts, the "cool" but evidently well-pleased politician rose from his favorite seat at the *Journal* office, a painted bentwood hickory armchair, seized the dispatch in his hands, read it slowly, and only then confided: "I felt sure this would come when I saw the second ballot." After congratulations all around, Lincoln announced: "I must go home. There is a little short woman there that is more interested in this matter than

I am." Then he pressed through a rapidly thickening swarm of well-wishers already filling the street outside the *Journal* office to offer him congratulations, joking as he headed in the direction of his house a few blocks away: "Boys you had better come and shake hands with me now that you have an opportunity—for you do not know what influence this nomination may have on me. I am human, you know."[86]

Looking on approvingly at this frenzied scene were the two Springfield Republican editors who for years had promoted Lincoln so loyally: Edward Baker and William Bailhache. Now their small and otherwise unremarkable country newspaper office had witnessed history.

Lincoln's newspaper friendships—and obligations—were about to ex-

"ET TU, GREELEY?"

The *Tribune* editor slays Seward in *Vanity Fair*'s June 1860 *Julius Caesar* parody, *"Et Tu, Greeley?"* Mounting the pedestal is the new—and noticeably dark-skinned—presidential nominee Lincoln. Below him a bearded Henry Raymond, as Mark Antony, looks on in despair.

pand. A taste of things to come arrived within days. One of the first to send congratulations to the newly minted nominee was William Schouler, onetime editor of the *Boston Atlas*, who still contributed occasional articles to Republican papers in and about town. "I am neither an office seeker or the son of one," he took pains to point out in his letter. That was because he already occupied a political office, and meant to hold on to it. He was serving as adjutant general of Massachusetts at a salary of $1,800 a year, he explained. And as he made clear, he anticipated that a change in administrations would bring no commensurate change in what he boasted was "not a mere ornamental position." [87]

The Republican press had done its work in behalf of Lincoln; now, months before Election Day, it was apparently time for Lincoln to go to work in behalf of the Republican press.

In return, Lincoln would demand from Republican journalists unconditional loyalty in print—along with hard work on direct grassroots politics—"*organizing* every election district," as he put it to a prominent Pennsylvania editor, even if it meant "counting noses one by one." [88]

Horace Greeley had already done his work—and more, at least according to one eyewitness at Chicago, who claimed the editor had done nothing less than balance the ticket at the convention. Following Lincoln's nomination, fellow delegates surrounded Greeley and asked, "Who is it best to bring forward for Vice-President?" Greeley replied: "The friends of Mr. Seward are very sore, and they must have their own way as to Vice-President." Pressed to name a candidate who could placate the Seward faction, "Mr. Greeley put his hand to the side of his mouth and in an undertone said, 'Hamlin of Maine.'" [89]

Hannibal Hamlin was chosen as Lincoln's running mate that afternoon.

CHAPTER EIGHT

I Can Not Go into the Newspapers

Republican editors throughout the North—even the politically myopic Horace Greeley, who suddenly faced significant danger of being marginalized by the party—quickly rallied behind Abraham Lincoln, although not before some of their Eastern brethren engaged in a furious debate over who deserved blame for William Seward's humiliation at Chicago. Three weeks after the convention, Kansas editor Mark Delahay tried assuring the newly anointed candidate that "the Raymond and Greeley quarrel should not hurt us much"—at least "not in NY." [1] But as the internecine newspaper war raged, Democratic editors pounced. Citing abundant evidence of morning-after remorse among Republicans, the opposition press did its best both to plant seeds of doubt about Lincoln's competence and to incite fears about his party's antislavery agenda.

Leading that effort, as usual, was James Gordon Bennett. Denouncing Lincoln's nomination as "absurd, improbable and incredible," the *Herald* wickedly claimed that astonished Democrats first greeted the news as some kind of "hoax, played off by some wag on the Little Giant." In the *Herald*'s brutal estimation, Lincoln was "rough timber . . . slovenly . . . an uneducated man—a vulgar village politician, without any experience worth mentioning in the practical duties of statesmanship, and only noted for some very unpopular votes which he gave while a member of Congress." [2]

Bennett could not resist reminding readers as well that Lincoln had visited New York but once—and then, for a fee to orate at Cooper Union. For good measure, Bennett lumped Lincoln together with Horace Greeley:

> The conduct of the Republican Party in the nomination is a remarkable indication of small intellect, growing smaller. They pass over Seward, Chase and Bates, who are statesmen and able men, and they take up a fourth-rate lecturer, who cannot speak good grammar, and who, to raise the wind, delivers his hackneyed, illiterate compositions at $200 apiece. Our readers will recollect that this peripatetic politician visited New York two or three months ago on his financial tour, when, in return for the most unmitigated trash, interlarded with coarse and clumsy jokes, he filled his empty pockets with dollars coined out of Republican fanaticism. If, after he becomes President of the United States, the public finances should fall, he can set out on a lecturing mission through the country, taking Horace Greeley along with him.[3]

Henry Raymond, trying his utmost to conceal his disappointment over the convention's choice, left Chicago not to return home, but dutifully to journey to Springfield together with Thurlow Weed, as members of the delegation assigned to notify Lincoln officially of his nomination. The visit proved disheartening. The laconic candidate did little to convince Raymond that he was ready for the presidency. "No one doubts that he has all the intellectual ability, the honesty of purpose, and the fixedness of political principle essential to the high position for which he is in nomination," the *Times* soon opined. "The only apprehension which any of his friends entertain is that he may lack the iron firmness of will and the practical experience of men of factions, which the passing crisis will render indispensable in a Republican president."[4]

Back home, Greeley squirmed as Democrats and embittered Seward Republicans alike circulated the charge that the *Tribune* editor bore primary responsibility for the convention defeat of the New York favorite son they still believed to be best qualified to be president. Bennett had the most sport of all, tormenting Republicans by asserting that Seward (whom he still detested) was "a far better man in every way than Abe Lincoln." The *Herald* reported that Greeley had not only "killed" the front-runner in Chicago, but that his grateful admirers had repaid him by launching a subscription "to buy Greeley a new suit of clothes to replace his present seedy raiment." (Bennett pledged his own contribution of five cents.) Bennett also invented the rumor that Greeley had supported Edward Bates in Chicago in the expectation that he would himself become the Missourian's running mate "as soon as Bates was out of the woods."[5] An infuriated Thurlow Weed reported to his own Albany readers that Greeley was actually overheard before he left Chicago exulting, "Now I am even with Governor Seward." On May 22, Greeley tried responding to the cascading charges with a lengthy editorial defending his actions in Chicago, vowing support for the Republican ticket, and indignantly maintaining that he truly believed the conservative Bates had been the best available man.[6]

This was all too much for Raymond, who replied with his own scathing indictment of Greeley in the *New York Times*. Mocking his rival editor for attempting "to be the historian of his own exploits," Raymond sarcastically charged that by displaying "the generosity which belongs to his nature, and which a feeling not unlike remorse may have stimulated into unwonted activity, he awards to others the credit which belongs transcendently to himself"—that is, for defeating Seward at Chicago. "Mr. Greeley had special qualifications, as well as a special love, for this task," Raymond editorialized, "to which none of the others could lay claim. For twenty years he had been sustaining the political principles and vindicating the political conduct of Mr. Seward through the columns of the most influential political newspaper in the country. He had infused into the popular mind, especially throughout the Western States, the most profound and thorough devotion to the anti-slavery sentiments which had given character to Mr. Seward's public career." Once in Chicago, however, Greeley had "labored personally with delegates as they arrived" to warn them of Republican defeat in November should Seward be nominated. And then Raymond unleashed a true bombshell: none of this treachery surprised the New York delegation, he charged, because Greeley had been secretly plotting against Seward since 1854.

"Being thus stimulated by a hatred he had secretly cherished for years, protected by the forbearance of those whom he assailed and strong in the confidence of those upon whom he had sought to operate," Raymond continued, "it is not strange that Mr. Greeley's efforts should have been crowned with success." To Greeley alone, Raymond concluded with a flourish, belonged "full credit for the main result of the Chicago convention, because his own modesty will prevent his claiming it,—at all events until the new Republican administration shall be in position to distribute its rewards."[7]

At first, a stunned Greeley responded feebly to the attack, counter-charging that by visiting Springfield and then Auburn (to console Seward), his *Times* rival had not only been "paying court alike, to the rising and the setting sun," but that he had returned to New York displaying "his constitutional addiction to crooked ways."[8] But Raymond's sensational charge that Greeley had dedicated himself to destroying Seward years earlier would not fade away. When New Yorkers began clamoring for the evidence, Seward himself provided it, returning the dispositive six-year-old letter to its beleaguered author. Greeley had little choice but to make public the damning proof himself. On June 14, the *Tribune* published the full text of the private missive he had sent to Seward back in 1854 "dissolving" their so-called "partnership." Greeley tried to cushion himself from the expected outcry by accompanying it with the claim that in the years since he had "uttered more praise with less blame" for Seward over the years "than of any other living statesman."[9]

The press had a field day. The latest Raymond-Greeley-Weed feud inspired a barrage of newspaper comments around the country, and many of their derogatory barbs were aimed at Greeley. The *Philadelphia Pennsylvanian* called it "a deep disgrace that the newspaper profession should present such instances of venality, ingratitude, and shamelessness." The *Cleveland Herald* clucked that "Ambition for personal political office has ruined many an editor," while the *Cincinnati Enquirer* tried reminding readers that Greeley was a "positive power in this country, more potent than all the Republican politicians put together."[10]

The debate only intensified. In another long and venomous column, Raymond skewered Greeley yet again, reminding *Times* readers that the "Philosopher" had based his 1854 grudge not on a dispute over doctrinal issues, but over the expectation of naked political reward and financial benefit for his newspaper. Greeley had lusted for the office of lieutenant governor that year, Raymond pointed out, not because "he thought himself peculiarly well-fitted for it, but because 'he wanted to have all his enemies on him at once, as he was tired of fighting them piecemeal,' and because his running would have . . . 'helped his paper.'" Pillorying his longtime adversary with undisguised relish, Raymond added attacks on Greeley's character, his personal habits, and his editorial style alike:

> We would be the last to underrate the services which Mr. Greeley has rendered to his party. But we cannot quite agree with him in thinking that any party

is bound to require such service by running a candidate . . . merely for the sake of bringing his enemies into compact shape and "helping his paper." This is more of a sacrifice than any political party can fairly be expected to make—a good deal more than Mr. Seward's friends demanded on his behalf at Chicago.

Mr. Greeley's letter suggests sundry other topics of discourse, upon which, however, we forbear to enter. In regard to his own profession, for example, we presume he has learned effectually,—though at some personal cost,—that even "milk and water" is a more palatable daily beverage for the average public taste than aquafortis [nitric acid]. . . . Readers of newspapers are human beings after all, and prefer being treated with some degree of respect, even when they do not happen to concur in sentiment with an Editor, who, even if he not be an office-seeker, may possibly have personal reasons of his own for seeking to dragoon them into conformity. It is a very bad matter to coerce a whole community, and the attempt indicates quite as little wisdom, as it generally secures of success.[11]

Always a hard man to shame, the resilient Greeley responded by ignoring the uproar and taking up the Lincoln banner as if he had been waving it for years. Somehow, in the space of just a week and a half, Greeley miraculously transformed himself from Seward spoiler to Bates delegate to Lincoln enthusiast, with hardly a word to justify his conversions. A young New York artist named Thomas Hicks, commissioned to travel to Springfield to paint a portrait of the newly minted nominee, happened to be visiting the *Tribune* office when the editor burst in from the Republican convention still "stained with the dust and grime of travel." When the staff gathered around begging for firsthand reports of the drama in Chicago, Hicks remembered, Greeley seized from his coat pocket a daublike woodcut depicting what the painter described as "a very plain man"—the latest portrait of Abraham Lincoln. Holding it aloft "with an air of triumph" as if "Honest Abe" had been his first and only choice for president, Greeley unselfconsciously declared: "There, I say, that is a good head to go before the people."[12]

By autumn, Greeley was touting Lincoln's candidacy as if he had invented it—and as if the nominee not only supported, but exemplified, the ideals that the editor had been advocating for decades. "Abraham Lincoln illustrates our position and enforces our argument," the *Tribune* declared in October. "His career proves our doctrine sound. He is Republicanism embodied and exemplified. . . . That he split rails is of itself nothing; that a man who at twenty was splitting rails for a bare living is at fifty the chosen head of the greatest and most intelligent party in the land, soon to be the head also of the nation—this is much, everything." Bravely, if unrealistically, Greeley even urged pro-Union Southerners to dare to vote Republican. If those with the "manly courage" to do so found themselves menaced at the polls, or permitted to cast their ballots only to see them "refused" or "destroyed," Uncle Horace assured them, "your duty is performed."[13]

Not every antislavery editor experienced such a swift conversion. Although Frederick Douglass's upstate abolitionist monthly still boasted far fewer readers than the widely circulated New York City dailies, no editor came closer to comprehending the truth about the 1860 convention results than this uninhibited freedom fighter, who, unlike white editors, advocated for abolition without any thought of personal or political reward. Writing in June, Douglass lavished praise on Seward and echoed the almost universal surprise at the choice of Lincoln. But he went on to describe the Republican candidate as "a man of unblemished private character" with "a cool, well-balanced head" and "great firmness of will." Lincoln could yet boast no great "literary culture"— here, Douglass underestimated him—yet he was admirably "industrious," "frank," and "honest." Douglass accurately concluded that Lincoln's "friends cannot yet claim for him a place in the front rank of statesmanship, whatever their faith in his latent capacities. His political life is thus far to his credit, but it is a political life of fair promise rather than one of rich fruitage."[14] Lincoln, who took no visible part in the New York newspaper kerfuffle over Greeley's schemes or his own qualifications, simply waited in Springfield for the Republican East Coast editors to finish letting off steam so they could return to what he regarded as their principal mission: that of ending Democratic rule in Washington by publishing propaganda aimed at boosting his own candidacy.

Stephen Douglas experienced far more frustration than his longtime Republican rival in uniting his party—and its press—behind his presidential aspirations.

He had begun the campaign season as the overwhelming favorite for the Democratic nomination. Writing in 1859, author Mary J. Windle spoke for many when she described Douglas as an inevitable "future President, with the White House . . . as much his future as the Tuileries that of the Imperial infant, or Windsor Castle that of the Prince of Wales."[15] But Southern Democrats were not quite ready to grant Douglas the deed to the Executive Mansion. Seething that the party platform failed to include a plank protecting slavery in the new territories, and blaming Douglas's Popular Sovereignty for inhibiting slavery's expansion, they refused to rally behind the Little Giant. When the Democrats convened in Charleston in April 1860 to select their standard-bearer, delegates endured fifty-seven inconclusive roll calls in a futile effort to choose a nominee. Douglas led on every round of balloting, but never mustered the two-thirds majority the Democratic Party then required to anoint national candidates. (Bennett stubbornly—and unsuccessfully—supported Buchanan for a second term, inspiring a series of cartoon attacks, one of which showed the editor as a barber lathering the president's hair into the shape of a dunce cap.)

With the delegates hopelessly deadlocked, Douglas men called for an adjournment and proposed reconvening at Baltimore in June—a strategy that temporarily salvaged Douglas's presidential hopes but as a consequence wrecked the Democratic Party. In Baltimore, Douglas finally won nomination, but Southern extremists stormed out of the hall and called for a convention of their own. There they chose John C. Breckinridge of Kentucky to stand for the White House on a separate Southern Democratic ticket. Further complicating the already muddled race was yet another convention in Baltimore, which brought together a coalition of former Know-Nothings and conservative old-line Whigs unprepared to rally behind the antislavery Republicans. Calling themselves the Constitutional Union Party, they awarded their own presidential nod to former U.S. senator and cabinet officer John Bell of Tennessee.

The breakup of the Democratic Party—"secession" by the Southerners, wags called it—gave many Republicans confidence from the start that they could not be beaten in November. His feud with Greeley temporarily at bay, Henry Raymond not only predicted a Lincoln triumph but added: "We think it not at all unlikely that Mr. Douglas himself fully shares this opinion." By the end of June, *Chicago Tribune* editor Charles Ray wrote Lincoln to exult: "It is early yet; but it will do you no harm to begin to consider what shall be the quality and cut of your inaugural suit. It does not seem to me that you have anything else to do in the campaign."[16] William Cullen Bryant, describing himself as "an old campaigner, who has been engaged in political controversies for more than a third of a century," was more practical, advising Lincoln that "the vast majority of your friends . . . want you to make no speeches, write no letters as a candidate, enter into no pledges, make no

promises, nor even give any of those kind words which men are apt to interpret into promises."[17]

Lincoln followed this advice and did nothing at all to advance his
candidacy—at least publicly—for the next six months. While "Wide-Awake"
clubs marched in support of his candidacy throughout the North, the Republican nominee waged his entire campaign by allowing political surrogates
and copacetic editors to speak in his behalf, sending occasional political instructions to supporters around the country, posing for new photographs
and paintings designed to introduce him to the national electorate, chatting
amiably with the occasional visiting journalist (relatively few correspondents
ventured to remote Springfield), and monitoring both the newspapers and his
constantly increasing volume of mail. The Republican press did its full share.
Supporters introduced a new special weekly called *The Rail Splitter*, whose
first edition introduced the lyrics to a rousing new campaign song called "Lincoln and Liberty," and featured a rough but appealing sketch of the self-made
nominee, dressed in homespun clothing, wielding an ax to chop wood.[18] The
presentation proved a harbinger of messages to come: party organs would
strive to emphasize Lincoln's log cabin origins and frontier upbringing, and
discuss the divisive slavery issue as seldom as possible. Whatever wire-pulling
the candidate did was conducted behind the scenes.

By contrast, facing abandonment by the bloc vote on which Democrats
had long counted from Dixie, Douglas had little choice but to break precedent
and take to the campaign trail in his own behalf. Anticipating charges that he
was desperate for office, he set off on a long and circuitous trip through the
South and up the Eastern seaboard by claiming he was off to reunite with his
ailing mother—who actually lived in more directly accessible upstate New
York. Naturally, wherever his trains paused to take on fuel, Douglas managed
to deliver speeches to local supporters. Greeley branded him "Douglas the
Wanderer," and cartoonists had a field day mocking "Stephen in Search of
His Mother," depicting him in one particularly emasculating caricature as a
dwarflike man-child enduring a spanking from the symbolic "mother" of the
nation, "Columbia."[19] Douglas's exertions did little to change the political
equation North or South of the Mason-Dixon line and moreover exacted a
heavy physical toll on the hard-drinking candidate.

Of course, the Douglas team also pursued the more traditional campaign
maneuvers long practiced by political parties and loyal journalists. His organization distributed pamphlets, speeches, and exclusive news through three offi-

cial newspaper organs—the Springfield *State Register*, the *Chicago Times*, and the *Washington States and Union*—soliciting support, editorial and financial alike, from Democratic editors nationwide. Chicago editor James Sheahan issued a pro-Douglas campaign biography, which the New York publishers Harper & Brothers promoted as its "prominent spring book."[20] The efforts did little good. Although Douglas confidently instructed the *Register*'s Lanphier to "open the canvas with vigor and energy,"[21] the candidate's once solid Northern Democratic press support began crumbling in mid-campaign. As one supporter soon warned from New York: "The most influential papers here are against us, or what is worse, Janus-faced."[22]

Even worse news for the Little Giant came from Chicago, where in midsummer the long-loyal James Sheahan abruptly sold the *Times* to Cyrus McCormick. "The sheriff was at the door, & we had to sell or be sold," Sheahan explained to his downstate colleague Charles Lanphier. It did not matter that the replacement editor was "an inflated ass," and the new owners "*against* us on Doctrine, and *for* Breckinridge every where except in Illinois." Douglas, who had supported Sheahan through political squabbles and financial setbacks alike, pouring his own money into the *Times* to keep it alive, was understandably furious. But an equally resentful Sheahan, vowing to bow out of politics forever, put much of the blame for the death of the *Times* on the senator's shoulders, implying that whatever help Douglas had provided had been insufficient.

"Douglas has been cruel in his conduct towards me," Sheahan complained at one point to Lanphier, who summoned the beleaguered Chicagoan to Springfield at the end of August so he could "provide the assistance of his pen during the present canvas."[23] The downstate job did little to heal Sheahan's resentments. "In the matter of the book of which I had hopes," he maintained of Douglas, "he wantonly interfered to my injury. I owe him nothing in any way."[24] In the final chapter of his Douglas biography, Sheahan had barely hinted at these festering frustrations, acknowledging that his 528-page opus was "voluminous" but adding, "to do full justice" to the subject "would require four times the space." The editor certainly turned out to be wrong in predicting that the "remarkable" Douglas was "the only man in his own party whose nomination for the Presidency is deemed equivalent to an election."[25]

Notwithstanding these seismic shifts, and aside from Douglas's desperate personal journey eastward, the presidential campaign remained for the most part conducted in and by the press. Unlike their Democratic counterparts, however, Republican editors never wavered on Lincoln. Newspaperman John Locke Scripps produced the first extended (if sanitized) description of Lincoln's personal virtues in a May 1860 profile for the *Chicago Tribune* (in which enterprise the writer now held a business interest). Scripps grandiosely described the Republican nominee as "a gentleman of modest means and simple tastes . . . a regular attendant upon religious worship" and "a scrupulous teller of truth." Lincoln reportedly read and approved the text before publication and it was probably at his later request that its pamphlet edition omitted a tidbit about his once using an expletive to denounce a crooked political deal.[26] The candidate subsequently provided Scripps with a long autobiographical sketch, which the journalist used as the basis for a pamphlet issued by the *Chicago Tribune* and co-published as a *New York Tribune Tract* by Horace Greeley.[27]

Lincoln certainly won the war of campaign "lives," an image-making battle he needed to dominate since he was far less known to the public than Douglas. By and large these efforts represented the work of newspapermen, not professional historians or biographers. In June, David W. Bartlett, a Washington correspondent for both the *New York Independent* and Bryant's *New York Evening Post* who had written a campaign biography of Republican presidential candidate John C. Frémont four years earlier, produced the first cloth-bound Lincoln life story.[28] It quoted the "Unanimous Commendations of the Press" in response to Lincoln's nomination (certainly based on highly selective research), and featured some two hundred pages of the candidate's speeches. Just three weeks after the Republican convention, *Harper's Weekly* carried an advertisement for the Bartlett book, calling it " 'Honest Old Abe,' First in the Field," and the most "reliable and authentic" of the "many 'Lives of Lincoln' " already in circulation. Gilt-edged editions were offered for one dollar.[29] The *Cincinnati Daily Gazette's* Joseph H. Barrett published a Lincoln biography, too, and from the hand of Ichabod Codding, a radical abolitionist clergyman and editor of the *American Freeman*, came another life story that timid moderate Republicans did little to promote.[30]

That same year, a then unknown twenty-three-year-old reporter for the *Ohio Journal* produced one more campaign biography entitled *The Life and Public Services of Hon. Abraham Lincoln, of Illinois, and Hon. Hannibal Hamlin, of Maine* (Lincoln's running mate). It proved the first of 103 books that its young author, William Dean Howells, went on to publish during his long literary career. Its historical importance, however, arose from the fact that Lincoln himself scrupulously read the text in advance, and offered handwritten corrections—all of them minor—before publication. True to the traditions of the period, Lincoln never publicly acknowledged his cooperation with any of the newspapermen who introduced him to the public through the medium of the campaign biography, especially Howells. To so admit would have betrayed an unseemly ambition for high office. At one point, the candidate declared that he had "scarcely been so much astounded at anything" as by the "public announcement" by Howells's publisher that the work was "authorized by me." Lincoln had not objected to interviews and editing, he conceded. "But at the same time, I made myself tiresome, if not hoarse, with repeating . . . that I *authorized nothing*—would be *responsible for nothing*."[31] For his part, Howells soon complained: "I never had any report of the book's sales, but I believe my *Life of Lincoln* sold very well in the West, though in the East it was forestalled by the books of writers better known."[32]

Not to be outdone in the press world's effort to introduce the candidate (and generate revenue thereby), Thurlow Weed saw to the publication of a 278-page collection of speeches by Lincoln, Seward, and other prominent Republicans.[33] And in addition to the *Tribune Tract* by Scripps, Horace Greeley published what he called a "convenient" and "indispensable" *Political Text-Book*, a guide to the 1860 race bulging with election statistics and speeches by the presidential and vice presidential candidates, all of it supposedly free of "partisan bias," but not surprisingly testifying to the justice of the Republican cause. Priced at one dollar per copy, and relentlessly promoted in a series of daily page-one advertisements in the newspaper, the guidebook went through eleven editions before Election Day.[34] Greeley also issued a *Tribune Almanac and Political Register*, filled with useful political data alongside benign advertisements for "porous plasters" and pianofortes.[35] Greeley profited handsomely from this publishing boom, not only from his own work, but from a slew of paid advertisements that publishers of rival biographies placed in the weekly and semiweekly editions of the *Tribune*, eager to reach Greeley's vast Republican audience.

By campaign's end, some 200,000 copies of various Lincoln biographies were in circulation in at least two languages, English and German. Lincoln's future private secretary, John Nicolay, firmly believed the "copious pamphlet and newspaper biographies in which people read the story of his humble beginnings, and how he had risen, by dint of simple, earnest work and native genius, through privation and difficulty . . . play[ed] no small part in a political revolution of which the people at large were not as yet even dreaming."[36]

• • •

Lincoln's one major concession to the increased burdens that came with his new political status was the hiring of his very first personal staff—of one. Shortly after his nomination, the candidate invited the twenty-eight-year-old, German-born John Nicolay to serve as his secretary. The slender Nicolay, whose frown of a mustache and pointy little beard did little to disguise his youth, agreed to a monthly salary of seventy-five dollars, to be paid by the Republican State Committee.

Lincoln had known the young newspaperman for several years; he had earlier recommended him to Horace Greeley for a job with the *New York Tribune* (a request Greeley ignored). More recently, Nicolay had been working for one of Lincoln's close political allies as Clerk of the Illinois secretary of state's office, a gathering place for many Republican political professionals that was located in the same State Capitol building where Lincoln began occupying a temporary office after his nomination. The secretary of state himself proposed his trusted employee to Lincoln, and with no one else in mind, the nominee agreed.

While Lincoln and his new secretary appeared to have little in common, they in fact shared many interests. For one thing, both men liked (and wrote) maudlin poetry. Nicolay had scribbled in an unpublished verse in 1851: "There comes an hour of sadness / In which I feel alone; When life appears but madness, / When I feel that joy has flown." The lines bore eerie similarity to a nostalgic ode Lincoln had penned some five years earlier, entitled, "My Childhood Home I See Again," which spoke of the "lone survivors" of his former prairie community, including one old acquaintance who had gone mad: "A human-form, with reason fled, / While wretched life remains." Just one year after writing his poem, Nicolay obtained a patent for "a device for improvement of Printing Presses." Lincoln, too, held a patent. They became the only politician and chief aide to share that distinction.[37]

More important to Lincoln was the fact that Nicolay boasted journalistic experience and could handle newspaper correspondence in his behalf. Nicolay had served during the 1850s as editor of the Pittsfield, Illinois, *Pike County Free Press*. By 1857 he was working as an "authorized correspondent and business agent" for St. Louis's Republican paper, the *Missouri Democrat*. Two years later, one influential friend urged Nicolay to launch "another daily in Springfield," arguing in a slap at the *Illinois State Journal* that "there is no competent paper at here at present." The approaching presidential election seemed "the most fitting occasion to get up a new establishment which can deal blows" to the opposition. With Nicolay at the helm as "one of the Editors of the new concern," and the proposed paper striving to be "racy, sensible, and pertinent," his admirer predicted that it would attract "many thousand subscribers."[38] Nicolay rejected the offer, but his recently acquired job with Lincoln did not inhibit him from continuing to submit freelance articles to various other newspapers. Only a few weeks before joining the campaign, Nicolay had drafted an editorial calling for Lincoln's nomination for the presidency. "He maintains the faith of the fathers of the Republic," read the endorsement. ". . . In his hands, the Union would be safe."[39] It was the closest thing to a perfect job application any journalist could ever have submitted. Nicolay had also attended the Chicago convention as a political correspondent for the *Missouri Democrat.*[40]

As the candidate probably knew, Nicolay had been "greatly disappointed" when he was not invited to write the Lincoln biography assigned to the equally untested William Dean Howells, although Nicolay later generously admitted that Howells had "performed his task much more worthily than I could have done."[41] As consolation and more, the fiercely loyal Nicolay now found himself in control of Lincoln's calendar and correspondence, eventually handling visitors who ranged from well-known pre-convention favorites like Bates and Chase searching for cabinet posts, to influential journalists seeking

The once and future journalists who served as Lincoln's private secretaries beginning with the 1860 campaign (from left to right): John G. Nicolay, John M. Hay, and William O. Stoddard.

influence, to rustic strangers content merely to shake hands with the once impoverished country youth who had now risen so high. Lincoln soon found he could depend on Nicolay not only to handle this influx of guests but also to pick out important letters from his growing daily mailbag and when necessary draft adroit responses, especially to the screeds that came pouring in from important Republicans eager to offer advice or request favors.

In short order, the burden of managing Lincoln's visitors and mail grew too great for even the tireless Nicolay to handle alone. The campaign then added an assistant secretary to the staff: the delicately handsome and profoundly gifted John M. Hay, only twenty-two. A relative of one of the candidate's longtime Springfield friends, Hay had no comparable journalistic experience—he was a Brown-educated aspiring lawyer—but boasted personal charm to spare and a genuine flair for writing. At the suggestion of one of his professors, Hay had sent the *Providence Journal* a firsthand report on Lincoln's activities in Springfield during the convention.[42] Soon he was not only helping Nicolay answer correspondence, but submitting fresh newspaper pieces under the rather precious nom de plume, "Ecarte," a coy play on a voguish two-man card game called écarté. Thus, Nicolay and Hay not only functioned respectively as office manager and correspondence clerk; they served also as official, if anonymous, propagandists, the equivalents of what today would be called campaign press secretaries.

If candidate Lincoln passed the summer and fall rather quietly in Springfield, back in New York the national presidential campaign waged in his name came to resemble outright warfare. The canvass brought out both the best and the worst from the big three editors, who behaved predictably in print, only with more energy, and occasionally more venom, than ever. Republicans Greeley and Raymond outdid each other in heaping encomia on Lincoln, although the *Times* did temper its enthusiasm for a few weeks while its editor recovered from his shock and chagrin over Seward's defeat. Meanwhile the supposedly independent but incurably racist Bennett, as scheming and unmanageable as ever, began issuing ominous warnings about what he increasingly regarded as a likely victory by the "Black Republicans."

For the first time, or so the evidence suggests, Lincoln took a personal interest in getting Bennett on his side—or, at the very least, off his back. In mid-June, the candidate's most powerful local newspaper ally, Chicago's Joseph Medill, attempted, clearly with Lincoln's blessing, to forge a neutrality deal with the volatile *Herald* publisher. Ostensibly in New York on a business trip, Medill somehow learned that Bennett was, as he put it, "not unwilling to 'dicker' terms" for muzzling his incessant criticism of the Republicans. As Medill sunnily alerted the nominee by mail, Bennett was said to believe Lincoln to be "the strongest man the Reps could have nominated . . . honest, capable, not dangerously ultra, thought you would make a good president." Medill planned to rendezvous with Republican national committeeman from Illinois Norman Judd, also visiting New York at the time, and finalize a strategy for approaching the elusive Bennett.

Lincoln was no doubt intrigued (though if he ever replied to Medill in writing, the evidence has not survived). "I'll have a preliminary meeting with his 'Satanic Majesty' before [Norman] Judd arrives," Medill informed Lincoln on June 19, "and ascertain his state of mind &c. &c. We deem it highly important to spike that gun; his affirmative help is not of great consequence, but he is powerful for mischief. He can do us much harm if hostile. If neutralized a *point* is gained." Moreover, Medill was sure he knew how to win Bennett over: with flattery. "We think his terms will not be immoderate. He is too rich to want money. Social position we suspect is what he wants. He wants to be in a position to be invited with his wife and son to dinner or tea at the white house, occasionally, and to be 'made of,' by the big men of the party. I think we can afford to do that much." [43]

Medill went on to hold two meetings with Bennett, but the two men struck no deal. The editor told his visitor that he thought Lincoln was "a man of good and honest intentions and would try to do [his] duty faithfully." But he feared he "would fall into the hands of bad advisors." As Medill recalled Bennett's crude words, "the first time . . . you caught a runaway nigger, and sent him back to slavery, you would raise the d—l in your party." At this, Medill reported, "the old Satanic laughed loud and boisterously." The *Herald* editor also worried aloud that Lincoln owed too large a political debt to Bennett's nemesis, Horace Greeley ("I assured him that Greeley had not been for you, that you were no favorite of his"). The sessions ended with Bennett telling Medill, "we could beat your man Lincoln, if we would unite, but I think it would be better for the country to let him be elected. I'll not be hard on him." [44] Breaking his word as usual, the editor soon began urging Douglas supporters to switch to Breckinridge in a last minute "fusion" effort to unite the "Democracy," defeat Lincoln, and save both the Union and the commercial vitality of the city. Stepping up its attacks on "the radically revolutionary character of the black republican party and its Presidential candidate," the *Herald* was soon likening "the public declarations of Lincoln" to "the bloody acts of John Brown" and, perhaps worst of all, to "the diatribes of Greeley."[45] It would not be the last time Abraham Lincoln or his surrogates tried and failed in their efforts to court James Gordon Bennett.

Bennett shamelessly played class and race cards in his autumn 1860 effort to demonize the Republicans. Lincoln's election, the *Herald* prophesied in one such outburst, would result in bankruptcy for local hotels, theater owners, and wagon makers dependent on Southern patronage, and cause financial ruin to tailors, shoemakers, and milliners reliant on slave-harvested cotton ("will you risk the bread you eat for the negro and his worshippers?"). On Election Day itself, Bennett published a hysterical fusillade of items designed to inflame white voters. In one, the *Herald* reported that an African American had recently dared to eat chestnuts on a public streetcar, refusing orders for his ouster and telling the conductor when he disembarked in his own good time that "after the 6th of November they'd show white folks how to treat colored people." Warned Bennett: "There is not the slightest doubt of it; and if the black republicans only keep on they will have no difficulty in establishing the long mooted question that a white man is really as good as a nigger."[46]

In the very same edition, Bennett predicted that Lincoln's election would lead to black suffrage. "Already," the paper reported, "the waiters and whitewashers and bootblacks have grown impudent in anticipation of the bright prospect before them." Bennett asked whether any "decent white man" would "vote himself down to the level of the negro race?" Not yet finished with its last-minute outburst, the *Herald* warned Irish- and German-born laborers that if Lincoln won, "you will have to compete with the labor of four million emancipated negroes." Bennett could not have been clearer in issuing these warnings: "Let every man who has a vote to cast," he brayed, "cast it against Lincoln, and for the Union—against disorder, and the destruction of all our commercial relations." In the most bizarre of his Election Day stunts, Bennett actually announced that a "special trance medium" had assured the paper that George Washington himself had come back from the dead to warn New York voters to "put down sectionalism and to crush out fanaticism." That the séance he described had not produced an outright endorsement of Breckinridge was perhaps the only truly surprising aspect of the report.[47]

For all his hostility, Bennett was never one to let his biases stand in the way of providing his readers with the best news coverage. The *Herald* spared no expense in covering the campaign. At one point the paper attached a reporter to William Seward's extensive late September speaking tour, following the New York senator all the way to Springfield to cover his eagerly anticipated meeting with Lincoln (who struck the *Herald* correspondent who glimpsed him for the first time as less "repulsive looking" than his recent portraits). After interviewing the Republican nominee, more importantly, the reporter suggested that Lincoln had "a good, strong mind, and an honest intellect."[48] By summer, the *Herald* began providing readers with occasional feature stories about Lincoln, filed from Springfield—the kind of coverage neither the pro-Lincoln *Times* nor the *Tribune* ever bankrolled.

Not that editorial hostility toward Lincoln ever subsided at the *Herald*'s New York headquarters, and on one particular occasion it caused the nominee considerable embarrassment. The episode unfolded three weeks after his nomination, when a restless Lincoln found himself intrigued by an invitation from Kentucky politician Samuel Haycraft that he make a campaign appearance in the hostile Southern state that the nominee nostalgically referred to as "the place of my nativity." Lincoln responded to the idea by joking: "Would not the people Lynch me?" Then he ill-advisedly shared his witticism with a reporter from the *Herald*. To Lincoln's dismay, the correspondent pounced on the story on August 8, rather malignantly interpreting Lincoln's remark as evidence that he genuinely feared "the invitation was a trap laid by some designing person to inveigle him into a slave State for the purpose of doing him harm."[49]

Soon Stephen Douglas and the Democrats took up the attack. Lincoln had been careless in this rare instance, speaking on the record when he should have kept his own counsel. What was more, he proved unusually thin-skinned when criticized. But he was no coward, and he knew that attacks on a candidate's manhood could cause significant political damage. So he quickly dashed off several indignant but surprisingly clumsy letters insisting on a retraction—precisely the kind of overwrought response Bennett no doubt hoped to incite. To Samuel Haycraft, Lincoln wrote: "Thinking this Herald correspondence might fall under your eye, I think it due to myself to enter my protest against the correctness of this part of it. I scarcely think the correspondent was malicious; but rather that he misunderstood what was said."

Unwilling to confront Bennett directly—probably a wise decision—Lincoln nonetheless viewed the problem seriously enough to forward his concerns to the secretary of the Republican National Committee, Senator George G. Fogg of New Hampshire, who had taken up residence at a New York hotel for the campaign. "I am annoyed some by the printed paragraph . . . taken from the N.Y. Herald," Lincoln began, pasting in a copy of the offending paragraph in case Fogg had not yet seen it. "This is decidedly wrong. I did not say it. I do not impugn the correspondent. I suppose he misconceived the statement. . . . I have, *playfully*, (and never otherwise) related this incident several times; and I suppose I did so to the Herald correspondent, though I do not remember it. . . . Now, I dislike, exceedingly, for Kentuckians to understand that I am charging them with a purpose to inveigle me, and do violence to me. Yet I can not go into the newspapers. Would not the editor of the Herald, upon being shown this letter, insert the short correction, which you find upon the inclosed scrap? Please try him unless you perceive some sufficient reason to the contrary." The so-called "scrap" contained a precisely worded third-person correction that Lincoln improbably hoped would be published verbatim: "We have such assurance as satisfies us that our correspondent writing from Springfield, Ills, under date of Aug. 8—was mistaken in representing Mr. Lincoln as expressing a suspicion of a design to inveigle him into Kentucky for the purpose of doing him violence. Mr. Lincoln neither entertains, nor has intended to express any such suspicion." [50]

Fogg obliged by calling at the *Herald* and, "in the most diplomatic way of which I was master," making the case for publishing Lincoln's third-person correction. Bennett "expressed himself very kindly disposed towards yourself *personally*," Fogg reported back to Springfield, echoing Medill's earlier impressions, "and of course very far from wishing to misrepresent you." He would print "any *correction* desired"—but only if it appeared over either Lincoln's signature or Fogg's. To issue it "*editorially* or by his *correspondent*," Bennett insisted, "would be to acknowledge the *Herald* or its *correspondent* in error. . . . That was the best, and all he could do." Fogg's advice was that Lincoln let the matter lie; he did not believe "the '*correction*' he offers, would *pay*." Illinois Republican Norman Judd, who was still in New York, concurred, and Lincoln ultimately backed off. "You have done precisely the right thing in the matter with the Herald," he wrote Fogg a few days later. "Do nothing about it. Although it wrongs me, and annoys me some, I prefer letting it run it's [*sic*] course, to getting into the papers over my own name." [51] Once again, a high-level negotiation between a Lincoln representative and James Gordon Bennett had ended in frustration for the candidate.

Lincoln never did get the satisfaction he desired from the *Herald*. Although Samuel Haycraft replied that he would be "pleased" to "make a statement to the paper," Lincoln rejected this approach, too. A week later the nominee wrote again to insist rather unconvincingly that his only interest in suggesting a correction had been "to assure you that I had not, as represented by the Herald correspondent, charged you with an attempt to inveigle me into Kentucky to do me violence."[52] Temporarily embedded *Herald* reporter Simon P. Hanscom—who was either an ardent Lincoln enthusiast or an "unscrupulous" schemer, depending on whose opinion the candidate was willing to accept—went on to produce some friendly articles for the paper in October, maintaining from his Springfield perch that Lincoln was no radical.[53] But the Kentucky episode had taught the president-to-be a valuable lesson: fighting newspaper editors for the last word—especially independent newspaper tycoons like James Gordon Bennett, whose principal goals were broad circulation and white supremacy—was a losing proposition.

Meanwhile, the overtly anti-Lincoln press did its own job relentlessly, assailing not only the candidate but his newspaper supporters as well. A Douglas journal in Pennsylvania complained at one point that the Republican dailies overflowed with "columns of childish trash." According to a like-minded Nebraska paper, big-city Easterners were so used to collecting waste from the "basement stories of outhouses" that they were pursuing their "old habit of pitching night soil" for their morning editions. The Democratic *Boston Herald* labeled the Republican press "inhuman monsters, practicing all sorts of rascality."[54]

For their part, Greeley and Raymond may not have committed the funds or personnel to provide coverage of Lincoln in Springfield, but they did more than provide editorial support at home: both also took to the stump to advocate publicly for the ticket. As ever, Greeley could be competitive even when working in behalf of others. When poet-editor William Cullen Bryant of the *Evening Post* composed a new Lincoln campaign song, the *Tribune* editor promptly did likewise, of course with inferior results.[55] The peripatetic Greeley's campaign tours took him into Connecticut and upstate New York, among other places. Wherever he went, he drew large crowds straining to hear his thin voice. In July, as Cincinnati lawyer Richard M. Corwine told Lincoln, Greeley's appearance "was made the occasion of a very handsome demonstration for our Cause . . . large & spirited." In October a Wall Street businessman suggested that Lincoln authorize a "public recognition" of Greeley's service to the campaign. "I know that New York has an immense population, and that no one man alone can shape public opinion in it so as to determine it's [sic] vote," wrote Elliott F. Shepard, "but I also know that Horace Greeley, more than any other one man has done and is doing this."[56]

Greeley would have agreed. Sounding as exhausted as Lincoln had been during his post–Cooper Union speaking tour five months earlier, Greeley wrote to his friend Bayard Taylor in August: "There is no rest for me till after the Presidential Election. I must write and speak incessantly, tho' so weary that I can hardly stand."[57] Meanwhile Bennett showcased his supposed political indifference—and arrogance—by hosting a "grand reception" in New York to honor a visiting Japanese delegation, at which his wife conspicuously adorned herself with a reported "$100,000 worth of diamonds and jewelry."[58]

Greeley and his fellow Republican editors also "appeared" involuntarily: that is, lampooned in anti-Lincoln campaign cartoons that went on sale in the summer and fall. Though designed to mock Lincoln as a bumpkin, such images primarily attempted to saddle him with the political baggage that came from association with outspoken liberals like Greeley. The preeminent New York printmaking firm of Currier & Ives, practically the *Tribune*'s next-door neighbor in the area just south of City Hall Park, issued a number of these anti-Lincoln cartoons. And quite a few of them included Greeley as a main character. In one painfully racist example, *"The Nigger" in the Woodpile*, the figure of Lincoln sits atop a bonfire-shaped log rail "platform," attempting to conceal a grinning African American trapped within to represent the lurking slavery issue. However clumsily, the print revealed an inescapable truth: Republican editors indeed preferred to steer clear of the volatile slavery issue in 1860, and instead emphasize Lincoln's inspiring personal story. Thus Greeley, wearing his trademark battered hat, long coat, frayed trousers, and white chin whiskers, can be seen in the cartoon telling a representative of "Young America": "I assure you my friend, that you can safely vote our ticket, for we have no connection with the Abolition party, but our Platform is composed entirely of rails split by our Candidate."[59] The lithography firm made the same point with *Letting the Cat Out of the Bag*, which portrayed Greeley, Raymond, and Lincoln all trying to repel a fierce black cat (labeled "Spirit of Discord") who escapes from the "Republican Bag" with the encouragement of antislavery zealot Charles Sumner. "What are you doing, Sumner!" Greeley cries, "you'll spoil all! she ain't to be let out until after Lincoln is elected!" To many Americans of the period, the composition reflected a growing fear that

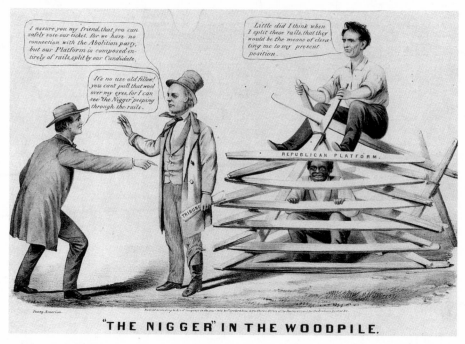

"THE NIGGER" IN THE WOODPILE.

Greeley and Lincoln try to hide the supposedly radical Republican platform beneath a "woodpile" made of Lincolnian log rails. It conceals a cruelly caricatured black man representing the combustible slavery issue.

Greeley and his fellow Republican journalists were conspiring to conceal their candidate's latent radicalism.[60]

In yet another print, Currier & Ives's *The Rail Candidate*, Greeley was back on view together with a black man carrying a squirming Lincoln astride the slavery plank of the Republican platform—in this case formed out of a single, uncomfortable-looking log rail. And in yet another, the editor appeared as a showman introducing an "illustrious individual"—one of Barnum's most retrograde sideshow attractions, the cruelly exploited dark-skinned child known as the "What Is It?"—as "our next candidate for the Presidency."[61] In *The Republican Party Going to the Right House* (rather than the White House), Greeley was again depicted transporting Lincoln aboard a rail, this time toward a lunatic asylum, declaring: "Hold on to me Abe, and we'll go in here by the unanimous consent of the people." And in *Political Blondins Crossing Salt River*, Greeley topples off a rail suspended over a raging stream, assuring fellow Republicans he will survive because "a bag of wind won't sink."[62]

Perhaps no campaign cartoon better illustrated the ramped-up collaboration between editors and politicians that election year than *The Great Exhibi-*

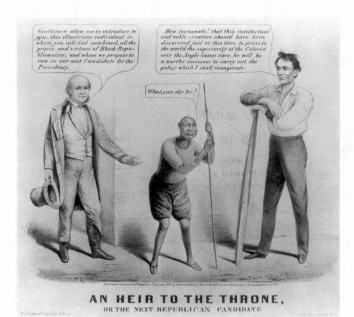

In an image designed to warn racist white voters that Republicans secretly planned to make blacks the equals of whites, Greeley introduces White House nominee Lincoln to "the next Candidate for the Presidency," an exploited P. T. Barnum attraction from Africa, advertised as less than human, and known as the "What Is It."

Greeley is an organ grinder, Lincoln his silenced monkey, in a print charging Republicans with concealing plans for abolition. At right, "Little Villain" Henry Raymond and his former boss, James Watson Webb, raise funds for the campaign.

tion of 1860. This particular Currier & Ives print found Greeley as an organ grinder (his music box labeled "New York Tribune"), with Lincoln as his comically oversized pet monkey, dancing obediently to the editor's tune, his waist tied like a puppet to Greeley's finger and his lips padlocked shut to keep him from saying anything new or controversial. What set this print apart was the inclusion of both James Watson Webb and Raymond, the former shown as a grizzled old man collecting campaign contributions in a tambourine labeled "Courier and Express"; the latter depicted as a bearded dwarf wearing short pants and a vest marked "New York Times," and carrying a miniature hatchet as he grasps Webb's hand and declares: "I'll stick fast to you General, for the present, because I have my own little axe to grind"—meaning his abiding resentment over Seward's defeat at the Republican convention.[63] Old grudges died hard, in images as well as words, so Currier & Ives made the Republican newspaper wars fodder for humorous commentary, taking Greeley's allegedly pernicious influence over Lincoln to new comic heights. One can only assume that James Gordon Bennett took his exclusion hard. He had last appeared in a separate-sheet political cartoon back in 1856, when he was shown attempting to bribe newly elected president James Buchanan.[64]

The editors' efforts on the stump, and their appearances in the graphic arts, may not have changed many votes. But they likely helped spur a gigantic voter turnout—some 80 percent of eligible white males nationwide—which was deemed crucial to Republican success in swing states like Indiana and Pennsylvania. On Election Day, November 6, excitement gripped New York as the vote count began, especially at the city's newspaper offices, where district tallies trickled in throughout the long evening. "Such crowds as were gathered around the doors of the Times, Tribune and Herald," Raymond's paper reported, "are only to be seen on these quadrennial occasions of the country's salvation or destruction." Onlookers "climbed on each other's shoulders and stood on each other's heads in a vain attempt to peer into the second story editorial room windows. Curiosity, apprehension, exultation—these and all other emotions, were as plainly stamped on each individual countenance as the Eagle on a quarter."[65]

When the final tallies were counted, Abraham Lincoln earned the most lopsidedly sectional victory in American history, carrying every Northern state but New Jersey, but winning not a single electoral vote from the South. From distant Oregon, where Lincoln edged out runner-up Breckinridge by some two hundred out of fourteen thousand total votes cast, the victor's old friend, former Springfield editor Simeon Francis, wrote the victor to "congratulate you on the results of this election," and, in a sign of things to come, to take his place at the front of the line of journalists who expected to be rewarded for their loyalty. "My hopes, long entertained, [are] so far un realized," he announced, reminding Lincoln: "I do believe our success . . . carried the state and California—not, however, without much and hard labor." (Before long, he was writing again with his first, but not last, specific request: that his brother-in-law be retained at his federal job in New London.) [66]

Lincoln's exclusively Northern plurality emboldened many Southern politicians and journalists to insist they would not be bound by the result. Yet there were no true political alternatives. Stephen Douglas amassed the second-highest total of popular votes, but won only twelve electoral votes to Lincoln's 180. Breckinridge swept the Deep South, and Bell prevailed in three Border Slave States. Yet in winning, Lincoln accumulated only 40 percent of the total ballots nationwide—the second-smallest popular plurality in American history. As for hotly contested New York state, Lincoln won outright thanks to a huge plurality north of Westchester; but whatever national influence Horace Greeley and Henry Raymond had labored to earn, it could be argued that when it came to the North's most important city, the irascible James Gordon Bennett still reigned supreme in his influence over Democrats: in voter-rich Manhattan, Lincoln collected barely a third of the popular vote.

The outcome aside, the 1860 campaign enriched all the papers. The *Herald* ended the year with seventy thousand daily subscribers; Greeley now claimed 75,000 daily and more than 200,000 weekly readers. Whatever his onetime misgivings, Greeley reveled in the Lincoln triumph, not surprisingly interpreting it as a personal vindication. Appearing at Manhattan's Stuyvesant Institute, he declared the Republicans "not a man-worshipping party," but an organization committed to Union and against slavery. In a way, the editor could now back up such claims with raw numbers: since the Republican ticket had won so few municipal votes on Election Day, Greeley could argue that he was now more popular in New York City than Lincoln was.[67] Nonetheless, Lincoln had the last laugh on all the newspapers. When a visiting *Herald* reporter asked him if he had any message for Bennett, he joked with the confident swagger of a winner: "Yes, you may tell him that Thurlow Weed has found out that Seward was not nominated at Chicago." [68]

Perhaps half in jest, half in earnest, Bennett now suggested that Lincoln ought to do the right thing and appoint Greeley to his cabinet (he certainly would have been delighted to see his competitor leave New York). The notion gained more serious traction when Philadelphia newspaperman John Wein Forney wrote Lincoln on November 12 to urge him not to "pass by the eminent deservings of the rare talents, and the high and commanding position, personal and political, of Mr. Greeley." His "speeches, like his editorials, are read and admired by all men," Forney attested, and gave him "an influence among the masses which no public position could increase, and which long years of partisan persecution have not lessened." Added Forney: "I do not know whether he expects to be included in the selection of your immediate counsellors, I do not know what his friends may ask of him—I speak only the sentiments of one who, having for years been opposed to him politically, and still objecting to many of his principles—regards him as the first journalist in America, and as eminently entitled to the thanks of his party for the vigor, the courage, and the integrity of his general course." [69]

Greeley, however, insisted he wanted no part of the cabinet—a sentiment that dovetailed neatly with Lincoln's reluctance to consider him. That did not mean that Greeley's lust for office had cooled. Indeed, very much thirsting for a political comeback, he set his sights on a different prize: the U.S. Senate seat from New York still occupied by William Seward, but destined to become vacant if the incumbent decided to join the Lincoln administration. The possibility placed Greeley in an awkward position, for he had no desire to see Seward attain higher office; yet only if Seward took the prime cabinet post as secretary of state would his Senate seat open up. "I *would* like to go to the Senate," Greeley confided to his friend, journalist Beman Brockway, "and *would not* like to go into the Cabinet." As he explained, "I belong to *The Tribune*, and as a Senator would continue to work for it, while as a Cabinet man I could not"—a remarkably frank assertion that underscored the fact that politics and journalism remained all but interchangeable. Within the week, an increasingly frustrated Greeley added: "I am sure I can do nothing more to make myself U.S. Senator, and I am not even sure that I would try very hard if sure of success." Nonetheless, Greeley continued to cast his eye on the prize, and before long made clear that he expected Lincoln to support his latest quest for office. [70] The editor of the *New York Tribune* was destined for political rebuke yet again. In the end Lincoln showed more interest in recruiting and rewarding John Wein Forney than Horace Greeley.

• • •

In the aftermath of the presidential election, the New York newspapers began paying attention not only to the prospects of a Lincoln presidency—and cabinet—but also to the unmistakable secession rumblings that began emanating from the South. "The revolution is marching apace," an alarmed James Gordon Bennett fretted in early November, "and as news of Lincoln's election spreads through the South, the echo comes back telling of a rising feeling in favor of secession and resistance."[71]

For months, the *Charleston Mercury* had been defiantly urging secession should the "Abolitionist" Lincoln win the White House. Now it bluntly proclaimed that his victory meant "disunion." The paper's firebrand owner, Robert Barnwell Rhett, was the quintessential Dixie-style politician-journalist, a onetime congressman and U.S. senator who emerged during the post-election period as the Deep South's preeminent agitator for separation. Rhett's was a formidable voice. Even the pro-Union *New York Illustrated News*, the youngest of the city's prospering picture weeklies, conceded of this "journalistic standard bearer of secession" that "his style combines both nerve and sinew." Now Rhett editorialized that the Southern states faced "the crisis of their fate," noting that "nothing is needed for our deliverance but that the ball of revolution be set in motion."[72] In this opinion, Rhett was not alone. A Georgia editorial similarly warned: "We have met the enemy, and they have conquered." And a Richmond paper likened Lincoln's election to "a declaration of war."[73]

In response, Raymond's cautious *Times* declared: "We are not surprised,— nor in the least alarmed,—at the symptoms of resentment and the movements toward secession which greet the news of Lincoln's victory in the Southern States." Dixie's angriest editors, he predicted, would certainly "denounce the Union and proclaim their determination to withdraw from its obligations. . . . But we have entire faith in the final subsidence of these waves of popular frenzy." Greeley, who republished the *Mercury*'s threat in his own paper just a few days after the election, similarly questioned the "unmistakable impress of haste—of passion—of distrust of the popular judgment." But he taunted all too dismissively that "the South could no more unite upon a scheme of secession than a company of lunatics could conspire to break out of bedlam."[74] Better that the Southern states leave the Union anyway, he insisted, than for the government to yield an inch on slavery. It was not the first or last time

Greeley and Raymond underestimated popular sentiment. Bennett proved no more prescient, but far cruder, when he complained that "nigger worship has ruined churches, ruined parties and now is ruining the whole country."[75]

In a way, Raymond's and Greeley's delusional overconfidence was understandable, because it was based in part on a professional assessment of their Southern counterparts' supposedly limited influence. The pro-secession press spoke loudly, but after all, the total circulation of all sixty-six daily newspapers in the future Confederate States of America remained comparatively tiny—little more than the combined readership of the *New York Herald* and *New York Tribune*—and could hardly wield as much influence, the Northern editors miscalculated, as their own papers. Greeley dismissed them as "silly gasconading journals."[76] Besides, Southern newspapers were far from unified in urging separation from the Union in the immediate aftermath of Lincoln's election. Yet in a breathtakingly short time, a matter of weeks, secession fever escalated into an epidemic, fanned by an increasingly radicalized Deep South press. As Greeley later described the situation, clinging to his view that the secession movement did not truly represent Southern sentiment, "a violent, unscrupulous, desperate minority . . . conspired to clutch power and wield it for ends which the overawed, gagged, paralyzed majority at heart condemn." Even Greeley admitted that "the 'sprinkle' swelled into a cascade, the cascade into a river, which inundated and reddened the whole breadth of our country."[77]

Although some Southern unionist publications tried for a time to stem the tide ("Is it wise so long to anticipate evils very likely never to come?" asked one North Carolina paper), the fire-eaters quickly overwhelmed the moderate voices. In the face of a growing public opinion avalanche, editors who preached restraint and patience were "miraculously" converted, or replaced at their posts by journalists committed to a more aggressive agenda, some even forcibly silenced.[78] For example, when one Corinth, Mississippi, editor tried cautioning against separation, he was "surrounded by infuriated rebels, his person threatened with violence, he was broken up and ruined forever, all for advocating the Union of our fathers."[79] The editor of the *Nashville Democrat*, which Greeley called "the best Union paper in Middle Tennessee," fled the city in terror, his wife forced to follow soon thereafter, "afraid that if she stayed after the election . . . she should not be able to escape at all."[80] Northern correspondents stationed in the South faced rude questioning from self-appointed "Vigilance Committees," and were routinely accused of fomenting slave insurrections and driven out of town. When one self-described "*attaché*" from the *New York Herald* arrived to cover the situation in Columbia, South Carolina, in December 1860, "an excited, vulgar, unruly, ignorant crowd" confronted him, forced him into a local doctor's office for questioning, tore through his belongings in search of incriminating documents, and peppered him with suspicious queries like: "Ain't you an abolitionist," and "Did you vote for Lincoln?" [81]

In the case of another menaced Unionist journal, the *Richmond Dispatch*, its editor tried only briefly to urge readers to "take time to consider" an appropriate response to the admitted "calamity" of Lincoln's election. Many Virginians, it argued, hoped and anticipated that the newly elected president would issue a statement of conciliation. When such assurances did not come quickly, the paper performed a sudden about-face and commenced urging that Virginians wait no longer for the president-elect to give "a sign," adding: "The outrage perpetuated is great, and cannot be wiped out by the failure of Lincoln to commit an 'overt act.'" [82] The Northern press was not alone in underestimating secession sentiment in the Deep South. Ohio journalist Donn Piatt believed that for far too long Lincoln himself felt the movement merely "a political game of bluff, gotten up by politicians, and meant solely to frighten the North." [83]

Defeated but unbowed, Stephen Douglas, heading home after his grueling campaign swing through the South, tried making one last appeal to Southern editors who had yet to succumb to secession fever. Writing from New Orleans, he insisted that "the mere election of any man to the Presidency by the American people, in accordance with the Constitution and the laws, does not itself furnish any just cause or reasonable ground for dissolving the Federal Union." [84] The comments appeared in the *Missouri Republican*—a Democratic paper—on November 17. They did little to stem disunion momentum in the Deep South.

On December 20, a convention at Charleston formally voted to take South Carolina out of the Union, the first state to secede. Remembering that the Palmetto State had tried leaving the Union once before, during the Jacksonian era, the *Tribune* calmly editorialized, "If she chooses to be without the advantages of the Union, which her sister States enjoy and will continue to enjoy, the loss is hers, and the advantages—so far as the saving of some heavy expense is concerned—are ours. . . . Only let the State continue to pay the regular duties on imports, and keep her hands off the [federal] Forts, and she can secede as long as she pleases." Once again, Greeley miscalculated secession fever, but another view of the crisis was taking shape at his newspaper as well: the editor was now preparing himself, and his readers, for the departure of the entire South, and without regret. "How far can secession go?" the paper asked on December 22, "and, second, if it should happen to be successful, is it not just possible that the North may feel disposed not to go over the ground a second time, even for the sake of bringing the seceders back again?" As Greeley later described his position, "the North could do without the South, and the South could do without the North."[85] Lincoln's two private secretaries maintained that Greeley's "damaging vagaries" encouraged the South "to hope for peaceable disunion." As a result, argued John Nicolay and John Hay, "the timid grew more despondent, the traitors bolder, and the crisis almost became a panic."[86]

James Gordon Bennett, by contrast, almost immediately understood that the South Carolina action represented "The Great Crisis of the Age," though he placed much of the blame on Northern antislavery Republicans. The *Herald* called on Lincoln, "if he understands his duty to his God and his country, and has the courage" to speak, to "declare himself independent of all factions, creeds, or partisan feelings of any sort," adding: "We want a President for the whole country—not for Vermont." Bennett could not resist taking a swipe at Republican journals in general, and Greeley in particular, for "grasping at straws" by suggesting that New York and New England could survive unscathed without the South. "The Massachusetts factories," argued Bennett fantastically, "with the aid of the South, merely give a living to their own population, far inferior to that which South Carolina gives her slaves."[87] At least Bennett grasped the importance of Union—even if only as a means of protecting local access to slave state trade.

Rhett's *Charleston Mercury* did not even wait until the morning after South Carolina secession to announce the momentous news of secession to its readers. On the very afternoon the convention reached its historic decision—within a breathtaking fifteen minutes, according to some accounts—the paper rushed out a single-sheet broadside extra proclaiming in supersized bold type: "THE UNION IS DISSOLVED." Only two hundred copies came off the press in its initial run, followed by another two hundred the following day—hardly enough to meet frenzied local demand for the souvenirs.[88] Yet

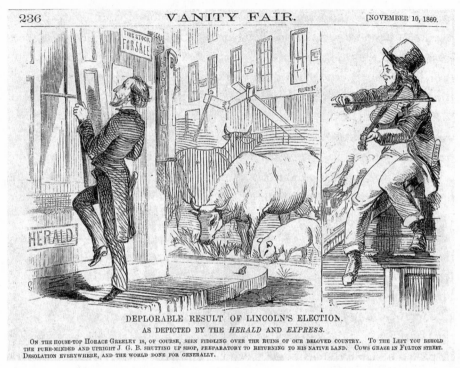

DEPLORABLE RESULT OF LINCOLN'S ELECTION.

AS DEPICTED BY THE *HERALD* AND *EXPRESS*.

ON THE HOUSE-TOP HORACE GREELEY IS, OF COURSE, SEEN FIDDLING OVER THE RUINS OF OUR BELOVED COUNTRY. TO THE LEFT YOU BEHOLD THE PURE-MINDED AND UPRIGHT J. G. B. SHUTTING UP SHOP, PREPARATORY TO RETURNING TO HIS NATIVE LAND. COWS GRAZE IN FULTON STREET. DESOLATION EVERYWHERE, AND THE WORLD DONE FOR GENERALLY.

In this post-election caricature from *Vanity Fair*, Greeley (right) greets Lincoln's election by "fiddling over the ruins of our beloved country," while Bennett (left), envisioning that New York would now become a wasteland, boards up the *Herald*.

rare as the broadside was even then—it instantly became a valuable collector's item—a local group calling itself the "Palmetto Boys of the Palmetto State" proved willing to part with one, dispatching a precious copy to President-elect Lincoln at Springfield, more as a defiant threat than a memento. In an attempt to "give the deed of a most malignant enemy the guise of a friendly act," one of his visitors observed, Lincoln tried assuring his worried eldest son that "it must have been intended for a Christmas gift." [89] It would not be the only anonymous warning to reach Lincoln during the dangerous interregnum between his November election and March inauguration.

Christmas found the defeated Stephen Douglas back in Washington, worrying no less than his successful presidential opponent that the Union they both loved might be on the brink of destruction. Total dissolution seemed more likely than ever once Mississippi, Florida, Alabama, Georgia, and Louisiana joined South Carolina by seceding in January and February—all expressing in their justifications an unwavering commitment to preserving and protecting the institution of slavery, which Lincoln's election, they insisted, threatened to destroy. As he had done so often during his long but, in the end, frustratingly disappointing political career, Lincoln's lifelong rival chose to express his concerns publicly through the press. In a long letter to his closest friend in journalism, Springfield editor Charles Lanphier, obviously meant for publication, Douglas poured out his fading hopes for compromise and peace. *"We can never acknowledge the right of a State to secede and cut us off from the Ocean and the world, without our consent,"* he began. Then, typically, he assumed his customary partisan tone to warn: "The fact can no longer be disguised that many of the Republican Leaders desire war & Disunion under pretext of saving the Union."

Like an old bantam rooster not quite ready to give up dominance over his flock, Douglas concluded: "I am for the Union, and hence am ready to make any reasonable sacrifice to save it."[90] By then, however, President-elect Lincoln had firmly decided that he would offer no gestures to mollify secessionists if they required compromise that would extend slavery westward. In the end, Douglas's warnings proved too little, too late. His plea appeared in print, but went unheeded. Few readers would have guessed that his desperate message to Charles Lanphier would also prove to be one of the last letters the exhausted Little Giant would ever write, to a journalist or to anyone else.[91]

CHAPTER NINE

Lincoln Will Not Talk with Anyone

Ignoring the growing clamor for reassurances that he posed no threat to slavery where it existed, Lincoln rigorously maintained his policy of "masterly inactivity" during the long wait between his election in November 1860 and his inauguration four months later in March 1861. This was the tense period known to history by Henry Adams's enduring descriptive phrase, the "Great Secession Winter," and it indeed grew into a season of frustrating discontent for journalists increasingly desperate for news from the president-elect.

Successfully resisting calls to conciliate the growing number of seceding states and their pro-slavery advocates in the press, Lincoln attempted to remain as invisible as he had made himself during the presidential campaign. But he also exercised strong behind-the-scenes leadership on two major priorities: enticing representatives of his diverse political coalition (and perhaps a few Southern Unionists) into his cabinet, and preventing unacceptable compromise by lame ducks and old fossils in Washington. When veteran leaders from North and South called for a Peace Convention devoted to finding compromise terms to end the crisis before the inauguration, Lincoln secretly but firmly instructed his closest allies in the capital to discourage any concessions on slavery extension. As he wrote Illinois senator Lyman Trumbull, "the tug has to come, & better now, than any time hereafter." [1] Meanwhile Lincoln publicly occupied himself by welcoming to Springfield cabinet aspirants like Edward Bates and Salmon Chase.

For a man pledged to say nothing new and controversial, especially to newspapermen, Lincoln nevertheless managed to maintain a lively and skillful correspondence with influential editors during the Secession Winter. Not all of them earned the courtesy of a reply—at least as far as we know, for only a handful of responses have survived—but that did not inhibit dozens from sharing their unsolicited views with him, particularly when it came to recommending candidates for patronage spoils.

The editor of the *Philadelphia Evening Bulletin*, for example, wrote to endorse Pennsylvania's controversial Simon Cameron for a cabinet post. The proprietors of several Minnesota papers wrote in behalf of Stephen Miller as the state's "unanimous choice" for surgeon general, a recommendation endorsed a month later by the pioneering woman editor Jane Grey Swisshelm of the *St. Cloud Journal*. The proprietors of the *Kingston* (New York) *Journal*, the *Rockford* (Illinois) *Forum*, and the *Toledo Blade* all proposed judicial candidates, while the editor of the *Wisconsin State Journal* urged Lincoln to name William P. Dole as commissioner of Indian Affairs (he did).[2]

Other editors were less specific in their expectations. One Ohio journalist asked only that a friend get "a position in one of the Departments at Washington, or elsewhere." A newspaperman from downstate Illinois wanted "any favor you may do" for a "fellow citizen."[3] Lincoln's German newspaper partner Theodore Canisius asked that an old Alton friend be named consul to Liverpool, based only on his "energetic" labors in behalf "of the republican party and especially of Mr. Lincoln."[4] Similar pleas arrived from newspapermen from San Jose, California, to Oneida, New York—and inevitably from both Greeley and Raymond, who wrote in February and March to urge appointing, respectively, favored candidates for surveyor of the Port of New York and American consul in Le Havre. Prematurely, but flatteringly, Raymond addressed each of his letters to "The President."[5]

Where policy matters were concerned, Lincoln continued to resist committing his views to writing lest they be published and misconstrued. And soon enough such concerns were validated when various newspapers either misunderstood or deliberately misinterpreted his position on slavery. From his cramped temporary office at the Illinois State Capitol, Lincoln did begin crafting the occasional confidential letter to keep important but anxious editors informed and in line. On one such occasion, late in November, he wrote

Raymond to complain when a conciliatory post-election speech by Senator Lyman Trumbull failed to garner positive coverage in Republican newspapers, and worse, had been misunderstood in the opposition's. "Has a single newspaper, heretofore against us, urged that speech [on readers] with a purpose to quiet public anxiety?" asked a frustrated Lincoln. "Not one, so far as I know. On the contrary the Boston Courier and its' [sic] class, hold me responsible for the speech"—true enough, for he had drafted part of Trumbull's statement— "and endeavor to inflame the North with the belief that it foreshadows an abandonment of Republican ground by the incoming administration; while the Washington Constitution, and its' [sic] class hold the same speech up to the South as an open declaration of war against them."[6]

Northern editors were not shy about sharing advice. John D. Defrees of the *Indianapolis Atlas*—who served also as the powerful chairman of the Indiana State Republican Committee—warned Lincoln in December that "secession feeling (tho' not so extensive as the newspaper accounts make it) exists to a much greater extent than the people of the West are willing to believe possible." But when Defrees suggested that Republicans respond by endorsing what he called "genuine popular sovereignty to the people of our Territories—not the Douglas sham," Lincoln shot down the objectionable idea. "I am sorry any republican inclines to dally with Pop. Sov. of any sort," he lectured Defrees. "It acknowledges that slavery has equal rights with liberty, and surrenders all we have contended for."[7] Defrees's wavering did not prevent Lincoln from considering the influential editor for the position of U.S. Government Printer.

Shortly before Christmas, Horace Greeley wrote a long policy letter of his own in an attempt to clarify his maddening insistence that while no state "can secede at pleasure from the Union, any more than a stave may secede from a cask of which it is a component part," if "seven or eight contiguous States (not one small one) were to come to Washington saying: 'We are tired of the Union—let us out!' I should say, 'There's the door—go!'" Worried about Lincoln's safety on his upcoming inaugural journey, Greeley also urged the president-elect to travel south via pro-Union Wheeling, and "with a very strong force."[8] Lincoln held his tongue. Writing to his sweetheart, a New York reader named George Peckham observed: "Lincoln seems quite conservative in his views which I am glad to see—but Greeley is doing his best to make trouble—your Wide Awake friends will find him out some day."[9]

Just before South Carolinians met for their secession convention in December 1860, the president-elect did, however, write to Greeley's newspaper rival Thurlow Weed to share his views on the constitutionality of secession— or lack of it—remarkably enough marking the first time Lincoln ever commented on the inflammatory but crucial subject. As Lincoln put it, "no state can, in any way lawfully, get out of the Union." Lincoln sent another note to the *Courier and Enquirer*'s James Watson Webb to assure him that he also opposed abandoning federal installations in the hostile South. "I think we should hold the forts, or take them," he confided in a letter marked as private, "as the case may be." And when William Cullen Bryant advised Lincoln to resist Weed's efforts to promote Seward for the cabinet, the president-elect ambiguously replied: "I promise you that I shall unselfishly try to deal fairly with all men and all shades of opinion among our friends." The strain showing, he added: "I can only say I shall have a great deal of trouble, [and] do the best I can." [10]

More newspaper advice arrived when Nathaniel Paschall, editor of the pro-Democratic *Missouri Republican*, implored Lincoln anew to make a conciliatory statement to Southerners. In response, the president-elect reminded Paschall that the Southern press already had access to all the assurances they needed: "I could say nothing which I have not already said, and which is in print and accessible to the public," Lincoln insisted. "Please pardon me for suggesting that if the papers, like yours, which heretofore have persistently garbled, and misrepresented what I have said, will now fully and fairly place it before their readers, there can be no further misunderstanding." [11]

Lincoln reacted even more indignantly when during the same mid-December period, Henry Raymond forwarded a letter he had received from Colonel William C. Smedes, whom he described as "an able, wealthy, influential gentleman of Mississippi." Smedes regarded Lincoln as "disastrous" for Southern Unionists like himself, believing "he is pledged to the extinction of slavery, holds the black man to be the equal of the white, & stigmatizes our whole people as immoral & unchristian." The allegedly moderate Smedes did not mince words. "I would regard death by a stroke of lightning to Mr Lincoln as but a just punishment from an offended Deity," he fumed, particularly because of "his infamous & unpatriotic avowals . . . made on the presentation of a pitcher by some free negroes to Gov. [Salmon] Chase." According to the Mississippian, Lincoln had committed the egregious sin of appearing at a racially integrated public event honoring the Ohio politician. A baffled Raymond hoped that Lincoln would at least "find time to say a word about the *silver pitcher speech*" to help the editor craft his own "comments on these matters" should a response become necessary. In Raymond's opinion, "Union men at the South *stand in need of backing* . . . and it seems to me important that we should open the door for them as wide as the hinges will let it swing."[12]

Instead, Lincoln, who had never attended any event like the one Smedes described, exploded in rage over the charge. "What a very mad-man your correspondent, Smedes is," he fumed in an attempt to kill the story before it gained traction. Assuming the third person to provide Raymond with the text of a formal denial if required, he added stiffly: "Mr. Lincoln is not pledged to the ultimate extinctinction [sic] of slavery; does not hold the black man to be the equal of the white, unqualifiedly as Mr. S. states it; and never did stigmatize their white people as immoral & unchristian; and Mr. S. can not prove one of his assertions true." Moreover, as Lincoln added for good measure, he was "never in a meeting of negroes in my life; and never saw a pitcher presented by anybody to anybody." A few weeks later, after Mississippi seceded, Smedes justified Lincoln's outrage by writing him directly to gloat: "The union of these American States is actually dissolved. . . . You will be installed President over a part only of the 'United States.'"[13]

Despite this troubling exchange, which exposed the perils inherent in either replying to or ignoring newspaper comments, Lincoln continued to share his thoughts with newspapermen only rarely, and almost always confidentially. On the other hand, he occasionally met in person with the prominent editors who journeyed to Springfield in the teeth of winter determined to see and influence him. Thurlow Weed was the first to invite himself, two weeks after the *Herald* prematurely declared: "Poor Weed. His glory is departed— his metal is broken—his pride is humbled—his self reliance is gone—the air of conscious superiority no longer graces him." In fact, Lincoln not only welcomed but encouraged the visit of the "prince of the New York lobbyists." As one of Lincoln's closest confidants had alerted Weed in advance: "Mr. Lincoln would be very glad to see you. . . . Your coming to Springfield may make newspaper talk, but he says he don't care for that, if you don't."[14] Weed used his visit to press Seward's claim to a cabinet post, and also urged the president-elect to nominate Southerners to fill other high positions—in addition to Greeley's onetime convention choice, Edward Bates, whom Lincoln had already resolved to appoint.

By December, however, following several unsuccessful overtures to Upper

South ex-Whigs, Lincoln concluded that he could not invite other Southerners into the cabinet after all. Not surprisingly, he provided his explanation in his long-accustomed manner: through a thinly disguised anonymous editorial in the *Illinois State Journal.* There is no doubt of its authorship; a surviving draft in Lincoln's hand proves that the president-elect crafted the opinion himself:

> We see such frequent allusion to a supposed purpose on the part of Mr. Lincoln to call into his cabinet two or three Southern gentlemen, from the parties opposed to him politically, that we are prompted to ask a few questions.
>
> 1st. Is it known that any such gentlemen of character, would accept a place in the cabinet?
>
> 2—If yea, on what terms? Does he surrender to Mr. Lincoln, or Mr. Lincoln to him, on the political difference between them? Or do they enter upon the administration in open opposition to each other?
>
> What is the understanding on these questions?[15]

The editorial—"known to have emanated directly from the President elect," the *New York Herald* reported, and published for the first time in his "recognized organ"—had its desired effect. It ended all talk of further Southern representation in the cabinet, though it left vexingly open the unanswered calls for compromise.[16] That issue came to the forefront again at the end of the year, when Lincoln agreed to sit down with yet another journalistic powerhouse, his old acquaintance, sixty-nine-year-old Duff Green. At outgoing president James Buchanan's behest, the onetime Jacksonian—Lincoln's old Washington "landlord" from back in his congressional days—showed up in Springfield determined to convince his fellow Kentuckian (and distant relative by marriage) to reconsider his resistance to further conciliation.[17] The famously blunt Green quickly got down to business: he wanted Lincoln to put something in writing to endorse a constitutional amendment that would guarantee the survival—and potentially the expansion—of slavery in return for an end to the secession movement. What was more, Green proposed dramatically carrying such a letter to Washington himself. This put Lincoln in a bind. Although Duff Green was past his prime as a power broker, he was a hard man to refuse; besides, he still counted many admirers, particularly in the Border Slave States whose Union loyalties Lincoln wanted to ensure, Kentucky first among them. So the president-elect complied with the request—after a fashion.

Two key Western editors who unsuccessfully urged Lincoln to clarify his policies before the inauguration: Indiana's John Defrees (left), who received a plum patronage job in the administration; and Kentuckian Duff Green (right), who abandoned the Union and supported the Confederacy.

"Gen. Duff Green is out here endeavoring to draw a letter out of me," Lincoln reported to Senator Lyman Trumbull on December 28. "I have written one." The text turned out to be almost exactly what Green hoped for. While it expressed Lincoln's Whiggish aversion toward constitutional amendments of any kind, it conceded that the American people deserved "a fair opportunity of expressing their will" regarding slavery compromise. Lincoln went even further on another volatile issue, renouncing any "lawless invasion, by armed force, of the soil of any State or Territory, no matter under what pretext, as the gravest of crimes" (a pledge he would later forgo). But rather than hand this potentially explosive statement to the volatile Green, Lincoln instead mailed it off to Senator Lyman Trumbull in Washington, instructing him to withhold it from the public if "you conclude that it may do us harm." The strategy worked. The sentiments remained unpublished, but the mere crafting of them had been enough to get Green out of Springfield before he could communicate any damaging complaints to the press. Only later did the outmaneuvered veteran editor tell Lincoln: "I regret your unwillingness to recommend an amendment to the constitution which will arrest the progress of secession." [18]

Since news of his recent visit had already appeared in print, Green now issued a threat: "I have deemed it expedient to publish a statement which will probably appear in the N.Y. Herald of tomorrow . . . framed as to give no offence to you." Green's statement appeared as promised, and proved benign, almost admiring. The *Herald* reported that Green "speaks of Lincoln with much respect, and believes that he sincerely wishes to administer the government in such manner as to satisfy the South." Green did add that Lincoln believed "secession is rebellion, and is resolved to use force to suppress and punish it." Only at the end of this long interview did Green assign blame for the crisis squarely on the North, insisting: "All that the South demands is their equal rights within the Union, or independence out of it." Once again, Lincoln's deft press manipulation had averted a political catastrophe. As for Green, he ultimately pledged his loyalty to the South and spent most of the war wisely, but futilely, urging the Confederacy to industrialize.[19]

Lincoln might not have survived the interregnum with his political power and personal following intact had it not been for a most unlikely source of reassurance: James Gordon Bennett's always unpredictable *New York Herald*. In mid-November, his pocketbook as deep as ever, and his eye as always focused on increasing circulation, Bennett assigned his German-born reporter Henry (born Heinrich) Villard, a disappointed onetime Seward backer, to plant himself in Springfield and provide regular dispatches to New York on the president-elect's activities.

Villard arrived in town expecting to dislike Lincoln. Indeed, he had privately admitted that he did not comprehend how such an "uncouth, common Illinois politician" had triumphed over Seward, a man he believed "the foremost figure" in the nation.[20] Over the next three months, however, the young correspondent's almost daily dispatches grew in warmth and appreciation. Before long, Villard was sympathetically conveying the brave and resolute manner in which Lincoln was bearing the burdens of a challenging period marked by treason and disunion on an unprecedented scale. More than any other journalist of his time, Villard constructed key pillars of what would emerge after the Civil War as part of the Lincoln legend: the beleaguered man of patience, wisdom, and unfailing humor.

Revolted as he was at first by the spectacle of "importunate office-seekers" crowding the hallways outside Lincoln's office in quest of self-advancement, Villard came to appreciate his ability to "submit to this tribulation." The journalist marveled at the president-elect's unique way of pleasing almost all visitors with his sometimes "grotesque joviality," for as Villard discovered,

Lincoln had a funny story for almost every caller, and "it would be hard to find one who tells better jokes, enjoys them better and laughs oftener than Abraham Lincoln."[21] As Villard reported, Lincoln learned to juggle a constant stream of visitors, mail, sittings for artists, and the vexing challenges of building a cabinet and scuttling the secession movement—all without making statements for the public record. "The idea that the President elect takes all visiting scribblers of more or less obscurity into his heart and makes them the repositories of his mind is so preposterous," Villard wrote on December 8, "that none but the greenest of their readers should be taken in with it. . . . The truth is that Mr. Lincoln has not talked and will not talk with anyone." Yet after a while, Villard emerged as Lincoln's voice, or at least the best reflection of his future policies. "I venture to say," the *Herald* correspondent accurately predicted in late January, "that one of the first acts of his administration will be to reinforce Fort Sumter should Major Anderson and his gallant band be found still holding out" at the federal garrison in Charleston Harbor.[22]

Although Villard never earned a byline for his copy, the stories themselves achieved enormous circulation. Because the *Herald* was contractually obligated to share its reports with other members of the Associated Press, Villard's dispatches often ended up published—sometimes on the same day as the *Herald* ran them—on the pages of the rival *New York Times*, the daily published by a man Bennett still derided as "Little Raymond."[23] For three full months, until February 1861, Villard operated as the only reporter in the nation regularly covering Abraham Lincoln—uniquely privy to exclusives, and well positioned to provide material for many newspapers at once. He was a one-man press pool. As Cincinnati correspondent Murat Halstead testified, "I know that the President regarded him with a warm affection."[24]

It is easy to understand why. By mid-December Villard was admitting: "Having closely observed him since the election, and well noted the impressions left upon him by the secession phases of the present imbroglio, I dare say that there are dormant qualities in 'Old Abe' which occasion will draw forth, develope [*sic*] and remind people to a certain degree of the characteristics of 'Old Hickory.'" Villard became convinced that Lincoln "honestly means to sink the man in the public officer, the partisan in the patriot, the republican in the faithful executor and protector of the federal laws in every state of the republic."[25]

If Villard never stopped objecting to the amount of time Lincoln was forced to devote to patronage matters, he surely came to the eventual realization that among those reaping the greatest rewards were fellow journalists. John L. Scripps, for example, whose principal qualification for office was the authorship of his 1860 Lincoln campaign biography, secured appointment as postmaster of Chicago at an annual salary of $1,500. Joseph Lewis of the pro-Republican *Chester County* (Pennsylvania) *Times*—remembered (at least by Lincoln) as the first newspaperman to publish a campaign life— was named commissioner of internal revenue. And yet another journalist-turned-biographer, Joseph Barrett of the *Cincinnati Commercial*, became commissioner of pensions.

Henry Villard of the *New York Herald* filed dispatches on Lincoln from Springfield throughout the 1860–1861 Secession Winter. His respect for the president-elect grew with each report.

New York journalist Henry Bowen, who helped organize Lincoln's visit to Cooper Union, eventually won appointment as a revenue collector in Brooklyn. New Haven editor James F. Babcock, who had hosted Lincoln during his post–Cooper Union speaking tour through New England, secured the coveted job of collector of the Port of New Haven, and newspaper veteran George Fogg, who had looked after Robert Lincoln during his terms at Exeter, became minister to Switzerland. Other diplomatic posts went to Rufus King of the *Milwaukee Sentinel* (minister to Rome), W. S. Thayer of the *New York Evening Post* (consul to Alexandria), and Rufus Hosmer of the *Michigan Republican* (Consul to Frankfort). Postmasters' jobs went to Peter Foy of the *Missouri Democrat*, A. W. Campbell of the *Wheeling Democrat*, George Dawson of the *Albany Evening Journal*, and to staff members of the *Dayton Daily Journal*, *Cleveland Leader*, and *Buffalo Times*.

At Thurlow Weed's urging, *New York Evening Post* assistant editor John Bigelow became American consul in Paris, an appointment enthusiastically welcomed by U.S. Minister-designate William Dayton, who wanted "a gentleman accustomed to the use of the pen." [26] The long-loyal William Bailhache of the *Illinois State Journal* aspired successfully to an army quartermaster's post. Another onetime editor, Connecticut's Gideon Welles (founder of the *Hartford Times*), got the biggest plum for New England: appointment to the cabinet as secretary of the navy. And despite Lincoln's qualms about his integrity, Pennsylvania publisher-turned-politician Simon Cameron became secretary of war. And then there was that German first among equals, Theodore Canisius.

Few newspapers produced as many presidential appointees as the *New York Tribune*. James E. Harvey became minister to Portugal, while James S. Pike won the post of minister to The Hague, and the paper's former business manager, Thomas McElrath, earned a prestigious place at the Customs House. With rumors continuing to swirl around Horace Greeley's own ambitions for political reward, the *Herald*'s Frederic Hudson wickedly observed that "it became the talk in newspaper circles that the *Tribune* would be depleted of its writers in consequence of the necessity of the new administration for suitable men to send abroad as ministers, *chargé d'affaires*, and consuls." Greeley huffily maintained that no "appointment of any correspondent of the *Tribune* to any 'clerkship' or other office at Washington was either sought, desired, or acquiesced in by us, and, if any such infidelity to our service has existed, it must have been very rare." The numbers argued otherwise. As the *Philadelphia Argus* smirked in February, "The black-republican papers are quarreling like cats and dogs over the prospective spoils at Washington."[27] Not that such rewards to friendly journalists were unusual or unexpected. In the South, journalist John B. Jones, who had once labored on a John Tyler campaign extra, soon found himself happily recruited to serve as a clerk in the Confederate War Department.[28]

That is not to say that every ambitious pro-Republican journalist received immediate or automatic spoils from Lincoln. One example was the twenty-five-year-old newspaperman William Stoddard, who later claimed distinction as the first editor to endorse Lincoln for the presidency—disputed by some historians since—in the *Central Illinois Gazette* in May 1859, just a month following Lincoln's informal first visit to his office. After the election, Stoddard worked assiduously to win a job on the future president's staff, visiting Lincoln in Springfield to press his case, and then, when he heard nothing further about an appointment, writing in frustration to the president-elect's law partner, William Herndon: "Should he honor me with his confidence I will set about the duties of my office with a degree of enthusiastic pride in their performance. . . . I have reason to fear that I shall really need some position—

you know how lucrative a business editing a country weekly is." Admitting
that his request was "bold, even presumptuous," Stoddard offered "to begin"
the job "'on trial,' as the Dutchman took his wife." [29] Still, Stoddard did not
secure a Washington post until July 1861—and then had to settle for appointment to the staff of the Interior Department, though on permanent loan
to the executive mansion to sign presidential land patents. The White House
budget would not allow for three private secretaries. (Eventually Stoddard
took charge of the president's correspondence, and went on to write a shelf of
books about his experiences as Lincoln's so-called third secretary.)

Lincoln also balked when the *Illinois State Journal*'s Edward L. Baker
recommended their "mutual friend" Harrison Fitzhugh as commissioner of
public buildings. It was not only that Fitzhugh hailed from Springfield, which
in the president-elect's view needed no further representation in Washington,
but because Lincoln suspected that his wife, Mary, who would have to work
closely with the next commissioner on White House maintenance matters,
might "object" to the appointment (in fact she favored someone else). As a
matter of fairness, Lincoln generally showed a reluctance to award fellow
Illinoisans. So much so that by January 1861 the *Chicago Tribune*'s Joseph
Medill angrily predicted that "there will not be one *original Lincoln* man in
the cabinet," only "competitors and enemies." The embittered editor, who
had expected to wield more influence on the incoming chief executive, wrote
to his partners: "Thank heaven we own and control the Tribune. We made
Abe and by G—we can *unmake* him." [30]

Before departing from Springfield to assume the presidency, Lincoln secluded
himself in a second-floor storeroom above his brother-in-law's dry goods shop
on Springfield's Capitol Square, and there began hammering out a draft of
his forthcoming inaugural address—a speech that had assumed enormous
importance in part owing to Lincoln's protracted pre-inaugural silence. The
date he began writing was February 4, 1861.

His self-imposed isolation proved impossible to sustain. On the very same
day he began turning his attention to what he knew would be the most widely
scrutinized oration of his career, the "Old Gentlemen's" Peace Convention
formally gaveled into order in Washington to propose its own set of Union-
preserving compromises before Lincoln could take office. Halfway across the
country, meanwhile, representatives from the six of the first seven seceded

states convened in Montgomery, Alabama, to create the Confederate States of America, electing Jefferson Davis as its first president. Lincoln could not help but take serious notice of both developments, as they were breathlessly reported the following morning in the Springfield and Chicago newspapers.

Real distraction arrived the next day, February 5, when Horace Greeley barreled into Springfield, ostensibly to deliver a previously scheduled nonpolitical lecture, "America West of the Mississippi." The town seemed to hold its collective breath in anticipation of fireworks likely to ignite at the one-time Edward Bates delegate's inevitable reunion with Lincoln. The tension only increased when the editor failed to present himself as expected at the president-elect's headquarters. A standoff ensued. "He stood on his dignity and awaited the approach of Mr. Lincoln, instead of approaching," Henry Villard acidly observed in a *Herald* article entitled "The Tribune Philosopher in Springfield." As Villard reported: "During the entire morning and a portion of the afternoon . . . Horace sat in his room in patient expectation of seeing the gaunt Presidential form loom up in his door." [31]

Never a stickler for protocol, Lincoln broke the impasse at around 4 P.M. and strolled over to call on the editor at his hotel. "What a sight the meeting of these two awkward and homely, but remarkable personages, must have afforded," Villard speculated. "What a treat to have listened to their exchange of advice and opinion, unrestrained as that must have been, from their common, characteristic, frank bluntness." In a more serious vein, even without access to the summit, Villard reported that "Greeley urged a strict adherence to an anti-compromise policy and is said to have received gratifying assurances. His opinion as to Cabinet and other appointments were freely solicited." All that Greeley's own *New York Tribune* ever provided its readers about the summit was a brief item coyly reporting: "A friend who has just had a prolonged and confidential interview with Mr. Lincoln, at Springfield, writes us that Mr. L. *is invariably opposed to all Compromises, no matter in what sense.*" [32] Whether Greeley or Lincoln also addressed the renewed whispers that Greeley indeed wanted a place in the cabinet, perhaps as postmaster general, no one knows.

Not content with conveying the Greeley sighting straightforwardly, the *Herald* followed up a few days later with an editorial crowing that the "Spruce street philosopher" was to be "left out in the cold" in his quest for influence. "The other day," Bennett snarled, "Greeley resolved to combine business with pleasure, and pick up a few dollars by a lecture in St. Louis. He started for that city, but, hearing that it was probable the Missourians would mob him, he turned tail and commenced running for dear life with the old white coat streaming out behind. . . . Where he is now we cannot say—probably he has not yet stopped in his 'wild career.' " [33]

None of these reports conveyed what surely weighed most heavily on Greeley's mind during his visit: the latest humiliation in the editor's long and fruitless quest to achieve high office. It was no wonder that he had locked himself in his hotel room. On the very day he arrived in Springfield, the New York state legislature convened in Albany to choose a successor to Senator William Seward, who had signaled his willingness to become Lincoln's secretary of state. And Greeley knew by the time he arrived in Springfield that absent a last-minute political miracle, he seemed destined for defeat yet again. Declining to lobby legislators personally, Greeley insisted: "I have expressed no wish but that the best man shall be put forward," even though he knew that the man he judged "best"—himself—was unlikely to prevail.[34]

For weeks, Greeley had inspired serious consideration in the race for Seward's seat, though he might have accurately assessed his slim chances by confiding that his candidacy worried "the Fire-Eaters who have been taught to believe me a decidedly vicious and dangerous Negro."[35] In fact, the decision turned on politics, not principle. Regarding Greeley's election with no less dread than did the South, Thurlow Weed and his supporters plotted to repay him for his disloyalty to Seward by promoting antislavery attorney William M. Evarts for the seat (while claiming "without doubt" that Weed "could have been elected himself" had he chosen to enter the race).[36]

Lincoln, who wanted no part of this latest reopening of the long-running Seward-Greeley feud, tried staying aloof from the process. Then, a Westchester County legislator named Benjamin F. Camp (who happened to be a *Tribune* stockholder) began whispering, after returning east from his own visit to Lincoln in Springfield, that the president-elect in fact preferred Greeley for the Senate and, what was more, wanted the editor to take control of all federal patronage in the Empire State. A livid Weed promptly wrote to Lincoln to complain that Camp was misrepresenting him "abominably," and that his "falsehoods" would almost certainly fool "some who are sharp for office & credulous." Weed simultaneously warned Lincoln advisor David Davis: "If Greeley gets into the Senate it will be because members are made to believe that Mr Lincoln desires it!" Davis in turn urged the president-elect "to set yourself right in this matter" and dispatch a message to Weed confirming his neutrality. Striving to keep all of New York state's leading Republican editors at bay, Lincoln wrote Weed on February 4 to confess that he had indeed expressed "kindness towards Mr. Greely" to Camp, "which I really feel, but with an express protest that my name *must* not be used in the Senatorial election, in favor of, or against any one. Any other representation of me, is a misrepresentation."[37]

By the time the message reached Weed, New York state's 115 Republican legislators had already caucused to consider a Senate nominee. For all the opposition mounted against him, Greeley came agonizingly close to victory. On the first three ballots taken on February 2, he and Evarts took turns leading the pack of candidates (with Henry Raymond earning one or two symbolic protest votes on each round). By the fourth roll call, Greeley took a slight lead, 43–41, with the jowly Albany jurist Ira Harris suddenly emerging from the pack of also-rans with 22 supporters. But the *Tribune* editor failed to win an outright majority on ballot six, and again began trading leads with Evarts on subsequent roll calls. Greeley's widest margin opened after the eighth inconclusive ballot: 47 votes for the editor, to 39 for Evarts and 19 for Harris—still no majority for any candidate.

Then, just before the ninth roll call, Weed dramatically instructed his loyalists to switch candidates, and Harris suddenly surged into the lead over Greeley 49–46, with all but 12 legislators abandoning Evarts in a blatant effort to stop the *Tribune* editor. The move succeeded. On the tenth and decisive ballot, Judge Harris won an absolute majority—60 votes to Greeley's 49—and the caucus moved to make his selection unanimous. Since Republicans held an absolute majority in the State Assembly and Senate and planned to vote for senator as a bloc, the caucus results all but guaranteed that Harris would be chosen by the full legislature when the formal election took place on February 5. Calling the outcome "patriotic," Raymond crowed that while many Republican legislators "cherished feelings for a favorite editor," they "disapproved of his secession sentiments, and were unwilling to trust him with a seat in the United States Senate."[38]

Putting a brave face on its editor's defeat, the *Tribune* hailed Harris (while Greeley remained on the road) as "an uncompromising friend of the principles which triumphed in the recent Presidential contest." The *New York Times*, on the other hand, bluntly reported that "friends of the State are consoled that Mr. Greeley was not nominated," predicting that the "Tribune will discover, in our opinion, ere long, that while the Republicans of the State appreciate fully the zeal and fervor which it brings to the advocacy of Republican principles, they are not prepared to join in its denunciations of Gov. Seward or its exultations over Mr. Weed." [39]

Rubbing salt into the defeated candidate's stinging wounds, the *Herald* editorialized: "Alas! poor Greeley, after all he has done and suffered for the republican party, is thrown overboard in the republican caucus at Albany. This is most ungrateful. No man has contributed so much to the party's success. He has turned his old white coat inside out and outside in half a dozen times to serve it." Labeling the unresolved Greeley-Weed rift as "The Irrepressible Conflict in the Black Republican Party," Bennett reported that Greeley was "so angry at his defeat for the Senatorship that he has made up his mind to 'devote his paper to the amiable purpose of breaking up the republican party or of turning it into an abolition party' "—a charge meant to further isolate Greeley as a radical. At least acknowledging the challenge facing "Old Abe" due to "rows among his friends and the machinations of his enemies," Bennett described the president-elect as "about the most unfortunate individual out of jail on the face of the earth." [40] By then, Lincoln must have agreed.

Undeterred by his latest rebuke, Greeley managed to compose a detailed three-page letter to Lincoln the very day after their Springfield meeting, declaring afresh that he wanted "nothing for myself," but insisting that the "anti Weed Republicans" of New York simply had to be satisfied in the matter of federal jobs, especially "in view of Mr. Seward's position in the cabinet." With breathtaking arrogance, Greeley proposed that the incoming president actually make a list of all "the offices local to New York and of such share of the Foreign and Washington appointments as may be fairly apportioned to our state," and then indicate which jobs he wanted to assign of his "own volition." The remainder would then be chosen alternately by Greeley and Weed factions one by one "till the list is completed." And then, Greeley promised, "you may dispose of New York at a single sitting and avoid the bitter heart burnings which are likely to follow any presumption that one side or the other has the dispensing of Federal patronage in our State."

To this scheme Greeley added a postscript identifying several favorites—including his indiscreet ally Benjamin Camp of Westchester—whom he wanted rewarded even before the "list" was prepared. In a final stroke of audacity, Greeley offered a self-serving account of recent political history by reminding Lincoln that in his view, "we took the course which led to your nomination." [41] Even so, Greeley continued to insist: "There is no office in the gift of the Government or of the People which I either hope, wish, or expect ever to hold." [42] It was finally possible to believe that Horace Greeley's own political ambitions were dead at last.

Somehow, Lincoln found time amid this latest political brawl to finish what he proudly called the "First Edition" of his inaugural speech. Then he quietly brought his handwritten manuscript to the offices of the *Illinois State Journal* and there asked general manager William Bailhache to do what he had done so often over the years (with varying degrees of accuracy): to typeset his speech so it could be read easily in public. The editor printed twenty copies, one each for "the gentlemen Lincoln had selected as members of his Cabinet," and others for his "Presidential advisers." [43] Bailhache proved his usefulness in other ways as well. At around this time, he complained editorially that the sectional conflict was worsening because so few Southern readers enjoyed access to Northern newspapers. "The people of the South do not know us," the *Journal* pointed out. "They are not allowed to read Republican papers down there." [44] The implication—insupportable, of course—was that if exposed to their news columns, Southerners might actually relent on secession. The next best thing to exerting influence, perhaps, was serving as official presidential typesetter and printer of the inaugural message.

Aside from Bailhache, Lincoln told only his private secretary about the secret endeavor. It was John Nicolay who testified that Bailhache gave "a trusty compositor" a "case of type, locked himself in a room of the Journal office, and remained there until the document was set up, the necessary proofs taken, and the form secure in the office safe until Mr. Lincoln could correct and revise the proofs." [45] Lincoln proceeded to review the first result, make corrections, and return it to Bailhache for a second printing, repeating the process one more time, and finally leaving the office with a third edition, eight printed pages long. Lincoln asked Bailhache to run off about a dozen copies so he could distribute texts to friends for their comments. [46]

"Perfect secrecy was maintained," Nicolay proudly remembered, "perfect faith was kept. Only the persons authorized knew that the work was being done." After Lincoln left the sparely furnished, perpetually cluttered newspaper office—for the last time in his life—with inaugural address in hand, employees emptied the type racks containing his inaugural speech, leaving no record of their effort. With that, Lincoln's lifelong relationship with the *Journal* finally ended, just as his greatest challenge, from political, military, and journalistic forces alike, was set to begin.

On February 9, Henry Villard reported that Lincoln would be departing his hometown for Washington within "three times twenty-four hours." The *Herald*'s wise and hardworking young Springfield correspondent summed up Lincoln's future this way: "A more enviable, but at the same time more delicate and hazardous lot than that accorded to Abraham Lincoln never fell to any member of this nation. The path he is about to walk on may lead to success, glory, immortality, but also to failure, humiliation, and curses upon his memory."[47]

"Mr. Lincoln leaves for Washington this morning for the purpose of assuming the position of President of the United States." So the *Illinois State Journal* reported with uncharacteristic restraint in a brief item published on February 11, 1861. After covering Abraham Lincoln's farewell remarks at the Springfield railroad station at eight o'clock that morning, the paper added more expansively: "We have known Mr. Lincoln for many years; we have heard him speak upon a hundred different occasions; but we never saw him so profoundly affected, nor did he ever utter an address which seemed to us as full of simple and touching eloquence, so exactly adopted to the occasion, so worthy of the man and the hour."[48]

Ironically Lincoln's impromptu parting words—punctuated by his closing lamentation, "Friends, one and all, I must now bid you an affectionate farewell"—might never have achieved their reputation for sublimity had the *Journal* version of the address, transcribed on the platform in a cold drizzle and rushed into print for the next day's edition, endured as the sole record of his remarks. It very nearly did. Astonishingly, after all his years of attentiveness to reporters, Lincoln failed on that historic morning to alert the correspondents scheduled to travel with him to Washington that he intended to speak publicly before his departure. A day earlier, in fact, he had specifically notified them that he would say "nothing warranting their attention" when he left town.[49] So it happened that before the president-elect boarded his special train, the largest pack of journalists ever to cover an inaugural journey crowded into their assigned seats early to get out of the rain, unaware that Lincoln would pause outside the caboose, doff his hat, and address some final thoughts to his neighbors after all—out of their hearing.

Of course Henry Villard of the *Herald* was part of that press contingent, by now well established as the reporter who knew Lincoln best. Joining the corps as well were Joseph Howard, Jr., of the *New York Times*, O. H. Dutton of Greeley's *Tribune*, and T. C. Evans of the *New York World*, all recently arrived in Springfield so they could leave town with the incoming president and travel with his party to the capital. The *Chicago Tribune* assigned Henry M. Smith, the *Cincinnati Gazette* sent W. G. Terrell, the *Philadelphia Inquirer* dispatched Uriah Hunt Painter, and *Frank Leslie's Illustrated Newspaper* credentialed its talented sketch artist Henri Lovie. Other papers would not be deprived of firsthand reports. Determined to miss no detail of what promised to be a dramatic cross-country journey, the Associated Press sent no fewer than five correspondents: J. R. Drake, S. D. Page, J. H. A. Bone, A. W. Griswold, and Theodore Stager. Deputy presidential secretary John Hay, who had continued to file pro-Lincoln dispatches for the *Missouri Democrat* throughout the Secession Winter, qualified as a traveling correspondent as well: as usual, he served during the inaugural journey as both an aide and a reporter.[50]

Fortunately, this retinue overheard just enough of Lincoln's Springfield farewell to realize at once that they had missed a major story. As soon as the train lurched out of town, Villard visited the presidential "saloon" car and asked Lincoln to provide the press pool with his text so reporters could belatedly transmit it by telegraph at the first stop. Lincoln, however, had no text to give him. He had spoken extemporaneously—and not with perfect grace, as the Springfield transcript would later show—but he agreed to reconstruct the speech for the journalists now. As the train steamed toward Indiana, the president-elect took pencil in hand and commenced writing in an increasingly shaky scrawl as his car lurched along the tracks, rocking as it picked up speed. Then, perhaps made queasy by the effort, he handed the task over to secretary John Nicolay, who took dictation for a few sentences more. Inexplicably—was Nicolay writing too slowly?—Lincoln then reclaimed the page and finished the text himself. What Lincoln ultimately handed Villard was a vastly improved, highly polished version of the spontaneous goodbye he had delivered moments earlier. As recrafted, it was not only a testament to the orator's gift for captivating hearing audiences, but also to his consummate skill at massaging such remarks for adaptation by the press. Most memorably of all, his original "Friends, one and all, I must bid you an affectionate farewell" emerged far more eloquently as "To His care commending you as I hope in your prayers you will commend me, I bid you an affectionate farewell." For his own report on Lincoln's impromptu farewell speech, Villard made no mention of his missed opportunity to hear it firsthand, instead adding a flourish as if he had witnessed not only Lincoln's remarks but the crowd's reaction: "As he turned to enter the cars three cheers were given."[51]

Had Lincoln been able to control his message with equal success for the duration of his inaugural journey, he might well have entered Washington and begun his presidency with his reputation at an all-time peak. But after nearly a year of unaccustomed silence, Lincoln soon showed that he was out of practice as a public speaker. Over the next few days, the president-elect sounded bellicose at Indianapolis ("Doctor Lincoln," commented the *Herald*, was not the first "political quack who has killed his patient through combined stupidity and ignorance"); oversanguine in Columbus (he "did not know what he was saying," Bennett insisted of the performance), and inexplicably focused on corollary tariff issues in Pittsburgh (offering "crude, ignorant twaddle," even Villard admitted).[52]

In a sense, it did not much matter what Lincoln said on the trip, or how he said it. In reports published in pro-Republican newspapers like the *New York Times* and *New York Tribune*, Lincoln inevitably appeared as a restrained leader well aware of the perils facing his fractured country, and consistently rising to the occasion with homespun, practical, and, in some instances, inspiring calls for calm and patience. To the press long aligned with the opposition Democrats, the reemergent Lincoln seemed more like an embarrassing comedian joking his way across the country, unwilling or unable to confront the grave crisis at hand. Journals in each two-paper city along the inaugural route affirmed these partisan sentiments: Republican papers in Indianapolis, Columbus, and Pittsburgh hailed the president-elect's less-than-sterling performances, while their pro-Democratic counterparts lacerated him even more brutally than he deserved. If Lincoln harbored any thought that the ongoing secession nightmare and the approach of inauguration day might unite Northern press support for his administration, he quickly learned he was mistaken.

Judging solely from the unfiltered transcripts of all his recorded remarks—more than a hundred public utterances, when all was said and done—the inescapable truth was that Lincoln did not really regain his oratorical footing until he reached Trenton, New Jersey, a week and a half after his departure from Springfield. The Republican press never admitted as much, but the incoming president did little until then to build public confidence as he made his way toward the national capital, even if his welcomes were mostly warm. Toward the end of the journey, even the loyal John Hay seemed disappointed. In one dispatch filed with the *Missouri Democrat* after the inaugural caravan reached upstate New York, Hay reported: "The greatest, richest and most powerful of the states has slapped the President upon the shoulder emphatically, told him to 'go it,' and be sure of at least one 'backer.' The state will keep its word. The question is, will 'Old Abe' go it?" If some of Hay's inaugural journey reports often seemed equally irreverent, they were marks not of disloyalty but of professional frustration. In each city, the official press corps monopolized the telegraph lines to file their daily reports. Forced to send his own stories by post, Hay had no choice but to make them vivid and offbeat. They featured, he admitted, "incidents of the sort not written in the chronicles of that natural enemy of the scribe, whose letters go by mail—the telegraph reporter," adding: "Accursed be his memory, forever and a day."[53]

On February 15, Lincoln's train paused at the tiny hamlet of Girard, Ohio, where an uninvited, curious-looking passenger boarded, clutching a gripsack and comforter as he entered the press car. "He wore that mysteriously durable garment, the white coat," John Hay caustically observed, "and carried in his hand a yellow bag, labelled with his name and address, in characters which might be read across Lake Erie." Here again was none other than the editor of the *New York Tribune*, still wandering through the countryside in search of news, influence, and lecture income. "No little sensation was produced . . . by the unexpected appearance on the train of Horace Greeley, equipped with a valise and his well known red and blue blanket," Henry Villard reported. Entering "the reporters' car," Greeley tried explaining that he believed he had boarded the regularly scheduled train east, a story that failed to convince the other journalists riding in what may have been the most gaudily decorated conveyance ever to pass through the countryside.

John Nicolay quickly ushered Greeley to Lincoln's private car, where the president-elect "came forward to greet him" and introduced him for the first time to Mrs. Lincoln. Thus Greeley enjoyed his second face-to-face conference with the president-elect within just ten days. Their conversation, however, went unrecorded. And then, after about twenty miles, the editor disembarked at one of his onetime stamping grounds: Erie, Pennsylvania. As usual, Greeley had caused a stir. It was not for nothing that the Cleveland *Plain Dealer* described him at the time—half disrespectfully, half admiringly—as the "drab-coated, white-hatted Philosopher" who enjoyed unlimited access to Lincoln because he had "made him President."[54]

Like Greeley, Henry Villard soon abandoned the entourage as well. Declaring himself "sick of the 'traveling show,'" and no doubt believing he would hear nothing further of importance from the man of the hour, the correspondent peeled away from the press corps once Lincoln reached New

York City on February 19. Making his way through the narrow hallways and overcrowded warrens that the *Herald* still called home, the indefatigable reporter asked James Gordon Bennett "to be relieved" of his assignment and the editor reluctantly agreed.[55] With Villard's departure, the *Herald*'s extraordinary months of day-to-day Lincoln coverage came to an end. Just a few days later, as it happened, Villard missed the most dramatic story of the entire journey. But so, too, for that matter, did the rest of the press contingent, through no fault of their own.

But first Lincoln labored mightily to make a good impression in the newspaper capital he had virtually taken by storm just a year earlier with his Cooper Union speech. This time, approbation in New York seemed harder to achieve. Even the smallest details of his greeting were hotly disputed by partisan correspondents, with the *Times* reporting an "immeasurable outpouring of the people," and the *Herald* insisting that the unenthusiastic crowds were far sparser than the "impenetrable" masses who had welcomed the Prince of Wales to the city just a few months before.[56] It was no wonder that journalists were barred from Mayor Fernando Wood's subsequent reception in Lincoln's honor, at least until one correspondent pushed his way inside by arguing, "Reporters aren't among the nobodies, you know."[57] Political divisions were no less tense. Wood had recently proposed that the city "disrupt the bonds which bind her to a venal corrupt master" and consider an open alliance with the Confederacy, an idea applauded by the *New York Daily News*, a paper conveniently operated by the mayor's brother Ben. To the *New York Illustrated News*, however, Wood's initiative signaled a policy of "Every man for himself. . . . If we are to have a political scramble, the Mayor of New York will go in for a big share of the spoils."[58]

After joining editors Thurlow Weed and James Watson Webb for a breakfast with anxious New York merchants on February 20, Lincoln confidently faced down Wood at the public levee at City Hall. Replying from across a desk once used by George Washington, the president-elect made it clear: "There is nothing that can ever bring me willingly to consent to the destruction of this Union, under which not only the commercial city of New York, but the whole country has acquired its greatness." The ship of state would be saved, he vowed, "without throwing the passengers and cargo"—his apt metaphor for the bitterly divided seaport—"overboard."[59]

Following an equally resolute but far more eloquent speech the next day before the New Jersey state legislature at Trenton, a reenergized Lincoln arrived in Philadelphia on February 21 for what promised to be the most stirring event of his entire trip: an emotionally charged flag-raising ceremony on Washington's Birthday outside the birthplace of American liberty, Independence Hall. Before he could rest up for the predawn ritual, however, Lincoln received distressing news from a visiting railroad detective named Allan Pinkerton: a credible assassination plot awaited him when his train reached the first Southern city on its itinerary, Baltimore. With reluctance, Lincoln agreed to alter his publicly announced travel plans and journey in secret to Washington overnight—bypassing Baltimore entirely, except for an unavoidable late-night, crosstown detour to change railroad lines. The decision may have saved Lincoln's life, but it nearly killed his reputation.

That evening, toward the end of a reception in his honor at Harrisburg, the president-elect slipped away to begin his clandestine trip, accompanied only by his longtime friend and bodyguard Ward Hill Lamon, and leaving the entire press corps behind. To avoid recognition along the way, Lincoln substituted a soft plug hat for his signature stovepipe. Correspondents went to bed that night in Harrisburg unaware that their quarry had escaped their scrutiny. Pinkerton agents cut telegraph lines to prevent their communicating the news should they somehow unearth it before Lincoln arrived safely in Washington. The following morning, angry journalists awakened to learn that the object of their attention had vanished.

Once allowed to do so, the reporters initially reported the developments forthrightly, leaving commentary to their editors—with one major exception. Joseph Howard of the *New York Times* had not come halfway across the country to be denied his right to observe the journey's final leg. He exacted his revenge in print. On February 25 the *Times* published his fictional account that Lincoln had stolen through Baltimore disguised in "a Scotch plaid Cap and very long military cloak so that he was entirely unrecognizable." Though the story was maliciously and obviously fabricated, Lincoln's press opponents pounced on it. To the always critical *Herald*, the new president had "crept into Washington" like a "thief in the night." When Greeley attempted to excuse the president-elect by insisting, "Mr. Lincoln may live a hundred years without having so good a chance to die," Bennett shot back: "We have no doubt the *Tribune* is sincerely sorry at his escape from martyrdom."[60]

In the weeks to come, newspapers North as well as South mocked Lincoln unforgivingly, accusing him of rank cowardice. "We do not believe the Presidency can ever be more degraded by any of his successors than it has been by him," reported the *Baltimore Sun*. But the papers had no compunction about supplying its readers with all the details. "*The New York Times . . .* furnishes the wondering world with ample details of the Lincoln hegira," the *Sun* proclaimed. "We are not disposed to deprive our readers of one jot or tittle of the outrageous romance with which the *Times* entertains its own."[61] "Mr. Lincoln's night ride to Washington will make hereafter a splendid incident for the theatre," Bennett commented, "while his Scotch cap will be as famous as the green turban of the Prophet, and his long military cloak be placed with the uniform of Washington in the Patent Office." The *Herald* declared that it would be better now "for Old Abe to cut Washington altogether, and return to New York, where he can be inaugurated magnificently under the auspices of Barnum."[62]

When the daily press exhausted its arsenal of critical words, illustrated weeklies like *Vanity Fair* and *Harper's* filled the void with humiliating pictures, portraying Lincoln in an array of ridiculous disguises, including beribboned tams and plaid kilts.[63] Surely the Scottish-born James Gordon Bennett must have taken special delight in—or umbrage over—the rash of images showing the despised "Black Republican" escaping danger by passing himself off as, of all things, a Scotsman. Newly hired *New York Times* editorial writer John Swinton (himself a native Scot) joked that Bennett "could dance the Highland fling, play the bagpipes, toss the caber, wield the claymore for his clan, sport an eagle's feather in his bonnet, climb the cloud-capped crags, or demean himself like Robbie Burns—all with equal facility. For these things, and others yet, he may be said to have done for a long time in the *Herald*."[64]

During the days leading up to his inauguration, Lincoln hoped to seclude himself at one of Washington's private homes, far from office seekers and influence peddlers. Fortuitously—in view of the Baltimore uproar—editor Thurlow Weed had learned of this plan when the inaugural procession stopped in Albany, and strongly objected, insisting that the president-elect was now "public property" and ought to register with his family at a public hotel where he could be seen by all, confident and unafraid. "The truth is, I suppose I am now public property," Lincoln echoed, "and a public inn is the place where people can have access to me."[65] The Lincoln party ended up at the most conspicuous Washington hotel of all, Willard's, just down the street from the White House, a far cry from the cramped boardinghouse on

Capitol Hill where the Lincoln family had lived in a single room twelve years earlier—and one far more likely to attract newspapermen to its thronged and smoke-filled lobby.

Moreover, as Lincoln soon learned, the Peace Convention was at the time conducting its deliberations in a former church next door, only recently annexed by Willard's. This time, however, Lincoln would not commit the same social blunder he had made in paying court at Greeley's hotel in Springfield. He would not call on the delegates; he would wait for the delegates to call on him. They did so on the evening of February 23, filing into his hotel suite around 9 P.M. for handshakes and conversation—a good deal of it less than friendly. Lincoln answered patiently when several Southerners accused him of being the aggressor in the secession crisis. The tense conversation inevitably turned to newspapers. "Your press is incendiary," thundered James Seddon, the convention's Southern manager. "It advocates servile insurrection, and advises our slaves to cut their masters' throats. You do not suppress your newspapers. You encourage their violence."

"I beg your pardon, Mr. Seddon," Lincoln calmly interrupted. "I intend no offence, but I will not suffer such a statement to pass unchallenged, because it is not true. No Northern newspaper, not the most ultra, has advocated a slave insurrection or advised the slaves to cut their masters' throats. A gentleman of your intelligence should not make such assertions. We do maintain the freedom of the press—we deem it necessary to a free government. Are we peculiar in that respect? Is not the same doctrine held in the South?"[66] No one could have predicted it at the time, but if Lincoln truly believed in absolute freedom of the press in February, he would come to think quite differently by July.

Although most of Lincoln's many subsequent visitors at Willard's were politicians and military men, few were surprised when prominent journalists followed, including Ben Perley Poore, who had known the president-elect during his congressional days. After "a cordial greeting" and "some pleasant reminiscences," Lincoln showed Poore the working copy of his inaugural address, exacting a promise that Poore would not allow its contents to "get into print." The veteran editor never went back on his word, but remembered well—and for the benefit of his readers—that Lincoln's copy of the address had been "put in type by his friend, the local printer" in Springfield—meaning Bailhache and Baker—and now boasted the president-elect's own inserts for emphasis, each designated with a handwritten "typographical fist."

Another press notable made his way to Lincoln's suite as well. "Horace Greeley stopped at Willard's (of course) . . . and attracted much notice," the *New York Illustrated News* informed its readers shortly before the inaugural. "His good natured, generous face, his unassuming manners, and especially his well known great coat, and broad-brimmed hat, made him a man of conspicuousness and mark. Besides which he was the editor of the *Tribune*, a fact enough in itself to emblazon any one for all time, and render him immortal for all eternity." The friendly paper reported Greeley "wandering about the public rooms, and along the lobbies and corridors of the great hotel, mostly busy with his own thoughts, and, not to speak it ill-naturedly, doing a little internal speculation upon his prospects of official employment." [67]

At one point, a Southerner approached Greeley inside the hotel and loudly berated him, charging that the *Tribune* had become "an engine of great mischief" and its editor "a Northern fire-eater, and an abolition bloodsucker." According to the *Illustrated News* correspondent who witnessed this scene, "our good Horace" was left with "his face full of smiling benevolence, and his hands in his great coat pockets—evidently tickled with the lecture, and not at all abashed. Our artist," the report ended, "who saw the whole thing, put it into pencil, and we have put it into engraving, and hope the public will like it."

HORACE GREELEY AND A SOUTHERNER. See page 310.

Greeley confronts a Southerner—or vice versa—in an incident captured by a *New York Illustrated News* artist inside the crowded lobby of Willard's hotel during the tense days leading up to Lincoln's 1861 inauguration.

Greeley's presence did not escape the gaze of visiting Southern journalists, either. On inauguration day, the *Charleston Mercury* reported yet another Greeley sighting at Willard's, but far less sympathetically. "His broad-brimmed hat was set back on his head, his cravat twisted to one side and above his collar, and his bosom exposed. As he slouched along in his ungainly rhinoceros way, a half drunken New Yorker stopped him." Greeley, stouter than in his early days, but still "thinskinned and smooth and fair as a baby," was fresh from "his last interview with Old Abe," at which, the *Mercury* reporter conjectured, the editor had made a final attempt to influence Lincoln in the still unresolved questions regarding the cabinet. Just moments later, the correspondent watched the inaugural parade begin along Pennsylvania Avenue. The *Mercury* reporter claimed to notice a "rickety Jersey wagon . . . much adorned with flags, and I observed that one of them was torn, so that all the stars remained while some of the stripes were missing. . . . This is ominous."[68]

Unlike the *Illustrated News*, New York's other picture weeklies took suspicious note of Greeley's apparently renewed influence on the incoming administration. *Frank Leslie's Budget of Fun* portrayed him in one cartoon as a liveried White House doorkeeper, forcibly keeping Seward out of the mansion by declaring, *"so many of our customers don't like you!"* In contrast, but no less critically, *Vanity Fair* portrayed Seward and Thurlow Weed comfortably ensconced inside the president's office, urging Lincoln to beware of "sharpers," while a frustrated Greeley struggles to break past the chained door to gain entrance. On the eve of the inauguration, the *Budget of Fun* attempted to explain Lincoln's safe arrival in Washington from Baltimore by showing him entering the White House crouched inside a steel safe, protected by soldiers, Wide-Awake marchers, and Horace Greeley, uncharacteristically brandishing an upthrust sword and carrying a pistol in his belt. For months, cartoons and caricatures that assailed Lincoln for wasting his precious time on patronage placed Horace Greeley at the head of the line of hungry aspirants for "Government Pap."[69]

On March 4, 1861, luxuriantly bearded, Lincoln delivered his long-awaited inaugural address before a crowd of thousands massed on the plaza outside the east front of the U.S. Capitol. Whether or not Greeley had read and commented on the oration in advance is not known. But several others had, including incoming secretary of state William Seward and Lincoln's longtime political rival, Stephen Douglas. Both men had urged the president-elect to be as conciliatory as possible, and in the days before the swearing-in, Lincoln had obligingly toned down his more defiant original language. Nonetheless, he vowed unmistakably in his speech "to hold, occupy and possess the property and places belonging to the Government." To Southerners who had insisted since December that the federal government must abandon Fort Sumter in Charleston harbor, that remark alone amounted to a declaration of war, even if Lincoln ended the oration with an eloquent plea for peace: "We are not enemies, but friends—We must not be enemies. Though passion may have strained, it must not break our bonds of affection. The mystic chords of memory, stretching from every battle-field, and patriot grave, to every living heart and hearthstone, will yet swell the chorus of the Union, when again touched, as surely they will be, by the better angels of our nature." [70]

Good nature seldom found its way into the party newspapers. When it came to reporting and analyzing the inaugural address, it was political business as usual—but with the volume ratcheted up to a new intensity, and with sectional pride and racial divisions now inflecting the commentary. Bitterly condemning the new president for offering to enforce the Fugitive Slave Act in return for the abandonment of secession, Frederick Douglass, for example, called the pledge "revolting," adding: "It was . . . weak, uncalled for and useless for Mr. Lincoln to begin his Inaugural Address by thus at the outset prostrating himself before the foul and withering curse of slavery." [71] By contrast hailing the speech for its "moral vigor" and "calm firmness," the ever loyal *New York Times* insisted: "Mr. Lincoln's Inaugural Address must command the cordial approval of the great body of the American people." Praising it for "a sagacity as striking as its courage," the *Tribune* agreed: "The Address can not fail to exercise a happy influence upon the country. The tone of almost tenderness with which the South is called upon to return to her allegiance, can not fail to convince even those who differ from Mr. Lincoln that he earnestly and seriously desires to avoid all difficulties and disturbance." [72]

Of course no such approval came from the South—or even from Democratic papers in the North. Lamenting the "crude performance" for a "careless *bonhomie*" and "resolve to procrastinate," Bennett's *Herald* lacerated Lincoln's address as "neither candid nor statesmanlike," and lacking "in dignity or patriotism." In Bennett's analysis: "It would have caused Washington to mourn, and would have inspired Jefferson, Madison, or Jackson with contempt. . . . It would have been almost as instructive if President Lincoln had contented

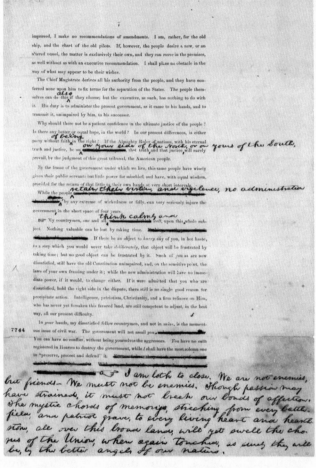

Lincoln had his inaugural address typeset by the *Illinois State Journal* before leaving Springfield, later adding handwritten changes, including this new ending, indicated by an artfully drawn pointing finger.

himself with telling his audience . . . a funny story and let them go. His inaugural is but a paraphrase of the vague generalities contained in his pilgrimage speeches, and shows clearly, either that he has not made up his mind respecting his future course, or else that he desires, for the present, to keep his intentions to himself."

Most Southern newspapers, however, insisted they understood Lincoln perfectly. The usually moderate *Richmond Whig* objected to the speech's "coercive" tone, predicting: "Let Lincoln carry out the policy indicated in his Inaugural, and civil war will be inaugurated forthwith throughout the length and breadth of the land." Condemning the address even more fiercely for reflecting "an impulse that hastens to the precipice," the *Charleston Mercury* branded its author "King Lincoln" and "the Orang-Outang at the White House," and decried the praise the speech earned in most Northern journals. "The Abolition-Republican papers are delighted with the Inaugural," complained the *Mercury*. "With cruel admiration, they call it a 'State Paper.'" To the *Mercury* it was more like "the tocsin of battle, but the signal for our freedom." The headline for its March 9 report bristled with indignant resolve: "Waiting for War to Begin."[73]

Henry Raymond spoke for many Republican editors when he took that dare. Expressing "the strongest and most confident hopes of the wisdom and success of the new Administration," Raymond ended his editorial by praising Lincoln's inaugural address with what turned out to be an equally ominous warning: "If the Union cannot be saved on this basis and consistently with these principles, then it is better that it should not be saved at all."[74]

President Abraham Lincoln holding one of his favorite and most consistently supportive newspapers, the *Washington Chronicle,* photograph by Alexander Gardner, Sunday, August 9, 1863.

PART TWO
UNCIVIL WARS

CHAPTER TEN

Wanted: A Leader

————————⊙————————

If the new president ever enjoyed a "honeymoon" period free from press criticism, it ended almost as soon as it began. Within weeks of the inauguration, Washington correspondents began besieging the administration with complaints about lack of access to official information and worse, occasional interference by the government in their pursuit of news. The friction prompted the Associated Press to call for a meeting to demand "good manners and common sense" from administration officials.[1] In response, the War Department insisted it simply wanted reports of its activities kept out of any Northern dailies that Southern officials might get hold of. There was reason for concern. When the new Confederate secretary of war, LeRoy Walker, urged his region's own newspapers to "forbear from the transmission and publication" of "intelligence . . . detrimental to our great cause," he let slip that his office had indeed obtained "valuable information" from the "medium of the enterprising journals of the North."[2]

The *New York Times*, which ignored the AP invitation, lost patience with Lincoln for its own, entirely political, reason, and barely a month after the president took office. In a withering April 3 editorial headlined "Wanted—A Policy," Henry Raymond charged that "our Government has done absolutely nothing, towards carrying the country through the tremendous crisis which is so rapidly and so steadily settling down upon us. It allows everything to *drift*." Lincoln, Raymond demanded, "must go up to a higher level than he has yet reached," stop wasting "time and strength in feeding rapacious and selfish partisans," and "adopt a policy of action" before people "lost heart" and confidence. "In a great crisis like this," the lecture concluded, "there is no policy so fatal as that of having no policy at all."[3]

It was no coincidence that just two days earlier, Secretary of State Seward had presented Lincoln with a breathtakingly presumptuous memorandum complaining in almost identical language that the administration was "yet without a policy either domestic or foreign." Seward then added, as if to nominate himself as savior, "Either the President must do it himself," or "devolve it on some member of his Cabinet." A conspiracy was afoot. Not only had Seward and Raymond obviously coordinated their private and public criticism of the president, but Raymond now rushed to Washington at Seward's request to be present at his anticipated coronation as a kind of de facto prime minister. Once in the capital, the editor hoped to be ideally positioned to telegraph a detailed exclusive announcing Seward's new powers. Arriving at midnight, Raymond spent the next four hours conferring with the secretary of state at his home while anxiously awaiting Lincoln's response. At one point, the editor summoned his Washington correspondent to the Seward mansion and confidently instructed him to draft a front-page report on Seward's elevation and to leave ample room for an enthusiastic editorial once the president, as expected, blinked.[4]

Neither article ever saw the light of day, for Lincoln outmaneuvered them both. With cool agility, he deflated the coup attempt by welcoming Seward's "advice," but insisting that, where making policy was concerned, "*I* must do it." The president managed not only to put the secretary of state firmly in his place but to humble the *New York Times* in the bargain. A disappointed Raymond sent a terse dispatch to New York conceding the scheme's collapse. It read: "Nothing more." If it was true, as rumored, that Raymond was tired of the newspaper grind and harbored hopes for a glamorous overseas appointment, perhaps as consul to Paris, the Seward imbroglio robbed him of his chance. Lincoln was no longer willing to reward him.[5]

The real "tremendous crisis" came a few weeks later in Charleston, and it changed everything. The Confederate attack on Fort Sumter on April 12, 1861, tectonically altered not only relations between the Union and the seceded Southern states, but between the federal government and the Northern press—and also between these long-partisan newspapers and their suddenly, overwhelmingly patriotic readers. After enduring some thirty-four hours of bombardment from the shoreline, Sumter's commander, Major Robert Anderson, lowered his tattered flag and surrendered the federal fort to the Confederacy on April 14. Then, to his good fortune, he led his garrison onto a ship bound for the nation's newspaper capital: New York.

There, just hours earlier, a local journalist-turned-poet first learned of the Sumter attack after leaving the opera around midnight and starting down Broadway on foot toward the Brooklyn-bound ferry slips. The stunning news arrived in the usual clamorous way. "I heard in the distance the loud cries of the newsboys who came presently tearing and yelling up the street," the eyewitness, Walt Whitman, testified. He snatched up a copy of one of the extras, and began devouring the Sumter report beneath street lamps flickering above a nearby hotel. Within minutes, thirty or forty people crowded around Whitman, imploring him to read the story aloud because the newsboys had run out of papers.[6]

In Washington, acting boldly in response to the bombardment while Congress remained dispersed in its customary post–inaugural day recess, Lincoln made news of his own by calling for 75,000 volunteers to "re-possess the forts, places, and property which have been seized from the Union." Four days later, he ordered a naval blockade of Confederate ports, and early the next month asked the states for yet another 42,000 soldiers and sailors for lengthier enlistments than required of the original ninety-day militia.[7] Lincoln's proclamations reassured his doubters in the North, but triggered waves of criticism in the Southern press, and helped propel Virginia, Arkansas, Tennessee, and North Carolina into the Confederacy. Calling for "vengeance on the tyrants who pollute the capital of the Republic," the *Richmond Whig* predicted that Jefferson Davis would soon occupy the White House, urging Lincoln to be "in readiness to dislodge at a moment's notice." Some of Washington's conservative editors might well have welcomed Davis there: both of the divided city's onetime pro–Stephen Douglas dailies "raised the disunion standard" no less vehemently than their colleagues across the Potomac.[8] In journalism, as in the country at large, a North-South fault line was emerging to supplant the Republican-Democratic divisions of years past.

Leading the patriotic charge in the North was the temporarily placated *New York Times*, which boasted even as the first shells were raining on Sumter that its Charleston correspondent George H. C. Salter (who wrote under the name "Jasper"), had been arrested "as a Federal spy . . . imprisoned for twenty-four hours, and then sent out of the city . . . destitute of funds."[9] Energized by these events, Raymond predicted that Lincoln's call for volunteers would send a "thrill like an electric shock throughout the land, and establish the fact that we have a Government." The South would soon "learn that Northern people are not cowards."[10]

The once pacifistic Horace Greeley came to believe, at least he so maintained after the war, that Lincoln made a "grave mistake" only in "underestimating the spirit and power of the Rebellion." Had the president "invited the people to assemble on a designated early day" in towns across the North rather than calling for a mere 75,000 volunteers, Greeley unrealistically maintained, "not less than One Million able-bodied men would have thus enrolled themselves." Instead, "what should have been a short, sharp struggle was expanded into a long, desultory one."[11] At the time, Greeley kept his disappointment to himself. Privately, he wrote Lincoln to urge "that the war for the Union" be "prosecuted with emphatic vigor," adding: "All are confident that the result will justify our fondest hopes."[12] Publicly, he joined the chorus for war with enthusiasm, calling on loyal Northerners to "unite on the common ground of resistance to treason" and assailing "imbecile apologists" for the slave system.[13]

At first, James Gordon Bennett, who was almost certainly the "imbecile apologist" to whom Greeley referred, remained unmoved by all this saber-rattling, even though his own Southern correspondents had been menaced in the South, too ("I escaped with my life only by assuming a disguise," *Herald* reporter Charles H. Farrell claimed after fleeing Pensacola).[14] Learning that Lincoln was weighing the termination of mail service to the seceded states, Bennett complained that the move would cause "serious damage" not only to the South, but "to the North also"—undoubtedly calculating his own potential circulation losses. Criticizing what he called a "causeless and senseless appeal to arms," Bennett insisted that "the people of this metropolis owe it to themselves, to their material and political interests, to their social security and to the country at large, to make a solemn and imposing effort in behalf of peace." But when he called for a public meeting to protest government "coercion," the rival *Times* demanded to know: "Is there to be no limit to the Herald's open advocacy of treason and rebellion?"[15]

Bennett had woefully underestimated the popular outrage in response to the assault on Sumter—and particularly to the insult that befell the American flag that waved there until shot down—twice—by Confederate shells. "That was the period," future general Jacob D. Cox recalled, "when the flag—*The Flag*—flew out to the wind from every housetop." Cox noted that "in New York, wildly excited crowds marched the streets demanding that the suspected or the lukewarm should show the symbol of nationality as a committal to the country's cause," adding: "He that is not for us is against us, was the deep, instinctive feeling." [16]

Bennett learned that bitter lesson the hard way. By April 15, the American flag could be seen floating "from all the principal newspaper offices" in Manhattan with the notable exception of Bennett's headquarters on Nassau Street. At the *Herald*, the flag's "absence seemed to excite the public indignation," Raymond almost gleefully reported. According to another of Bennett's infuriated contemporaries: "If the flag of the United States had been trailed in the mud of Nassau Street, followed by hooting ruffians of the Sixth Ward, and the symbol of the Rebellion has floated in its stead from the cupola of City Hall . . . it would not have cost this isolated alien one pang,—unless, perchance, a rival newspaper had been the first to announce the fact. *That*, indeed, would have cut him to the heart." [17]

Later that tense day, braving a chill rain, "an excited crowd filled the sidewalk" outside the *Herald*, "and gazing up at the windows . . . indulged in various expressions of dislike to that establishment." Frightened employees armed themselves and summoned help. Bennett himself was "pursued and hooted in the street." Then, after a phalanx of police deployed outside the building, a "Committee of gentlemen" called on the besieged editor and strongly "suggested that, if he wished to save his 'institution' from attack, he must display the Stars and Stripes" at once. Not until 4:30 P.M. did the crowd spy a newsboy racing toward the building, a flag folded under his arm. Minutes later, a limp "American ensign" finally appeared from one of the paper's upper-story windows. Disappointed protesters emitted a mixture of "groans and cheers" at this "tardy compliance with the wishes of the people." Only after what the *Times* ridiculed as Bennett's "sudden conversion" did the "multitude" gradually disperse. [18]

They soon took their anger elsewhere. The next afternoon, lawyer George Templeton Strong was working at his desk when he suddenly heard strange "unwonted sounds" coming from outside his window on Wall Street. Peering down, he saw "a straggling column of men running toward the East River." Strong's first impulse was that "they were chasing a runaway horse, but they soon became too numerous to be engaged in that." The crowd instead surrounded the office of the nearby, pro-Democratic *Journal of Commerce*, which had editorialized that the South ought to be allowed to leave the Union in peace. Strong heard some muffled "outcries," then "the black mass was suddenly in motion with waving hats." A line of policemen came running down the street, and the crowd reluctantly moved on, "cheering lustily." Strong later learned that the demonstrators, "mostly decently-dressed people, but with a sprinkling of laboring men," marched next to the Democratic *Express*, *Day-Book*, and *Daily News*, "requiring each to put up the flag," too. Other marchers headed across the river to demand the *Brooklyn Eagle* do the same. "Flagmania," as the *Tribune* dubbed the phenomenon, had engulfed the entire New York newspaper world.[19]

Bennett's own "sudden conversion" was only beginning. Although he blamed the *Times* and *Tribune* for exciting "a mob to the committal of acts of violence," he proclaimed the very next day that the time had "passed" for "public peace meetings, in the North," instead vowing: "War will make the Northern people a unit." The "actual presence of war cuts short all debate and closes the argument." And any "discussion of the right and wrong in this matter" had become "a waste of time." Bennett was never one to cling to a lost cause. War, which only twenty-four hours earlier had to Bennett posed the threat of economic disaster for New York, now would surely "result in a happy revival of business in this city and all over the North."[20]

For his part, refusing even to acknowledge that other New York editors had preceded him in praise of Lincoln's response to Sumter, Bennett as usual chose to go on the offensive against his rivals: "Our military chieftains of the

The New York press lords at the start of the Civil War. From left to right: James Gordon Bennett, Horace Greeley, and Henry J. Raymond.

Courier and *Tribune* are jubilant; the little whisperers of the *Times* . . . seize the occasion to ventilate their petty malice and spleen against their neighbors."[21] This time his competitors tried denying him the last word. When Mayor Fernando Wood issued a proclamation of his own, calling on New Yorkers to maintain order and respect property and person, Republican editors charged that the "ridiculous message" was designed to protect deserving targets like the mayor's friend Bennett. Reminding readers that the treacherous Wood had only weeks earlier advocated that the city secede from the Union, Greeley thundered that if "any journal issued within the limits of the Jeff. Davis Confederacy" had published such a decree, "its editors . . . would at once be strung up to the handiest lamp-post or some convenient limb of a tree." Greeley pronounced himself delighted that the "journals lately parading the ranks of the Secessionists with scarcely disguised exultation, have been suddenly sobered."[22] This salvo prompted Bennett to protest, "we cannot see the propriety of minor journals like the *Tribune* . . . pitching into the Mayor's proclamation. When a public man issues an unobjectionable document he should not be abused."[23] No one could accuse Bennett of lacking gall.

Now the *Herald* editor went on the offensive, audaciously seizing upon a patriotic cause of his own to champion: the briefly disputed reputation of Major Anderson, the officer who had surrendered Fort Sumter. As it happened, Anderson arrived in New York on April 19, the anniversary of the Battles of Lexington and Concord, carrying the Sumter flag with him, and unfurling it at a patriotic rally at Union Square. Imbued by holiday patriotism, New Yorkers gave him a hero's welcome—but not before another of the city's newspaper editors questioned his conduct at Charleston Harbor. When James Watson Webb labeled Anderson "the vilest traitor the world ever saw," it was Bennett who most indignantly countered that "Major Anderson has proved himself a brave and faithful officer." Further embracing the president—whom he had subjected to relentless criticism for months—as the only proper arbiter of such matters, the *Herald* insisted that Lincoln was "better qualified to form a correct judgment in the case than even our Wall street contemporary, with all his learning and experience in military affairs."[24] Bennett rescued his battered reputation, perhaps even his business—by all but wrapping himself in the flag he had earlier shunned. Where measuring public opinion was concerned, Bennett still boasted the magic touch.

Lincoln was not unappreciative of the *Herald*'s sudden support; because of its unsurpassed circulation in Europe, the president considered it vital. So he dispatched Thurlow Weed, who had not spoken to the "Satanic Majesty" in three decades, to confirm Bennett's willingness to back the war. Lincoln chose the Albany editor for the mission, he told Weed, because he had experience "belling cats."[25] Bennett confirmed his extraordinary about-face by summoning correspondent Henry Villard to his office. There he assigned the writer who had covered Lincoln back in Springfield to travel to Washington and tell the president that "the *Herald* would hereafter be unconditionally for the radical suppression of the Rebellion by force of arms, and would advocate and support any 'war measures' by the Government," particularly if the administration agreed to offer his son, James Gordon Bennett, Jr., a commission as a navy lieutenant. Though Villard believed his employer "utterly selfish," he agreed to carry the message to the White House. Before they parted, the editor added that he also wished Villard to visit Secretary of the Treasury Salmon Chase, and offer him his personal yacht as a "gift to the Government for the revenue service." The man who just days earlier had advocated laying down arms was now prepared to supply them. Villard agreed to the mission, the younger Bennett became a lieutenant in the naval service, and the elder Bennett rewarded his correspondent with a raise in salary to thirty-five dollars a week.[26]

Bennett's somersault proved no less acrobatic than Henry Raymond's, for the *Times* editor now did yet another about-face and resumed hurling criticism the president's way, notwithstanding the otherwise unifying effect of the Sumter attack. Only ten days after the surrender, Raymond picked up where he had left off on April 3, this time accusing the administration of lacking not only a policy, but a chief. In a way, the editor's frustration was understandable. On April 19, a pro-Confederate mob had attacked Massachusetts troops as they passed through Baltimore en route to the defense of Washington. Four soldiers died in the melee, earning distinction as the first Union martyrs of the Civil War.[27] Then, to Raymond's chagrin, Union forces abandoned the Gosport Navy Yard near Norfolk, torching it before its evacuation so Confederates could not make use of it, and surrendered the antislavery landmark of Harpers Ferry, also without firing a shot. Now, in an editorial outburst published on April 25 under the headline, "Wanted—A Leader," Raymond demanded courage—or change.

"In every great crisis," the blistering new opinion piece began, "the human heart demands a leader that incarnates its ideas, its emotions, and its aims. Till such a leader appears, everything is disorder, disaster and defeat. The moment he takes the helm, order, promptitude and confidence follow as the necessary result. When we see such results, we know that a hero leads. No such hero at present directs affairs. The experience of our Government for months past has been a series of defeats. It has been one of continued retreat." The administration, Raymond again charged, was still spending far too much time dealing with patronage matters, and not enough on restoring the Union. Arguing that a "holy zeal" now animated "every heart," Raymond asked, perhaps in one final effort to "nominate" Seward for president: "Where is the leader of this sublime passion? Can the Administration furnish him?" If federal officials could not correct their "constitutional timidity" and "innate reluctance . . . to face the horrors of war," then "let them earn the gratitude of the people by . . . laying their ambition on the altar of their country"—in other words, by yielding authority to others willing to fight.[28]

Lincoln had endured his share of press criticism over the years, but even for him this was beyond the pale. Never much for keeping records, he showed his displeasure on this occasion by clipping the offending *Times* article and filing it, along with similarly critical recent columns, with a handwritten label that underscored his anger: "Villainous articles." Wisely, he expressed none of his outrage directly to Raymond. Instead he worked to bring the *Times* chief closer into his orbit. Lincoln invited Raymond to Washington, where he poured on the rustic charm, confiding the enormous pressures he faced in filling up patronage vacancies in the North while facing down disloyalty in the South. After their White House meeting, Raymond accepted the president's extraordinary excuse that he "wished he could get time to attend to the southern question" but for the fact that "the office-seekers demanded all his time." The editor remembered sympathetically, even fondly, that Lincoln likened himself to "a man so busy in letting rooms in one end of the house, that he can't stop to put out the fire that is burning the other."[29] Thereafter the *Times* was far more supportive of the administration.

Raymond exacted his only measure of compensation by besieging the president with "rapacious and selfish" patronage recommendations of his own—adding to the very burden he had earlier charged was taking too much of the chief executive's precious time. One aspirant for a foreign consulate earned a face-to-face meeting with Secretary of State Seward simply because, as Lincoln scribbled, "You see he has a note from H. J. Raymond. Give him an interview." When a congressman-elect from New York later sought Lincoln's aid on "a matter of political importance," Lincoln urged him to consult the editor of the *Times* first. "Raymond," he said, "is my *Lieutenant-General* in politics. Whatever he says is right in the premises, shall be done."[30] Apparently it no longer seemed to matter, as Raymond had previously complained so bitterly, that Lincoln was wrong "to fritter away the priceless opportunities of the Presidency in listening to the appeals of competing office-hunters."[31]

Opportunities soon ran out entirely for Lincoln's longtime political nemesis, Stephen Douglas. Weeks earlier, offering conspicuous public gestures to promote unity, he had held the new president's hat outside the Capitol during his swearing-in, escorted Mrs. Lincoln to the inaugural ball, and taken to the Senate floor to heap praise on his old rival's inaugural address.[32] Then, when the Illinois state legislature announced it would go into special session on April 23 to discuss the crisis, Douglas's loyal Springfield press defender Charles Lanphier urged the senator to rush home to calm escalating antiwar sentiment, as if no one else in public life possessed the influence do so.

Douglas thereupon embarked on a tiring journey west, pausing at stops along the way to warn crowds against "the new system of resistance by the sword and bayonet to the results of the ballot-box." The loser of the recent presidential election repeated his message along a route that amounted to an ironic retracing of Lincoln's recent inaugural journey—but in the opposite direction. Reaching Springfield, he received a hero's welcome in the same State Capitol chamber where Lincoln had delivered his anti-Douglas "House Divided" address three years earlier. Now, with the "house" indeed split, Douglas railed not against Lincoln, but against Southerners disloyal to "the government established by our fathers."[33]

The senator reported to Lincoln that "the state of feeling" in Illinois was "much less satisfactory than I could have desired or expected when I arrived." Still, he hoped "for entire unanimity in the support of the government and the Union." In what turned out to be his final letter to the *State Register*'s Charles Lanphier, he wrote: "The prospects are gloomy, but I do not yet despair of the Union. We can never acknowledge the right of a State to secede and cut us off from the Ocean and the world, without our consent."[34] It was perhaps his finest moment.

Worn to the bone by his exertions, Douglas staggered back to his Chicago residence on May 1, and almost immediately took to his bed suffering from a bout of rheumatism compounded by what appeared to be typhoid fever.

For a time he rallied, then relapsed. With the national press reporting almost daily on his fluctuating condition, Douglas took a final turn for the worse at the end of the month. A few days later, the decades of exuberant campaigning and hard drinking took their ultimate toll. On June 3, the Little Giant died, just forty-eight years old.[35] His lifelong competition with Abraham Lincoln—in both politics and the press—was over. Yet the *New York Times* gave no quarter in announcing the "sad news." Acknowledging that Douglas's name "will have a prominent place in history," Henry Raymond could not help reminding readers that the "measures which he in the main originated" lay "at the foundation of our present complications." Raymond conceded only that it was "greatly to be regretted that he could not have been spared to take part in the struggle in the origin of which he was so prominent an actor."[36]

Lincoln refused to take part in any Republican press effort to blame his old rival for the crisis he alone now shouldered. Rather, in a magnanimous show of respect—the equivalent of holding Douglas's hat, and more—he ordered the White House and all federal offices in Washington draped in black for thirty days.

In Washington, a long-established newspaper tradition was in its death throes as well. For generations, presidents had designated one capital newspaper or another as their official "organ"—the recipient of exclusive announcements and lucrative government printing orders. Now a revolution was at hand. Effective with Lincoln's inauguration on March 4, Congress had upended the custom by establishing the first U.S. Government Printing Office. More than 350 federal workers would soon assume responsibility for publishing most of the nation's executive, legislative, and judicial records. As consolation, any officially designated newspaper "organ" could still earn profitable government advertising, as well as reputation-building access to administration scoops. Even during the tense hours when Confederates began aiming their artillery against Fort Sumter, Lincoln found time to attend to this obligation—and in something of a surprise, to alter it further.

The large, established journals like the *National Intelligencer* (now under the management of James C. Welling, veteran publisher William Seaton's new partner) and the pro-Democratic *National Union* would continue to earn official advertising placements by virtue of "having the largest permanent subscription." In a remarkable shift from tradition, however, Lincoln decided to reward a newcomer to the city's journalistic pantheon: the tiny *National Republican*. The daily had been founded just a few weeks after the presidential campaign by an abolitionist survivor of two separate mob attacks by pro-slavery Washingtonians.

Though the paper was now less influential than in previous years, its designation sent a clear signal about the new president's sincere antislavery sentiments. The *National Republican*'s novice editor, Lewis Clephane, had once served as business manager for the *National Era*, the now defunct abolitionist paper mobbed back in Lincoln's days as a congressman. More recently, Clephane had operated a pro-Republican Wide-Awake political club in Washington, which barely survived another violent attack soon after Lincoln won the election. On November 26, a defiant Clephane converted the Wide-Awake headquarters into a newspaper office and there launched the *National Republican*. Now Lincoln repaid him for his loyalty and sacrifice. "In virtue of his authority to designate at discretion one newspaper in the city of Washington for the publication of notices and advertisements from the Executive departments," went the April 11, 1861, order, ". . . the President designates the 'National Republican.'" As further reward, the administration also named Clephane postmaster of the District of Columbia.[37]

As it turned out, Lincoln would not use Clephane as his exclusive mouthpiece after all. The new president quickly learned that there was far more advantage in doling out information to the more widely read Washington dailies, one story at a time. For the rest of his presidency, Lincoln used the District's newspapers selectively and informally—occasionally pitting one against the other in quest of the best coverage—feeding the New York press with stories released first to the Washington editors and all but terminating the "party organ" tradition that had thrived unchanged since the age of Jackson.

Before long, Lincoln began to favor one Washington-based journalist in particular: that wily political chameleon John Wein Forney. The forty-three-year-old publisher of the *Philadelphia Press*, a former Buchanan and Douglas Democrat, had already spent twenty-five years in the newspaper trade, in the course of which he had exacted political rewards dating back to the Polk administration. In late 1859, Forney had established a second paper, a Washington weekly called the *Sunday Morning Chronicle*, and began spending most of his time in the national capital. Now he filled his new paper with flattering comments about the Lincoln administration. He made sure to secure his first face-to-face appointment with the new president less than two weeks after Lincoln's inauguration.[38] The reasons for the editor's political reawakening, not surprisingly, involved political patronage—not only what the editor could secure for others, but what he could earn for himself. Within a year, Forney converted the weekly *Chronicle* into an equally pro-administration daily.

"Forney had the loftiest ambitions," conceded his lieutenant John Russell Young. But he "never learned—or at least never applied—the lesson which Bennett seared into the hearts of the generation,—that the world must fear before it followed, that there is a great deal of the dog in what people call public opinion, and that it must be well flogged before you have the comfort of its affection." Forney "never came [in]to his own," Young believed, because he tried too hard for "recognition," rather than influence.[39] Unlike Bennett, and even crusaders like Greeley, Forney yearned to be liked.

To his dismay, Forney had recently lost his patronage sinecure as clerk of the U.S. House of Representatives. As he remembered with gratitude, Lincoln thereupon "called in person upon a number of Senators and asked them to vote for me for Secretary of that body"—an even better job, paying $3,600 a year. As soon as the Senate returned for its special session, Lincoln made his preference for Forney clear to an old Illinois ally, Orville H. Browning, the man recently appointed to fill out the unexpired senate term of the late Stephen Douglas. Just five days after Browning arrived in Washington to take up his new duties, he received an invitation to visit Lincoln in the White House, where, among other issues, the president "expressed [to] me a wish that Forney should be elected Secretary of the Senate. Said he had rendered very important services to the administration, acting in good faith with it, and doubted whether the support of Pennsylvania could be secured without him." A few days later, Browning assured the president, "I think we can elect him." The Republican caucus chose Forney on July 15, with Browning confiding in his diary, "I voting for him on the recommendation of the President & others, knowing nothing about him myself. Never having even seen him to know him." In return, Forney commenced bombarding Lincoln with praise—along with patronage suggestions of his own. (Such arrangements were hardly unusual. The president's longtime supporter Horace White of the *Chicago Tribune* became clerk of the Senate Military Affairs Committee.)[40]

To further reward Forney, the State Department gave the *Chronicle* at least $4,776.34 in advertising during a single year of the war.[41] For the administration, it proved a sound investment. With Forney, Lincoln secured two advocates for the price of one, for the editor continued to publish his pro-administration paper in Philadelphia. Forney used his widening access in the capital to launch a new Washington gossip column for the *Press*, entitling it: "Occasional." Lincoln not only read it; he "occasionally" wrote for it. Although he had sworn off anonymous journalism years earlier, he could not help ghostwriting items for the new feature. Forney sent one of these unsigned tidbits to Secretary of War Simon Cameron on August 16, proudly identifying it as the "President's article." Loyal to the end, Forney devoted not a word in his two-volume memoirs to the open secret of Lincoln's resumed dabbling in journalism.[42] The number of items Lincoln contributed during his White House years has never been calculated and likely never will be; they were, after all, anonymous. Though his efforts may have been less promiscuous than some modern historians have suggested, they were almost certainly more commonplace than his collected works suggest.

Forney entertained lavishly and, some said, drank, talked, and fawned too much. A Democratic journal back in Pennsylvania complained that Forney's newspapers began "gravitating with constant . . . approaches to Black Republicanism" in order to "entitle it to its reward from the Abolitionists." Journalist George Alfred Townsend labeled Forney "one of the most timid men that ever filled a dictatorial place like editor. It partly arose," Townsend believed, "from his nursing office-seeking on one knee and a newspaper on the other." Even Horace Greeley, seldom timid about promoting his political ambitions through the press, complained that Forney did so clumsily, failing to serve as both "an independent journalist and an office-holder," and adding disparagingly: "Any journalist who holds an office writes in a straight [*sic*] jacket."[43]

The observation may have been apt, but a penchant for fawning did not make Forney less of a force in the federal capital. Rather, it brought him as close to the leading personality of the day as any editor in the country. Greeley, Raymond, and Bennett, who remained in New York through much of the war, enjoyed far less direct access to Lincoln. For his part, Forney left no doubt about his indebtedness to his new presidential patron. As he later wrote of Lincoln: "He was most considerate of the feelings and deservings of others."[44] What Forney believed he deserved were political rewards, and he got them—recommending appointees to serve from Washington to Colorado—in one case blatantly accompanying his most recent request with a clipping of

John Wein Forney, editor of the *Washington Chronicle*, Lincoln supporter, patronage recipient, and ultimately semi-official administration "oracle."

his latest editorial criticizing administration "fault finders."[45] In many ways, Forney became the administration's "official organ" after all.

Also expecting significant reward was James Watson Webb, another newspaper editor who had advocated for Lincoln's election in 1860, although with how much impact was open to question. By the time the new administration came to power, Webb's glory days were behind him. Still, even aging editors past their prime expected political recognition for loyal service long rendered, and the pugnacious old ex-Whig was no exception. In May, Lincoln obliged by offering the editor he respectfully called "General" the job of U.S. minister to Turkey, but Webb evidently thought the posting beneath him, and declined it. His political debt thus paid, Lincoln might have dropped the matter there, but in June he proposed nominating Webb for a South American post instead ("Brazil will strengthen me," Webb had pleaded with Lincoln, ". . . and add to my usefulness"), and this time the crusty old newspaperman accepted. Before departing for Rio, Webb sold his enterprise to the *New York World*, and after more than thirty years in business the *Courier and Enquirer* ceased to exist. James Gordon Bennett's most persistent and vitriolic press enemy earned not only a plum diplomatic post, but the enormous sum of

$100,000—a record price for a newspaper. Declaring him "dead and buried," Bennett smirked of his longtime enemy: "we shall sadly miss his fuss and feathers." [46]

In his mid-April recruitment and blockade proclamations, Lincoln had sought to stave off criticism that he had exceeded his authority by calling Congress back into session to ratify his executive initiatives—but not until July 4, by which time, he believed, his new policies would seem irreversible, particularly in the warm glow of Independence Day *amor patriae*. In the meantime, he labored to build an army and navy along with a loyal Republican government, continuing to give respectful consideration even during the mounting military crisis to job recommendations from leading journalists. [47] Then, two days before the House and Senate reconvened, with anti-Union sentiment on the rise in Maryland, Lincoln ordered General Winfield Scott to "suspend the writ of Habeas Corpus" wherever "resistance occurs" along the route carrying federal troops between New York and Washington. It was the latest in a series of suspensions aimed at inhibiting further secession. The outcry from the Democratic papers in Baltimore was predictable, swift, and loud. Forney spoke for most Republicans by expressing "universal confidence in the administration." [48]

On July 4, the president sent his eagerly anticipated special session message to Capitol Hill. Even without the opportunity to orate in person (tradition of the day required presidents to submit, but not perform, their congressional communications), Lincoln rose to the occasion with a "speech" filled with sparkling phrases. Written in plain language designed to resonate not only with Congress but especially with the Northern people through the press, it offered legal, moral, and practical arguments for armed resistance to the rebellion. In Lincoln's view, the revolt constituted a challenge not only to "the fate of these United States," but "to the whole family of man . . . whether"—and here he deployed a phrase to which he would memorably return two years later—". . . a government of the people, by the same people—can, or cannot maintain its territorial integrity, against its own domestic foes." [49]

Offering an impassioned justification for suspending habeas corpus, Lincoln denied violating his oath, asking at one point: "Are all the laws, *but one*, to go unexecuted, and the government itself go to pieces, lest that one be violated?" Emphasizing this critical question, he added: "Must a government, of necessity, be too *strong* for the liberties of its own people, or too *weak* to maintain its own existence?" He accused the "movers" of secession and rebellion of "insidious debauching of the public mind," and, once again reiterating this argument, of "drugging the public mind of their section for more than thirty years."

Fire-eaters, Lincoln charged at one point, had "sugar-coated" outright treason. The colloquialism had prompted former Indiana journalist John Defrees—recently named U.S. government printer—to march to the White House to complain that such language "lacked the dignity proper to a state paper." Lincoln calmly responded: "Defrees, that word expresses precisely my ideas, and I am not going to change it. The time will never come in this country when the people won't know exactly what *sugar-coated* means . . . I think I'll let it go." Defrees also tried editing the text, deleting what he regarded as surplus commas; Lincoln put them all back.[50] Yet another veteran editor had been put in his place by the new president.

On the subject of civil liberties, Lincoln insisted in his message that he had curtailed them only with "the deepest regret." He "could but perform this duty," he argued, "or surrender the existence of the government." A "dangerous emergency," he maintained, required the imposition of an executive authority to which he assigned a novel new name: the "war power."[51] His own "sugar-coating" came seven paragraphs from his conclusion: "This is essentially a People's contest. On the side of the Union, it is a struggle for maintaining in the world, that form, and substance of government, whose leading object is, to elevate the condition of men—to lift artificial weights from all shoulders—to clear the paths of laudable pursuit for all—to afford all, an unfettered start, and a fair chance, in the race of life."[52] Focused on the niceties of composition, Defrees and other journalists failed to perceive in the message the groundwork for imminent challenges to freedom of the press.

In many circles, Lincoln's eloquence fell on deaf ears. Perhaps still pining for a Seward coup, the *New York Times* proclaimed the message such a "painful jumble" it concluded that it must have been faultily transmitted over the telegraph. In Confederate and Border Slave States, Lincoln's message aroused outright denunciation. The Baltimore newspaper *The South* spoke for many pro-secession editors when it branded its author "the equal, in despotic wickedness, of Nero or any of the other tyrants who have polluted this earth."[53] From the opposite perspective, Frederick Douglass despaired that the message made "no mention" of slavery, anguishing: "Any one reading the document, with no previous knowledge of the United States, would never dream from anything there written that a slaveholding war [is] waged upon the Government, determined to overthrow it." Almost alone among these observers, one-time Seward supporter George William Curtis of *Harper's Magazine* perceived the extraordinary talent behind the message, hailing it as "wonderfully acute, simple, sagacious, and of antique honesty!" Soon to take up an important new post as editor of *Harper's Weekly*, Curtis added this of the president: "Some of us who doubted were wrong." [54]

Less than three weeks after the president's muscular declaration of power, the raw recruits of the Union army marched confidently toward Manassas, Virginia, some thirty miles southwest of Washington, to meet the untested Confederate army in battle. "Forward to Richmond! Forward to Richmond!" blared the *New York Tribune* under the banner headline: "The Nation's War-Cry." In the paper's bold, capitalized words—which Greeley had not authored himself (he was recovering from a knee injury at his Chappaqua farm when they were first published)—"The Rebel Congress must not be allowed to meet there on the 20th of July! BY THAT DATE THE PLACE MUST BE HELD BY THE NATIONAL ARMY!" Greeley may not have originated the challenge, but he did keep it on page one, unchanged, for eight consecutive weeks. During that time he vowed it would be "the Tribune's sole vocation to rouse and animate the American people for the terrible ordeal which has befallen them." As Thurlow Weed sneered: "Mr. Greeley assumed command of our armies, reiterating his orders day after day in italics and capitals." [55]

The "orders" were easier issued than accomplished. At age seventy-five, commanding general Winfield Scott was too old and infirm to lead troops; he assigned the task to the West Point–trained Ohioan Irvin McDowell. The Confederate military leadership boasted only slightly more experience: P. G. T. Beauregard, who had overseen the April attack on Fort Sumter, led the principal Confederate army at Manassas, and West Point–educated Mexican War veteran Joseph E. Johnston led a powerful reenforcement from the Shenandoah Valley. Confederate President Jefferson Davis, a West Pointer with Mexico experience of his own, felt anxious enough about the situation to rush to the front, too, prepared to take overall field command himself if necessary—though he arrived on the scene too late to do so.

To many residents of nearby Washington, the approaching encounter

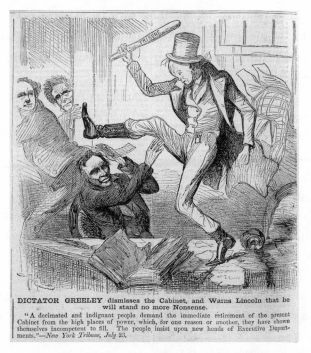

DICTATOR GREELEY dismisses the Cabinet, and Warns Lincoln that he will stand no more Nonsense.

"A decimated and indignant people demand the immediate retirement of the present Cabinet from the high places of power, which, for one reason or another, they have shown themselves incompetent to fill. The people insist upon new heads of Executive Departments."—*New York Tribune, July 23.*

"Dictator" Greeley attempts to run the war—by ousting Lincoln's cabinet—in an August 1861 cartoon from *Harper's Weekly.*

proved equally irresistible. On Sunday, July 21, hundreds of excursionists packed picnic baskets and headed to the front to enjoy the widely expected Union triumph. Encamping themselves on hillsides where they could view what they assumed would be a quick rout, they toasted early reports of federal gains. Late that afternoon, however, Rebel forces counterattacked, and Union lines broke. The retreat turned into a rout when roads became so clogged that troops trampled over both picnickers and their overturned food hampers. Panic-struck civilians fled for their lives. Edward House of the *New York Tribune* described the scene as a "perfect frenzy." [56]

As House's presence attests, Washington's overconfident spectators were not the only civilian witnesses to the Union debacle. For the first time since the Mexican War, a cadre of journalists assembled en masse to cover battle action for the newspapers. This "great swarm of correspondents" had descended on Washington earlier that month, where the initially collegial atmosphere quickly grew competitive in anticipation of imminent military action. In the words of one of the first to arrive: "Any officer who will descant on the war is certain to have a circle of listeners, notebook in hand, and when the fountain has run out or shuts up, off they rush to the telegraph office or the writing-rooms, which are filled with chroniclers of the gossip of the hour." John Wein Forney dubbed the newly arrived gaggle "the gentlemen of the ravenous pen." [57]

The talented reporters who crossed the Potomac bridges in mid-July and headed to the battlefront on horseback or in wagons included House and Warren of the *Tribune*, the debonair Edmund Stedman of the *World*, Henry Villard and William B. Shaw for the *Herald*, Richard C. McCormick of the *Evening Post*, and representing the *Times*, no fewer than four correspondents, including Joseph Howard (author of the Scotch cap calumny), former Confederate prisoner George Salter ("Jasper"), and leading the contingent, editor Henry Raymond himself. And these were just the New York correspondents. On the scene as well were Lincoln's friends Charles Ray and Horace White of the *Chicago Tribune*, plus John Russell Young of Forney's *Philadelphia Press,* and Charles ("Carleton") Coffin of the *Boston Journal,* not to mention a reporter and a messenger for the AP, and illustrator Alfred A. Waud, on assignment for the *New York Illustrated News* (artist-correspondents like Waud would eventually produce enough drawings to inspire some seven thousand wartime woodcuts in the weekly press). [58] Of all these "war correspondents," only McCormick and Raymond—the latter while visiting Europe during the Austro-Sardinian War in 1859—were known to have ever seen, much less reported on, a military battle. General McDowell, for his part, was delighted that his expected triumph would be recorded by such a huge press corps, for victory would surely make him immortal. "I have made arrangements for the correspondents to take the field," he informed the reporters, remarking that they should "wear a white uniform, to indicate the purity of their character." [59]

McDowell directed this particular witticism to one of the most gifted—but ultimately one of the most despised—battlefield correspondents of the entire Civil War: William Howard Russell of the *London Times.* Russell not only reported the Union defeat; he all but shouldered the blame for it. As it turned out, his painful experiences here would establish benchmarks for access by—and limits on—all the journalists who went on to cover the conflict.

Russell had no idea what obstacles awaited him when he crossed the ocean for America. A friend of Dickens, Trollope, and Thackeray, the plump, flamboyant, and supremely confident Russell was already the most celebrated journalist in the world, having earned global fame covering the Crimean War. For the seven years before his arrival, most reports from America had been supplied to the *London Times* by a New York lawyer named J. C. Bancroft Davis, nephew of historian George Bancroft. For a time, young Davis's anti-slavery views seemed to dovetail perfectly with his paper's 1860 editorial declaration: "If we have paid a sincere homage to the rising greatness of America, it has not been to that which the Southerners are so anxious to conserve but that which they are striving to destroy."[60]

The *London Times* was avidly read on both sides of the Atlantic even though its editions were nearly two weeks old by the time they reached the United States (and American news equally outdated by the time it got to England). By early 1861, the world's most influential daily apparently decided it could no longer rely on a partisan American to supply it with American news, especially after London-based managing editor Mowbray Morris concluded that Lincoln's alleged early timidity called to mind "Pontius Pilate—washing his hands of the affair and leaving both action and responsibility to whoever chose to take them." Now Lincoln had become a dictator, Morris informed Davis, and "ought to be whipt down the steps of the great house at Washington." When his American correspondent failed to adjust his coverage accordingly, Morris decided that his readers deserved a new reporter, as he bluntly advised Davis, "who has not been mixed up with your domestic politics, and whose sympathies are not engaged in the struggle now going on." In mid-March, Bancroft Davis dutifully took himself to the Manhattan docks to greet his paper's new war correspondent. Enter William Howard Russell.[61]

Russell spent a few heady days in New York, where he made the acquaintance of American journalists like Henry Raymond, Herbert Bayard Taylor, Greeley's top deputy Charles Dana, and some nameless person whom the anti-Semitic Englishman dismissed as a "clever & humorous . . . Jew ed[ito]r."[62] Russell failed, however, to conquer the city as easily as he expected. Charging that "shrewd as he is," the new arrival had fallen in with "a knot of practical jokers," Horace Greeley objected when one of Russell's early dispatches maintained that "New York would do anything rather than fight." Should he remain "perverted in favor of a bad cause," Greeley railed, Russell's future reports were "sure to recoil upon himself, and to lose him the esteem in which he is so generally held."[63] Nonetheless, when Russell moved on to Washington, Secretary of State Seward greeted him like a visiting potentate, promptly inviting him to the White House to meet President Lincoln at a diplomatic reception. There, the Englishman caught his first glimpse of the "tall, lean man, considerably over six feet in height, with stooping shoulders, long pendulous arms, terminating in hands of extraordinary dimensions, which, however, were far exceeded by his feet." [64]

"He was dressed in an ill-fitting, wrinkled suit of black," Russell observed, "which put one in mind of an undertaker's uniform at a funeral." Above a "sinewy muscular yellow neck" adorned with "a rope of black silk . . . knotted in a large bulb" rose "a great black mass of hair, bristling and compact like a riff of mourning pins." In Russell's perceptive view: "A person who met Mr. Lincoln in the street would not take him to be what—according to the usages of European society—is called a 'gentleman' . . . but at the same time, it would not be possible for the most indifferent observer to pass him in the street without notice." [65]

"Mr. Seward then took me by the hand," Russell attested, led him over to Lincoln, "and said—'Mr. President, allow me to present to you Mr. Russell of the London *Times*.' On which Mr. Lincoln put out his hand in a very friendly manner, and said, 'Mr. Russell, I am very glad to make your acquaintance, and to see you in this country. The London *Times* is one of the greatest powers in the world—in fact, I don't know anything which has much more power,—except perhaps the Mississippi. I am glad to know you as its minister.'" Lincoln enlivened their subsequent conversation with "two or three peculiar little sallies," and Russell went away "agreeably impressed with his shrewdness, humour, and natural sagacity." [66]

The very next day, Mary Lincoln invited Russell back to the White House for dinner, where the journalist heard the president tell another funny story, this time about a drunken Irishman. Later he met General Winfield Scott (who drank warm claret, seemingly oblivious to a serenade blaring outside his window). [67] Even with the doors of official Washington thrown open to him, however, Russell could not resist irreverence. He confided to his diary that the overdressed Mrs. Lincoln looked "preposterous." And when Russell posed for his own photograph adorned with the customary American copyright declaration—"Entered by Mathew Brady According to an Act of Congress"—he invented the lascivious tale that when the rustic president was shown a similarly stamped Brady image of his wife, he protested: "I really cant stand this. I wont have Mrs. Lincoln 'entered by Brady' according to an act of Congress or not." [68]

Following a hastily arranged fact-finding tour of the South, where Russell recoiled at the horrors of slavery, the correspondent returned to the federal capital, secured a horse and rig, and then joined his American counterparts at

Manassas. There he, too, witnessed the Union rout, later contending, "had I been able to file a despatch that night I would have stated that McDowell had been repulsed and that a panic had ensued among a portion of his troops."[69] Yet in the vivid report he ultimately did transmit, Russell stated precisely that and more, describing hysterical Union soldiers crying out "with the most vehement gestures, 'Turn back! turn back! we are whipped!'" Russell painted a portrait of leaderless amateurs fleeing in fear and confusion over ground "strewed with coats, blankets, fire-locks, cooking tins, caps, belts, bayonets," all asking "where General McDowell was."[70] Russell cautioned his London editors to publish his damning observations alongside a factual account of the battle, but the *Times* ignored him and ran his critique alone.

Though he added fuel to the fire by reporting over the next two days on the "unseemly and disgraceful" conduct of the defeated Union troops back in Washington ("streets were thronged with disorderly soldiers congregated round the drinking saloons"), Russell later acknowledged that authorities quickly restored order there, instilling a new determination that seemed "deeper than that which had taken place when the North was aroused by the echoes of the bombardment of Sumter."[71]

The praise proved too little, too late, even after Lincoln appeared to place the blame for Bull Run and its aftermath where it belonged by relieving McDowell of command. When the "latest," already outdated, copies of the *London Times*—bearing Russell's unflinching account—arrived in the United States by ship a few weeks later, many readers concluded that the correspondent had done more than simply chronicle the battle. Perhaps in an insidious attempt to encourage British recognition of the Confederacy, critics charged, he had exaggerated his mortifying charge that Union troops behaved shamefully under fire, and that trained officers proved helpless to rally them. Anglophobe James Gordon Bennett responded by branding Russell a "snob correspondent" whose "sole pride and vocation" was to "deride, sneer at, and vilify everything and everybody." In the resulting furor, Russell, almost as much as the Union high command, bore the brunt of public outrage, so much so that his editor worried that "some enraged patriot will shoot him through the head for telling disagreeable truths."[72] Fanning the flames, Count Adam Gurowski, a Washington gadfly who made his living by translating European newspapers for the State Department, whispered that "over a glass of whiskey," Russell actually boasted "that the *Times* intended to destroy the Union!" Stung, the correspondent protested, "I never drank a glass of whiskey

London Times American reporter William Howard "Bull Run" Russell, the most famous war correspondent in the world.

or anything with him in my life," but his answer failed to appease detractors.[73]

Russell took the mounting criticism seriously, though he also basked in the resulting attention. "There is every chance of my being the best abused man in the U.S., and that means the world," he boasted in the August 22 edition of the *London Times*, "for telling the truth as I see it."[74] The most famous war correspondent on the planet soon acquired a derisive and unshakable new nickname: "Bull Run Russell." Although Horace Greeley offered that "it was not too late for Mr. Russell to write something about this country worthy of his better genius," the "Forward to Richmond" crowd had found in the *London Times* correspondent an ideal scapegoat for a Union military failure that Russell had merely reported.[75] Forgotten in the ruckus was that Greeley himself had dispiritedly called Bull Run "the shipwreck of our grand and heroic army."[76]

General William Tecumseh Sherman, who helped contain the Union panic at Bull Run but loathed all journalists, foreign and domestic, confided to his wife that the correspondents who shied away from acknowledging the chaos that reigned at Manassas lacked the "moral courage to tell the truth."[77] Truth, however, was not what Northern readers wanted to hear after the federal catastrophe. It might be said that no other battle of the Civil War—certainly no loss—ever aroused as much emotional uproar as Bull Run. Antiwar newspapers would soon learn this bitter lesson for themselves.

For a time, Russell's fellow British journalist, Edward Dicey of the *Spectator*, tried defending his compatriot. Dicey complained that with "utter unscrupulousness," Bennett's *New York Herald* in particular made Russell "the object of the most rancorous abuse . . . partly, because he had given personal offense to the editor, by declining his invitations; still more, because he had given offence to the American public."[78] (Bennett had urged that Russell be "belched forth from the community"; in turn, Russell judged Bennett "so palpably a rogue—it comes out so strongly in the air around him, in his eyes & words & smell & voice that one pities the cause which finds him a protagonist.") Jealousy from American reporters was perhaps inevitable, but at least one fellow English correspondent, Frederick Edge of the *London Morning Star*, contradicted Russell, too, insisting that he had witnessed Union "heroism" at Bull Run. Russell dismissed Edge as a "revolting mucus."[79]

It was no small accomplishment for any journalist to become persona non grata in America; even the unscrupulous and unlikable Bennett had long maintained his power and curious appeal. Russell, however, somehow managed to evolve into a pariah, for which he bore no small share of the blame, at least according to Ben Perley Poore. For one thing, except for pro-Confederate English illustrator Frank Vizetelly, whom he befriended, Russell did too little to win admirers among his fellow journalists. He privately assailed the *Chicago Tribune* over its "ludicrous" accounts of his activities, dismissing editor Charles Ray as "a fat elderly man" who "saw nothing of what I saw!" He stirred resentment by using his expense account to host ostentatious "supper parties," and his leisure time to stage "private theatricals." Then he feuded with *Harper's Weekly*, insisting he had never authorized its artist Theodore Davis to travel with him into the South (where the New York pictorial weekly was considered toxic).[80] Thereafter Russell grandly resolved "to have no words with any representatives of the local press as the falsehoods & misrepresentations which are the certain results are monstrous."

Although Russell thought *New York Tribune* correspondent Edward House "a nice fellow," he continued to arouse the enmity of House's boss, Horace Greeley, largely because Russell simply failed to comprehend the fact that slavery had caused the war, and instead clung to what Greeley labeled "the mistaken idea prevailing in England concerning the nature of the present American difficulties." Rather than offer an olive branch, Russell huffed to *London Times* editor-in-chief John T. Delane: "Horace Greeley is the nastiest form of narrow minded sectarian philanthropy, who would gladly roast all the whites of South Carolina in order that he might satisfy what he supposes is a conscience but which is only an autocratic ambition which revels in the idea of separation of the South as the best recognition of its power."[81]

Among American editors, Henry Raymond stood virtually alone in commending Russell for giving "a clear, fair, and perfectly just and accurate, as it is spirited and graphic, account of the extraordinary scenes which passed under his observation. Discreditable as those scenes were to our Army," Raymond admitted, "we have nothing in connection with them, whereof to accuse the reporter. He has done justice alike to himself, his subject, and the country." [82] Raymond's voice was worth more than most on this matter, for he had witnessed Bull Run himself. On the subject of William Howard Russell, however, even the *New York Times* proved without influence.

Within the Lincoln administration, only the crafty secretary of war, Simon Cameron, seemed willing to forgive Russell and continue confiding in him. Reminiscing with the reporter one evening—no doubt over alcoholic refreshments—about his own start as a newspaper "printer . . . at 10 d[olla]rs. a week" back in Pennsylvania, Cameron shared a fact of American life that the London correspondent should already have absorbed. It fell on deaf ears. "He says the press rules America," Russell noted. "I dont think it does[.] I'm certain it oughtn't." [83] A few months later, under a barrage of escalating press criticism over allegations of ineptitude and corruption, Cameron himself would prove the point by losing his job. In January 1862, Lincoln replaced him as secretary of war and exiled him to distant St. Petersburg as American minister to Russia.

Henry Raymond filed his own initial report from the Manassas vicinity after a preliminary skirmish on July 18, writing in the first person, as any celebrity editor might. With an eye on his local readership, he focused at first on New York regiments whose families would surely crave reports about their activities at the front. ("I went out with the centre column. . . . The Sixty-ninth Regiments of New-York were thrown to the right," went one such report.[84]) Like other reporters covering the first battle of the Civil War, Raymond sought no advance information from the Union high command, and used no sources to confirm or deny rumors. And although he owned a great city newspaper, he was no less reliant than his fellow journalists on the telegraph for transmitting dispatches to his paper. In this case, the nearest telegraph operated out of Washington, hours from the front, but Raymond had brought a "runner" with him to carry his stories to the capital, where they could be transmitted to New York.

Hoping to make the first edition of the next morning's paper when the real battle began on July 21, Raymond sent his messenger galloping off with a dispatch early that afternoon. The copy read, in part: "I write this at 2-1/4 o'clock, and am compelled to close in order to avail myself of a special messenger to Washington. The fight is still going on with great energy. The rebel batteries have again commenced firing upon us, and their balls and shells fall thick upon the road and in the field which I had selected as my observatory." The eventual outcome, Raymond conceded in his dispatch, "is not certain at the moment I write." No nom de plume for this writer; he confidently signed his report: "H. J. R."[85]

Less than an hour after his messenger rode off, however, the real "outcome" became painfully apparent. As the tide of battle turned, Raymond scribbled an updated story acknowledging Union defeat, but in the tumult was unable to secure another messenger. The editor had no choice but to retreat to Washington himself along with the battered and dispirited federal troops, revised dispatch in hand. He did not arrive at the capital telegraph office until late that steamy night, looking "sun-burned, dusty, and hardly recognizable." There, the exhausted but determined editor handed in his new account of the Union rout, but the telegraph operator on duty took it upon himself to refuse to transmit it, claiming it would not be in the national interest to wire such a humiliating account.[86]

What Raymond did not know was that, as soon as the initial reports of McDowell's defeat reached Washington, General Scott ordered that all further news from Manassas be kept off the wires for at least a day. Scott was no novice at censorship. Earlier, he and Secretary of State Seward had prevented Washington journalists from wiring the names of Massachusetts soldiers killed in an anti-Union riot that had broken out as they passed through Baltimore.[87] Scott soon insisted that no accounts of troop movements go out over the telegraph without his specific approval.[88] When that arrangement proved unwieldy he imposed rules that precluded correspondents from reporting or predicting any movements by the army. Bull Run brought out the iron glove. "We desire it to be distinctly understood that we are not in the *slightest* degree responsible for what, if done deliberately by us, would be branded a wanton and reckless trifling with the feelings of the public," huffed the *Times* a few days later. ". . . It was an act of the government—and not the conductors of the *Times*—who suppressed the facts of this most important case."[89] It would not be the last time censorship would deny the public access to vital war news. Telegraph censor Alfred Talcott later told a congressional investigating committee that Scott had forbidden him to wire any news about the Confederate victory at Manassas.[90]

Not until July 26, by which time Raymond presumably returned to New York by train to take control of the story back at his desk, did the *Times* publish a full report on the Union catastrophe. For four full days until then, unless they consulted friends or rival newspapers that published the truth first, its readers were led to believe that the Battle of Bull Run had ended with a Union victory.

One New York–based *Times* reporter never forgot the effect on local residents "when the first dirty newsboy whirled through the streets shrieking at the top of his ominous voice, 'Defeat of the Union Army.' . . . It was regarded as a smart commercial fraud, which ought to be put a stop to by the police." By noon, its revised headlines had convinced most New Yorkers that a disaster had indeed occurred, leaving readers "panic stricken"—and no doubt less sanguine about the reliability of their newspaper.[91] Professional as ever, Raymond ate humble pie—and worried aloud about British opinion—by reporting frankly that "the first and foremost thought in the minds of a very large portion of our people after the repulse of Bull Run was, "What will Russell say?"[92]

No truly accurate audit can ever be made to calculate the size of the army of newspapermen that subsequently mobilized to cover the rest of the Civil War—both from government epicenters in Washington and Richmond and alongside Union and Confederate troops in the Eastern and Western Theaters of combat. The numbers were simply too vast, the range of publications too broad, and the printed records too immense. Indisputably, however, the war's Bohemian Brigade ranked as the largest cadre of war correspondents ever to take to the field anywhere in the world up to that time.

Their supply of information nourished an insatiable demand. The public appetite for battlefield news proved boundless from the outset. As Oliver Wendell Holmes, Sr., put it: "We must have something to eat, and the papers to read. Everything else we can give up. . . . We all take a pride in sharing the epidemic economy of the time. Only *bread and the newspaper* we must have."[93] Even before the war started in earnest in July 1861, all three major New York dailies dispatched correspondents to Southern cities, sometimes under cover of disguise, to take the temperature of anti-Union sentiment. The *New York Times*'s George Forrester Williams, for one, passed himself off as an English tourist when he turned up in Richmond, later escaping safely to Washington but only one step ahead of suspicious Confederates. A colleague made it back to the North only by traveling through Virginia by night.[94] Their exploits thrilled New York readers.

Like William Howard Russell, these reporters soon achieved considerable fame of their own. Horace Greeley sent the talented writer Samuel Wilkeson to become his Washington bureau chief, but both that journalist and his celebrated editor were soon eclipsed by battlefield correspondents who provided the *Tribune* with vivid, almost daily details of military engagements—and casualties—to a breathless home-front public. Wilkeson, the son of a well-known Buffalo politician and the father of two boys who eventually served in the Union army, went on to earn his own greatest renown by escaping from his desk job and taking the field to write about battles himself.

Henry Raymond found his own star correspondents in men like William Swinton (brother of John Swinton, one of his New York associate editors) and the intrepid Lorenzo Livingston Crounse, who committed himself to "the single object of getting the news, and getting it first, too."[95] The *Times* retained a twenty-nine-year-old freelance newspaper veteran named Franc Bangs Wilkie to cover the Western Theater for the paper after learning that Wilkie had usefully attached himself to the First Iowa Infantry as its embedded correspondent. When Wilkie encountered difficulty collecting the promised $7.50 per column (plus expenses) from New York, he began publishing his reports concurrently in the *Dubuque Herald* to make ends meet. Known by the pen name "Galway," Wilkie covered the Battle of Wilson's Creek, Missouri, among other early Union setbacks, earning headlines of his own when he was imprisoned as a spy after crossing Confederate lines in pursuit of a story.[96]

It proved difficult for Wilkie and other reporters operating in the West to dispatch timely copy to New York. Transmission sometimes required days-long horseback rides to the nearest telegraph office, followed by the wiring of news that was already cold. Typically, reports from the Western Theater did not reach Eastern newspaper readers for a week or more. Critics sneered that Wilkie was particularly slow to see his coverage into print; he loved describing the action, but was not too reliable about getting stories to his editors.

That kind of sloppiness would never do for the *Herald*. James Gordon Bennett wisely named the well-organized Frederic Hudson to supervise his paper's battlefront coverage from New York. Hudson later asserted that he employed some sixty-three different correspondents during the course of the war. "Never did any journal in any country maintain so vast an expenditure for news," journalist James Parton agreed in 1866. ". . . A reporter returning from the army laden with information, procured at lavish expense, was received in the office like a conqueror coming home from a victorious campaign, and he went forth again full of courage and zeal, knowing well that every man employed on the Herald was advancing himself when he served the paper well."[97]

Veteran journalist Ben Perley Poore agreed that most battlefield reporters were "quick-witted, plucky young fellows, able to endure fatigue, brave enough to be under fire, and sufficiently well educated to enable them to dash off a grammatical and picturesque description of a skirmish." But because most were relegated to the rear, there to await scraps of news, the curmudgeonly Bostonian sniffed, "There were honorable and talented exceptions, but the majority of those who called themselves 'war correspondents' were mere scavengers."[98]

Imperfect and untimely it may occasionally have been, but comprehensive war coverage reached more readers than ever, and at a staggering financial cost to the publishers. *Herald* correspondent Sylvanus Cadwallader was probably not exaggerating when he claimed that, early in the conflict, he often had a special railroad locomotive at his disposal to speed stories north when the telegraph wires were monopolized by the military.[99] Another of Bennett's hirelings secured a pass "to accompany naval expeditions in any staff capacity," almost anywhere on the rivers and seas regardless of cost.[100] The *Herald* claimed that during a single week in the summer of 1861, it allocated $1,000 just for receiving telegraphic news from sources other than the Associated Press. Indeed, the cost of sending a two-thousand-word dispatch just from Washington to New York usually ran around $100. The *Herald* later estimated that overall it spent between $500,000 and $750,000 covering the four years of war.[101] For titans like Bennett, money was no object. Major events often inspired editions boasting bonus pages, and the *Herald* soon routinely adorned its front pages with battle maps. The *Herald* and *Times* introduced the novelty of stacking headlines and subheads atop major stories, so busy readers could almost instantly get the sense of the main news, as if reading a handbill, before diving into the dense text. The professionals called these big, bold titles "banks" or "decks."

Newspapers unable to afford staff to position at every flash point in the field of war often relied on the New York correspondents for adaptable reports. According to one account, George Smalley's original report on the Battle of Antietam for the *New York Tribune* eventually appeared in some 1,400 newspapers nationwide.[102] Bennett was justified in reminding readers that his own reporters always covered battlefield action in person. "Bombs burst above their heads, and cannon balls whiz past their noses and scatter their papers," he boasted. "This gives their letters such vivid, graphic interest. . . . Homer and Milton did very well for old times; but the present age requires the HERALD's staff." [103]

Raymond and Greeley could not muster the financial resources to invest so heavily in battlefield coverage, but each still managed to deploy some twenty correspondents at any given time. "What a busy place the editorial office of the *Times* was!" marveled correspondent William Swinton of this period. ". . . We were constantly receiving packages from correspondents at all points of the compass, special dispatches from the front, or from many a front, official documents or advices; covert news from army officers, visits from wire-pullers or pipe-layers, information from the departments at Washington, and gratuitous suggestions from men of all sorts and conditions." [104] Its roster of reporters included Adam Badeau and Joseph Howard. Most prominent of all were the principal correspondents for the Eastern Theater: the onetime preacher Crounse and the daredevil Swinton.

Charles Dana, succeeded by the young Boston abolitionist Sydney Howard Gay (once Dana left the paper in 1862 to accept a job in the War Department) managed coverage for the *New York Tribune*. Greeley's correspondence corps boasted hardworking professionals like William A. Croffut, Albert Deane Richardson, and at least one female reporter, Jane Grey Swisshelm. If the *Tribune* never managed to field quite as large a battlefield contingent as Bennett or Raymond, Greeley's own editorial commentary exerted perhaps the greatest influence. Greeley worried at first that the burdens of war coverage would break him financially. "We are all poor as John's turkey," he confided in June 1861, adding: "Advertisements are scarce as saints, and don't threaten to be plentier." The *Tribune* survived, raising its prices to cover costs, seeing circulation expand, and by August installing its first stereotype press, which made it possible for an entire broadsheet page to be printed on a single plate. [105] Most Union commanders trusted Greeley's reporters more than any other correspondents; one general even assigned a *Tribune* correspondent to transmit orders and messages during battle. [106]

Non–New York papers endeavored as best they could to keep pace. Continuing to manage *Philadelphia Press* coverage from his perch in Washington, for instance, John Wein Forney authorized his deputy John Russell Young to spend the considerable sum of twenty-five dollars a day to secure war news for his home paper.[107] Forney's rival *Philadelphia Inquirer* meanwhile found a new audience among soldiers in the field by sending newsboys to hawk copies in army camps. Papers that for generations had shunned Sunday publication on moral grounds now unashamedly introduced Sabbath editions to keep pace with a war that knew no days of rest. The Western dailies soon wearied of relying on the East Coast–based Associated Press for news that often appeared first in New York and Boston. ("Telegraph fully all news you can get," the *Chicago Times*'s Wilbur Storey alerted his correspondents, "and when there is no news send rumors."[108]) Their publisher soon organized a Western Associated Press to speed more reliable stories to Chicago and other outposts more quickly. Such was the demand for news, even in the economically deprived South, that a Confederate News Association sprang up by 1862 to make sure that news of battlefield victories made its way expeditiously into the new nation's daily papers.

Many famous Civil War–era bylines later faded into obscurity, but they were widely read and broadly recognized during the conflict and, in many cases, long after. Typical of the breed of battlefield correspondents who collected their observations for postwar reminiscences, the *Herald*'s George Alfred Townsend later produced a highly popular memoir of his wartime experiences. The *Times*'s William Swinton wrote several (famously describing Bull Run as the battle that "made known that the contest was to be a war, not a 'sixty days' riot").[109] So did the reporter once assigned to cover Lincoln in Springfield: Henry Villard, who switched from the *Herald* to the *Tribune* mid-war.

Like the raw Union recruits he first covered in July 1861, the experienced Villard cut his teeth as a battlefield correspondent at Bull Run—and nearly paid for the experience with his life. During the early hours of the fray, a famished Villard paused with the *Tribune*'s Edward House to pick ripe cherries at an abandoned Manassas farmhouse. Suddenly a swarm of Confederate shot began riddling the trees, sending twigs, leaves, and fruit splashing onto their upturned faces. After that close call, Villard boasted with affected sangfroid, "the music of bullet, ball, and grapeshot never had much terror for me." Villard found himself severed from McDowell's headquarters during the chaotic Union retreat. "My newspaper instinct was fully aroused," he remembered. "I saw a chance of outstripping the rival correspondents with a report of the battle by reaching Washington as quickly as possible." Villard still had a horse at his disposal, so he cantered his way through the retreating mass of soldiers toward the capital and there supposedly filed the very first report on the disaster published in New York. Bennett ordered an extra edition to feature the exclusive.[110] Villard fared much better under fire than the *Tribune*'s bookish Adams Hill, who reportedly fled from the battlefield in a panic after a bullet came dangerously close to his skull during a preliminary skirmish. His fellow war correspondents never let him forget that he had shown the feather under fire.

In a pinch, the *Tribune* and most of its rival papers could rely on dispatches from the Associated Press, whose own cadre of wartime correspondents, supervised by Washington bureau chief Lawrence Gobright, probably exceeded in number even that of the *Herald*. The seasoned Gobright had been covering the national capital since the age of Jackson, and no matter how furious the bloody fighting became over the next four years, always joked that the "battles" he once covered inside Capitol Hill committee rooms were far more brutal than those he later observed on the fields of war.[111]

Eventually, the full roster of wartime journalists grew to gigantic proportions. In the 1950s, the enterprising historian J. Cutler Andrews identified the names of some 350 different war correspondents who worked in the field for Northern newspapers alone between 1861 and 1865, and tracked the work of another ninety-five who labored for newspapers published in the Confederacy.[112] The actual number was undoubtedly far greater.

No newspaperman ever expressed more hysteria over the Bull Run catastrophe than Horace Greeley. The editor who, in rapid succession, had urged Lincoln to accept dissolution of the Union without war, but then to march aggressively to Richmond, took on yet another role after the Union army fled from Manassas: that of hand-wringing penitent. Bull Run nearly unhinged him.

Until the battle, Greeley had devoted much of his Lincoln correspondence to setting himself up as the sole arbiter of New York patronage—chiefly, he unconvincingly maintained, "to consolidate and strengthen the friends of the Administration" in the metropolis. Back in April, just as Raymond began publicly expressing disappointment in the president, Greeley wrote Lincoln confidentially in an effort to prevent the Raymond-Seward clique from filling either of the two biggest federal vacancies in the city: the plum jobs of collector and surveyor of the port. However timely the appeal, and whatever his recent displeasure with Raymond, Lincoln was not ready to empower Greeley alone. The president dismissed the editor's proposal with a Western-style comment: "Greely," he drawled, misspelling the editor's name, was ". . . in favor of having the two big puddings on the same side of the board." [113]

After Bull Run, Greeley turned on Lincoln. The federal defeat drowned out earlier thoughts of capturing Richmond, and rekindled the editor's earlier instinct that the North should let the South secede. To his credit, he abjured from stating his anxieties editorially, but in a feverishly written July 29 confidential letter to the president, Greeley left little doubt that he again preferred abandoning the fight, and moreover would hold Lincoln responsible for any further bloodletting. The editor signed his morbid letter, "Yours, in the depth of bitterness."

This is my seventh sleepless night—yours too, doubtless—yet I think I shall not die, because I have no right to die. I must struggle to live, however, bitterly. But to business.

You are not considered a great man, and I am a hopelessly broken one. You are now undergoing a terrible ordeal, and God has thrown the gravest responsibility upon you. Do not fear to meet them.

Can the Rebels be beaten after all that has occurred, and in view of the actual state of feeling caused by our late awful disaster? If they can—and it is your business to ascertain and decide—write me that such is your judgment, so that I may know and do my duty.

And if they *cannot* be beaten—if our recent disaster is fatal—do not fear to sacrifice yourself to your country. If the Rebels are not to be beaten—if that is your judgment in view of all the light you can get—then every drop of blood henceforth shed in this quarrel will be wantonly, wickedly shed, and the guilt will rest heavily on the soul of every promoter of the crime. I pray you to decide quickly, and let me know my duty.

If the Union is irrevocably gone, an Armistice for thirty, sixty, ninety, 120 days—better still, for a year—ought at once to be proposed with a view to a peaceful adjustment. Then Congress should call a National convention to meet at the earliest possible day. And there should be an immediate and mutual exchange or release of prisoners and a disbandment of forces.

I do not consider myself a judge of any thing but the public sentiment. That seems to me every where gathering and deepening against a prosecution of the war. The gloom in this city is funereal for our dead at Bull Run were many, and they lie unburied yet. On every brow sits sullen, scowling, black despair.

. . . This letter is written in the strictest confidence, and is for your eye alone. But you are at liberty to say to members of your Cabinet that you *know* I will second any move you may see fit to make. But do nothing timidly nor by halves.

Send me word what to do. I will live till I can hear it at all events. If it is best for the country and for mankind that we make peace with the Rebels at once and on their own terms, do not shrink even from that. But bear in mind the greatest truth—"Whoso would lose his life for my sake shall save it," do the thing that is the highest right, and tell me how I am to second you.[114]

Lincoln never replied to this tortured missive, and certainly never told Greeley "what to do." If he ever shared the letter with his cabinet, as its author advised, no evidence survives.[115] Instead, Lincoln sealed it with a piece of red ribbon and filed it away in his desk, telling not a soul about its existence. Hidden or not, it surely had the immediate impact of reducing Lincoln's confidence in Greeley. Not only was the editor's loyalty now in question; so was his stability.

Not for another three years did the president disclose the letter's contents to anyone. When he finally did so it was in April 1864, when Lincoln came "loafing" into his White House office late one night expressing gratitude to Greeley for a useful bit of recent editorial praise. Something in it suddenly reminded the president of the editor's three-year-old diatribe, and as his secretaries, John Nicolay and John Hay, looked on, Lincoln fished it out of his pigeonhole desk, untied it, and challenged his aides to "decipher" Greeley's infamous scrawl—a "discursive cryptograph," according to one contemporary. After Hay staggered his way through the message, reading aloud, he looked up in astonishment and declared it "the most insane specimen of pusillanimity that I have ever read." Then Nicolay added that if it was ever published it would ruin Greeley, predicting: "Bennett w[oul]d. willingly give $10,000.00 for that." As he retied the tape round the papers, Lincoln glanced up and replied almost wistfully: "I need $10,000 very much but he could not have it for many times that."[116]

Horace Greeley may have been ready to surrender in 1861, but Abraham Lincoln was not; not even when federal forces endured another humiliating defeat at the Battle of Ball's Bluff, Virginia, on October 21. Only forty-nine Union men died in the fighting, but among the casualties was Lincoln's close friend Colonel Edward Dickinson Baker, for whom the future president had named his late son, Eddy. Overcome with grief, Lincoln ordered a White House funeral for Baker, but the family's only public expression of mourning came from his precocious ten-year-old son, Willie Lincoln, who composed what the boy called "my first attempt at poetry," a tribute (probably sent along by his father) published in the administration organ, the *National Republican*: "There was no patriot like Baker, / So noble and so true; / He fell as a soldier on the field, / His face to the sky of blue."[117]

In late August 1861, news reached Washington that another famous military figure, Union general John C. Frémont, commander of the Department of the West, had taken the extraordinary initiative of banning slavery in Missouri—without notifying, much less seeking authorization from, the president. Like everyone else in the capital, Lincoln learned the startling news from the press. The general's action cheered antislavery advocates, but posed a major challenge to the president's cautious approach to the slavery issue, not to mention his prerogatives as commander-in-chief. The *Times, Herald*, and *Tribune* had expressed few misgivings over General Benjamin F. Butler's earlier declaration that slaves fleeing into Union lines should be considered "contraband of war—that is, property subject to seizure and protection by the army." But to Lincoln's mind, Frémont had taken a dangerous, not to mention unauthorized, step forward.[118]

The dashing Frémont was a national celebrity in his own right: an explorer known as the "Pathfinder of the West," a former U.S. senator from California, and the Republican Party's first presidential candidate back in 1856. But Frémont was proving something of a disappointment as a commander of the sprawling and volatile territory he was assigned to supervise at the outset of the war. Critics blamed him for the Union loss at the Battle of Wilson's Creek on August 10, placing his reputation in jeopardy. Frémont responded on August 30 by ordering the confiscation of all Rebel property in Missouri—including slaves, whom he unilaterally declared "free men."[119]

Fearful that Frémont's proclamation would "alarm our Southern Union friends, and turn them against us," particularly in crucial Kentucky, Lincoln responded by asking the general to "modify" his order to apply only to those residents actively engaged in supporting the Confederacy. The politically insensitive Frémont resisted, forcing the president to revoke the order publicly. As Lincoln explained to Orville Browning: "I think to lose Kentucky is nearly the same as to lose the whole game. Kentucky gone, we can not hold Missouri, nor, as I think, Maryland.[120] When Frémont failed to go on the offensive militarily, Lincoln felt he had no choice but to relieve him of his command.

Not surprisingly, the Frémont affair provoked an outcry from many of Lincoln's closest pro-freedom press supporters. The *Chicago Tribune*'s Joseph Medill, for one, complained privately that his old friend's decision "cast a funereal gloom over our patriotic city," adding: "It comes upon us like a killing June frost—which destroys the comming [*sic*] harvest. It is a *step backwards*."[121] In a rare show of unity, both the *Missouri Democrat* and the *Missouri Republican* expressed support for Frémont's initiative, as did Greeley, Raymond, and even Bennett. The New York *Anglo-African* protested in especially heartbreaking terms that "the reverse at Bull Run was a slight affair compared with the letter of Abraham Lincoln, which hurls back into the hell of slavery the thousands in Missouri rightfully set free by the proclamation of Gen. Frémont."[122] Greeley glumly urged his Washington editor, Samuel Wilkeson, to assure Lincoln that he would support the administration "by silence whenever I cannot do it by words, because I believe its fall would involve that of the government. . . . If I can stand such letters as Lincoln's to Fremont, they need not fear my breaking with them on any personal ground whatever."[123]

Still, Lincoln held his ground, even if he privately agreed with the assessment that soon appeared in the *New York Times*: "The proclamation of Gen. Fremont brings us to a new chapter in the war of rebellion."[124] That chapter as yet had no clear ending.

William Howard Russell returned to Washington in September, ready to report on further military action, but his English colleague, the *London Spectator*'s Edward Dicey, elected to return home. Dicey had seen enough of America—just enough, in fact, to inspire a book about his experiences here. Unlike Russell, however, he had come to believe that the American press was "a tolerably fair—probably the fairest—exponent of American opinion." Dicey cautioned only that the unceasing competition, particularly among New York's newspapers, offered "proof of the absence of high mental culture in the United States."

"Day after day," Dicey noted with dismay, "there is a sort of triangular duel between the editors of the *Herald*, the *Tribune*, and the *Times*, in which personalities, or what in any other papers would be considered gross libels, are freely bandied to and fro." Worst of all, "in this warfare, the *Herald* being utterly, instead of only partially, unscrupulous, comes off an easy victor." Dicey conceded that Bennett was unethical and reckless, but added: "The real cause . . . of the *Herald*'s permanent success, I believe to be very simple. It gives the most copious, if not the most accurate, news of any American journal. It is conducted with more energy, and probably more capital; and . . . written with as rough common sense, which often reminds me of the [London] *Times*. It has too, to use a French word, the *flaire* of journalism." As Dicey marveled, "I have seen two people reading the *Herald* for one I have observed reading any other newspaper." [125]

"Of course, if I chose," Dicey hastened to add, "I could pick out hosts of eccentricities, and what we should call absurdities, in American journalism. The larger and, I hold, the truer view is, to look upon the American press as a vast engine of national education, not overdelicate in its machinery, but still working out its object. As such, it is, indeed, the press of a great and free people." [126]

Those freedoms were about to be subjected to their greatest challenge ever.

CHAPTER ELEVEN

Freedom of the Press Stricken Down

———◆———

Although he restrained himself from saying so at the time, and was, in fact, nearly hysterical for peace, Horace Greeley later maintained: "Mr. Lincoln did not fully realize that we were to have a great civil war till the Bull Run disaster. I cannot otherwise explain what seemed to many of us his amazing tameness."[1]

If Lincoln's so-called timidity ever really existed, it vanished quite soon after that battle—at least toward a new foe he judged to be nearly as dangerous as armed Rebels: antiwar, anti-administration, anti-recruitment newspaper editors. Against these foes, the Union government commenced an additional war, which Greeley eventually came to support almost as ardently as the fight to restore the Union. Months earlier, Lincoln may have assured delegates to the Washington peace conference that even in the wake of secession, he still believed a free press "necessary to a free government."[2] But outright rebellion altered his thinking on the subject, especially after the July battle that was supposed to end the Civil War in a single afternoon. For his part, Greeley may have believed that, following the Bull Run defeat, Lincoln "still clung to the delusion that forbearance, and patience, and moderation, and soft words would yet obviate all necessity for deadly strife."[3] But the record suggests otherwise. Following Bull Run, the administration turned its attention not only to forging weaponry and raising more troops, but also to quelling home-front newspaper criticism that the president, his cabinet advisors, and, more surprisingly, many Northern newspaper editors, believed was morphing from tolerable dissent into nation-threatening treason.

In the wake of this tightened oversight, some Democratic war opponents tried arguing that constitutional guarantees of free speech and free press must remain absolute no matter what the danger of an armed revolt. Even Lincoln's friend Edward Baker, in one of his final speeches in the U.S. Senate before accepting his fateful military commission, insisted that neither the eradication of slavery nor the preservation of the union justified threats to "the liberty of the press."[4] Critics pointed out that the First Amendment unequivocally guaranteed: "Congress shall make no law . . . abridging the freedom of speech, or of the press." And Congress never did. This did not inhibit the administration from determining that in an unprecedented case of rebellion, and under the powers the president had claimed in order to crush it, military necessity superseded constitutional protection, and contingency trumped the organic assurances of freedom of expression within the Bill of Rights.

Based on this argument, the administration began conducting—or, when it occurred spontaneously, tolerating—repressive actions against opposition newspapers. At their most unobjectionable level, the safeguards were initially meant to keep secret military information off the telegraph wires and out of the press. But in other early cases, censors also prevented the publication of pro-secession sentiments that might encourage Border States out of the Union. In an anonymous dispatch for the *New York Examiner*, presidential clerk William Stoddard probably spoke for the White House in complaining that, cut off from their usual sources, "the legion of daily newspaper reporters" roamed "the streets and camps . . . pouncing, with hawk-like avidity, upon every poor little stray item which, in their palmier days, they would have scorned to notice."[5] And some of those "items," the administration believed, should remain secret.

Eventually the military and the government began punishing editorial opposition to the war itself. Authorities banned pro-peace newspapers from the U.S. mails, shut down newspaper offices, and confiscated printing materials. They intimidated, and sometimes imprisoned, reporters, editors, and publishers who sympathized with the South or objected to armed struggle to restore the Union. For the first year of the war, Lincoln left no trail of documents attesting to any personal conviction that dissenting newspapers ought to be muzzled. But neither did he say anything to control or contradict such efforts when they were undertaken, however haphazardly, by his cabinet officers or military commanders. Lincoln did not initiate press suppression, and remained ambivalent about its execution, but seldom intervened to prevent it.

Did press dissent really pose an existential threat to national security? Probably not, certainly not in the free, loyal Northern states. But a frightened Northern public and most pro-Republican editors not only failed to object to the more paranoid view, they encouraged it, even when it triggered outright violence against newspapers. Perhaps, for these supportive editors, the additional appeal of reducing the Democratic competition seemed irresistible.

The military laid the foundation for press censorship well before Bull Run. Unable to read, much less censor, every newspaper published in the country, it acted promptly to control both the source and distribution points for news. Soon after the April attack on Fort Sumter, it cut the telegraph wires between Washington and Richmond. Then the administration banned the use of the postal service and other exchange routes in and out of the rebellious states. National papers with large circulations in the South—particularly the *Herald*—suffered considerably as their Southern readership dwindled. Soon all of Washington's telegraph wires, the standard medium for transmitting news from city to city, fell under military control—as Henry Raymond had learned to his consternation after Bull Run. In the aftermath of the federal defeat there, a season of official crackdowns on individual newspapers commenced. The cascading hostility toward pro-peace, pro-slavery journals made the angry crowd that menaced the *Herald* offices after Sumter seem like a band of carolers by comparison.

Suppression fever flared up first in an area of Northern Virginia that fell quickly under Union control. Once again it was a "desecrated" flag that stimulated the eruption. On May 24, a young Lincoln protégé, the dashing Zouave colonel Elmer Ephraim Ellsworth, marched his colorfully attired men into Alexandria determined to tear down an offending Confederate flag from atop one of the town's seedier hotels. Ellsworth captured the banner, but paid with his life when the innkeeper blew open his chest with a shotgun as the colonel descended the hotel staircase. As the first Union officer killed in the Civil War, Ellsworth became an instant martyr—his "memory . . . revered, his name respected," mourned the *New York Times*.[6]

With the rallying cry "Avenge Ellsworth" on their lips, Federal troops

soon occupied the entire Washington suburb. Union colonel Orlando Will-
cox then ordered the *Alexandria Gazette* to publish a proclamation declaring martial law. Rather than comply, editor Edgar Snowden shut down the
paper, whereupon Union soldiers seized the office, smashed property, and
allegedly stole valuables. A precedent had been established. Snowden lay low
until October, when he launched a new journal called the *Alexandria Local
News*, vowing that the venture would focus on "the truth, as far as that can be
reached." Union forces kept their eye on Snowden, and his comeback proved
fleeting. When, later that year, Union troops seized the rector of an Alexandria church merely for omitting the customary prayer for the president,
Snowden denounced the arrest as an "outrage." Soldiers responded by setting
fire to the headquarters of the *Local News*. The beleaguered editor suspended
operations yet again, only to reopen the old *Gazette* in 1862. Two years later
he would be arrested himself.[7]

Situations like these became commonplace in most of the volatile Border
Slave States where Union commanders struggled to prevent pro-slavery interests from mounting secession efforts. In Maryland, for example, Lincoln
authorized each military commander "to arrest, and detain, without resort to
the ordinary processes and forms of law, such individuals as he might deem
dangerous to the public safety."[8] The broad order by no means exempted
journalists. When, that summer, the pro-secession *Baltimore Exchange* editorialized that "the war of the South is a war of the people, supported by
the people," while the "war of the North" was "the war of a party . . . carried
out by political schemers," military authorities shut down the paper, arrested
editors W. W. Glenn and Francis Key Howard—the latter, a grandson of
the author of the National Anthem—and shipped them off to prison without trial. Howard's surviving personal papers suggest that authorities may
have acted prudently in his case: the records included secret resolutions in
which Baltimore leaders pledged violent support for the Confederacy.[9] He
remained in detention, his case unresolved, for months, and for a time he was
confined at Fort McHenry in Baltimore harbor, the very installation whose
bombardment half a century earlier had inspired his grandfather to write
"The Star-Spangled Banner." Howard also spent time at that most notorious
of press dungeons, New York's Fort Lafayette, and later wrote an unrepentant
memoir about his lengthy confinement entitled *Fourteen Months in American
Bastilles.*[10]

In short order, acting under instructions from Secretary of War Cameron, federal marshals suppressed four more of Baltimore's anti-Union journals and imprisoned a number of their proprietors. "The secession organs in Richmond were not more unscrupulous or desperate in their attempts to undermine and overthrow the Government at Washington than these same in Baltimore," the *New York Times* cheered. Henry Raymond's only complaint was that it cost the federal government millions of dollars "to repair the mischief of the un-muzzled organs of treason in Baltimore."[11] That there was some truth to the suspicions of treason among local newspapermen was confirmed when onetime reporter J. B. Jones, making his way through the city en route to Richmond, reassuringly found *Baltimore Sun* editor Arunah Abell to be "an ardent secessionist."[12] In September, emboldened federal authorities arrested yet another Maryland editor, Daniel Deckart, for publishing a "disloyal sheet" in Hagerstown. Deckart ended up confined for more than a month at Washington's dank Thirteenth Street prison.[13]

Inevitably, suppression fever, like the war itself, spread west, particularly to Missouri and Kentucky, two Border States where Union loyalty was decidedly a fragile sentiment. During the post–Bull Run summer, as strategically crucial Missouri teetered on the brink of secession—in the end it never left the Union but remained a fierce battleground—commanding general John C. Frémont moved under martial law to consolidate control over the press. In one early action, the army suppressed the pro-Confederate *St. Louis State Journal* and arrested its editor, Joseph W. Tucker. Back in New York, the *Times* again showed no sympathy for such brethren. Raymond pointed out that the "the chief Western organ of the Southern conspirators" had "given itself up to stimulating the mob of St. Louis to sedition and bloodshed, and inaugurating the reign of anarchy in the city and State."[14] Federal troops also sacked the *Cape Girardeau Eagle*, closed down the *Hannibal Evening News*, and padlocked newspapers in smaller Missouri outposts like Warrensburg, Platte City, Osceola, Oregon, and Washington.[15]

A politician destined to be embroiled in later free speech controversies—Democratic congressman Clement L. Vallandigham of Dayton, Ohio—responded to these shutdowns with a vow to introduce federal legislation "to secure the freedom of speech and of the Press." The initiative received little support. Raymond continued to mock the theory that "organs of treason" could be protected to publish at will. "The United States is now AT WAR with Secessionism," he editorialized. ". . . Whatever ministers to it must be destroyed; whatever stands in the pathway of our triumph must be over-

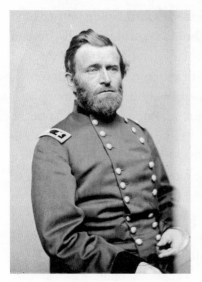

General Ulysses S. Grant—before he became a successful military commander, an early enforcer of Union newspaper suppression.

thrown." The *Times* adamantly rejected the "vague notion afloat that freedom of speech carries with it some special and peculiar sanctity."[16]

Less than a week after that comment appeared in print, one of the newly minted generals under Frémont's command acted to suppress a newspaper in yet another Missouri district. His name was Ulysses S. Grant. On August 26, Grant moved not only against grocers supplying food to secessionists, he also ordered the shutdown of the *Booneville Patriot*, published some forty miles from his Jefferson City headquarters. "Bring all the printing material, type &c with you," he directed his troops. "Arrest J. L. Stevens and bring him with you, and some copies of the paper he edits." Stevens was no more entitled to civil rights, Grant maintained, than the other "obnoxious" Confederate sympathizers. "Give secessionists to understand what to expect if it becomes necessary to visit them again." Just a week later, Grant reported that "some of the despatches" earmarked for telegraphing "by one of the Newspaper correspondents" accompanying his army were "so detrimental to the good of the service that I felt it my duty to suppress them," too.[17]

For a time, the assault on the pro-slavery, pro-Confederate press in Missouri continued unchecked—and at both Washington and New York editorial desks, unchallenged. That same month, the military closed down two more St. Louis papers, the *War Bulletin* and the *Missourian*, charging that both were "shamelessly devoted to the publication of transparently false statements regarding military movements in Missouri." When the St. Louis *Christian Advocate* came to the papers' defense, the provost marshal warned its editors to adhere to its identity as "a religious paper" or face "the discipline of the department," too.[18] Military censorship tightened further when the army "seized and destroyed" the *St. Louis Daily Evening News*, and briefly detained editor Charles G. Ramsay for criticizing Frémont's failure to rescue a federal garrison at Lexington, Missouri.[19] "We are under a reign of terror," an anonymous correspondent protested to Postmaster General Montgomery Blair after

Ramsay's arrest. ". . . Will our President countenance such tyranny?" [20] Blair dutifully forwarded the warning to Lincoln, but the president offered neither comment nor relief.

By September, suppression fever reached the Bluegrass State. On the 9th, an angry Union loyalist from nearby Indiana named Charles Fishback inflamed matters by sending Secretary of State Seward a batch of recent editorials from the *Louisville Courier*, a paper that Horace Greeley had earlier branded "a Secession Press." Was it not "about time," Fishback implored Seward, that "the editor were an occupant of Fort Lafayette or some other suitable place for traitors? The people are getting tired of sending their sons to fight rebels while such as this editor, more mischievous by far than if armed with muskets, are allowed to furnish aid and comfort to the enemy unmolested." [21] On the 18th, three days after a cabinet meeting at which the matter may well have come up for discussion, the Post Office obliged by banning the *Courier* from the U.S. mails. The following day, federal authorities raided the newspaper's offices and took several employees into custody, including assistant editor Reuben T. Durrett, whom they charged with publishing "editorials of the most treasonable character."

It was not a banner day for free speech in Kentucky. Also seized as a traitor on September 19 was the state's former governor, Charles S. Morehead, along with one Martin W. Barr, who, it was alleged, "used his position as telegraph agent for the Associated Press to advance the insurrectionary cause." [22] The case of the ex-governor of course dominated the news, relegating the Durrett arrest to the background. In fact, because Durrett was linked to the detention of so important a politician, it became one of the first press arrest cases in which Lincoln involved himself directly, though not, as it turned out, sympathetically.

The *Courier*'s racist but pro-Union owner, George D. Prentice, promptly acted to absolve himself from his employee's views but also tried to exert influence to liberate him. Prentice had previously called on Kentucky to remain neutral, and typically expected the president to bestow patronage influence on him in return. Now he wrote Lincoln twice in one day to urge leniency for Durrett. Perhaps he was "a secessionist," Prentice conceded, "but he has never done any harm in our community. . . . I would rather give a portion of the brief remnant of my life than have his confinement protracted." Lincoln remained unmoved. He coolly scribbled on the back of Prentice's plea: "sent to Fort Lafayette by the military authorities of Kentucky and it would be improper for me to intervene without further knowledge of the facts than I now possess."[23]

The "further knowledge" soon arrived—of a decidedly condemnatory nature—courtesy of pro-Union Kentucky Democrat Joseph Holt, secretary of war under Buchanan, but now working tirelessly to keep his home state from seceding. Holt informed Lincoln that Durrett had indeed "done everything to incite the people of Kentucky to take up arms against the General Government," adding: "His arrest has rejoiced the hearts of the Union men, and his discharge . . . would in my judgment be a fatal mistake." Holt enclosed a cache of Durrett "paragraphs," in one of which the journalist asserted that Kentucky was "under no obligation to remain in the Union, but under many to leave it."[24] Durrett remained in confinement, and Lincoln rewarded Holt's loyalty by naming him judge advocate general of the Union armies.

Undaunted, Durrett's sympathizers pressed on for his release through other channels. To no avail, they wrote to Secretary of the Treasury Chase on October 10, arguing that Durrett was a "harmless man" who "hardly knew which side he was on," and again petitioned Lincoln for mercy by pointing out that his confinement had left the journalist's family "financially ruined." Only in October did Lincoln finally tell Seward: "I am willing if you are that any of the parties may be released"—that is, if the president's reliable Kentucky allies James Guthrie and James Speed agreed that "they should be." Yet not until Durrett himself wrote Seward in December to protest his innocence and complain bitterly about conditions in prison was his case finally reopened. Seward finally relented, ordering the journalist's release providing he agree to do nothing "hostile to the United States."[25]

Durrett swore to a standard oath of allegiance on December 9 and at last became a free man—after ten weeks inside a series of federal prisons without trial—and only after Prentice again reminded Lincoln of "the importance of the Journal as an agency in this struggle." For good measure, Prentice added that he could sustain the paper only if Lincoln awarded him contracts to supply the army with weapons, animals, and food. Few 1861 suppression episodes better illustrated the dangers facing Border State editors who opposed the Union, or the rewards expected by those who supported it. At least Lincoln could console himself in the belief that "I understand the Kentucky arrests were not made by special direction from here."[26] This was small consolation to Durrett, who was still languishing in prison when his employer began securing lucrative government contracts.

Equally chilling incidents took place in Northern states that had voted strongly for Lincoln in 1860, and posed no danger of abandoning the Union. Though unsanctioned by the government, these attacks, most of them spontaneous, were seldom restrained by local authorities, and rarely punished by local courts. Nearly all the aggression reflected shame and fury over the humiliation at Bull Run. In much the same way official Washington attempted to place undeserved blame for that fiasco on the *London Times*, residents of Northern towns and villages long accustomed to tolerating both Republican and Democratic newspapers now unleashed their pent-up rage on Democratic newspapers that questioned military recruitment or mocked the soldiers' performance on the battlefield.

On August 19, Edward Everett, the still respected Massachusetts statesman who had stood unsuccessfully for vice president on the 1860 Constitutional Union ticket, published a widely reprinted article assailing "Northern Secession Journals." Everett insisted that it was "an absurdity . . . under the venerable name of the liberty of the press, to permit the systematic and licentious abuse of a government which is tasked to the utmost in defending the country from general disintegration and chaos." [27] Perhaps it was no coincidence that the very next day, a mob destroyed the office of the *Sentinel*, a Democratic weekly published in Horace Greeley's old training ground of Easton, Pennsylvania. Around the same time, another infuriated crowd invaded and sacked John Hodgson's pro-Democratic, antiwar *Jeffersonian* in West Chester. The mob pitched Hodgson's printing press out the window, hurled subscription records into the street, and christened the pile of papers and account books with the contents of a chamber pot. The assailants, unconvincingly described by the local Republican paper as unknown strangers "from the country," were never brought to justice. [28]

Another dramatic Pennsylvania suppression incident—this of the official variety—involved a supposedly "obnoxious" Philadelphia publication called the *Christian Observer*, whose Presbyterian affiliation did not inhibit its openly pro-secession, pro-slavery bias. "Such piety," complained another paper, "is the worst act of infidelity to God and the cause of good government, and has been tolerated too long." [29] Authorities did not much worry about the *Observer's* influence on Philadelphians, but the paper enjoyed substantial readership in nearby Maryland. A month after Bull Run, its feisty, sixty-six-year-old editor, Amasa Converse, published what he claimed was an authentic letter from an unnamed Virginian charging that Union forces recently on the march there had committed "gross, brutal, fiendish, demonic outrages" meant to "ravage the country, pillage the houses and burn them, outrage the women, and shoot down for amusement . . . even children." [30]

That was all the provocation federal authorities needed. Just before noon on August 22, a U.S. marshal stormed the headquarters of the *Christian Observer*, confiscated type, and evicted staff. Converse appealed the suppression case directly to Lincoln, claiming he was but a poor old man who had always promoted "harmony, good will," and "the preservation of the Union," adding: "I cannot believe that you would justify the proceeding if you knew the facts." But the editor's protest—that "every American citizen wherever he might be, and however humble," should be "more secure than in any other part of the Globe, in his rights of speech person and property"—fell on deaf ears. With no hope of reopening in Baltimore, Converse picked up and relocated to the Confederate capital of Richmond—so much for being a good Union man—where he reestablished his paper in friendlier surroundings. Lincoln never replied to the editor's insistence that "freedom of the press I have always believed was one of the great bulwarks of our national safety." [31] On the contrary, by refusing to intervene on his behalf, Lincoln implicitly

Early targets of Union press crackdowns: Francis Key Howard (left), imprisoned at Fort McHenry; and Amasa Converse (right), driven from Philadelphia.

accepted the argument that national safety required that hostile journals like the *Christian Observer* be muzzled—especially if they enjoyed substantial circulation in the Border Slave States he was trying to keep within the Union.

This ultimately proved to be administration policy even if the "disloyal" newspapers were published as far from the Mason-Dixon Line as New York. By late July, even the anti-Republican *Herald* was deploring what Bennett called "the licentiousness of expression" rampant in the city's "secessionist papers." [32] In rare form, Bennett assailed the "pious and oily old hypocrite" who ran the *New York Journal of Commerce*, and lambasted the "weeping and wailing Jeremiah of the *Daily News*" for expressing "unspeakable horror" over "the warlike usurpations of Abraham Lincoln . . . which are all moonshine." Never one to miss an opportunity to stick the knife into Henry Raymond, he added: "The little fidgety tricksters of the *Times*, although they no longer demand that 'Honest Abe Lincoln' shall be superseded in his office . . . can still discover nothing but rottenness and roguery at Washington." [33]

August proved the cruelest month for New York's anti-administration sheets. On the 16th, a federal grand jury for Manhattan's Southern District filed a "presentment"—in legal terms, a formal notice of suspected illegality—with the U.S. Circuit Court. It inquired whether "certain newspapers" in the city, ". . . in the frequent practice of encouraging the rebels now in arms against the Federal government" had overstepped freedom of the press and now deserved "the employment of force to overcome them." The document identified five specific targets. All of them supported the Democratic Party, opposed Lincoln, and questioned the need to recruit volunteers to put down the rebellion: N. R. Stimson's pro-Confederate *New York Day-Book*; James H. Van Evrie's white supremacist *Freeman's Journal*; the pro-Democratic *Brooklyn Eagle*; Gerard Hallock and William C. Prime's anti-Republican *Journal of Commerce*; and the *Daily News*, the Democratic organ run by the prosecession mayor's own brother, the newly elected Democratic congressman Benjamin Wood. [34] Announcement of the presentment proved remarkable enough to find a place in the annual *Confederate States Almanac*, a publication otherwise devoted to Southern battlefield victories. [35]

The grand jury foreman who signed his name to the document, a prominent Manhattan broker named Charles Gould, was animated by something other than his interpretation of the Constitution. A well-to-do Seward admirer, Gould had become a humanitarian activist on war matters, organizing Union rallies and campaigning for an improved ambulance corps to correct the "cruel and criminal neglect of maimed men" at Bull Run. In other words, Gould was a loyal Republican through and through—a political warrior for the Union. Administration censors could not have hoped for a better advocate.

As if to prove the point, Gould later signed a public letter "supporting the Government in prosecuting the war" and criticizing "unjust attacks of a portion of the press" that undermined those efforts.[36] On at least one other petition, Gould's name appeared alongside that of Henry Raymond. Although fellow New York elite George Templeton Strong disliked Gould—he thought him the "embodiment" of "corrupt, mercenary, self-serving, sham-patriotism"—Strong judged the grand jury action against newspaper "nuisances" wholly "consolatory." To such loyalists, Northern pro-peace newspaper editors ranked no higher in mid-1861 than Southern traitors.[37]

Gould and his fellow grand jurors were not alone in these sentiments. Raymond, too, agreed, branding the five papers charged as "open and avowed advocates of secession," and there was abundant evidence in print that he was correct. The virulently racist Van Evrie, author of an 1854 tract that judged "Negroes" an "inferior race" and slavery their "normal condition," had recently insisted in the *Freeman's Journal* that abolitionist "madmen" in Washington had no right to wage war without congressional approval, and that "no outward pressure of the bayonet can . . . 'save the Union.'" The *Day-Book* had similarly railed against the "coercive policy" of "the rash and foolish Lincoln." And Ben Wood's *Daily News* had savaged "the dictatorship of 'Honest Old Abe'" and his "Bloody Administration." Recently, Wood had likened Lincoln to Henry VIII and warned that his policies would provoke "murder, massacres," and "negro insurrection." The City's Common Council responded by voting to withhold municipal advertising from the *Daily News*, but the mayor—editor Wood's brother—vetoed the bill.[38]

The Bull Run defeat took the debate beyond politics. "The Grand Jury are aware that free governments allow liberty of speech and of the Press to their utmost limit," Gould conceded in the August 16 presentment, "but there is necessarily a limit. If a person in a fortress or an army were to preach to the soldiers submission to the enemy, he would be treated as an offender. . . . If the utterance of such language . . . through the Press is not a crime, then there is great defect in our laws, or they were not made for such an emergency." The panel urged the judge to guide them toward the logical next step: bringing formal charges against the Democratic editors.[39]

Official Washington did not wait for the court to rule (in fact, the presiding judge never formally responded to the presentment). The very same day, Lincoln announced stringent new rules banning all "commercial intercourse" with the Confederacy, an order widely interpreted to apply to distributors of all products, including news.[40] Apparently concluding that the new ruling together with the Gould presentment were sufficient grounds for punitive action, the New York City postmaster declined to accept the five named dailies for further mail shipments to subscribers. Then on August 21, Postmaster General Blair made the order national by totally banning all five from the U.S. mails, declaring them "dangerous, from their disloyalty."[41]

When the *Daily News* tried to subvert the order by shipping papers south by railroad, government agents boarded incoming trains and confiscated the bundles. "The Marshal could not have known of anything peculiarly obnoxious to censure in that particular issue of the paper," commented the *Times* after two thousand copies were "hauled off in a furniture car" in Philadelphia. ". . . We are brought to the conclusion, therefore, that the Daily News is condemned, by reason of its general political tone, and that the Administration is resolved to prohibit its circulation in certain districts." Yet this disturbed Henry Raymond not at all. Proof that the *News* meant to give "aid and comfort to the enemy," he reported, was "the fact that most of the packages seized here are directed to places in Maryland, Delaware, Kentucky and Missouri, where there are thousands of disaffected people, who need but an evidence of sympathy from the North to precipitate secession." The only "surprise" about the seizure, contended the *Times*, was the fact "that the Administration has so long forborne to defend itself against the fanatical insurrectionary crusade of the secession papers published in loyal States." Lincoln left no fingerprints on the *News* crackdown, but certainly knew about it as it was occurring: he received at least one telegram from Philadelphia alerting him to the ongoing confiscation. A few days later, Raymond rejoiced anew when a U.S. marshal in upstate New York seized another eleven hundred copies of the *News* circuitously bound for Louisville via Albany.[42]

News editor Benjamin Wood tried fighting back, ludicrously insisting he had "spoken of the President and his Cabinet . . . only in terms rigorously and studiously respectful" while "mobs have been instigated against us by a vitiated rival Press, and the mother tongue exhausted upon us in coarse abuse and in misrepresentations of our sympathies and our motives." As for his Republican press colleagues, Wood charged, they had made themselves "notorious as mere panderers to popular passion and partisan interests. The loss to the American nation of its liberty and its honors—the horrors of civil war and our national degradation—are to be laid at their door." The "sword has been drawn," Wood charged, "against liberty of speech and liberty of the press and a venal, bigoted Court has dared to threaten, here in our midst, the most plainly outspoken and truthful journals of the metropolis with indictment." [43]

Wood's protests did nothing to calm the uprising. Later that month, the War Department further tightened the noose by issuing General Orders No. 67. Citing an 1806 law that made "giving intelligence to the enemy" a crime punishable by death, the new directive "absolutely prohibited" the "writing, printing or telegraphing" of intelligence "respecting the operations of the army, or military movements on land or water, or respecting the troops, camps, arsenals, intrenchments, or military affairs." Violators faced imprisonment, court-martial, even execution. For good measure, the department issued the names of 154 additional newspapers it considered dangerously opposed to the war. Regarding the watch list as a badge of honor, the *Day-Book, Daily News,* and *Journal of Commerce* published all 154 titles—as did Bennett's *Herald.* When the *Journal of Commerce* complained that the administration aspired to "extinguish the liberty of the Press throughout the United States quite as effectively as it has been done under any of the Governments of the Old World," the *Times* bristled: "Society always reserves an eminent right to protect itself against such licentious use of privilege of printing as tends to destroy its framework, and introduce immorality, confusion and anarchy . . . we are at a loss to see what right of the Press should shield the Journal of Commerce from the penalty of a crime against society." [44]

Rather than perceive a general threat to a free press, some pro-war newspapers saw instead an opportunity to quash contrary views and irksome competitors. It was that newly minted patriot, James Gordon Bennett, who made one of the strongest of all the arguments for widening the dragnet, noting that thus far, for the most part, antiwar journals were merely being identified, not shuttered, while at the same time Confederate authorities were cracking down on their own dissenting press voices far more harshly. "Under the dominion of Jeff. Davis, no voice and no newspaper is allowed to whisper a word in favor of the Union. Life, liberty, conscience, and everything there are under a reign of terror which can only be compared with that of the first French Revolution. In the loyal States, on the other hand . . . the supporters and emissaries of this rebellion are still allowed a very large margin of liberty

or license injurious to the public cause. . . . We hope that our Northern secession newspaper managers will soon find it most adviseable [*sic*] to give up
their bad cause and its reasonable affiliations in every shape and form. Let
them steal off and look for relief under the government of Jeff. Davis, if they
cannot sustain that of the United States in this crisis, for they who are not for
our government are against it."[45]

Bennett and Raymond were not alone in questioning the right of anti-
Union newspapers to free-press protection. The *Philadelphia Evening Bulletin* also hailed the New York shutdowns, and added that the suppression of
the hometown *Christian Observer* had been "a wise and judicious step," too.
Urging that its local press be subjected to even deeper scrutiny, the *Bulletin*
demanded to know: "Does every paper rejoice over the success of our arms
and sorrow in our sorrow? Let the matter be looked into." Future censorship must be unrelenting, the *Bulletin* insisted, for wily editors cleverly com-
mingled "sentiments about patriotism, religion, humanity, bloodshed, mercy
and the like, the whole together meaning no more or less than *treason.*" Over
the next few days, the *Bulletin* rattled the cage. Unpatriotic newspapers were
doing more to threaten "destruction of the Union than a dozen Bull Run
defeats. . . . Is the United States Post Office to be desecrated to the treasonable use of assisting to demoralize its own people, weaken the hands of the
Government, and render war so unpopular that all volunteering will cease?"

When the pro-disunion *Philadelphia Evening Argus* closed its doors before it, too, could be suppressed, the *Bulletin* gloated: "The list of killed or
wounded among the Democratic newspapers is constantly swelling." To critics who argued that "the freedom of the press is a palladium of liberty," the
Bulletin offered this striking response: "If they are encouraging those who are
making war against it; if they are doing their utmost to trail our flag in the
dust—it is perfectly idle to talk of the freedom of the press . . . *a traitor has
no rights.*"[46] Here the *Bulletin* hinted at something few other papers were willing to admit: Democratic affiliation alone had become almost tantamount
to treason. On the other hand, Republican fealty, as local editor John Wein
Forney had learned to his advantage, attracted official favor. In that vein,
Jesper Harding, publisher of the pro-Lincoln *Philadelphia Inquirer*, earned
appointment during the crackdowns as collector of internal revenue for the
City of Brotherly Love, while Forney continued to urge additional patronage
aspirants on the White House. To one disgusted Richmond journalist, "the
servile press" in the "Yankee states" had created a truly unholy alliance with

the "Lincoln Government to suppress freedom of speech throughout Yankee-dom. In proportion to the atrocity of each violation of liberty are the shouts of these slaves of despotism." [47]

Although he arrived at the conclusion that censorship was justified with more difficulty and less enthusiasm, Horace Greeley, too, eventually began warning against the "Dangers of Too Much Toleration." Though he cautioned New Yorkers not to take the law into their own hands, and questioned whether a minor daily like the *Daily News* could truly stir a "mutiny," Greeley ultimately conceded that it was "possible to be too tolerant in the fear of abridging freedom." Suppression that in peacetime might constitute "persecution," he declared, amounted in wartime to "precaution." The Constitution guaranteed freedom of the press, but common sense required "all who would exercise it" to understand "that abuses of it will subject the offenders to punishment." [48] The comment prompted Bennett to suggest that Greeley's post–Bull Run criticism of Winfield Scott should be treated as treason as well. "The only way to stop his mischief," the *Herald* sneered, "is to suppress the publication of the *Tribune*, which has done and is doing a thousand times more good to the enemy than the *Daily News* and all its tribe have ever done or could ever do." [49] Suppression had become a byword. Bennett's mock threats against the *Tribune* never gained traction, but facing seizure and censure with no support from pro-administration editors, the *New York Daily News* had little choice but to shut down. Unable to reopen his paper for two years, editor Wood focused his attention on his congressional duties and directed his literary talents toward producing a turgid anti-suppression novel he called *Fort Lafayette; or, Love and Secession.* [50]

In fact as well as fiction, the Fort Lafayette of Wood's title, a grim citadel squatting just off the Brooklyn coastline, became "home" to so many unindicted Confederate and pro-Confederate war prisoners—editors along with blockade runners—that it acquired a new nickname: the "American Bastille." By mid-September, authorities added to its growing population of journalists the *New York Daily News*'s Philadelphia correspondent, William H. Winder (brother of a Confederate general), incarcerating him for "treasonable communication with the enemy" after he called on Pennsylvania citizens to resist joining the army. [51] Winder later produced an exposé of his own: a book called *Secrets of the American Bastille.* [52]

After Thurlow Weed conducted a tranquil 1861 inspection tour of Fort Lafayette, the *New York Times* rosily maintained that the facility was "very comfortable . . . more like a hotel than anything else, where the proprietor is rather strict." [53] Missouri editor Reuben Durrett no doubt came closer to the truth when he complained to Secretary of State Seward that at Fort Lafayette he "was compelled to sleep upon a bag of straw half a foot shorter than myself without a pillow and blanket," and that "the food given me there was raw pork, tough beef and bread . . . served upon a board table which the dirty cook swept with the same broom with which he swept the floor." [54]

Despite the growing threat of exile to the Brooklyn purgatory, some press resistance continued. Unwilling to bow to pressure, James A. McMaster tried to continue publishing the New York *Freeman's Journal*. On September 14, however, formally charged by Seward with "editing a disloyal newspaper," McMaster was arrested (after a struggle) in his office and imprisoned at Fort Lafayette, where he remained for a month until agreeing to swear to the oath of allegiance. [55] There he may have met, among other fellow journalists, such recent arrivals as Henry A. Reeves, editor of Long Island's *Green Port Watchman*, ambiguously charged with publishing "secessionist teachings." Detectives seized him in September as Reeves attempted to flee by boarding a train bound for upstate New York. That same day, a Burlington, New Jersey, newspaper contributor named James W. Wall joined the fort's prison population, too, arrested after writing a letter criticizing Postmaster General Blair for his "high-handed, unconstitutional act in stopping certain newspapers from being circulated through the mails." [56] Though Wall was the son of a U.S. senator (a friend of Blair's father, no less, during the days when the elder Blair served as publisher of the *Washington Globe*), kinship could not save him from serving thirteen days at the American Bastille without formal charge. It did not help his case that he had also contributed "obnoxious and dangerous" columns to the *New York Daily News* that allegedly "exulted over the defeat of the U.S. troops at the Battle of Bull Run." [57] In October, officials in upstate Malone, New York, arrested editor Francis D. Flanders (along with his attorney brother, Joseph) and shipped him to the fort as well, after his *Franklin Gazette* editorialized that "the Southern States had a right to secede." Local Unionists complained that the twins were inhibiting efforts to recruit volunteers. [58] Francis's wife took over the paper after his arrest.

Before the turbulent 1861 summer ended, the *New York Day-Book* suspended its daily edition, prompting the *Times* to rejoice (taking a swipe at Bennett in the bargain): "No newspaper in the country, except possibly the Herald and News, did more to encourage the Southern people to plunge into the Maelstrom of secession, by . . . misrepresenting the sentiment of the North, than the Day Book."⁵⁹ *Day-Book* editor N. R. Stimson later resumed publishing, but only his weekly edition, finally owning up to its retrograde principles by renaming it *The Caucasian*. But the postal ban limiting its widespread circulation remained in effect.⁶⁰

Facing similar ruin, the *Brooklyn Eagle* recanted and reformed its editorial policy. Playing the role of sacrificial lamb, managing editor Henry McCloskey resigned in September, falling on his sword in his farewell editorial: "Having so long exercised the unrestrained expression of opinion which American citizens have enjoyed, he may have transcended the limits within which the present national administration is disposed to confine political discussion." After McCloskey's departure, Irish-born Thomas Kinsella took over as editor, and in one of his first editorials, maintained: "The pretence that we desire to subjugate anybody but rebels, is now amply refuted."⁶¹

Meanwhile, another grand jury in neighboring New Jersey filed a present-ment of its own with the federal circuit court at Trenton. Following New York's lead, it charged five allegedly disloyal Garden State papers—the *Newark Evening Journal*, *Warren Journal*, *Hunterdon Democrat*, *New Brunswick Times*, and *Plainfield Gazette*—with "thwarting" the government's efforts at "self-preservation." While the jurors stressed, "We cherish a due respect for freedom of the press," they called on readers at the very least to "withhold patronage" of the papers.⁶² The editor of the largest of these, the antiwar New-ark daily, managed to escape formal prosecution—but only until 1864, when authorities arrested him for treason. Nor was the widening purge limited to English language newspapers. Yet another grand jury, this one in Westches-ter County, New York, issued a presentment recommending the suppression of two local German papers, the *National-Zeitung* and the *Staats-Zeitung*. And back in Manhattan, angry residents circulated a petition denouncing the French language *Courier des Etats-Unis*. Not even Lincoln's home state of Illinois was immune from suppression fever. There, a Republican daily in Peoria successfully agitated to ban the anti-administration German language *Demokrat* from the U.S. mails.⁶³

Perhaps most chilling were the unauthorized, unofficial, and largely un-punished attacks on journals and journalists by civilians and frustrated sol-diers in the North, even in New England. In Connecticut, such a fate awaited editors William Pomeroy and Nathan Morse of the *Bridgeport Daily Adver-tiser and Weekly Farmer*, who had argued in May that the South was "resisting

a rebellion; one initiated by the Abolitionists and Republicans of the North!"
Much criticism followed—from resident celebrities like showman P. T. Barnum and inventor Elias Howe, among others—but initially no censorship or
violence. That was before Bull Run. On August 24, a month after the battle,
a crowd of five hundred Unionists disrupted a pro-South "Peace Meeting" in
suburban Stepney, then stormed back to downtown Bridgeport and broke
into the offices of the *Daily Advertiser.* The marchers hurled printing presses
and type into the street, and stomped them into scrap. Co-editor Morse escaped unharmed only by crawling to safety through a third-floor window.
Not far away, expecting a similar uprising, armed men stationed themselves
inside the offices of the Democratic *Hartford Times,* "determined to defend
it while life lasted," and vowing to sack the three local Republican papers if
attacked.[64]

In early August, a New Hampshire regiment returning from Bull Run
leveled the antiwar *Democratic Standard* in Concord, burning its property in
the street. A similar invasion destroyed the *Bangor Democrat* in Maine after
that paper likened the secessionists of 1861 to the revolutionary patriots of
1776 and urged readers to oppose "this unholy and unjustifiable war." Editor
Marcellus Emory was eating his dinner about half a mile away when he heard
the first clanging of fire bells. "After finishing my meal," he recounted, "I set
out to return to my office. Soon after I met two gentlemen in a buggy, who
informed me that my office had just been sacked, and all my property thrown
into the street." Hastening to the scene, Emory found a mob of two thousand
men "engaged in heaping my tables, stands, cases and other material" into a
large fire burning in the middle of Market Square." When he plunged into his
ransacked headquarters in an attempt to secure his account books, he heard
"demonic cries for my blood . . . 'Hang him! Tar and feather him! Kill him.'"
With four years' toil "swept away" by "mob violence," the editor mourned:
"Thus hath the freedom of the press been stricken down here in Maine, not
from any patriotic impulse, but through the wicked instigation of a band of
politicians who would willingly subvert all law and order for the maintenance
of a mere party dogma."[65]

The most harrowing New England incident of all occurred on the evening of August 19, when rowdies in Haverhill, Massachusetts, stormed the
home of Ambrose Kimball, editor of the *Essex County Democrat.* There they
disarmed him, hauled him off to a local inn, and threatened him with bodily
harm unless he recanted his antiwar editorials. Kimball refused, so his at-

tackers stripped him to his undergarments, swathed him in tar and feathers, and dragged him through town tethered to a wooden rail—an old vigilante tradition, but now a brutally ironic desecration of the symbol of opportunity closely associated with the country's rail-splitter president. After toting Kimball through the streets and back to his newspaper office, his assailants demanded that he give three cheers for the Union, and then deposited him at the hotel where the humiliation had begun. There, a defeated Kimball finally fell to his knees, held up a trembling hand, and meekly declared: "I am sorry that I have published what I have, and I promise that I will never again write or publish articles against the North, and in favor of secession, so help me God." Indifferent local authorities took months to bring charges against six of the ruffians involved in the attack, and when they finally did so, the town of Haverhill rallied to their defense. No one was ever punished. Kimball abandoned his paper and emigrated to Iowa.[66]

If other Northern editors felt any bond with these hideously persecuted fellow professionals, they rarely expressed solidarity. In fact, the Republican press continued applauding such crackdowns, at least the official ones. Just weeks after predicting that the press would not "regard in silence or obsequi-

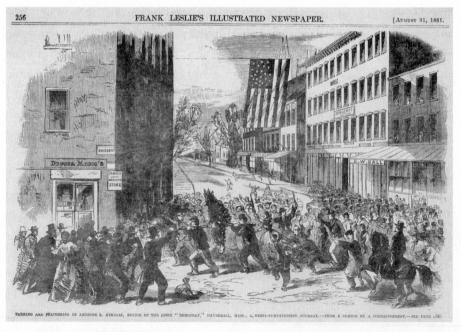

The tarring and feathering of Massachusetts Democratic editor Ambrose Kimball—a cause célèbre given national exposure when it was portrayed in *Frank Leslie's Illustrated Newspaper* on August 31, 1861.

ously applaud" the administration, but would instead act "the school master, exposing and commenting upon every act that does not come up to . . . the standard which competency demands," the *Times* judged the New York *Journal of Commerce* "guilty of exciting a riot in our streets and apologizing for the mob." No "right of the Press," the *Times* reiterated, "should shield" it "from the penalty of a crime against society." [67] Branding the *Daily News* "that most pestilent of secession sheets," the *New York World* (still a Republican paper) added that "every newspaper that" approved of secession "be regarded as the accomplices of treason." And the *Chicago Tribune* questioned the very concept of "absolute freedom of the press" during a rebellion. "Until the war is over," it argued, "we must be content to accept whatever the altered conditions of the times and the country may demand as a requisite of national salvation." [68]

Many Democratic journalists fell silent once the crackdowns began in earnest, surely fearful of reprisals. The most notable exception was George Wilkes, whose New York sporting paper, *Spirit of the Times*, remained critical of Lincoln without censure. Wilkes may have simply been too inconsequential to persecute: he was popular around town, but given his paper's focus on horseracing, not particularly influential. His ability to escape the 1861 press dragnet suggests that it was never systematic or comprehensive—rather the result of sporadic outbursts of ill will. To William Howard Russell, it was a distinction without a difference. The English correspondent expressed shock that so many "leading statesmen" of America seemed to consider that "Liberty of the Press was a nuisance carried to its present extent, that universal suffrage demanded limitations & had outgrown the bounds set to it by the fathers of the country." [69] But even the world-famous Russell dared not express these sentiments in print; he merely shared them in a private letter to his London editor.

Had the country—loyal Republican journalists especially—risen up immediately to oppose or merely question unchecked newspaper suppression, the outbreak might have ended aborning, or become less widespread, indiscriminate, and acceptable. An outcry might have inspired legislative or executive remedies designed to establish boundaries on free expression that differentiated dissent from sedition and specified penalties for violation. Instead, in the shock and humiliation that followed Bull Run, the idea took hold in the North that any paper encouraging disunion or discouraging enlistment deserved to be silenced by whatever means might be at hand—even if the sentiment encouraged gangs of ex-soldiers, often fueled by liquor, to try atoning for their failures on the battlefield by striking out against home-town editors who supposedly dishonored their service. Raymond of the *Times* spoke for many unconcerned publishers when he argued: "The temporary surrender of these rights is a small price to pay for their permanent and per-petual enjoyment."[70] For a time, those rights nearly evaporated, while the leaders of the newspaper profession looked the other way or overtly defended the new constraints.

Their overall lack of indignation constituted either the most masochis-tic period in American press history, or a sign of genuine consensus that without some level of oversight—up to and including the constant threat of suppression—the country itself might not survive the war. Even censorship hawk Henry Raymond never signaled an eagerness to surrender constitu-tional protections, only a willingness "to waive those rights for a time, in order to save the Constitution and the Government." Raymond insisted that there was "no danger to freedom or to personal liberty from this. When the exigency which compels their suppression has passed away, the people will demand their restoration."[71]

It may also be argued that the Lincoln administration exercised *less* news-paper control than it might have imposed during so widespread a civil war. The government never attempted to impose formal limits on dissent, or to suggest precisely where criticism ended and treason began. In one sense, the administration's overheated but disorganized response to newspaper dissent unleashed what might be called the "Salem Witch" hunt of the Civil War: a summer-long hysteria that spread wildly before healers knew quite how to control either the cause or effect of the panic. Even at its fever pitch, however, early Civil War–era press suppression was marked by a series of uncoordi-nated, case-by-case outbreaks, as evidenced by how many different federal agencies had their hands in the 1861 crackdowns: the Post Office (to secure the ban on mailing antiwar papers), the State Department (which held official responsibility for domestic security until February 1862), Treasury (called on occasionally to intervene), Interior (to enforce postal bans), and the War Department (along with the army), not to mention the courts. Everyone seemed partially in charge of the issue, yet no one seemed to be in full con-trol. It comes as little surprise that Lincoln learned of Cameron's "suspension of the Baltimore newspapers" indirectly from Seward—and only after they occurred.[72] At first, save for new Post Office and telegraph strictures, no over-arching policy or authority formally governed questions of freedom of the press, beyond the broad "war power" Lincoln had ascribed to himself in his July Message to Congress.

The outcome might have been far worse for antiwar journals. Had Lincoln and his counselors sat down around the cabinet table to explore a government-wide response to press dissent—and there is no evidence they ever did—they might perhaps have aimed for the total destruction of the antagonistic Democratic Party press, once and for all. Instead, it was "Wanted: A Policy" all over again—or perhaps evidence of a good deal more restraint than Lincoln is often given credit for.

Because of the absence of any organized pogrom against press freedom, the Democratic press eventually recovered from the censorship panic of 1861, in time to exert significant influence over the vigorously contested off-year elections of 1862, and then to report—and, some charged, provoke—the anti-draft riots of 1863. Many shuttered newspapers reappeared. Although military and postal authorities tried for a time to prevent the West Chester, Pennsylvania, *Jeffersonian* from reopening after it was sacked, a federal court in Philadelphia ruled by October that the paper had committed no outright treason and could resume publication. In January 1862 the court relaxed the postal ban that kept the paper from its subscribers, and the *Jeffersonian* resumed its caustic criticism of the Lincoln administration. The following year, it won a judgment of more than $500 for damage to its property during the attack, despite complaints by the local Republican paper that "had the government listened to the counsels of such presses as *The Jeffersonian*, Jeff Davis would now occupy the capitol at Washington and the rebel flag would float over the Keystone state."[73]

Even in bitterly contested Missouri, pro-Confederate journals rebounded. Several of the papers shut down in August 1861 resumed publication not long thereafter. As many as six anti-administration journals continued to operate unchallenged during and after the first wave of suppression. Meanwhile Confederate forces operating in Missouri began systematically sacking pro-*Union* papers, hauling off the printing press of one such journal all the way to Arkansas. That October in Tennessee, antislavery editor William "Parson" Brownlow closed down his *Knoxville Whig* one step ahead of arrest by the Confederate army. If nothing else, newspapers were targeted by both sides in the conflict.[74]

Press censorship and suppression—though they would continue, off and on, throughout the war—never again approached the witch-hunt peak reached in the summer of 1861, when some two hundred newspapers and their editors were identified, menaced, arrested, imprisoned, humiliated, bankrupted, mobbed, or sacked. That the panic of 1861 did not escalate into the permanent elimination of a free press in the United States was something of a miracle. In fact, many newspapers flourished during the Civil War, vastly increasing their coverage, circulation, and influence, and in some cases earning huge profits in the bargain. Inquisitive reporters still turned up everywhere—both in Washington and at the front—asking inconvenient questions, attempting to file unauthorized dispatches, testing the scrutiny of official censors, and competing to secure unsanctioned scoops. There was no escaping them. Rather than kill the press during the Civil War, the conflict and the Lincoln administration in effect gave it new life—especially if its practitioners were pro-Union and pro-Republican.

Union loyalty helped secure, but did not always guarantee, entrée for journalists. To be sure, some officers gave preferential treatment (along with access to useful information) to friendly reporters who could be relied upon to produce flattering coverage. These publicity-hungry aspiring heroes operated almost in the antique tradition in which politicians granted exclusives to loyal "organs." In return, such officers expected their favorite reporters to "puff" their reputations in print. John Wein Forney, for example, introduced John Russell Young to General Nathaniel Banks in late 1861 as "a young man of brilliant abilities." Forney did not bother mentioning that Young had successfully covered the Battle of Bull Run. Instead he stressed what seemed far more important: that he was "thoroughly devoted to the cause, and knows how to keep a secret."[75]

Other commanders, especially those subjected to frequent criticism, made life for journalists uncomfortable, if not unbearable. For most battle-tested officers, reporters more often attracted suspicion than appreciation. Commanders worried that journalists might inadvertently put them in peril by reporting where they were encamped—or heading. Once published in the North, such seemingly banal information could easily be spirited to Richmond by Confederate sympathizers and then deployed to plan attacks. Reporters learned the hard way that not every general was willing to trade information for flattery.

In the fall of 1861, a newly assigned *Cincinnati Commercial* war correspondent named Florus B. Plympton discovered this painful lesson for himself when he approached one of the most press-wary military leaders of the entire war, William T. Sherman, at a railroad station north of Louisville. Plympton blithely handed the moody Union general his letters of introduction, one of them signed by Sherman's own brother-in-law, Thomas Ewing, Jr.

Plympton probably did not know that Sherman had been nursing antipathy toward the press for years. Back in 1856, a local journal had published, from rooms just a few floors above Sherman's own San Francisco banking office, what the future general considered "falsehood and malice" designed to injure local financial institutions. Sherman stormed upstairs, confronted the editor, told him "I could not tolerate his attempt to print and circulate slanders in our building," and warned him that "if he repeated it, I would cause him and his press to be thrown out of the windows." Sherman proudly remembered that the editor "took the hint" and relocated.[76]

Now, five years later, Sherman gave but a cursory glance to Plympton's documents, and then made a theatrical show of checking the time on his pocket watch. Looking up to glare at the reporter, the general snarled: "It is eleven o'clock; the next train for Louisville goes at half past one; take that train; be sure you take it; don't let me see you around here after it is gone."

Staggered, Plympton tried reasoning: "But, General, the people are anxious and it's not my business to tell anything but the truth of what I see here."

To which Sherman shot back: "We do not want the enemy any better informed about what is going on here than he is. Make no mistake about the train."[77]

Unfortunately for Sherman, Plympton's paper had the last word. An opportunity for revenge arose in October, when the *New York Tribune* reported that during a military summit, Sherman had pleaded for 200,000 new men in order to hold Kentucky for the Union, a request his superiors considered irrational. The high command responded by transferring Sherman to St. Louis, feeding rumors that his mania for reenforcements had expanded into a full-scale nervous breakdown. This gave the *Cincinnati Commercial* the chance to get even. On November 16, describing Sherman as "a perfect monomaniac on the subject of journalism," the paper openly questioned his mental fitness to lead troops. Sherman sank into a depression, prompting the *New York Times* to report that his "disorders" might render him ineligible for command, "perhaps permanently." On December 11, the *Commercial* threw the harshest light yet on the commander's emotional struggles by publishing a follow-up story under the blaring headline, "General William T. Sherman Insane." Sherman, the paper reported, had gone "stark mad." He had wildly overestimated opposition forces and irresponsibly suggested evacuating all Union troops from Kentucky. "It seems providential," came the conclusion, "that the country has not to mourn the loss of an army through the loss of the mind of a general into whose hands was committed the vast responsibility of the command in Kentucky."[78]

Since it was now winter, and the armies on both sides were idle, Sherman took the opportunity to exile himself to his home "to allow the storm to blow over somewhat." But as he bitterly recalled, the "newspapers kept up their game as though instigated by malice." Other Northern papers picked up the "insanity" story and spread it nationwide. When Sherman protested the persecution to Murat Halstead, editor of the *Cincinnati Commercial*, Halstead "cavalierly" replied that the general's mental condition was "one of the news-items of the day," and merited all the coverage it had provoked. If Sherman had a correction to offer, Halstead volunteered to print it—"as though I could deny such a malicious piece of scandal affecting myself," the general seethed.[79] Eventually, the press tired of the story on its own, but its impact haunted Sherman for months. In his own frank estimation, he did not regain his reputation until he helped Ulysses S. Grant achieve Union victory at the Battle of Shiloh in April 1862.

At the time, however, Sherman's anger and shame were not enough to convince his superior officers to punish the offending journal, whose editor, Halstead, it was no doubt pointed out, was reliably pro-Republican and pro-Lincoln: as far as censorship was concerned, an untouchable. "The newspaper reports are certainly shameless and scandalous," General Henry W. Halleck consoled Sherman in December, "but I cannot agree with you, that they have us in their power 'to destroy us as they please.' I certainly get my share of abuse, but it will not disturb me."[80] It disturbed Sherman, however, and his hatred of reporters only intensified. As Halstead later put it, in quite an understatement, Sherman "was not one of those generals who cultivated the press." And when he expressed his hostility, Halstead noted, he "had a way of stating things that stung and stuck."[81]

In late autumn 1861, stung by recent battlefield defeats and feeling exhausted and beleaguered after five decades in military service, Winfield Scott retired to

West Point. To succeed him as general-in-chief, Lincoln appointed a man less than half Scott's age: George B. McClellan, a vainglorious popinjay who had been scheming to force out Old Fuss and Feathers for months. McClellan immodestly described his task as nothing less than "converting the unorganized, defeated, and dispirited remains of McDowell's Bull Run command into the Army of the Potomac . . . *ab infinito*—out of nothing." [82]

Ill-advisedly, McClellan directed one of his first offensives not against the Confederacy but against the *New York Times*, shockingly accusing Henry Raymond of treason. In a December 1861 letter to Secretary of War Cameron, the general charged that in recently publishing "a map of our works on the other side of the Potomac, & a statement of the composition of the Divisions in that same locality," the *Times* was "clearly giving aid and comfort and information to the enemy." McClellan called it "a case of treasonable action, as clear as any that can be found." In his view, "the interests of our arms, require the suppression of this treasonable sheet, & urgently recommend that the necessary steps to suppress the paper may be taken at once." [83]

Cameron had no choice but to forward the outrageous complaint to Raymond for his comment, but made sure to add in a conciliatory cover note: "Feeling assured that no such motives as those indicated in his letter, dictated the publication I have taken this mode of advising you of the importance and necessity of avoiding a similar inadvertency in future." An indignant Raymond fired off a reply to the secretary, sneering that there had been no "inadvertency" at all: the map in question had been copied from a lithograph sold openly at Willard's Hotel, and the rest of the so-called secret information gleaned from reports published in other newspapers. "I repel in the strongest terms every intimation contained in Gen. McClellan's letter," Raymond protested, that the *Times* had published any of this material "with any treasonable intent, or with any design, purpose or thought of either aiding the enemy or embarrassing the army under his command." [84] Not surprisingly, the *Times* went unpunished. George McClellan had lost his first battle.

Not one to abandon his aspiration to control the press, McClellan had proposed an all-new system of voluntary press censorship. Grandly summoning the press corps to his headquarters on August 2, he convinced representatives of the *Tribune, Herald*, and nine other papers to agree to "refrain from publishing, either as editorial or correspondence . . . any matter that may furnish aid and comfort to the enemy"—that catch-basin phrase again. In return, McClellan offered "facilities for obtaining and immediately transmitting all information suitable for publication"—in other words, better access to telegraph wires during and after battles.[85]

Lawrence Gobright of the Associated Press, one of the correspondents who met with the general that day, willingly signed the document. "It agreed that all the correspondents of the press would carefully abstain from publishing all news concerning army movements," he explained, while the army promised to "furnish every facility to the press to procure correct information." Adams Hill of the *Chicago Tribune* initially believed the journalists had agreed "to cooperate with the censor of the press. . . . We were to publish nothing in relation to military movements, but might publish everything in relation to battles." But when Union forces suffered another humiliating defeat on October 21 at Ball's Bluff, Hill complained that his dispatches were "not allowed to go over the wires until two or three days afterward."[86] The press thereafter considered the contract with McClellan breached.

McClellan, an avowed Democrat incurably suspicious of pro-administration journals, meanwhile undertook a secret effort to gain the support of James Gordon Bennett and the copacetic *Herald*, sending word to New York that he wanted the editor to identify a specific battlefield correspondent to receive his exclusive confidences. "I am anxious to keep Mr. B. well posted," he wrote, "& wish to do it fully—ask how far I can go in communicating important matters." McClellan might more profitably have taken a lesson from his future opponent Robert E. Lee, who shared his adversary's impatience with journalists, but seemed sympathetic to their legitimate needs. "I am sorry . . . that the movements of the armies cannot keep pace with the expectations of the editors of the papers," Lee remarked to his wife. "I know they can regulate matters satisfactorily to themselves on paper. I wish they could do so in the field." But then he added this conciliatory object lesson: "No one wishes them more success than I do & would be happy to see them have full swing." McClellan—indeed most of the Union military command, not to mention the civilian Lincoln Administration—would probably have disagreed.[87]

The momentous year of 1861 ended with a crisis of the diplomatic kind—one that excited a press storm in its wake. It began on November 8, when Captain Charles Wilkes, the overzealous commander of a Union blockading ship patrolling the waters north of Cuba, detained a British mail steamer, the *Trent*.

As Wilkes knew, the ship was transporting two newly named Confederate diplomats, James Mason and John Slidell, who had recently slipped past the Union blockade en route to London and Paris, respectively, to take up overseas posts as advocates for European recognition of the Confederacy.

Wilkes arrested both men and took his prisoners to the mainland for detention, and their capture came close to engulfing the United States in a world war. British politicians and newspapers threatened an armed response unless American authorities released Mason and Slidell, sent them on their way, and issued a formal apology. It was not just that a Union vessel had seized members of the traditionally immune diplomatic corps (though the Lincoln administration did not recognize the Confederacy as a sovereign nation entitled to name ambassadors). Far more importantly, at least to England, a United States ship had interfered with a British vessel sailing under Her Majesty's colors. To many in Great Britain, even those who opposed slavery, this violation of international law constituted grounds for military retaliation.[88]

At first, Northern newspapers, including the *New York Times*, urged defiance—until Lincoln made it clear, as he is said to have put it, that the Union could only fight "one war at a time." A previously bellicose Seward came to his senses and began counseling conciliation. His friend Henry Raymond got the message, too. By mid-December, he editorialized that "if, upon mature reflection, the law should be against us, we shall, in a similar spirit, make the proper reparation."[89]

Scottish-born James Gordon Bennett, however, showed no desire to pacify the English he so despised. For weeks, he kept his Anglophobic warmongering at a fever pitch. Although Great Britain's secretary of state for the colonies believed that Washington would eventually release the Confederate diplomats, he admitted that with "the mob and the Press manning the vessel, it is too probable that this atonement may be refused."[90] For good measure, Bennett accused William Howard Russell of engaging in lucrative insider financial speculation during the "*Trent* Affair," prompting the harassed correspondent to lament: "If I am ever in another Bull's Run you may depend on it I never get out of it alive. . . . I'm the only English thing they can vent their anger on, & the [London] Times is regarded as so dead against the North that everyone connected with it in the North is exposed to popular anger."[91]

On November 25, noting that Bennett's diatribes were "being copied far and wide," Raymond charged that "the New-York Herald is doing infinitely more to advance the rebel cause abroad than all the agents, official and unofficial, who have gone thither upon that service. For the last two months, its columns have teemed with denunciations, threats and insults, to the English Government, which, coupled as they are with an ostentatiously fulsome support of the Administration, are universally regarded there as indicating a settled purpose on the part of the Government to provoke a war with England." Asked Raymond: "Is it at all surprising that language like this, habitually used, with every conceivable phrase and form of malignant exasperation . . . should arouse a bitter hostility against the cause of the Union among the people of England?"[92]

The increasingly political *Frank Leslie's Illustrated Newspaper* also saw rank opportunism behind Bennett's militancy. "The *Herald* was, but a short time ago, entirely in the interest of the South," it pointed out. ". . . The conversion of the paper was effected with weathercock celerity, and it is now as vituperative in behalf of Mr. Lincoln as it used to be against him; but its dearest sympathies are with the slavery men, and it still keeps up volleys of slang against all who desire the abolition of the slave system."[93] Bennett's inconsistencies prompted Thurlow Weed to visit the White House, where he warned Lincoln that "the course of the *Herald* was endangering the government and the Union." Always looking to his opponents' better angels, Lincoln told Weed he was sure that "if Mr. Bennett could be brought to see things in that light, he would change his course." In this regard, Lincoln was too optimistic.[94]

Relentlessly fanned by Bennett, the crisis festered unresolved until the day after Christmas, when, their backs to the wall, Lincoln and Seward finally agreed to release the envoys, but without specifically admitting to a violation of international law. The British had hoped for a more abject apology, perhaps a financial settlement, but accepted America's reversal. Mason and Slidell sailed for Europe and Lincoln endured no worse punishment than the embarrassment of backing down from a fight. Throughout 1861, the administration had proven much more successful at fighting journalists than at battling Rebel armies and standing up to hostile foreign governments.

As it turned out, McClellan's recent and rather clumsy effort to control the press corps not only collapsed, but stimulated unexpected consequences. One was a centralization of government control over the telegraph. Back on October 22, 1861, Assistant Secretary of State Frederick Seward had prohibited "all telegraphic dispatches from Washington, intended for publication, which relate to the civil or military operations of the government." [95] Now, in early 1862, Lincoln's newly named secretary of war, Edwin Stanton, went a step further, moving official telegraph operations from McClellan's headquarters to a library next to his own office in Washington. There, for the next three years, Lincoln would be an almost daily (and nightly) visitor to await official news as it arrived from the front.

The relocation may have been convenient for the president, but it proved inhibiting for the press, just as the secretary of war intended. In February, Stanton named Edward S. Sanford, president of the Atlantic Telegraph Company, as "military supervisor of telegraphic lines and offices in the United States"—in other words, chief censor—and issued General Orders No. 10, codifying administration control over "any or all the telegraph lines in the United States, their appendages and appurtenances." [96] On the flip side, Stanton was not above courting loyal journalists—or hiring them. When Horace Greeley abruptly dismissed his managing editor, Charles Dana—because Greeley "was for peace [and] I was for war," Dana remarked—Stanton promptly named Dana assistant secretary of war. [97]

Just a few weeks after his confirmation, Stanton showed that he meant business where censorship was concerned by moving to suppress the openly pro-Confederate Baltimore paper *The South*. The secretary of war ordered commanding general John Adams Dix to "Seize and take possession of the paper" and then to arrest publisher Samuel Sands Mills and editors Thomas W. Hall and Thomas H. Piggott. Hall, who had the dubious honor of being hauled away by the famous detective Allan Pinkerton, was charged with "openly and zealously advocating the cause of the insurrection and largely contributing to unsettle and excite the public mind." He spent months in a series of military prisons, permitted to see his wife only "in the presence of an officer." Then in June, Stanton—purportedly with Lincoln's blessing— ordered the arrest of Charles C. Fulton of the *Baltimore American* merely for planning to publish details about a recent presidential meeting. Thrown into Fort McHenry, "the depot for traitors" as he called it, the anguished Fulton appealed to Lincoln "for a hearing and prompt release in behalf of my family." As he insisted, he had "risked both life and property in defending the Union cause" in a hostile city. Deaf to his protests, Stanton insisted for a time that Fulton be confined "closely . . . communicating with no one." [98]

Stanton's show of uninhibited zealousness, followed by the arrival of a petition from leading citizens of Boston reminding Congress that "the Administration has no right . . . to attempt any limitations whatever of the freedom of the press," prompted an inevitable, perhaps overdue response: a full-scale congressional investigation that unexpectedly entangled the president and his family.[99] In early 1862, the House Judiciary Committee began hearings into the question of whether "telegraphic censorship of the press has been established in this city" in contradiction of the Constitution, and, if so, whether censorship had been used "to restrain wholesome political criticism and discussion." The committee called a number of witnesses from the government and the military, along with journalists suddenly willing to complain under oath that they indeed feared using "severe language" against Lincoln and had been prevented from wiring the truth about Union battle losses. The testimony eventually ran to more than a thousand handwritten pages.[100]

Some of the interviews proved chilling. Telegraph superintendent H. Emmons Thayer all but boasted that he had censored reports of cabinet meetings, regarding them as "private business" meant to "embarrass the Government." Asked point-blank during one session if he had ever had "any dispatches suppressed at the telegraph office," Simon Hanscom of the *New York Herald* openly admitted: "I have had a great many . . . a great deal of trouble with the Govt. in regard to the censorship of the press." Hanscom hastened to point out that he perceived no "malice" in the censorship, suggesting that many of the readers at the telegraph office "didn't seem to comprehend the business they had in charge." The correspondent also admitted that he tried repeatedly to get around the indistinct rules. Told he "must not write anything about Cabinet meetings no matter what the subject was," Hanscom tried to slip one such article through Colonel Sanford anyway, reporting that Lincoln and the War Department differed on the issue of admitting escaped slaves into Union lines. The censor informed the reporter that "he couldn't send it, and couldn't give me any reason for not sending it. I got vexed." Individual dispatches might be banned in their entirety—like Hanscom's initial report on the resolution of the *Trent* affair—or "the censor would dash his pen over a paragraph, and frequently such an erasure would destroy the entire sense of an article." Concluding that, where reporting news was concerned, it was better late than never, the *Herald* correspondent testified that he ultimately found his way around the rules by sending his dispatches to New York by mail.[101]

Adams Hill, whose rumored flight from Bull Run had made him a laughingstock among his colleagues, got the committee's serious attention with a similar story. He had once tried to wire a scoop reporting that Assistant Secretary of the Navy Gustavus V. Fox had journeyed to New York to inspect a newly built mortar fleet poised to steam south. The telegraph censors refused to send it, implying that the report would give away Union technological and deployment secrets. Even David Bartlett, a pro-administration correspondent from the *New York Evening Post* who had written a laudatory 1860 Lincoln campaign biography, testified that, like Henry Raymond, "I was interfered with . . . the morning after the battle of Bull Run," but thereafter chose "to be on good terms with the censor" and "had few dispatches stopped." That is, until he tried to report the news of Simon Cameron's ouster from the cabinet. Bartlett rushed his scoop to the telegrapher, he reported, "but he refused to send it." [102] Such testimony showed that censors routinely interfered not only with military, but also with government news.

During his turn in the witness chair, Samuel Wilkeson, Washington editor of the *New York Tribune*, broadened this complaint by testifying: "I am not allowed to send anything over the wires which, in the estimation of the censor, the Secretary of State, or the Assistant Secretary of State, shall be damaging to the character of the administration, or any individual member of the Cabinet," or injurious to "the reputation of the officers charged with the prosecution of the war." It had become clear not only that the State Department was actively involved in domestic censorship, but that the naive telegraph operators themselves were empowered to rely on their own limited judgment without supervision. To Wilkeson, the rules constituted a net cast too widely. "I was not allowed to mention by telegraph the simple fact that Mason and Slidell were surrendered," he testified. But like Simon Hanscom, he had sent his suppressed reports by post, adding triumphantly, "unless they go to the mails & search out my letters they cannot prevent the publication of what they suppress by telegraph." [103]

Not all the witnesses cooperated. After refusing to appear voluntarily, William McKellar, former managing editor of the now shuttered *New York Daily News*, was dragged from his Harlem bed one morning by two detectives who served him with a subpoena, searched him, and forcibly escorted him to Washington to testify. There, although he had only recently published a signed farewell editorial, he perjured himself to the committee, insisting he had never read, much less written, for his paper. McKellar claimed he had served only as the head of the *News*'s business department, retained none of the records that might have shed light on the paper's alleged disloyalty, and had nothing to do with its editor, Congressman Benjamin Wood. [104]

On the other hand, Lawrence Gobright of the Associated Press had "no comment to make of the censor," recalling not a single instance in which his straightforward dispatches had ever been suppressed. As he proudly told the committee, taking a swipe at the newspaper reporters with whom he often competed, our "business is merely to communicate facts . . . not to make any comments." The pro-Lincoln Gobright volunteered: "I would not throw a straw in the way of the successful prosecution of this war. I have not done so, and I would not." [105]

Summoned to defend the oversight policies from a government perspective was Frederick Seward, son of the secretary of state, and the official identified by many resentful witnesses as the power behind telegraphic censorship— until supplanted by Stanton. Yet Fred, to whom uncertain telegraph censors occasionally did bring controversial dispatches for further inspection, flatly denied that he played such a role. All he would confirm was that restraints had been put in place not only on reports of troop movements, but "in regard to any action of the Govt, and giving intimation of it where it might reach the enemy prior to the time the Govt intended to have it published." [106]

This particular revelation was perhaps less incriminating than it sounded,

Managers of Union telegraph censorship in Washington: Undersecretary of State Frederick Seward (left); and later, Edwin M. Stanton (right), newly appointed secretary of war.

for the younger Seward was delicately alluding to an episode of "intimation" that had embarrassed the administration just a few months earlier: a news leak of what was considered epic proportions. "The struggle of today, is not altogether for today—it is for a vast future also." So Lincoln had majestically concluded his first Annual Message to Congress on December 3.[107] The only problem was that, in an unprecedented breach of protocol, the inspiring words had appeared in the *New York Herald* that very morning—hours before they were scheduled to be read aloud in House and Senate. The incident set Washington tongues wagging, with many insiders suspecting that someone in the White House must have provided the *Herald* with an advance text.

Precisely how James Gordon Bennett obtained the president's message remains a mystery. But at the time, eyes focused on the so-called "Chevalier" Henry Wikoff, a sometime diplomat who functioned as a secret source and occasional, uncredited, *Herald* contributor. Born in Pennsylvania, Wikoff had spent so much time abroad that he seemed vaguely foreign—attractively so, to men and women alike. Even John Wein Forney gushed about the "shrewd" Wikoff's ability to "talk of love, literature, and war" with equal ease, and Forney was not the only credulous Washington insider to succumb to the "cosmopolite's" charm.[108] While that shrewd judge of character Lincoln disliked him (Bennett once felt compelled to apologize to the president if "Mr Wikoff gave you any trouble" about some "small matter"),[109] the "Chevalier's" circle of admirers soon came to include Henry Villard—nobody's fool—and, ultimately, the president's wife, Mary. William Howard Russell smirked that by November 1861, "that disgusting Wikoff" had become "master of ye situation at ye White House." Although Russell believed Mary Lincoln to be as "loyal as steel to . . . Lincoln the First," he judged her "accessible to the influence of flattery," and, he implied, to the promise of money to fund her extravagant spending.[110] By December, some in Washington whispered that Wikoff had charmed the Annual Message out of the first lady, perhaps in return for an actual bribe.

Summoned before the House Judiciary Committee on February 10, the "Chevalier" refused to provide satisfactory answers, whereupon its members ordered him thrown into the Old Capitol Prison until he was ready to cooperate. General Daniel Sickles, Wikoff's friend, attorney, and fellow Bennett intimate, then appeared to offer the committee a preposterous explanation: White House gardener John Watt had glimpsed the president's manuscript in the mansion's library (however distant that second-floor chamber stood from

Watt's outdoor post), where he miraculously committed it to memory and later recited it word for word to Wikoff. No one could doubt that Wikoff had been in and around the mansion at the right time; on December 3, he even wrote an unctuous note to the president on White House stationery suggesting that as "a compliment to Mr. Bennett" he should provide the editor with an advance copy of his message. "This compliment was always paid Mr B by the last President," he advised, "& it can hardly be denied that it is deserved as much & more from Your Excellency." Yet Senator Orville Browning had no doubt that "the President's message had been furnished to Wycoff [*sic*]" by Mary.[111]

Lincoln himself may have come to suspect his wife's complicity. The very day after Wikoff refused to testify to Congress, at least according to veteran journalist Ben Perley Poore, the president rode up to Capitol Hill himself to urge Republicans on the investigating committee "to spare him disgrace" and drop the matter altogether. Since Lincoln's beloved son Willie was at the time clinging to life at the White House—he would die of typhoid fever just a week and a half later—the congressmen expressed no desire to add to his sorrows. The gardener's "improbable story was received," Poore recalled, "and

Suspected of leaking the president's 1861 annual message to the *Herald*: Mary Lincoln (left) and her friend "Chevalier" Henry Wikoff (right).

Wikoff was liberated."[112] The president thereupon banned the troublemaker from the White House, by one account physically tossing him out the door. Completing the purge, Lincoln declared that Watt, then on leave from the army to work in the White House gardens, was "not needed," and ordered him returned to his regiment.[113]

But Lincoln surely knew who bore the principal guilt for the scandal. When, late in September, the persistent "Chevalier" brazenly petitioned the president for a pass to accompany a naval vessel down the Potomac "as a reporter for the Herald," Lincoln refused to accommodate him. Explaining his decision to Bennett, Lincoln was careful to avoid mention of the Annual Message affair; Wikoff's request, he insisted, had simply arrived too late at night to justify awakening the secretary of the navy. "I write this to assure you," Lincoln told Bennett, "that the administration will not discriminate against the Herald, especially while it sustains us so generously, and the cause of the country so ably as it has been doing."[114] The ban applied to Wikoff alone— not the newspaper for which he worked—that is, the president implied, as long as the *Herald* sustained the administration. Lincoln never mentioned Wikoff's name in writing again.

Mary Lincoln surely knew how close she came to public exposure. Months before the purloined letter incident, she had reached out to flatter the powerful Bennett, thanking him for "the kind support and consideration, extended towards the Administration, by you, at a time when your powerful influence would be sensibly felt." In her rambling prose style, clogged as always with an overabundance of commas, she added: "In the hour of peace, the kind words of a friend are always acceptable, how much more so, when a 'man's foes, are those of their own household' . . . rights are invaded and every sacred right, is trampled upon!" Mary's reference to foes within the "household" may have applied to the fractured Union, or to her own White House coterie, Wikoff and Watt included; she did not specify. She was merely grateful "in my own individual case, when I meet, in the columns of your paper, a kind reply, to some uncalled for attack, upon one so little desirous of newspaper notoriety, as my inoffensive self."[115]

Abraham and Mary Lincoln were not the only observers to notice how thoroughly Bennett's *Herald* had altered its once hostile editorial policy since it first tasted the anger of the mob back in April 1861. Visiting English writer Anthony Trollope, whose own novels abounded with brawls of the kind in which Bennett had once specialized, concluded that despite "the largest sale of any daily newspaper," the *Herald*'s violence-prone editor was now "absolutely without political power," having "truckled to the Government more basely than any other paper." Trollope thought the situation a matter of just deserts for what he regarded as the most offensive of the "tyrannical and overbearing" American newspapers, one for which "vituperation" had long been a "natural political weapon." But "since the President's ministers have assumed the power of stopping newspapers which are offensive to them," Trollope charged, "they have shown that they can descend to a course of eulogy which is even below vituperation." [116] What Trollope failed to understand is that by introducing such innovations as front-page battlefield maps, and by adding extra reporters and bonus pages to cover major events, the *Herald* was in fact attracting more readers than ever, benefiting from its new understanding with the White House, and prospering accordingly. If he was guilty of "treason," Bennett chortled, it certainly paid handsomely. James Gordon Bennett never cared about political power for its own sake, but only as a means to economic success. And according to those standards, by 1862 he was more powerful than ever.

Questioned about the Annual Message scandal during his own interrogation by the committee in late January 1862, the rival *Tribune*'s Samuel Wilkeson proved as reluctant as Frederick Seward to reveal any knowledge of the affair. He hinted only that he would never "quarrel" or "complain" about losing an exclusive story when the "source of that news was obtained from women." Pressed to reveal whether he believed that the document in question had been obtained from "Members of the President's family," Wilkeson stammered: "Yes, sir. I suppose the *Herald* had relations with the female members of the Prests. family & gave that paper an advantage over the rest of us." [117] By then Bennett's "advantage" had grown so strong that, however his information was obtained, one of Greeley's assistant editors conceded: "The *Herald* is constantly ahead. We are obliged to copy from it." [118]

In the end, not only did the accusations against Mary Lincoln remain unreported, the House committee entirely dropped its distracting side inquiry into the leaking of the Annual Message. It did, however, conclude in its March 20 final report that unobjectionable news reports had indeed been swallowed up in the teeth of widespread telegraphic censorship; that the censors had interfered not only with "military information which might be of advantage to the rebel authorities" but also with "numberless" dispatches "of a political, personal, and general character"; and that what began as an agreement between the press and General McClellan had widened into a much broader system of censorship "controlled by the Secretary of State."

Insisting that "Government interference" should be confined to "what may legitimately be connected with the military and naval affairs of the nation," the committee strongly recommended that in the future the telegraph be "left as free from government interference as may be consistent with the necessities of the government in time of war." Members urged passage of a specific resolution declaring that "the government should not interfere with the free transmission of intelligence by telegraph" unless the information was objectionable or if the military required priority use of the telegraph for its own "legitimate purposes."[119] The proposal proved ambiguous enough to inhibit the Republican-dominated full House from enacting any legislative remedy. The censors were left in charge without further oversight.[120]

In the midst of the hearings, as if to send a message of his own on the subject, Secretary of War Stanton issued a strict new order to Washington's chief of police: "All newspaper editors and publishers have been forbidden to publish any intelligence received by telegraph or otherwise respecting military operations by the United States forces. . . . If violated by any paper issued to-morrow, seize the whole edition, and give notice to this department that arrest may be ordered." In another announcement issued that same day, Stanton declared that the president had taken possession of all telegraph lines throughout the United States. Any paper guilty of using the telegraph to publish military news not approved by "the official authority" would be excluded from using the wires or the railroads to transmit future news.[121] While Congress and the press were busy hashing out the limits of access to and transmission of the news, the secretary of war had staged a successful interoffice coup and seized control of censorship operations from the secretary of state—and he did so with Lincoln's acquiescence. When Stanton asked the president for more discretion in controlling the Bureau of Ordnance and "perhaps some others"—possibly meaning the telegraph system—Lincoln replied: "The Secretary of War has my authority to exercise his discretion in the matter."[122] Stanton did precisely that.

No one seemed immune from the resumption and consolidation of the censorship dragnet, even the administration's most loyal friends in the press. On March 17, 1862, just three days before the committee was scheduled to issue its formal findings, the War Department punctuated its claim to total oversight by closing down John Wein Forney's *Washington Sunday Chronicle*, of all newspapers, for publishing a report on military movements in violation of General Orders No. 67. Only when the editor offered profuse regret and explained that the news had been brought to him very late the previous night, that the edition went to press without his customary editorial supervision, and that he would be certain to "carefully guard against a recurrence," did the War Department permit the *Chronicle* to reopen after a day in rare silence.[123]

Stanton had served notice that whatever Congress thought about the arbitrary censorship rules previously enforced by Montgomery Blair, Simon Cameron, or George McClellan, or overseen by the father-and-son team of William and Frederick Seward, and investigated by the House Judiciary Committee, he was now in full control and had no reluctance about suppressing even Lincoln-friendly newspapers.

Toil and trouble: *Vanity Fair* likens the troublesome
New York editors to "The Three Beldams."

For his part, Lincoln struggled mightily to remain above the fray. Ben Perley Poore and other leading correspondents turned up in the White House one day to convince him that "the surveillance of the press" had become "as annoying as it was inefficient," resulting in "innocent sentences which were supposed to have a hidden meaning" being "stricken from paragraphs which were then rendered nonsensical"—all in the name of censoring supposedly classified information that was readily available throughout both Washington and "Dixie."

To this complaint Lincoln answered with one of his distracting funny stories. When two of the "angry journalists" persisted in their protests, demanding that the president return to the subject they wanted to discuss, Lincoln "listened in his dreamy way" and then commented: "I don't know much about this censorship, but come down-stairs and I will show you the origin of one of the pet phrases of you newspaper fellows."

Lincoln was referring to the growing vogue for the idiomatic French catchphrase "*revenons à nos moutons*"—roughly translated as, "let's get back to the subject at hand," but literally meaning, "let's return to our sheep." Leading his bewildered visitors down several staircases and into the White House cellar, the president "opened the door of a larder, and solemnly pointed to the hanging carcass of a gigantic sheep."

"There!" Lincoln exclaimed to the startled reporters with a smile, "now you know what '*Revenons à nos moutons*' means." Pointing proudly to the huge slab of meat, he enthused: "It was raised by Deacon Buffun at Manchester, up in New Hampshire. Who can say, after looking at it, that New Hampshire's only product is granite?" [124] What this perplexing demonstration had to do with press censorship none of his visitors could fathom. But his comments successfully terminated the meeting without further argument.

Journalists constantly hungry for news, though perpetually wary of government interference, learned as the war progressed that Lincoln's own chief product often amounted to silence, deflection, and disinformation, and that when he did not want to get back to the point, the adroit president did not "*revient à ses moutons*." Rather, he avoided the subject at hand.

CHAPTER TWELVE

Slavery Must Go to the Wall

——————◆——————

Just after New Year's Day 1862, Horace Greeley returned to the national capital—once again not to report news, but to make it—after the Washington Lecture Association invited him to deliver the latest in a series of anti-slavery talks at the Smithsonian Institution. Part-time *Tribune* correspondent William Croffut helped stage the events. But first he had to lobby skeptical Smithsonian officials to make its large amphitheater available for the series. Astonishingly, its secretary fretted that his Southern regents, including Jefferson Davis himself, might object. Greeley seized the chance to lecture, "especially," he joked, "as I have already earned the reputation of being the poorest public speaker in America."[1]

Greeley was particularly eager that Lincoln hear his talk, so Croffut visited the White House to ask whether the president might attend. "Yes, I will," Lincoln impulsively replied, turning to his assistant secretary to ask: "I can get away, can't I, Hay? I never heard Greeley, and I want to hear him. In print every one of his words seems to weigh about a ton; I want to see what he has to say about us."[2]

"Horace Greeley . . . has come down here to marshal the hosts of the grumblers," John Hay soon reported far less enthusiastically in one of his anonymous newspaper columns—adopting the latest nickname for the *Tri-*

bune editor: the Grumbler. "No man denies his honesty, no man questions his disinterestedness. He is not a candidate for any office within the gift of the people or President. He grumbles because he is an honest old fanatic, and does not agree with the Administration."[3]

Hay may not have known that, Greeley's "grumbling" notwithstanding, Lincoln was then in the midst of a quiet effort to repair his strained relations with the editor. Although he had never replied to Greeley's hysterical letter of the previous summer, Lincoln grew confident enough in his restored stability to enter into an informal agreement at the end of 1861 to supply administration-sanctioned news stories to the *Tribune* through a third party. One of the middlemen was pro-Union Southerner James R. Gilmore, who had just founded a new magazine called the *Continental Monthly.* Under the nom de plume "Edmund Kirke," Gilmore had also written a recent anti-slavery novel that greatly impressed the president, who remarked that the author genuinely "knew the South" and, moreover, thought like a "lawyer or jurist"—high praise from a man who never read fiction, not even *Uncle Tom's Cabin.*[4] (Perhaps Lincoln admired Gilmore's *Among the Pines* because it featured the optimistic prediction: "Free the Negroes by an act of emancipation, or confiscation, and the rebellion will crumble to pieces in a day.")[5]

When Gilmore journeyed to New York to tell Greeley of his plans for the magazine, the *Tribune* editor asked him whether he believed he could ever win Lincoln's confidence. Gilmore was not sure, but had recently enlisted a pledge for help from an administration confidant, former Kansas governor Robert J. Walker, who in the 1850s had attempted to navigate the "Bleeding Kansas" storm with integrity. "Robert J. Walker!" Greeley exclaimed. "Why, he's the greatest man we've had since Ben Franklin."[6] Greeley was eager to know whether Gilmore might be able to direct Walker "from time to time" to elicit Lincoln's "views on certain lines of policy" for the *Tribune.* On this score, Gilmore remained skeptical: he believed Lincoln to be a "hear-all-and-say-nothing sort," but asked Greeley what he might expect as a reward in return for alerts from the White House. Greeley then proposed what he called a "double harness" arrangement "of mutual help to each other." If Gilmore could provide him with "prompt information . . . when allowable," then Greeley would "materially" support the start-up magazine.[7]

Under the terms of the deal, Greeley agreed to contribute to, as well as advertise in, Gilmore's fledgling publication. The administration would pass news to Walker. Then Walker would spirit the information to Gilmore, who in turn would transmit it to the *Tribune*. The arrangement was bound to fail—it was simply too complicated to sustain, and the administration inevitably proved highly selective about what it shared for Greeley's benefit—but for a time, the editor noticeably relaxed his criticism of Lincoln and instead focused his chronic impatience for victory (and abolition) on the battle-weary George McClellan, who spent the early weeks of 1862 maddeningly bedridden in Washington with typhoid fever. Greeley accused McClellan of dithering, and came close to charging him with treason.

Thus, by the day of his January 3 Washington appearance, Greeley had at last become something of an administration insider by proxy. That evening, in the company of three cabinet secretaries—Chase, Welles, and Attorney General Edward Bates (Horace Greeley's bizarre first choice for president two years earlier)—the president headed to the redbrick Smithsonian "castle" to hear the editor's oration. Organizers ushered Lincoln to an honored place on the speaker's platform and seated him right next to Greeley. The two men were back onstage together—just as they had been at Cooper Union in New York—but this time reversing their earlier roles, with Greeley now on the rostrum and Lincoln perched behind him barely an arm's length away, a silent observer. The large audience, including, some claimed, two-thirds of Congress and a number of Frémont admirers hostile to the president, kept both the speaker and his most famous listener in sight throughout the evening.

William Croffut, for one, observed that Lincoln looked careworn. "He was never handsome," he conceded, but now, sadly, seemed "more cadaverous and ungainly" than ever, "sallow . . . weary and sad."[8] Greeley agreed that Lincoln's face was now "seamed with thought and trouble."[9] Greeley looked different, too. Paunchier now, he had lost most of his hair, and the white strands that remained stood out in all directions in scraggly wisps. His bald pate and pale cheeks remained as smooth as a baby's, but now he sported an odd new tonsorial affectation: a corona of white whiskers somehow sprouting below his chin, from his neck, like a wildly unkempt ruff. Greeley had long given cartoonists a virtual arsenal of trademarks with which to parody him—baggy pants, overflowing pockets, long coats, battered top hats, blanketlike shawls, and weather-beaten gripsacks. Now he had refreshed even this bag of tricks with his new neck hair, and artists enjoyed a field day making him look odder than ever.

As a public philosopher, however, Greeley was no laughing matter. Adopting as his lecture subject "The Nation," Greeley commenced with the witty admission that he remained a "peculiar institution" in Washington, but hoped that Union military successes might soon make it possible for him to raise his voice farther south. Turning serious, he argued forcibly against compromise on abolition. "We must emerge from this struggle essentially free," he loudly declared in his whinny of a voice. "And now, if the Union is to be restored, it is only on the basis of freedom . . . *it is time to look the enemy in the eye.* . . . Compromise is impossible." [10] As he pronounced those sharp words, the speaker turned around as if to address Lincoln personally. "A more dramatic scene has seldom been witnessed by any popular assembly," Croffut testified. The crowd responded with a "wild and prolonged cheer." [11]

When the pro-Frémont audience rose to greet Greeley's conclusion with a standing ovation, Lincoln remained conspicuously seated, his face frozen in an expressionless mask. Bennett's *Herald* denounced the entire spectacle as "a shrewd dodge on the part of our white-coated philosopher to get a hearing from 'Honest Old Abe.'" [12] All Lincoln would concede afterward to the abolitionist Indiana congressman George W. Julian, who sat on his other side that night, was: "That address was full of good thoughts. I would like to take the manuscript home with me and carefully read it over some Sunday." Whether he ever found "some Sunday" to do so remains unknown. From Greeley's Washington correspondent Homer Byington, however, an exasperated Lincoln demanded to know: "What in the world is the matter with Uncle Horace? Why can't he restrain himself and wait a little while?" With or without Lincoln's encouragement, however, the fight over slavery was about to take center stage alongside the fight for the Union. [13]

Around this same time, still hoping to salvage his foundering career in America, *London Times* correspondent William Howard Russell undertook one final campaign to woo his detractors. He treated Raymond, Forney, Greeley, Seaton, and Bryant to "the best dinners I could give them . . . and laid it on frightfully. . . . The result was that I only increased the hostility of those who were not invited." [14]

From Bennett, who was intentionally excluded from this roster, Russell insisted he would accept only a full apology for his many "gross & unprovoked attacks." Receiving none, Russell contented himself with his exaggerated belief that he had made Bennett "eat so much dirt" because "The [London] Times would not quote the Herald in future & that thus the European noto-

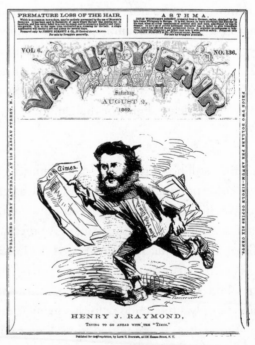

Greeley the lecturer, acknowledged—and ridiculed—in a March 1862 *Vanity Fair* cover story, and Raymond dismissed as a mere newsboy a few months later.

riety on which he prides himself" was "injured if not totally destroyed." A few weeks after Greeley's lecture, Russell sulked that it would be his rivals' "great triumph to drive me away." Soon he discovered that he could no longer secure interviews with prominent officials. They had become "fearful of being attacked in the press if they are pointed out for any civility to me."[15]

"You must either go to the front or come home," his editor finally advised him from London in late March. Despite Russell's problems, the paper still expected stories to be filed from America. Worse, Secretary of War Stanton acted in April to revoke and reevaluate all existing press credentials, threatening to arrest any reporter who attempted to visit the front without fresh certification. The department never disclosed the official reason. When journalists objected, Stanton modified his order to apply only to foreign correspondents whom he could not "punish . . . if they gave aid to the enemy."[16]

Sensing, no doubt correctly, that this latest purge was aimed specifically at him, Russell lodged a protest with the War Department. He received no answer. Russell then appealed directly to the president, calling on him at the White House and eliciting a one-sentence letter—in which Lincoln ambiguously urged that "if any charges should come against Col. Russell let us give him a hearing before acting." The embattled correspondent remembered that the vague assurance "at first gave me hopes" that the president would overrule Stanton, but "the next day [he] informed me he could not take it upon himself to do so." Perhaps Lincoln had decided to heed a recent warning about Russell from Congressman Elihu Washburne: "I think his sympathies are all with the rebels, and he expresses himself entirely confident that we cannot subdue the rebellion. I have no doubt he is doing all he can to get his govt. to recognize the negro confederacy."[17] According to Ben Perley Poore, Lincoln told William Seward: "This fellow Russell's Bull Run letter was not so complimentary as to entitle him to much favor."[18] Yet Russell pugnaciously insisted to Charles Sumner—one of "innumerable Senators" to whom he pleaded his case—"I write for the English people, not for the American people."[19]

No doubt fearing just such declarations of independence and immunity, Stanton reacted with an iron fist: he could not close the *London Times*, but he could close it off from Union war news. A defiant Russell booked passage for the front anyway, but when he tried to embark by sea, authorities forcibly put him off the boat.

With neither a valid pass nor a means to enter the war zone, with no defenders left in the army or the government, and few sources willing to confide in him, Russell had little choice but to abandon his assignment and return to England. He did so in April. In one of his final comments from America, he proclaimed: "There is more in Lincoln than you would imagine." But Russell never got to report on the president's next three years in office. Instead he exacted revenge for what he regarded as his unwarranted banishment by compiling his American notes and publishing them in London the following year in a sensational book entitled *My Diary North and South.*[20]

Russell's departure from American soil deprived the conflict of one of its most incisive observers. In lobbyist Sam Ward's opinion, by ousting him, the Union foolishly "tomahawked" its own most potentially influential overseas eyewitness, at a time when the government desperately needed England's support, or at least, neutrality.[21] Less obviously, but perhaps even more significantly, Russell's exile cemented government control over information about the conflict, foreign and domestic alike.

On March 6, 1862, two months after hearing Greeley wave his freedom banner at the Smithsonian, Lincoln reclaimed center stage on the issue, sending a Special Message to Congress pledging the government "to co-operate with any state which may adopt gradual abolishment of slavery, giving to the state pecuniary aid, to be used by such state in it's [*sic*] discretion, to compensate for the inconveniences public and private, produced by such change of system." The proposal constituted Lincoln's first concrete effort to launch America on a path toward abolition: a national order for gradual emancipation, to be enforced at the state level, but financed with federal funds. The measure would not end slavery everywhere, or even ban it anywhere immediately, but Lincoln optimistically believed that if embraced, the plan would secure Union loyalty in the Border States and perhaps even end the war "at once."[22]

Editorial reaction followed within a day, bringing the expected kudos from Republican newspapers and praise even from Bennett. Clearly pleased, Lincoln preserved laudatory clippings from five New York papers: The *Times*, *Tribune*, *Herald*, *World*, and *Evening Post*—all wholeheartedly supportive save for one *Times* item that questioned the government's ability to finance such an undertaking. On March 9, John Nicolay entered Lincoln's office "to read to the President the most recent Tribune and Herald articles concerning his emancipation message—both papers continuing to warmly endorse it."[23] Still irked over the misgivings expressed by the *Times*, Lincoln showed his secretary a copy of a letter he had just sent off to Henry Raymond.[24] The president was not about to let the profligacy charge stand unanswered.

"I am grateful to the New-York Journals, and not less so to the Times than to others," Lincoln began, "for their kind notices of the late special Message to Congress." Then Lincoln confided his objection to the article in question. "Your paper . . . intimates that the proposition, though well-intentioned, must fail on the score of expense. I do hope you will reconsider this. Have you noticed the facts that less than one half-day's cost of this war would pay for all the slaves in Delaware, at four hundred dollars per head?—that eighty-seven days cost of this war would pay for all in Delaware, Maryland, District of Columbia, Kentucky, and Missouri at the same price? Were those states to take the step, do you doubt that it would shorten the war more than eighty seven days, and thus be an actual saving of expense[?]" Lincoln wanted not only the last word on the subject, but also a correction. "Please look at these things," he concluded his letter, "and consider whether there should not be another article in the Times?"[25]

As so often resulted when Lincoln reached out directly to editors, the personal touch worked wonders. Raymond replied within the week: "You will have seen long before this reaches you . . . that the Times has published several articles in support of your special message. As soon as I saw the one to which you allude, I telegraphed to the office to sustain the message *without qualifications or cavil*, and I believe the paper has done so since. . . . I regard the message as a master-piece of political wisdom and sound policy."[26]

Meanwhile Lincoln continued his effort to build bridges to the Grumbler. The crafty president coveted Greeley's continued backing for his Border State initiative, but wanted the *Tribune* to temper its editorial enthusiasm so as not to make his initiative seem threatening to the affected Border States. Greeley, too, had thrown full support behind the "wisdom" of Lincoln's proposal, terming it "one of those few great scriptures that live in history and mark an epoch in the lives of nations and of races." Of course, Greeley also seized the opportunity to excoriate Bennett for the "cheat and sham" of praising both Lincoln and his pro-slavery foes in Congress. Greeley also blasted Raymond for the "mistake" of doubting whether the plan could succeed.[27] "If I were to suggest anything," Lincoln soothed Greeley, "it would be that as the North are already for the measure, we should urge it *persuasively*, and not *menacingly*, upon the South." Greeley responded to assure the president, "I am sure you will find great patience in the country as well as in Congress with regard to all action respecting slavery if it can only be felt that *things are going ahead.*" [28]

Typically, Greeley wanted something in return for his moderation: Lincoln's support for the latest congressional initiative to ban slavery in the District of Columbia—the fulfillment of a dream both men had harbored since introducing similar bills of their own while serving in Congress together more than a decade earlier. The idea was again before the House and Senate, and this time, with most Southern representatives gone and no longer voting, it stood a good chance of enactment if Lincoln agreed to sign it. When Lincoln cautioned that he still believed, as he had back in 1850, that District-wide emancipation ought to be subject to a referendum of its white citizens, Greeley even dropped the objections he had raised to that proviso back in their House days. "I will advocate it in the Tribune if you desire it," Greeley pledged. He hoped for passage by the symbolic deadline of July 4. Their latest rapprochement also meant, as usual, that Lincoln resumed tending to Greeley's patronage recommendations. [29]

Perhaps emboldened by both Raymond's latest reassurance of support and Greeley's new pledge of restraint, Lincoln accelerated his efforts against slavery. In April—three months earlier than Greeley had hoped—the president approved the newly passed bill abolishing slavery in the nation's capital. "That I should live to see the President of the United States deliberately advocating Emancipation," wrote Frederick Douglass in his monthly paper, "was more than I ever ventured to hope." [30] In short order, Lincoln also made good on his party's 1860 platform pledge to prohibit slavery expansion, signing a law that once and for all outlawed the institution in the Western territories. Still, abolitionists continued to press for more widespread action. Lincoln meanwhile yearned for battlefield successes that would bolster his authority to act more decisively, but antislavery forces actually regarded the bleak military situation as an opportunity. As Greeley told the president: "The stagnation of the grand Army has given life to all manner of projects which would be quiet if the War had been going vigorously on." [31] Unlike Raymond, Greeley believed Lincoln should strike boldly against slavery everywhere, and sooner rather than later.

Where was Henry Raymond in March 1862 when his New York staff published the critical editorial that provoked such a strong response from the president? He was back in Albany, serving yet another term in the New York

State Assembly, unable to resist the call of politics even during wartime.[32] His latest and last sojourn as a state legislator ended after a single session. A few weeks later, Raymond headed off to a different battleground—electing to travel south to cover George McClellan's long-awaited offensive against the Confederacy.

McClellan had devised an ambitious—and, as it turned out, wholly unwieldy—plan to seize Richmond. The "Young Napoleon" transported more than 100,000 men and fifteen thousand animals by ship to Fort Monroe at Hampton Roads, Virginia, and from there began slowly marching them up a tongue of land between the York and James Rivers, intending to capture the Confederate capital from the southeast. From the start, Lincoln feared that the scheme would leave Washington exposed to attack, but he reluctantly consented to McClellan's strategy. At least his recalcitrant general was finally proposing to use his army somewhere, anywhere.

After Bull Run, Raymond had supposedly put his days as a war correspondent behind him, but he could not resist again journeying to the front to witness what he and other Northern editors believed might be the campaign that ended the rebellion. Raymond went on to file a succession of hopeful dispatches from the Peninsula, several of them predicting the capture of Richmond without resistance, but eventually he came to realize that McClellan had bogged down hopelessly, his advance reduced to a crawl. Indeed, convinced by faulty intelligence that he was vastly outnumbered, the overcautious McClellan paused so often to dig in that he gave the enemy ample time to rally to the defense of its capital.

Worse, the general still seemed more hostile to the press than to the Rebels. McClellan repeatedly fired off telegrams to Stanton in Washington to complain about unauthorized leaks and violations of his tight restrictions on newspaper coverage. The general became particularly outraged when he learned that, barred from reporting his army's movements, several enterprising Philadelphia and New York journalists (the *Herald* alone boasted at least two dozen correspondents on the Peninsula) took to obtaining the latest copies of the Richmond dailies—which bulged with useful details of his army's activities—and shipping them north so their editors could extract and reprint the information.

For a time, Raymond enjoyed his time on campaign. He bivouacked at a nine-dollar-per-week farmhouse along the Chickahominy River, sharing a room with young *Herald* correspondent George Alfred Townsend. There he regaled the younger journalist with stories about covering war in Europe, and lobbed frank barbs about rivals like Greeley (jealous of his political success, claimed Raymond) and Townsend's own boss, Bennett (a "monstrous blackguard"). Raymond tried but failed to convince Townsend to abandon the *Herald* and join the *Times* at a higher salary. Townsend, who believed Raymond suffered from "a predilection for 'Bohemia'"—the voguish term for a reporter's life on military campaign—nonetheless praised him as "an indefatigable correspondent."[33]

Eventually, the lack of newsworthy military progress, coupled with decreasing access both to and from McClellan's headquarters—the army established a rigorous new censorship operation at Fort Monroe—increased Raymond's restlessness. The memory of the general's outlandish effort to suppress the *Times* for treason a few months earlier remained raw. Frustrated, Raymond published some mildly critical commentaries from the front (noting, for example, the "high spirits" of the Rebels at the May 4–5 Battle of Williamsburg),[34] and eventually concluded that McClellan was unlikely to give him any future advantage. This became increasingly the case once Lincoln began advancing his emancipation initiatives back in Washington. McClellan believed the war should be waged to restore "the Union as it was," with slavery intact, and recoiled at the idea at commanding an army of liberation for blacks. In late June, with the enchantment of Bohemia gone, Raymond decided to return to New York. It was the last time the editor would report directly from a battlefield. His paper exacted a bit of revenge by alerting its readers that, as McClellan stalled against the real enemy, a distracting "little side war" raged uncontrollably "between the newspaper correspondents and the military."[35]

One journalist who remained on the scene on the Peninsula complained in the *Chicago Tribune* a month later that the remaining correspondents were "puffing" McClellan: "The amount of lying that has been sent abroad on the wings of the press and telegraphed to mislead and delude the country is enormous." When the press began blaming the latest military reversals not on the general but on the War Department, the Chicago paper regarded it as poetic justice for Edwin Stanton's sometimes brutal attempts to control even indisputably loyal, well-meaning journalists. As the *Tribune* reminded its readers of Stanton: "He commenced his career by an unjust and crazy warfare upon them—a warfare wholly without purpose, without system, without excuse. His campaign was directed against his friends. From the arrest of Forn[e]y . . .

strange fanaticism has marked his conduct toward the loyal American press. If they now have their revenge on him, it may be said that 'turn about is fair play.' "[36] But some readers never did learn the truth about the Union army's lack of progress in Virginia. By August, ever-supportive of McClellan, Bennett was blaming *New York Tribune* leaks for the military setbacks on the Peninsula. "We wish the disgrace," insisted the *Herald*, "to fall where it belongs."[37]

For his part, Henry Raymond returned to the front only one more time—the following January—when he received notice to claim his soldier-brother's body in Belle Plain, Virginia, after the Battle of Fredericksburg. Assuming his brother had been killed in action, Raymond promptly embarked on the mournful journey, but when he got there, found to his shock and joy that his brother was alive and well. It seemed that the telegraph operator had garbled the message: Raymond had been summoned to meet not his brother's corpse, but his *corps*. The incident may have taught the editor yet another valuable lesson about the unreliability of dispatches by wire.[38]

By far the biggest news story to come out of the stalled 1862 Union offensive was the March 9 battle between the ironclad vessels USS *Monitor* and CSS *Virginia* at Hampton Roads. Northern and Southern competition to put an iron warship into naval service had hardly been a secret. For months, the press had breathlessly reported rumors about secret construction projects on both sides. Reflecting undisguised concern that Union ship designers were losing this vital race, the *Times* even ran a public notice urging that proposals for new "iron-clad steam vessels-of-war" be sent to the Navy Department.[39]

Then on March 8, the newly refitted Confederate ironclad *Virginia* steamed into Hampton Roads and, impregnable to return fire, wreaked destruction on the helpless, all-wooden federal fleet. Fortunately for the Union, the quickly built, more technologically advanced, and far sleeker *Monitor* arrived on the scene from Brooklyn just hours after the *Virginia*'s rampage. The following day, the two ironclads met in one-on-one combat and fought to what amounted to a draw—though the mere fact that the smaller *Monitor* halted the *Virginia*'s brief reign of terror was hailed as a victory in Northern newspapers.

Lincoln, who had intuitively encouraged fast-track construction of the *Monitor*, rushed down to the front after the battle to get a firsthand look at the modern marvel. There, both the president and the "cheesebox on a raft" attracted further attention from reporters, including celebrated author Nathaniel Hawthorne. "It could not be called a vessel at all," Hawthorne dismissed the *Monitor* in the *Atlantic Monthly.* "It was a machine . . . for lack of a better similitude it looked like a gigantic rat-trap." Hawthorne, who retained an admiration for Franklin Pierce, the dignified former president who had appointed him to several federal offices, had a similar reaction when he applied his "ambitious vein of description" to the current chief executive (Ben Perley Poore, "note book in hand," joined the rare interview). Hawthorne produced such a frank description of the homespun Lincoln that his *Atlantic* editor deleted it from the published article, going so far as to apologize in a footnote: "The sketch appears to have been written in a benign spirit . . . it lacks *reverence.*"[40] A resentful Hawthorne confided, "what a terrible thing it is to try to let off a little truth in this miserable humbug of a world."[41]

Unfortunately for the Union side, the *Monitor-Virginia* duel proved the high point of the Peninsula Campaign. By midsummer, Raymond was back home and McClellan on his way to failure at the hands of a freshly promoted Confederate general who ascended to top command after the Battle of Seven Pines on May 31. The "new" Confederate defender was a previously overlooked, fifty-five-year-old veteran named Robert E. Lee. He had been ignored by the press for so long that even Richmond's *Southern Illustrated News*, in belatedly publishing his portrait in December, remained unaware that Lee's hair had turned snowy white and that he had grown a soon-to-become iconic beard; its outdated front-page woodcut showed Lee dark-haired and clean-shaven save for the black mustache he had worn during the Mexican War. As McClellan busied himself organizing an orderly retreat from the Virginia Peninsula, the *New York Times* concluded that the Union's "military and naval operations seem everywhere to have come almost to a dead end."[42]

So, nearly, did the administration's recently improving relationship with Horace Greeley. In late March, Greeley launched a series of heated attacks on one of Lincoln's favorite companions, his old Illinois law crony Ward Hill Lamon, now serving under a presidential appointment as marshal of the District of Columbia. The gigantic "Hill," as the president called him, was a treasured member of the White House inner circle, not only a friend and occasional bodyguard, but one of the few intimates capable of deploying a joke or song to snap Lincoln out of the grip of melancholy. In taking him on, Greeley ran a huge risk of permanently alienating the president.

Lamon was also a loyal Republican, but critics like Greeley believed that in his official post as a federal marshal he had become overly enthusiastic about pursuing and confining fugitive slaves who streamed into Washington seeking protection. General James Wadsworth, the new military commander of the District, complained to the president in the strongest terms that Lamon was detaining fugitives in the Washington prison on only the flimsiest of suspicions. Congressional Republicans agreed, threatening to abolish the post of marshal altogether and require the election of a sheriff. Lamon was clearly no Benjamin Butler when it came to contraband slaves, and reports of his unseemly zeal outraged Greeley, who published a series of attacks on the marshal.

In April, Lamon responded by filing a libel suit against the *Tribune* editor. James Gordon Bennett chortled, "H.G. is beginning to reap the reward of his labors. He finds that impudent and unwarranted assaults upon honest officials for partisan purposes may not always escape punishment. He will probably ere long pay a compulsory visit to the District, if he should not . . . fly the country."[43] Instead, on April 8, four days after a grand jury indicted him for "malicious libel of public officers," Greeley admitted to his bureau chief, Samuel Wilkeson: "I stay away from Washington because I'm afraid to go thither. If there was the least chance of a fair trial I of course would not mind going, but there isn't. Lincoln has disgraced himself so much by appointing . . . [that] vagabond Marshal; that I presume there is no chance that he will ever remove him."[44] He never did.

The president did, however, eventually negotiate a truce that spared both Lamon and Greeley further confrontation and embarrassment. After Lamon dropped the libel suit at the end of 1862,

Ward Hill Lamon, marshal of the District of Columbia—and longtime friend of Lincoln—who sued Greeley for libel in 1862.

Greeley thanked Lincoln for his "interposition," confessing that he could not have found either the time or money to stand trial in the capital. Yet the editor could not stop himself from smugly adding: "Still, that suit has done me good service. It has saved me several journeys to Washington on other folks' business,—business to me most irksome, yet which I could not have refused without offense; yet which I could not be expected to undertake at the expense of a month or so in your crowded and not too cleanly jail." [45] Lincoln was no doubt gratified that Lamon's lawsuit had at least kept the unmanageable Greeley out of the city for the better part of a year. As for General Wadsworth, until his transfer in September he continued to pressure Lamon to liberate confined African Americans, but Lincoln never publicly admonished his old friend over the issue. [46] The War Department ultimately ordered Wadsworth's successor as military commander of the District of Columbia to bow to civil law on such matters—meaning to the ultimate authority of Ward Hill Lamon.

During the Peninsula Campaign, Lincoln had confronted not only McClellan's inertia but one more attempt by a field commander to seize the initiative, and the commensurate publicity, on emancipation. On May 9, General David Hunter, one of the officers who had acted as a bodyguard during Lincoln's inaugural journey, unexpectedly declared enslaved people in his department—embracing South Carolina, Georgia, and Florida—to be "forever free." Ten days later, responding just as he had to the earlier Frémont proclamation, Lincoln revoked the order, insisting that the freedom power "I reserve to myself," not to "commanders in the field." [47]

The *New York Herald* responded to this latest incident with a stinging editorial demanding an immediate overhaul of the "mismanaged" War Department. Seward and Chase had backed off from "the nigger business," Bennett railed. "Who then remains? Only Secretary Stanton, to whom both Seward and Chase have thrown their dirty linen—the newspapers and the niggers." Inaccurately, Bennett believed Stanton had urged Hunter to issue his emancipation order as a kind of stalking horse. Now the editor warned Lincoln that if he did not oust Stanton from office, the president might be forced from his. Bennett's ugly diatribe prompted another of those ingenious personal replies from Lincoln, who gently thanked the editor "for the able support given by you, through the Herald, to what I think the true cause of the country, and also for your kind expressions towards me personally." Lincoln offered only the mildest of rebukes: "I wish to correct an erroneous impression of yours in regard to the Secretary of War. He mixes no politics whatever with his duties; knew nothing of Gen. Hunter's proclamation. . . . I wish this to go no further than to you, while I do wish to assure you it is true."[48]

Once again, another of Lincoln's masterful private letters to an editor had its desired salutary effect. Bennett replied that he believed Stanton to be "a gentleman and a patriot" after all, adding: "Be assured it has been my constant desire ever since this unhappy war broke out to aid and assist your government in all its wise and important measures—Your success in the terrible crisis has been wonderful, and I have no doubt now of a successful and brilliant termination to the struggle. . . . On many occasions I have found myself groping in the dark in endeavoring to sustain your administration, but generally try to come out right." Bennett even proposed a "short visit in Washington in order to have a full and confidential conversation with yourself." A relieved Lincoln managed to dodge Bennett's latest request for a face-to-face meeting, but resumed paying attention, of course, to the editor's patronage appeals.[49]

Not everyone proved willing to cheer Bennett's support for the administration. Boston Republican Edwin Wright reminded the president of the "*negrophilism*" of "the old traitor of the N.Y. Herald." And New Yorker James W. White warned that the *Herald* was still "doing infinite mischief . . . stirring up all the hatred and bitterness that it can in a manner the most malignant," adding: "No act of stern justice would be hailed by more satisfaction by all the loyal people of New York than the suppression of the *Herald*."[50]

The paper's latest rants also prompted reform-minded minister William Goodell, editor of the small New York weekly *Principia*, to caution Lincoln that Bennett's "pestilent sheet" could never be fully trusted. Controlled by "well known Secession-Sympathizers" who continued to use it to alienate "the ignorant and most vicious and evil-disposed portion of our city populace," Goodell warned, the *Herald* remained capable of endangering peace and safety in the city. Loyal New Yorkers had neither forgiven nor forgotten "that the *Herald* was preparing to raise the Confederate flag, on the fall of Fort Sumpter, that it had long been openly pleading the Confederate cause, for the purpose of carrying into effect Mayor Woods [*sic*] exhortation to the citizens of New-York to Secede." Circumstances since may have compelled Bennett to "hoist the Union flag, and, in a degree, to change the tone of his paper." But "whether flattering or threatening the Administration, his one evident aim is to control or influence it, in the interest of the Confederacy, or, if unsuccessful, to overthrow it by violence."[51] Ignoring these alarms, Lincoln continued to court Bennett; in a crisis, he confidently believed he could control him.

Then the *Tribune* made its own misgivings public. Conceding Lincoln's authority to rule on all military matters, including emancipation decrees by renegade generals, Horace Greeley nonetheless called on the president "to consider and act upon the manifest necessity of having a definite, unvarying, clearly understood policy with regard to this subject." The Gilmore news agreement notwithstanding, Greeley was again losing patience with the president. Exiled from Washington, the frustrated editor put his famous literary flair on display to declare, with more accuracy than Lincoln would yet publicly admit: "Slavery, and its doom, is sure. Every gun fired in this struggle, no matter on which side, no matter what else it hits or misses, lodges a ball in the carcass of the writhing monster. Man may hesitate or vacillate, but the judgment of God is sure, and under that judgment Slavery reels to its certain downfall."[52]

Not long after Greeley's prophetic words appeared in print, Lincoln decided to look to an old warrior for advice on the frustrating military situation. Late in June, he embarked on one of his exceptionally rare trips outside Washington to consult McClellan's predecessor, Winfield Scott, at his retirement home at West Point. It was the only way Lincoln could again engage Old Fuss and Feathers, for the bloated veteran no longer had the stamina to travel. More than willing to suspend protocol and travel north for the visit, Lincoln may have particularly relished the chance to escape the relentless Washington press corps for a few days. For this, his only presidential trip to New York state, Lincoln took with him the outspoken General John Pope, rumored to be lurking in the wings to succeed McClellan if the Peninsula Campaign collapsed. Correspondent George Townsend, who knew both men, observed that Pope "had all of Mr. Lincoln's garrulity (which I suspect to be the cause of their affinity), and none of that good old man's common sense."[53]

Lincoln caught the capital's newsmen completely off guard with his unannounced outing, which remained cloaked in secrecy even after it commenced. Slipping out of Washington aboard a private railroad car, he arrived in New York City around 1 A.M. on June 23, and changed trains there undetected by Gotham's dailies, too. Not until the 24th did the *Tribune* finally break the story, announcing almost sheepishly: "It is stated on the authority of passengers from West Point today that President Lincoln and General Pope arrived at Cozzen's Hotel, West Point, at an early hour this morning, and the fact that a special train passed over the Hudson River Railroad after midnight leaves little reason to doubt the truth of the report."[54] Wondered the acerbic *Herald*: "Has Old Abe taken another clandestine flight in Scotch cap and military cloak?"[55]

The reading public never learned the details of Lincoln's five-hour conference with Scott. The general wrote up a summary of the meeting, but shared it with Lincoln alone.[56] The only thing the president ever said publicly about his mission provided instead a bizarre public acknowledgment of the government's hard policy on an entirely different matter: newspaper censorship. Despite all his years in the political arena, Lincoln remained uncomfortable speaking extemporaneously. So when a small but insistent crowd finally caught up with him while he paused to change trains in Jersey City on June 25, he agreed to speak but went decidedly, perhaps intentionally, off topic, apparently still delighted that he had outwitted all the reporters who made it their habit to follow his every move. This time, however, journalists were on hand to transcribe every word.

"When birds and animals are looked at through a fog they are seen to disadvantage," Lincoln began his disjointed greeting to the puzzled knot of well-wishers, "and so it might be with you if I were to attempt to tell you why I went to see Gen. Scott. I can only say that my visit to West Point did not have the importance that has been attached it. . . . The Secretary of War, you know, holds a pretty tight rein on the Press, so that they shall not tell more than they ought to, and I'm afraid that if I blab too much he might draw a tight rein on me."[57] On this occasion, Lincoln "blabbed" hardly at all.

As always, the president told the press exactly what he wanted them to hear, and not a word more.

Once back in Washington, Lincoln not only reshuffled the army high command, he also attempted to rekindle recent antislavery momentum by summoning Border State congressmen to the White House to press his compensation plan. The officials listened respectfully, but after caucusing independently, voted overwhelmingly to reject the president's offer.

"Can you enlighten the people in regard to the real object and purpose of the Administration at Washington in relation to the Rebellion?" an impatient reader calling himself "Enquirer" wrote Horace Greeley after this latest emancipation initiative collapsed. With the "great army of the Potomac" now "hid away," the "President with full power to act, & with a force, ever ready and willing & anxious to be called upon and by & through which the rebellion could be crushed suddenly and surely"—meaning African-American recruits—"hangs back, hesitates, & leaves the country to drift away to certain destruction." The *Tribune's* managing editor, Sydney Howard Gay, forwarded the complaint to the White House, noting ominously, "I am receiving daily many similar letters. . . . I do not publish them because I know they would exercise a most serious influence upon the public mind." Lincoln responded by inviting Gay to "come and see me at once; and, if possible, bring your correspondent with you." But "Enquirer" decided "it would be a mere waste of time & money" to undertake such a trip. Besides, he sneered, "I understand the policy is now finally settled that none but white men are to be allowed to give their lives for the preservation of the country. This is our weakness as it is the strength of the rebels, and with this policy we shall fail in the end." [58]

Lincoln often let such expressions of disrespect roll off his back—even though White House clerk William Stoddard complained that criticism from "prominent portions of the New-York press" was then "without parallel in the history of American journalism." As Stoddard viewed matters, "The conservatives, falsely so called, seem to be in an agony of fear lest the President is on the eve of launching the country into a war of rapine, pillage and destruction. The fanatical radicals are in a foaming rage because he makes provision for the carrying out of his proposition to the Border States representatives." [59]

Whipsawed by Border State resistance, conservative mistrust, and Republican impatience, not to mention military inertia, a frustrated Lincoln contemplated his next move. Inevitably, he turned his thoughts to executive action under the war power. Even before reading "Enquirer's" observations, he had commenced writing the first draft of a presidential decree that would cite military necessity to ban slavery in all the seceded states. Emancipation was now at hand.

Lincoln reverted to a familiar technique to introduce his bombshell plan: the precisely timed newspaper leak. On July 17, the day after Congress passed the bold but largely unenforceable Confiscation Act, intended to free, shelter, and perhaps colonize slaves held by disloyal Southerners, the well-informed *New York Times* advised its readers: "It seems not improbable that the President considers the time near at hand when slavery must go to the wall." Raymond was on to something. The president would "not conserve slavery much longer," John Hay echoed in a confidential July 21 aside to a prominent antislavery activist. "When next he speaks in relation to this defiant and ungrateful villainy it will be with no uncertain sound."[60] The very next day, Lincoln prepared to unleash that sound with a force he knew would be heard around the world.

On July 22, 1862, the president called his cabinet into session and read aloud the brief document he had recently been drafting: an order aimed at destroying slavery in all the Rebel states, whether individual slave owners were actively disloyal or not. Based on the Confiscation Act, which impractically left enforcement to federal courts that no longer sat in the Confederacy, Lincoln proposed giving the liberating power to the armed forces. His text concluded with the momentous vow that, as of January 1, 1863, "all persons held as slaves within any state or states, wherein the constitutional authority of the United States shall not then be practically recognized, submitted to, and maintained, shall then, thenceforward, and forever, be free."[61]

Lincoln did not follow custom that day by formally polling his ministers. As he remembered it: "I said to the Cabinet that I had resolved upon this step, and had not called them together to ask their advice, but to lay the subject-matter of a proclamation before them."[62] Huddled around their conference table, however, the officials refused to be silenced. Attorney General Bates at once objected to Lincoln's idea on legal grounds—he doubted the president had the power to confiscate slaves in Confederate territory, even as a war measure. Postmaster General Montgomery Blair warned that the summertime initiative carried enormous political risk for the autumn; the proclamation, he prophesied bluntly, "would cost the Administration the fall elections."[63] Lincoln regarded these objections as unsurprising and unconvincing, for Bates and Blair were the most conservative members of the cabinet, and both hailed from slave states, Missouri and Maryland respectively.

The president held his ground even after Treasury Secretary Salmon Chase, the longtime antislavery advocate from Ohio, shockingly suggested that Lincoln merely give generals in the field the authority they needed "to organize and arm the slaves" themselves.[64] Only when Seward came up with

Francis Carpenter's painting *The First Reading of the Emancipation Proclamation* featured a copy of the *Tribune* in the foreground (lower left corner). Greeley viewed the painting at the White House in 1864 and suggested improvements.

an unexpected rationale for delay did Lincoln listen. Such a radical move after so disastrous a military campaign on the Peninsula, argued the secretary of state, would "be viewed as the last measure of an exhausted government . . . our last *shriek*, on the retreat." Here was "an aspect of the case," Lincoln admitted, that he had "entirely overlooked." Bowing to Seward's counsel, as he later told a visiting artist, "I put the draft of the proclamation aside, as you do your sketch for a picture, waiting for a victory." [65]

The wait proved far longer than he had hoped. Lincoln occupied his time expanding and refining his text, working at his summer retreat north of downtown Washington and occasionally jotting down a few words at the War Department telegraph office while awaiting success from the front that might lay the groundwork for its announcement. For a time, emancipation remained Washington's best-kept secret.

Meanwhile, the president launched an elaborate campaign—through the press—to prepare white America for the thunderbolt that was burning a hole in his desk drawer. To some observers, especially in retrospect, the statements emanating from the White House that summer constituted a campaign of dissimulation bordering on deceit. As clumsy as some of these messages sounded even at the time, however, they in fact served to prepare the country's divided, and arguably bigoted, white majority for black freedom, even if at some cost to Lincoln's subsequent claim to high reputation as a liberator.

Lincoln had reasons to tread carefully, even surreptitiously. For one thing, he anticipated strong resistance to emancipation from the Border States, even though they would be exempt from the proclamation. He feared further opposition from within the army, particularly from Democratic officers like McClellan who had insisted they would not fight for black freedom. And Lincoln expected a fight from Democrats in conservative Union strongholds like New York, where poor white immigrants feared an influx of free black workers who might compete with them for future jobs. To stress the constitutionality of his order, and also to reassure the more racist elements of his fragile Union coalition, Lincoln determined to couch emancipation in terms of "military necessity" rather than social benevolence.

The effort commenced on July 30, when Forney's *Philadelphia Press* called outright for presidential action against slavery. It is difficult to imagine that one of Lincoln's closest press confidants was not in on the secret plan. Crafted as if to urge the president toward a policy that Forney likely knew Lincoln had already decided upon, the editorial amounted to a trial balloon not only for emancipation but for black recruitment as well: "A million able-bodied men await but our word to ally themselves with us bodily, as they are with us in heart," Forney wrote. "A magnificent black blister as a counter irritant! . . . Will we use it? Or shall we go on for another year paying bitterly in blood for our culpable irresolution? . . . The cause is too great to permit such namby-pambyism." Those who understood the inner workings of the administration no doubt suspected at once that the editorial constituted a leak authorized—perhaps even worded—by Lincoln himself.[66]

Then on August 14, the president summoned a delegation of free black men to the White House. This was in one sense a milestone in racial progress; no president had ever before invited a group of African Americans to any official conference at the executive mansion. But the historic cordiality eroded quickly. When Lincoln entered the room, his visitors no doubt noticed that a reporter stood at his side to record his words. The president proceeded to launch into a stinging lecture to the delegation—clearly meant not only for his stunned audience at the White House, but for newspaper readers who would soon have the transcribed words before them in print. Admitting that "your race suffer very greatly . . . many of them by living among us," Lincoln told his visitors that "ours suffer from your presence. In a word we suffer on each side. If this is admitted, it affords a reason at least why we should be separated."[67] His proposed solution was voluntary emigration to Central America or Liberia—an old idea, but undoubtedly a fresh disappointment to guests who had arrived at the White House expecting news on emancipation, not colonization.

Lincoln could not have been surprised that his blunt speech did little to convince free African Americans to abandon the United States, although he may have been shocked by the hostility it elicited from the black community beyond Washington. Frederick Douglass, who had been barnstorming the country to advocate immediate abolition, reacted with fury when he read the published version of Lincoln's remarks in the press. The president was guilty of adopting "the language and arguments of an itinerant Colonization lecturer," Douglass editorialized, "showing all his inconsistencies, his pride of race and blood, his contempt for Negroes and his canting hypocrisy." As Douglass reminded Lincoln, *slavery* had caused the war, not *slaves*. "Mr. President, it is not the innocent horse that makes the horse thief, not the traveler's purse that makes the highway robber, and it is not the presence of the Negro that causes this foul and unnatural war, but the cruel and brutal cupidity of those who wish to possess horses, money, and Negroes by means of theft, robbery, and rebellion." [68]

Lincoln never responded to the criticism, probably confident that his emancipation order, when it came, would ease Douglass's hostility. Besides, though addressed to blacks, Lincoln's White House remarks were above all aimed at whites: designed to convince them that he was no particular friend of African Americans, and leaving the impression that any action he might take against slavery would not, if he could help it, include the amalgamation of millions of slaves. Overall, Lincoln was no doubt pleased by the blanket coverage. Once Republican papers printed and praised the remarks, Lincoln's conservative ally, Senator Orville Browning, assured the president that the effort had made him so "*strong* among the people"—meaning, of course, white people—that he could safely "do anything which your full and unbiased judgment shall decree necessary to give success to our arms, and crush the rebellion." Besides, Browning added, the "only grumblers are a few radicals of the Tribune persuasion, and a few other radicals of the pro slavery school—the latter, dissatisfied because the war is not solely for the protection of slavery, the former because it is not solely for its extermination." [69] Browning was certain that military success would drown out all such carping. Perhaps General Pope, now leading the Union army in Virginia in place of McClellan, could regain the offensive against Lee.

By mid-August, however, the situation in the field remained stalemated, and Horace Greeley, as unpredictable as ever, and no doubt resentful over the legal troubles that still kept him from Washington, decided to strike his own blow for freedom. In a long, blistering editorial entitled "The Prayer of Twenty Millions"—the most savage assault he had ever launched against the president—Greeley charged that Lincoln had been "strangely and disastrously remiss in the discharge of your official and imperative duty with regard" to emancipation, and maddeningly unwilling "to fight Slavery with Liberty." In the *Tribune*'s withering estimation, Lincoln remained "unduly influenced" by "fossil politicians" from the Border States. He was woefully insensitive to loyal Southerners "writhing under the bloody heel of treason," and unconscionably blind to the sufferings of escaped slaves rushing in increasing numbers into the protection of Union lines. Warning that "all attempts to put down the Rebellion and at the same time uphold its inciting cause" were "preposterous and futile," Greeley demanded that Lincoln cease "fighting wolves with the devices of sheep." The time had come, the editor proclaimed, to embrace the "emancipating provisions of the Confiscation Act."[70] Emancipation would generate hundreds of thousands of new fighting men. For a brief time, the

HORACE GREELEY. "Mr. President, 'do you propose to ignore, disregard, and in effect defy' these twenty millions here present, whom I command?"

A pox on all their houses: this cartoon assailing Greeley's 1862 "Prayer of Twenty Millions" editorial mocks the editor, the president (left), and the supposedly inferior African Americans Greeley proposes to liberate.

editorial apparently stunned the president. When his old Illinois friend Leonard Swett appeared at the White House, Lincoln showed him recent *Tribune* articles that seemed to suggest that "the President and all the men in his Administration were a sett [*sic*] of 'wooden heads' who were doing nothing and letting the country go to the dogs. 'Now,' said he, [']that represents one class of sentiment.[']"[71]

Two days later, Lincoln responded with a widely reprinted letter coolly setting out his priorities in a style notably devoid of Greeley's histrionics. Few of Lincoln's appeals to the people through the press ever earned such widespread circulation, commentary, or lasting fame. Yet why and how he came to write it have been thoroughly misunderstood almost from the day it first appeared in print. On its most basic level, the reply proved a master stroke if only because it confided a policy he had yet been unable or unwilling to announce publicly. As Lincoln now explained to Greeley—and the nation:

> I would save the Union. I would save it the shortest way under the Constitution. The sooner the national authority can be restored; the nearer the Union will be "the Union as it was." If there be those who would not save the Union, unless they could at the same time *save* slavery, I do not agree with them. If there be those who would not save the Union until they could at the same time *destroy* slavery, I do not agree with them. My paramount object in this struggle *is* to save the Union, and is *not* either to save or destroy slavery. If I could save the Union without freeing *any* slave I would do it, and if I could save it by freeing *all* the slaves I would do it; and if I could save it by freeing some and leaving others alone I would also do that. What I do about slavery, and the colored race, I do because I believe it helps to save the Union; and what I forbear, I forbear because I do *not* believe it would help to save the Union. I shall do *less* whenever I shall believe what I am doing hurts the cause, and I shall do *more* whenever I shall believe doing more will help the cause. I will try to correct errors when shown to be errors; and I shall adopt new views so fast as they shall appear to be true views.[72]

Although he added an ameliorating coda—"I have here stated my purpose according to my view of *official* duty; and I intend no modification of my oft-expressed *personal* wish that all men every where could be free"—Lincoln's declaration was otherwise consistent with his recent remarks to the Washington freedmen. But he had subtly expanded them by introducing the idea of freeing "some" slaves if such an act could win the war and save the Union—the very plan Lincoln had already determined to pursue.

Lincoln's genius for synchronized press manipulation was never more apparent—nor was his capacity to exact a little publicly inflicted vengeance. Though addressed to Greeley and couched as a private reply, the president twisted the knife by feeding the text first to the *Washington National Intelligencer*, where the letter appeared on Saturday, August 23, as the paper's lead item. (Obviously delighted, Lincoln clipped the story and retained it for his files.) The paper's editor, James Welling, had been recruited to join the venerable paper by co-publisher Joseph Gales, back in 1851, and had emerged during the war, following Gales's 1860 death, as its principal editorial force, especially once owner William Seaton entered his seventies.[73] Although Seaton praised him as a professional of "high moral and conscientious character," Welling, like the paper's original owners, had no compunctions about working for the government and the press simultaneously. He quickly became assistant clerk of the Court of Claims, and the paper, long sympathetic to slave owners and hostile to Lincoln, grew more friendly toward the administration.[74] Still, the choice of the *Intelligencer* to break such an important story must rank as one of Lincoln's odder public relations decisions. Perhaps he wanted his restrained words to be announced first by a paper not known for its antislavery zeal. Or possibly, Lincoln selected a conservative paper merely to taunt the progressive Greeley. But one cannot help thinking that after spending so much time, so futilely, during his Congressional days, trying to break into the pages of this powerful Washington newspaper, Lincoln took special pleasure in making the *Intelligencer* dance to his tune at last. Welling himself claimed no special relationship with the president, insisting benignly years later: "The letter came into my hands from the fact that I was one of the editors of the *Intelligencer*, to which Mr. Lincoln sent it for publication."[75]

As usual, Lincoln's timing proved exquisite. The following morning, Sunday, his letter reappeared in newspapers throughout the country, but not in Greeley's, for the *Tribune* still did not publish on the Sabbath. Greeley would have his reply, but not directly, not quickly, and certainly not exclusively. And as Welling noted, the rollout of the "pithy and syllogistic" message helped Lincoln "to take the whole country into his confidence."[76] Acknowledging the sheer brilliance of the strategy, Welling noted: "The anti-slavery passions of the North, which had hitherto been kicking in the traces," he noted, "were now efficiently yoked to the war chariot of the President."[77]

Even overtly anti-emancipation journals reacted well to the Union-first tone of Lincoln's response, with the customarily hostile *New York Journal of Commerce* predicting that it would "touch a response in every American heart." Albany editor Thurlow Weed, who still hoped Lincoln would not "divide and destroy the North" by striking against slavery too hastily, conceded that the president's letter to Greeley (whom Weed still actively loathed) "warmed the hearts, inspired the hopes, and touched the patriotism of the people," adding his crucial blessing for emancipation in the future: "Let whatever strengthens our cause, or weakens the Enemy, be done."[78] Greeley himself acknowledged that the "manifesto was exultingly hailed by the less radical portion of his supporters," though he sulked, "I never could imagine why."[79] He tried securing the last word with a rejoinder, assuring Lincoln "that nothing was farther from my thought than to impeach in any manner the sincerity or the integrity of your devotion to the Union." But he maintained that the president could not "safely approach the great and good end you so intently mediate by shutting your eyes" to slavery. "The Rebellion is strengthened, the national cause is imperilled, by every hour's delay to strike Treason this staggering blow."[80]

Although the general public did not realize it at the time, there was a good deal more to this epic struggle between masterful political writers, and the long-ignored details offer further evidence of Lincoln's rare gift for directing "public sentiment." Here was no ordinary case involving an editorial that inspired a reply. More accurately, the episode constituted a duel of public messages, each timed to earn political and historical credit for freedom. Before either composition appeared in print, a backstory unfolded behind the scenes.

On August 18, just two days before Greeley published his editorial, the *Tribune*'s information procurers Robert Walker and James Gilmore arrived at the White House for a conference with Lincoln. Before the meeting began, the well-placed Walker whispered to Gilmore: "I have good news for you, but it must be strictly confidential,—the Emancipation Proclamation is decided upon." Secret or not, under the terms of the three-way news-sharing agreement put in place a few months earlier, Gilmore owed such scoops to the *Tribune*.

As Gilmore now reminded Walker, "all of Mr. Greeley's impatience would be removed if he knew these facts." But Walker cautioned: "We had better ask Mr. Lincoln. I have suggested it, but he has been fearful Greeley would leak out." During their meeting, the president considered Gilmore's advice that he alert Greeley to his emancipation plans, but replied: "I have only been afraid of Greeley's passion for news. Do you think he will let no intimation of it get into his paper?" Besides, as Lincoln pointedly reminded his visitors, "I infer from the recent tone of the *Tribune* that you are not always able to keep Brother Greeley in the traces." When the president pressed Gilmore further on why Greeley had lately become so "wrathy," his visitor suggested that it was the "slow progress of the war" and "your neglect to make a direct attack upon slavery." Now, Gilmore reported, Greeley had embarked on writing an "appeal to the country, which will force you to take a decided position." When Lincoln then suggested that Greeley should come to Washington himself to discuss matters face-to-face, Gilmore offered the remarkable admission that the famous editor feared the president's ability to influence the press. Greeley "objected," Gilmore confessed, "to allowing the President to act as advisory editor of the *Tribune*." [81]

"I have no such desire," Lincoln fired back. "I certainly have enough now on my hands to satisfy any man's ambitions," adding: "Does not that remark show an unfriendly spirit in Mr. Greeley." [82] No one left a record of how the conversation ended, but Gilmore's revelations would have hardly inspired the president to take Greeley into his confidence.

Gilmore later claimed that he did not arrive back in New York until the day Greeley's "Prayer of Twenty Millions" appeared in print, but he never denied that he might have managed to share his advance knowledge of emancipation as soon as he could transmit the news. But even if Gilmore did not do so immediately, Lincoln had also confided his emancipation plans to *Tribune* managing editor Sydney Howard Gay, though impatient abolitionist Wendell Phillips still cautioned Gay: "If the proclamation of Emanc. is possible at any time from Lincoln (which I somewhat doubt) it will be wrung from him only by fear." [83] From whichever source he heard the stunning news, Greeley reacted by publishing the Phillips letter and also rushing into print his own "Prayer of Twenty Millions." His plan was not merely to encourage Lincoln to issue an emancipation order, but to position himself to earn personal credit when the inevitable order was announced.

The vulpine Lincoln remained a step ahead. Greeley may have cynically rushed his "Prayer of Twenty Millions" into print as soon as he received the tip that emancipation was imminent, but Lincoln had already drafted his "paramount object" text as a public message justifying his forthcoming emancipation decree. Once the opportunity arose, he simply converted it into a letter to Greeley. War correspondent Whitelaw Reid confirmed this sequence of events in a now-forgotten dispatch two days later for the *Cincinnati Gazette*. Reid revealed that the president had read a "rough draft" of his "paramount object" statement aloud to at least one friend "some days" before Greeley's editorial ever appeared. "So novel a thing as a newspaper correspondence between the President and an editor excites great attention," Reid reported of the result, knowingly adding: "The *National Intelligencer* in publishing the letter reads Greeley a lesson in good manners." [84]

The outmaneuvered Greeley eventually came to believe, too, that "Mr. Lincoln's letter had been prepared before he ever saw 'Prayer,' and that this was merely used by him as an opportunity, an occasion, an excuse, for setting his own altered position—changed not by his volition, but by circumstance—before the country." Greeley grandly added: "I'll forgive him anything if he will issue the proclamation." [85] It is hard to judge who proved craftier in this affair: the editor who knew emancipation was imminent but then, eager for credit, publicly demanded it anyway; or the president who had already decided to proclaim emancipation but now argued that he would do so only if it would restore the Union. The prize for nerve ultimately went to Lincoln, for while Greeley's editorial called on him only to enforce the Confiscation Act, the president replied as if the editor had demanded the broader executive order he was planning. "I do not see," Greeley later admitted, "how these points can have escaped the attention of any acute and careful observer." [86]

More importantly, Lincoln's "reply" mollified conservative Unionists, inspiring James Gordon Bennett to chirp, "It shows that the incessant hue and cry of our abolition radicals for a proclamation of emancipation does not disturb the equanimity or shake the honest convictions of Abraham Lincoln." [87] But not everyone appreciated Lincoln's reply to Greeley. Antislavery diarist Adam Gurowski lamented: "Mr. Lincoln is the standard-bearer of the policy of the New York Herald," likening him to Pierce and Buchanan. "You cannot refine Mr. Lincoln's taste, or extend his horizon," added Ralph Waldo Emerson when he read Lincoln's reply. "He will not walk dignifiedly through the traditional part of the President of America, but will pop out his head at each railroad station and make a little speech, and get into an argument with Squire A. and Judge B. He will write letters to Horace Greeley, and any editor or exporter or saucy party committee that writes to him, and cheapen himself. But this we must be ready for, and let the clown appear." [88] On this occasion, Emerson badly underestimated the president.

It is little wonder that William Seward chose this moment to forward to the White House a letter from a rural citizen named Edgar Cowan, who offered this assessment: "Certainly to-day nine tenths of the Republicans are groaning over the tyranny exercised upon the Country by the N.Y. Tribune and its suite, and are looking to the Administration for deliverance in some unmistakeable [sic] form, so as to break the thrall and allow the Country press to follow its bent in support of the President." Lincoln surely found solace in Cowan's reminder that "no greater mistake was ever made than to suppose the newspapers are correct indices of popular opinion." [89]

Still striving for the upper hand, Greeley attempted to trump Lincoln one more time, fully armed now with James Gilmore's gossip from the White House. The very morning Lincoln issued his "paramount object" message, the *Tribune* published an entirely different story under the headline: "From Washington. The Abolition of Slavery. Proclamation of Emancipation by the President." Reporting that it had obtained the exclusive news "from so many sources that it can no longer be considered a state secret"—the unnamed sources of course being Gilmore and Walker—the *Tribune* announced: "Two or three weeks ago the President laid before his Cabinet a proclamation of Emancipation abolishing Slavery wherever in the 1st of next December the Rebellion should not be crushed." [90] Though the account muddled some of the details, including the date the order would take effect, it otherwise seemed the scoop of the century. [91]

As it turned out, Greeley had again overplayed his hand. Rather than attract the attention his editorial had generated, the national press ignored Greeley's report amid the avalanche of conversation and commentary on Lincoln's reply to the "The Prayer of Twenty Millions." In a typical accolade, the *New York Times* commented that Lincoln "could not have said anything more satisfactory to the country," adding a slap at Greeley: "It is in infinitely better taste, too, than the rude epistle to which it is an answer." Raymond directly charged his onetime employer with trying "to substitute his own conscience for Mr. Lincoln's in the present National perplexity. The President not yet seeing the propriety of abdicating in behalf of our neighbor, consoles him with a letter that assures the country of abundant sanity in the White House." [92] Few papers took the *Tribune's* emancipation exclusive seriously enough to republish it. Thus, as it turned out, Lincoln's letter served as a response not alone to the editorial of the 18th, but also to the premature news flash of the 22nd. It is no wonder that Greeley, who did not print Lincoln's "paramount object" letter until Monday the 25th, a day after the competition had done so, reportedly complained: "I can't trust your 'Honest Old Abe.' He is too smart for me." [93]

By August 26, even the more conservative Republican newspapers seemed to bow not only to the inevitability of emancipation, but, for all of their previously expressed reservations, the need for it. "When the proper moment shall arrive for such a step," the *Times* editorialized, "we believe the President will take it, and we do not believe he will be coerced into taking it a single day sooner than his own judgment tells him, it can be taken with effect, and made instrumental in preserving the Union." [94] Meanwhile, the administration continued to send out signals that the proclamation awaited only some Union victory as a trigger. On August 27, the *Chicago Tribune* concluded "from the tenor" of Lincoln's Greeley letter that "if the next battle in Virginia results in a decided victory for our army," a proclamation "will be forthwith issued." [95]

Just days later, however, General Pope suffered a crushing defeat at the Second Battle of Bull Run. The secret of emancipation may have begun leaking out, but the moment for its announcement was lost. Bryant's *New York Evening Post* lamented that it was "well known that the President had this proclamation ready some weeks" before and would have issued it sooner but for the latest "shameful" defeat at Manassas. The *New York Times* still hoped that when "the proper moment shall arrive for such a step, we believe the President will take it." A leader less firmly committed to liberty might have retreated from his commitments and folded his tent as quickly as the whipped Army of the Potomac. By this time, however, even the increasingly anti-Republican *New York World* acknowledged that "Proclamation Mania" had overrun the North. [96]

Lincoln's most mystifying effort to frame emancipation came a few weeks after the Second Bull Run catastrophe. On September 13, 1862, the president welcomed to the White House a three-man delegation of Christian ministers from Chicago. The clergymen had recently sent Lincoln an impassioned "memorial" urging "National Emancipation . . . without delay." [97] Having just learned that Confederate forces under Robert E. Lee had launched an invasion of Maryland, and that the Union army, restored to McClellan's command, was now approaching a potentially epochal confrontation, Lincoln was perhaps off his guard, and certainly more desperate than ever for the elusive battlefield victory that could unleash freedom, even if he had no reason on earth to be confident of the coming encounter.

Speaking from an armchair while his visitors took notes—suggesting that he well knew that his comments would eventually be published—Lincoln began the meeting by expressing a desire to understand God's will on emancipation, emphatically adding: *"And if I can learn what it is, I will do it!"* Then, conceding that slavery was at "the root of the rebellion" and that Southerners would have "been impotent without slavery as their instrument," Lincoln let loose with an exasperated outburst: "What *good* would a proclamation of emancipation from me do, especially as we are now situated? I do not want to issue a document that the whole world will see must necessarily be inoperative, like the Pope's bull against the comet!"—a reference not to the recently humiliated *General* Pope, but to a fifteenth-century Roman Catholic pope named Calixtus III, author of a famously impotent order banning what was to become known as Halley's Comet.[98] James Welling later maintained that Lincoln had expressed all these comments with a "festive humor."[99]

"Would *my word* free the slaves," Lincoln continued in this vein, "when I cannot even enforce the Constitution in the rebel States?" Then he reiterated the substance of his Greeley letter: "Understand, I raise no objections against it on legal or constitutional grounds; for, as commander-in-chief of the army and navy, in time of war, I suppose I have a right to take any measure which may best subdue the enemy. Nor do I urge objections of a moral nature, in view of the possible consequences of insurrection and massacre at the South. I view the matter as a practical war measure, to be decided upon according to the advantages or disadvantages it may offer to the suppression of the rebellion." Reiterated the president: "Whatever shall appear to be God's will I will do."[100]

After an hour more of discussion, the Chicago ministers departed, assuring their host "that God would reveal the path of duty to the President."[101] Lincoln's patient, complex effort to pave the way for public acceptance of emancipation ended rather anticlimactically. He had cited military necessity as the inspiration for any future action. He had emphasized—and exaggerated—his fading commitment to colonization. And now he had promised to seek divine guidance as his army took up positions to defend Maryland from Confederate invaders. Not surprisingly, the clergymen shared the story of their meeting as soon as they got home—in the press, of course—but their effort backfired, on Lincoln as much as themselves. The passage of time, fast-moving military developments, and slow-moving trains all conspired to render the ministers' revelations superfluous, and moreover to make Lincoln appear strangely indecisive, when their report finally appeared in print. In the interval, on September 15, the *New York Evening Post* predicted: "When success shall again have crowned our arms, this important document may be confidently expected." [102]

That long-awaited success finally came two days later, when Union and Confederate forces clashed at Antietam. In a delicious irony, it was that stubborn anti-emancipationist, George McClellan, who accomplished the victory Lincoln had entrusted to a higher power. McClellan eked out his bloody win on September 17, after which Confederate forces withdrew unmolested back into Virginia. It was victory enough. Announcement of the Preliminary Emancipation Proclamation came five days later—following another historic cabinet meeting at which Lincoln made clear that this time he would brook no objections. If the Confederacy did not end its rebellion by January 1, the commander-in-chief would end slavery there forever. He had made a pact with his "Maker," Lincoln gravely told his cabinet ministers, and God had "decided this question in favor of the slaves." [103]

So accustomed had he become to administration leaks that Treasury Secretary Chase searched that afternoon's newspapers for an early announcement of the proclamation, and pronounced himself "disappointed to find none." This was one story Lincoln did not dare release prematurely. Readers in Chicago thus awoke the next morning to a truly discordant set of stories: those from both the president and the local ministers. Lincoln no doubt knew that the clerics would publish a report of their meeting, but could not know precisely when—just as he could not have predicted the timing or outcome of the approaching military clash in Maryland. As matters transpired, McClellan's army prevailed while the ministers were making their way home. Although they quickly wrote up their report and submitted it to the *Chicago Tribune*, it became outdated the day it appeared. The *Tribune* published the clergymen's "what good would a proclamation from me do?" account on September 23— the very same morning it announced the proclamation itself.[104] Sometimes even Lincoln could not fully manage the press.

In his "peculiar, cautious, forbearing, and hesitating way," Frederick Douglass nonetheless cheered when he first heard the news, this "slow, but we hope sure" president had, "while the loyal heart was near breaking with despair, proclaimed and declared . . . *Thenceforward and forever free*. . . . The careful, and we think, the slothful deliberation which he has observed in reaching this obvious policy, is a guarantee against retraction." [105] As a columnist for a West Coast–based African-American paper similarly realized, all of Lincoln's preparatory statements, however unsatisfying or even offensive they seemed originally, now assumed clarity as part of a logical progression toward emancipation. It was evident "by close observation," declared the *Pacific Appeal*, that "there could be seen a constant under-current in favor of freedom." [106] Frederick Douglass's only complaint was that the proclamation gave Confederates a hundred days to abandon the rebellion before forfeiting their right to own slaves.

The mainstream Republican press rejoiced at the announcement. Typical was the reaction of Lincoln's old hometown newspaper, the *Illinois State Journal*, which hailed the proclamation as second in historical importance only to the Declaration of Independence, noting: "True patriots of every name rally around the President." A nervous Lincoln remained unsure that all of those "patriots" would now fight to free the slaves as well as to restore the Union. As he confided to Vice President Hannibal Hamlin, "commendation in newspapers and by distinguished individuals is all that a vain man could wish . . . but breath alone kills no rebels." [107]

His concerns proved justified. Onetime "War Democrats" who had supported the fight to restore "the Union as it was" protested vigorously, with Bennett, animated by warnings from his field correspondents that the order will "give us a Military Dictator," charging that Lincoln had caved in to "our shrieking and howling abolition faction." The reaction was even louder from Peace Democrats. The president's longtime enemies at the *Chicago Times* denounced the proclamation as "an act of bad faith to every conservative man in the North . . . a monstrous usurpation, a criminal wrong, and an act of national suicide." New York's once-suppressed *Day-Book* demanded to know: "Shall the working classes be equalized with Negroes?" The *London Times*, whose support Lincoln coveted in hopes of heading off British diplomatic recognition of the Confederacy, charged that the "nefarious" president had done his best to "excite a servile war in the States he cannot occupy with his arms." And the *New York World*, under new Democratic ownership, charged that the proclamation was unconstitutional, based on "that higher law—that is to say that open defiance of law—which has distinguished emancipation agitators from the beginning." When Lincoln quietly issued another proclamation a few days later widening suspension of habeas corpus, editorial criticism from all parts of the divided country only intensified. "Not content with proclaiming all the negroes of the South free, and inviting them to engage in a war with their masters," howled the *Richmond Dispatch*, "the ruler of Yankeedom has issued another proclamation declaring martial law throughout all that interesting region of the country. . . . Those who were once his fellow citizens, are now his timid and abject slaves." [108]

Lincoln had hoped that emancipation would unleash "a stampede of 'loyal blacks' deserting their rebel masters," the *Washington Intelligencer* reported, but no doubt spoke with authority when it conceded: "We have reason to know that his own faith is weak on this point." [109] The *New York World* was even blunter. "Massa Greeley," it chortled a month after the preliminary proclamation was made public, "where's your nine hundred thousand warriors?" [110] Lincoln must have been sorely tempted when his former press partner Theodore Canisius wrote from his desk at the Viennese consulate to recommend "General Baron Lenk"—the "most prominent artillery officer of the Austrian army," according to the former Springfield editor—who now wished to volunteer his services to the Union cause. "Men like the General we ought not to refuse," wrote Canisius. Ultimately, Seward talked Lincoln out of offering a commission to someone "from abroad." The president would have to wait patiently for his African-American "warriors" after all. [111]

If Lincoln's faith in the public response to emancipation weakened during the summer of 1862, it nearly evaporated altogether that autumn. Election season ignited a popular revolt against the president, the proclamation, and the Republicans, just as Montgomery Blair had prophesied. To be sure, political parties in power customarily lost congressional seats in off-year canvasses, but considering that the North was committed to a fight to save the Union itself, and that voters in Confederate states did not even participate, the results proved as surprising as they were discouraging. Not that savvy observers like Bennett failed to prophesy what he called "a glorious triumph . . . over our radical abolition disorganizers." As New York City voters headed to the polls in November, Bennett confidently invited Horace Greeley to a "*fete competre*," requiring only that his rival "be mum on the nigger question and make his appearance in neat and clean apparel." Once the results became clear, Bennett hailed the "Conservative Revolution" as a "rebuke" to Lincoln. [112]

When all the votes were counted, twenty-two Republican House incumbents lost their seats—even the speaker. The total Democratic gain, including pickups in formerly independent districts, amounted to twenty-eight. The Republicans retained control of the House and preserved their majority in the Senate, but surrendered the governorships of New Jersey and New York as well as state legislative majorities in Indiana and Pennsylvania. The next House delegation from Lincoln's home state of Illinois, once 5–4 Democratic but enlarged in accordance with population growth, would now tilt Democratic by a margin of 9–5. The president's friend Orville Browning lost his Senate seat, and even Lincoln's own home congressional district elected a Democrat to his onetime seat in the House of Representatives. It was a thorough drubbing, and while Lincoln was willing to accept responsibility, he believed there was blame enough to share—particularly with the press.

Admitting that "the ill-success of the war had much to do" with the Democratic comeback, a disappointed Lincoln also believed, "Our newspaper's [*sic*], by vilifying and disparaging the administration, furnished them all the weapons to do it with." [113] Left unsaid was an extraordinary implication: Lincoln and his party had done nothing to discourage free expression during the off-year elections. Newspaper shutdowns had decreased, and press criticism widened, unchecked by censorship. A commander-in-chief in time of rebellion had not only allowed popular elections to proceed as scheduled, remarkable in and of itself, but had permitted the uninhibited resumption of a partisan war of words in the country's press.

In the newspaper capital of the nation, earlier the scene of newspaper suppression on an unprecedented scale, New York Democrat Horatio Seymour, now governor-elect, had campaigned openly on an antiwar platform. Seymour's victory not only embarrassed Lincoln in a state he had won two years earlier, it automatically transformed the new governor into a viable challenger in the 1864 presidential contest. (After the vote, Lincoln dispatched Thurlow Weed to caution Seymour that no national candidate could ever succeed in the loyal states without demonstrating a thorough devotion to the Union.) In Henry Raymond's opinion, Seymour remained a man "trusted by traitors." [114]

Horace Greeley, convinced that Democrats had triumphed in the off-year elections because so many thousands of Republican-leaning New York soldiers were away at the front, unable to cast ballots, for once agreed with the *Times*: "That *all* Seymourites are disloyal, we never said nor believed," he editorialized. "That the disloyal are nearly or quite all Seymourites, we do know." Then Greeley warned the president that "the Country cannot endure another month's inaction in our Armies." The war for the Union, he insisted, "must be fought out speedily and resolutely or it will die out. Defeat will be a calamity, but delay is ruin." [115] This time Lincoln sent Greeley no reply. But in a breathtaking show of nerve, especially in the wake of so strong an electoral rebuke, the president fired George McClellan and replaced him with General Ambrose E. Burnside.

Henry Raymond shared his own post-election analysis with Lincoln on November 25, offering shrewd advice on how best to craft the January 1 final Emancipation Proclamation so as to alarm as few conservatives as possible. It should, Raymond maintained—almost as if he had been reading Lincoln's mind—be couched as "a *military weapon* purely & exclusively." Any attempt "to make this war *subservient* to the sweeping abolition of Slavery," he warned, "will revolt the Border States, revolt the North and West, invigorate and make triumphant the opposition party, and thus defeat *itself* and destroy the Union." An emphasis on military necessity, on the other hand, would prevent "cavils on points of legality and constitutionality," stay "the public odium and dissension inevitable in a more sweeping and less guarded movement," and "free just as many slaves and thus attain the same practical results" as a decree designed for "those who deem the *mode* of more importance than the result itself"—meaning reformers like Greeley.[116]

Whether Raymond genuinely influenced Lincoln, or merely echoed the president's own inclination to proceed just as the editor advised, remains difficult to ascertain. All Lincoln promised Raymond in his acknowledgment of December 7 was to "consider and remember your suggestions." But when he began composing his final proclamation, this supremely talented writer in fact suppressed his proven gift for lofty expression. Instead, he created a dry, legalistic document that one liberal European newspaperman dismissively likened to "the trite summonses that one lawyer sends to an opposing lawyer." The journalist's name was Karl Marx.[117]

No one leaked the Annual Message to Congress that Lincoln sent to Capitol Hill on the first of December 1862—but not for want of trying. Lincoln always "acted on the fear that his annual messages might, if supplied to the press, find their way into print in advance of delivery," remembered the AP's Lawrence Gobright.[118] This time, however, no Wikoffs lurked in the White House library to dispatch a premature text to James Gordon Bennett or anyone else.

The morning of its scheduled release, Gobright did hasten a note to presidential secretary John Nicolay, who was slated to carry the message to Capitol

Hill for John Wein Forney to read aloud to the Senate. The Associated Press manager did not want Forney to enjoy both that privilege and an exclusive, too. "I will be on the lookout for you at the door of the Senate, after you shall have delivered the Message to Congress," Gobright scrawled. "Please have two copies for me in the envelope, for the better convenience of transmission."[119]

Forney, who had already asked Lincoln to extend him a similar courtesy, wrote the White House the same morning to vow that he would not only "do justice to the message in reading," but expected that his paper, rather than the Associated Press, would secure earliest access to the text. His *Washington Chronicle* was now a daily—just as Lincoln had strongly urged—and as a devoted administration mouthpiece, Forney now believed he should always be the first to publish the president's words. He, too, asked Nicolay to hand over a copy of the Annual Message, promising, "it shall see no mortal eye but mine."[120]

On this occasion, no doubt recalling the humiliating scandal of the previous December, Lincoln kept his message a closely guarded secret. Even so, Forney's absolute loyalty did not crack. A few days later he instructed his editor John Russell Young to run an "Occasional" item supporting the message's renewed call for Border State compensated emancipation, hinting that its "facts were furnished from the highest authority." If it came from Lincoln himself, it was not the first or last time the president had authored an anonymous piece for Forney.[121]

"Fellow-citizens, *we* cannot escape history," Lincoln declared in that annual message, defending both emancipation—scheduled to take effect in a month—and his stubborn plans to promote gradual abolition in the loyal slave states and voluntary colonization for free African Americans. "In *giving* freedom to the *slave*, we *assure* freedom to the *free*—honorable alike in what we give, and what we preserve. We shall nobly save, or meanly lose, the last best, hope of earth. Other means may succeed; this could not fail. The way is plain, peaceful, generous, just—a way which, if followed, the world will forever applaud, and God must forever bless."[122]

Lincoln was far too battle-scarred to expect the entire newspaper world to bless even one of his finer (if most schizophrenic) literary achievements, devoted both to embracing freedom and ridding the country of those freed. In the end, Republican newspapers praised the message (the *Times* hailing it as "concise, clear, and perspicuous," and Greeley pitching in with reservations only about Lincoln's compensation plan). To no one's surprise, Democratic journals assailed it. The reaction in the African-American press was generally negative as well. "As free colored men, we thank Mr. Lincoln for nothing," bristled the *Weekly Anglo African*, "when he asks Congress to provide the expatriation of such of us as may be desirous to leave the country. We are decidedly of the opinion that we will stay." The always unpredictable Bennett was critical for other reasons. "We have always admired the President as a joker," he taunted, "but we never imagined that he could so aptly blend exquisite humor and practical common sense in an official document." Worst of all, Bennett reported "no public curiosity" over Lincoln's words. Instead, he noted "a prevailing anxiety to hear the latest news from the army." [123]

That news came less than two weeks later, and it proved disastrous. The African-American weekly *Pacific Appeal* had ushered in the final month of 1862 by expressing the hope that Lincoln would "not yield to pro-slavery pressure, by the modification or withdrawal of his great mandate for emancipation" no matter what happened on the battlefield. But when Union forces under Burnside suffered a devastating battlefield defeat at Fredericksburg, Virginia, on December 13, at a cost of more than twelve thousand casualties, no editor, black or white—indeed no American in any profession—remained altogether sure that Lincoln retained the power or conviction to make his proclamation final. The staggering loss had an air of farce to it: correspondents who staggered back to Washington in its aftermath were forbidden for a time from reporting it. "The rule was," Lawrence Gobright bitterly commented, "we must not let the enemy know what was taking place, as if the enemy did not already know he had fought a battle." [124]

As New Year's Day—the deadline for final emancipation—approached, the only thing certain was that the competition for news—especially now that it involved the biggest story of the century—would proceed as usual. "The New York Editors are anxious, if possible, that your Proclamation, if ready, may be telegraphed to the Associated Press this afternoon or evening," Indiana congressman Schuyler Colfax nagged Lincoln on December 31, "so that they can have it in their New Year's morning newspapers with Ed[itoria]l. articles on it." Colfax, a faithful Lincoln supporter who at the age of sixteen had begun contributing what Greeley had called "invaluable" antislavery articles to the *Tribune*, was in line to become the next House speaker, so his advice mattered. "You are aware," he pointed out to the president, "that, as no papers are printed throughout the land the morning of New Year's, if this is not done, it will not be published in any morning paper till Jan 3rd, robbing it of its New Year's character." [125]

Lincoln considered the request—even pondered sending an advance text to James Gordon Bennett as well. "It is important to humor the Herald," he advised Nicolay. "Is there any objection to [correspondent Simon] Hanscoms [*sic*] telegraphing the proclamation?" In the end, however, neither the Associated Press nor the New York papers earned an advantage, not even Greeley or Raymond, each of whom believed he merited the exclusive in return for years of antislavery advocacy. Instead, late on New Year's Eve, the editors received a disappointing alert from Nicolay: "The Proclamation cannot be telegraphed to you until during the day tomorrow."[126]

By then Lincoln undoubtedly had come to the realization that his order ultimately would generate a response well beyond the realm of mere news reporting. For the first time in his life, he looked beyond ephemeral journalism to validate his place in history—although it did take a journalist to help him see the light. On December 30, John Wein Forney sent Philadelphia portrait painter Edward Dalton Marchant to the White House armed with the editor's personal introduction. Marchant, Forney's letter revealed, had been "empowered by a large body of your personal and political friends to paint your picture for the Hall of American Independence. . . . There is no likeness of you at Independence Hall. It should be there."[127]

As it turned out, Forney was the only newspaperman whose advice Lincoln took to heart in those fraught hours leading up to final emancipation. At the editor's well-timed recommendation, Marchant began three full months of work inside the White House creating a romanticized portrait of Lincoln signing the proclamation with a feathered quill such as the founding fathers might have used to approve the *first* Declaration of Independence. In the background of the canvas, the chains on a statue of "Liberty" were portrayed as symbolically shattering.[128]

Here was the kind of heroic interpretation that Bennett, Raymond, and Greeley, even at their most flattering, could never have provided.

CHAPTER THIRTEEN

Sitting on a Volcano

———————— ◦◦◦ ————————

As the clock ticked down toward the midnight hour for freedom, Reverend Henry Highland Garnet ascended the pulpit at New York's Shiloh Presbyterian Church to lead a New Year's Eve worship service—what the *Times* called "a grand jubilee" for "the colored people of this City . . . in anticipation of the Emancipation Proclamation."[1] Garnet planned for his congregation to pray together until word arrived from Washington that Lincoln had indeed signed the final document. None of his parishioners could doubt that, on this historic night, the abolitionist preacher, born a slave, deserved at least some of the credit for the momentous decree now at hand.

Yet toward the end of the emotional service, Garnet generously made clear that he believed that credit should be shared—with a crusading white journalist who had also opposed slavery for a generation. When Garnet spied a pale, white-whiskered man shambling down the church aisle, he interrupted his sermon to announce that a true abolitionist hero had just entered the house of worship—someone who had "done more to destroy the vile institution of Slavery than any man in the country. . . . I allude to Hon. Horace Greeley." The congregation rose and began to cheer and chant Greeley's name.

But then Garnet noticed that the new arrival was applauding as well. The minister motioned for quiet, then admitted: "A gentleman right here before me looked so much like Mr. Greeley that I thought it was him, but when I mentioned Mr. Greeley's name, he clapped as hard as the rest, and then I saw my mistake."[2] Garnet laughed, and his congregants joined in the merriment. "Nobody would be ashamed to look like him," the minister offered. To which a voice from the pews called out: "Some of the most eminent writers have called Mr. Greeley handsome"—followed by more laughter.[3] It was not so much that Greeley was not inside Shiloh Church that night. It was the fact that his attendance would have surprised no one. For all his personal peculiarities and inconsistencies on secondary issues, the *Tribune* editor had never wavered in his fight against slavery. Had Greeley joined this or any other "midnight hour" worship service on the eve of emancipation, he would have been welcomed as a hero.

As it happened, Lincoln did not sign the final proclamation until the following afternoon. In Washington, Bishop H. M. Turner had fortuitously scheduled his own worship service for the evening of January 1. Well before sunset, parishioners filled every last seat at his Israel African Methodist Church. Turner was astounded when an overflow crowd packed into the churchyard outside, oblivious to the winter cold. Then the bishop had an inspired idea. Remembering that he had witnessed an emotional public reading of the preliminary proclamation back in September, he determined to obtain a copy of the final decree and recite it to his congregation. Turner knew exactly where to secure one: from the nearest evening newspaper office. So began his dramatic quest:

> I hurriedly went up to the office of the first paper in which the proclamation of freedom could be printed, known as the "Evening Star," and squeezed myself through the dense crowd that was waiting for the paper. The first sheet run off with the proclamation in it was grabbed for by three of us, but some active young man got possession of it and fled. The next sheet was grabbed for by several, and was torn into tatters. The third sheet from the press was grabbed for by several, but I succeeded in procuring so much of it as contained the proclamation, and off I went for life and death. Down Pennsylvania Ave. I ran as for my life, and when the people saw me coming with the paper in my hand they raised a shouting cheer that was almost deafening. As many as could get around me lifted me to a great platform, and I started to read the proclamation. I had run the best end of a mile, and was out of breath, and could not read. Mr. Hinton, to whom I handed the paper, read it with great force and clearness. While he was reading every kind

of demonstration and gesticulation was going on. Men squealed, women fainted, dogs barked, white and colored people shook hands, songs were sung, and by this time cannons began to fire at the navy-yard, and follow in the wake of a roar that had for some time been going on behind the White House. Every face had a smile, and even the dumb animals seemed to realize that some extraordinary event had taken place . . . the jubilation that attended the proclamation of freedom by His Excellency Abraham Lincoln, I am sure has never been surpassed, if it has ever been equaled.[4]

Not everyone was jubilant. "The deed is done," lamented the *Chicago Times* two days later, "the deed which unites the people of the South forever in their rebellion; which converts the war from a constitutional contest for the integrity of the Union to an unconstitutional crusade for the liberation of three millions of negro barbarians." An example of "administrative madness," echoed the *New York World*. But like Reverend Garnet, the racist *World* gave credit—or blame—where it was due: "The *Tribune* has its wild and wicked will."[5]

While Republican journalists like Greeley applauded, and African-American editors exulted ("a day for poetry and song," rejoiced Frederick Douglass), the Democratic press united in furious opposition to the Emancipation Proclamation, especially to its call for black recruitment. It was a measure of both increased confidence and tolerance that administration and military authorities did little to suppress such newspaper attacks, or persecute the editors who lobbed them. Despite their criticism, most anti-administration, anti-emancipation, and antiwar newspapers survived unmolested throughout 1862 and early 1863, emboldened enough to advocate for the supposedly loyal opposition during local election campaigns and to assail Lincoln's proclamations of September and January.[6]

There were exceptions to the cease-fire. Sporadic censorship did break out from time to time, and from coast to coast, a chilling reminder that tolerance went only so far. Back in February 1862, Secretary of War Stanton had served up a reminder of his powers by imprisoning a *New York Herald* correspondent in Washington for alleged "treason and complicity with the enemy." A gloating Henry Raymond endorsed the "justice" and "propriety" of arresting any Bennett employee, assuring *Times* readers that the government still remained innocent of wholesale "interference with the freedom of the Press."[7] Raymond himself had yet to embrace black recruitment, but he was a Republican. No one menaced him when he questioned the proclamation's call for African-American troops or argued that the decree might more wisely have been issued as a purely military order to eliminate the possibility of Supreme Court review.[8]

Democratic editors received no such benefit of the doubt, and doubts about Union loyalty often generated harsh consequences. Around the time Lincoln signed the District of Columbia emancipation act, General Benjamin Butler suppressed the daily *True Delta* in recently conquered New Orleans. On another occasion, Butler lost patience with a chaplain who doubled as a war correspondent for the *New York Evening Post*. After berating him as a "hypocrite," Butler sentenced him to spend hours inside a live-munitions storage tent, where the slightest move would have blown him to pieces.[9] In the Far West, officials shut down the "incendiary" *Oregon Democrat* in March 1862, and later shuttered the *Los Angeles Star* for providing "aid and comfort to the enemy" after it railed against "the utter folly and wickedness of the Emancipation Proclamation."[10] In Iowa, press suppression broke out in Burlington, where a Democratic editor was hauled off to prison.[11] For some, these isolated, small-town crackdowns were insufficient. When the anti-Lincoln *New York Express* denounced the proclamation in September, an agitated A. W. Spies wondered "how, is rebellion to be crushed while such insulting traitorous papers are allowed to be freely circulated among the people?" In a blistering letter to Secretary of State Seward, Spies vowed: "Tens of thousands in New York now stand ready to enter the printing establishments of several papers and break the heads of the editors, and are only restrained by its unlawfulness and are waiting for our weak & pukish Govt to do the needful to them."[12]

Though elections had proceeded as scheduled in the fall of 1862—something of a miracle, under the circumstances—and Democratic newspapers had enjoyed their say about the candidates without interference, the threat of censorship was never far from the surface. Whether the constant worries about intimidation muffled the Democrats' strength or motivated them to the polls, however, no one could say with certainty. Confidence could not have reigned among Democratic editors when New York Democratic congressman Benjamin Wood found himself under investigation by the House Judiciary Committee for allegedly communicating "important intelligence to the rebels." Vehemently denying the charges, Wood insisted: "I have never communicated, and have never attempted to communicate, directly or indirectly, any important intelligence, or any intelligence, to any person, within the lines of the Southern Confederacy, whether in arms, or others." [13] To have said otherwise would have exposed his *Daily News* to another shutdown.

On January 27, 1863, in one post-election case that did unleash an uproar, General Robert Schenck, commander of the army's Middle Department, suppressed the pro-Democratic *Philadelphia Evening Journal* and ordered the arrest of publisher Albert D. Boileau. "It had been recently very violent in its abuse of the administration," attested a local pro-war diarist named Sidney George Fisher, "and was distributed in large quantities among the Army . . . which is thought to be very demoralized." [14] Authorities seized Boileau at his home and hustled him off to Fort McHenry in Baltimore a week after his daily merely published an editorial comparing President Lincoln's 1862 Annual Message to the one just issued by his Confederate counterpart Jefferson Davis—"a comparison," according to the *Journal*, "quite damaging to the intellectual capacity of the Federal President." [15] Assailing the Emancipation Proclamation, the *Journal* further sneered: "Who but a fool believes that the Union can be restored by such means?" [16]

Although the scathing comments were the work of an editorial writer, and may have been published without Boileau's knowledge, General Schenck held the publisher responsible. [17] Boileau's arrest ignited an avalanche of protest from the state's Democratic newspapers—some charging it was retaliation for their party's success in the recent state elections, others condemning it as a "hellish" act of kidnapping. Even administration mouthpiece John Wein Forney expressed concern about the manner of Boileau's seizure, alluding to Shakespeare's *Hamlet* to complain in the *Washington Chronicle* that it had been carried out "in the dead waste and middle of the night." [18] One of the imprisoned editor's most ardent defenders turned out to be Amasa Converse, the graybeard Philadelphia editor whose *Christian Observer* had been run out of town by federal authorities two years earlier. On Lincoln's fifty-fourth birthday, as it happened, Converse editorialized from his new base in Richmond to laud Boileau for maintaining "the liberty of speech and the press" in the face of Lincolnian suppression. Converse could not help reminding readers that no one had come to his defense when his own paper suffered a similar fate back in 1861. [19]

Such was not the case this time. The Boileau affair exploded into a political nightmare for Republicans, fueling charges of federal power run amok. Democratic legislators, journalists, and jurists had a field day questioning the legality of ignoring civil procedure in a loyal Union state whose courts were fully functioning. A federal judge in Philadelphia even proposed indicting the marshals who had arrested the editor. Democrats in the State Assembly introduced a bill to forbid the federal government from transferring any future prisoners out of the state. One legislator charged that the Boileau arrest was an act of vengeance for his paper's earlier criticism of General Schenck's military failures, no justification for "destroying the tranquility of a domestic fireside and invading the dearest rights of man." The legislator, who took note that Lincoln had done "nothing" to make his own views clear after the arrest, added melodramatically that Boileau's daughter had reacted to his arrest by going into convulsions.[20] Eventually the state's Republican governor, Andrew Curtin, had no choice but to suggest that Congress pass a law requiring speedy, impartial trials for those charged with treason.

Boileau turned out to be the wrong hero for any sustained campaign against suppression, for he apparently had little interest in editorial content and no intention of becoming a martyr to freedom of the press. After languishing at Fort McHenry for six days, he offered up an almost embarrassingly abject apology for the editorial "and other criticisms of like dangerous character," and vowed not to write, print, or publish any future articles "tending to the support or encouragement of the rebellion."[21] Then, shortly after regaining his freedom, Boileau cut his ties to the *Evening Journal* altogether and was heard from in the press no more. But his successors at the paper intensified their criticism of the Lincoln administration, convinced—correctly as it turned out—that the Boileau affair made it unlikely that Pennsylvania's Democratic editors would again be spirited to remote federal forts without a fair trial. Other Keystone State newspapers would face suppression in the future, but no editor would ever again be transported out of its jurisdiction.

Around the same time as the Boileau affair, the House Judiciary Committee belatedly asked Postmaster General Blair to justify his long-standing policy of denying objectionable newspapers access to the U.S. mails. No doubt speaking for the entire Lincoln administration, Blair proudly responded that freedom of the press was not a "license that is guaranteed." In a frank defense of his actions, Blair argued that newspapers could no longer "aim blows at the existence of the government, the Constitution, and the Union, and at the same time claim its protection."[22] War Department solicitor William Whiting, whose legal opinions Lincoln respected, was also heard from on the suppression issue in 1863. In his influential pamphlet, *War Powers of the*

President, he argued: "If freedom of the press cannot be interfered with, all our military plans may be betrayed to the enemy." In Whiting's view, the "Civil Rights of Loyal Citizens in Loyal Districts are modified by the Existence of War." Confederates believed—and behaved—no differently. In September 1863, Georgia troops sacked the offices of the *North Carolina Standard* in Raleigh, after which its supporters retaliated by destroying the printing press at the rival *State Journal*—and all over a gubernatorial election.[23]

Like a disease tamed but not cured, instances of suppression fever had bubbled up even as Lincoln was scribbling his earliest emancipation draft the previous summer—in, of all places, the president's own home state. Illinois was under no particular threat from either Confederate armies or sympathizers, but in July 1862, without generating much attention, military authorities there banned the circulation of the *Quincy Herald*, asserting that its anti-Union editorials encouraged the Rebels. This was followed by the arrest of the staff of the *Paris Democratic Standard*. Around the same time, a mob sacked the offices of the anti-administration *Bloomington Times*. Facing a similar fate, the editor of the *Jerseyville Democratic Union* abandoned his paper and fled town. Under such threatening conditions it was perhaps understandable that the late Stephen Douglas's onetime press advocate, James Sheahan, formerly editor of the *Chicago Times*, devoted his new job at the *Chicago Morning Post* to "supporting the war policy of the government without giving up the democratic point of view."[24] Like Douglas, Sheahan was a Unionist first. And extolling Unionism seemed the only way an "opposition" paper could now survive in Illinois unmolested.

Sheahan's former paper was now operating under the management of virulent antiwar Democrat Wilbur Storey, who had assumed the helm at the *Chicago Times* in 1861 with the financial backing of Cyrus McCormick of reaper fame and fortune. Storey launched his new career as a provocateur by declaring: "It is a newspaper's duty to print the news, and raise hell."[25] Crucial to Storey's hell-raising was a virulent racism and an unrelenting hatred of a president he called an "irresolute, vacillating imbecile."[26] The paper's hostility intensified in March 1863, when Congress passed and the president signed the nation's first Conscription Act. The equally hostile *New York Caucasian* responded with the headline, "Lincoln to Be Impeached."[27]

Like the racist *Caucasian*, the *Chicago Times* unequivocally opposed the draft and indeed any military recruitment, especially of African Americans. In response, pressure from pro-administration forces mounted against the West's leading "Copperhead" newspaper—"Copperhead" being the serpentine new term for Peace Democrats opposed to the war, emancipation, and involuntary military service. In early 1863, both the local YMCA and the Chicago Board of Trade launched boycotts of the *Times*. Then the Chicago & Galena Railroad banned its sale on all trains. And by February, two military commanders in Tennessee prohibited it from circulating in their encampments.[28] Unwilling to tone down his attacks, Storey defiantly intensified his criticism when General Ambrose Burnside, now commanding the Department of the Ohio, launched a broad new effort to curtail dissent within his jurisdiction. Burnside's latest crackdown was aimed specifically at muzzling the outspoken Copperhead politician Clement Vallandigham. The ex-congressman (and onetime newspaperman) had long and vocally opposed the "despotism" of "King Lincoln" and what he called the "wicked and hazardous experiment" of waging war without congressional consent.[29] In the wake of Democratic gains throughout the state in the 1862 elections, an emboldened "Valiant Val" now contemplated a race for Ohio Governor in the fall of 1863.

Almost at once, his nascent campaign collided with the new effort by Burnside to restrict dissent. On April 13, Burnside issued General Orders No. 38, banning all public statements sympathetic to the enemy.[30] General Milo S. Hascall, serving in nearby Indiana, immediately interpreted the order as an invitation to silence the Democratic press in that state, too. "All newspapers and public speakers that counsel or encourage resistance to the Conscription Act, or any other law of Congress passed as a war measure," he announced, would be "treated accordingly." Though Hascall left big-city journals alone, he soon shuttered small Democratic papers in the towns of Winamac, Columbia City, and Huntington, while bullying many more into silence.[31] Only when Indiana's Republican governor raised objections was the general's campaign halted. Military authorities eventually transferred Hascall to the Army of the Ohio, but not before his own General Orders No. 9 quieted press dissent in Indiana.[32]

Meanwhile, eager to test the limits of Burnside's offensive, Vallandigham arranged to address a Democratic rally at Mount Vernon, Ohio, on April 30. There he provocatively denounced Lincoln and the war he insisted was being waged for "the freedom of the blacks and the enslavement of the whites."[33] Six days later, in the middle of the night, Burnside's soldiers dragged Vallandigham from his Dayton home and placed him under arrest even as the town's church bells tolled in sympathy.[34] The arrest set off a small riot. An incensed mob set fire to the pro-Republican *Dayton Journal*. When a pro-Confederate "butternut" tried to slice the hose being used to douse the blaze, Union troops shot him dead. This latest outbreak of violence prompted Burnside to arrest the editor of the Democratic *Dayton Empire*. Union soldiers tore "the insides out of" that paper's headquarters.[35]

Convicted after a quick hearing before a military tribunal at Cincinnati, Vallandigham was ordered to be confined in a military prison for the duration of the rebellion, but on May 19, Lincoln commuted the sentence and banished his critic to the Confederacy, hoping he would disappear.[36] A month afterward, inflamed Ohio Democrats indeed chose the exiled Vallandigham as their candidate for governor. "Free Speech! Free Press! Free Men!" roared the *New York Herald* in announcing his nomination.[37]

One Ohio newspaper that supported Vallandigham—the aptly named *Columbus Crisis*—paid a stiff price. Even earlier, a mob had tried unsuccessfully to burn down its offices. After editor Samuel Medary announced his backing for the exiled Vallandigham's gubernatorial candidacy, a Union general banned the paper from the mails. Worse threats followed, especially after Medary vowed to continue his campaign for "the liberty of the press" by practicing it "freely." When a pro-Vallandigham Ohio army captain tried to distribute the paper to his troops, he was arrested. The following year, even though his influence was on the wane, Medary, too, was arrested for "conspiracy against the Union." He died before facing trial.[38]

For weeks, Lincoln worried anxiously about the tense Ohio situation, especially once sympathy for Vallandigham metastasized beyond the Buckeye State. In one example, outraged Democrats convened a mass meeting in mid-May at Albany, Thurlow Weed's home base. They issued a series of resolutions denouncing the administration over the Ohio crackdown, particularly its disregard for "the liberty of speech and of the press," forwarding a copy to Lincoln on the 15th.[39] The president pondered his response for nearly a month.

Unfortunately for Lincoln, the fallout from the Vallandigham affair meanwhile triggered the most controversial incident of press suppression to date. It surprised no one that the *Chicago Times* had lambasted Burnside and Lincoln over Vallandigham. But Burnside shocked nearly everyone when he foolishly escalated the crisis by ordering the paper padlocked and its gun-toting editor arrested. The governors of both Indiana and Illinois had each implored the

War Department in Washington to take action against the paper, but few expected the blow to come from the commander of the Department of the Ohio. Yet on June 1, Burnside issued an order not only banning delivery of the *New York World* from his district and closing down the *Jonesboro Gazette*, but authorizing the suppression of the *Chicago Times* "on account of the repeated expression of disloyal and incendiary statements."[40] Two days later, while Lincoln was still weighing his answer to the Albany Democrats, an officer representing Burnside warned Wilbur Storey not to print his next day's edition. That night, the truculent editor instead locked his doors and set his press to work. At 5 A.M., a detachment from nearby Camp Douglas—named for the late senator, the onetime object of the paper's affection—stormed the office, ousted its staff, stopped the presses, hauled stacks of freshly printed morning editions into the street, and shredded them. The army declared operations suspended and occupied the building.[41]

The shutdown of the *Chicago Times* unleashed a firestorm of protest—more than Burnside (who had acted without the authority of Stanton or Lincoln) expected, and certainly more than the president desired at this sensitive moment. A bipartisan group of municipal leaders quickly urged Lincoln to

Squaring off over press freedom in Chicago: General Ambrose E. Burnside (left), who ordered the shutdown of the *Chicago Times*, and its Copperhead editor, Wilbur Storey (right), who resisted it.

overturn the order; on June 4, Senator Lyman Trumbull and Chicago congressman Isaac Arnold—both Lincoln allies—worriedly forwarded the petition to the White House. That same day, the Illinois General Assembly passed a resolution condemning the suppression as "destructive of those God-given principles whose existence and recognition for centuries . . . have made them as much a part of our rights as the air we breathe." Although Chicago's newly established, pro-Republican Union League defended the shutdown ("prosecute the blatant spouters of Treason," it demanded),[42] and Kansas editor Mark Delahay reacted by telling Lincoln he had been "too Easy and lenient with . . . Traitor News papers,"[43] their support was drowned out by dissenting voices. A crowd of some twenty thousand angry citizens rallied in the Windy City to express their anger, spinning rumors that they were planning to get even by sacking the pro-Lincoln *Chicago Tribune*.[44] "Why should the Chicago *Times* be suppressed," James Gordon Bennett mischievously wondered, "and the New York *Tribune*, which is a thousand times more dangerously treasonable, be permitted to rave on unrebuked?"[45]

With the crucial Ohio election approaching, and the Albany dissidents still awaiting an answer to their protest, Lincoln wanted nothing less than a distracting side debate over freedom of the press in Chicago. This time he acted decisively—and retreated. On June 4, even as sixteen carloads of Union troops set out by rail from Springfield to Chicago to put down any potential street revolt, Lincoln informed Stanton that "additional dispatches" had convinced him that "we should revoke or suspend the order suspending the Chicago Times."[46] The paper resumed publication; the Burnside occupation had lasted but thirty-seven hours. As Lincoln later told Isaac Arnold, the petitions from angry Chicagoans had "turned the scale in favor of my revoking the order." Henry Raymond, speaking for the many Republican editors who sincerely believed that this instance of suppression had gone too far, hailed the revocation as "a just and timely act" and strongly cautioned against any repetition.[47]

Raymond did not, however, join a bipartisan group of fifteen New York editors who convened a special emergency meeting at the Astor House on June 8 to devise a uniform policy on the limits of press dissent ("each individual Editor must exercise his own judgment and act accordingly," Raymond insisted).[48] The diverse group included proprietors of anti-administration journals like the *Daily Argus*, the *Journal of Commerce*, and the *Caucasian*, along with liberal editor Theodore Tilton of the *Independent* and a group rep-

140   VANITY FAIR.   [June 27, 1863.

THE HAND-WRITING ON THE WALL.

SHOWING THE TERRIBLE APPARITION SEEN BY THE WEAK-KNEED EDITORS OF NEW-YORK, IN CAUCUS ASSEMBLED.

New York editors who drafted a press freedom code in the wake of the Chicago shutdown face "The Hand-Writing on the Wall"—the looming shadow of Lincoln pointing their way to imprisonment at Fort Lafayette.

resenting the city's ethnic papers: the *Staats Zeitung,* the *Jewish Messenger,* and the *Irish American.*[49] The editors not surprisingly elected the most prominent man among them as chairman: Horace Greeley. Under his stewardship, the editors hammered out a six-point resolution conceding "the rights and duties of the press in a time like this," acknowledging the illegality of inciting treason or rebellion, but questioning "the right of any military officer to suppress" a journal "printed hundreds of miles from the seat of war." Newspapermen had no more privilege "to incite, advocate, abet, or uphold or justify treason" than other citizens, the statement declared, but the press still enjoyed the constitutional right "to criticize freely and fearlessly the acts of those charged with the administration of the Government, also those of their civil and military subordinates."[50]

While Greeley made the summit meeting his paper's lead story the next day, Raymond and Bennett (who also boycotted the conference) ignored it in their own editions. It was too much to hope that the big three could really sit down around one table, much less agree on policy. Worse, the *New York*

Evening Post, whose representative did attend the meeting, dissented from the final declaration, preferring "a more decided recognition of the right which the constitution unquestionably confers upon the government to protect itself and the nation in times of 'invasion and insurrection,' even to the disregard of the courts and the infringement of personal liberties."[51] Unbowed, *Argus* editor Elon Comstock forwarded a copy of the resolutions to Lincoln. Comstock heard nothing in response, and neither did Greeley.[52] The inability of the city's eternally competitive major editors to come together around the crucial issue of press freedom doomed the June 8 summit to the status of historical footnote. Had Greeley been able to woo Bennett and Raymond to attend the Astor House conference and endorse the resolutions hammered out there, press suppression might have been dealt a fatal blow. Instead, the war between the military and the newspapers raged on.

The *National Intelligencer* refused to let the controversy die, either. More devoted to the Union cause than to antislavery *or* absolute freedom of the press, the paper condemned the now reopened *Chicago Times* on June 6 for its long history of retrograde journalism. That very day, Lincoln seized the opportunity to dissent, composing an unsigned letter to the editor that hardly disguised his authorship. "Being an Illinoisian [*sic*]," it began, "I happen to know that much of the article is incorrect." Lincoln rosily recalled James Sheahan's prewar *Chicago Times* as the "ablest" paper in the Democratic fold, pointing out that "since Senator Douglas' death, Mr. Sheahan left the Times, and the Times since then, has been identified with the Times before then, in little more than the name." A clumsily edited version of the letter appeared in the *Intelligencer* that same day. Mutilated or not, Lincoln had once again gotten his message across. However harsh the slap at political editor James Welling and the *Intelligencer*, it was clear that the president was making an effort to keep Chicago's James Sheahan loyal to the Union in a city where administration support seemed to be wavering. Lincoln had also allowed the rogue *Chicago Times* to reopen, made certain that insiders understood that he regretted its current editorial policies, but stressed the difference between partisan and what he considered unpatriotic journalism. Now he was free to turn his attention to the Albany Democrats.[53]

As he had done the previous year in response to Greeley's "Prayer of Twenty Millions," Lincoln crafted his latest statement as a private letter to Democrat Erastus Corning, but made certain it reached the *New York Tribune* and other Republican papers to ensure the most sympathetic reception. It was the longest and toughest statement Lincoln had yet offered to justify the "war power," and pulled no punches in defending press suppression. The president still believed that traitors, "in their own unrestricted effort to destroy Union, constitution, and law, all together," had for too long assumed that "the government would, in great degree, be restrained by the same constitution, and law, from, arresting their progress." [54]

Now Lincoln charged that "under cover of 'Liberty of speech' 'Liberty of the press' and '*Habeas corpus*,'" traitors "hoped to keep on foot amongst us a most efficient corps of spies, informers, supplyers, and aiders and abettors of their cause in a thousand ways." To demonstrate that wartime censorship would cause no long-term harm, the president harked back to some "pertinent history" involving his old political enemy Andrew Jackson. Lincoln recalled with the sudden enthusiasm of a convert that after the Battle of New Orleans, the general, too, had imposed martial law and suppressed the press. Noting that "liberty of speech and the press" had suffered no permanent "detriment" at Jackson's hands, Lincoln made the case for his own far-reaching, but temporary, authority to suppress constitutional rights in order to save the Constitution itself. He was as certain that harsh oversight would cease when the rebellion ended as he was sure that no man "could contract so strong an appetite for emetics during a temporary illness, as to persist in feeding upon them, through the remainder of his healthful life." [55]

Lincoln's "Corning letter" quickly earned widespread distribution beyond Albany. The president's friends at the *Chicago Tribune* lost "no time in spreading before our readers the President's admirable reply." In Washington, Forney wrote effusively: "God be praised the right word has at last been spoken by the right man, at the right time. . . . It will thrill the whole land." And in New York, Greeley printed the letter "conspicuously," predicting it "will do much good." [56] Even Bennett called it "most interesting," though he congratulated "our Democratic fellow-citizens on the manifest good effects of the spirit, vigor and resolution with which they have compelled Mr. Lincoln to come before the aroused and indignant country with a defensive apology." [57] In rebuttal, the *New York World* bristled: "Was anything so extraordinary ever before uttered by the chief magistrate of a free country? Men are torn from their homes and immured in bastilles for the shocking crime of *silence*!" [58]

Attempting a rejoinder in behalf of Albany's Democrats, Erastus Corning insisted that "the American people will never acquiesce in this doctrine." [59] He was wrong. Corning's foundry may have provided some of the iron plate for the USS *Monitor*, but this time Lincoln had pierced his armor. The presidential message, printed in countless newspapers and republished in pamphlet form (including a "War Tract" from the *New York Tribune* that sold fifty thousand copies) dominated the national conversation, and for a time put the Vallandigham and *Chicago Times* matters on ice.[60] One of its several pamphlet editions—of which as many as half a million may eventually have circulated nationally—bore the quaint title of *The Truth from an Honest Man*, cannily reviving the president's "Honest Abe" image to add still more credence to the message.[61] The Corning letter, often remembered primarily as a defense of executive power, served many purposes at once. Issued just as rumors began swirling about another Confederate thrust into the North—perhaps this time into Pennsylvania—it also justified using force to suppress antiwar journalists like Philadelphia's Albert Boileau, not to mention Chicago's Wilbur Storey.

Actually, Lincoln never fully convinced himself that he acted wisely in revoking the shutdown of the newspaper that had hounded him for so long. A full year later, he was still admitting of the *Chicago Times* imbroglio: "I can only say I was embarrassed with the question between what was due the Military service on the one hand, and the Liberty of the Press on the other. . . . I am far from certain to-day that the revocation was not right."[62] One thing was certain: Lincoln had meant what he said in his Albany letter: newspapers that overstepped their bounds indeed warranted suppression. What remained unclear were the bounds themselves. At the end of June, General Schenck, perhaps emboldened by the Corning letter, acted without much publicity or objection to prohibit Baltimore's newspapers from publishing "extracts" from the anti-Lincoln *New York World*, *New York Express*, *Cincinnati Enquirer*, *New York Caucasian*—and of course the reopened *Chicago Times*.[63] Then in September, Schenck closed the *Baltimore Daily Republican* for printing a poem called "The Southern Cross," and banished its three proprietors to the Confederacy.[64] For his part, Chicago's Wilbur Storey stubbornly resumed his campaign against conscription. In July he published a notice provocatively entitled, "How to Resist the Draft," which recommended that dissenters collect funds to buy substitutes to serve in their place.[65]

In New York, Henry Raymond's *Times* seemed equally reluctant to join the anti-suppression bandwagon, but for a different reason: jealousy over Chicago's growing rivalry with the nation's largest city. Raymond continued to flog Storey's paper and to denounce Chicago itself, which he charged "surpasses Boston in conceit and self-idolatry." Determined to halt the city's rising influence, Raymond condemned its Republican and Democratic journals alike: "We can hardly remember a week since the present Administration came into office," he editorialized, "when the newspaper press of Chicago was not badgering it for want of sense or backbone." In Raymond's opinion, it was "time to put down the brakes on this too ambitious town." [66]

Bennett, too, attacked the Windy City's press wholesale, criticizing both the *Chicago Times* ("a mere party hack, representing a set of politicians the vilest and meanest in the Union") and the *Chicago Tribune*, branding both papers as "representatives of a corrupt city, whose social depravity . . . is a byword throughout the land." Predictably, Bennett could not help but harp, yet again, on the indignities he had personally endured after Sumter, when, he reminded readers, "mobs . . . under the leadership of the attaches of the [New York] *Tribune*, visited various newspapers with a view to their intimidation." Perhaps now, he declared, the "people are at last awakened to the necessity of vindicating the bill of rights." [67] Yet no such awakening followed.

A few weeks after the Chicago and Albany brouhahas, the president dutifully remembered that he must not only justify press crackdowns, but reward press supporters. The promise of such rewards remained as vital as the threat of suppression to fulfilling the goal of retaining influence and power. As a reminder of the fragile state of the entire industry, financially stressed by the costs of war coverage, the *National Intelligencer* nearly went out of business for want of "official advertising." [68] Although the other, smaller Washington paper that Lincoln had earlier designated as his official organ had recently received nearly $600 in advertising orders from the War Department alone, delayed payments threatened its survival, too. "I wish you would allow the Republican (my paper as you jokingly call it) to be paid for advertising," the president chided Secretary of War Stanton. "The non-payment is made a source of trouble to me." [69] Stanton may have considered Lincoln's loyalty to "his" *National Republican* a joke, but to the country's humorist-in-chief it was no laughing matter. Nor was the crucial Ohio gubernatorial campaign. The *Republican* won its request for payment, but on October 13, Vallandigham lost his comeback race in a rout. A gratified Lincoln had every reason to feel that his insistence on drawing the line between freedom of expression and treason had been vindicated.

The *Chicago Times* incident proved an exception. Lincoln seldom interfered directly when military commanders like Burnside or Sherman took out their aggressions on hostile reporters. That he admired combative generals—on both sides of the war—became more apparent than ever after Forney's pro-administration *Washington Chronicle* marked the death of Confederate foe "Stonewall" Jackson in May with an editorial hailing "his heroism, his bravery, his sublime devotion, his purity of character," adding: "He is not the first instance of a good man devoting himself to a bad cause." After reading the glowing article, Lincoln unexpectedly wrote Forney: "I wish to lose no time in thanking you for the excellent and manly article in the Chronicle on 'Stonewall Jackson.'" Never before or after did Lincoln praise an enemy combatant so extravagantly—especially in the press. Coincidentally, the very next day, the president rejected as "embarrassing" William Cullen Bryant's plea to reinstate the German-American general Franz Sigel.[70] Unlike Jackson, Sigel did not win battles. For a time, Lincoln did defend Ambrose Burnside's feisty successor, Joseph Hooker, even after the press accused the new Union commander of harboring dictatorial ambitions. At a White House reception, Henry Raymond recalled, "the President put his hand on my shoulders and said in my ear, 'Hooker does talk badly, but the trouble is, he is stronger with the country today than any other man.'"[71]

Hooker did not remain in favor for long. In May 1863, "Fighting Joe" mismanaged his army into another catastrophic Union defeat, at the Battle of Chancellorsville, and Lincoln lost confidence in his flamboyant general (even after fatal, accidental fire by his own sentries deprived the Confederacy of their formidable "Stonewall"). Hooker, eager to retain his command, fretted that the president was receiving negative reports about him from hostile journalists, particularly after rumors swirled that he had slipped into Washington without leave after Chancellorsville. "You need not believe any more than you choose of what is published in the Associated press dispatches concerning this Army tomorrow," a nervous Hooker wired Lincoln on June 26. Lincoln replied the next day to assure him: "It did not come from the newspapers, nor did I believe it."[72] But the president no longer believed in Hooker, especially after Robert E. Lee followed up his Chancellorsville victory by launching an invasion into Pennsylvania—his course charted, some hinted, by reading the daily reports about Union positions published in the Philadelphia papers. In response, on June 26, federal grand jurors in Washington brought charges of treason against William W. Harding, the second-generation publisher of the *Philadelphia Inquirer*, for printing "information concerning the army movements to the aid and comfort of those engaged in the rebellion against the United States."[73] But news continued to leak. Lee learned that General

J. E. B. Stuart had failed to obey orders to join his invasion force only by reading detailed reports about Stuart's ride around the federal army in the Baltimore and New York papers, when it was too late to do anything about it.[74] It was also too late for Hooker. At the end of June, with his confidence in the commander gone and Lee marching north, Lincoln relieved Fighting Joe and replaced him with Pennsylvania's own George Gordon Meade.

In the end, press indiscretion was not enough to tilt the Pennsylvania invasion to the Confederates.[75] In a matter of days, Meade fended off Lee's furious assaults at Gettysburg. Later, the victorious general exacted revenge by expelling *New York Times* correspondent William Swinton, not only because he, too, supposedly revealed troop movements, but also because Swinton criticized Union officers, Meade included.[76] Meade's ire was not based, as some asserted, on his embittered reaction to criticism that he failed to pursue Lee's retreating army after Gettysburg—although correspondent Whitelaw Reid reported that Lincoln believed "Lee's escape the greatest blunder of the war."[77] Rather, "Snapping Turtle" Meade's hostility to the press dated back to Antietam, where he had ridiculed one correspondent for not knowing the difference between a division and a corps, and confided to his wife that he was sure that resentful reporters would deny him "credit for these last battles."[78] Meade subsequently ordered the arrest of William Kent of the *New York Tribune* for filing stories "full of malicious falsehoods," and would also have arrested Thomas Cook of the *New York Herald* for writing that Lincoln planned to relieve Meade, had not Cook left camp for Washington just before the general ordered his provost marshal to seize him.[79]

Notwithstanding Meade's aversion to reporters, the Battle of Gettysburg produced a torrent of celebratory press coverage in the North (a "splendid triumph," declared the *New York Times*).[80] Not all of the accounts from the South proved accurate. "Today Maryland is ours," the *Vicksburg Daily Citizen* lied in an article prepared on July 2, "To-morrow Pennsylvania will be." One Richmond paper reported exuberantly that the Confederate army had routed the Union and taken forty thousand Union prisoners, branding Northern reports of Lee's retreat "a Yankee lie."[81] In at least one instance, however, the battle inspired pure poetry. The talented Samuel Wilkeson, now working for the *New York Times*, undertook to cover the battle, knowing that his own son was serving there. Wilkeson arrived at Gettysburg on the steamy evening of July 1, only to learn that his boy had been gravely wounded by an artillery shell, then left behind in a field hospital when Union forces retreated from

Barlow's Knoll. The younger Wilkeson died that night. "Who can write the history of a battle whose eyes are immovably fastened upon a central figure of transcendentally absorbing interest," Wilkeson anguished in a brave story published a few days later, "—the dead body of an oldest born, crushed by a shell in a position where a battery should never have been sent, and abandoned to death in a building where surgeons dared not to stay?" In a sublime coda elevating journalism to the realm of scripture, Wilkeson concluded:

> My pen is heavy. Oh, you dead, who at Gettysburgh [*sic*] have baptized with your blood the second birth of Freedom in America, how you are envied! I rise from a grave whose wet clay I have passionately kissed, and I look up and see Christ spanning this battlefield with his feet and reaching fraternal and lovingly up to heaven. His right hand opens the gates of Paradise—with his left he beckons these mutilated, bloody, swollen corpses to ascend.[82]

Did Abraham Lincoln read these words? No one knows, though the report certainly won enough acclaim to have invited the president's attention. If he did see Wilkeson's story, one phrase in particular may have genuinely inspired him. With his own "new birth of freedom" declaration, Lincoln would soon consecrate all the soldier graves at Gettysburg.

As for Meade, apparently he learned little from his early, unpleasant experiences with the press. A year after Gettysburg, he authorized a severe act of disrespect in punishing Philadelphia journalist Edward Cropsey for making supposedly "libelous statements calculated to impair the confidence of the army in their commanding officer." Before banishing him beyond his lines, Meade forced Cropsey to march through camp carrying a sign reading, "Libeler of the Press," the kind of humiliation ordinarily reserved only for cowards and traitors. Meade boasted to his wife that the "sentence" was carried out "to the delight of the whole army, for the race of newspaper correspondents is universally despised by the soldiers."[83] Assistant Secretary of War Charles Dana, though a former newspaper editor himself, witnessed the episode and remembered only that Meade had been "much distressed" by the criticism that provoked it.[84]

Journalists, however, reacted to the insult by conspiring to ignore Meade in their subsequent dispatches, except to report his failures. Although Meade continued to command the Army of the Potomac, eventually under Grant, journalists began treating him as if he no longer existed. Later, the first generation of wartime memoirs, many compiled by former war correspondents, did likewise. Unlike the equally press-averse William Sherman, who became so successful he could not be ignored, Meade's hostility to journalists contributed to his future invisibility, good service notwithstanding. After 1863, the reporters who had been his victims virtually wrote him out of the Civil War.

Such a fate did not befall the Union general who harbored the fiercest contempt for the press. As early as April 1862, "Cump" Sherman, as he was known to his family, complained to his brother, Senator John Sherman, that newspapermen who criticized his conduct at the Battle of Shiloh were cowards who fled at the first sign of attack. A few weeks later, the general's wife advised the senator: "Cump has opened a regular warfare upon the correspondents, whom he detests, so we must henceforth be content to see him vilified by them."[85] In June, General Sherman issued a frank and bitter letter to one of his political accusers: "I am not surprised when anonymous scribblers write and publish falsehoods, or make criticism on matters which they know nothing about or which they are incapable of comprehending. It is their trade. They live by it. Slander gives point and piquancy to a paragraph and the writer being irresponsible or beneath notice, escapes punishment."[86] No general hated the press more passionately than this victim of earlier newspaper slanders about his sanity.

Sherman was no doubt delighted when, in August 1862, General Grant ordered him to arrest Warren P. Isham, the Memphis correspondent of the *Chicago Times*. Although no formal charges were ever filed—Isham's offense was variously rumored to be revealing that Confederate ironclads had run the blockade, or being caught in a state of undress at a bordello—the real cause was more likely the fact that the reporter was the brother-in-law of the *Chicago Times*'s Copperhead editor, Wilbur Storey. Believing all "newspaper harpies" were "spies" and "should be punished as such," Sherman enthusiastically complied with the order. The general subsequently persecuted Samuel Sawyer, publisher of the Copperhead *Memphis Daily Appeal*, for filing a critical dispatch about a subordinate. In this case, Sherman exposed a genuine traitor. Yet Sawyer's editors, John R. McClanahan and Benjamin Dill, charged that "Lincoln's hireling minions would deprive us of the privilege of expressing at all times our earnest God-speed to the progress of Southern independence." The *Appeal* suspended publication in its home city and relocated first to Grenada, then Meridian, Mississippi, and finally to Atlanta, one step ahead of Union troops, shifting headquarters so often it became known as the "Moveable Appeal." [87] Ironically, *Appeal* correspondent John Linebaugh, assigned to cover the Army of Tennessee, later aroused the wrath of Confederate general Braxton Bragg and found himself in prison.[88]

As for Sherman, he wanted no further press coverage of any kind, if he could prevent it. In December 1862, he issued an order banning any civilians except transport crews from traveling with his army.[89] The following month, after suffering embarrassing setbacks near Vicksburg, he interfered with mail service out of his headquarters, delaying one of correspondent Franc Wilkie's unflattering reports to the *New York Times* by more than two weeks. Wilkie complained: "Had the commanding General W. T. Sherman and his Staff, spent half the time and enterprise in the legitimate operations of their present undertaking, that they have in bullying correspondents, overhauling mailbags and prying into private correspondence, the country would not now have the shame of knowing that we have lately experienced one of the greatest and most disgraceful defeats of the war." [90]

Lincoln, who was trying not to intervene in such matters, did make a gesture toward overruling one of Sherman's most sensational 1863 press suppressions: the general's overwrought effort to expel and, in an unprecedented

Accuser and accused: General William T. Sherman (left) ordered *New York Herald* correspondent Thomas Knox (right) court-martialed.

move, court-martial, a hostile reporter from the *New York Herald*. Correspondent Thomas W. Knox had recently attached himself to Sherman's army without authorization, then charged the general with "insanity and inefficiency" at the December Battle of Chickasaw Bluffs.[91] As Knox calmly told Sherman: "I had no feelings against you personally, but you are regarded as the enemy of our set, and we must in self-defense write you down."[92] Sherman, who thought Knox no better than a Confederate spy, threatened to resign if the president interfered with the reporter's prosecution, "not that I want the fellow shot," he emphasized, "but because I want to establish the principle that such people cannot attend our armies."[93] At the court-martial, Sherman testified against the reporter personally. He reacted with fury when the court cleared Knox of the most serious charges, declaring him guilty only of accompanying the army without permission—an offense that carried no criminal penalty beyond banishment from army lines.

New York Tribune correspondent Albert Deane Richardson believed Sherman hounded Knox out of a "morbid sensitiveness" to criticism. As he insisted to his managing editor, Sydney Gay: "An accredited journalist, in the legitimate exercise of his calling, has just as much *right* in the army as the commander himself."[94] Richardson did more than just complain to his home office. In another effort to combat censorship, he gathered signatures from fellow journalists in the field and then, accompanied by James M. Winchell of the *New York Times*, carried their "memorial" all the way to the White House and secured a meeting with the president. Instantly remembering their only previous encounter back in 1859, Lincoln jovially recalled Richardson as a onetime *Boston Journal* correspondent who was "out on the prairies with me on that winter day when we almost froze to death." The president ushered his visitors into seats, flung his leg over the arm of his chair, and regaled them with a funny story about an Indian who spoke defective English. The president then punned that if Longfellow had been right that "Lake Minne-haha" translated into "laughing water," then a creek Lincoln had once encountered called "weeping water" ought to be named "Minne-boohoo."[95]

Only after these jolly preliminaries ended did Richardson get down to business and present his petition. The president dutifully examined it, thought it over, and agreed to pardon Knox—but only if Grant approved. When Richardson protested that Grant would never humiliate his friend Sherman, Lincoln exclaimed: "I should be glad to serve you or Mr. Knox, or any other loyal journalist. But, just at present, our generals in the field are more important to the country than any of the rest of us, or all the rest of us. It is my fixed determination to do nothing whatever which can possibly embarrass any one of them. Therefore, I will do cheerfully what I said, but it is all I can do." Hearing no further objection, the president proceeded to write out the conditional pardon, handing it over to Richardson with "a little sigh."[96]

Sherman was livid when he read the text. Lincoln's order asserted that "Mr. Knox's offence was technical, rather than willfully wrong." Worse, the president proposed allowing the reporter to "return to Gen. Grant's Head-Quarters, if Gen. Grant shall give his express consent."[97] Grant, who suspected that Knox had indeed come to camp determined to "blast" Sherman's "reputation with the public," but wished to offend neither his commander-in-chief nor his subordinate, cleverly passed the decision down to Sherman himself; Grant would permit Thomas Knox's return only if *Sherman* consented.[98]

Oblivious to the politics—for Lincoln needed to keep Knox's boss, James Gordon Bennett, happy—Sherman dug in, sending the reporter the following message: "Come with a sword or musket in your hand, prepared to share with us our fate in sunshine and storm . . . and I will welcome you . . . but come . . . as the representative of the press, which you yourself say makes so slight a difference between truth and falsehood, and my answer is, Never."[99] The ban remained in force. Knox never forgave Sherman, but later came to regard their "little quarrel" as a " 'blessing in disguise,' in saving me from . . . twenty months in Rebel Prisons."[100] That was because by the time Knox wrote those forgiving words, his colleague and advocate, Albert Deane Richardson, along with twenty-one-year-old fellow *Tribune* correspondent Junius Henri Browne, had fallen into Confederate hands after jumping into the Mississippi River to escape a burning tugboat near Vicksburg. Captured by Confederates on shore, the two ended up confined inside a series of Southern prisons for months until managing a daring escape.[101]

Under ordinary circumstances, Confederate authorities might have paroled the reporters—after all, they were not enemy combatants—but Richardson and Browne were something worse to Southerners: Horace Greeley employees, and that alone seemed to justify harsh treatment at the hands of their captors, many of whom blamed the antislavery editor for the war. As the Atlanta newspaper *The Confederate* put it, such reporters were "our vilest and most unprincipled enemies—far more deeply steeped in guilt, and far more richly deserving death, than the vilest vandal that ever invaded the sanctity of our soil and outraged our homes and our peace. . . . We would greatly prefer to assist in hanging these enemies to humanity, than to show them any civilities or courtesies." By comparison, a *New York World* reporter seized in the same incident earned a quick parole after his editor sent a pro forma request for his release. The plea from anti-Lincoln editor Manton Marble, according to Richardson, proved as effective "as if it had been an order from Jefferson Davis."[102] On the other hand, Lincoln's efforts to liberate Richardson and Browne ("get them off, if you can," he instructed), urged on by Sydney Gay, were ignored.[103]

The disproportionate Confederate hostility to the *Tribune* mirrored the irrational anger of William Sherman toward nearly every journalist he encountered. Sherman never lost his often self-destructive hatred of "men who will not take a musket and fight, but follow an army to pick up news for sale."[104] Although he convinced himself that he was "no enemy of . . . freedom of the 'press' and 'speech,'" Sherman insisted on his right to regulate journalists covering his military campaigns. As he maintained with almost flagrant disrespect: "Mr. Lincoln and the press may, in the exercise of their glorious prerogative, tear our country and armies to tatters; but they shall not insult me with impunity in my own camp." Sherman believed in a free press, he said, but insisted journalists "be limited, else in bad hands they generate discord, confusion and war, resulting in military rule, despotism, and no freedom at all." Whether the ends justified Sherman's means has been debated ever since.[105] As his fame expanded, however, the administration's inclination to rein him in shrank. Not a soul in Washington reprimanded Sherman when he told another Memphis editor in October 1863: "Freedom of speech and freedom of the Press, precious relics of former history, must not be construed too large. You must print nothing that prejudices government or excites envy, hatred, and malice in a community . . . my first duty is to maintain 'order and harmony.'"[106] Few doubted that Sherman's notion of "order" precluded frank observations by a free and unfettered press. But he was too valuable to the Union war effort to earn any rebuke more substantial than the president's reminder that he had gone a bit too far with the Thomas Knox case.

While Lincoln maintained his laissez-faire attitude toward Sherman's press crackdowns, he proved far more intolerant when less successful generals went too far in constraining newspapermen, especially demonstrably loyal ones. William McKee, for example, editor of the long-sympathetic St. Louis *Missouri Democrat*, fared far better than Thomas Knox when he, too, challenged the assumption that press freedom reigned in the Western Theater. McKee did nothing worse than obtain and publish the president's May 27, 1863, letter appointing General John M. Schofield commander of the Department of the Missouri and urging him to negotiate the "pestilent quarrel" among pro-Union men in that state.[107]

Instead Schofield mounted a new quarrel with the press. Overreacting to the leak, Schofield demanded that McKee identify his source. When the editor refused even to respond, Schofield ordered him arrested. Protests poured into the White House, one of which blasted Schofield's action as "an insult to the supporters of the Union and the government."[108] Lincoln gently reproached his general on July 13, advising him that while he had not technically violated press freedoms by detaining McKee, his severity was likely to irritate local citizens. "I fear this loses you the middle position I desired you to occupy" in Missouri, the president wrote. "I care very little for the publication of any letters I have written"—this from a man who made so certain his major letters were published and praised in sympathetic newspapers!—"Please spare me the trouble this is likely to bring." When Schofield resisted, Lincoln tried conceding that there had indeed been "an apparent impropriety," while insisting, "it is still a case where no evil could result, and which I am entirely willing to overlook."[109] McKee went free, his source protected. As Lincoln cautioned Schofield—in a manner meant to clarify his policy on martial law in all the volatile Border States—"Let your military measures be strong enough to repel the invader and keep the peace, and not so strong as to unnecessarily harass and persecute the people."[110] Never did Lincoln offer a clearer summary of his overarching attitude on freedom of the press in wartime.

Late in September, the president faced one more irritating press controversy in Missouri, another consequence of Schofield's heavy hand. By this time, Lincoln believed, "no organized military force in avowed opposition to the general government" still existed in the state. Yet he had just received complaints from Union men there that Schofield persisted in menacing its opposition voices. Determined to avoid new confrontations in the region, Lincoln instructed the general to do no more than "compel the excited people there to leave one another alone." Schofield was ordered to arrest only "individuals, and suppress assemblies, or newspapers, when they may be working *palpable* injury to the Military in your charge; and in no other case will you interfere with the expression of opinion in any form, or allow it to be interfered with violently by others."[111] Lincoln's order certainly left the door ajar for future press censorship, but as Schofield learned, only victorious generals earned the power to suppress journalists unchecked.

Just one day after writing his exasperated July 13 letter to General Schofield on the McKee case, Lincoln scribbled a frantic message to his eldest boy, Robert, then lodging at the posh Fifth Avenue Hotel in New York en route home to Washington after finishing his latest semester at Harvard. Asked the worried father: "Why do I hear no more of you?" [112]

The lost or unspoken answer was that the young man was trapped—or perhaps thrilled to find himself—in the middle of the most horrific urban convulsion in American history. On July 13, as the military prepared to draw the names of the city's first conscripts, Manhattan erupted in anti-draft violence. Born of resentment over the new law's escape clause—the wealthy could avoid the draft by hiring a substitute or paying the U.S. Treasury $300—the protest quickly cascaded into a bloody, full-blown rampage. Blaming African Americans for both the draft and the war, rioters directed unspeakable violence against the unarmed local black population, women and children included, devastating the city's small community of color.

Dependably Republican newspapers—along with Bennett's *Herald*—had supported the draft wholeheartedly. Although Bennett objected to the $300 opt-out provision, he argued that "we need all the soldiers we can obtain" and overoptimistically reported "the good feeling that has everywhere marked the first drawings." But Joseph Medill more accurately reported to Lincoln from Chicago that he had "never witnessed greater hostility to any public measure." [113] Just as Medill feared, New York's Copperhead dailies assailed the draft as unconstitutional and discriminatory, and, according to the Republican papers, succeeded in stirring up murderous resentment in the city's poor white neighborhoods.

Knowing full well that the reply would be "black freedom," Manton Marble's *New York World* nonetheless posed this incendiary question: "To what use is this new army to be put?" The draft will ignite "manifestations of popular disaffection," Marble predicted. "It is impossible to tell what shape it will assume." Benjamin Wood's *New York Daily News* was even blunter: "A free people will not submit to the conscription." The draft was "an outrage upon all decency and fairness." Noting ominously that "violence and bloodshed have already marked the cause of [draft] enrollment in the West," the *News* warned: "There is a lurking mischief in the atmosphere that surrounds this unwelcome stranger as it now prepares to make its forcible entry across our thresholds. There are symptoms of a wide-spread inclination to extend to it a harsh greeting." On July 4, New York governor Horatio Seymour fanned the flames. In a roaring Independence Day speech, Seymour all but urged violent resistance, offering the rallying cry: "Remember this, that the bloody and treasonable and revolutionary doctrine of public necessity can be proclaimed by a mob as well as by a government."[114]

Nine days later, on July 13, just as the governor had prophesied, a mob attacked the provost marshal's office on Third Avenue as officials prepared to commence drawing names for the draft.[115] By the time Robert Lincoln received his father's urgent message to hasten to Washington, crowds had already sacked and torched the office, stormed uptown toward the southern end of the new Central Park, then pillaged their way down Manhattan's West Side. That afternoon, a largely Irish-American mob heartlessly set fire to the Colored Orphan's Asylum on Fifth Avenue and Forty-third Street. For a time they trapped more than two hundred helpless children inside the burning building, permitting them to escape only after forcing them past a gauntlet of jeering hecklers. Reverend Henry Highland Garnet, host of the city's joyful, integrated "midnight hour" church service just six months earlier, became a target as well. His home would certainly have been sacked had his daughter not had the presence of mind to cut his nameplate off their front door.[116] If the rioters learned that the hated president's own son was in the vicinity, his life would have been endangered, too.

The Civil War had finally come to New York. Robert Lincoln eventually made his way safely to Washington, but up to five hundred people, many of them people of color, died in the four-day-long atrocity, chased and beaten to death on the streets, forced off the docks to drown in the rivers, genitally mutilated, or strung from lampposts and incinerated. The rioters targeted property as well, invading the homes and shops of prominent Republicans, looting and plundering, and menacing black-owned dwellings and "colored" churches. Outnumbered city police and unheeded Catholic priests proved powerless to stop the violence. George Templeton Strong watched one band of "Irish blackguards" attack Mayor George Opdyke's home on Fourteenth Street. Strong felt somewhat cheered when a group of passing "gentlemen" rushed to the scene and used "their walking sticks and their fists" to disperse "the popular uprising (as the *Herald, World,* and *News* call it)." A furious

Strong predicted that for encouraging riot—which it certainly did not—the *Herald* would be "doomed henceforth to obscurity and contempt." Then he ominously prophesied: "*Tribune* office to be burned tonight." [117]

Indeed, within hours, the rioters turned their fury on Newspaper Row. "Down with the *Tribune*!" came a loud voice from Printing House Square as a mob massed outside the paper. "Down with the old white coat that thinks a naygar as good as an Irishman!" [118] Inside, Horace Greeley, no doubt wearing just such a trademark coat, worked away obliviously at his desk. As the threat mounted, managing editor Sydney Gay finally rushed to his boss's side. "The authorities have taken no steps for our defence," he cried. "The *Evening Post* has armed its building; we must do the same if it is to be saved. This is not a riot, but a revolution."

"It looks like it," Greeley calmly replied. "It is just what I have expected; and I have no doubt they will hang *me*; but I want no arms brought into the building." Then the editor rose from his desk and announced that he was going out for his usual evening meal. "If I can't eat my dinner when I'm hungry," he declared, "my life isn't worth anything to me." With that, Greeley stepped outside and coolly walked through the milling crowd and safely on to a nearby restaurant, white coat and all. [119]

Late that night, some 125 employees returned to the paper to await the inevitable attack from the "bloodthirsty vagabonds." Venturing into the thronged street at one point, Greeley biographer James Parton heard one "bull of a man" declaiming in a distinct Southern accent: "What's the use of killing the niggers? The niggers haven't done nothing." Then, gesturing violently toward the upper floors of the *Tribune*, the man shouted: "*Them* are the niggers up there." Someone hurled a rock toward one of the windows, but it struck a shutter and tumbled harmlessly back to the street. Parton then raced to the nearby City Hall police station and begged for protection. By the time a contingent of five patrolmen ran back with him across the park to the paper's defense, "stones were flying fast," shattering the *Tribune's* windows. The police tried restraining the mob, but the rioters shoved them aside, rushed forward, and broke into the building's ground-floor "counting room." Only when an officer outside fired a gun into the air did the invaders retreat back into the street and disperse, leaving in their wake shards of glass, smashed furniture, scattered papers, and a few smoldering fires. At least they had not reached the editorial rooms upstairs, or found their way down to the printing presses. [120]

The danger was postponed, but not eliminated. A sudden thunderstorm helped disperse what was left of the mob—"undoubtedly they had a natural dread of water as well as soap and towels," mocked journalist Charles Congdon.[121] But the next day, another menacing crowd assembled in the square, and staff members—they were reporters, after all—learned from a credible source that a second assault on the *Tribune* would begin soon. Somehow, James Gilmore managed to slip outside and secure an emergency audience with General John Wool, from whom he obtained a permit to secure arms. Gilmore then ferried across the river to the Brooklyn Navy Yard, where Admiral Hiram Paulding provided him with wagonloads of "bombshells" to defend the paper. The establishment whose editor had refused weapons the day before now fortified itself with a supply of lethal grenades and a cannon loaded with grapeshot and canister.

When Greeley discovered that, against his express wishes, his newspaper had been turned into an arsenal, he demanded that the "brimstone pills" be removed. "Take 'em away, take 'em away," he squawked in his high-pitched voice. "I don't want to kill anybody, and besides they're a damn sight more likely to go off and kill some of us." But his staff informed him that the building was now subject to martial law under the command of a Colonel Adams, and that it might help matters if Greeley left the building. "The mob knows he is here," Adams agreed, "and if he stays it is likely they will attack us." Sydney Gay ordered a carriage, and finally, after protesting that he could easily take a streetcar home—then glancing out the window and conceding of the mob, "Well, they *are* a hard-looking set"—Greeley slipped out a side door and departed to safety. Meanwhile, in the erroneous belief that the *Tribune* editor resided at a town house on Twenty-ninth Street, another mob had stormed the vicinity and nearly torn to shreds a lookalike it mistook for the editor.[122] To Gilmore, Greeley showed "a very high order of bravery" that day. "He knew that he was marked out as a special victim by at least ten thousand ruthless ruffians, who, had they laid hands on him, would have given him short shrift and a short rope from the nearest lamp-post; and yet he came and went as usual, and with no regard whatever for his personal safety. He evidently felt that the trial day of his life had come, and had made up his mind to meet it like a man."[123]

Tribune correspondent Whitelaw Reid arrived in town just in time to join the ranks of defenders. "Muskets were provided for every employee," he testified. "The floor of the editorial room was littered with hand grenades, and extra bayonets were lying about on the desks like some new pattern of mammoth pen-holders. Arrangements for pouring a volume of scalding steam into the lungs of anybody attempting to force an entrance had been perfected." [124] Meanwhile, the mob began milling again in the summer heat, as if waiting for a signal or a leader. Suddenly a gang of three times its size materialized out of City Hall Park and joined the surging crowd. Shouted orders were heard, but then, just before the next attack could begin, a large contingent of city police dramatically emerged from the dark and began beating the rioters into submission. From the upstairs windows, a *Tribune* editor could hear the awful "tap, tap, tap, of the police clubs on the heads of the fugitives." [125] The *Tribune* had escaped destruction again.

At *Times* headquarters just north of the *Tribune* building, Henry Raymond was not about to allow his paper's gleaming new five-story tower to meet the same fate as the draft office, orphanage, or *Tribune* counting room. Together with Leonard W. Jerome, one of his principal investors, Raymond took to the second floor, armed with two newfangled Gatling guns he had obtained from the army. Raymond and Jerome pointed them into the street from the northern windows where they could easily be seen throughout Printing House Square, leaving no doubt that the editor would deploy the deadly "revolving cannons" against any rioters who threatened his establishment.

As backup, Raymond ordered several employees to aim rifles in the same direction. Street-level doors were locked shut. Raymond's newfangled "*mitrailleuses*" were "capable of one hundred discharges per hour . . . so as to rake Chatham and Centre Streets" in the event of an attack. Unlike "Fort Greeley," which "barricaded" its windows with "bales of printing paper" for protection, casting the establishment into darkness, the *Herald*'s Fredric Hudson reported that Raymond ordered the *Times* building "brilliantly illuminated" so no secret assault could be launched under cover of night. According to at least one eyewitness, Raymond had another useful "weapon" at his disposal: the presence of the *New York Daily News*'s Democratic editor, Benjamin Wood, who took up a position in the doorway and implored the roving gangs of rioters to spare the *New York Times*. [126] Raymond's personal involvement helped his building survive unscathed. Later, while regretting what he casually dismissed as the *Tribune*'s "trifling loss," Raymond took credit for dispatching some of his own employees to spare Horace Greeley further damage. "We have not always agreed with our neighbor on political policies," Raymond declared in a show of unity, but "when such an issue is forced upon us journalists, they must make it their common cause." [127]

Otherwise, Raymond then "poured a galling fire into the ranks of the mob," as his earliest biographer put it, not with gunfire, but through a fusillade of editorials that increasingly condemned James Gordon Bennett and other Democratic editors for showing too much tolerance for Governor Seymour and especially the mob. "The *Herald* characterizes it as the people and the *World* as the laboring men of the city," Raymond howled. "It is ineffably infamous." [128]

By July 16, a full day before Union troops belatedly arrived in the smoldering city to restore order, it was back to business as usual for the New York newspapers, with Bennett, Greeley, and Raymond resuming their sniping at each other. They even felt safe enough to quarrel over silly issues—whether or not, for example, the *Tribune* editor had hidden himself away at his favorite eatery during the period of greatest danger, scribbling editorials on greasy menus. Republican editors also debated the extent of their Democratic counterparts' guilt. For his part, Bennett defiantly wondered whether "Copperhead" or "niggerhead" (Republican) newspapers deserved principal blame for the riots. Bennett could not resist the opportunity to gloat a bit that Greeley had finally tasted the kind of mobbing he had once "proposed for us." [129]

The anti-draft riots may have ravaged and embarrassed New York, but at least for a time they showcased the city's newspapermen at their courageous best. Despite the genuine danger they faced, neither the *Times* nor the *Tribune* missed a deadline or postponed an edition. Even as mobs congregated threateningly outside their doors, their reporters continued to fan out through the city to cover the story of the riots. Their presses never stopped humming.

The riots also gave New York's pictorial weeklies the chance to escape from the shadows cast by the powerful dailies. They were unavoidably late in reporting the event—coverage did not appear until their August 1 issues. But *Harper's Weekly*, for one, used the intervening time well to craft a judicious editorial response, and create compelling pictures, which the dailies were neither equipped nor staffed to offer their readers.

In addition to defending conscription as a public duty, *Harper's* took exceptional care to caution against condemning the "perversity of the Irish race" for the riots. The weekly took pains to hail the brave Irishmen who helped save the displaced children of the burning Colored Orphan's Asylum, and heaped praise on Archbishop John Hughes and "the entire Roman Catholic priesthood to a man" for condemning the outbreak. Instead, *Harper's* assigned blame where nearly all Republican papers believed it belonged: on "the despicable politicians and their newspaper organs"—Democrats who, they claimed, incited the mob.[130] "They denounced Mr. Lincoln as an imbecile tyrant," the weekly charged. "They denounced the war as a needless, fratricidal, and abolition war. . . . Under these circumstances," *Harper's* asked, "who can wonder at riots breaking out?" The Democratic press was guilty of nothing less than "malignant partisanship" designed to make "political capital on the government."[131]

Most irresistibly of all, *Harper's* offered a two-page centerfold adorned with ten woodcut engravings of some of the most grisly scenes of horror— including the lynching and burning of "a Negro in Clarkson Street," the beatings of policemen, soldiers, and innocent civilians, and prominently, the *Charge of the Police at the "Tribune" Office.* The weekly may have warned against blanket condemnation of the Irish, but the rioters it depicted falling under the blows of police nightsticks bore the unmistakable physical attributes common in stock caricatures of Irishmen: square-topped plug hats and simian facial features, including bulbous noses reddened by whiskey. Such clichéd and incendiary portraiture did little to support the narrative advanced by the paper, but likely evoked greater interest. To *Harper's* readers, who subscribed to the weekly specifically because of its prominent and timely illustrations, pictures spoke infinitely louder than words. By calling for tolerance

Charge of the Police at the "Tribune" Office: Harper's Weekly depicts New York draft rioters threatening Greeley's headquarters, portraying the attackers as Irish thugs.

while visually portraying the Irish as thugs (and the thugs as Irish), *Harper's* had it both ways, as it did on most issues of the day. After all, it routinely provided not only topical sketches of the battlefront, but toxic cartoons that just as often lampooned Abraham Lincoln as Jefferson Davis. Appearing to be nonpartisan and offering strong support for the war leavened by frequent pictorial criticism of the president, *Harper's* earned a large readership and an even larger legacy.[132]

Soon after the riots, Greeley emissary James Gilmore spent three hours at the White House trying to convince Lincoln that Horatio Seymour had seditiously plotted the entire outbreak. He did not want the Democratic governor to escape unscathed. Sounding much like his *Tribune* benefactor, Gilmore proposed a patronage-oriented solution to get to the bottom of things: why not appoint his future father-in-law as a special investigator? Lincoln demurred. Having conspicuously withheld military assistance for days, he would continue leaving the matter to local authorities. "You have heard of sitting on a volcano," the president explained. "We are sitting upon two. One is blazing away already, and the other will blaze away the moment we scrape a little loose dirt from the top of the crater. Better let the dirt alone, at least for the present. One rebellion at a time is about as much as we can conveniently handle." [133]

With his dramatic letters of 1862 and 1863—ostensibly to Horace Greeley and Erastus Corning, but also strategically released to the newspapers to reach far wider audiences—Lincoln in some ways wrote the big three New York editors out of the equation when it came to molding public opinion. At the very least, he reduced the editors' influence. In doing so, he revolutionized the art of presidential communications. Greeley, Raymond, and Bennett may have continued commenting on Lincoln's statements, but when the president spoke out in print, their own editorials often seemed more like sidebars. Lincoln had come to realize that he could control "public sentiment" best by bypassing the editors and going directly to their readers. Rather than resume making time-consuming public speeches, he transformed the so-called public letter into a weapon of mass communication.[134]

One opportunity to speak in person, however, proved irresistible. In late summer, the citizens of Gettysburg, burdened with the horrific task of burying the thousands of dead who fell during the July 1–3 battle, had devised an ambitious plan to create a National Soldiers' cemetery not far from the scene of some of the worst of the second day's fighting. Now they were ready for the official dedication. Organizers did not ask the president to deliver the principal oration, however. That honor went to the venerable Edward Everett, whose landmark 1861 defense of press suppression no doubt remained fresh in Lincoln's mind.

"A few appropriate remarks" were all that Gettysburg officials wanted from the president, since Everett was to be the main attraction.[135] But the stubborn legend which holds that Lincoln sloughed off the opportunity, or left preparation of the speech to the last minute—perhaps even scribbled it on the train ride to Pennsylvania—is unsupported by the facts. Perhaps aware that creating a short address required even more effort than crafting a long one, Lincoln went to work on his talk in early November.

He knew precisely how to begin it. Four days after the battle ended, he had spoken extemporaneously to serenaders gathered to rejoice over the victory on the White House lawn. "How long ago is it?—eighty odd years," he had begun, "since on the Fourth of July for the first time in the history of the world a nation by its representatives, assembled and declared as a self-evident truth that 'all men are created equal.'" The following morning, those rambling words appeared in all three New York dailies—the *Times*, *Tribune*, and *Herald*—and Lincoln may have blanched when he read them. But the thought behind them was valid. He resolved to express it more felicitously. Eventually it came into sharper focus in Lincoln's exordium: "Four score and seven years ago, our fathers brought forth a new nation, conceived in liberty and dedicated to the proposition that all men are created equal." For his closing, Lincoln might have remembered Samuel Wilkeson's elegiac post-battle obituary to his fallen son, whose blood, he had written, "baptized . . . the second birth of Freedom in America." In the president's deft hands, the nation would now be dedicated to "a new birth of freedom." Lincoln had lost neither his prodigious memory for press reports nor his abundant gift for rewriting.[136]

On Sunday, November 8, Lincoln headed to Alexander Gardner's Washington photography gallery to pose for a new suite of portraits. The Gettysburg dedication was only eleven days away, and the event was likely very much on the president's mind. Had the president written his own speech yet? wondered *Sacramento Bee* correspondent Noah Brooks, who claimed he accompanied Lincoln to Gardner's that day. Yes, came the reply, "but not yet finished." His draft was brief—"or, as he emphatically expressed it, 'short,

short, short.'"[137] Atop the small table at which he sat for the cameras, at least according to Brooks, lay an envelope supposedly containing an early printing of Everett's remarks, thoughtfully dispatched by the famous orator so Lincoln might avoid topics that would be covered in the main address. Whatever its contents, Lincoln did not open the envelope he brought to the gallery that day; the Gardner sitting ended too quickly. But the package can be seen in several of the resulting photographs, lying on the draped table at his side, not far from Lincoln's massive right hand. Gardner's studio had not always been so efficient. At a visit to inaugurate the enterprise three months earlier, Lincoln had enough waiting time between poses to unfold and read the latest edition of the *Morning Chronicle.* Sharp-eyed Lincoln admirers who obtained copies of that day's mass-produced portraits would have easily been able to identify the paper's logo on one pose in particular (and perhaps even spot the horsefly clinging to the president's trousers).[138]

Lincoln embarked for Gettysburg the day before the November 19 ceremony, along with a retinue of civil and military celebrities larger than any that had accompanied him since his inaugural journey. Among the passengers were John Nicolay and John Hay, who made sure that a corps of supportive reporters joined the traveling party. When he arrived in the village, Lincoln retired to the private home of David Wills, the local judge who had invited him to

Horace Greeley studies his own *New York Tribune* in a photograph taken in 1863. By this time both Lincoln and Greeley—each once noted for eccentric garb—dressed with fashionable dignity.

the event, determined to use whatever time he had left to revise his remarks. Meanwhile, his two secretaries headed over to visit John Wein Forney, also in town for the dedication, "and drank a little whiskey with him." As Hay observed: "He had been drinking a good deal during the day and was getting to feel a little ugly and dangerous," particularly on the subject of Montgomery Blair, whom he wanted fired from the cabinet. Forney's managing editor, John Russell Young, soon joined the group. Forney was still "growling about Blair" when the president stepped outside of the nearby Wills house to pronounce "half a dozen words meaning nothing" to a knot of well-wishers. The response was unenthusiastic and Lincoln withdrew to return to his work upstairs.[139]

The celebrants were growing tipsier and louder by the minute. Nicolay now devilishly proposed that Forney deliver an oration of his own, and searched for a band to serenade him and some reporters to write down his words. "He still growled quietly and I thought he was going to do something imprudent," Hay recorded in his diary. Forney mumbled, "if I speak, I will speak my mind," and asked that congenial "recorders" be on hand to transcribe what he said.

Forney's Gettysburg address commenced a few minutes later, after the editor took another swallow of liquor and the knot of "recorders" summoned to the scene squatted expectantly in an entryway, writing tablets at the ready. Forney was by now in a foul mood. "My friends," he began, to a round of applause, "these are the first hearty cheers I have heard tonight. You gave no such cheers to your President down the street. Do you know what you owe to that Great man? You owe your country—you owe your name as American citizens." In a way, Forney was making sense, even if he was slurring his words. "He went on blackguarding the crowd," Hay recalled, denouncing pro-slavery Democrats, then resuming his paean to Lincoln, "that great, wonderful mysterious inexplicable man; who holds in his single hands the reins of the republic; who keeps his own counsels; who does his own purpose in his own way no matter what temporizing minister in his cabinet sets himself up in opposition to the progress of the age."

On and on Forney went, until finally he ran out of steam. "That speech must not be written out yet," John Russell Young nervously instructed the "recorders." "He will see further about it, when he gets sober." (The Associated Press devoted a few lines to the address anyway.) The party then launched into a loud rendition of "John Brown's Body" and retired for the night, while inside the Wills house on the town square, the object of Forney's adulation continued laboring over the two pages of manuscript he was trying to massage into an elegy. No one knows whether Lincoln went to bed that night. The unrelenting noise from drunken revelers thronging the streets must have made it difficult, even impossible, to sleep.

Nor is anyone certain whether Forney managed to get himself to the cemetery the following day for the ceremonies, or if he did, whether a massive hangover clouded any reliable observations about the president's performance. Fortunately, a large contingent of journalists from all over the country assembled near the speaker's platform, and John Hay himself took notes and ultimately provided Forney with a superb report of the ceremony.[140] None of the reporters attempted to record Edward Everett's two-hour-long oration, for the great man had supplied it to the newspapers in advance. All the correspondents needed to do was watch in awe as he intoned the entire marathon speech from memory.

Long practice had taught Lincoln that while his piercing voice could carry only a few hundred feet, newspapers could spread his words to the entire country. When his turn finally came, the reporters were ready—or were they? Disagreement broke out later about whether Lincoln, too, spoke without notes, or whether, as others recalled, he removed his manuscript from his breast pocket and began reading from it. Or perhaps he grasped the sheets but spoke without referring to them at all? Whatever the case, the skilled orator may (or may not) have failed to arouse an audience exhausted by Everett's stem-winding lecture. Just two minutes after he began, Lincoln resumed his seat—to silence, applause, an ovation? Reports differed on that point, too. A startled John Russell Young, who had been distracted by the desperate efforts of a photographer trying to arrange his camera in front of the platform—he never managed to take the president's picture—realized he had failed to make a shorthand record. From the second row of press benches, he blurted out to Lincoln in an audible voice to ask "if that was all." The president glanced at Young and answered: "Yes, for the present."[141]

Lincoln's friend Ward Hill Lamon, who served as master of ceremonies for the event, later complained that both the audience and the press corps failed to appreciate Lincoln's masterpiece. "The marvelous perfection, the intrinsic excellence of the Gettysburg speech as a masterpiece of English composition," he maintained, "seem to have escaped the scrutiny of even the most scholarly critics of that day, on this side of the Atlantic." Lamon contended that "the discovery was made . . . by distinguished writers on the other side," particularly the *London Spectator*, *Saturday Review*, and *Edinburgh Review*—all of which in fact did not extol the address until long after pro-administration domestic papers did.[142] In fact, no one did more to create the myth of Lincoln's "flat failure" at Gettysburg—the president's own words, at least according to Lamon—than the irrepressible marshal of the District of Columbia. "The speech will not *scour*," a distressed Lincoln allegedly told his old friend after he spoke. Lamon agreed: the address "fell on the vast audience like a *wet blanket.*"[143]

Again, the facts speak otherwise. No one will ever settle the debate over whether Lincoln's most famous speech was rhapsodically or indifferently received. But we at least know for certain that when he concluded, the president made certain that Joseph Ignatius Gilbert, the lucky young Harrisburg reporter hired for the day to cover the event for the Associated Press, got to examine the president's handwritten manuscript to check it against his shorthand transcription. Gilbert later admitted that, standing directly below the platform, he had become so fascinated by Lincoln's "intense earnestness" that he had "unconsciously stopped taking notes" just as Lincoln "glanced up from his manuscript with a faraway look in his eyes as if appealing from the few thousands below him to the countless millions whom his words were to reach." [144] As a result, Gilbert desperately needed to check his imperfect shorthand record against the president's copy.

Lincoln readily complied, knowing that most papers around the country would pick up Gilbert's report. The AP stringer then inserted the word "Applause" wherever he had heard the crowd clapping. At the end he wrote: "Long continued applause." By Gilbert's original account, the crowd had interrupted the speech to clap hands six times, though he later recalled that Lincoln earned "no outward manifestations of feeling." As Gilbert explained it in 1917: "His theme did not invite holiday applause, a cemetery was not the place for it, and he did not pause to receive it." Aside from this incongruity, Gilbert's shorthand account also suffered from several errors. The phrase "unfinished work" came out as "refinished work," "government" of, by, and for the people, as "Governments." [145] As a consequence, many newspapers throughout the country garbled their reprints as well—even though stenographers enjoyed "an excellent light" aboard the presidential special returning them to Washington, "around which," John Hay observed, "busy as bees, they com-

Joseph Ignatius Gilbert, the young Associated Press reporter who transcribed Lincoln's Gettysburg Address.

pared notes and transcribed their phonographic reports for the papers for which they were laboring." [146]

Editorial commentary varied, too, but it would be a mistake to accept Lamon's assertion that it took the foreign press belatedly to remind readers (and Lincoln) of the greatness of the Gettysburg Address. For one thing, the *London Times*, not surprisingly, lambasted the speech, charging that the "imposing ceremony" at Gettysburg was "made ludicrous by some of the luckless sallies of that poor President Lincoln." [147] In actuality, domestic press reaction to Gettysburg broke quickly—and, as most reports of the day invariably did—strictly along party lines. Republican papers extolled Lincoln's address enthusiastically, while Democratic papers—perhaps sensing that the speech represented the opening salvo in a forthcoming campaign for a second term—criticized it mercilessly. Thus the *Chicago Times* asserted: "The cheek of every American must tingle with shame as he reads the silly flat and dishwatery utterances of the man who has to be pointed out to intelligent foreigners as the President of the United States." But readers of the pro-administration *Chicago Tribune* read the contrary prediction: "The dedicatory remarks by President Lincoln will live among the annals of the war." [148] Just a few days earlier, the Gettysburg master of ceremonies, Ward Hill Lamon, had visited the White House to read aloud "a slip from the Chicago Tribune in which they very strongly advocate A. L. for his own successor." That politics was in the air as the ceremony neared was confirmed when Lamon pronounced the laudatory post-Gettysburg editorial "an utterance . . . stimulated by the prospect of a new Administration paper being started in Chicago pledged against grumbling." [149]

Of course, Forney's *Philadelphia Press* hailed Lincoln's effort as an "immortal speech." But in Ohio, the battered *Columbus Crisis* mocked Lincoln's "*of* the people, *by* the people, and *for* the people" coda, reminding readers still mourning Clement Vallandigham's recent political defeat that government power belonged to states, not presidents. [150] Few Confederate papers bothered to acknowledge Lincoln's speech at all; an exception was the *Richmond Enquirer*, which reported that his hosts had limited the president to a "small compass, lest he should tell some funny story over the graves of the Immortals." [151]

Most remarkably of all, none of New York's big three—the *Times*, *Herald*, or *Tribune*—bothered to assess Lincoln's remarks. Instead, while they lavished considerable space on reporting the ceremonies, and dutifully printed

Lincoln's brief speech in full, they focused far more attention on Everett's keynote, relegating the presidential address to the status of a footnote. The highest compliment the *Times* paid to Lincoln was to paraphrase his speech as if to excuse its lack of attention to it, noting that all the Gettysburg orators "seem to have considered, with President Lincoln, that it was not what was said here, but what was done here, that deserved their attention." The Gettysburg Address was the biggest Civil War story Greeley, Raymond, and Bennett missed.[152]

By one account, at least as measured in column inches, Republican papers devoted five times more space to Lincoln's Gettysburg remarks than did their Democratic counterparts.[153] If Edward Everett dominated the next day's press coverage nearly everywhere, it was because the wily old orator, past his prime or not, had planned things so well. Still, this was one instance when the first draft of history deserved and received major revision. Everett himself generously told Lincoln afterward that he wished he had come "as near to the central idea of the occasion, in two hours, as you did in two minutes."[154] Not even the well-practiced tradition of feeding advance information to the press could diminish Lincoln's Gettysburg Address, or add luster to Everett's. Lincoln's greatest speech may not have evolved into national "gospel," as historian Gabor Boritt has pointed out, until the early twentieth century.[155] But most Republicans who read accounts of the address in 1863 understood that their president had triumphed, even if the New York press remained strangely oblivious.

Everett had tried for a different result. He had arranged early distribution for his speech because he still believed, as he had once put it, that the "newspaper press of the United States is, for good or evil, the most powerful influence that acts upon the public mind."[156] In two hours or two minutes, Lincoln could not have expressed it better himself.

The year 1863 came to a close with the usual press clamor for advance texts of another address, Lincoln's Annual Message to Congress, still considered the most important presidential "speech" of any season. "We are very anxious to have an early Copy," John Wein Forney began his own annual message to John Nicolay, ". . . but I would not, for the world, embarrass the President, or lay him open to the charge of partiality. Do the best you can, and this will oblige.[157]

Lincoln stubbornly kept the text secret until its delivery date, but, in a move that stunned journalists and legislators alike, accompanied the official message with a proposed Proclamation of Amnesty and Reconstruction, offering rebellious states a path to armistice if they embraced black freedom. Then he added the vow: "While I remain in my present position, I shall not attempt to retract or modify the Emancipation Proclamation nor shall I return to slavery any person who is free by the terms of that proclamation." The president concluded by dedicating his message to the armed forces, including black soldiers—"the gallant men, from commander to sentinel . . . to whom, more than to others, the world must stand indebted for the home of freedom disenthralled, regenerated, enlarged, and perpetuated." [158]

Partisan press analysis followed, as always. Greeley's *Tribune* saluted Lincoln's "wise humanity and generous impulses." [159] John Nicolay, who witnessed the reading on Capitol Hill, reported that Congress responded to the message "as if the millennium, had come." But the *Richmond Examiner* predictably labeled its author "a Yankee monster of inhumanity and falsehood." [160]

"The rebel borders are pressed still further back," Lincoln reported of the war effort that day. ". . . The crisis which threatened to divide the friends of the Union is past." [161] But the crisis atmosphere that perennially divided the Northern press remained unresolved, still simmering, and destined to reignite during the election year of 1864.

Two weeks before the end of the year 1863, the *New York World*'s increasingly anti-emancipation, anti-Lincoln editor, Manton Marble, told Horace Greeley he could "expect nothing from the *Tribune*'s fairness, justice or generosity towards me or the paper of which I am the editor." Greeley would not have disagreed; as the country lurched toward a presidential election year, the New York papers geared up for the editorial battle of the century. Joseph Medill of the *Chicago Tribune* spoke for many Republican papers when he bravely predicted in December: "Mr. Lincoln is in no sort of danger from rivals. . . . Let him push forward the war on an anti-slavery basis and the people will give him more time to finish up his job." [162]

Not if Marble and the Democratic press had anything to do with it.

CHAPTER FOURTEEN

No Time to Read Any Papers

———————————◆———————————

The Civil War generated an endless supply of news, but not all of the nation's newspapers thrived—or even survived. This proved particularly so in the South. There, a once robust two-party political culture vanished. With President Jefferson Davis set to serve his six-year term unchallenged until 1867, and with no intervening national election campaigns to arouse the reading public, regional newspapers built on political values understandably lost not only readers, but their very reason for existing. Of course, the dramatically shifting Confederate political landscape was not the only reason for their decline. Economic hardship played perhaps the biggest role of all.

Ultimately, the South's once thriving newspaper industry became a casualty of the Civil War, but its decline occurred not for lack of eager readers, but rather due to a dearth of manpower and resources. One problem was near-universal white conscription, which deprived many Confederate papers of their editors, writers, and compositors—for "printing," a veteran of the *Richmond Inquirer* explained unselfconsciously in 1864, "is one of the few mechanical arts practiced [only] by free white men in the South, it requiring a greater degree of education than is permitted to slaves." Another problem was paper itself—that is, the lack of it, or when obtainable, its sometimes comical inconsistency. Even the perennially optimistic *Confederate States Al-*

manac admitted midway through the war that a Southern newspaper might be "short enough for a pocket handkerchief one day, and big enough for a paper tablecloth another."[1]

The South boasted only a fraction of the nation's paper mills before the war began, and fewer still once Union forces began occupying significant portions of its territory. Eventually, the paper supply dwindled to a trickle. The ever-scarcer stock grew expensive and inferior—made from rags or straw and stubbornly resistant to ink. As one Savannah editor lamented, "we are reduced to printing on paper, which, half the time, nobody can read." Most journals had no choice but to curtail their frequency and proportions, sometimes publishing on slips "little larger than lawyer's foolscap." In the wake of such shortages, many papers closed down altogether. A Baton Rouge editor, forced to suspend publication in 1862, used his final issue to promote himself for a new career: "The editor of this paper being now out of employment, owing to a temporary suspension of the same is anxious and willing to do something for a livelihood . . . [and] has no objection to serving as a deck-hand on a flat-boat, selling ice-cream, or acting as paymaster to the militia."[2]

That newspapers might have retained significant influence was widely understood at the time. Recognizing their morale-boosting power, federal forces often made sure to oust pro-Confederate editors from whatever towns they seized, and to encourage the establishment of pro-Union papers in their place.[3] By 1862, Henry Raymond noted with pride the appearance of Unionist dailies in the Carolinas, Florida, Louisiana, Tennessee, and Virginia. "These presses undoubtedly are doing, and will continue to do, a great deal of good," he declared. "It was by the falsehoods of the rebel Press that the rebellion was stimulated . . . and it must be largely through the efforts of a loyal Press that the power and love of the Union will be restored."[4]

Although supply shortages and military setbacks caused many established Southern newspapers to still their presses, a few stubbornly held on. Papers published in the Confederate capital managed to survive, although some Richmond dailies were eventually reduced to publishing on single sheets. Ironically, because they operated so near to Washington, copies often found their way into the White House. "Here are some newspapers from Richmond, just received," William Seward wrote Lincoln in a note accompanying one such bundle in late 1862. "I have marked an article in the Enquirer about 'Straggling.'"[5]

In May 1863, Lincoln acknowledged the reliability—or at least the availability—of the Confederate capital's journals by asking General Hooker: "Have you Richmond papers of this morning? If so, what news?"[6] Around the same time, reports from embattled Vicksburg arrived at the White House courtesy of the *Richmond Dispatch*.[7] But Lincoln knew better than to trust everything he read in the Confederate press. It was believed that many of them intentionally distorted news both to keep morale high in the South and in the expectation that Yankee papers would reprint the falsehoods and demoralize Northern readers. As Grant closed in on "the Gibraltar of the Confederacy," General Sherman complained that "the conductors of the Press of the Northern States as now conducted, are as much the Enemies of our Common Country as the Armed Rebels whose sentinels now walk in bold and manly defiance on the opposing heights of Vicksburg." As usual when it came to press matters, Sherman missed the point. Lincoln was far more concerned when the *Richmond Sentinel* exaggerated the strength of Confederate resistance there, and reported that Sherman had been seriously wounded. When General Daniel Butterfield shared with Lincoln the latest reports holding that Union forces were "demoralized," Lincoln astutely replied: "The news you send me from the Richmond Sentinel of the 3d must be greatly if not wholly incorrect."[8] The president knew that newspaper accounts must not only be studied, but occasionally refuted.

A few Deep South papers stubbornly held on. In South Carolina, it took what it called a "horrible and brutal" hundred-day Union siege to force the *Charleston Courier* to suspend publication. Somehow the paper soon reopened with a smaller format. Even when the city prepared to surrender, the *Courier* mustered the professional discipline to declare: "As journalists . . . we are called upon to restrain our feelings."[9]

Remarkably, several new periodicals actually opened for business in the Confederacy during the war—and remained in operation at least for a time. A new Confederate Press Association also came into existence, even as Union forces progressively destroyed the telegraph lines vital for their transmissions. The association offered news at particularly generous discount prices to sympathetic Border State papers that relocated to the Confederacy after fleeing from their home cities in the wake of Union crackdowns. In 1863 the association even elected refugee Memphis editor Benjamin Dill to its board of directors.[10]

Back in Richmond, publishers E. W. Ayres and W. H. Wade debuted the *Southern Illustrated News* in 1862, optimistically calling it "Not a luxury, but a necessity." The paper managed to celebrate a succession of Confederate military heroes, making no secret of its own crushing obstacles by regularly advertising for artists and supplies. When both these resources evaporated, the *News* began to appear irregularly, its final edition reaching readers in early 1864. A newspaper that in peacetime might have competed for prestige with New York pictorial newspapers like *Harper's* and *Leslie's*, instead perished for want of the essentials any newspaper needed to sustain itself: paper, ink, and staff.[11]

Desperate but resourceful, some Southern newspaper publishers took to issuing one-sided editions printed on any material their proprietors could secure—including wallpaper. Even amid such humiliating deprivation, one crippled paper that had once advocated strongly for secession and rebellion now refused to offer an "apology for the . . . color and quality of the paper." Its rainbow variety, it proudly maintained, merely reflected "the hardships of war."[12]

None of these "wallpaper editions" earned more enduring fame than those published in Vicksburg during the 1863 siege. For two months beginning in May, the federal fleet, operating under the overall command of Ulysses S. Grant, shelled the "Hill City" day and night. The bombardment drove starving citizens underground, where they took up residence in caves. Cave dwellers hardly constituted the most reliable newspaper customers—they had other necessities foremost on their minds—but one local journal somehow continued to survive: the *Vicksburg Daily Citizen*. Publisher J. M. Swords consumed his ordinary paper stock by early June, but on five occasions during the final days of the siege managed to publish single-sheet editions on the backs of wallpaper fragments. Some of the wallpaper boasted rose-and-purple brocade designs, others pink-and-red floral patterns. Swords used what he could get.

On July 1, the publisher began preparing what turned out to be his final issue. The isolated Swords was by then so out of touch that he featured long-outdated news of General Lee's "brilliant and successful" triumph against Hooker at Chancellorsville two months earlier. Three days later—on Independence Day—with the ranks of the city's defenders eroding due to disease and starvation, the Confederates surrendered Vicksburg to General Grant. In that final edition, Swords had mocked "the great Ulysses—the Yankee Generalissimo" for expressing "his intention of dining in Vicksburg . . . and celebrating the 4th of July with a grand dinner and so forth." Taunted the *Daily Citizen*: "Ulysses must get into the city before he dines in it. The way to cook a rabbit is 'first catch the rabbit.'"

Then catch "the rabbit" Grant did—making sure to feast on the *Vicksburg Daily Citizen*. Once, Grant had closed down opposition newspapers within command. This time, he made sure a hostile paper stayed open. Swords fled town ahead of the surrender, while the metal type was still in its racks for the latest and, as it turned out, last edition. Union conquerors not only seized the office, but with some former civilian printers apparently in their ranks, rewrote and reset one of its front-page stories before putting it on press. Rare surviving July 2 wallpaper editions of the *Vicksburg Daily Citizen* conclude with the following acerbic update—the Union conquerors' last laugh on a once thriving local newspaper and its readers:

> Two days bring about great changes. The banner of the Union floats over Vicks-burg. Gen. Grant has "caught the rabbit"; he has dined in Vicksburg, and he did bring his dinner with him. The "Citizen" lives to see it. For the last time it appears on "Wall-paper." No more will it eulogize the luxury of mule-meat and fricasseed kitten—urge Southerner warriors to such diet nevermore. This is the last wall-paper edition, and is, excepting this note, from the types as we found them. It will be valuable hereafter as a curiosity.[13]

Soldiers in the field, on both sides, thirsted for news throughout the conflict, and this was especially so for those who signed up for the longest enlistments, and stayed away from home for the lengthiest stretches. Many craved reports on home-front political wars even as they faced a deadly war of their own. Even prisoners could not do without news, and some took to creating "papers" of their own, even if they had to produce them laboriously by hand. In 1865, a group of Confederate officers confined to the Union prison at Fort Delaware produced four copies of a meticulously hand-lettered journal they entitled *Prison Times*. It featured advertisements for fellow captives who specialized in tailoring, shaves, and shoe repair "at reasonable rates," along with notices about the prison musical association and debating society.[14]

Even—especially—when far from their families, most literate soldiers continued to yearn for occasional glimpses of their hometown papers. Demand never abated. Union Colonel Alfred McCalmont, a former newspaperman who commanded various Pennsylvania regiments during the war, remembered that when his men were stationed at camps along the Rappahannock River in Virginia, they would gather every afternoon to meet the train bearing "the morning papers of that day." In September 1863, McCalmont wrote to his brother to thank him for sending an additional "puff" via mail. But the general thought the praiseworthy article "in bad taste, very much overdone and calculated to do a man more harm than good," adding: "I do not care much for such things. . . . I am, almost indifferent to newspaper blame or approbation, because I helped to edit one a number of years, and know how little there is of true value in anything they say."[15] Most officers, however, yearned for such hometown praise.

Eastern-bred officers like McCalmont had an especially hard time keeping up with the press when they were stationed in the distant West. Embedded correspondents there were a common sight on campaign, but actual newspapers became rarities. "I received the two papers and was very glad to get them," soldier Charles Edwin Cort wrote home from Kentucky in 1862. "We do not get much news. I would like to get the Republican once and a while and some of the Chicago papers. The Cincinnati papers are poor concerns, we can get them once a day for 5 cts. the same day they are dated."[16] For sailors, because they served on ships that often operated far from land, news became even scarcer, and if it somehow made its way aboard, staler. Yet when the paymaster on the USS *Monitor* received an outdated *Chicago Tribune* from his wife as a Christmas present in 1862, William Frederick Keeler exulted, "it was like meeting an old acquaintance." Less than two weeks later, as the *Tribune* and other papers reported, the iconic Union ironclad went to the bottom off Cape Hatteras.[17] Making news of their own, the paymaster and a few others miraculously managed to escape.

With an appreciation for news no less ardent than Keeler's, a Union surgeon serving in Virginia who believed newspaper correspondents "a nuisance as a general thing" because "two thirds of their stories are untrue," nevertheless looked forward to evenings, when he could "pull off my coat, creep under my blanket, read the *New York Herald* . . . and then to sleep."[18] Expressing similar enthusiasm, Wisconsin private Guy Taylor wrote his wife from the Eastern Front in 1864: "There is now a noose boy that comes with papers everyday for 5 cents we can get a paper so the boys get more reading now than they did." A surgeon from the 85th New York was equally grateful for the arrival of his newspaper so he could use it as an "improvised" tablecloth for a dinner beside a "cheerily-burning campfire."[19] Even those who could barely read and write somehow knew that the press served a purpose—like soldier Hillory Shifflet, who haltingly wrote to his wife from Chattanooga asking for "a par of yourn gloves," adding, "the best way to send it is to do it up in a nusepaper."[20]

Much as they thirsted for information, soldiers knew that their hometown papers, however rare their appearance in camp, sometimes brought with them an obnoxious point of view. Even on campaign, soldiers remembered which editors they most loathed—and most blamed for their own situations. Writing from Tennessee, one Indiana soldier told his wife that the only way for the Union to win the war was to drive the Rebels "into the Gulf of Mexico and the Negroes into hell." Then he added, "and if that won't do it we will have to hang old Greeley and a few more of the Abolitionists." [21] An equally pro-Democratic soldier, David Meyers, complained to his brother: "I suppose you have seen how they tried to stop the *Chicago Times* from coming into military Distribution. The reason of that was simply because it tells the truth." [22] In an eerie reflection of civilian newspaper strife, Ohio captain Benjamin F. Sells found himself arrested in 1863 for distributing copies of the Copperhead *Columbus Crisis* to his troops. [23]

Other soldiers made gestures to distance themselves from Democratic-leaning journals, especially those widely believed in the ranks to be disloyal. When in October 1862 a group of enlistees objected to an article posted in

Correspondents of the *New York Herald* gather at a Union encampment beside their "N. Y. H. Headquarters" wagon. The *Herald* put more journalists in the field than any paper.

the *American Volunteer*, they broke into its Carlisle, Pennsylvania, headquarters, "injured the presses and threw the type into the streets." [24] During the 1862 Peninsula Campaign, a captain observed one of his men picking up an unexploded Confederate shell. After emptying it, he "put into it a copy of the New York Herald, when after plugging he fired back again to the enemy, where I presume it has been received and *contents noted*." [25] But the lively *Herald* also counted many admirers. For a time, Bennett's men operated what amounted to newsstands at several army camps, selling papers to soldiers. No Northern paper reached more troops in the field. But none enjoyed greater confidence among the Union high command than the *Tribune*. When James Parton wrote to General Benjamin Butler in January 1865 scolding him because New Yorkers "were disappointed this morning in opening their *Herald*, *Times*, and *Tribune*, not to find therein your report of the Wilmington expedition," and James White reminded Butler that he had "promised to send" his report "to the *Tribune*," the general felt obliged to explain that the War Department had forbidden him to share the information. "*I have done my duty*," he added.[26]

Shortly after the Battle of Gettysburg, two enterprising reporters, the brothers William Conant Church and Francis Pharcellus Church, both correspondents for the *New York Times*, moved to fill what they saw as a void. They established the weekly *Army and Navy Journal and Gazette of the Regular and Volunteer Forces*, a private venture despite its name, established "in obedience to an insistent demand for an official organ for members of the American Defense and those connected to it." The *Times* soon acknowledged that the paper managed "to supply what hitherto we had been without—an organ devoted to the military and naval history and organizations of the United States"[27]—and one that reflected no obvious political orientation except support for the troops. Soldiers paid ten cents per copy or five dollars for an annual subscription. Major John Chipman Gray wrote to his friend John Codman Ropes that a recent *Army and Navy Journal* "résumé" of the hard Union fighting in Virginia "was really exceedingly well done and put some little order into the confusion of the daily newspapers."[28] So did the special newspapers issued for the behemoth Sanitary Fairs organized throughout the North to raise funds to support sick and wounded soldiers. Few of these extravaganzas lacked for their own daily publications.[29] War, and even the suffering and charity it inspired, all proved good for the newspaper business.

Civilian papers would nonetheless play an especially significant role in camp during the election year of 1864. Soldiers followed the political campaign through their favorite papers, whenever available, and for good reason: for the first time, men in uniform were widely encouraged to return home on furlough to cast ballots, or alternatively to vote in the field. A new battle raged—this time between Democrats and Republicans in the ranks. In this atmosphere, former newspaperman McCalmont, now stationed in Pennsylvania, did nothing to hide his strong support for the Democrats. He stood firm, he boasted, even when a "Republican correspondent volunteered to give me a puff in a Philadelphia paper" in return for a ten-dollar loan.[30]

While soldiers on both sides yearned for news, Abraham Lincoln found a new way to shield himself from it: by largely abandoning his lifelong addiction to reading the papers every day. Copies of the latest editions were never far from his office or mind, but the harried president eventually began delegating the task of perusing them to his staff. He still might take a newspaper along to a photographer's gallery to fill the long, empty moments between camera exposures. But he no longer read them routinely, cover to cover, day after day. And he no longer recited their stories aloud to anyone within earshot—as he had done so routinely, and to some, so irritatingly—during his days as a lawyer back in Illinois.

"After he gave up reading them," testified White House clerk William Stoddard, "we had a daily brief made for him to look at, but at the end of a fortnight he had not once found time to glance at it, and we gave it up."[31]

Unless major issues dominated the print conversation, Lincoln's appetite for devouring the news abated. By 1864, he confided to a visitor that he could "find no time to read any papers."[32] His new, self-imposed insulation provided Lincoln with a way to distance himself from the press even as he increased his direct contact to its readers through his public letters—not to mention the regular office hours he maintained throughout the war in order to see ordinary Americans in person. "I call these receptions my '*public-opinion baths*,'" he told journalist Charles G. Halpine in 1863, ". . . for I have but little time to read the papers and gather public opinion that way."[33]

"Heaps of newspapers" still continued to arrive at the White House every day, Stoddard remembered, complaining that "we have to buy the newspapers we really need and read, like other people, but a host of journals, all over the country, supply the White House gratis. Open them if you wish to learn how the course of human events, and of the President in particular, is really influenced. How very many of these sagacious editors have blue-and-redded their favorite editorials, and have underscored their most stinging paragraphs!"[34]

Unable to inspire a reaction to their columns, frustrated correspondents and their pro-administration editors often sought face-to-face private meetings with the president. "That is because they fear lest Mr. Lincoln may otherwise fail to be duly impressed," Stoddard sneered. "He might even not see their points! His first complete failure was an attempt he made to watch the course of public opinion as expressed by the great dailies East and West." In Stoddard's view, it was no great loss; the editors had begun "dancing around the situation in such a manner that no man can follow them without getting too dizzy for regular work."[35] Ironically, Lincoln's growing indifference brought him closer to Washington journalists, for it compelled them to seek him out and build their relationships with him.

One long-term guest who also took note of the president's growing indifference to newspapers was the young New York artist Francis Bicknell Carpenter, who spent six months at the White House in 1864 working on his ambitious painting, *The First Reading of the Emancipation Proclamation*. Given the run of the mansion to make sketches, Carpenter enjoyed repeated opportunities to observe Lincoln and his staff as they conducted daily business. Carpenter could recall only a single occasion during all his time there when he noticed Lincoln "engaged in looking over the contents of a journal, which he had casually taken up." Otherwise, Carpenter testified, "it might have dampened the patriotic ardor of many ambitious editors" had they known that their products were often "appropriated by the servants . . . and rarely, or never, reached the one they were preeminently intended to enlighten as to his duty and policy."[36]

The painter did often spy newspapers strewn about "the Secretaries' quarters." These included Forney's *Philadelphia Press* and its rival, the *North American*, as well as: Baltimore's *Sun* and *American*; Boston's *Advertiser*, *Journal*, and *Transcript*; the Chicago *Tribune* and *Chicago Journal* (but not the hostile *Chicago Times*); the Cincinnati *Gazette* and *Commercial*; the *Missouri Republican* and *Missouri Democrat*—for both of which John Hay contributed his occasional uncredited editorials—and no fewer than six newspapers from New York City: the *Times*, *Tribune*, *Herald*, *World*, *Evening Post*, and *Independent*.[37] But only occasionally did a few titles make it into the president's inner office. "The Washington dailies,—the 'Chronicle,' 'Republican,' and 'Star,'—were usually laid on his desk," the painter attested, "and I think he was in the habit of glancing at the telegraphic reports of these; but rarely beyond this. All war news of importance, of course, reached him previous to its publication. He had, therefore, little occasion to consult newspapers on this account. The Private Secretaries . . . kept him informed of the principal subjects discussed editorially in the leading organs of the country." [38] Chief of staff John Nicolay corroborated this observation, admitting: "Excepting the Washington City Dailies, in which he carefully reads the telegraphic dispatches, the President rarely ever looks at any papers, simply for want of leisure to do so." [39]

This did not inhibit longtime Lincoln ally Joseph Medill from writing testily to Nicolay after learning that the president "had not seen a copy of the Chicago Tribune for four months." Bristled the editor: "If it miscarries we will have that corrected. If he does not want it—declines to read it—we will discontinue sending it." Nicolay assured Medill that the paper continued to be "received very regularly, opened and kept with other papers on the newspaper table in *my* office [emphasis added]," noting, "it is very regularly examined by myself, and especially sought after by the Western men who happen here." Rather than place the *Tribune* "under ban at the Executive Mansion," Nicolay soothed Medill, Lincoln would be "very glad to receive it here so long as in your kindness you may please to send it"—that is, without charge.

But Lincoln's secretary did not leave matters there—knowing that the president's onetime official Chicago organ had recently fired off some cranky editorials about military conscription. "I can assure you of what you ought to be able to guess," Nicolay added icily,

> that the President's task here is no child's play. If you imagine that *any man* could attempt its performance, and escape adverse criticism, you have read history in vain, and studied human nature without profit. But was it not to be expected that those of the President's friends, who knew him long and intimately—who understood his integrity and his devotion to the country and the cause entrusted to his charge—would at least abstain from judging him in the blindness of haste, and condemning him in the bitterness of ill-temper? . . . I desire to continue reading the Tribune—reserving only the privilege of finding as much fault with it as it finds with the Administration.[40]

Undeterred, Medill made his way to Washington together with a Chicago delegation to lodge his opposition to the draft in person. A "public-opinion bath" must have been in full swing the day the editor tried to gain entry to the White House, for Medill retreated back to his rooms at Willard's hotel and peevishly wrote to Lincoln: "Not having either time or inclination to hang round waiting rooms among a wolfish crowd seeking admission to your presence for office contracts or personal favors, I prefer stating in writing the substance of what I would say verbally." [41] Notwithstanding the disobliging note, Lincoln summoned Medill and his delegation back to the mansion, where the reunion proved less than cordial. After the visitors tried making their case against conscription, Lincoln erupted at them: "You ought to be ashamed of yourselves. . . . Medill, you are acting like a coward. You and your *Tribune* have had more influence than any paper in the Northwest in making this war. You can influence great masses, and yet you cry to be spared at a moment when the cause is suffering. Go home and send us those men." [42]

Lincoln proved far more tolerant when it came to another longtime Illinois press supporter, Thomas Pickett, editor of the tiny *Rock Island Register*. Pickett's early support for Lincoln's presidential ambitions had been repaid with a plum, $700-per-year job as official agent for the local army quartermaster's department—an increasingly popular patronage assignment for struggling editors eager to make some money off the war. [43] But in March 1863, the town's Democratic paper accused Pickett of using the job to line his own pockets through the inflated sale of timber and stone. Protesting his innocence, Pickett appealed to Nicolay to bring his case before the president, arguing: "Our republicans think it is a queer state of affairs if a copperhead editor, acting on his malicious feelings, can have the power to remove a loyal man from office." [44] Before Lincoln could review the matter, however, Pickett lost his position "without chance to be heard," prompting a hurried telegram to the president himself. While the editor awaited word from the White House, he organized a petition campaign to Secretary of War Stanton. The flurry of letters had their desired effect. Lincoln intervened on April 20, writing to the Rock Island postmaster to ask that this "old acquaintance and friend of mine" be allowed to give testimony in his defense. Pickett eventually won his reinstatement. [45]

Boasting even closer personal and political ties to the president, William Bailhache of Lincoln's old Springfield "organ," the *Illinois State Journal*, believed himself entitled to similar vindication when he, too, came under attack at home. Early in the war, grateful for his years of support, Lincoln had named Bailhache assistant army quartermaster for Springfield with the rank of captain. But in May 1863, no fewer than thirteen hometown Republicans bombarded the president with complaints that Bailhache had proven corrupt. Included among the alerts was a letter from Lincoln's longtime banker, Jacob Bunn, who had noticed Bailhache's accounts bulging at a suspicious rate. By the end of the month, Lincoln wearily instructed the accusers to select a successor from among a list of other local Republicans. Transferred to a "subordinate position" in the field, an angry Bailhache urged his co-publisher, Edward Baker, to send Lincoln a "good strong remonstrance (or go & see him in person)" and tender his resignation from the service. He could not believe "Mr. Lincoln ever intended I should be thus used in order to please his 'life-long friends.'"[46]

Baker indeed made the long journey to Washington, where he claimed that Lincoln expressed "the kindliest feelings" toward the ousted quartermaster. But Baker undoubtedly devoted most of his White House visit to arguing in behalf of an altogether different "victim": his own father-in-law, Ninian Edwards, who was married to Mrs. Lincoln's older sister. Despite familial ties, Edwards had recently lost his own army job as Springfield commissary of subsistence in the same purge that sank William Bailhache—in Edwards's case, accused of helping Democrats to prosper from his contracts, a believable enough charge since he had supported Stephen Douglas in 1860. Making matters even more complicated was the fact that editor Baker had contracted with his father-in-law to supply the rations that Edwards, in turn, distributed to the army, allegedly at a profit. It was an arrangement that invited corruption. Baker's visit did nothing to reduce the president's displeasure, especially when, just hours after the editor's departure, Lincoln discovered yet another letter from Springfield "renewing the pressure upon me" to resolve the dispute. Lincoln had heard enough. He told Baker: "The appeal to me in behalf of Mr. Edwards and Mr. Bailhasche [sic], for a hearing, does not meet the case." The president still had no "reason to suspect" either man's guilt, and doubted they would face formal charges. But his other old friends had been "harassing" him for two years "because of Mr. E. & Mr. B." Though the president still thought they were "without dishonesty," he believed they easily "could have saved me from this, if they had cared to do so."[47] Lincoln reassigned Ninian Edwards to Chicago, and kept Bailhache in limbo.

Two months later, many of these same neighbors invited the president to return to Springfield to address a giant Union rally in his old hometown. Lincoln ultimately decided that he could not spare the time to undertake the lengthy journey—and perhaps had no enthusiasm for visiting while Republican friends there remained at each other's throats. Instead, he decided to craft another of his "public letters" to be read aloud in Springfield and circulated to the national press. But the Bailhache affair refused to go away.

Now back home in Springfield, Edward Baker wrote the president one more time to ask that Lincoln find his partner a commensurate quartermaster's job elsewhere, noting, "I cannot believe you 'intended' to disgrace our mutual friend." When no offer came by October, Bailhache's wife sent the president a long letter of her own, demanding that her husband not only be restored to his old position, but actually promoted—to "show his enemies that you still retain confidence in him." [48] William Bailhache received no promotion, and more troubles followed. To Edward Baker's chagrin, a group the editor labeled "enemies and slanderers" now launched an additional "inquisition" into his own alleged skimming. Melodramatically citing "the memory of all the by-gone devotion and persevering friendship I have ever shown him (*when devotion and friendship were valuable to him*)," Baker asked former senator Orville Browning to intervene with Lincoln to save him from "disgrace." [49] As far as the president was concerned, however, the case was closed.

More obscure editors with less call on Lincoln's loyalty continued to bring their own views to the president's attention, even if they had to resort to writing self-promoting introductory letters to gain an audience. Stoddard maintained that these desperate overtures seemed more an effort to impress Lincoln than to influence policy, and that, in any event, their missives seldom aroused any interest. Editorial criticism, often scathing, poured in unabated, but for the most part Lincoln increasingly let the attacks roll off his back. Ward Hill Lamon noted that "Mr. Lincoln persistently declined to read the harsh comments of the newspaper press." On one occasion, the president made a point of quoting Daniel Webster to suggest that he had grown a thicker skin. As Lincoln declared of his newspaper detractors on that occasion, "we can afford to pass them by with the dying words of the Massachusetts statesman, 'we still live.'" Then he added: "I am sure they don't worry me any, and I reckon they don't benefit the parties who write them." [50] Frank Carpenter seconded this sentiment, testifying: "Violent criticism, attacks, and denunciations, coming either from radicals or conservatives, rarely ruffled the President." [51]

Lincoln sometimes behaved otherwise as the war dragged on. He may have given up reading newspapers on a daily basis, but was almost certain to react strongly when well-meaning or malignant correspondents sent him offensive clippings through the mails. One such backlog of critical editorials came to the president's attention, after Reverend Henry Ward Beecher, acting in his new capacity as an editor of the *New York Independent,* began sounding what Carpenter called "editorial . . . bugle blasts" against the administration. Criticism from that progressive weekly was nothing new. Just a few weeks before the dedicatory ceremonies at Gettysburg, the paper's principal editor, Theodore Tilton, had sent Lincoln "an abusive editorial in the Independent & a letter stating he meant it in no unkindliness."[52]

Although Lincoln resisted the temptation to follow the weekly paper's latest denunciatory series as it appeared in print, a package eventually arrived at the White House overflowing with sample clippings. "One Sunday," artist Carpenter observed, "Lincoln took them from his drawer, and read through them to the very last word." When he finished, his face "flushed up with indignation," and he hurled the pile of papers to the floor, quoting the Book of Kings to exclaim of Beecher: "Is thy servant a *dog*, that he should do this thing?" Within seconds, however, Lincoln's dark mood evaporated, "leaving no trace behind of ill-will toward Mr. Beecher."[53] The *New York Tribune's* Albert Richardson confirmed Lincoln's forgiving nature. "Ignorant of etiquette and conventionalities, without the graces of form or of manner," as he described him after his 1863 visit, the President showed a "great reluctance to give pain" and evidenced "a beautiful regard for the feelings of others"—even newspapermen.[54]

The "wiry, sallow, silent-stepping" Lawrence Gobright of the Associated Press, whom William Stoddard dubbed "the censor of all war rumors," was one journalist who enjoyed frequent access to the president, although not always productively.[55] Gobright thought Lincoln "generally courteous," but "sometimes distrustful of newspaper people." Wary of leaks, "whenever he did impart any item of news, especially relating to events of the war," Gobright recalled, Lincoln was "extremely cautious in his narration." Yet the president was occasionally himself guilty of whispering important news too soon. Even in those cases, according to Gobright, Lincoln always seemed "astonished to find the keen-scented correspondents publishing important matters in advance of the time designated by himself."[56]

Hard as he tried to be circumspect, the ever-friendly Lincoln often caught himself in the midst of revealing too much to reporters. With Albert Richardson and the *New York Times's* James Winchell he was convivially chatting about military affairs one day when he suddenly stopped short and exclaimed:

"I am talking again! Of course, you will remember that I speak to you only as friends; that none of this must be put in print!"[57] Journalists seldom violated such admonitions, even if the unspoken rules of the profession required that interview subjects declare their comments to be off the record before, not after, confiding them.

In August 1863, Gobright implored the president to provide him with an advance copy of the remarks he was preparing for the upcoming mass meeting in Springfield. Lincoln had decided to mail the text home with the instruction that his old friend James C. Conkling read it aloud at the rally.[58] Gobright immediately sensed its newsworthiness. But Lincoln refused to comply with his request, insisting: "I can't do it, for I have found that documents given to the press in advance are always prematurely published." (To another journalist on the same scent, Lincoln reiterated that he found "the practice of furnishing advance copies to newspapers to be a source of endless mischief.") Somewhat offended, Gobright protested that his agency had never issued official documents "before their proper time."[59]

"I can't help that," Lincoln waved him away. "I have always found what I say to be true."

"Well, Mr. President," came Gobright's indignant reply, "it is your property, and you have a right to dispose of it as you choose. Good day."

Lawrence Gobright, wartime Washington bureau chief of the Associated Press.

The following morning, Gobright discovered to his dismay that extracts from the message had been published in John Wein Forney's *Washington Chronicle*, one of the journals, the Associated Press manager fumed, "to which the President was in the habit of first turning his attention," and in this instance involving "the same letter which he was so fearful of being published prematurely!" Gobright stormed back to the White House and demanded that one of the staff secretaries explain the slight. It was meekly explained that some "enterprising editor" had somehow obtained a copy of the message and released it without authorization. While Gobright seethed over the slight, Forney endured a tongue-lashing from the president for leaking the message, and in turn attempted to cover his tracks by blaming Gobright, informing Lincoln that the *Chronicle*'s version of the text had come directly from the Associated Press. Typically, Forney offered to make up for the lapse by promising: "To-morrow we will republish it, accompanied by a strong editorial endorsement." (Lincoln was probably not overly disappointed when the loquacious Forney decided to embark on a long, health-restoring visit to Europe the following summer, although he declined Forney's request that he supply him with letters of introduction to European friends; he had none, the president explained.[60])

The president's mood did not improve when he discovered that the text on which he had labored for so many weeks had come out mangled in the initial reports that appeared in the newspapers. "I am mortified this morning to find the letter to you, botched up, in the Eastern papers, telegraphed from Chicago," Lincoln angrily wired James Conkling. "How did this happen?" Conkling, who unconvincingly claimed that he received this disturbing telegram in the midst of the very event at which he was preparing to read the president's remarks, replied sheepishly that he was "mortified" as well. He admitted that while he had indeed sent the text to the Western Press Association in Chicago before the event, he had left "strict injunctions not to permit it to be published before the meeting." He hoped at least that "no prejudicial results have been experienced as the whole letter was published the next day."[61]

Indeed, Lincoln soon reveled in the attention the letter generated through subsequent newspaper reprints punctuated by editorial praise in Republican papers nationwide.[62] His most passionate defense of black recruitment, the message climaxed with Lincoln's vivid warning to his former neighbors that when peace returned, "there will be some black men who can remember that, with silent tongue, and clenched teeth, and steady eye, and well-poised bayonet, they have helped mankind on to this great consummation; while, I fear, there will be some white ones, unable to forget that, with malignant heart, and deceitful speech, they have strove to hinder it."[63]

"It hits, as his written efforts always do, the very heart of his subject," Henry Raymond, no particular friend of black recruitment, applauded in the *New York Times*. ". . . Those of us who favor the war are bound to consent to all available means for its effective prosecution, and to form their judgment by the military judgment solely." Added Raymond of Lincoln: "The very best proof of his fitness for his recent weighty responsibilities is to be found in the fact that he has a soul possessed of this magnanimity, and a mind capable of these conceptions of patriotic duty." In an unusual show of unity, Horace Greeley concurred, editorializing: "The most consummate rhetorician never used language more put to the purpose." [64] Lincoln was never more successful in controlling the newspapers than when he wrote newspaper copy himself.

Despite his inability to read the press as closely as he had before entering the White House, Lincoln still occasionally looked to newspapers for information he was unable to obtain through official channels. "You probably wonder what interest I can find in talking to a newspaper correspondent," Lincoln told *New York Times* reporter George Forrester Williams. As the president explained: "I am always seeking information, and you newspapermen are so often behind the scenes at the front, I am frequently able to get ideas from you which no one else can give me." [65] Such proved precisely the case when young *New York Tribune* correspondent Henry E. Wing somehow made his way past enemy lines in Virginia and walked seventy-five miles to Washington to update Lincoln on Ulysses S. Grant's progress at the Wilderness—where communication lines had been severed. When the two were alone, Wing reported to the president: "General Grant told me to tell you, from him, that whatever happens, there is to be no turning back." Lincoln was so overcome with gratitude at this report that he embraced Wing with his "great strong arms" and planted a kiss on the reporter's brow. [66]

Lincoln proved only slightly less grateful for good political news, especially from distant areas. Around the time he issued his "Conkling letter," Lincoln anxiously wired the Republican *Cincinnati Gazette*: "Please send me your present posting as to Kentucky election." Editor Richard Smith replied with the reassuring report: "The union state ticket is elected by a very large majority." Even the anti-administration *Louisville Journal* had so conceded, Smith added, though the opposition paper claimed "of course that the democrats were intimidated." [67]

Knowing that well-connected journalists like Smith occasionally received news before he did, especially late at night, Lincoln often proved willing to receive Washington "scribblers" at all hours. On one such occasion, a pair of correspondents got word that the Union had captured Charleston. Although it was past 11 P.M., they rushed to the White House in search of confirmation, but on arriving learned from the doorkeeper that Lincoln had gone to bed. The visitors insisted that he be interrupted, assuring the guard that the president would want to hear the report they had for him. The doorkeeper reluctantly headed upstairs to check, then returned to tell the reporters they could indeed proceed to the private quarters—provided they understood "they would see the President in a style of costume in which no other visitors had ever seen him."

Entering his bedroom, they found the uninhibited commander-in-chief "with no clothing on excepting his shirt. He invited his guests to be seated, and he himself took a chair. He inquired as to the date of their news; and on being informed, said he had three days later intelligence," and that their news was incorrect. The visitors fumbled their apologies, and as they withdrew, solemnly asked Lincoln to excuse them for "disturbing his slumber." The president insisted "it made no difference and good-humoredly bade them good night, with a profound bow." At this gesture, the mortified journalists fled, remembering Lincoln's appearance "as not only novel but ludicrous."[68]

Gobright glimpsed a quite different side of Lincoln when he knocked at the president's office door one evening during the 1863 Vicksburg siege. "I have nothing new," Lincoln at first muttered impatiently. Then he looked up at his visitor and confessed: "I can't sleep to-night without hearing something; come, go with me to the War Department, perhaps Stanton has something." Together, the two walked over to the nearby telegraph office, where Gobright looked on with fascination as the operator handed Lincoln the latest dispatch from the front. The president looked "nervous;" his hands and legs "shook violently" as he grasped the wire, his face turning "ghastly" pale. Lincoln strained to make out the report in the "imperfect" gaslight, and then moaned, "Bad news, bad news," quickly adding: *"Don't say anything about this—don't mention it."* As it turned out, the disheartening report proved inaccurate; no disaster had befallen Union troops at Vicksburg after all. As relieved as he was to receive the correction, Lincoln now grew agitated that his earlier distress might inspire a disobliging story of its own. Turning to Gobright, he urgently reiterated, "don't say anything about this."[69]

Lincoln intentionally said a great deal to Albert G. Hodges, editor of Kentucky's influential *Frankfort Commonwealth*. On April 26, 1864, Hodges visited the White House to express disapproval over the growing deployment of black troops in his home state, where slavery remained legal and racial prejudice strong. According to Orville Browning, who also attended the meeting, Lincoln began the session in much the same way he had launched his meeting two years earlier with the African-American freedmen: by asking if he could "make a little speech." This time, however, his guests were "much pleased" with what they heard. Hodges asked for a copy of the remarks so he could publish them. The president casually replied that he had not found the time to write them down, but advised Hodges "to go home and he would write him a letter in which he would give, as nearly as he could all that he had said to them orally."[70] A few days later, Lincoln composed and dispatched to Hodges what Senator Browning at once recognized as a "well written and excellent paper."

"I am naturally anti-slavery," it memorably began. "If slavery is not wrong, nothing is wrong. I can not remember when I did not so think, and feel." And yet, Lincoln went on, he fully understood that the presidency never gave him the constitutional authority to "act upon this judgment and feeling." That is, until civil war forced him to choose whether "to lose the nation, and yet preserve the constitution."

In Lincoln's homespun view: "By general law life *and* limb must be protected; yet often a limb must be amputated to save a life; but a life is never wisely given to save a limb." Under this theory, he argued, emancipation became "an indispensable necessity"—as did "arming the blacks"—to save the life of the nation. Finally, Lincoln introduced one of his most famous justifications for his revolutionary policies: a higher power had animated his decisions. "I claim not to have controlled events, but confess plainly that events have controlled me," he insisted. And if God now willed that the country remove the "great wrong" of slavery, "impartial history will find therein new cause to attest and revere the justice and goodness of God."[71]

That Lincoln had grown determined that these words quickly reach Kentucky's newspaper readers became apparent when, eighteen days later, with no response yet in hand, he impatiently telegraphed Hodges to inquire: "Did you receive my letter?"[72] Lincoln need not have worried. The text soon appeared in Hodges's daily, and quickly thereafter in papers nationwide. Horace Greeley lauded the president's "rare quality, the ability to make a statement which appeals at once, and irresistibly, to the popular apprehension." Much pleased, Lincoln endorsed the *Tribune* editorial in a bold hand, "Greeley on the Hodges Letter," and kept it in his files.[73] While James Gordon Bennett reprinted it without comment, Henry Raymond cheered: "The letter of President Lincoln to the editor of the *Frankfort Commonwealth* is a new and admirable specimen of his ingenious character, and of his remarkable aptness in stating the truth."[74]

The newspapers' version of "the truth" often evoked frustration and fatalism from Lincoln, but sometimes laughter as well. John Hay recalled the president entering his office one Sunday, picking up a stray paper, and reading "the Richmond *Examiner's* recent attack on Jeff. Davis. It amused him. 'Why,' said he 'the Examiner seems ab[ou]t. as fond of Jeff as the [New York] World is of me.'"[75] Lincoln often used humor to vent his frustrations with opposition papers. When he overheard Frank Carpenter telling Mary Jane Welles, wife of the secretary of the navy, that newspapers were not always reliable, the pun-loving president interjected: "That is to say, Mrs. Welles, they '*lie*,' and then they '*re-lie*'!" On another occasion, a delegation tried to interest Lincoln in a newfangled repeating gun that functioned without the escape of gas. After a successful demonstration, Lincoln remarked, "Well, I believe this really does what it is represented to do. Now have any of you heard of any machine, or invention, for preventing the escape of 'gas' from newspaper establishments?"[76] One especially "violent" newspaper attack merely reminded the president of a story about an immigrant "fresh from the 'Emerald Isle.'" Filled with terror at the loud but harmless sound of "a grand chorus of bullfrogs," the Irishman was consoled by his friend: "And sure, Jamie! it is my opinion it's nothing but a '*noise*'!"[77] So, he implied, was newspaper criticism.

Lincoln never held a formal news conference, and save for the 1862 White House visit by Nathaniel Hawthorne, granted journalists no major interviews. Instead, he left instructions that when reporters called at the White House, their cards or messages be brought into his office even if he was in session with the cabinet. He occasionally interrupted meetings to invite correspondents inside for quick private chats, as eager to receive news as to share it. Or he sent word that the press visitors should wait until he could receive them. When he was simply unable to admit reporters, he often scrawled replies on the backs of their notes or visiting cards. William Stoddard believed that Lincoln felt it his duty to consider reporters' questions "with extreme courtesy," and to set them right "as a duty" when they made errors in print. But he seldom warned correspondents in advance of any "news-error" they might be "falling into."[78] Much had changed. For years, Lincoln had devoted his time to visiting journalists at newspaper offices throughout Illinois, eager for their attention and friendship. Now newspapermen were coming in droves to *his* office, seeking attention from him.

Among Lincoln's 1864 White House press visitors was Theodore Tilton of the *Independent*, who brought with him a legendary guest: no less than the father of abolitionist journalism, William Lloyd Garrison. It was a significant milestone. No previous president had ever received the fifty-eight-year-old founder of *The Liberator*, and Tilton later reported: "His reception of Mr. Garrison was an equal honor to host and guest." When the antislavery hero reported that, en route through Baltimore, he had been unable to locate a Baltimore jail where he was once confined, Lincoln smiled: "Well, Mr. Garrison, when you first went to Baltimore you couldn't get *out*; but the second time you couldn't get *in*!"[79]

Ben Perley Poore recalled that Lincoln was "always ready" to be helpful to "those correspondents in whom he had confidence."[80] One morning, as Lincoln was adjourning a cabinet meeting devoted to discussing a recent military victory, the president cheerfully called out to the waiting reporters, "Walk in, walk in; be seated, take seats." As they filed into his office, one of the correspondents attempted to pose a question. "I know what you have come for," Lincoln good-naturedly interrupted him, "you want to hear more about the good news. I know you do. You gentlemen are keen of scent, and always wide awake."

"You have hit the matter precisely, Mr. President: that's exactly what we want—the news."

Leaning back in his armchair and stretching his long legs onto the top of his cabinet table, Lincoln declared to his visitors: "I've already told this story half a dozen times, but I'll tell it again, as you haven't heard it." Then, as the scribes recorded his words, Lincoln related the latest news from the front. He seemed "more than ordinarily cheerful" that day, one of the journalists recalled. "He was happy" when he was able to communicate positive stories.[81]

One journalist who seemed to make Lincoln happier than most was Noah Brooks, a thirty-two year-old Washington correspondent for the *Sacramento Daily Union*. Brooks became a presidential favorite following his arrival in the capital in late 1862. Writing under the nom de plume "Castine"—the name of his Maine birthplace—Brooks's sympathetic reports quickly caught the president's attention. The following year, the correspondent was rewarded with a coveted extra job as a clerk in the House of Representatives. By late 1864, Brooks had become such a regular presence at the White House that—at least according to his own reckoning—Lincoln began entertaining the idea of naming him his new private secretary should he win a second term.[82] Both

Nicolay and Hay, exhausted from years of grinding toil and sick of constant squabbles with Mary Lincoln, were eager for other assignments, while Stoddard, in ill health, headed west that September to become a federal marshal in Arkansas.

Brooks, who eventually filed more than two hundred "Castine" dispatches for the *Sacramento Union*, was shocked when he caught his initial glimpse of the president in church—the first time he had cast eyes on him since encountering him at Springfield years earlier. "The change in his personal appearance was marked and sorrowful," Brooks noted. ". . . His eyes were almost deathly in their gloomy depths, and on his visage was an air of profound sadness. His face was colorless and drawn." To Brooks's surprise, Lincoln almost immediately summoned him to the White House. "Do you suppose I ever forget an old acquaintance?" the president happily exclaimed when they shook hands. "I reckon not." [83]

Brooks claimed he went on to see Lincoln privately once or twice a week for the next two and a half years—perhaps an exaggeration, though many of his "Castine" reports do show that he was often in the right place at the right time to observe the president. Of course he unfailingly supported administration policy. He endorsed black recruitment and applauded conscription, going so far as to remind readers that the much hated $300 buyout clause would at least fatten the federal Treasury. In April 1863, Brooks got to accompany Lincoln, his "able and noble" wife, and their son Tad on a morale-boosting visit to General Hooker's military headquarters in Virginia. In October, he was among the first to float the notion that Lincoln hoped for—and deserved—a second term. And in November, Brooks published a surprisingly intimate view of life inside the White House. It offered a novel peek at how the president conducted business in his private office, as well as glimpses into what Brooks claimed was an entirely happy private life in the family quarters. In perhaps the first public hint that he coveted Nicolay's job, Brooks dismissed the incumbent secretaries as "snobby and unpopular," and lavished further praise on his chief advocate, Mary Lincoln, calling her "the best and truest lady in our beloved land." [84]

Naturally, Brooks had plenty to say about how the president dealt with rival newspapers—on both the wholesale and retail levels. Not only did he comment on Lincoln's ongoing attempts to influence Washington's more unsympathetic correspondents, he reported a particularly amusing 1863 incident in which the president asked his Irish coachman to "go out and get the morning

Noah Brooks, Washington correspondent for the *Sacramento Daily Union* under the nom de plume "Castine," and aspirant to become the president's next private secretary.

newspaper." When the servant failed to return, "the anxious President went out himself and invested five cents in a *Morning Chronicle.*" It was later revealed that the coachman thought it beneath his dignity to run errands. Lincoln's response came the following morning. Though he said nothing, he repaid his driver's "hauteur" by ordering up the presidential carriage at 6 A.M. and assigning another servant to ride down Pennsylvania Avenue in the passenger seat to buy a newspaper while the "mortified coachman" sat in the driver's box.[85]

Lincoln also shared deeply personal thoughts with Brooks—or so the correspondent later maintained. It was to the journalist that the increasingly religious president allegedly confided: "I have been driven many times upon my knees by the overwhelming conviction that I had nowhere else to go." Later Lincoln added: "I should be the veriest shallow and self-conceited blockhead upon the footstool if, in my discharge of the duties which are put upon me in this place, I should hope to get along without the wisdom which comes from God and not from men."[86] These revelations Brooks saved for his post-assassination articles and memoirs, undoubtedly embellishing them with florid language the plainspoken Lincoln likely never used.

Far easier to believe was Brooks's recollection that Lincoln had an almost childlike habit of regaling visitors with any "sharp saying" he had uttered during the day, taking "simple-hearted pleasure in considering some of his best 'hits.'" Once, in December 1864, Lincoln began proudly telling Brooks what he had just said to two insistent visitors seeking pardons for their husbands, Confederate prisoners of war confined at Johnson's Island, Ohio. At each of their interviews, Lincoln remembered, the ladies testified that their husbands were religious men. Lincoln ultimately gave in and ordered their release, but not without offering the wives a lecture. It was at this point in the story that the president interrupted himself and decided to commit the incident to writing in the third person, scribbling on a piece of stiff boxwood he balanced on his knees as Brooks looked on. Signing it and handing the finished manuscript to his guest, he declared: "Here is one speech of mine which has never been printed, and I think it worth printing."

THE PRESIDENT'S LAST, SHORTEST, AND BEST SPEECH.

On thursday of last week two ladies from Tennessee came before the President asking the release of their husbands held as prisoners of war at Johnson's Island. They were put off till friday, when they came again; and were again put off to saturday. At each of the interviews one of the ladies urged that her husband was a religious man. On Saturday the President ordered the release of the prisoners, and then said to this lady "You say your husband is a religious man; tell him when you meet him, that I say I am not much of a judge of religion, but that, in my opinion, the religion that sets men to rebel and fight against their government, because, as they think, that government does not sufficiently help *some* men to eat their bread on the sweat of *other* men's faces, is not the sort of religion upon which people can get to heaven!" [87]

Brooks did not seem to realize that the germ behind this epistle was in fact seven years old, originated by Lincoln during his final debate with Stephen Douglas in 1858. Since it was the closest thing to a press release Lincoln had ever issued, Brooks made sure it was published in the *Washington Chronicle* the following morning.[88] A few months later, Lincoln would repurpose the sentiments yet again for his second inaugural address.

On still another visit to the president's private office, Brooks found himself staring in wonder at Lincoln's cluttered desk, whose pigeonholes bulged with alphabetized files labeled with important names, including those of several generals and, not unexpectedly, Horace Greeley. Brooks noticed one curiously identified compartment. "I see you looking at my 'W. & W.,'" Lincoln finally said. "Can you guess what that stands for?" When Brooks failed to come up with an answer, Lincoln explained "with a merry twinkle of the eye, 'that's Weed and Wood—Thurlow and Fernandy.' Then he added with an indescribable chuckle, 'That's a pair of 'em!'" [89]

As that comment reminded Brooks, Lincoln always had the most difficulty with—and the most time for—the New York editors, particularly Manhattan's big three. Welcoming a visiting reporter from the *New York Herald* once, the president declared: "You gentlemen of the press seem to be pretty much like the soldiers, who have to go wherever sent, whatever may be the dangers or difficulties in the way. God forbid I should by any rudeness of speech or manner, make your duties any harder than they are. . . . If I am not afraid of you, it is because I feel you are trustworthy." [90] As Lincoln boasted that day, doubtless hoping that his reassuring words would reach James Gordon Bennett himself: "The press has no better friend than I am—no one who is more ready to acknowledge . . . its tremendous power for both good and evil." [91]

The fragile administration truce with the pro-war, but anti-emancipation, *Herald* was frequently put to the test. In the fall of 1863, Bennett profoundly embarrassed the White House by puffing the story that Lincoln had sent his garrulous Jewish chiropodist, Isachar Zacharie, on a mission to Richmond to explore an armistice. Though in truth it was no more than an expedition to measure Union loyalty among the Confederate capital's Jews, the anti-Semitic Bennett made Lincoln's trust in Zacharie seem odious. The doctor, who loved publicity and knew Bennett well enough to remember the last time he encountered him, was at least partially responsible for the leak, though he expressed shock at seeing the story in print. "I was amazed on reading the Herald News-paper to find the article," he disingenuously assured his most famous medical patient. "I pledge to you that I have not lisped a word respecting this matter. . . . I have not seen Mr. Bennett or any one connected with the Herald for the last six months." [92]

That same year, the celebrated Shakespearean actor James Hackett made public a letter from Lincoln in which the Shakespeare-loving president un-inhibitedly identified his favorites among the Bard's plays and soliloquies. Perhaps aware that Hackett was a longtime friend of his rival Henry Raymond, Bennett pounced on the letter, editorializing: "Mr. Lincoln's genius is wonderfully versatile. No department of human knowledge seems to be unexplored by him. He is equally at home whether discussing divinity with political preachers, debating plans of campaigns with military heroes, [and] illustrating the Pope's bull against the comet to a pleasure party from Chicago. . . . It only remained for him to cap the climax of popular astonishment and admiration by showing himself to be a dramatic critic of the first order, and the greatest and most profound of the army of Shakespearean commentators." When Hackett wrote Lincoln to apologize for inadvertently giving the *Herald* an opportunity to taunt him, Lincoln assured him he need not worry. Shrugging off his long years of experience as a target of newspaper mockery, Lincoln sighed: "I have endured a great deal of ridicule without much malice; and have received a great deal of kindness, not quite free from ridicule. I am used to it."[93]

Among the major New York editors, Henry Raymond remained the most steadfast supporter of the administration. Greeley's *Tribune* may have been "the most widely read Republican journal of the country," newspaperman A. K. McClure acknowledged, but Raymond was the only "leading journalist of New York" on whom Lincoln could consistently "rely for positive support."[94] In turn, the *Times* owner felt free to besiege Lincoln with repeated recommendations that he find jobs for his friends and his friends' friends.[95] Their relationship was also social. At William Seward's urging, Lincoln welcomed Raymond to the White House at Christmas 1863.[96] And the following May, when Secretary of War Stanton refused to approve a pass for *Times* correspondent Edward A. Paul to cover the Army of the Potomac, Lincoln intervened by reminding Stanton: "The Times I believe is always true to the Union, and therefore should be treated at least as well as any."[97]

In this one unusual case, however, the prickly Stanton got his back up and refused to follow orders. "The Times is treated by this Department precisely

The curious case of war correspondent E. A. Paul: Lincoln instructs Secretary of War Stanton to treat the *New York Times* cordially, but Stanton refuses to grant the *Times* reporter a pass to cover the army. The test of wills played out entirely on the back of Paul's original letter to the president.

as other papers are treated," he bristled. "No pass is granted . . . to any paper except upon the permission of General Grant or General Meade. Repeated applications by Mr Forney and by other editors have been refused on the same ground as the Times until the correspondent is approved by the Commanding General. This is the regulation of all the armies and the Secretary of War declines to do for the Times what is not done for other papers." Paul in turn protested that Stanton had entirely missed the point: Meade had already granted him a pass, yet Stanton not only declined to endorse it, but upbraided Paul "in stronger language than is necessary to repeat" for going over his head to the president. Raymond then took the case to John Nicolay, insisting that the *Times* was experiencing continuous difficulty "getting any correspondents into the field . . . while special pains seem to have been taken to give the World, Herald, &c. all possible facilities. Mr. Stanton's treatment of me in this matter is perfectly inexplicable. . . . I am not aware of having ever given him cause for the resentment & hostility he seems to feel toward the *Times*." Precisely how Lincoln won the skirmish over E. A. Paul's credentials remains unknown, but within a few months the correspondent was successfully filing reports to the *Times* from the front in the Shenandoah Valley. Notwithstanding Stanton's politically tone-deaf hostility, Raymond cemented his position as Lincoln's most loyal New York press advocate—and before long, his latest biographer.[98]

Nonetheless, Lincoln did not always do as Raymond advised, either. In August 1864, the editor joined Thurlow Weed and New York senator Edwin Morgan to petition for the release of one Louis A. Welton, recently imprisoned at Fort Delaware. Raymond, who had read and believed Welton's protests of innocence, insisted that "his pardon would be an act of *justice*." After looking into the matter, Lincoln reported back that the prisoner in question had in fact entered Union lines "with a contract to furnish large supplies to the rebels" and "was arrested with the contract in his possession." Now Welton was obviously trying "to escape by telling a very absurd and improbable story." Cleverly turning final judgment over to his New York correspondents, Lincoln concluded: "Now, if Senator Morgan, and Mr. Weed, and Mr. Raymond, will not argue with me that I *ought* to discharge this man, but will . . . simply request me to do it, I will do it solely in deference to their wishes." Two weeks later, speaking for the gullible trio, Morgan withdrew the request for clemency.[99]

Horace Greeley was in some ways tougher to manage than even Bennett.

Though he and Lincoln shared many values and had known each other for parts of three decades, Greeley remained the hardest of the editors to predict and the most difficult to please. The editor vacillated endlessly between advocating aggressive war and demanding speedy peace, all the while maintaining his unwavering hatred of slavery and unquenchable lust for patronage power and high office. Although Indiana congressman George Julian maintained that Lincoln had "the most profound personal respect for Mr. Greeley, and placed the highest estimate upon his services as an independent writer and thinker," Secretary of the Interior John P. Usher probably came closer to the truth when he remembered that the "complaints and criticisms" that filled the pages of the *Tribune* "very much annoyed" the president.[100]

Yet Greeley was also capable of coming to Lincoln's defense when his help was least expected. In March 1864, the *Tribune* reported that Mary Lincoln's pro-Southern half-sister, Martha Todd White, had abused a presidential pass by smuggling medicines and other contraband into the Confederacy. The paper added fuel to the fire by asserting that "the chuckling of the Rebel press over her safe transit with Rebel uniforms and buttons of gold was founded in truth." The embarrassing story prompted John Nicolay to alert Greeley that out of respect for the editor's "authority the Copperhead newspapers" were now circulating the story, which the president's chief of staff insisted was false. Submitting a correction, Nicolay asked: "Will you be so kind as to publish the enclosed, or its equivalent, in the editorial columns of *The Tribune*?" Nicolay's version of the story maintained that Mrs. White's presidential pass had not exempted her from the "usual" baggage inspection, and that in fact her luggage had been searched and no contraband discovered. While Greeley had by then determined to fight against Lincoln's renomination, he replied, "I shall of course publish the enclosure. . . . Though I am an earnest one-term man, I want to publish all the truth I can get and as few falsehoods as possible."[101]

Frederick Douglass recalled that Lincoln "seemed to feel very keenly the reproaches" that Greeley "heaped upon him for not bringing the war to a speedy conclusion." Although Douglass was by this time the leading spokesman for the nation's African Americans, he was in another sense one more of the elite newspapermen who enjoyed access to the president, certainly the only editor of color. Lincoln invited him to the White House to discuss black recruitment and the sensitive topic of equal pay for "colored" troops. "In all my interviews with Mr. Lincoln," Douglass later testified, "I was impressed with his entire freedom from popular prejudice against the colored race."[102]

Unlike Bennett, Greeley, Raymond, or Douglass, the ideally situated John Hay owned no newspaper. Yet Hay managed to function throughout the war as the closest thing to an official press spokesman in Lincoln's employ. While serving on the White House staff, Hay avidly continued his journalistic career, posting feature stories for the St. Louis papers and, until it became a Copperhead sheet, the *New York World*. His dispatches extolled administration policy and occasionally offered forthright criticism of the press corps. Thus Hay may have been speaking for the White House when he observed: "There has never been an age so completely enthralled by newspapers as this. They have begun to be taken as the absolute reflex of the will of the people and the earnest thought of a nation." To Hay, "their utterances meet with an attention absurdly out of proportion to their importance."[103] Savvy as he was about the newspaper business, Hay and his fellow White House secretaries never quite pierced the armor of either partisan journalism or the deeply personal rivalry that had kept New York City's three principal editors at each other's throats for more than a decade.

Moreover, Lincoln and other press watchers in the administration remained unsure about the extent to which the big New York dailies reflected national, or at least Northern, public opinion. "We in Washington have so little faith in the New-York newspapers, as indices of the real public feeling," William Stoddard complained in one of his own anonymous press reports in 1862, "that we are at a loss what the people really think." As Stoddard lamented of Gotham's editors, "they can neither understand nor appreciate an honest man who is in earnest."[104] But they had to be cultivated.

Even from his perch in Philadelphia, John Russell Young seemed aware that the New York relationships were far more complex than Stoddard comprehended. The real explanation for the three editors' inconsistent attitudes toward the president, he suggested, had more to do with their own bitter rivalry than with administration policy. Each of New York's three reigning press lords, Young believed, hated each other far more than they ever cared about Lincoln: Bennett, still the "sinister . . . lawless, eccentric influence . . . breathing wrath upon all who would not bow down and worship"; Greeley, the "resolute, brilliant, capable, irresponsible, intolerant" idealist convinced that "disputation was the higher duty of man"; and Raymond, who relished "the joy of a fight," yet possessed "no skill in discussing . . . moral consequences." Raymond himself came close to agreeing with this assessment when he admitted that, however vehemently the press might criticize politicians, the newspaper trade was designed not to reform society but to earn money. "There is nothing," he maintained, "of less consequence to a public man than what the papers printed about him yesterday,—nothing of more consequence than what they may print about him to-morrow." [105]

In this remark, Raymond may have sold himself and his accomplishments short. Although he was no match for Bennett when it came to conniving, or for Greeley when it came to crusading, Henry Raymond retained an instinct for political power that his competitors could never match. Not for nothing was Raymond dubbed Lincoln's "Lieutenant-General in politics."

As surely as Washington morphed into a military fortress during wartime, it also became a well-supplied center of incoming and outgoing news. "There is probably no city in the Union," Noah Brooks marveled in mid-1863, "where the daily newspaper pabulum of the people is so varied as in Washington. From dusky morn till dusky eve we have a fresh relay of printer's ink, and a continuous and strident cry from the newsboys salutes each waking ear." Even so, Brooks dismissed Seaton and Welling's staid *Intelligencer* as "an ancient fossil," and Forney's newer *Chronicle* as a "Greek chorus" that automatically cheered all of Lincoln's "intentions or opinions . . . as the height of wisdom, skill, and ability." [106]

Forney continued to ride high until his hiatus in Europe, but on the last day of 1864, Seaton ended his decades-long ownership of the *Intelligencer* and sold the paper to the firm of Allen, Coyle, and Snow, who then converted it into an overtly pro-administration daily. James Welling promptly departed from the staff as tongues wagged over the sudden transition. But Washington became a consummate newspaper town not only because of its own array of morning and afternoon papers. As residents of the political and military center of gravity, its civilians, soldiers, public officials, and lobbyists consumed imported, out-of-town newspapers as avidly as they devoured their food and liquor at local hotels. As early as 1842, Greeley had promised that the *Tribune* would be "delivered each morning" to Washington subscribers, and he had kept his word, in peace and war. [107] Early each day, newsboys crowded the city's railroad depot to await trains bearing the incoming Baltimore and Philadelphia dailies, then rushed copies to eager readers on Capitol Hill and at Willard's hotel. By afternoon, when the New York papers arrived, the newsboys again grasped for bundles and began racing through the streets shouting the "savage whoop" of "New York *Erald*, *Times*, *Tribune*, and *Wurruld!*" [108]

By then, many prominent out-of-town newspapers had established news bureaus in the brick buildings near the White House along Pennsylvania Avenue, and north along Fourteenth Street. The area around Willard's abounded with satellite offices representing the nation's major dailies. Washington headquarters for the *Times*, *Tribune*, *World*, and *Boston Advertiser* clustered in structures usefully adjacent to the Western Union office. Their boldly lettered signs transformed the once sleepy neighborhood into a humming nerve center for political journalism. Here was more of an authentic "Newspaper Row" than existed even in Manhattan. The invigorating atmosphere inspired journalists Henry Villard, Horace White, and Adams Hill to establish a "Washington standpoint" of their own opposite Willard's: a new, independent feature service to supply stories to newspapers that lacked their own capital bureaus. [109] Calling their new press agency "the beginning in this country of the news syndicates," Villard quickly signed on as subscribers the *Chicago Tribune*, *Missouri Democrat*, *Cincinnati Commercial*, and *Boston Advertiser* to the tune of fifteen dollars a week each. [110] But in mid-1864, the three correspondents almost paid for their enterprise with their liberty.

The crisis that nearly destroyed Villard, White, and Hill in Washington began in New York, and originally involved two entirely different journalists, one of them the outspoken voice of the Copperhead Democrats, Manton Marble, the twenty-seven-year-old editor of the *New York World*. Marble had learned his craft at the *Boston Journal* before moving to New York to work for the antislavery *Evening Post*. He landed a job as night editor of the then-pro-administration *World* soon after it acquired the *Courier and Enquirer*. When the *World* faltered in April 1862, Marble borrowed money to buy it. He kept the paper in print, but by September his note came due, and he scoured the town in search of investors to keep it afloat. By one account, Marble first tried wooing conservative Republicans, perhaps even Thurlow Weed. When these efforts foundered, Marble agreed to sell shares to a group of anti-Lincoln Democrats, including ex-mayor Fernando Wood, Democratic National Committee Chairman August Belmont, and Samuel L. M. Barlow, a pro-slavery lawyer and longtime friend of presidential aspirant George McClellan. Marble sealed the deal by agreeing to support Democrat Horatio Seymour for New York governor in 1862. Several *New York World* staff members quit in protest. [111]

Marble's expedient political conversion transformed him almost overnight into New York's loudest anti-administration voice. He proved far abler than the raving editors at fringe papers like the *Daily News* and far harder to muzzle, though he predicted soon after rebranding the *World* that if he continued publishing anti-Lincoln editorials, "it will be at our peril." [112]

At the outset, the recapitalized paper supported prosecuting the war, as long as it meant "holding on to the Constitution with the same unyielding persistence," meaning opposition to administration initiatives to free slaves. [113] Eleven days after issuing that warning, Marble was shocked to learn that Lincoln had announced his Emancipation Proclamation, "for the Constitution confers on the federal government no power to change the domestic institutions of the States." [114] The expanded suspension of habeas corpus triggered further denunciation—particularly after investor Belmont founded the Society for the Diffusion of Political Knowledge in February 1863, and Marble began helping the anti-Lincoln organization draft an outpouring of hotly partisan pamphlets. The Vallandigham arrest that year Marble regarded as "a high handed assumption of despotic powers." [115] A month later, Marble learned from Democratic Ohio congressman Samuel "Sunset" Cox that General Burnside had banned the *World* from his military district. Cox told Marble that vendors were giving copies away "as waste paper." [116] Marble responded by intensifying his vitriolic attacks on Lincoln.

When the ax finally fell a year later, Marble's splenetic editorials ironically had nothing to do with the crackdown. In the predawn hours of May 18, 1864, an Associated Press messenger delivered to all its subscriber newspapers in New York—including the *World*—copies of the president's latest proclamation. Or so it appeared. The authentic-looking document urged a national day of "fasting, humiliation and prayer," hinted darkly about "the general state of the country," and called for

Manton Marble, virulently anti-administration editor of the *New York World*, published a bogus presidential proclamation in 1864, igniting a new crackdown against the press.

a breathtaking 400,000 new volunteers.[117] With Ulysses S. Grant enduring a bloodbath of casualties in a struggle to subdue Robert E. Lee in Virginia, the proclamation seemed a cry of desperation—an admission that to prevail, the Union required both divine intervention and a huge infusion of fresh troops. It was major news.

Presidential proclamations always arrived at the city's newspaper offices in the same routine manner. After their receipt at the New York AP over government-sanctioned telegraph wires, a clerk copied them using "manifold paper"—a recently perfected precursor to carbon paper. By inserting tissue-thin sheets of yellow paper between a manifold's waxy leaves, a copyist could simultaneously produce multiple copies. Once finished, the office manager dispatched runners to transport the resulting "flimsies" to every newspaper at once. Something about this particular message, however—perhaps its baroque literary style, the lateness of the hour, or the fact that messengers seemed to vanish seconds after delivering them—aroused suspicion at most night desks. Nearly all the town's papers opted not to publish the text before checking further with Washington—where officials instantly branded the proclamation a fraud. The *Tribune*, which had closed its editorial offices for the night by the time the "messenger" arrived, later chortled that the gullible *Herald* ran off twenty thousand copies of its morning edition with the proclamation featured before realizing its error, stopping the presses, and destroying the run.[118]

Two unlucky dailies, however, both of them allied with the antiwar Democrats—the *World* and the *Journal of Commerce*—fell for the hoax and printed the verbatim text in their May 18 issues. Though he later branded the forgery "an infamous outrage," *Journal of Commerce* editor William Prime insisted that the proclamation was "a perfect imitation of Associated Press dispatches in the minutest details."[119] Whether its publication was an accident or an act of partisan malice did not matter to Richard Yates, governor of Illinois, who anxiously wired Lincoln: "Is the proclamation in New York World . . . a genuine document? Please answer immediately." Lincoln quickly assured his old friend: "If any such proclamation has appeared, it is a forgery."[120] Yates's concern was understandable. Only a year earlier, another call for troops had unleashed draft riots, not only in New York, but in towns across the North.

To his credit, when Manton Marble realized that he, too, had been duped, he quickly announced a reward of $500 to apprehend and prosecute the forger. The gesture proved too little, too late, to save either him or his newspaper. The very day the proclamation appeared, after a hasty emergency meeting at the War Department—during which Seward and Stanton both urged a strong response—Seward issued a statement "to the public" branding the purported proclamation "an absolute forgery." [121] Then Stanton drafted, and the president signed, the only direct order Lincoln ever issued to close down a newspaper or arrest an editor, and sent it to General John Adams Dix, the New York–based commander who had helped put down the city's anti-draft disturbances in 1863:

> Whereas, there has been wickedly and traitorously printed and published this morning, in the "*New York World*" and New York "*Journal of Commerce*," newspapers printed and published in the city of New York—a false and spurious proclamation, purporting to be signed by the President . . . of a treasonable nature, designed to give aid and comfort to the enemies of the United States, and to the rebels now at war against the Government, and their aiders and abettors: you are therefore hereby commanded forthwith to arrest and imprison in any fort or military prison in your command, the editors, proprietors and publishers of the aforesaid newspapers. . . . You will also take possession by military force, of the printing establishments of the "*New York World*," and "*Journal of Commerce*," and hold the same until further order, and prevent any further publication therefrom. [122]

Although a flabbergasted Dix delayed executing the instructions—prompting several impatient reminders from Stanton in Washington—his troops finally seized and shuttered the two Democratic newspapers at ten o'clock that night, arresting both Marble and Prime, detaining them at army headquarters, and making plans to transport them by boat to the dreaded Fort Lafayette.

Within hours, in a repetition of the bipartisan outrage expressed after the 1863 shutdown of the *Chicago Times*, several New York papers rallied to Marble's and Prime's defense. Early on May 19, Sydney Gay of the *Tribune*, Erastus Brooks of the *Express*, and Frederic Hudson of the *Herald* telegraphed Lincoln jointly to argue that the hoax could easily have "succeeded in any daily newspaper establishment in this city," and that Marble and Prime "were innocent of any knowledge of wrong." Now that all editors, publishers, and news agents had placed themselves on high alert, Gay and his colleagues added, future hoaxes were unlikely. Their urgent recommendation was that the president "rescind the order under which the World and the Journal of Commerce were suppressed."[123]

Democratic papers nationwide rushed to express outrage, with the *Boston Commonwealth* snickering that Lincoln would surely "be punished in the 'World' to come." Even Republican editor William Cullen Bryant called the suppression "a violation of the constitutional guarantees of freedom of the press." Not everyone agreed. Henry Raymond maintained that Marble and Prime remained culpable regardless of whether they had fallen for the hoax out of "malice or neglect," arguing: "How does liberty of discussion involve the name of forging the name of the President of the United States? Such a forgery has been committed. The two papers named have given currency to it."[124]

Marble and Prime barely avoided deportation to the American Bastille, but not until Saturday, May 21, were they allowed to reopen their newspapers. Since neither issued Sunday editions, they did not resume publication until Monday the 23rd. Fortunately for the beleaguered Democratic editors, two days earlier General Dix had identified the author of the counterfeit proclamation as Joseph Howard, Jr., the same onetime *New York Times* correspondent who three years earlier had invented the libel that Lincoln wore a Scotch cap disguise to slip through Baltimore. Now employed as an associate editor by the *Brooklyn Eagle*, Howard had apparently devised the scheme for an entirely apolitical reason: to make a financial killing. He believed that news of a massive troop call-up would signal military desperation and cause the stock market to plummet. Then Howard could move in and buy gold, whose price was sure to soar in the resulting panic. Before the hoax came to light and prices plummeted, he could sell at a profit.

Gideon Welles leaped to the conclusion that the culprit was one "of a pestiferous class of reckless sensation-writers for an unscrupulous set of journalists who inform the public mind." The navy secretary had little good to say about any member of the Fourth Estate. "Scarcely one of them," he fumed, "has regard for truth, and nearly all make sure of their positions to subserve selfish, mercenary ends. This forger and falsifier Howard is a specimen of the miserable tribe."[125] Nonetheless, Welles regretted that Lincoln moved so harshly against the two New York papers, blaming Seward and Stanton for exciting him into overwrought retaliation. "The seizure of the office of the *World* and *Journal of Commerce*," he confided to his diary, "was hasty, rash, inconsiderate, and wrong, and cannot be defended. They are mischievous and pernicious, working assiduously against the Union and the Government and giving countenance and encouragement to the Rebellion, but were in this instance the dupes, perhaps the willing dupes, of a knave and wretch." Welles was hardly the only government official to object. At least two congressmen introduced resolutions of inquiry, and even Nicolay and Hay later admitted that the shutdowns were indefensible. Welles glumly predicted that the arrests would "weaken the Administration and strengthen its enemies." [126]

Especially if Marble had anything to say about it. Once he regained his freedom and his presses, the vengeful editor took the first opportunity to issue a long, denunciatory protest—using Lincoln's own "public letter" format to vilify him. Published under the bold, stacked headline, "Popular Rebuke of the Military Raid on the Press. THE 'WORLD' MOVING AGAIN," Marble's message to the president began with a methodical defense of the actions he had taken once he realized his night staff had been duped into typesetting the fake proclamation. Later, "printers and pressmen" were "brought from their homes and beds to put in type and publish the news of our misfortune." The sale of morning editions was promptly halted, he insisted, and a boat bound for Nova Scotia en route to Europe to distribute the May 18 issue was detained at the docks—though the War Department believed that Marble actually intended to dispatch the shipment even though he knew the proclamation was bogus. "But to characterize the proceedings as unprecedented," Marble lectured Lincoln, "would be to forget the past history of your administration; and to characterize them as shocking to every mind, would be to disregard the principle of human nature from which it arises . . . do not imagine that the people of this city or state, or country have ceased to love their liberties, or do not know how to protect their rights. It would be fatal to a tyrant to commit that error here and now." To Marble, Lincoln was no better than King Charles I, who was "doubtless advised to, and applauded for, the crimes by which he lost his crown and life." [127]

The *World* has "been ungagged," diarist George Templeton Strong commented, and "vomits acid bile most copiously . . . full of protest and fury . . . suggesting, *inter alia*, a parallel between Uncle Abe Lincoln and Charles the First! One might as well compare dirty little penny-a-lining Marble with Catiline." Strong wondered: "Will this most novel suggestion tempt Honest Old Abe to cultivate a peaked beard and long curls and to extend his shirt collar into a wide area of ornamental lace?" [128] Republican papers, divided over the original suppression order, now united to condemn Marble's "impudent" letter to the president.

Marble left no doubt that he believed the suppression of the *World* was politically motivated. "Had the *Tribune* and *Times* published the forgery," he demanded of the president, "(and the *Tribune* candidly admits that it might have published it and was prevented only by mere chance) would you, sir, have suppressed the *Tribune* and *Times* as you suppressed THE WORLD and *Journal of Commerce*? You know you would not." Marble insisted that Governor Seymour prosecute Dix and all the officers who had acted against him, a course of action that posed the threat of a constitutional crisis. Seymour obliged by ordering New York district attorney "Elegant" Oakey Hall, himself a onetime newspaperman, to launch an inquiry. A grand jury convened, but in June refused to indict.[129] Reluctant to drop the matter, the governor pressured Hall to issue a warrant for Dix's arrest. The case was heard before City Court Judge A. D. Russell—although at Lincoln's instructions Dix refused to appear: he was "not to relieve himself of his command or be deprived of his liberty for obeying an order of a military nature which the President of the United States directs him to execute." Not until July did the district attorney give up and drop the charges.[130]

JOSEPH HOWARD, JUN., THE FORGER.

Joseph Howard, Jr., of the *Brooklyn Eagle* forged the counterfeit presidential proclamation in 1864 and ended up in Fort Lafayette. Three years earlier, the same reporter had invented the story that President-elect Lincoln had sneaked through Baltimore in disguise.

Still the imbroglio refused to die. Unlike Marble and Prime, the real culprits, Joseph Howard and a cohort, *Brooklyn Eagle* reporter Francis Mallison, did end up at Fort Lafayette, and languished in confinement there for months. Not until August did Henry Ward Beecher, an old friend of the Howard family, ask for mercy, offering Public Printer John Defrees the lame excuse that "Joe" had been "the tool" of a "man who turned states evidence and escaped." Defrees forwarded Beecher's plea to Lincoln, who three weeks later instructed Stanton: "I very much wish to oblige Henry Ward Beecher, by releasing Howard; but I wish you to be satisfied when it is done—What say you?" Stanton replied, "I have no objection if you think it right—and this a proper time." The president issued an order freeing the reporter on August 23: "Let Howard, imprisoned in regard to the bogus proclamation, be discharged."[131]

Defrees then urged Lincoln to release Mallison as well, pointing out that since he was a Democrat (Howard was actually a Republican), the latter's parole was "being used to shew that the President uses his power for party friends."[132] In this case it took a remorseful letter from Howard himself— admitting that Mallison had been "comparatively subordinate in the affair" and assuring Lincoln of "sincere regret at my folly"—to earn presidential clemency. It helped that the chastened Howard, too, believed "that certain 'Democratic' stumpers are making a handle of his continued confinement, taking the absurd ground that he is held on account of his Democratic affiliation." On September 20, Lincoln ordered Stanton: "Let Mallison, the bogus proclamation man, be discharged."[133]

Yet Lincoln never stooped to explain, much less apologize for, the arrests and shutdowns in New York—or, as Marble put it, to "confess and repair your mistake" and "make reparation for the wrong you have done."[134] In fact, the evidence suggests that the president not only tolerated, but perhaps encouraged, a far wider crackdown at the time, believing the forged proclamation to be a much more dangerous hoax than he ever publicly admitted. For the very night before the *World* published Howard's forgery, the president had been working on an authentic proclamation that indeed called for more troops—300,000 more, to be precise—by either enlistment or conscription.[135] The sudden appearance of the Howard forgery unleashed panic within the White House and among the cabinet: fear that someone may have leaked a genuine proclamation, and one for which Lincoln had not yet laid the needed political and press groundwork. James Gilmore was told that while the *World* announcement was "a fabrication," Lincoln "had decided to call for 300,000 in July, but not before." Now he had good reason to fear that what appeared to be its premature leak might incite another deadly anti-draft riot in New York—worst of all, in an election year.[136]

Seward and Stanton did far more than convince the president to suppress the *World* and *Journal of Commerce*. Though, as it was later shown, Howard alone had forged the spurious document, using a stylus that Mallison stole from the *Tribune*, the administration expanded its initial crackdown. That same day, Stanton ordered General Dix to seize and occupy the New York offices of the new Independent Telegraph Company, which had recently begun service as an alternative provider of the official dispatches carried for the AP by the American Telegraph Company. The War Department monitored traffic on the AP, but not on the Independent lines. Although it was the Associated Press that had inadvertently wired the bogus proclamation west, the agency remained unpunished while the entire New York staff of the Independent Telegraph wound up at Fort Lafayette. The administration also closed down its offices in Baltimore, Harrisburg, Pittsburgh, and Philadelphia (where it was called Inland Telegraph), and began dragging various employees to Washington for questioning.[137]

Not yet satisfied that he had identified the source of what he still believed might have been a dangerous security breach, Stanton ordered his aide Major Thomas Eckert to invade the Washington bureau of the Independent Telegraph Company as well. Under his direction, authorities seized the Twelfth Street premises, searched the files, closed down the operation, interrogated its operators, including superintendent James N. Worl, and shipped the lot of them to the Old Capitol Prison in a drenching rain. Finally, Stanton inexplicably ordered the shutdown of the guiltless little news syndicate operated in the capital by Henry Villard, Adams Hill, and Horace White. On May 19, White endured intense interrogation, Hill was placed under "observation," and the loyal Villard, incredibly, ended up briefly imprisoned.[138] If Stanton could not control news at the point of publication, then he would suppress it at its point of origin—even if in this case, the sources he identified were not in the slightest way complicit in the proclamation hoax. Not for days were the wholly innocent Independent Telegraph operators released. Stanton tried atoning for his brutal haste by offering the fledgling operation the privilege of linking its lines to the War Department, as telegraph operator David Homer Bates remembered, "so that a share of the Government telegraph business might be given to them."[139]

If Joseph Howard, Jr., Francis Mallison, Henry Villard, Adams Hill, and Horace White—or even Manton Marble and William Prime—ever knew for a fact that Abraham Lincoln was working on a genuine proclamation calling for hundreds of thousands of new men to come to the aid of Ulysses Grant in Virginia, they never admitted so. Yet all of them paid a heavy price for a coincidental hoax that inspired Abraham Lincoln's one and only direct curtailment of a free press. What happened next was almost as extraordinary as the temporary relaxation of censorship that had followed the crackdowns during the 1861 summer of rage. With a presidential election fast approaching, the government once again retreated from the wave of harsh oversight. Military secrets remained under strict ban, but political censorship became off limits. Freedom of the press made another comeback in war-torn America.

In a kind of ironic coda, Lincoln finally issued his proclamation on July 18. It called not for 300,000, or even 400,000 new volunteers—but half a million![140]

Just weeks after the New York newspaper shutdowns, and while the latest suppression controversy was still dominating the political conversation, Republicans headed to their presidential nominating convention at Baltimore. For several months leading up to that event, Lincoln's path to a second term had been frustrated by opposition from within his party—fanned by the blatant exertions of Horace Greeley to derail his candidacy and find a substitute to run in his place, an effort that had nothing to do with fears about tyranny and press suppression.

As early as mid-1863, in much the same determined way he had pressed his successful effort to block William Seward at Chicago four years before, Greeley sent James Gilmore to Murfreesboro, Tennessee, to see if General William Rosecrans might be interested in making the race. Rosecrans not only rejected the overture, but admonished Gilmore, "you are mistaken about Mr. Lincoln. He is in his right place."[141] (Gilmore loyally reported his secret mission to the president.) Even Greeley was forced to admit that Lincoln still exerted an almost mystical tug on many voters: "The People think of him night & day and pray for him & their hearts are where they have made so heavy investments."[142] Nonetheless, the editor remained convinced that Lincoln should be denied a second term, and stepped up his search for an antislavery alternative. Although his opposition has often been ascribed to his belief that he did not think Lincoln could be reelected, there is no doubt that Greeley opposed Lincoln over policy differences as well. "I wanted the war driven onward with vehemence," the editor unconvincingly tried explaining a few years later, "and this was not in his nature."[143]

In a *Tribune* editorial published in late February entitled "Opening the Presidential Campaign," Greeley argued that Lincoln had failed to prove himself "so transcendentally able" as to preclude consideration of men like Treasury Secretary Chase or Generals Benjamin Butler, John C. Frémont, or even Ulysses Grant. "We freely admit Mr. Lincoln's merits," the editorial continued, "but we insist that they are not such as to eclipse and obscure those of all the statesmen and soldiers who have aided in the great work of saving the country from disruption and overthrow." [144] The pro-Lincoln editor of the Erie, Pennsylvania, *Gazette* warned Simon Cameron—in a letter the ex–war secretary promptly shared with the president—that "Greeley of the Tribune is manifesting his usual want of judgment." [145] Greeley had yet formally to propose an alternative, but for now it was anyone but Lincoln. A few weeks later, Greeley punctuated his discontent by attending a Frémont rally at Cooper Union.

With Greeley's encouragement, the ambitious Chase stepped up his own maneuvering to wrest the Republican nomination from the president. On September 29, 1863, Greeley wrote the treasury secretary to vow, "if in 1864 I could *make* a President (not merely a candidate) you would be my first choice." Three days later, Greeley sent his friend, *Tribune* stockholder Benjamin Camp, to visit Chase in Washington, after which Chase breathlessly confided to his diary that Camp "proposed plan for collecting public sentiment in my favor as candidate for Presy." [146] But the boomlet collapsed in March, and Chase resigned from the cabinet in embarrassment, proving no match for Lincoln in wooing support from politicians and journalists alike.

Like Rosecrans, Grant soon made it clear that he, too, wanted no part of a challenge to his commander-in-chief, so Greeley resumed promoting Frémont. Still a darling of the progressive, so-called Radical wing of the Republican Party, Frémont emerged as a viable third-party candidate after a convention of disaffected Union men, war Democrats, and German-American admirers met in Cleveland on May 31 and nominated him by acclamation. Evidently Greeley did not take the third-party movement seriously, for he continued to lobby the Republican organization to dump Lincoln at Baltimore. On the eve of the national convention, Greeley was still warning: "Mr. Lincoln is already beaten. He cannot be elected. And we must have another ticket to save us from utter overthrow. If we had such a ticket as could be made by naming Grant, Butler or Sherman for President, we could make a fight yet." [147]

No real competition materialized. By the time the Republicans, now united under the banner of the National Union Party, gaveled into order at Baltimore in early June, Lincoln's nomination was a foregone conclusion. And it was not Horace Greeley but Henry Raymond, the new chairman of the party, who won the most "boisterous applause" at the convention, just as Greeley had in 1860. Delegates shouted their approval when Senator Edwin D. Morgan proposed a platform plank calling for a constitutional amendment banning slavery. But they broke out into "yells and cheers unbounded as soon as the beloved name of Lincoln was spoken."[148]

As soon as the convention adjourned, New York *Independent* editor Theodore Tilton headed from Baltimore to Washington to visit the president and report to him on the gathering. At the White House, he told Lincoln how especially pleased convention delegates had been when they first heard Morgan introduce the resolution to end slavery. Interrupting him, the president claimed his own share of credit for the initiative. "It was I who suggested to Mr. Morgan that he should put that idea into his opening speech," the president proudly pointed out. He was not about to let an antislavery editor return home believing that another leader had originated the momentous recommendation. Fully convinced, Tilton called it "the very best word he has said since the proclamation of freedom" and published the news.[149]

Lincoln may have stayed home during the Baltimore convention, but he had worked his political magic from a distance to push what would become the Thirteenth Amendment to the Constitution and he wanted the press to know it.

CHAPTER FIFTEEN

Long Abraham a Little Longer

James Gordon Bennett spent most of the 1864 election year openly excoriating Abraham Lincoln in print, while Horace Greeley labored to undermine the president more surreptitiously—plotting to replace Lincoln at the top of the Republican ticket even after the convention renominated him. Republican chairman Henry Raymond, on the other hand, publicly advocated for Lincoln's candidacy, while fretting privately that it could not succeed.

For his part, Lincoln labored with extraordinary patience and skill behind the scenes to get New York's two powerful, but perennially feuding, Republican editors committed to his reelection. And he toiled with particular dexterity to defang Bennett's supposedly independent but consistently pro-Democratic *Herald*. As always, the intense maneuvering played out against the backdrop of the editors' insatiable appetite for political reward and their irreconcilable antipathy toward each other. The challenge for Lincoln in late 1864 proved enormous.

Merely attending to the Big Three's often conflicting patronage expectations proved no easy matter—and the balancing act became more fraught when other editors demanded their share of influence, too. In June, William Cullen Bryant protested when his publisher, Isaac Henderson, lost his post as a navy agent and endured the humiliation of arrest for alleged "frauds on the government." Lincoln not only defended the dismissal (though he assured Bryant that due process would be respected), he seized on the occasion to lecture the antislavery patriarch with uncharacteristic irritation. "While the subject is up," he wrote Bryant, "may I ask whether the Evening Post has not assailed me for supposed too lenient dealing with persons charged of fraud & crime? and that in cases of which the Post could know but little of the facts?" Bryant could only thank Lincoln for confirming his reputation for "equity and love of justice," and assure him that the *Post* had never consciously offered an "assault" on his "public conduct."[1] Bryant would remain firmly in the president's corner for the rest of the campaign.

In early spring, however, Henry Raymond's upstate ally (and Greeley enemy) Thurlow Weed signaled patronage expectations of his own. Weed let the president know that he felt unappreciated and ignored, a complaint the perplexed Lincoln could not wave off without risking political damage. "I have been both pained and surprised recently at learning that you are wounded because a suggestion of yours as to the mode of conducting our national difficulty, has not been followed," Lincoln wrote him on March 25, "—pained, because I very much wish you to have no unpleasant feeling proceeding from me, and surprised, because my impression is that I have seen you . . . apparantly feeling very cheerful and happy. How is this?"[2]

In a conspicuous show of respect, Lincoln sent John Nicolay all the way to New York City to hand-deliver this conciliatory letter directly to Weed at the Astor House. "He read it over carefully once or twice," Nicolay reported back, "and then said he didn't quite understand it." Weed's only recent gripe had involved federal patronage at the U.S. Customs House in New York, not the "national difficulty." He (and William Seward) wanted Salmon Chase ally Hiram Barney ousted from his lucrative job as Collector of the Port of New York, and they warned that if the president did not expunge such "weak" and "intriguing" appointees, some of whom "had been engaged in treasonably aiding the rebellion," their presence would jeopardize Republican success in the forthcoming elections. Weed and Raymond eventually got their wish, but only after another visit to New York by Nicolay, and another secret conference, this time at the offices of the *New York Times*. As long as Lincoln had brought up the "national difficulty," however, Weed seized the opportunity to advise him that the entire cabinet ought to be reshuffled, for Welles was a "cypher, Bates a fogy, and Blair at best a dangerous friend."[3]

That Lincoln humored Weed may have reflected an abiding respect for the party boss, or perhaps an ongoing need to placate all the Empire State editors who sometimes seemed more determined to defeat each other than to beat the Democrats. Lincoln apparently satisfied Weed, at least for a while, because no further grousing came from the Albany powerhouse that campaign season—even though his first choice to replace Barney, Abram Wakeman, failed to get the coveted job.[4] It would not be the last time the president would misinterpret a letter from the so-called Wizard of the Lobby. Denied the right to collaborate with Weed in naming a new collector, Raymond resumed peppering the White House with other patronage recommendations.[5]

Unlike Republican papers, whose loyalty to Lincoln sometimes wavered over the issue of federal vacancies, the Copperhead press differed with the president on fundamental issues, and aired its grievances harshly and unrelentingly throughout the campaign. In perhaps the most infamous example, beginning in April and for five continuous months, the *New York World* hammered away at the scabrous charge that during an inspection trip to Antietam back in 1862, Lincoln had callously urged his traveling companion, Ward Hill Lamon, to sing a comic song as the two strolled among the dead and wounded still littering the battlefield. "The American people are in no mood to re-elect a man to the highest office," the *World* howled a few weeks after Lincoln's nomination, "whose daily language is indecent, and who, rising over the field of Antietam, when thirty thousand of his fellow citizens were yet warm in their freshly made graves, could . . . call for the negro song of 'Picayune Butler.'"[6] The paper punctuated its attack with a comic ditty of its own: "Abe may crack his jolly jokes / O'er bloody fields of stricken battle, / While yet the ebbing life-tide smokes / From men that die like butchered cattle."[7]

Even though the libel was at first confined to the pages of hostile Democratic sheets like the *World*, it was repeated often enough to prompt one concerned pro-war Democrat to warn Horace Greeley in April that the story must be "authentically contradicted." Looking on the bright side, the correspondent hoped that "if the charge can be disproved," then other members of his party would "forsake the fortunes of Mac the Unready"—meaning George McClellan, the likely Democratic nominee for president—for surely even Peace Democrats would "not support a party resorting to such brutal charges."[8] Typically, Lincoln resisted the impulse to respond, even after Lamon warned him that he was being "painted as the prime mover in a scene of fiendish levity more atrocious than the world had ever witnessed since human nature was shamed and degraded by the capers of Nero and Commodus."[9]

"Let the thing alone," Lincoln insisted. "If I have not established character enough to give the lie to this charge, I can only say that I am mistaken in my own estimate of myself. In politics, every man must skin his own skunk. These fellows are welcome to the hide of this one. Its body has already given forth its unsavory odor." [10]

Then on September 9, the *World* issued the most scurrilous version of the story yet. This time it alleged that McClellan, Lincoln's host on the day in question at Antietam, had heroically attempted to halt the inappropriate serenade by telling the president: "Not now, if you please. . . . I would prefer to hear it some other place and time." [11] The latest report prompted yet another fevered letter of concern, this time addressed directly to Lamon, insisting that the "damaging" report must be denied once and for all. Lamon hastened back to the White House armed with his own draft response to the *World*. Still, the president hesitated. "I would not publish this reply," he told Lamon after reading it. "It is too belligerent in tone. . . . If I were you, I would simply state the facts as they were . . . without the pepper and salt." Then Lincoln unexpectedly offered, "Let me try my hand at it." [12] Taking up pen and paper, he began ghostwriting a letter to the editor himself.

In the version of the Antietam episode Lincoln crafted that day: "Neither Gen. McClellan or any one else made any objection to the singing; the place was not on the battle field, the time was sixteen days after the battle, no dead body was seen during the whole time the president was absent from Washington, nor even a grave that had not been rained on since it was made." Though the account radiated with his unique literary style, the president asked Lamon to sign his own name to it. [13] But inevitably, Lincoln's characteristic "better angels" again took hold, and he told his friend, "I dislike to appear as an apologist for an act of my own which I know was right. Keep this paper, and we will see about it." The statement was not made public after all. A frustrated Lamon, who later explained that he had volunteered comic songs near Antietam only to bring his friend out of a "spell of . . . melancholy," was never allowed that entire campaign season to express his belief that "Mr. Lincoln was as incapable of insulting the dead . . . as he was of committing mean and unmanly outrages upon the living." [14]

Emboldened and unchallenged, the *World* and the city's other Democratic papers stepped up their attacks. The Antietam episode enjoyed relentless additional exposure, inspiring publication of a slanderous cartoon entitled *The COMMANDER-IN-CHIEF conciliating the SOLDIER'S VOTES on the Battle*

Field. The lithograph depicted a heartless Lincoln ignoring the bleeding troops strewn across the landscape as he asks Lamon to "sing us 'Picayune Butler,' or something else that's funny." In a significant break with tradition, the *New York World* itself engineered publication of this and several other campaign cartoons, three of them warning of an "abolition catastrophe" should Lincoln win a second term. A fourth portrayed Lincoln, Greeley, and other Republicans burying the last vestiges of the "Constitution, the Union, Habeas Corpus, Free Speech, and Free Press" in order to promote their secret goal of racial equality.[15] Until publication of these ferocious caricatures, campaign prints had always been commercial products, issued by publishers seeking profits, not political advantage. Now, for the first time, a party newspaper had coordinated production not only of editorial invective, but also caricatures, and, as would soon be revealed, a mischievous book project as well.

The bizarre book venture was an elaborate hoax masterminded by the race-obsessed *World* to ensnare the president into supporting a mock proposal for white-black amalgamation. The broader goal was to make the supposedly genuine "threat" of black equality the key scare tactic in the race to deny the president a second term. But for the book ploy to succeed, the *World* assumed Lincoln's gullibility, and few enemies ever triumphed by underestimating him. The plot began unfolding when Bromley & Company, the same printers assigned to issue the paper's anti-Lincoln cartoons, published the ninety-page tract by *World* correspondents David G. Croly and George Wakeman. Entitled *Miscegenation: The Theory of the Blending of the Races*, the deadpan text was crafted to outrage Negrophobic Democrats by soberly designating the Civil War as a struggle for "the blending of the white and the black" to achieve social harmony.[16]

The authors, in truth flagrant bigots, next dispatched a copy of their incendiary booklet to the White House, straightforwardly asking Lincoln for his endorsement. Had he offered praise for the publication, the *World* planned to use it as proof of the president's latent enthusiasm for race mixing. Instead, suspecting at once that a fraud was afoot, Lincoln tossed both the request and the book into his files and never replied, hinting to friendly journalists that he had foiled an attempt to draw him into a dangerous intrigue. Not to be outdone, while the *World* itself refrained from overtly promoting Croly and Wakeman's *Miscegenation*—preferring that readers conclude that the book had appeared spontaneously—editor Manton Marble encouraged like-minded Copperhead publications to hail it. In a supreme show of self-confidence, the publishers even advertised the volume in William Lloyd Garrison's abolitionist paper, *The Liberator*. The *World* did arrange the uncredited publication of a *Miscegenation* lithograph visualizing the dangers of a "millennium of abolitionism" in a Lincoln-led future. The image showed the president cordially bowing to a mixed-race couple, while in the background white liverymen drive black passengers in a carriage. And here was a caricatured Horace Greeley as well. The anonymous artist portrayed the Old Philosopher eating ice cream alongside a black woman.

Though he deftly sidestepped the *Miscegenation* plot, Lincoln continued to endure ferocious attacks from the white supremacist New York press. John Van Evrie, publisher of the *New York Weekly Day-Book*, a paper founded on the ashes of the onetime daily the administration had suppressed back in 1861, produced a screed of his own entitled *Subgenation*. Though cast as an earnest rebuttal to the outrages proposed in *Miscegenation*, it is unlikely that its author was not aware that the *World's* book was a hoax, or that his response was certainly designed to perpetuate the controversy it ignited. Arguing perversely that the Southern states which had denied the so-called "lower races" their rights had as a result incubated the most "democratic ideas," Van Evrie's book charged Lincoln with hatching a secret plan to erect a new government "founded on miscegenation," and asked voters: "Shall we allow him to do so?" [17]

In the same vein, the *New York Daily News* fanned the flames by warning that, despite Lincoln's supposed enthusiasm for amalgamation, white women would never consent to reproduce with black men because "the negro's body is disagreeably unctuous, especially . . . when under the strong 'emotional' excitement so certainly produced on his animal nature if permitted to follow her with lascivious glances." [18] In a no less repugnant report, the *New York Freeman's Journal* complained that "filthy black niggers . . . now jostle white people and even ladies everywhere, even at the President's levees." [19] Such inflammatory articles harped on a common theme: Lincoln's reelection would pollute America by making blacks the equals of whites, and encouraging interracial sexual congress.

When he was not assailing Lincoln and the "*national humiliation*" of military stalemate, Manton Marble predictably aimed barbs against Greeley, taunting him as "the great agriculturalist" who has "beaten his plowshare into a bayonet." [20] By October, the *World* darkly hinted that Greeley had "lost all moral control over the insubordinate type-setters, the eccentric model-farmers, the moon-struck poets, the free-lovers, the socialists, the long-haired abolitionists, and the other human beings of all colors of political doctrine . . . who make up that unhappy family known as 'The Tribune Association.'"[21]

The *World* meanwhile solidified its role as the official national organ of the Democrats. When the party ill-advisedly postponed its national convention from July 4 to August 29, a move that left too little time for the fall campaign, it was to Marble that George McClellan confided his displeasure at the delay; the general petulantly threatened to refuse to have his "name used" as a candidate until he was formally nominated.[22] Once the campaign did get under way, the *World* tried making up for lost time with a series of hagiographical pieces puffing McClellan's military record, accompanied by a barrage of renewed attacks on his opponent. "Lincoln has been as dishonest as he has been unjust in his treatment of General McClellan," went a typical editorial in late September. In another salvo, Marble charged Lincoln with "four years of usurpation, of lawless, reckless, mis-government." And in a series of

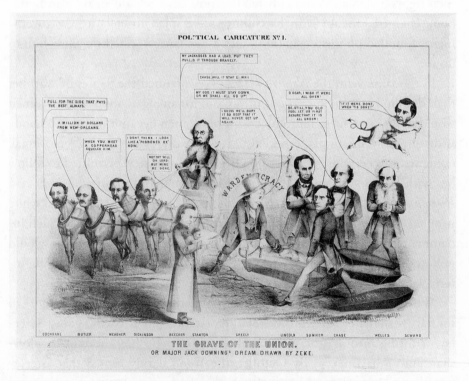

Greeley (center) helps lower the coffins of Union, Habeas Corpus, and Freedom of the Press into "The Grave of the Union" in an anti-Lincoln 1864 campaign print engineered by the *New York World*.

front-page stories that ran through autumn, Marble bombarded readers with provocative headlines: "Why Mr. Lincoln Should Be Removed from Office," "Mr. Lincoln's Plot to Disenfranchise Maryland," "The South to Be Throttled and the Negroes Freed," "Abraham Lincoln: Is He Honest? Is He Capable?" and "McClellan Is the Hope of the Nation."[23]

In these and other front-page stories, the *World* accused Lincoln of such sins as relentless partisanship, corruption, abuse of power, spiking the national debt, encouraging violence against Democrats, abetting fraud in local elections, and approving "Postoffice espionage." Lincoln, Marble charged, based his presidency on "no principle [and] no respect for law."[24] In September, the *World* sensationally charged that New York Republicans had staged a shocking "Miscegenation Ball" at party headquarters, at which mixed-race couples allegedly cavorted on the dance floor—a report that in turn inspired yet another anti-Republican cartoon. The potential for a politically damaging scandal prompted Greeley's *Tribune* to denounce "the scoundrelly *World*" for encouraging it.[25] When not portraying Lincoln as a dangerous radical, Marble mocked him as a crude jester. Just before Election Day, the *World* again put its contempt into rhyme: "There is an old joker named Aby— / Who, it must be confessed, is a gaby; / He sickens the folks / With his malaprop jokes / Till they vow to get rid of old Aby."[26]

That such unabashedly vicious coverage emanated from New York unchecked in 1864 certainly demonstrated an extraordinary and seldom acknowledged shift in the political culture. Earlier that year, Judge Advocate General Joseph Holt had left little doubt that he believed that anti-administration editors like Marble and Wood posed a genuine threat to the Union. They poisoned the "community," Holt complained, "a large part of whom, styling themselves democrats, and professing strong attachment to the constitution and government of the United States, adopted the opinions and prejudices speciously inculcated by the widely circulated New York press, hostile to the administration and its principal measures for conducting the war." Holt believed that "such newspapers, denouncing the draft as unconstitutional, and calling on the people to oppose it were read at public meetings . . . and there appears to be reason for the belief that some honest and patriotic men were deceived by them." Despite such concerns, for the most part, the previously restrained free press again operated freely throughout the heated presidential race, a condition for which Lincoln has received too little credit.[27]

No record exists of any official decision to relax censorship and suppression during the political campaign, but the absence of any renewed crackdown strongly suggests a new tolerance. There were exceptions. General Lew Wallace did suppress two antiwar Baltimore papers in September—the *Loyalist* and the *Evening Post*—prompting Manton Marble to warn his readers that should Lincoln be reelected he would surely impose similar restrictions everywhere, and "throughout the term of his natural life." [28] And in August, a pro-Democratic Maine editor was indicted for treason in the federal courts for writing an anti-draft editorial entitled "More Victims for the Slaughter Called For"—but also, court papers hinted, for consorting with foreign agents in a scheme to furnish "arms munitions and supplies of war and fitted out armed vessels for the prosecution of . . . war against the United States." [29] But these cases were the exceptions, not the rule.

Proof of the administration's otherwise unwavering commitment to an unshackled press during election season could be found in its tolerance of an editor who had nearly been confined to Fort Lafayette earlier in the year: Marble himself. Lincoln had previously vowed that he would restrict press freedom only when it endangered the troops or the Union itself. During the campaign, he proved his sincerity by tolerating unrestrained political attacks in the Democratic papers. Having confounded many of his critics merely by allowing the election to proceed during a rebellion, Lincoln now demonstrated his faith in the right of the people to choose their leaders, even during civil war, by accompanying that decision with a commitment to unrestricted press coverage as well.

Further evidence of this election-year tolerance came when prospects looked bleakest for Republicans. In August, the *New York Tribune* writer James Gilmore managed to secure and publish an interview with Jefferson Davis, one of the few profiles of the Confederate president to appear in the North during the war. The fact that it promoted Davis's hope for a negotiated peace infuriated some of Lincoln's friends, who feared that war-weary voters would unseat him if he resisted a credible proposal to stanch the bloodshed. "What business had these fellows with such a subject?" fumed Navy Secretary Gideon Welles. "They place the President . . . at a disadvantage in the coming election." [30] Welles clearly did not know that the president not only sanctioned publication, but endorsed the periodical Gilmore proposed for its appearance. For when Lincoln learned that the audacious Gilmore had conducted his interview with Davis, he welcomed the journalist to the White

House with a hearty, "I'm glad you're back," and an impatient, "What is it,—as we expected?"

"Exactly so," came Gilmore's reply. "There is no peace without separation. Coming down on the boat, I wrote out the interview to read to you when you are at leisure."

"I am at leisure now," answered Lincoln impatiently. So Gilmore read his proposed press report aloud at the executive mansion. When he was finished, Lincoln asked eagerly, "What do you propose to do with this?"

"Put a beginning and an end to it, sir, on my way home, and hand it to the *Tribune.*"

"Can't you get it into the *Atlantic Monthly*?" countered Lincoln. "It would have less of a partisan look there."

"No doubt I can, sir," Gilmore replied, "but there would be some delay about it."

"And it is important that Davis's position should be known at once," Lincoln agreed. "It will show the country that I didn't fight shy of Greeley's Niagara business without a reason; and everybody is agog to hear your report. Let it go into the *Tribune.*"

In the end, the two men came up with yet another plan: place a brief report about Davis's insistence on independence in a Boston newspaper, then a longer story later in the *Atlantic.* Not content with dictating the release of information and the exclusion of Horace Greeley one final time, Lincoln added a request for further control: "Send me the proof of what goes into the *Atlantic.* Don't let it appear till I return the proof. . . . This may be worth as much to us as half a dozen battles." [31]

Gilmore escaped further criticism, but that is not to say that spontaneous outbreaks against newspapers did not occur during the year. Among the more than thirty papers sacked by mobs in 1864 were the *Fairfield* (Iowa) *Constitution and Union,* the (Meadville, Pennsylvania) *Crawford Democrat*, and the *Chester* (Illinois) *Picket Guard.* Civilian mobs did their most pernicious work in Ohio, while federal authorities focused on slave states like Maryland, Missouri, and Kentucky—for example banning all Democratic papers (save the *Missouri Republican*) from circulating in Memphis in October. However chilling, compared to the suppression fever of 1861, such outbreaks remained rare in 1864. [32]

Meanwhile, Lincoln continued to face political flare-ups ignited by journalists from his own party. During the summer, Chicago postmaster John L.

Scripps initiated a re-election challenge to the president's friend, sitting congressman Isaac Arnold, and allegedly used his own hundred postal appointees to promote his candidacy among local Republicans. The outraged incumbent fired off a letter of protest to Lincoln, who had appointed Scripps to his plum job back in 1861. "Is it right or fair," demanded Arnold, "that the power of the government should be used to crush one who has sustained the administration as faithfully as I have?" Lincoln drafted a carefully written letter to Scripps, omitting specific names and merely reporting the "complaint" that the postmaster was using his "official power" to defeat a congressman with whom he was "well satisfied." Lincoln proposed a "correct principle" to guide both of the aspirants to the coveted seat: "all our friends should have absolute freedom of choice." Arnold almost gleefully reported that Scripps received the note "in a storm of rage & passion . . . said it was an insult" and branded as "untrue" the charge that he had "used his office" to promote his candidacy. Pressed to publish a "general circular" advising all postmasters against political activities, Lincoln withdrew from the controversy altogether. In the end, neither Arnold nor Scripps won the congressional seat. The Republican nomination fell to yet another onetime editor, John Wentworth.[33]

James Gilmore's interview with Jefferson Davis was hardly the most potentially subversive press gambit undertaken that campaign summer. That dubious honor belonged to Gilmore's imprudent backer Horace Greeley. Like many Republicans, Greeley wanted an end to both slavery and war; but unlike most, he oscillated between one exclusive aspiration and the other, adding to his reputation for grandiose waffling. By mid-1864 the formerly hawkish Greeley suddenly concluded that an exhausted North above all wanted a cessation of hostilities. And he believed he had found a means to achieve that goal. For more than a year, the editor had been quietly discussing peace with a shady antiwar Democrat from Maine named William Cornell "Colorado" Jewett, who now proposed bringing Northern and Southern leaders together for an armistice parley. Greeley not only endorsed the idea, but for a time proposed (mainly to irk Secretary of State Seward) that European powers assume the role of arbitrators. Then the editor changed course yet again and began suggesting that he himself might be the best negotiator for the North.[34] The urge to prove he was a better diplomat than the secretary of state he despised must have been for Greeley irresistible.

On July 7, Greeley wrote Lincoln to report what he believed to be a major breakthrough: Jewett had reached neutral territory, Niagara Falls, Canada, with so-called Confederate ambassadors in tow, all supposedly armed with full authority from "J.D."—meaning Jefferson Davis—to negotiate for peace. Greeley now urged that the emissaries be granted safe passage to Washington to confer with Lincoln. "I entreat you, in your own time and manner," the editor prodded him, "to submit overtures for pacification . . . which the impartial must pronounce frank and generous." His lecture to Lincoln concluded with a blunt assessment of the national mood no less desperate in tone than his suicidal letter after Bull Run: "I venture to remind you that our bleeding, bankrupt, almost dying country longs for peace—shudders at the prospect of fresh conscriptions, of further wholesale devastations, and of new rivers of human blood." [35]

Greeley accompanied this outburst with a "Plan of Adjustment" he proposed submitting to the negotiators. It called for an immediate cease-fire in return for a renunciation of secession and an end to Lincoln's effort to abolish slavery, offering total amnesty and restored citizenship for Confederates, as well as a national convention to ratify all terms. Greeley even threw in the unaffordable offer of $400 million in federal funds to compensate Rebel owners for their freed slaves. And he proposed full representation for the seceded states in the House of Representatives—even though this last concession would certainly doom congressional approval of a constitutional amendment banning slavery everywhere, a hallmark of the National Union Party platform. The man who had prayed for emancipation on behalf of "twenty millions" was now signaling a willingness to cancel or at best delay the freedom he had so ardently advocated.

Deeply annoyed, Lincoln told his friend, Illinois house speaker Shelby M. Cullom, that Greeley was beginning to cause him "almost as much trouble as the whole Southern Confederacy." [36] And, indeed, Greeley's schemes did pose a real political threat, for Lincoln knew he could not appear to reject any serious peace proposal out of hand, even one that had virtually no chance of success. As the president groused to New York secretary of state Chauncey M. Depew, Greeley clearly meant to "influence the peace sentiment of the North, to embarrass the administration, and to demoralize the army," and in those goals proved "successful." The entire mission, Lincoln sensed, was a "subterfuge" aimed at sabotaging his prospects for reelection. [37] Then the president hit on a way to outmaneuver the editor. In a stroke of sheer public relations

FUN.—August 13, 1864.

NIAGARA DOVES.

Uncle Abe :—" SAY, GREELEY, WHAT 'AVE YOU BROUGHT BACK !"
Dove Greeley :—" NAREY NOTHINK, NUNKEY !"

"Niagara Dove" Greeley admits to Lincoln that he has brought "narey
nothink" home from the aborted 1864 Canada peace conference.

genius, Lincoln decided that rather than repudiate the overture outright, or
permit the emissaries to travel south to Washington, in full view of the capital's press corps, he would instead encourage Greeley to travel north and engage Confederate officials himself at Niagara Falls. "I just thought I would let
him go up and crack that nut for himself," he drawled.[38] Although Lincoln
believed that the initiative could never succeed ("Don't you worry; nothing will come of it," he assured Toledo congressman James M. Ashley), he
shrewdly calculated that empowering Greeley would both shift responsibility
for the outcome and suck the air from the peace-at-any-price balloon.[39]

Further calling Greeley's bluff, the president sent John Hay by ship to New
York to visit the *Tribune* office and provide the editor with official passes guaranteeing safe conduct to Canada for all participants in the proposed conference. Suddenly balking, Greeley told Hay that he now believed himself "the

worst man" to negotiate for peace, whining that rival "newspapers would be full" of invective if he failed. The editor tried wriggling out of the assignment with yet another communication to Lincoln: would it not be better for the Confederate negotiators to head straight to Washington and parley directly with administration officials? But the president coolly insisted that Greeley was not "to *send* me a letter but to *bring* me a man, or men" willing to talk, if such men could be identified at Niagara, adding: "I am disappointed." Lincoln now hit on a way to turn the tables. "I not only intend a sincere effort for peace," he alerted Greeley, "but I intend that you shall be a personal witness that it is made."[40] Trapped in a web of his own spinning, Greeley had no choice but to proceed to Canada. Although just back in Washington from New York, Hay raced north again to join the summit. Lincoln wanted Hay to keep a watchful eye on the unpredictable editor and the Confederate representatives alike.

Hay brought yet another surprise for Greeley to Niagara Falls. Lincoln had crafted his own statement of conditions, aimed at restraining Greeley and distancing himself from the talks themselves—and above all, to preserving emancipation. As his new "To whom it may concern" instructions made clear to the editor: "If you can find, any person anywhere professing to have any proposition of Jefferson Davis, in writing, for peace, embracing the *restoration of the Union* and *abandonment of slavery*, what ever else it embraces, say to him he may come to me with you, and that if he really brings such proposition, he shall, at the least, have safe conduct, with the paper (and without publicity, if he choose) to the point where you shall have met him" [italics added]. Greeley "didn't like it," Hay confided.[41] The editor had suddenly come to the conclusion that imposing any conditions at all, especially these, would imperil negotiations. But it was too late. As far as Lincoln was concerned, there could be no peace without freedom.

To the surprise of no one on either side of the war, Greeley's peace mission to Canada imploded almost as soon as it began. Shadowed by Hay, he did meet briefly with three of the emissaries, J. P. Holcombe of Virginia, George Sanders of Kentucky, and Jacob Thompson of Mississippi—Hay dismissing one as "a seedy looking rebel with grizzled whiskers" and another as "a tall solemn spare false looking man with false teeth false eyes & false hair"—but the delegates readily admitted that they had no real authority to negotiate. Their hesitancy turned to outrage when Greeley asked Hay to share Lincoln's "To whom it may concern" letter. The memo, they bristled, amounted to "a rude withdrawal of a courteous overture." To accept its preconditions, they huffed, would be akin to submitting to conquest, and "the generation was yet unborn which would witness such submission." Echoing the Confederate position, the *New York Daily News* likened Lincoln's terms to "the caprice of a foolish girl trifling with her submissive lover."[42]

Just as Greeley feared, and as Lincoln surely expected, perhaps even hoped, the *Tribune* editor did not escape the debacle without his own share of rebuke. As one of the Confederate emissaries complained of the reluctant ambassador: "It must be confessed that Mr. Greeley, in his hysterical, deluded, and quixotic course in this affair, cuts a shabby and pitiable figure." Not only had Greeley exhibited none of his "usual frankness and straightforwardness in these goings-on," the critic charged; he had violated the code of chivalry, criticizing his own government by "bitterly" reproaching Lincoln and insisting that "nine tenths of the whole American people, North and South, are sick of slaughter and anxious for peace on almost any terms."[43]

When one Southern negotiator added insult to injury by bidding farewell to the *Tribune* editor with the remark, "I wanted old Bennett to come up but he was afraid to come," a thoroughly deflated Greeley sputtered: "I expect to be blackguarded for what I have done. . . . I am not allowed to explain. But all I have done has been done under instructions." In Gideon Welles's analysis, once Lincoln insisted on "the abolition of slavery as one of the conditions [for peace], a string in Greeley's harp was broken." To Welles's delight, Lincoln's hard line on slavery "embarrassed Greeley and defeated a wily intrigue."[44] In retrospect, the escapade seemed to many observers nothing more than a sham incited by the Rebels—and relying on Greeley as their dupe—intended to coax war-weary voters from the Lincoln reelection camp. But the galling "result," Lincoln soon pessimistically observed, "is that he is still attacking me for needlessly prolonging the war."[45]

The mortified editor meanwhile returned home to New York pondering a way to save face. Convinced that Lincoln had sent him off on a hopeless adventure while blocking any possibility for genuine negotiations, Greeley embraced a new scheme he thought would salvage his reputation. In an effort to fix blame for the Niagara Falls disaster squarely on the president, the *Tribune* seconded Henry Raymond's August 4 proposal that the entire Lincoln-Greeley correspondence on the peace negotiations be made public. After Raymond called for its publication—doing so only to help vindicate the president, unaware it contained Greeley's unsettling rant against the war—

Greeley disingenuously told Hay, "I have no special desire to see it in print, but certainly not the least objection." Suddenly finding himself back on the defensive, Lincoln replied, "With the suppression of a few passages in your letters, in regard to which I think you and I would not disagree, I should be glad of the publication. Please come over and see me." But in a breathtaking show of disrespect, Greeley refused the invitation. He would "come to Washington whenever you apprise me that my doing so may perhaps be of use," he stiffly replied, but a visit now was sure to incite "further mischief" at the hands of the editor's "bitterest personal enemies" in the administration. "What, then, can I do in Washington?" he demanded to know. "Your trusted advisors nearly all think I ought to go to Fort Lafayette for what I have done already." [46]

The president had little choice but to send Greeley the full file of their correspondence. But he also made clear he would consent to its publication only if Greeley agreed to a few editorial deletions—which the president boldly marked in red pencil. "The parts of your letters which I wish suppressed," Lincoln bluntly explained, perhaps carefully choosing that ominous word to remind Greeley that entire newspapers had been shut down for less, "are only those which, as I think, give too gloomy an aspect to our cause, and those which present the carrying of elections as a motive of action." But Greeley was adamant. "I do not feel disposed to let my letters to you go to the public with such suppressions as you indicate," he protested. ". . . I prefer . . . *not* to print the correspondence, unless as it was written." To cover all contingencies, Lincoln dispatched another set of the letters to the loyal Raymond, while still recommending it not appear in print. As the president saw matters, "it is better for *me* to submit, for the time, to the consequences of the false position in which I consider he has placed me, than to subject the *country* to the consequences of publishing these discouraging and injurious parts." Greeley came close to the truth when he concluded his next note to Lincoln: "I fear my chance for usefulness has passed." [47] With cunning rather than force, the president had finally managed to "suppress" one of his harshest and most dangerous Republican critics.

Ultimately, fragments from the letters found their way into the nation's press after all, and a six-page pamphlet version appeared by August 15, all of which at least omitted Greeley's inflammatory "dying country" lament. No red pencil could obliterate the overall political damage caused Lincoln by Greeley's ill-advised, ill-timed quest for peace. The *New York Evening Post* spoke for many pro-war newspapers when it labeled the affair "inexpressibly sickening." Marble's *New York World* chortled that if the Niagara Falls escapade had not been "too serious for laughter," it would "go into convulsions."[48] In a more ominous vein, the *Cincinnati Enquirer* spoke for many angry Democrats when it charged that Lincoln's "To whom it may concern" letter had at last revealed the president's true abolitionist tendencies. "Every soldier" killed in future battles, the paper put its readers on notice, "will lose his life not for the Union, the Stars and Stripes, but for the negro." In this opinion, Chicago editor Joseph Medill concurred. He thought the letter would encourage "Copperheads to get an enfilading fire on us," because Lincoln had effectively proclaimed "the war was waged to free negroes." As a result, Medill gloomily predicted, "our political prospects do not look bright." This flurry of anti-Lincoln editorials did not go unnoticed in the Confederacy. In fact, peace negotiator Clement Claiborne Clay of Alabama—who for unknown reasons had absented himself from the actual meeting with Greeley and Hay—concluded that the attacks might prove damaging enough to doom Lincoln at the polls and thus bring peace and independence to the South after all. As Clay reported to the Confederacy's secretary of state, Judah P. Benjamin, on August 11: All the Democrat newspapers "denounce Mr. Lincoln's manifesto in strong terms, and many Republican presses (and among them the New York Tribune) admit it was a blunder. Mr. Greeley was chagrined and incensed by it, as his articles clearly show. I am told by those who profess to have heard his private expressions of opinion and feeling, that he curses all fools in high places."[49]

On August 19, Lincoln summoned his cabinet to the White House to report on the "particulars" of the aborted Niagara Falls conference and the publication of his Greeley correspondence. He told his ministers that he hoped, at least, that the debacle "will shut up Greeley, and satisfy the people who are clamoring for peace."[50] Welles remembered the president explaining that "though G. had put him in a false attitude, he thought it better he should bear it, than that the country should be distressed by such a howl, from such a person, on such an occasion." Welles took solace from the hope that the scandal might once and for all end Lincoln's attempts to woo Greeley—a man, Welles insisted, to whom the president had "clung too long and confidingly." Welles was not the only advisor who believed that, much as Lincoln and Greeley still had in common—their backwoods origins, a common genius for communication, and a shared passion for free labor—there were now far more issues dividing than uniting them.[51]

At the end of the cabinet meeting, Lincoln could only agree. Greeley had become "an old shoe," he grimly admitted, "—good for nothing now, whatever he has been." Of course the president proceeded to explain the aphorism. "In early life, and with few mechanics and but little means in the West, we used to make our shoes last a great while with much mending, and sometimes, when far gone, we found the leather so rotten the stitches would not hold. Greeley is so rotten that nothing can be done with him. He is not truthful. The stitches all tear out." [52]

If that were so, cabinet members and friends alike wondered, why not reply to the weakened editor publicly, just as Lincoln had so successfully done in response to Greeley's "Prayer of Twenty Millions" two years earlier? Indeed, the president confessed to one visitor that Greeley's conduct "annoyed" him "probably more than anything which happened during his administration." As the guest implored, "Why don't you publish these facts in a card? They will be printed in every newspaper in the United States. The people will then understand exactly your position, and your vindication will be complete." Lincoln pondered the suggestion for only a moment before explaining: "Yes, all the newspapers will publish my letter, and so will Greeley. The next day he will take a line and comment upon it, and he will keep it up, in that way, until, at the end of three weeks, I will be convicted out of my own mouth of all the things which he charges against me. No man," the president concluded, "whether he be private citizen or President of the United States, can successfully carry on a controversy with a great newspaper, and escape destruction, unless he owns a newspaper equally great, with a circulation in the same neighborhood." [53]

Instead, Lincoln simply stopped corresponding with the editor of the *New York Tribune*. "Poor Greeley is nearly played out," Gideon Welles later observed with unconcealed joy. "He has a morbid appetite for notoriety. Wishes to be noted and forward in all shows. Four years ago was zealous—or willing—to let the States secede if they wished. Six months later was vociferating, 'On to Richmond.' Has been scolding and urging forward hostile operations. Suddenly is for peace, and ready to pay the Rebels four hundred millions or more to get it." Welles probably spoke for the entire administration when he summed up the veteran editor this way: "He craves public attention. Does not exhibit a high regard for principle. I doubt his honesty about as much as his consistency. It is put on for effect. He is a greedy office-hunter." [54]

Earlier that summer, without invitation, Greeley had indeed paid a visit to

Washington, even summoning the nerve to call at the White House to have a look at artist Francis Carpenter's *First Reading of the Emancipation Proclamation*, then hanging on temporary exhibit at the mansion. Greeley could always be counted on to tout his own role in the historical drama the picture celebrated, and he spent a good deal of time that day peering closely at the canvas for evidence of his own acknowledgment. Carpenter remembered that the editor's initial comments "were not particularly gratifying," and at first attributed it to his being "near-sighted." Greeley insensitively remarked that the engravings in his own recently published Civil War history, *The American Conflict*, far surpassed Carpenter's artistry. Then, in a moment of inspiration, the painter drew Greeley's attention to the image of a newspaper he had introduced within the foreground of his canvas, "symbolizing," Carpenter patiently explained, "the agency of the 'Press' in bringing about *Emancipation*." The painter pronounced that the accessory "was studied from a copy of the 'Tribune.'" Hearing this, Greeley brightened noticeably. "I would not object," he declared, "to your putting in my letter to the President on that subject."[55]

Then, as Greeley occupied himself in reappraising the painting, Carpenter bounded up to the president's office on the second floor of the White House to inform him that the editor had unexpectedly turned up "below stairs," and might usefully be flattered if Lincoln paid his respects. Lincoln barely glanced up from his work and then icily replied: "Please say to Mr. Greeley that I shall be *very* happy to see him, at *his leisure*."[56] Greeley would not call on Lincoln, and Lincoln would not invite him up. The breach was complete.

Lincoln now felt most comfortable when he was able to address issues directly to the people through the press, without the intervention of editors like Greeley. With his previous messages to Conkling, and Corning, and of course to Greeley himself, Lincoln had transformed newspapers into personal sounding boards, introduced language ordinary Americans could understand, and broke past traditional barriers that had long separated presidents from the people. He could now afford to cut Greeley off.

Another potentially useful opportunity for outreach arose shortly after the Niagara Falls episode, when Charles D. Robinson, the Democratic but pro-war editor of Wisconsin's *Green Bay Advocate*, read the recently published Lincoln-Greeley correspondence. Concerned that it had too casually introduced a radical new policy, Robinson wrote to ask the president for an "interpretation" of his sudden insistence that peace could not come "unless accompanied with an abandonment of slavery." The Wisconsin newspaper-man had long taken at face value Lincoln's assertion, as expressed in his reply to the "Prayer of Twenty Millions," that if he could save the Union without freeing any slaves, he would do so. Now the president's improvidently published "To Whom it may concern" letter had clearly identified emancipation as a prerequisite for peace. "This puts the whole war question on a new basis," Robinson fretted, "and takes us War Democrats clear off our feet, leaving us no ground to stand upon." [57] Here was a chance for Lincoln to publish a rationale for his refusal to contemplate peace without black freedom.

In the draft he prepared for a reply, Lincoln acknowledged the Union-first tone of his 1862 Greeley letter, but reminded Robinson that it had also contained the vow: "I shall do *more* whenever I shall believe *doing* more will help the cause." As Lincoln saw matters, the situation had since changed, and now indeed required *more*. "The way these measures were to help the cause, was not by magic, or miracles," he pointed out, "but by inducing the colored people to come bodily over from the rebel side to ours. . . . Take from us, and give to the enemy, the hundred and thirty, forty, or fifty thousand colored persons now serving us as soldiers, seamen, and laborers, and we can not longer maintain the contest." Lincoln concluded with a startling offer: "If Jefferson Davis wishes, for himself, or for the benefit of his friends at the North, to know what I would do if he were to offer peace and re-union, saying nothing about slavery, let him try me." [58] Lincoln no doubt thought there was little danger that Davis would indeed "try" him on such terms.

Nevertheless, he prudently put the Robinson manuscript aside, waited for some time to elapse, probably shared it with confidants, and then reconsidered it. Whatever the reason, since no record of a final letter exists, Lincoln presumably decided not to send it after all—although some of its sentiments soon leaked out in the press. The Niagara Falls affair may have temporarily knocked Lincoln off balance, leaving him so uncertain about popular sentiment that he backed away from deploying his most potent communications innovation: the public letter.

For most of the summer of 1864, the presidential race played out against the bloody backdrop of frustrating military stalemate and achingly high, relentlessly reported casualties on the battlefield. The clamor for peace continued unabated. With the Democratic convention postponed, Lincoln and his first-term record dominated the conversation for months—and generated a torrent of press criticism. "Mr. Lincoln had his periods of depression," John Wein Forney admitted of this period. The Washington editor was present when reports of carnage at the Battle of the Wilderness arrived at the White House in May. Lincoln reacted with "an outburst of uncontrollable emotion," crying out: "My God! my God! . . . twenty thousand poor souls sent to their final account in one day. I cannot bear it! I cannot bear it." Forney never told his newspaper readers of the episode. Nor did he reveal that he found Lincoln in an even darker mood a few nights later, "ghastly pale" with "dark rings . . . round his caverned eyes." Holding up a volume of Shakespeare, the president murmured: "Let me read you this from 'Macbeth' . . . it comes to me to-night like a consolation: 'To-morrow, and to-morrow, and to-morrow/ Creeps in this petty pace from day to day, / To the last syllable of recorded time; / And all our yesterdays have lighted fools / The way to dusty death. Out, out brief candle! / Life's but a walking shadow; a poor player, / That struts and frets his hour upon the stage, / And then is heard no more: it is a tale / Told by an idiot, full of sound and fury, / Signifying nothing.'"[59]

Four years earlier, Lincoln had kept himself aloof from the sound and fury of the campaigns by relying on old speeches and new campaign biographies to make his case to the people. Tradition had not changed since, and the president kept close to the White House during the summer and fall of 1864, turning down speaking invitations ("I believe it is not customary for one holding the office" or "being a candidate for re-election," he told the host of one rally), and instead sending a letter to be read aloud to attendees. As in 1860, he encouraged surrogates to orate, and editors to write, in his behalf. Lincoln did hit upon one ingenious new way to "campaign" without appearing to do so: by making informal appearances on the White House grounds to greet battle-scarred army veterans with inspiring reminders of why the war was worth fighting. With reporters invariably on hand to transcribe these gems and see to their publication, the seemingly casual remarks had the full impact of campaign speeches. "We are striving to maintain the government and institutions of our fathers," Lincoln told one Ohio regiment, "to enjoy them ourselves, and transmit them to our children and our children's children forever." And then, in an obvious slap at his critics, he added: "I beg of you not to allow your minds or your hearts to be diverted from the support of all necessary measures for that purpose, by . . . inflammatory appeals made to your passions or your prejudices. . . . Nowhere in the world is presented a government of so much liberty and equality. To the humblest and poorest amongst us are held out the highest privileges and positions. The present moment finds me at the White House, yet there is as good a chance for your children as there was for my father's." Those remarks promptly appeared in the *New York Tribune,* as did similar morale-building lectures to soldiers, black freedmen, and other visitors.[60]

One formerly potent campaign weapon all but vanished from his arsenal. Not surprisingly, fewer Lincoln biographies appeared in 1864 than in 1860: there was less demand now, far less need to introduce a candidate who had become the best known man in the country. New life stories did come from former *Sandusky Daily Register* editor Orville J. Victor and from Philadelphia journalist David Brainerd Williamson, along with an updated edition of his 1860 Lincoln biography by Joseph H. Barrett.[61] But these were the exceptions, not the rule. Unquestionably the most influential title among this spare new round of biographies appeared under the byline of Henry J. Raymond.

From its inception, Raymond's *History of the Administration of President Lincoln* was officially sanctioned—and aided—by the White House. By February, its publisher, James C. Derby, sent John Nicolay "a sett [*sic*] of proof sheets" so "errors in name or incident" could be corrected.[62] When in March the president issued a poorly publicized letter thanking a New York workingmen's group for its support, Derby assured Nicolay that he would add "Mr. Lincoln's admirable words" to "the Volume of Gov. Raymond." And the following month, Raymond determined to include the president's unpublished wartime messages to McClellan prodding the sluggish general into action, noting that they "would add greatly to the usefulness of the History of Your Administration which I am compiling." After *New York Times* war correspondent William Swinton brought copies to New York, Derby predicted that the administration would be pleased "to read how Gov Raymond's [manuscript] squelches 'Little Mac.' "[63]

Later that April, Derby thanked Nicolay for a "revise of the Gettysburgh Speech," too, signaling that after neglecting Lincoln's masterpiece when it was first delivered the year before, Raymond had determined to feature it in his new book. The alliance among the White House, the *Times,* and Raymond's publishing house—down to the smallest detail of research, distribution, and cost—was never clearer than when Derby encountered difficulty procuring some "hard to get" back issues of the *New York Tribune* that Raymond needed for research. When an unnamed stranger offered to sell the old papers for twenty-five cents a copy, five times their street value, Derby actually felt compelled to ask Nicolay to authorize the expenditure, asking "how high shall I go in payment of same[?]" The collaboration intensified further once Raymond's book appeared in May. The publisher asked the White House to send him "the names of such *Lincoln* men, as will interest themselves in its Circulation,—in Washington, Illinois & everywhere." That the book was still, for Derby, a commercial venture, became apparent when he fretted about competition—one "miserable catch penny" biography that appeared around the same time, he reported dismissively, as well as a "hotch-potch [of] 'Old Abes [*sic*] Jokes'"—neither project, like his, written by the editor of the *New York Times* and blessed, financed, and distributed by the White House.[64]

A sympathetic recounting of Lincoln's life with an emphasis on his White House record, Raymond's book overflowed with orations, proclamations, and Lincoln's now famous newspaper letters ("the most remarkable state papers of modern times," claimed one advertising circular). Raymond ended the tome with a restrained but patriotic case for not changing horses in midstream: "If . . . the measures which President LINCOLN has inaugurated for quelling the rebellion and restoring the Union, are permitted to work out their natural results, unchecked by popular impatience and sustained by public confidence, we believe they will end in re-establishing the authority of the Constitution, in restoring the integrity of the Union, in abolishing every vestige of slavery, and in perpetuating the principle of democratic government upon this continent and throughout the world."[65] Acknowledging Raymond's ability to write "without much emotion" but "always without fatigue," the *New York World* smirked: "If the cause of Mr. Lincoln shall appear weak in the hands of so shifty and versatile and, truth compels us to say, so really able an advocate, it must be intrinsically weak indeed."[66]

The 492-page opus, which enjoyed what its publisher called "a moderate sale,"[67] proved to be but one of Raymond's signal contributions to the campaign. Few journalists ever assumed such enormous political responsibilities at such a high level. Not only did Raymond wield the gavel at the party's June convention at Baltimore, he also became a Republican candidate for Congress from New York, conducting his own election campaign while speaking throughout the state in behalf of Lincoln.[68] Finally, Raymond cemented his position as the administration's official journalist by assuming the powerful role of chairman of the National Union Party's Executive Committee—in effect, the political boss of the newly rebranded Republicans. The onetime Greeley acolyte had come a long way, and no one (but Greeley) seemed to take exception. Raymond's multitude of political and editorial responsibilities amounted to business as usual in the fully integrated world of press and politics—albeit at the highest level yet attempted. Besides, Raymond's new status could be called fitting and proper for another reason, for the co-owner of the *New York World*, August Belmont, concurrently served as chairman of the *Democratic* National Committee.

Raymond took his responsibilities as Republican leader seriously. Taking on the role of fundraiser-in-chief with relish, he made it clear that he expected employees of the federal customs houses, along with those working at the Treasury, War, Navy, and Post Office departments, to ante up with contributions to Lincoln's campaign. Perceiving no conflict of interest in the demand, Raymond explained to cabinet officers, "we must have the whole power and influence of the government this coming fall, and if each Department will put forth its whole strength and energy in our favor we shall be successful." Stanton and William Pitt Fessenden—Chase's successor as secretary of the treasury—readily agreed to place a levy on their subordinates, but Welles, who continued to suspect that Raymond was a Seward agent masquerading as a Lincoln supporter, contended that it was improper for "an assessment . . . to be laid on certain officials and employees of the government for party purposes." [69]

Caustically acknowledging that "parties did strange things in New York," Welles expressed particular outrage when Raymond attempted to launch his fundraising efforts by assessing workers at the Brooklyn Navy Yard. "I am amazed that Raymond could debase himself so far as to submit such a proposition," the navy secretary fumed, "and more that he expects me to enforce it." Warned Welles: "They would remove any man who is not openly with us and of our party organization" and "would employ no doubtful or lukewarm men in the yard, whatever may be their qualifications or ability in their trade." Unmoved, Raymond responded by insisting that the fundraising appeal actually be expanded to include other Union navy yards as well. Welles blustered that he "could not be instrumental in any such abuse," and that he would have said the same thing to Raymond himself, "had he possessed the manliness to call on me." But Raymond found Welles to be "unapproachable, a wall that he cannot penetrate or get over." So the editor ignored him and pressed his plan directly with Lincoln and other, more receptive, members of the administration.[70]

Well into September, Welles waged his lonely fight to keep the Navy Department beyond the reach of politics. By mid-month he broke entirely with the *Times* editor over the fundraising issue. "Raymond has in party matters neither honesty nor principle himself," he raged in his diary, unwilling to make his concerns public, "and believes that no one else has. He would compel men to vote, and would buy up leaders. Money and office, not argument and reason, are the means which he would use." Welles feared that Raymond, trained in "the vicious New York school of politics," was "working upon the President secretly, trying to poison his mind and induce him to take steps that would forever injure him." It took another month more for Welles to realize he was waging an unwinnable campaign. Lincoln sympathized with the secretary's scruples, but made it obvious that he favored "not interfering," which was tantamount to blessing the fundraising scheme Raymond introduced. In October, Lincoln solidified political control over the Brooklyn Navy Yard by asking Welles to assign one of its ships to head off to meet the Mississippi Squadron and gather absentee votes from sailors for the forthcoming election.[71] The policy was soon replicated by all the squadrons, and as an initiative designed to maximize Republican turnout at sea, was the equivalent of allowing soldiers to vote in camp.

Raymond may have won the fundraising battle, but even while waging it, came alarmingly close to concluding that he—and Lincoln—would lose the entire political war. In August, just two weeks after the Niagara Falls debacle, Raymond suddenly expressed the same desperate yearning for peace at any price that his rival Greeley had advocated earlier. The only differences were that Raymond lacked a Niagara-like platform, and also prudently kept his concerns out of the public eye. As party chairman, however, his dire prognostications for the fall election had to be taken more seriously than any outburst by Greeley.

The political and military situations had suddenly grown murkier. On July 30, Grant had suffered a rare, humiliating defeat at Petersburg. True, on August 5, Union admiral David G. Farragut triumphed at Mobile Bay. But that very day, leaving little time for celebration, Horace Greeley allowed two Radical Republican leaders, Senator Benjamin Wade of Ohio and Representative Henry Winter Davis of Maryland, to use the pages of the *Tribune* to condemn Lincoln for his recent pocket veto of their Reconstruction plan.

Lincoln favored a more lenient and flexible blueprint for readmitting seceded states to the Union—one that would require only 10 percent of the voting population to swear their allegiance to federal authority (the Wade-Davis bill insisted on outright majorities). In the "Wade-Davis Manifesto," as published in the *Tribune*, the authors declared it "their right and duty to check the encroachments of the Executive on the authority of Congress." No doubt motivated in part by the legislators' decision to announce their manifesto exclusively in a rival newspaper, the *Times* condemned it as "a treacherous and malignant attempt to stab a President whom they profess to support."[72]

Agitated by this new assault on Lincoln from the radical wing of his own party, Raymond warned his readers on August 10 that "Democrats everywhere are very confident of victory in the pending Presidential canvas." Then, two weeks later, on August 22, the editor and chairman took up a piece of official Union Party Executive Committee letterhead and poured forth his morose and brutally frank doubts to the president, fashioned more in the hand-wringing spirit of Horace Greeley than he probably realized. Democrats had still yet formally to anoint their candidate for president, but the Republican chairman appeared ready to surrender to the opposition on policy matters. "I am in active correspondence with your staunchest friends in every State," Raymond informed Lincoln, "and from them all I hear but one report. The tide is setting strongly against us." Illinois, Pennsylvania, and Indiana were all leaning Democratic. Disappointed over "the want of military successes," and certain that future peace overtures would be rejected, Raymond warned, the Northern electorate was ready to rebel, too.

"Nothing but the most resolute and decided action on the part of the government and its friends, can save the country from falling into hostile hands," a desperate Raymond insisted. His astonishing solution was that Lincoln now publicly abandon emancipation as a precondition for armistice. The president must appoint a commissioner to negotiate with Jefferson Davis "*on the sole condition of acknowledging the supremacy of the constitution,*" Raymond implored, "—all other questions to be settled in a convention of the people of all the States."[73] Word of Raymond's misgivings sped all the way to Ohio, where Lincoln ally Richard Corwine darkly predicted that "Weed & Raymond would urge Lincoln to withdraw and that they had assurances of success because Seward had said, and Lincoln concurred in it, that the latter had *no* prospect of being elected." Corwine was sure that the two editors were actively scheming to replace Lincoln at the head of the ticket with

General Benjamin Butler.[74] Thurlow Weed then reported to William Seward that Lincoln's "re-election was an impossibility," adding that "nobody here doubts it. . . . Mr. Raymond, who has, just left me, says that unless some prompt and bold step be now taken, all is lost." Seward promptly shared the dire letter with the president.[75]

As Lincoln saw it, not only his own survival, but that of the Union and emancipation, now hung in the balance. Displaying the same restraint he had exhibited in response to earlier doomsday warnings, Lincoln held off on responding to his doubters, though it was clear that Raymond's and Weed's messages depressed him. On the very day he likely received both letters, August 23, and perhaps with their glum assessments in mind, Lincoln asked the members of his cabinet to sign, sight unseen, a memorandum conceding that "it seems exceedingly probable that this Administration will not be re-elected." The document pledged cooperation with his successor in order "to save the Union between the election and the inauguration; as he will have secured his election on such ground that he can not possibly save it afterwards." The following day, just as he had done earlier with Greeley, Lincoln seemed to invite Raymond to "obtain, if possible, a conference for peace with Jefferson Davis, or any person by him authorized for that purpose." Appearing to abandon his long-standing insistence on peace only with slavery ended, Lincoln drafted a letter authorizing the *Times* editor to propose that "upon restoration of the Union and the national authority, the war shall cease at once, remaining questions to be left for adjustment by peaceful modes."[76]

Lincoln meant this dare to signal no abandonment of his commitment to freedom. That became evident when around the same time he invited Frederick Douglass to the White House. There, the president asked Douglass to draft a plan to spread news of the Emancipation Proclamation southward to as many enslaved people as could be reached before March, when a new Democratic administration would certainly nullify it. Douglass obliged with a detailed proposal to assign agents to hasten "squads of Slaves . . . within Union lines." In Douglass's view, the meeting provided "evidence conclusive on Mr. Lincoln's part that the proclamation, so far as he was concerned, was not effected merely as a 'necessity.'" But as Douglass lamented to Theodore Tilton in late October, Lincoln said nothing publicly "in this Presidential canvass for the reason that Republican committees do not wish to expose themselves to the charge of being the 'N—r' party."[77]

At around the same time, August 25, Lincoln summoned Raymond and the members of the Republican National Committee to another White House meeting, which cabinet members Seward, Stanton, Welles, and Fessenden joined. Although he had scuttled the Greeley peace gambit by empowering the *Tribune* editor to make a fool of himself publicly, Lincoln wished to handle the circumspect Raymond privately, sensitively, and with the kind of effort he knew worked best with the more loyal and conservative *Times* editor: personal persuasion along with what the president had early in his career called "cold, calculating reason." Fresh from his uplifting session with Douglass, Lincoln convinced Raymond that any new peace initiative, especially one without freedom guaranteed, would be an error of historic proportions. To send a commission to Richmond, he convincingly argued, "would be worse than losing the presidential contest—it would be ignominiously surrendering it in advance." Bowing to both logic and pressure, Raymond pledged not to advocate for peace after all, even if it meant that the administration might indeed go down to defeat. The editor left the White House "encouraged and cheered," and "Lincoln's experimental letter thereafter slept undisturbed, in the envelope he placed it, for nearly a quarter of a century." [78]

Then, just a week after Raymond's forlorn predictions reached Lincoln's desk, fate—in the ironic form of news from that most unapologetic enemy of the press, General William T. Sherman—dramatically intervened to upend the political equilibrium. First, on August 31, George McClellan, as long expected, finally secured the Democratic nomination for the presidency, albeit saddled with a party platform that even some Democrats thought overeager for peace at any price. Much worse for Lincoln's newly anointed opponent, McClellan enjoyed barely twenty-four hours in which to dominate the news. The very next day, Confederate defenders surrendered Atlanta, and Sherman's victorious army moved in to occupy that fiercely contested city. Breathless newspaper coverage of Atlanta's capture all but eclipsed the McClellan story, turning the tide of the military and political wars simultaneously. Renewed Union "confidence" and "prestige," exulted the *New York Times*, would now "surely spread its infection." [79] Frequent critic Theodore Tilton of the *Independent*, admittedly "never . . . a partisan for Mr Lincoln's re-election," now wrote John Nicolay to crow: "If the President has *not* said he was 'a beaten man,' he will hereafter have *no* occasion to say it. We are going to win the Presidential election. The divisions are going to be healed. I have never seen such a sudden lighting up of the public mind as since the late victory at Atlanta." [80]

After years of hostility, the press now began showering accolades on Sherman, with Bennett's *Herald* calling him "one of the great men of the time," and even the general's longtime nemesis, the *Cincinnati Gazette*, hailing his Atlanta triumph as "the blast of a war trumpet." Not until Election Day, when an Indianapolis reporter dared to hazard a guess as to the size of Sherman's force as it prepared to march to the sea—an estimate promptly reprinted in the Richmond newspapers—did Sherman erupt in his customary manner and demand that the correspondent be prosecuted. The press blackout that had preceded Sherman's capture of Atlanta now resumed in a new blaze of adverse publicity, but in another stroke of luck for Lincoln, did not commence until the very day ballots were being counted in the contest for president, when it was too late to impact the election. Voters thus never learned that Assistant Secretary of War Charles Dana, onetime managing editor of Greeley's *Tribune*, had urged Sherman to counteract news leaks by "publishing other paragraphs, calculated to mislead the enemy"—in other words, through a campaign of disinformation.[81]

Yet the final outcome of the presidential race was still far from settled. Lincoln's foes—from the Democratic and Republican sides alike, journalists as well as politicians—continued to plot against him. Greeley, as usual, led the assault from among the president's "friends." In early September, deaf to renewed public confidence in the administration and the army, Greeley, together with *Evening Post* veteran Parke Godwin and Theodore Tilton—notwithstanding the latter's enthusiastic recent note to John Nicolay—launched a quixotic campaign to rally the Republican faithful back into convention in Cincinnati in order to dump the president from the ticket.

The trio of editors went so far as to send letters to the nation's Republican governors provocatively inquiring whether "the interests" of party and country did not "require the substitution of another candidate in place of Lincoln." Loyal Republican leaders quickly distanced themselves from the ill-timed insurgency, while Lincoln supporters rushed to report the coup attempt to the White House. James Conkling, the Springfield neighbor to whom Lincoln had entrusted the public reading of his open letter on black recruitment the previous year, alerted the president that Illinois governor Richard Yates had received one of the letters from Greeley, Godwin, and Tilton "enquiring of him whether we can carry Illinois whether you can be elected and whether it would be advisable to nominate another candidate. The Governor will answer most emphatically that we can carry Illinois—that you can be elected and that it would not be advisable to put any other candidate in the field." Vowed Conkling: "We shall carry the State by a large majority, if we can keep clear of these faint hearted, weakkneed politicians who are afraid of the popularity of McClellan." [82] Wisconsin's James T. Lewis spoke for the majority of Republican governors when he wrote the trio of editors on September 7: "You ask . . . 'in your judgment is the re-election of Mr. Lincoln a probability'? Answer, I think it is a strong probability. . . . In my judgment the interests of the Union party, the honor of the Nation and the good of Mankind, demand that Mr. Lincoln should be sustained and re-elected." [83] Within days, Thurlow Weed jubilantly reported to William Seward that the "formidable and vicious . . . conspiracy against Mr. Lincoln" had collapsed in a "Fizzle." [84]

Just a week later, on September 17, John C. Frémont officially abandoned his third-party candidacy for the White House, calling on his followers to unite behind the president. Frémont's withdrawal capped a rare, glorious month for Lincoln in the press. On the 23rd, the president responded to—or, as some whispered, repaid—the Frémont faction by asking Postmaster General Montgomery Blair to resign from his cabinet. Perhaps as part of the same complex deal, Henry Winter Davis of Manifesto fame lost renomination to the House of Representatives. After surviving several undermining peace initiatives from the editors of both the *Tribune* and the *Times*, Lincoln, with help from the federal military, had finally united the party. As the once despondent Henry Raymond reported to Lincoln from party headquarters in mid-September, "Things look pretty well here." [85] Well enough for a remorseless Greeley to resume besieging Lincoln with requests for favors and renewed pressure for peace, "so anxious am I that not one needless drop of blood should be shed in this terrible struggle." [86] Still stubbornly ignoring the threat that his efforts posed to emancipation, Greeley continued pressing Lincoln to reopen peace talks with the Confederacy, summoning the pluck to advise him: "Above all let nothing be said or done which can touch the pride of the Southrons. They have fought splendidly, and should be treated magnanimously." Greeley ended this latest advice with a belated offer to come to Washington after all, if he "could do any good." Not surprisingly, Lincoln replied to no letters and extended no invitations. [87]

Scorned and ostracized, the ever-nimble editor responded with yet another dizzying about-face. Offering neither explanation nor apology for his latest transfiguration, he began promoting Lincoln's reelection as if he had been advocating it from the start. Not only did he commence editorializing in the president's behalf, he hatched an audacious scheme to sway the important soldiers' vote to the administration. At Greeley's urging, with John Nicolay's help, and with Chairman Raymond's acquiescence, the army assigned a colonel named Absalom H. Markland to distribute free of charge "such newspapers . . . as the National Committee may determine to circulate in the Army of the Potomac"—meaning only those journals that spoke in "very logical and argumentative speech in favor of our platform and against McClellan." [88]

The effort clearly proved successful, for within days the *New York World* was complaining: "The monopoly of the sale of the papers in General Grant's and Sheridan's armies is given with the distinct understanding that as few as possible of the Democratic papers shall be sold by them. . . . The only papers our soldiers are allowed to see are . . . all violent administration sheets, daily filled with calumnies on the Democratic party and its candidates." In the West, as Marble further griped, "by order of the military satraps, the opposition papers are suppressed outright within the military lines; so that there can be no mistake, the World, Chicago Times, Cincinnati Enquirer, etc., are specified by name as being excluded, and so our western armies can learn nothing of political matters except through the medium of the partisan sheets in the interest of Mr. Lincoln." [89] For military and civilian consumption alike, Greeley's own editorials were by month's end not only touting the president's reelection, but ridiculing talk of armistice as "folly or treason," and adding with a rare display of bellicosity that "the only effective Peace Commissioners" were Grant, Sherman, Sheridan, and Farragut. [90] (When the soldiers ultimately cast their ballots for president, Lincoln would capture four of every five votes.)

Outmaneuvered among the general's uniformed constituency, Democrats turned to civilian-based strategies Lincoln had successfully deployed four years earlier, including an attempt to corral ethnic support through the foreign language press. The plan seemed almost quaint in the wake of the blanket coverage now pouring off the presses of the widely read party-affiliated dailies. "How to take, to turn, and to satisfy an 'Editor,' is and always has been one of the most difficult problems," a German Democrat from Philadelphia, Max Langenschwartz, told George McClellan in September. The task was especially difficult, the McClellan supporter pointed out, if "one is unable to be preceded by an overwhelming force of *Bank-Checks*." Apparently, McClellan was less willing to invest in foreign language papers in 1864 than Lincoln had been in 1859. Yet Langenschwartz optimistically believed that journalists were susceptible to another form of persuasion: flattery. "He will now hoist our flag," the correspondent guaranteed after meeting the editor of what he termed "the most influential german paper in the State" on September 26, ". . . and that will be more useful than fifty public speeches could have done so quickly." [91]

Further details about this clumsy attempt to woo piecemeal German support for the Democrats are lost to history. But focusing on the one ethnic bloc that always dependably tilted Republican seemed an unwise investment of energy by McClellan forces. That officials from both parties continued to pay close attention to the foreign language press, however, was evidenced when Lincoln's Chicago friends urged that the *Illinois Staats Zeitung* "be dropped from those receiving advertisements of the War Department" in retaliation for "attacking the enrollment law, [and] the call for more troops." [92] Lincoln made sure that year also to reward smaller newspapers that had demonstrated consistent loyalty. During the campaign he saw to it that one of his most faithful journalistic supporters back home earned financial rewards for its backing. "The Journal paper was always my friend; and of course its editor the same," the president wrote in June in an endorsement meant to encourage local Republicans to buy notices in the Springfield daily. "If there is any special reason why it should not have a share of the advertising I do not know it." [93]

For reasons that had little to do with financial reward beyond the ever-higher profits he was earning from his own daily and weekly editions, James Gordon Bennett became the last of the big three New York editors to come to terms with the president's increasingly probable reelection. Editorializing in May, he had sounded not unlike Manton Marble in pillorying Lincoln for "blunders" and "criminalities" and dismissing Republican political prospects as "impossible." [94] Bennett spent the summer of 1864 skewering Lincoln's candidacy, proposing Grant as an alternative, and lauding the Democratic opposition. Complaining that there was "not an honest, fair-dealing Administration journal in New York City," Gideon Welles believed that the *Herald*, in particular, gave "tone and direction" to the rest of the antagonistic Gotham press. "When the *Herald* has in view to defame or put a mark upon a man,"

Welles recognized, "it commences and persists . . . [in] attacking, ridiculing, abusing, and defaming," until gradually another journal begins to echo "the slanders of the *Herald*" and "follows up the work."[95] In other words, Bennett's paper remained especially dangerous because its opinions were contagious.

Even though Lincoln had never bowed to Bennett's 1860 plea for social recognition in return for editorial neutrality, the president did appreciate the editor's post-Sumter show of patriotic ardor, and as the reelection campaign headed into the home stretch, refused to give up on the goal of winning the crafty editor's endorsement, or at least the softening his strident hostility. According to one of the president's closest Illinois allies, Bennett genuinely "wanted to support him" in 1864, and yearned only "to be noticed by Lincoln." One of the editor's friends pleaded that if Lincoln merely invited Bennett to the White House to "chat," then "his paper would be all right." It seemed a tiny price to pay, but still Lincoln resisted. "I understand . . . Bennett has made a great deal of money, some say not very properly," he mused, and "now he wants me to make him respectable." Though Lincoln had earlier opened the White House to another of his wife's half-sisters—this one the widow of a Confederate general, no less—he simply could not bring himself to extend an invitation to Bennett, a mark of the editor's outcast social status. Stubbornly, Lincoln agreed to receive him "if he came," as he would welcome any caller during public office hours.[96] But when in July Bennett unleashed a new torrent of criticism against both Greeley and Lincoln over the Niagara Falls fiasco, Lincoln decided to go courting after all, armed with a new approach designed to neutralize the *Herald* editor without formally receiving him.

As an intermediary, Lincoln chose the "affable" but wildly ambitious New York City postmaster, Abram Wakeman, the former Customs House aspirant who enjoyed close political ties to Raymond, Weed, and Seward. Wakeman, whose Manhattan home had been burned by arsonists during the 1863 antidraft riots, had proven his loyalty to the administration by working to prevent postponement of the Republican convention, a scheme Greeley and other Lincoln doubters had devised to bolster the chances of potential last-minute entries like Grant. In late July 1864, Lincoln sent Wakeman an expansive policy letter, pointing out that while the Confederacy's Niagara Falls delegates had never been empowered to negotiate on behalf of the Richmond government, they had indeed been encouraged by others to play a role in abetting Lincoln's antiwar political opponents. "Thus the present presidential contest," Lincoln concluded, "will almost certainly be no other than a contest between a Union and a Disunion candidate, disunion certainly following the success of the latter. The issue is a mighty one for all people and all time; and whoever aids the right, will be appreciated and remembered."[97]

Here was no ordinary explanation to a local postmaster, but rather a meticulously worded political message clearly meant for other eyes. In fact, Lincoln intended the statement—highlighted by the overt offer of "appreciation" in return for support—for none other than James Gordon Bennett, with whom it was soon shared. Three weeks later, Wakeman reported back to the president: "I have read it with proper explanation to Mr. B. He said, after some moments of silence, that so far as it related to him, 'It did not amount to much.'" Apparently, the editor expected a more "specific" promise of future reward. Now the game was on. Senator James Harlan of Iowa—an intimate whose daughter would soon become engaged to Lincoln's son Robert—told John Hay that "Bennett's support is so important especially considered as to its bearing on the soldier vote that it would pay to offer him a foreign mission for it." Although Lincoln hesitated, even Bennett's longtime enemy, Horace Greeley, trying to work his way back into the president's good graces even as he continued plotting to sabotage him, suggested to Bennett's friend, journalist William O. Bartlett, on August 30 that an overt deal was desirable. As Greeley viewed matters, "if the President should see the way clear to tend to the Editor of the Herald some important diplomatic post in recognition of his services to the country in sustaining the Union at all hazards, but especially in upholding the Draft, I think a very good and extensive influence would thereby be exerted."[98]

Lincoln devoted no further letters to the sensitive subject, but continued to send emissaries to Bennett to discuss an arrangement, even as he contended simultaneously with Greeley's subterfuge and Raymond's sudden doubts. On one of her own 1864 trips to New York, Mary Lincoln herself paid what was surely a carefully planned social call on Bennett and his wife. Later, Mary wrote directly to Wakeman, who had become one of her confidants, to urge him to step up the courtship of the *Herald* editor. "A little notice of them would strengthen us very much I think," she advised, demonstrating that she was in on the effort to win Bennett's support. As Mary coyly put it, her husband "appreciates a kind expression of Mr B's very much." When "the *World* dares to insinuate against us," she noted in contrast, "the public should take them in hand."[99]

Bennett's friend Bartlett soon began reporting secretly to the White

Almost an ambassador: James Gordon Bennett, as he looked in 1865, the year Lincoln offered him the post of U.S. minister to France.

House in person on the editor's evolving attitudes—and in turn working in New York to press Lincoln's case for reelection on Bennett. Finally, Bartlett broached the specific offer of a plum diplomatic post in return for peace with the *Herald*. ("I am from Washington, fresh from the bosom of Father Abraham," Bartlett declared to Bennett on November 4, adding carefully that Lincoln *"expected to do that thing as much as he expected to live."*)[100] Lincoln had sent word that he was prepared to name Bennett as minister to France, one of the choicest foreign assignments at his disposal.

Yet in the end it was the Democratic platform that influenced Bennett more than the gratifying promise of an overseas appointment. Its peace plank—demanding that "immediate efforts be made for a cessation of hostilities"—infuriated the reborn Unionist, and as soon as the Democratic convention adjourned the exclusively anti-Lincoln tone of *Herald* campaign editorials began shifting.[101] As summer yielded to fall, the paper began condemning appeasers and emphasizing its support for total Union victory. Though it never actually endorsed Lincoln, as some historians have erroneously contended, the *Herald* at least began lobbing equal doses of criticism at both presidential nominees, making a point of declaring with wholly uncharacteristic equivocation that the ultimate choice belonged to voters, not editors.[102]

Such benign posturing did not prevent "His Satanic Majesty" from spewing his pent-up bile at his newspaper rivals. Always particularly eager to ridicule his *Tribune* counterpart, Bennett gloated on September 23 that the "leading men of the republican party" had all "eaten humble pie, and are now making speeches for Lincoln," including Greeley, "in spite of his *Tribune* articles" (indeed Greeley was by then on an upstate political tour in Lincoln's behalf). In October, Bennett aimed his wrath at Democratic chairman August Belmont, charging that his work as New York agent for the Rothschilds had made him "rich as a Jew." (As the anti-Semitic Bennett well knew, Belmont himself was Jewish-born.) But when, in an act of desperation, Jefferson Davis proposed offering freedom to slaves who enlisted in the Confederate army, Bennett dropped his own long-standing opposition to black enlistment by conceding: "When such propositions come from Richmond, the negro soldier policy pursued by President Lincoln ceases to be a debatable question. He is vindicated by the Rebels themselves." Dutchess County, New York, Democrat Albert C. Ramsey—a onetime newspaper editor—still hoped Bennett might yet play a pivotal role in George McClellan's behalf in the final days of the campaign. Though Ramsey lobbied the editor and reported that "an excellent feeling now exists in the Herald office," he conceded that "Mr. Bennett doubts if we can succeed in November," as he frankly told McClellan weeks before the election. Ramsey well understood that the usually "impulsive" editor had become "very shy of committing his paper," but tried to talk McClellan into believing that the *Herald*'s refusal to endorse him could still prove helpful. "So far," Ramsey argued unconvincingly, "the apparent neutral course of the paper has aided us more than the most decided support of our side. This to be sure was accidental, but the most knowing of our opponents call it 'adroitness.'" Others probably agreed that Bennett's neutrality indeed helped—but Lincoln's Republicans, not McClellan's Democrats.[103]

Although Bennett put a scare into Republicans by receiving McClellan at his Manhattan estate late in the campaign (at Ramsey's urging), the editor dealt a crushing blow to Democratic hopes some two weeks before Election Day by demanding that the general further repudiate his party's peace plank. McClellan's expected refusal, as William Bartlett explained to Lincoln, was needed to pave the way for Bennett's "distinctly accepting you as satisfactory." Bartlett proudly rushed a copy of the paper's ambiguous next edition to Lincoln, describing "the *Herald* of this date" as "a model paper for our side," and adding that "Mr. Bennett told me yesterday that he had accomplished more for you than he could have done any other way, because he has carried his readers with him."[104]

In other words, there was to be no direct announcement of support for Lincoln. In fact, even while stepping up his criticism of "peace at any price" Democrats, Bennett continued to rail against what he called "Lincoln's misrule." And the *Herald* devoted considerable space to further attacks on the "baser instincts and passions of the party press" itself, pointing out that any voter making his choice based on the "scurrilous abuse" to which both candidates had been subjected would think McClellan a "double dealing traitor" and Lincoln "the most methodical and skillful demagogue in the United States." Bennett even praised Greeley for becoming less "savage and rampant" in his recent editorials—the result of the "moral suasion of the Herald," of course—but added that the pro-McClellan *World* remained guilty of "shocking depravity." On the eve of the election, the ambivalent Bennett aimed one final riposte at his old Republican foes, mocking Greeley as "a non-combatant on principle" who "cannot bear the report of a pistol without exhibiting every symptom of fright." Was Lincoln a tyrant and a "swindler" as the *World* charged—or was McClellan a traitor, as the *Tribune* maintained? In the end, Bennett admitted, "we have no hope of Paradise regained with this election. We have no fears of the destruction of the country with the success of Lincoln or McClellan. Each is a failure. . . . The choice, Old Abe or Little Mac, is rather a choice of evils than a choice of excellences." [105]

After so many years of outright hostility, Bennett's final "pox on all their houses" election eve editorial was perhaps viewed by the administration to be very nearly an endorsement. As Pennsylvania journalist A. K. McClure recalled: "Lincoln knew how important it was to have the support of the *Herald*, and he carefully studied how to bring its editor into close touch with himself." McClure hailed the effort—which he maintained included the "confidential tender of the French mission"—as "one of the shrewdest of Lincoln's great political schemes," even if McClure erred in recalling that it resulted in outright "support" from James Gordon Bennett. [106] In fact, one of the final *New York Herald* headlines before the day of political reckoning proclaimed: "The Only Hope of the Country Is the Election of McClellan." [107] If Lincoln traded Bennett a presidential appointment in return for a "cessation of hostilities," he got precious little in the bargain.

Whatever their final terms, Lincoln remained publicly "shut pan" about any patronage offer to Bennett, not even confiding it to cabinet officials like William Seward, who was bound to object to the appointment after enduring years of criticism from the *Herald* over both local and foreign policy issues. No wonder that in March 1865, when Gideon Welles admitted that a "rumor is prevalent and very generally believed that the French mission has been offered Bennett," he confidently added: "I discredit it." [108] Little did Welles know that, a month earlier, Lincoln had written secretly to Bennett to "propose, at some convenient and not distant day, to nominate you to the United States' Senate as Minister to France." Knowing that Congress was about to adjourn, and would need time to advise and consent on what might prove a controversial nomination, Lincoln waited anxiously for a reply. Finally, on March 6, in a letter carried to the White House by Bartlett, the editor turned down the job. Thanking the president for "so distinguished an honor," Bennett confessed "that at my age I am afraid of assuming the labors and responsibilities of such an important position," adding that "in the present relations of France and the United States, I am of the decided opinion that I can be of more service to the country in the present position I occupy." [109]

Perhaps Bennett never really wanted to become minister to France. Very likely, Lincoln never really wanted to send him there, unless he believed it would at least usefully separate him from his printing presses. In the end, both men earned no more, and no less, than what they had originally sought in 1864: Lincoln secured from Bennett a kind of hostile neutrality, while Bennett at last earned his long-sought gesture of presidential respect. Neither of these wary combatants ever expected more. Lincoln eventually named another newspaperman as minister: John Bigelow, co-owner of the *New York Evening Post*. But Mary Lincoln objected strenuously when other papers derided the Bennett offer as "one of Mr. L's 'last jokes.' . . . Lest he might consider, that it was intended as a *jest*," she told Abram Wakeman, "do not fail to express my regrets to him." Mrs. Lincoln, for one, was disappointed "that Mr B—did not accept." [110]

On Election Day, November 8, 1864, New York City's overwhelmingly Democratic voters again repudiated Lincoln—by a resounding two-to-one margin. The president narrowly retained the state's crucial electoral votes only by attracting huge support upstate. Stung by the local results, Greeley borrowed a page from the *Herald's* racist playbook by insisting that "the atrocious McClellan majorities uniformly rolled up in our City" had originated in "dens of debauchery, harlotry . . . crime" and "Irish grogshops." [111]

Party chairman Raymond, who telegraphed Lincoln at 9:40 P.M. on election night to concede, "Democratic majority in this city will be thirty four thousand," could take consolation from the fact that he himself handily won election to Congress from the Sixth District, amassing a five-thousand-vote plurality against three opponents; this despite the fact that Lincoln had refused to use his influence to urge another Republican out of the four-way race. All through the night, Republican editors dutifully kept Lincoln informed of voting trends in their home states. As eagerly as they had supported him during the campaign, they now wanted to be among the first to inform him of "their" success. When John Wein Forney wired early from Philadelphia that "the State was sure for Lincoln," and "by a decided majority," the president remarked, looking more solemn than joyous: "As goes Pennsylvania, so goes the Union, they say." At midnight, Horace Greeley telegraphed that New York would go to Lincoln "by about four thousand." Edward Baker of Lincoln's old Springfield mouthpiece, the *Journal*, sent word, "You have carried this state by at least twenty thousand." And from William Fishback and William McKee of the long-supportive *Missouri Democrat* came word that their state was safe by "about ten thousand." As more and more heartening results trickled in through the early hours of the morning, Lincoln finally allowed himself to say that "he felt relieved of suspense." It was Noah Brooks, though denied access to Lincoln's election night headquarters—perhaps by John Nicolay, aware by now that the *Sacramento Daily Union* correspondent was growing ever more ambitious for his job—who sent a hastily scrawled "table of election returns," probably the first complete account of the vote to arrive at Lincoln's desk.[112]

Did the municipal tallies for president suggest that the Republican editors had lost influence in New York, or that Bennett's pacification had failed to reduce Democratic hostility? Perhaps. But of far greater importance, on matters political, the three press titans had attempted to influence not just their Manhattan readers, but their national subscribers as well. And by trumpeting their preferences in the bellwether, undecided states, not just in their intractably Democratic home turf, Raymond, Greeley, and Bennett had all, in their way, helped Lincoln win a second term.

Despite his continued unpopularity in New York City, the final nationwide tally gave Lincoln an unexpectedly easy reelection triumph: a healthy 55 percent of the popular vote, majorities in twenty-two of the twenty-five Northern and Border States, and a lopsided electoral vote advantage of 212–21. The victorious Republican chairman expressed no surprise at the result. "It simply is a verification of what we have steadily declared from the outset," a jubilant Raymond concluded in the *Times*, "that the American people would stand by the Government as long as the Government stands by the flag." To the recently mollified *Herald*, the result assured that "the rebellion shall be put

768

Long Abraham Lincoln a Little Longer.

"Long ABRAHAM LINCOLN
a Little Longer"—artist
Frank Bellew's tribute to
the president's reelection—
appeared in *Harper's Weekly*
on November 26, 1864.

down by force of arms; that there can and shall be no compromise with Jeff. Davis, and that the Union in its integrity shall be maintained." Launching one final attack on the Democrats he had once supported, Bennett added: "Some of the over-credulous readers of the New York *World* . . . may be disappointed, but the knowing ones among the democracy knew that vain boastings and foolish promises would not carry the election." Horace Greeley could only agree. "We hold that the People have just decided," proclaimed the *Tribune*, that "*the* NATION SHALL LIVE AND THAT SLAVERY SHALL DIE— so much, and no more." [113]

Later that month, *Harper's Weekly* published a deceptively simple, wordlessly eloquent cartoon showing the rustic-looking, hyper-attenuated figure of Lincoln gazing at the viewer from a narrow, column-wide panel, one hand characteristically tucked inside his lapel, the other clutching the presidential election results. The caption spoke volumes: after another furious political battle waged in and by the press, it was to be "Long Abraham Lincoln a Little Longer." [114]

A few evenings after his triumph at the polls, Lincoln appeared in the second-story window of the White House to acknowledge a victory serenade. It was a celebratory occasion, but the president had something serious to say. "We can not have free government without elections," he told the festive crowd, no doubt proud not only of his victory but also of the license he had extended to the opposition press during the campaign, "and if the rebellion could force us to forego, or postpone a national election, it might fairly claim to have already conquered and ruined us." To a relieved Lincoln, the "undesirable strife" of the political campaign so relentlessly waged in the press had been worth the pain. "It has demonstrated that a people's government can sustain a national election, in the midst of a great civil war." Thinking perhaps of the newspapermen who had vilified him during the campaign, he closed by asking "those who have not differed with me, to join with me, in this same spirit towards those who have." [115]

But the fiercely partisan struggle had taken its toll on the weary president. "It is a little singular," he remarked sadly to John Hay as he waited for the results on Election Day, "that I who am not a vindictive man, should have always been before the people for election in canvasses marked for their bitterness." [116]

Lincoln had passed the three months between his first election and his inaugural journey in unbreakable solitude and calculated silence. But much had changed in four years. This time there would be no transition of power, no obligation to defer to a lame-duck incumbent, no need for silence. His policies vindicated, Lincoln remained visibly in charge, appearing frequently before the public and the press in the weeks leading up to his second swearing-in.

Surprisingly, though the hotly partisan political campaign had ended with success for Lincoln, federal forces now resumed menacing opposition newspapers in war zones. Union troops suppressed the Louisville *True Presbyterian* in December, banishing its editor, Reverend Stuart Robinson, to Canada. The preacher wrote to the president in December to protest the "foolish" shutdown of what he insisted was "a purely ecclesiastical journal." As Robinson conceded in the next breath, "I have not sustained your administration." But he added, "neither do I wish to be driven into opposition to it, as a political writer, in defence of freedom of the press & religion." [117] When Lincoln failed to acknowledge the plea, the exiled minister published a long, scathing, open letter to the president, charging that "a large part of the people regard your administration as signalized, beyond all constitutional governments of modern times, for its tyrannical contempt for personal liberty, freedom of speech, and of the press, liberty of conscience and freedom of religion." But Robinson's public plea fell on resolutely deaf ears. In something of a validation of the army's actions against the minister, a southern Indiana Presbyterian synod sought to ban its members from reading Robinson's newspaper. [118]

Although Horace Greeley's Canada peace mission had ended in confusion and humiliation in 1864, Lincoln now turned his attention to an ambitious mission of his own that must have seemed to some observers no more plausible, and no less perilous, than Greeley's: convincing the lame-duck House of Representatives to consider the constitutional amendment abolishing slavery—and, crucially, to do so before the Confederate army was subdued, or could initiate an attractive new proposal for peace without freedom.

Lincoln had several reasons to advocate for the amendment sooner rather than later. For one thing, the Emancipation Proclamation applied only to states engaged in rebellion against the federal government. Slavery therefore remained legal in most of the Border Slave States, and would remain so, Lincoln feared, if the war ended without a final, fatal attack on the institution. Maryland voters had narrowly voted to outlaw slavery in 1864, but its future in Delaware, Missouri, and Kentucky remained murky. If the Confederacy capitulated or sued for peace before slavery could be eradicated, the House might prove disinclined to advance a constitutional solution. However, should Lincoln convince dubious congressmen that vanquishing the rebellion depended upon destroying its root cause, he might yet accomplish peace and freedom together. Finally, Lincoln remained acutely aware that the power he had invoked to issue the proclamation had yet to be tested in the courts. "Nobody was more quick to perceive or more frank to admit the legal weakness and insufficiency of the Emancipation Proclamation than Mr. Lincoln," observed journalist James Welling.[119] A constitutional amendment would render the question moot. It would be "a king's cure for all evils," as Lincoln put it. "It winds the whole thing up."[120]

The raw politics, however, tilted against success. Had Lincoln been able to wait longer, he might have enjoyed a far easier time ushering the freedom amendment through Congress. The Senate had passed the measure quickly enough, but in late 1864 an initial House vote fell a few votes short of the two-thirds majority required to send it on to the states for ratification. The next House, swept into office on the coattails of the Lincoln landslide, would boast major gains for the president's party when it next gaveled into order in December 1865—or sooner, should Lincoln call the new Congress back into special session after his reinauguration—and would be so overwhelmingly Republican that the amendment was certain to sail through. Copperheads like Fernando Wood of New York had lost their bids for reelection and would not be returning to Washington. Victorious loyalists like Henry Raymond would be heading to the capital to support the administration. Still, with the end of the war now in sight, Lincoln convinced himself that he must push another floor vote during the lame-duck session, even if it meant that resistant outgoing Democrats were again compelled to participate.

If the president could somehow persuade enough lame ducks to support the amendment—if not through logic then with the promise of federal jobs once their terms ended—he believed he could change enough minds to secure the necessary "ayes." To help secure the required votes, Lincoln turned to a lobbyist urged on him by the unlikeliest of sources: Horace Greeley. Former *Nashville Gazette* editor William N. Bilbo arrived in Washington bearing a letter of introduction from Greeley attesting that he was "ready to do good service to our national cause." Lincoln put him to work trolling for congressional converts to the amendment, at one point getting the mysterious operative released from prison for what Bilbo called "the malicious or profoundly ignorant charge of being a Southern spy." [121] When floor debate opened, Greeley himself turned up in Washington in his role as presidential elector from New York, using his privileges as a former—albeit unelected—congressman to gain access to the House chamber, prompting anti-amendment Ohio Democrat Samuel "Sunset" Cox to pause in the midst of one floor speech to sarcastically welcome the "able and patriotic" visitor. [122]

Then that nettlesome old Jacksonian editor, Francis Preston Blair, Sr., the former postmaster general's father, undercut the momentum for freedom by reawakening the dormant effort for peace with the Confederacy. Lincoln bowed to the ex-journalist's initiative and allowed the seventy-three-year-old to proceed to Richmond to talk armistice with Jefferson Davis. The president harbored ample reasons to expect another failure, but also knew from Greeley's Canadian misadventure and Raymond's summertime jitters that too many otherwise reliably antislavery men remained willing to sacrifice emancipation for armistice if a cease-fire could save lives. Though the press at first learned little about Blair's trip, his initiative came close to sinking the Thirteenth Amendment. Although he reported nothing to Lincoln during his mission, Blair did confide in Horace Greeley, assuring him, "my faith is strong that we shall have a happy deliverance, and that soon," adding a few days later that "nothing can defeat an early peace unless technicalities or points of honor be employed by the selfish & unpatriotic in the South." [123]

As the House debate proceeded, accompanied by furious behind-the-scenes arm-twisting and almost breathless press coverage, Blair returned to Washington and informed the president that a new trio of authorized Confederate emissaries—this time including Vice President Alexander H. Stephens, the president's onetime Whig colleague in Congress—was heading to Washington to negotiate peace. Fearing that their arrival might convince wavering House Democrats that the war could be brought to a close with slavery intact after all, Lincoln cannily ordered the army to detain the commissioners at Fort Monroe, Virginia, and keep them there. Rumors of the emissaries' journey toward the capital reached the House floor anyway, prompting outcries for an explanation. Lincoln calmly responded, with perfect—if selective—honesty: "So far as I know, there are no peace commissioners in the city, or likely to be in it."[124] The floor debate on the Thirteenth Amendment resumed, and when the clerk called the question on January 31, the resolution sending it to the states passed the House with a handful of votes to spare. Within a day, Edward L. Baker, editor of Springfield's *Illinois State Journal*, wired Lincoln the joyful news that before any other state could consider, much less ratify, the amendment, it had "just passed both branches of our Legislature with great hurrah."[125]

In New York, Henry Raymond exulted, "The Southern people, with all their errors and delusions, do not longer imagine that slavery can be saved." Even Bennett declared himself "gratified at the success of this great measure." Of course he also claimed personal credit for its passage, "considering the earnest support which it has received through our editorial columns," and took an inevitable swipe at the administration by asserting that the amendment would at last end the confusion "resulting from the tinkering, illegal, and incongruous emancipation experiments of President Lincoln." Passage of the Thirteenth Amendment at least represented "progress in some direction," Bennett acknowledged, ominously adding: "Time will tell whether it is forward or backwards."[126]

The press had not only covered the House debate intently, but played a behind-the-scenes role in the sometimes questionable campaign for "ayes"— by *not* reporting the campaign for votes. Only later did journalist Whitelaw Reid claim that lobbyists hired to persuade lame-duck Democrats to vote for the amendment—presumably including ex-journalist Bilbo—had spent up to $50,000 on bribes. One House member whom Greeley lobbied personally was outgoing Connecticut Democrat James E. English, who had voted against the resolution in 1864. Now, about to depart Congress, English dreamed of a comeback as his party's nominee for governor. After Greeley intervened, English ended up supporting the resolution. The *Tribune* promptly hailed his support for "that most righteous Amendment" and urged grateful supporters "to vote for English this Spring."[127] Unforgiving Democrats denied their former congressman the gubernatorial nomination anyway.

A few days after the House vote, Lincoln hastened to Hampton Roads and there personally delivered the news to the three peace commissioners: slavery was on the path to certain destruction, and no deal for peace could be considered without black freedom recognized. No one made a record of the talks, but at one point Lincoln supposedly dangled the idea of compensating rebellious states for slaves already freed under the proclamation; and at another, responding to a lecture about parallels in the English Civil War, chuckled that all he could recall was that Charles I had lost his head. If the president indeed shared these thoughts, they came right out of comments previously made by journalists: Greeley's overgenerous terms for the Niagara Falls peace conference, and Manton Marble's threatening allusions to King Charles after reopening the *New York World*. To the end, Lincoln unashamedly got some of his best talking points from newspapermen. Perhaps he even took inspiration from the advice that came from the *Chicago Tribune*'s Joseph Medill: "Don't be in too much hurry for Peace. Don't *coax* the rebel chiefs, but pound them a little more." [128]

As far as coverage of the peace conference was concerned, a tight press blackout reigned, in the wake of which, *Times*, *Tribune*, and *Herald* correspondents outdid themselves in unsubstantiated speculation. Lincoln had always tried to oversee the dissemination of information about any peace negotiations even as he was conducting them.

Then in March, John Wein Forney, back from Europe and again at the helm of the *Washington Chronicle*, published his own predictions about the peace negotiations. The competition howled, angry at being scooped and, in some cases, worried that the president might give away too much to achieve peace at Hampton Roads. Even Noah Brooks, no less privy to official policy than Forney, complained. "At this time," he noted in the *Sacramento Daily Union*, "when the public, with a few factious exceptions, was resting confidently in the belief that Lincoln's wonderful sagacity and discretion would bring the country and himself out all right, the Washington *Chronicle*, in a series of double-leaded, sensational leaders, ablaze with all of the clap-trap of typographical ingenuity, showed that the editor, J. W. Forney, in his eagerness to be considered as the oracle of the President (rushing to the conclusion that Lincoln was going to obtain peace by compromise), had deliberately gone to work to prepare the public for the sacrifice of something vaguely dreadful, and dreadfully vague. These articles . . . were telegraphed all over the country, indorsed by Greeley . . . read by astonished and indignant thousands." [129]

Brooks need not have worried. The Hampton Roads conference ended without an agreement and the war entered its final days. Admitting to his readers that he had always believed in "an early Peace," Greeley, coming full circle from his negotiating days at Niagara Falls, now insisted that Union forces resume the fight "with energy and enthusiasm." In a similar vein, characterizing the peace conference as "wholly and utterly fruitless," Henry Raymond's *New York Times* reported after the Confederate envoys left Hampton Roads: "It is now fully realized that an energetic prosecution of the war opens the only path through which peace can be obtained." Bennett, too, saluted Lincoln for conducting the talks with a "frank manner" and "equal firmness," while as expected the *New York Daily News* condemned the president and his "faction of destructives" for refusing to trade armistice for recognition of Southern independence. Adding that the Confederate diplomats had abandoned their quest for peace out of resentment over Lincoln's "threats and insults," a Richmond newspaper vowed: "Our people will rise up behind him everywhere, more defiant and unsubdued than ever." [130]

By the time Lincoln made his way down Pennsylvania Avenue on the brisk, cloud-filled morning of March 4 to take the presidential oath of office for the second time, the only remaining question was, not whether, but when the Confederacy would submit. The Thirteenth Amendment was already on its way to ratification: in less than two months, eighteen of the twenty-seven required state legislatures had already voted to ratify. Although Lincoln had ample justification to claim credit for the approaching transformation of American society, he planned to display no conqueror's bravado that inaugural day. He would propose no specific vision for the national future beyond freedom and reunion, repentance and forgiveness.

The speech was shorter this time—750 words in all, the briefest inaugural address since Washington's second. Lincoln devoted much of it to describing how the war had unavoidably engulfed the continent, arguing that slavery had been its one and only cause, and that the entire country, North and South, must accept blame for its sinful existence—and endure the devastating judgments of a justifiably angry God. Then the national preacher abruptly softened his tone to conclude on an achingly beautiful note of compassion—pleading for "malice toward none" and "charity for all." [131]

Later that momentous day, onetime newspaper editor Frederick Douglass attended a post-inaugural reception at the White House—although, not surprisingly, he had to force his way in past guards who did their best to prevent him from entering; at one point they hurled him out of a first-floor window to get rid of him. When the president later spied him in the crowd, he called out in a voice, the abolitionist icon remembered, "heard all around" the East Room: "Here comes my friend Douglass." As Douglass approached, the president heartily added: "Douglass, I saw you in the crowd to-day listening to my inaugural address. There is no man's opinion that I value more than yours; what do you think of it?" More to the point, the president perhaps wondered, what would Douglass say or write about the speech?

Douglass's reply no doubt delighted him: "Mr. Lincoln, it was a sacred effort." Then, as Douglass disappeared into the throng, the president called after him: "I am glad you liked it." It was, as Douglass remembered it, "the last time I saw him to speak with him."[132]

Hungry as ever for press accolades, Lincoln allowed his eagerness for newspaper praise to get the better of him when it came to Thurlow Weed—misinterpreting another of Weed's letters, just as he had when the presidential race was first getting under way a year earlier. This time, in a note posted the day of the inauguration, Weed had written to commend Lincoln for an entirely different speech: his reply to the congressional committee that had officially informed him of his reelection four months before. It was "not only the *neatest* but the most pregnant and effective use to which the English language was ever put," Weed gushed. "Everyone likes a compliment," Lincoln gratefully replied on March 10. "Thank you for yours on my little notification speech, and on the recent Inaugeral [*sic*] Address. I expect the latter to wear as well as—perhaps better than—any thing I have produced; but I believe it is not immediately popular. Men are not flattered by being shown that there has been a difference of purpose between the Almighty and them." In this analysis, Lincoln proved correct. But Thurlow Weed had not written a word about the inaugural address.[133]

Others wrote a great deal about it, though not all the responses pleased Lincoln—perhaps explaining his eagerness to infer praise from Weed. Greeley thought Lincoln's majestic second inaugural lacked the "politic" and "humane" spirit of his first, worrying that its Old Testament–style brimstone (which preceded its pacific peroration) dangerously hinted at vengeance on the conquered Southern states ("This Haman shall hang on the gallows he erected for Mordecai," Greeley worried, quoting the Old Testament himself). Oblivious to Lincoln's soon-to-be-immortal closing lines, Greeley declared he would have preferred "manifestations of generosity, clemency, magnanimity." For his part criticizing its "glittering generalities," Bennett complained that Lincoln's speech furnished "no information as to his future policy." Like

Greeley, he insisted that "a fresh, unequivocal exhibition of the spirit which impelled the former Inaugural would have been politic and humane" and moreover "quickened and deepened the disintegration of the Rebel forces." [134] Among New York's big three, only Raymond hailed the "calmness" and "modesty" of Lincoln's oration, adding a comment that almost seemed meant as a warning to his hypercritical fellow editors: "We have a President who will be faithful to the end, let what betide. Let him be sustained with the same fidelity." [135] Just four days after the inaugural, Raymond asked for his expected rewards: he resumed peppering Lincoln with requests for federal jobs for those who had done "the greatest possible service during the last canvas[s]." [136] For the editor turned biographer turned party chairman, it was back to political business as usual.

Lincoln spent most of the early spring on something of a vacation at the Virginia military front, far from newspapers and newspapermen, following the army in the field and consulting with General Grant at his headquarters at City Point. Before departing Washington, however, the president enjoyed a relaxing visit from Henry Raymond, regaling the serious-minded editor at the White House with dialect stories he read aloud from a newly published book by the Toledo pro-Republican journalist David R. Locke—who doubled as a humorist under the pen name Petroleum V. Nasby. Lincoln simply adored his comic work. [137]

Just a few days later, on March 27, artist Albert Hunt caught a glimpse of Lincoln sitting cross-legged at a Virginia wharf, a copy of the *Richmond Dispatch* spread across his lap. Hunt hastily sketched the president, and handed the result to him as a souvenir. As it showed, here on the road, separated from the War Department telegraph and his secretaries' daily gossip about what the press was reporting, Lincoln had returned to his old habit of reading original newspapers himself.

Within a week the Confederate capital fell, and while Lincoln remained in Virginia, hundreds of *New York Herald* newsboys rushed through the streets of Washington "as fleet of foot and as breathless with enthusiasm as Malice with his fiery cross," hawking extra editions sped to the city from New York. Buried in the *Herald*'s April 3 issue was the more alarming news that against the cautionary advice of Secretary of War Stanton and others, Lincoln had "designed going himself to Richmond, and may have done so before now." [138]

Last portrait of Lincoln from life—sketched by Albert Hunt
at Union army headquarters, City Point, Virginia, March 27,
1865—showed the president reading a Richmond newspaper.

As it transpired, just as Stanton feared, the president did indeed make a stunning, unannounced entrance into the smoldering city the following day. Only hours had passed since Jefferson Davis and his government had fled and ordered its warehouses torched, after which Union forces marched in unopposed to occupy the capital. Now nearly in ruins, Richmond overflowed with angry Confederate deserters, along with anxious white civilians unsure of their future and a large black slave population suddenly, officially liberated under the terms of the Emancipation Proclamation. Lincoln's bodyguard later admitted of Lincoln's visit: "It seems to me nothing short of miraculous that some attempt on his life was not made." [139]

Accompanied only by his young son Tad and a small detachment of sailors, and fortuitously joined on the shore by a small knot of journalists who had just reached the city to report on its occupation, Lincoln strolled unexpectedly into town from the riverfront on April 4. What happened next was described by some eyewitnesses as a spontaneous outpouring of reverence—though the spontaneity may have been fueled by the reporters, eager to stoke a human interest story, who may have taken it upon themselves to alert the nearest African Americans that their "messiah" had arrived. Whether his admirers recognized Lincoln on their own or with the encouragement of the correspondents, first one, then a few more, and ultimately hundreds of freed slaves soon came pouring from the wharf to greet the man they regarded as their deliverer. As Admiral David Dixon Porter, who walked Richmond's streets with Lincoln that day, reported, "the colored race . . . seemed to spring from the earth. They came, tumbling and shouting, from over the hills and from the water-side."[140]

Overwhelmed by the frenzied welcome, Lincoln stopped in his tracks, not quite certain how to respond. As he stood frozen in place, worshipful African-American admirers reached for his hand or attempted to kiss the hem of his coat. One elderly man, as Porter remembered, "fell upon his knees before the President, and kissed his feet," prompting Lincoln to plead, "don't kneel to me. . . . That is not right. You must kneel only to God and thank him for the liberty you will hereafter enjoy."[141] Charles C. Coffin, who published one of the only accounts of the visit to appear in Lincoln's lifetime, never mentioned such an exchange. Whether it really occurred or not died with David Dixon Porter. Whether or not *any* words were exchanged, only with the greatest difficulty did Lincoln and his party inch along the thronged streets toward Union military headquarters at the onetime Confederate "White House."

Ignoring the riotous greeting, the *New York Herald* correspondent on the scene inexplicably focused instead on the humiliation of the "collapsed capital" and the president's visit to the Davis mansion, where he reported Lincoln nervously swiveling on his Confederate counterpart's chair and "running his hands frequently through his hair." The *New York Tribune*'s Richmond correspondent could not help commenting irreverently: "It is not known whether the occasion reminded Mr. Lincoln 'of a little story,' but it is to be presumed that it did."[142] As at Gettysburg, the New York journalists had again missed a story for the ages.

Word of Lincoln's self-effacing but triumphal entry into Richmond spread anyway. Thomas Morris Chester, an African-American correspondent working at the scene for Forney's *Philadelphia Press* on a story about Richmond's

notorious, now abandoned slave pens, witnessed at least part of the spontaneous demonstration, and later reported that "one enthusiastic negro woman"
greeted the president by exclaiming: "I know that I am free, for I have seen
Father Abraham and felt him." [143] The *Boston Journal*'s Coffin observed yet
another highly emotional scene: "An old negro, removing his hat to him with
tears of joy rolling down his cheeks." In response, "The President removed his
hat and bowed in silence." That small but momentous gesture, Coffin at once
recognized, "upset the forms, laws, customs, and ceremonies of centuries." [144]

Returning to City Point, Lincoln hoped to remain in Virginia long enough
to witness the end of the war, but instead, visibly buoyed by his trip to Richmond, returned to his own capital to prepare for peace and Reconstruction. A
few days later, on April 9, a chorus of church bells and cannon fire announced
to Washington the news of Lee's surrender to Grant at Appomattox. In New
York, diarist George Templeton Strong read the papers and happily observed:
"Even the *World* and *Daily News* say that Secessia is now conquered, crushed,
subjugated, and under our feet." [145]

The following evening a jubilant crowd swarmed to the White House,
called for Lincoln, and pleaded for a speech. As the *National Intelligencer*
reported, "bands played, the howitzers belched forth their thunder, and the
people cheered." [146] Haggard but exhilarated, the president eventually appeared at his usual perch inside the mansion's second-story window, but offered only a few words. He "would not say anything more," he teased one
correspondent on the scene, "lest the reporters should fail to quote him right
in the country." [147] In truth Lincoln wanted time to prepare a serious public
address on Reconstruction. He would speak more formally, he vowed to the
crowd, the following evening, and from the same spot. Lincoln's appearance
had been so unexpected, his comments so terse, that the *Herald* managed to
record and print only a portion of his remarks.

As promised, the president returned to the same window to deliver his formal address on the night of April 11. When he finished the oration, Lincoln
turned and thanked Noah Brooks for holding a candle aloft so he could
read his lengthy manuscript in the darkness. "That was a pretty fair speech, I
think," he chuckled afterward, "but you threw some light on it." Brooks, who
reported that the crowd greeted Lincoln with "cheer upon cheer, wave after
wave of applause," was surprised that the president's oration was "longer and
of a different character from what most people had expected," but thought "it

was well received." [148] That Brooks stood in for John Nicolay on this occasion surprised none of the wags who whispered that the journalist would soon replace the Teutonic "Cerberus" who had guarded Lincoln's gate for four years. Nicolay was away on assignment—and about to miss the most cataclysmic news story of the entire war.

Lawrence Gobright of the Associated Press witnessed the April 11 speech, too. "A large crowd gathered at the White House," he reported. When Lincoln appeared, "he was greeted with repeated cheers. . . . I had never seen him so quietly happy, as he complacently surveyed the throng before him. It seemed that his tall form had received an additional foot of stature." [149] One last time, the Democratic journalists responded negatively. Typically, the *New York World* criticized the presidential address for its "vagueness, indecision, and . . . *emptiness.*" But not every foe in the audience that night would have agreed that the president's proposals seemed vague. Among the crowd that heard Lincoln call for extending the "elective franchise . . . to the colored man"—that is "the very intelligent," and "those who serve our cause as soldiers"—was the incurably racist, pro-Confederate actor John Wilkes Booth. "Now, by God, I will put him through." Booth seethed to a companion at the scene. "That will be the last speech he will ever make." [150]

Three nights later, on Good Friday, April 14, Gobright was sitting alone in his office, "having filed, as I thought, my last dispatch," when shortly after 10 P.M. he heard the sound of rapid footsteps on the stairs, followed by a loud pounding on the door. Suddenly a breathless friend burst in, gasping the unimaginable news: he had been sitting in the audience watching a play at nearby Ford's Theatre when an assassin attacked the president. A shot was heard. A woman—perhaps Mrs. Lincoln—had screamed. John Wilkes Booth had leapt from the box to the stage, proclaiming revenge. And then the lifeless body of Lincoln had been borne outside and into a house across the street.

Hours later, when someone explored the contents of the stricken president's pockets, a wallet was found, stuffed with worthless Confederate currency—souvenirs, no doubt, from his recent triumphant visit to Richmond. Discovered, too, were relics Lincoln had obviously valued just as much: nine carefully cut newspaper clippings, several of which showered him with the kind of press acclaim for which he had battled his entire political life. "There is a general feeling," the often critical Henry Ward Beecher had said of Lincoln in one of the articles the president so carefully preserved, "that

PRESIDENT LINCOLN.

The large audience assembled last evening at the Academy of Music, to hear an address from Rev. Henry Ward Beecher, may be considered as fairly representing the most enlightened and intelligent population of Philadelphia. The welcome to Mr. Beecher was hearty, as it should have been. Every portion of his address was well received; but the loudest applause was given when he spoke in commendation of the course of the National Government in its prosecution of the war against the Southern rebels. An incidental allusion to General Jackson called forth some hearty plaudits. When they ceased Mr. Beecher, in his peculiar quiet way, said "Abraham Lincoln may be a great deal less testy and wilful than Andrew Jackson, but in a long race, I do not know but that he will be equal to him." The storm of applause that followed this seemed as if it never would cease. The turn given to the popular enthusiasm, by the mention of Lincoln's name alongside of Jackson's, was wholly unexpected. But the spontaneous outburst showed how strong a hold the President has upon the popular heart throughout the loyal North. As the time approaches for a new Presidential election, and people cast their eyes about for a candidate, there is no one so generally looked to as Abraham Lincoln. Other men may have the requisite talents and virtues; but none impress the people as being so well entitled to the next term of four years as the man who has so faithfully guided the republic through the terrible storms of civil war. There is a general feeling that after a term of war he is entitled to a term of peace; and that other men, military and civil, must defer their claims at least until the year 1868.

Abraham Lincoln had this favorable clipping in his wallet when he was assassinated on April 14, 1865.

after a term of war he is entitled to a term of peace." [151]

Gobright rushed to the telegraph office to send off "a short 'special,'" then raced with his friend to the theater a few blocks away. The building was now dark and empty, but the two made their way inside, upstairs, around the balcony, and into the flag-festooned private box where Lincoln had been enjoying a comedy barely an hour earlier. "When we reached the box," Gobright remembered, "we saw the chair in which the President sat at the time of the assassination; and, although the gas had for the greater part been turned off, we discovered blood"—not to mention the actual gun John Wilkes Booth had used to shoot the president. Gobright next tried to gain access to the house where Lincoln now lay dying, but was refused entry. Instead, as if living a nightmare, the Associated Press bureau chief stumbled back to his office to begin "writing a full account of that night's dread occurrences." Though his fingers were "nervous and trembling," he had a job to do. "I can never forget," Gobright later admitted, "the alarm, and horror of that night." [152] Gobright's report appeared the next day as the lead item in the *National Intelligencer*—the same paper whose attention Lincoln had so vainly sought during his first years in Washington as a congressman.

Transported by extra editions sped nationwide, then rushed to the streets, the horrifying news reached distant cities, and even the remote countryside, within hours. In Ridgefield, Connecticut, Anna Marie Resseguie, a young woman who had heard Horace Greeley lecture in her hometown ten years earlier, now reported sorrowfully to her diary: "The Tribune comes clad in mourning, announcing the awful intelligence that our president Abraham Lincoln was assassinated." [153] In upstate Canandaigua, New York, young Caroline Cowles Richards glanced out of her window just after breakfast on Saturday, April 15. "I . . . saw a group of men listening to the reading of a morning paper," she recalled, "and I feared from their silent, motionless interest that something dreadful had happened, but I was not prepared to hear of the cowardly murder of our President." [154] And in Philadelphia, rumors of Lincoln's death prompted Sidney George Fisher's wife to rush out to purchase a paper. She returned home, Fisher remembered, "and read to me, half crying & in a tremulous voice, the sad & terrible story." Fearing an outbreak of retribution against Lincoln's critics, the city's mayor called out the police to protect the city's sole, surviving Copperhead paper, *The Age*, from the possibility of mob attack. [155] From one end of the country to the other, North as well as South, Lincoln's murder and the search for his assassins filled nearly every page of every newspaper. The tragic story would remain the focus of their reports and commentary for weeks. Admitting to the "overburdening grief" that had afflicted the country so soon after Lee's surrender, even the long-hostile *New York World* admitted that the "splendor of our triumph is robbed of half its luster." [156]

For more than thirty years, Abraham Lincoln had labored to cultivate and captivate a succession of like-minded newspaper editors in a progression of ever larger cities. He had succeeded in securing their steadfast loyalty, yoking them to his own growing ambitions, and manipulating them on occasion to carry his message to a constantly widening sphere of readers. And for those same thirty years Lincoln had attracted the fierce enmity of opposition newspapermen from Springfield to Washington, all of them determined to thwart him. All the way up to the spring of 1865—even after the triumphant end of the bloodiest war in American history—their disapproving voices continued to fill as much newspaper space as the praise Lincoln had worked so hard all his life to secure.

Only with the sudden, violent death of the journalists' greatest subject and canniest manipulator did they finally speak with one voice.

As Lincoln's body returned to the White House to lie in state, the three major New York dailies that had covered Lincoln's national political career so relentlessly—and sometimes, so critically—now adorned their front pages with mournful black trim, posting thickly inked headlines that seemed not only to echo the growing chorus of national lamentation, but to echo each other as well.

"Our Loss. The Great National Calamity," bannered the *New York Herald*.

"The Great Calamity . . . The Nation's Loss," announced the *New York Tribune*.

"Our Great Loss . . . The National Calamity," headlined the *New York Times*, adding: "Party Differences Forgotten in Public Grief." [157]

They had quarreled bitterly over politics, split on slavery and abolition, squabbled over emancipation and black recruitment, and dueled over issues of war, peace, and indeed, over Lincoln himself, somehow managing, for all their distracting competition, to write the invaluable first draft of Civil War–era history.

Nothing before had ever truly reconciled them, much less inspired them to speak in one voice. But the war was over, slavery was dying, and Lincoln was dead, a martyr to union and freedom alike. Now, for the first time in so many years that no one seemed able to remember how long their feuds had lasted, James Gordon Bennett, Horace Greeley, and Henry J. Raymond had finally found something about which they could all agree.

We Shall Not See Again the Like

T he press survived the Civil War, and its major editors all outlived Abraham Lincoln—although in a few cases, not by much. After a brief period devoted to mourning the assassinated president, they resumed their decades-long quest to assassinate each other.

Of the three principal New York press titans of the age of Lincoln, Henry Raymond of the *New York Times* was the first to depart the scene. But not before he enjoyed an enormous literary success in the wake of the president's assassination. In just ninety days, Raymond updated his 1864 Lincoln campaign biography and republished it under a new title; the repurposed book sold 65,000 copies in just six months. Mary Lincoln, who faulted Raymond for opposing her campaign for a widow's pension, nonetheless judged the book "*the most correct* history . . . that has ever been written." [1]

Raymond's political career proved less rewarding. Not long after taking his seat in Congress in December 1865, he became embroiled in the toxic debate over the impeachment of Lincoln's White House successor, Andrew Johnson. Ever the loyal organization man, Raymond aligned himself with the small group of conservative House Republicans who refused to abandon the accidental president accused of thwarting Lincoln's plans to extend African-American rights. Even though the full House voted to impeach and the Senate acquitted Johnson after a trial, Raymond found himself ostracized by the progressive wing of his party, serving on in Washington with diminished influence, his command of the *Times* notwithstanding. He refused renomination for a second term, returned to his newspaper full-time, and in 1867 declined President Johnson's grateful offer of the job of minister to Austria.

When Raymond began experiencing "a paralytic tendency in the muscles of his right hand and wrist" the following year, the hardworking editor ignored the symptoms. On June 18, 1869, just a few hours after holding a pair of late-night meetings—one, appropriately enough, devoted to politics, the other to the paper—Raymond collapsed in the hallway of his Manhattan home, the victim of what was described as an attack of "apoplexy." He died early the following morning, only forty-nine years old. "It is beyond our power to estimate how greatly his editorial labors have influenced public opinion," his grieving wartime correspondent John Swinton declared in an obituary rushed into print the day after Raymond's death, ". . . but we believe that the scope and measure of his influence, as well as its beneficent character and results, have been worthy of journalism in the most exalted view of its purpose." Writing in the *Independent* thirty-one years later, Swinton reappraised Raymond as "a man of many talents rather than of special genius." Genius or not, the editor left a formidable estate valued at $450,000.[2]

Among the wartime big three, James Gordon Bennett of the pro-Democratic *New York Herald* alone remained maddeningly independent from, yet at the same time enormously influential on, organized politics. He never regretted his decision to refuse Lincoln's 1865 offer to send—or, as some saw it, to banish—him overseas as American minister to France. But within months of the assassination, he lost his appetite for running the daily paper he had created, and in 1866 turned over its reins to his playboy son James Jr., and retired to his upper Manhattan mansion. On occasion, he paid a sentimental visit to his newsroom or contributed an editorial, perhaps aware that his anointed heir had no intention of devoting the kind of single-minded energy to the enterprise that its founder had. Inevitably, the *Herald* began a slow but irreversible decline. Uncertain that his hard-won legacy would endure, the elder Bennett died of a stroke at his Washington Heights home on June 1, 1872, at the age of seventy-six. His longtime adversary Horace Greeley served as a pallbearer at his funeral.

"The *Herald* was his creation," Bennett's paper noted in tribute at his death, "the embodiment of his long cherished idea of justice, owing allegiance to no party and laboring singly for the advancement and happiness of the people." Left unmentioned was the founding editor's long opposition to emancipation, black equality, and nearly all Republicans. Even the *Tribune* acknowledged: "He had no aim other than to make a great and lucrative newspaper."[3] That Bennett's enterprise had proven lucrative neither Demo-crats nor Republicans could doubt. He died the wealthiest of the New York big three.

The *Tribune's* Greeley never found—and likely never sought—cures for either his lust for political office or his attraction to lost causes. In 1867, in one of the last and most famous instances of his obsession with ill-advised crusades, he joined twenty other prominent men who signed a $100,000 bail bond to free the imprisoned symbol of slavery and disunion: former Confederate president Jefferson Davis. Long a staple in caricatures as the quintessential progressive abolitionist, Greeley now found his name featured on the mass-produced *Bail Bond of Mr. Jefferson Davis . . . With all the Signatures Thereto*, a best-selling print in the South that helped elevate the leader of the onetime "slaveocracy" to the status of Lost Cause icon.[4] Pouncing on an opportunity to humble their suddenly vulnerable rival, fellow journalists unleashed a fresh torrent of criticism. Greeley now seemed, at least to some, nothing less than a traitor, and *Tribune* subscriptions plummeted. Undaunted, Greeley pub-lished his autobiography in 1868—an excellent account of his early life that offered only a cursory exploration of the Civil War years or his complex re-lationship with Abraham Lincoln. Beginning in 1870, Greeley gave employ-ment to Lincoln's gifted onetime assistant secretary (and unofficial press aide) John Hay.

During these years, Greeley unsuccessfully sought Republican nomina-tions for Congress and governor, and although he secured the party's nod to run for New York State comptroller in 1869, he lost the election to an incum-bent Democrat. Three years later, in 1872, opposed as ever to second terms for presidents, the editor broke with the country's greatest living war hero, President Ulysses S. Grant, and challenged him for the White House as the candidate of a new Liberal Republican Party. In so doing, Greeley accepted as well the endorsement of the Democrats whose policies he had opposed for three decades. A mass-produced campaign print of the day showed the Greek philosopher Diogenes discovering in Greeley his long-sought honest man—actually a precise, unacknowledged copy of a decades-old design that had earlier shown Diogenes discovering Honest Abe Lincoln. Such tributes did little to help the *Tribune* editor against the popular Grant. The electorate rejected Greeley by a wide margin, 56–44 percent; he lost his home state of New York by more than fifty thousand votes.

Crushed by the stinging defeat, and overwhelmed by the sudden death of his beloved wife just before Election Day, Greeley described himself as "the most utter, hopelessly wretched and undone of all who ever lived."[5] Shortly after writing those agonized words, he suffered a nervous breakdown and was committed to a Pleasantville, New York, sanitarium. There he died just a few weeks later at age sixty-one. He thus became the first and only White House candidate who failed to live until the electoral votes in his contest were officially cast. As a result, also uniquely, he earned not a single electoral ballot in his race for president. It marked a bizarre and tragic end for the eternally independent and unpredictable "philosopher" whose sudden demise was, in a way, no less surprising than his extended period of fame, success, and political influence.

"Abraham Lincoln and Horace Greeley were the most thorough[ly] *American* of all our leading characters in this generation," the celebrated minister Theodore Cuyler reminded readers after the editor's death. "Both sprang from obscurity; both were cradled in poverty; both worked their way up by sheer brain-work; both were excessively simple, democratic, and homespun in their manners and dress; both were awkward in gait; both abounded in quaint dry humor." Cuyler noted, too, a "sad resemblance in the tragic end of the two great patriots and philanthropists. The brain of one was pierced by a pistol ball; the brain of the other was pierced by an acute and deadly grief that killed as surely as any bullet ever fired. . . . We shall not soon see again the *like* of the great president and the great journalist."[6] Joining assorted dignitaries at Greeley's funeral were surviving newspaper contemporaries like Manton Marble of the *World*, George Jones, Henry Raymond's founding partner at the *Times*, and even Greeley's onetime mentor and longtime adversary, Thurlow Weed.

Shortly before his final breakdown, Greeley scrawled a last will transferring his $30,000 worth of shares in his paper along with other assets to his daughter. The Tribune Association then awarded controlling interest in the daily to staff editor Whitelaw Reid, and the paper continued to publish for nearly a half century more.

Today, two seated bronze statues of Horace Greeley still greet passersby in neighborhoods where the *Tribune* once flexed its journalistic muscle: John Quincy Adams Ward's sculpture in City Hall Park just north of what used to be Newspaper Row, dedicated in 1916; and Alexander Doyle's 1894 statue for the neighborhood where his paper moved after the *Tribune* founder's death—but which ironically came to be known as Herald Square.

• • •

With a few exceptions, most of the other editors who made their mark during the age of Lincoln maintained their expectations of lifelong political reward before fading into obscurity, beginning with both the friendly and hostile editors from his own hometown.

Until five years after the assassination, Lincoln's very first press supporter, Simeon Francis, founding editor of the *Illinois State Journal*, clung to the patronage job with which Lincoln had rewarded him for his political loyalty early in the war: army paymaster for Fort Vancouver in Washington Territory. Francis finally retired in 1870 with a handsome half-salary pension. He died two years later in Oregon in his seventy-sixth year.

His successor, scandal-plagued William Bailhache, sold his interest in the *Illinois State Journal* during the war and later relocated to New Mexico. Undaunted by the scandal that dogged him during the Lincoln years, he resumed his quest for political patronage. President Chester Alan Arthur named him a receiver of public moneys in 1881, but Bailhache left that post in 1885 and later headed farther west, eventually to San Diego, where he returned to the newspaper business. Remaining at Springfield, his onetime partner, Edward L. Baker, maintained his post at the *Journal* until his retirement from the paper in 1880, and then became U.S. consul at Buenos Aires. Baker died in 1897, Bailhache in 1905.

It was probably just a coincidence that five days after Lincoln delivered his canonical Gettysburg Address, his chief Springfield newspaper critic, Charles Lanphier of the *Illinois State Register*, announced that he would "leave the position which I have held for many years only from a desire to engage in other pursuits less conflicting and laborious. To my democratic hosts," he added, "I bid adieu in an editorial capacity to join them as a private Co-worker" in the battle "for peace, prosperity, and re-union under the Constitution." In other words, Lanphier left the newspaper business to become a full-time politician. Beginning in 1864, he served two terms as the elected clerk of the Sangamon County Circuit Court, but in 1872 lost a race to become Illinois state treasurer. Lanphier retired that year, but lived on to see the new century, dying in 1903 at the age of eighty-three.[7]

In 1974, dramatically changing economic circumstances compelled the two long-opposed independent Springfield dailies to merge into one paper. That year the *State Journal-Register* debuted, featuring on its new logo a prewar drawing of the man one of its halves had so long touted, and the other had so consistently opposed.[8] The paper has published ever since.

Henry Villard, the onetime Illinois correspondent for German newspapers who later filed such memorable stories about President-elect Lincoln for the *New York Herald*, and went on to cover the Civil War as a battlefield correspondent for Greeley's *Tribune*, afterward became the Washington reporter, then a foreign correspondent for Horace White's *Chicago Tribune*. In the 1870s he invested wisely in railroads, and became a wealthy business tycoon. Villard returned to journalism in 1881, buying the *New York Evening Post* and hiring his onetime boss Horace White as an editor. Villard died at his country estate at Dobbs Ferry in 1900 at the age of sixty-five. His Madison Avenue mansion, designed by the architects McKim, Mead and White before his business empire began to unravel, is today a New York City landmark, part of it the home of the Municipal Art Society. Villard's superb multivolume memoirs appeared posthumously.

Chicago newspaper veteran White, who had covered the Lincoln-Douglas debates, broke with his partners at the *Chicago Tribune* over the 1872 presidential election; White supported Horace Greeley. Following Greeley's defeat and death, White joined Villard in New York to help run the *Evening Post*, becoming editor-in-chief in 1899. After retiring four years later, White served on a New York state financial commission. He died at age eighty-two in 1916 after being run down by an automobile.

White's onetime *Tribune* colleague Dr. Charles H. Ray left the Windy City Republican paper in 1864 and the following year ran afoul of Union military authorities when he tried to open a potentially profitable trade with captured Southern cities in "calico, women's shoes, stationery & the like," and was compelled to petition Lincoln to provide authorization. Just two months before his death, the president reluctantly gave Ray permission to trade in noncontraband items, providing he obtained "the approval in writing of the Department commanders . . . and not without."[9] Ray later helped found the Chicago Historical Society. After failing in another business enterprise, he became editor and co-owner of the *Chicago Evening Post* in 1869, but died the following year at age fifty-nine.[10]

The third partner in the *Chicago Tribune* triumvirate, Joseph Medill, a Grant backer, resumed his role as publisher of the paper after White's ouster, serving in the post until his death in 1899 at age seventy-five. The founder of one of America's most enduring newspaper dynasties, two of his grandsons,

Joseph "Medill" McCormick and Robert R. McCormick, succeeded him at the *Tribune*, while another grandson, Joseph Medill Patterson, founded a successful tabloid in New York City, adopting for it the name of that wartime Copperhead journal, the *Daily News*. Medill's great-granddaughter, Alicia Patterson, became a newspaper publisher in her own right at Long Island's *Newsday*. For years, most of the family newspapers continued their editorial support for the Republican Party.

James W. Sheahan, late of the pro-Douglas *Chicago Times*, soldiered on at the Democratic *Chicago Post* until the month of Lincoln's death, when surprisingly he joined the paper he had spent years noisily contradicting: the *Chicago Tribune*. Sheahan went on to publish an 1868 history of Chicago, and several years later produced one of the first books about the 1871 fire. In 1883, not long after co-authoring a pamphlet about Chicago with his old press rival and current employer, Joseph Medill, Sheahan died at age fifty-nine.[11]

Sheahan's pistol-packing, Civil War–era *Chicago Times* successor, Copperhead editor Wilbur Storey, continued for a decade and a half to run the paper that Lincoln's army had briefly shut down in 1863, selling his interest only when failing health forced his retirement in 1877. The following year, he suffered a crippling stroke, and spent the last years of his life an invalid. Storey died at age sixty-four in 1884.

As for the other reigning New York editors of the Civil War period, William Cullen Bryant proved one of the few who walked away voluntarily from the newspaper business with his passion for political journalism subdued and his literary reputation intact. After serving for half a century as editor and part-owner of the *Evening Post*, the graybeard poet retired from the paper in 1878—but not before returning to his first love and publishing new free verse translations of Homer's *Iliad* and *Odyssey*. During a Central Park ceremony that same year honoring the Italian journalist-hero Giuseppe Mazzini, however, Bryant slipped and fell. He died of complications a few weeks later at the age of eighty-three. His *New York Post*, which has been continuously published since its founding by Alexander Hamilton in 1803, is now owned by Rupert Murdoch, who ironically bears far more resemblance in political philosophy and journalistic style to James Gordon Bennett than to William Cullen Bryant.

Albany editor and political boss Thurlow Weed, who owned nothing in New York City, it was mockingly said, except Henry Raymond, retired from both journalism and politics in 1867. Like Raymond, Weed's political influence had plummeted after his resistance to Andrew Johnson's impeachment. He spent his last five years living quietly in Manhattan, where he died in 1882 at the age of eighty-five. His autobiography, edited by his daughter and a valuable source for scholars, appeared two years later.[12]

Just after announcing his support for Samuel J. Tilden for the Democratic presidential nomination in 1876, Manton Marble abruptly sold the declining *New York World* to William Henry Hurlbut, a onetime Henry Raymond protégé, and retired from journalism in May—one step away from bankruptcy.[13] That same year, Marble was widely mentioned as a candidate for governor of New York, but failed to secure the Democratic nomination. His name resurfaced in 1885 as a potential nominee for U.S. secretary of the treasury after the Democrats returned to power under Grover Cleveland. When that prize eluded him, too, Marble was considered for a prime consular post, but again the former editor was passed over. Marble ultimately relaunched himself as a "publicist" in London, dying there in 1917 at the age of eighty-two.[14]

James Watson Webb, the hot-tempered former editor of the *New York Courier and Enquirer*, continued serving as U.S. minister to Brazil, the post to which Lincoln had appointed him, until 1869. Webb then returned to New York, dying there in 1884 at the age of eighty-two, convinced to the end that the North would have won the Civil War sooner had Lincoln made him a major general when the fighting first broke out.

Copperhead editor William Prime continued to operate his once virulently anti-Lincoln *New York Journal of Commerce* until 1893, when he sold the paper to William Dodsworth. Under the new name of *The Journal of Commerce and Commercial Bulletin,* the paper returned to its business roots and published without interruption into the 1990s.

The equally anti-Lincoln editor-politician Benjamin Wood, who, like James Gordon Bennett broke with General George McClellan in 1864 over the Democratic Party's peace platform, left the House of Representatives after three terms in 1865, served briefly in the New York State Senate, and returned for another two-year term in Congress in 1881. All the while, he continued at the helm of the *New York Daily News* until his death in 1900 at the age of eighty. The original *Daily News* went out of business shortly thereafter.

Theodore Tilton experienced marital difficulties in the early 1870s and sent his wife, Libby, for counseling with his longtime friend and onetime fellow *New York Independent* editor, Reverend Henry Ward Beecher. Apparently the charismatic minister's "counseling" went too far. In 1874, Tilton brought criminal charges against the famous minister for "criminal intimacy" with Libby, resulting in a sensational trial that drove America's Reconstruction battles off the front pages. When a jury failed to convict Beecher, and Brooklyn's Plymouth Church excommunicated his accuser, Tilton went into exile in Paris. He died there at the age of seventy-one in 1907.

Perhaps the state's most famous newspaper editor, Frederick Douglass had in August 1863 discontinued publication of his *Douglass' Monthly* after sixteen consecutive years in print to devote himself to recruiting black troops, and in anticipation of a military commission for himself that never arrived. "With a heart full and warm with gratitude to you for all you have done in furtherance of the cause of these to whom I devoted my life," Douglass closed his valedictory editorial by echoing the final words Lincoln had imparted to his neighbors when he left Springfield for the presidency: "I bid you an affectionate farewell."[15] When the Civil War ended two years later, Douglass became president of the Freedman's Savings Bank and, later, American chargé d'affaires in the Dominican Republic. Although he supported Grant's two bids for the presidency, Douglass in 1872 became the first African American to run (albeit symbolically, and without his consent) for national office (against the Grant reelection ticket) as the vice presidential candidate of the Equal Rights Party.

Four years later, on the eleventh anniversary of Lincoln's assassination, Douglass delivered a justly famous dedicatory address at the unveiling of Thomas Ball's Lincoln statue in Washington. Again paraphrasing Lincoln's words—this time the sentiments of his 1862 Annual Message to Congress—Douglass told the nation's African Americans, "In doing honor to the memory of our friend and liberator, we have been doing highest honors to ourselves."[16] Those who remembered that Lincoln had once adapted Douglass's "right makes might" phrase for his career-altering 1860 Cooper Union address no doubt believed that the rhetorical debt had finally been collected. Frederick Douglass died in 1895 at around seventy-seven years of age. Since he had been born a slave, no one, not even the great black leader himself, was ever sure of his precise birth date.

• • •

In the nation's capital, years before Ball's controversial "Emancipator" statue was unveiled, John Wein Forney, who had tried without success to win a cabinet post after Lincoln's reelection, sold the *Washington Chronicle* in 1870. He then returned to the city where he had launched his career in journalism, armed with a new federal patronage post: collector of the Port of Philadelphia. Ever searching for the next chance, Forney later rejoined the political party he had abandoned during Lincoln's presidency, again becoming a Democrat. He published two volumes of memoirs, which boasted a trove of firsthand reminiscences about Lincoln, and died in 1881 at age sixty-one.[17]

Forney's Washington rival for access to Lincoln administration news, James Welling of the *National Intelligencer*, became president of St. John's College in Annapolis after the war, then served as a professor of English at the College of New Jersey and finally as president of Columbian College—later known as George Washington University—in Washington. He was sixty-nine when he died in 1894.

Lawrence Gobright, longtime chief of the capital bureau of the Associated Press, testified before the military tribunal hearing the case of alleged Lincoln assassination conspirator Dr. Samuel Mudd. Later he covered Andrew Johnson's national get-acquainted tour for the AP. His memoirs appeared in 1869, but eight years later, Gobright ran afoul of the bureau and retired.[18] He died in 1881 at age sixty-five.

Noah Brooks, who might well have gone on to serve as Abraham Lincoln's White House secretary had the president lived for a second term, published his highly useful biography of Lincoln thirty years later, and began the new century with a book about the Lewis and Clark Expedition.[19] He was seventy-two years old when he died in Pasadena, California, in 1903.

Then there was the case of Theodore Canisius, the German-born editor who had entered into a discreet publishing partnership with Lincoln back in 1859 in Springfield, and who continued his career in government and diplomacy long after his benefactor's assassination.

After leaving the post to which Lincoln had named him—that of American consul at Vienna—Canisius held other consular positions in both Germany and England before beginning an extended tour as consul to the Samoan Islands. Canisius also produced a German-language Lincoln biography in 1867, which went through several editions over the years but failed to inspire an English translation. Never a good businessman, Canisius tried launching a sugar refinery, but enjoyed no more success than he had scored in the newspaper business. He returned to Chicago in fragile health in 1885, and died there that December, believed to be around sixty years old. Neither his books nor his obituaries made mention of the German-language weekly he had once co-owned with the leader he outlived by two decades; Canisius took that secret to the grave. His *New York Times* death notice mentioned only that the late diplomat had once been "acquainted with President Lincoln." [20]

Though Greeley and Bennett reconciled symbolically after the latter's funeral in 1872, both of these feisty old rivals surely would have objected violently had they lived to witness the 1924 merger of their once fiercely competitive newspapers to form the *New York Herald Tribune.* Later owned by John Hay Whitney, a grandson of Lincoln's assistant secretary, John Hay, the new paper went on to earn a reputation as one of the most brilliantly written dailies in the city. But in the 1960s, a newspaper era marked by costly labor strikes and intense competition from television news, the paper began suffering unsustainable losses in readership and revenue. In 1966, the struggling *Herald Tribune* merged once again—this time with the polyglot local dailies the *World Telegram and Sun* and the *Journal American*, forever obliterating the individual political traditions that had once informed the founding of each of those seven distinct, original titles. The new, consolidated *World Journal Tribune*, however, did not long endure. After only eight months, it closed its doors forever in May 1967—thereby putting a "30" on the entire epoch that had witnessed the founding of Ben Day's *Sun*, Manton Marble's *World*, James Gordon Bennett's *Herald*, and Horace Greeley's *Tribune.*

The *New York Times*, rescued from the brink of extinction in 1896 by onetime *Knoxville Chronicle* "printer's devil" Adolph Ochs—and still owned by his descendants (today published by his great-grandson Arthur Ochs Sulzberger, Jr.)—remains the only one of the three major New York dailies founded in the age of Lincoln to survive into the twenty-first century. In the decades since the Ochs family took control, the *Times* became and remains the most influential daily not only in the city, but in the nation, and one of the leading print and online news platforms in the world.

Today, just as it did during the Civil War, the *Times* again occupies the most modern newspaper headquarters in New York, a gleaming 2007 Renzo

Piano–designed glass skyscraper on Eighth Avenue at Fortieth Street. There, just outside the paper's sun-drenched executive boardroom on the tower's sixteenth floor, in a hallway otherwise dominated by sleek white tables and a modern black leather couch, publisher Sulzberger continues to devote a place of honor to a treasured, but discordant-looking relic from the age of the partisan political press: the quaint wooden lowboy secretary desk once used on Newspaper Row by the *Times*'s founder, Henry Jarvis Raymond.

ACKNOWLEDGMENTS

Awriter launches a new project hoping he can underwrite the cost of pursuing it. So my gratitude goes first to supporters who helped fund this undertaking. Warm thanks go to the Peter Jay Sharp Foundation, especially Norman Peck, and to the Lehrman Institute, in particular Lewis Lehrman, for their generosity and faith over nearly a decade.

The most generous and sustained support of all came from Roger Hertog, chairman emeritus of the New-York Historical Society, who asked me to serve as the Society's first Roger Hertog Fellow, enabling me to conduct research there and at many other places. It is an honor to carry his name in my job description.

I am much indebted to the scholars who read all or part of the manuscript and offered many ideas for its improvement. Thanks go first to Professor Emeritus Craig L. Symonds of the U. S. Naval Academy with whom I had the pleasure of editing a 2010 collection of *New York Times* Civil War coverage. Working on that earlier project fueled my enthusiasm for this broader study, which incorporates research we unearthed together. This time around, Craig reviewed every line of text, never faltering in his generous commitment even during periods that would have made postponement understandable.

In addition, that ninety-year-old wonder, Wayne C. Temple of the Illinois State Archives—born, like Lincoln's mother and myself on February 5 (somewhere between those two events, we often joke)—applied his encyclopedic knowledge to chapters focusing on Lincoln's Springfield years. And Civil War scholar John F. Marszalek improved sections relating to William T. Sherman and his volatile relationship with journalists. I also thank the inexhaustible Dr. Jonathan W. White of Christopher Newport University, who read the text and proposed terrific ideas for additions and illustrations. His thoughtfulness even extended through his initial sleepless nights as a first-time father.

Special gratitude goes to Princeton professor emeritus—and premier Civil War authority—James M. McPherson, along with Seward biographer Walter Stahr, for the gift of their unexpected, but truly essential readings and comments.

At the institutions where I conducted principal research, scholars and administrators alike proved unfailingly generous with their time and guidance. I must single out Michelle Krowl at the Manuscripts Division of the Library of Congress, who pointed the way to many relevant documents and again made possible my full access to the original documents in the Abraham Lincoln Papers.

In Springfield, Illinois, my thanks go to Daniel W. Stowell, director of the Papers of Abraham Lincoln, and to research specialist Marilyn Mueller. At the Abraham Lincoln Presidential Library & Museum, I am grateful to James Cornelius, knowledgeable curator of the Lincoln Collection, and his colleague Jennifer Ericson, as well as to director Eileen Mackevich, library services director Kathryn Harris, archivist Cheryl Schnirring, library associate Debbie S. Hamm, and audio visual specialists Mary Michals and Roberta Fairburn, most of whom have been there for me during many Lincoln endeavors. In another "Lincoln state," appreciation goes to my frequent collaborator Sara Vaughn Gabbard at the Friends of the Lincoln Collection of Indiana at Fort Wayne; to Ian Rolland, for generously backing the digitization of archives on which I relied for research; and to Jane Gastineau and Adriana Maynard at the Lincoln Financial Foundation Collection. For frequent good advice from the southern seat of the war, my gratitude to John Coski, historian at the Museum of the Confederacy in Richmond.

At the New-York Historical Society, I thank both president Louise Mirrer and chair Pam Schafler for their always warm welcomes, along with curators, librarians, and research specialists Linda Ferber, Jean Ashton, Jillian Pazereckas, Jeanne Gardner, Eleanor Gillers, and the ever resourceful Valerie Paley (who seems to know where every last document is stored), not to mention Dale Gregory, who creates such accessible public programs. I am similarly grateful to my Albany colleagues: former New York State Archivist Christine Ward, Carla Janowsky at the State Library, Mark Schaming of the State Museum, State Historian Robert Weible, and Robert Bullock, formerly of the State Archives Partnership Trust.

At the Lehigh Valley Heritage Museum in Allentown, Joseph Garrera showed me original post-assassination newspapers whose mournful headlines inspired the closing lines of this book. At the Lincoln Forum, an organization with which I have been proudly associated for twenty years, encouragement came from chairman Frank J. Williams, co-administrator Betty Anselmo, and treasurer Russell Weidman, who not only administered my research grants, but thoughtfully gave me a Frederick Douglass book once owned by his adored late wife Budge. Good advice and warm collegiality also came from my longtime Lincoln Group of New York friends, including Richard Sloan, Stan King, Henry Ballone, and Steve Koppelman. Additional thanks go to the staffs of the many other institutions where I conducted research: the National Archives, the Newseum, the Pennsylvania Historical Society, the New York Public Library, the Columbia University Libraries, the Richmond Public Library, the American Antiquarian Society, and the Chicago History Museum.

Private collectors and dealers are important resources as well. My friend Daniel Weinberg, proprietor of Chicago's Abraham Lincoln Book Shop, helped me find elusive titles crucial to my research and generously gave permission to publish his two photographs and one life sketch showing Lincoln with newspapers. Nathan Raab of the Raab Collection shared recently discovered Horace Greeley correspondence. Book dealer Chuck Hand of Paris, Illinois, remained faithfully on the lookout for rare publications, and Christopher Coover, manuscript specialist at Christie's, shared relevant catalogue entries. George Buss of Freeport, Illinois, Lincoln enactor and Stephen Douglas collector, provided a perfect early likeness of "The Little Giant."

Speaking of resources, the Frank and Virginia Williams Lincolniana Collection in Rhode Island remains one of the best private archives of Civil War–era material in the country, and thanks to Frank, one of the most accessible. My close friend for more than thirty-five years has never refused a plea to transmit an urgently needed document or source. Further opportunities to marvel at original material arrived closer to home. I thought I would never see, much less hold in my hands, Lincoln's original, handwritten letter in support of beleaguered editor Thomas Pickett, but my friend Tony Kushner allowed me to do so, for which I'm truly grateful.

The working journalists and editors of the Civil War era boast a number of descendants who still champion their heritage and retain valuable material and family memories. My gratitude goes to Michael Larocco for a peek at the Daniel Butterfield archive; to Brenda Molloy Paley, whose ancestor Joseph I.

Gilbert transcribed the Gettysburg Address; and to Beth Colley, descendant of Joseph H. Richards of the *New York Independent.* Sadly, Eleanor Stoddard, granddaughter of Lincoln's private secretary William O. Stoddard, died at age ninety-two just days after I handed in the manuscript, reminding me afresh of how generous she had been over the years in sharing materials from the Stoddard archive.

More inspiration came from publisher J. P. Leventhal, who issued the 2010 *Times* compendium, and Dwight Zimmerman, who mined the digitized archives on which I continued to rely for this project. I am grateful as well to *Times* veterans Mitchel Levitas and Alex Ward, who supervised that project together with an earlier one, *Lincoln and the Times,* for which I had the honor of working with the late, great David Herbert Donald.

I must also acknowledge the young researchers who aided me in nailing down quotes and finding documents and clippings. Principal gratitude goes to my primary research aide, the relentless Avi Mowshowitz, with additional thanks to Leland Chamlin and Win Rutherfurd. A special shout-out to Kraig Smith and Becky Schear of the Metropolitan Museum's Public Affairs department for using their off-hours to insert corrections and remind me that no matter how hard I try, I really don't know how properly to use the Internet.

My longtime senior colleagues at the Met often tease me about the time I devote to Lincoln, but this never detracts from the encouragement they have always shown me. Thanks again go to President Emily Rafferty and Director and CEO Thomas Campbell, as well as Librarian Ken Soehner and American Wing curators Morrison Heckscher, Thayer Tolles, and Elizabeth Kornhauser. And for being the best instant Latin phrase translator this side of Ancient Rome, I thank Philippe de Montebello as well.

I have profited enormously from discussions with fellow historians. For the pleasure of their company, conversation, and advice on this project, I thank: Jonathan Alter, Sidney Blumenthal, Gregory Borchard, Robert and Ina Caro, Ron Chernow, Henry Cohen, Alicia Cooper, William C. Davis, Peter Dickson, Paul Finkelman, Amanda Foreman, Guy Fraker, Norton Garfinkle, Doris Kearns Goodwin, Thomas Horrocks, James McPherson, David Mindich, Mark E. Neely, Jr., Matthew Pinsker, Ford Risley, James I. Robertson, Walter Stahr, John Taliaferro, Michael Vorenberg, Thomas Wheeler, Ted Widmer, Sean Wilentz, Douglas L. Wilson, Brenda Wineapple, Kenneth Winkle, and David Woodard.

Among those who invited me to deliver early talks on aspects of this book, which helped me shape the final study, I thank Jonathan White, who hosted a 2012 Christopher Newport conference on "Lincoln, the Constitution, and the Nation at War;" the Albany Law School and New York State Archives, which included me in its 2012 "Civil War on Trial" conference; and Marilyn Marcus of the Association of the Courts of New York State, who invited me to deliver the annual lecture named for the late husband of the esteemed emerita Chief Judge of the State Court of Appeals, Judith Kaye.

Hearteningly, over all the years that I worked on and discussed this book, I never encountered a print or broadcast journalist who failed to cheer the project. For their encouragement, thanks go to the following modern heirs to the Civil War "Bohemian Brigade:" Max Frankel, Joyce Purnick, Jill Abramson, Glenn Collins, Eleanor Randolph, James Barron, and Sam Roberts, all of the *New York Times;* Michael Goodwin of the *New York Post;* Rex Smith and Paul Grondahl of the *Albany Times-Union;* Ken Kurson of the *New York Observer;* Brian Lamb, Susan Swain, Steve Scully, Peter Slen, Russell Logan, and all my friends at C-SPAN; WAMC Radio CEO Alan Chartock, Jeffrey Brown of the *PBS News Hour;* television lions Charlie Rose and Gabe Pressman; Peter Dunn of CBS, along with his mentor and mentee, respectively, Dennis Swanson and Lew Leone; and the late and much missed Richard Heffner, for more than fifty years the host of PBS' *Open Mind.* At the Associated Press, I thank retired editor Richard Pyle, senior editor, vice president, and longtime friend Michael Oreskes; corporate communications officer Chuck Zoeller; writer Allen G. Breed; and director of corporate archives Valerie S. Komor, who asked me to speak during the run of the 2011 exhibition, "Long Remembered: The Associated Press with Lincoln at the First Inaugural and Gettysburg," and also opened the AP collection for research.

Special thanks go to Arthur Sulzberger, Jr., publisher of the *New York Times,* who shared his knowledge of Henry J. Raymond's armed defense of the paper during the 1863 Draft Riots and also gave me several opportunities to visit my favorite relic from that era: Raymond's own desk. Arthur's late father, "Punch" Sulzberger, was chairman of both the *Times* and the Met when I first arrived on the museum's staff. Punch shared his own trove of *Times* stories over the years, not to mention a copy of an 1870 Raymond biography—the first book I read for this project. Additional thanks go to current and former *Times* friends who have so often helped celebrate my books on the nineteenth-century press: Ethan Riegelhaupt, Lou Fabrizio, Alexis Buryck, Denise Warren, Barbara Jackson, and Nancy Karpf.

Lincoln never employed a public relations man—none existed in his day—but as one who once served in that capacity, for a somewhat later generation of public officials, I underestimate neither the craft nor its best practitioners. For their friendship and years of shared insights about the press and politics, I thank Howard Brock, Richard Edelman, Mortimer Matz, Martin McLaughlin, Ethan Riegelhaupt (again), Kevin Sheeky, William Cunningham, Ken Sunshine, and especially the late and much missed John O'Keefe, who, had he lived in the nineteenth century, would no doubt have induced Abraham Lincoln to wine and dine at the River Café in Brooklyn. Lincoln would have emerged from the experience a happier man.

Many public officials, past and present, have been equally enthusiastic about this book, especially my former boss, the inspiring Mario Cuomo and his extraordinary successor in Albany, Governor Andrew Cuomo. I am also grateful to President Bill Clinton for sharing his insights on this subject at several treasured encounters and for generously acknowledging my Lincoln work on many occasions. I have enjoyed my opportunities to discuss the nineteenth-century press with former Speaker of the House Newt Gingrich, Congressman Jerrold Nadler, New York City Comptroller Scott Stringer, and Manhattan Borough President Gale Brewer. Special thanks go to Senator Dick Durbin of Illinois, and his chief of staff, Patrick Souders, for giving me access to the Senate floor, where I saw and touched the desk where Congressman Preston Brooks nearly beat Senator Charles Sumner to death in 1856. Talk about Washington infighting!

Fortunately, no such disharmony reigns at my terrific publishing house, Simon & Schuster. It is hard to imagine being blessed with a more skillful or inspiring editor than Alice Mayhew. This is my third book for Alice, and with each successive project I become increasingly grateful for the opportunities to work with her. Her astute guidance—my occasional resistance notwithstanding—has made this a far better book. Further gratitude goes to Jonathan Cox of S&S for his additional help in organizing the project and its illustrations, to his successor Stuart Roberts, to indefatigable copy editor Fred Chase, to Julia Prosser and Maureen Cole of the PR team, and of course to publisher Jonathan Karp for his enthusiasm for the project. And I'm grateful as ever to my agent Geri Thoma, who has so ably represented me for more than twenty years.

Last but not least, I thank my family members for their abundant patience and help. Love and appreciation go to my brilliant daughters Meg and Remy (who ably proofread every page of manuscript), my gifted son-in-law Adam Kirsch, and my precious grandson Charles, who keeps me in my place and showers me with more affection than I deserve. My amazing mother Rose Holzer turned ninety-eight years young as I handed in this manuscript—a day after I marked my own sixty-fifth birthday—and much as I regret the Saturdays I had to postpone my usual weekly visits to her and my sisters Deanne and Susanne in order to press on with the book, her understanding reduced my customary level of Jewish guilt.

Above all, I want to express adoration and appreciation for Edith, my wife of forty-three years. For this project, we conducted much research side by side. We shared day after day at the Library of Congress, transcribing the papers of countless journalists and politicians and eyeballing blurry microfilm reels in the Newspaper Reading Room until we could barely see. Edith not only helped unearth many gems; her subsequent review of the first manuscript draft immeasurably improved the final book. Just as importantly, her constant care and feeding made it possible for me to survive twelve-hour workdays every weekend for more than four years—and then nursed me back to health after a hideous accident, a botched surgery, complications, and setbacks, so I could proofread galleys and keep the project on schedule. Edith is my sounding board for ideas, a shoulder to lean on when things are going in the wrong direction, and an honest critic whose approval means everything to me, as it has ever since high school. I could not possibly have written this book without her love and help, and only hope she's not too exhausted for the next one—whatever and whenever that may be.

NOTES

Abbreviations Used in the Notes

ALPLC   Abraham Lincoln Papers, Library of Congress.

ALPLM   Abraham Lincoln Presidential Library and Museum, Springfield, Illinois.

CW   Roy P. Basler, ed. *The Collected Works of Abraham Lincoln*, 8 vols. New Brunswick, N.J.: Rutgers University Press, 1953–55.

OR   *The War of the Rebellion: A Compilation of the Official Records of the Union and Confederate Armies*, 128 vols. Washington, D.C.: U.S. Government Printing Office, 1880–1901.

INTRODUCTION: A MORE EFFICIENT SERVICE

1   Quoted in Paul M. Angle, *"Here I Have Lived": A History of Lincoln's Springfield, 1821–1865*, orig. pub. 1935 (Chicago: Abraham Lincoln Book Shop, 1971), 85–86; Lincoln to Mary Owens, May 7, 1837, *CW*, 1:78.

2   For Springfield population shifts, see Kenneth J. Winkle, "The Voters of Lincoln's Springfield: Migration and Political Participation in an Antebellum City," *Journal of Social History* 25 (1992): 595–611.

3   *Sangamo Journal*, n.d., quoted in Angle, *"Here I Have Lived,"* 113–14.

4   William H. Herndon and Jesse William Weik, *Lincoln's Herndon*, ed. Douglas L. Wilson and Rodney O. Davis, orig. pub. 1889 (Urbana: University of Illinois Press, 2006), 231.

5   See Peter Bain and Paul Shaw, *Blackletter: Type and National Identity* (Princeton: Princeton University Press, 1998).

6   See Harry E. Pratt, *The Personal Finances of Abraham Lincoln* (Springfield, Ill.: Abraham Lincoln Association, 1943), 112; for the first modern report of Lincoln's investment in the German newspaper, see "A Bit of Staggering Information," *Chicago Tribune*, May 15, 1941.

7   Alexis de Tocqueville, *Democracy in America*, orig. pub. 1835–1839, ed. J. P. Mayer (New York: Harper Perennial, 1968), 517–18.

8   See Richard Rosenfeld, *American Aurora* (New York: St. Martin's, 1972).

9   It was a falling out with pamphleteer and journalist James Thomson Callender—imprisoned for sedition under Adams—that in fact led to the most humiliating episode of Jefferson's career. When Jefferson pardoned Callender but denied him the federal patronage job he coveted, the journalist exacted his revenge by publishing the first scandalous reports that Jefferson had fathered a child by his slave Sally Hemings. Quoted in Leonard W. Levy, ed., *Freedom of the Press from Zenger to Jefferson: Early American Libertarian Theories*, volume 1 of a 2-volume survey (Indianapolis: Bobbs-Merrill, 1966), 360, 371. In his own rise to power, not surprisingly, Jefferson was capable of praising newspapers—when they agreed with him. See Leonard Levy, *Jefferson and Civil Liberties: The Darker Side*, orig. pub. 1963 (Chicago: Ivan R. Dee, 1989), 48–55.

10   Edward Connery Lathem, *Chronological Tables of American Newspapers, 1690–1820* (Barre, Mass.: American Antiquarian Society and Barre Publishing, 1972), 31–35.

11   Gordon S. Wood, *The Idea of America: Reflections on the Birth of the United States* (New York: Penguin, 2011), 281.

12   Matthew Warshauer, *Andrew Jackson and the Politics of Martial Law: Nationalism, Civil Liberties, and Partisanship* (Knoxville: University of Tennessee Press, 1996), 33.

13   See Donald B. Cole, *A Jackson Man: Amos Kendall and the Rise of American Democracy* (Baton Rouge: Louisiana State University Press, 2004).

14   W. Stephen Belko, *The Invincible Duff Green: Whig of the West* (Columbia: University of Missouri Press, 2006), 104.

15   Ibid., 98–99.

16   One nineteenth-century account held that Green "denounced" Jackson as a "tyrant" for choosing Martin Van Buren, not John C. Calhoun, as his successor. See Lambert A. Wilmer, *Our Press Gang; or, A Complete Exposition of the Corruptions and Crimes of the American Newspapers* (Philadelphia: J. T. Lloyd, 1859), 20.

17   L. D. Ingersoll, *The Life of Horace Greeley, Founder of the New York Tribune, with Extended Notices of Many of His Contemporary Statesmen and Journalists* (New York: Union Publishing, 1873), 103–4.

18   Willard Grosvenor Bleyer, *Main Currents in the History of American Journalism* (Boston: Houghton Mifflin, 1927), 151.

19   Mark E. Neely, Jr., *The Extra Journal: Rallying the Whigs of Illinois* (Fort Wayne, Ind.: Louis A. Warren Lincoln Library and Museum, 1982), 3.

20   Joel H. Silbey, *The American Political Nation, 1838–1893* (Stanford: Stanford University Press, 1991), 54.

21   Lorman A. Ratner and Dwight L. Teeter, Jr., *Fanatics and Fire-Eaters: Newspapers and the Coming of the Civil War* (Urbana: University of Illinois Press, 2003), 11–12.

22   "The New York Herald from 1835 to 1866," *North American Review* 102 (April 1866): 374.

23   Anthony Trollope, *North America*, 2 vols. (London: Chapman & Hall, 1862), 2:427.

24   Ludwig Gall quoted in David M. Henkin, *City Reading: Written Words and Public Spaces in Antebellum New York* (New York: Columbia University Press, 1998), 133.

25   Elizabeth R. Varon, "Tippecanoe and Ladies, Too: White Women and the Party Politics in Antebellum Virginia," *Journal of American History* 82 (September 1995): 504.

26 Dr. Amos Willard French quoted in Wayne C. Temple, "The Linguistic Lincolns: A New Lincoln Letter," *Lincoln Herald* 94 (Fall 1992): 110.

27 *Illinois State Journal*, June 29, 1860.

28 Charles Eugene Hamlin, *The Life and Times of Hannibal Hamlin by His Grandson*, 2 vols. (Cambridge, Mass.: Riverside Press, 1899), 37

29 Quoted in Charles F. Wingate, ed., *Views and Interviews on Journalism* (New York: F. B. Patterson, 1875), 163.

30 See, for example, Louis M. Starr, *The Civil War's Bohemian Brigade: Newsmen in Action* (New York: Alfred A. Knopf, 1954).

31 The records are unavoidably imprecise because the database lacks such major publications as the *New York Times* and the *Chicago Press & Tribune*. Moreover, scanning the words "Lincoln" or "Douglas" yields false positives for people (and even ships and animals) with the same or similar names. But the numbers cited here have been painstakingly cleansed, and the trends they suggest are inescapable: Lincoln and Douglas received escalating press attention over the years, reflecting their growing prominence—and perhaps influencing it as well.

32 Roy Watson Curry, "The Newspaper Presses and the Civil War," *West Virginia History* 6 (January 1945): 226.

33 George F. Williams, quoted in "Bennett, Greeley, and Raymond. A Glimpse of New York Journalism Twenty-Five Years Ago," *The Journalist* 4 (October 2, 1886): 1.

34 May D. Russell Young, ed., *Men and Memories: Personal Reminiscences by John Russell Young* (New York: F. Tennyson Neely, 1901), 208. Young became Librarian of Congress during the McKinley administration.

35 Quoted in Ratner and Teeter, *Fanatics and Fire-Eaters*, 14.

36 Thomas Low Nichols, *Forty Years of American Life*, 2 vols. (London: John Maxwell & Co., 1864), 1:322.

37 "The New York Herald from 1835 to 1866," 378.

38 Lincoln's reply at the Ottawa debate, August 21, 1858, *CW*, 3:27.

ONE: THE TYPES ARE IN OUR GLORY

1 These descriptions, along with the coincidence of the two men's common rite of passage in mid–1831, were first noticed, and beautifully described, in William Harlan Hale, *Horace Greeley: Voice of the People* (New York: Harper & Brothers, 1950), 1–3.

2 Theodore L. Cuyler, " 'Uncle Horace,' " *The Temperance Record*, January 25, 1873, 40.

3 "By littles" is from the autobiographical sketch Lincoln prepared for John L. Scripps in June 1860, in *CW*, 4:62; the reference to "reading," is from a sketch prepared the previous December for Jesse W. Fell, *CW*, 3:511. For recollection of young Greeley, see James Parton, *The Life of Horace Greeley, Editor of "The New-York Tribune," from His Birth to the Present Time*, rev. ed. (Boston: James R. Osgood, 1872), 26.

4 *CW*, 4:62; Parton, *The Life of Horace Greeley*, 35–36.

5 Sarah Bush Johnston Lincoln interview, in Douglas L. Wilson and Rodney O. Davis, eds., *Herndon's Informants: Letters, Interviews, and Statements About Abraham Lincoln* (Urbana:

University of Illinois Press, 1998), 108; a "schoolmate" quoted in Parton, *The Life of Horace Greeley*, 26. Throughout, I have corrected the more egregious and distracting misspellings by Herndon's correspondents.

6   Wilson and Davis, eds., *Herndon's Informants*, 107.

7   Douglas L. Wilson and Rodney O. Davis, eds., *Herndon's Lincoln* (Urbana: University of Illinois Press, 2006), 512. This is the best annotated edition yet published of Herndon's controversial nineteenth-century Lincoln biography.

8   Quoted in Douglas L. Wilson, *Honor's Voice: The Transformation of Abraham Lincoln* (New York: Alfred A. Knopf, 1998), 62.

9   Robert Bray, *Reading with Lincoln* (Carbondale: Southern Illinois University Press, 2010), 44; Ida M. Tarbell, *The Early Life of Abraham Lincoln* (New York: S. S. McClure, 1896), 87.

10   Wilson and Davis, eds., *Herndon's Informants*, 426, 430, 512.

11   *CW,* 4:63–64; Earl Schenck Miers, ed., *Lincoln Day by Day: A Chronology, 1809–1865*, 3 vols. (Washington, D.C.: Lincoln Sesquicentennial Commission, 1960), 1:14–15.

12   William Dean Howells interview with Dr. John N. Allen, 1860, in David C. Mearns, ed., *The Lincoln Papers: The Story of the Collection with Selections to July 4, 1861*, 2 vols. (New York: Doubleday, 1948), 1:157.

13   There is still much mythology attached to Lincoln's life in New Salem. The best book remains Benjamin P. Thomas, *Lincoln's New Salem*, orig. pub. 1934 (Chicago: Lincoln's New Salem Enterprises, 1973). For Lincoln as village postmaster, see 94–101.

14   Horace Greeley, ms. autobiographical sketch dictated to Moses Cortland, April 14, 1845, Horace Greeley Papers, Library of Congress. In a postscript written in his own hand, Greeley, already infamous for his illegible penmanship, attested that he had asked his "boy" to copy the manuscript so it would exist in "readable characters."

15   Greeley autobiographical sketch; Horace Greeley, *Recollections of a Busy Life, Including Reminiscences of American Politics and Politicians . . .* (New York: J. B. Ford & Co., 1868), 39; Parton, *The Life of Horace Greeley*, 41; 2–4, 24.

16   Greeley, *Recollections of a Busy Life*, 61.

17   Ibid., 61–63.

18   Ibid., 75, 76.

19   Ibid.

20   Ibid., 81; William M. Cornell, *The Life and Public Career of Horace Greeley* (Boston: Lee and Shepard, 1872), 148.

21   "A Working Man's Recollections of America," *Knights Penny Magazine* 1 (1846): 99–100, consulted on http://historymatters.gmu.edu/d/5839.

22   Greeley autobiographical sketch.

23   Greeley, *Recollections of a Busy Life,* 82–87; Greeley autobiographical sketch.

24   Greeley, *Recollections of a Busy Life,* 88.

25   Greeley autobiographical sketch.

26   Simeon Francis to Allen Francis, ca. 1831, Francis Family Papers, ALPLM.

27   Andy Van Meter, *Always My Friend: A History of the State Journal-Register and Springfield*

(Springfield, Ill.: The Copley Press, 1981), 11–13; Josiah Francis to Charles Francis, May 4, 1832, Francis Family Papers, ALPLM.

28   Undated records in the Francis Family Papers, ALPLM.

29   Van Meter, *Always My Friend*, 7–9.

30   *Sangamo Journal*, February 23, 1832; Van Meter, *Always My Friend*, 13.

31   Van Meter, *Always My Friend*, 9, 13.

32   John G. Nicolay and John Hay, *Abraham Lincoln: A Biography*, 10 vols. (New York: The Century Co., 1890), 1:105.

33   *Sangamo Journal*, March 15, 1832; *CW*, 1:5–9.

34   *CW*, 1:8–9.

35   Speech in Congress, July 27, 1848, *CW*, 1:510.

36   *Sangamo Journal*, July 19, 1832. The author is grateful to historian Matthew Pinsker for bringing this story to his attention.

37   No copy of the handbill has ever been located. The story that Lincoln reprinted his *Journal* letter in this format was introduced by Lincoln's White House secretaries, later his biographers. See Nicolay and Hay, *Abraham Lincoln,* 1:105. The authors also contended that he "never took his campaigning seriously," but this is hardly believable.

38   The Abraham Lincoln Presidential Library and Museum has commissioned a computerized textual analysis of the *Journal*'s unsigned editorials in an effort to identify which can safely be attributed to Lincoln, but it remains to be seen whether the project can ever produce a unanimous consensus among scholars about their authorship.

39   Matheny quoted in Wilson and Davis, eds., *Herndon's Informants*, 430–31.

40   Quoted in Charles C. Patton, ed., *Glory to God and the Sucker Democracy: A Manuscript Collection of the Letters of Charles H. Lanphier*, 5 vols. (Privately printed, Illinois, 1973), 1:17.

41   The *Register*, quoted in Van Meter, *Always My Friend*, 109. The charge may have related to Lincoln's aborted duel with Democratic politician James Shields a few years later; see Chapter 2.

42   For Lincoln's pseudonymous work as a newspaper columnist, see Wilson, *Honor's Voice*, 175–78; Michael Burlingame, *Abraham Lincoln: A Life*, 2 vols. (Baltimore: Johns Hopkins University Press, 2008), 1:159–60; postal rates recalled in Thomas, *Lincoln's New Salem*, 95; *Beardstown Chronicle* episode in Wilson and Davis, eds., *Herndon's Informants*, 430.

43   Wilson and Davis, eds., *Herndon's Informants*, 374; A. W. Shipton, *Lincoln's Association with the Journal: An Address Delivered by A. W. Shipton, Publisher of the Illinois State Journal, at a Conference of Newspaper Publishers and Executives, Coronado, California, September 27, 1939*, pamphlet, Springfield, Ill: n.d.

44   George Henry Payne, *History of Journalism in the United States* (New York: D. Appleton, 1920), 256.

45   Frederic Hudson, *Journalism in the United States, from 1690 to 1872* (New York: Harper & Brothers, 1873), 430–31; see also James L. Crouthamel, "The Newspaper Revolution in New York, 1830–1860," *New York History* 45 (1964): 91–113.

46   David M. Henkin, *The Postal Age: The Emergence of Modern Communications in Nineteenth-Century America* (Chicago: University of Chicago Press, 2006), 42–50.

47   Frank M. O'Brien, *The Story of the Sun. New York, 1833–1918* (New York: George H. Doran, 1918), 11. The papers were the *Courier and Enquirer* and *Evening Post.*

48   Clarence Day, Jr., son of the *Sun* founder (also named Clarence, or "Clare") wrote the 1935 autobiographical book that inspired the hit play *Life with Father.* Quoted in Matthew Goodman, *The Sun and the Moon: The Remarkable True Account of Hoaxers, Showmen, Dueling Journalists, and Lunar Man-Bats in Nineteenth-Century New York* (New York: Basic Books, 2008), 23.

49   Ibid., 26. The *Sun* was not exactly the nation's first penny daily, but it was the first to succeed. Earlier, such papers as *The Bostonian* and the *Philadelphia Cent* appeared briefly, but quickly folded.

50   *New York Sun*, September 5, 1833.

51   O'Brien, *The Story of the Sun*, 38, 40, 50.

52   New York's Children's Aid Society was founded in 1854 largely to house and educate homeless newsboys.

53   [Isaac C. Pray], *Memoirs of James Gordon Bennett and His Times. By a Journalist.* (New York: Stringer & Townsend, 1855), 181–82. Day boasted of introducing high-powered printing presses in a speech in 1851, reprinted in part in Hudson, *Journalism in the United States*, 418. See also Michael Emery, Edwin Emery, and Nancy L. Roberts, *The Press and America: An Interpretive History of the Mass Media*, 9th ed., orig. pub. 1954 (Boston: Allyn & Bacon, 2000), 117.

54   *Memoirs of James Gordon Bennett*, 183.

55   New York Courier and Enquirer and *New England Magazine*, quoted in Allan Nevins, *The Evening Post: A Century of Journalism* (New York: Boni & Liveright, 1922), 137.

56   Hale, *Horace Greeley*, 21.

57   Bayard Tuckerman, ed., *The Diary of Philip Hone, 1828–1851*, 2 vols. (New York: Dodd, Mead & Co., 1889), 1:30, quoted in Payne, *History of Journalism*, 262.

58   Tuckerman, ed., *The Diary of Philip Hone*, 1:271.

59   *Philadelphia Public Ledger*, March 25, 1836, quoted in Henkin, *City Reading*, 110.

60   O'Brien, *The Story of the Sun*, 53–54.

61   *Memoirs of James Gordon Bennett*, 41. Despite its title, Bennett did not cooperate with this book. In fact, when Pray sent his latest proofs to the *Herald*, Bennett yelled at the messenger, "I don't want it! I won't have it," and threw the package into the hall (10–11).

62   Ibid., 43.

63   Don. C. Seitz, *The James Gordon Bennetts: Father and Son, Proprietors of the New York Herald* (Indianapolis: Bobbs-Merrill, 1928), 18–19; Douglas Fermer, *James Gordon Bennett and the New York Herald: A Study of Editorial Opinion in the Civil War Era, 1854–1867* (New York: St. Martin's, 1986), 13.

64   *Memoirs of James Gordon Bennett*, 45.

65   Hone Diary, quoted in Hale, *Horace Greeley*, 23, 63; Seitz, *The James Gordon Bennetts*, 76.

66   *Memoirs of James Gordon Bennett*, 45.

67   Noah wanted to create a Jewish homeland on an island in the Niagara River in upstate New York.

68   Oliver Carlson, *The Man Who Made News: James Gordon Bennett* (New York: Duell, Sloan & Pearce, 1942), 76–77, 79.

69   Beman Brockway, *Fifty Years in Journalism Embracing Recollections and Personal Experiences with an Autobiography* (Watertown, N.Y.: Daily Times Printing, 1891), 32.

70   Ben: Perley Poore, *Perley's Reminiscences of Sixty Years in the National Metropolis . . .* , 2 vols. (Philadelphia: Hubbard Brothers, 1886), 1:58; *Memoirs of James Gordon Bennett*, 134. See also Elwyn Burns Robinson, "The Dynamism of American Journalism from 1787 to 1865," *Pennsylvania Magazine of History and Biography* 61 (October 1937): 434–45.

71   Hudson, *Journalism in the United States*, 429.

72   Robinson, "The Dynamism of American Journalism from 1787 to 1865," 436.

73   Ibid.; entry from Bennett's "Diary of a Journey Through New York . . . July 12–August 18, 1831," New York Public Library.

74   *New York Herald*, 1836, quoted in James Melvin Lee, *History of American Journalism* (Boston: Houghton Mifflin, 1917), 197.

75   Hudson, *Journalism in the United States*, 432–33.

76   James L. Crouthamel, *Bennett's New York Herald and the Rise of the Popular Press* (Syracuse, N.Y.: Syracuse University Press, 1989), 21–22.

77   *New York Herald*, February 28, 1837, quoted in William Grosvenor Bleyer, *The History of American Journalism* (Boston: Houghton Mifflin, 1927), 191.

78   *Memoirs of James Gordon Bennett*, 468; *New York Herald*, November 26, 1841; Crouthamel, *Bennett's New York Herald and the Rise of the Popular Press*, 33.

79   Fermer, *James Gordon Bennett and the New York Herald*, 18–19.

80   See *The Death of Tammany and His Wife Loco Foco*, lithograph by H. R. Robinson, New York, 1837. Reprinted in Bernard F. Reilly, Jr., *American Political Prints, 1766–1876: A Catalog of the Collections in the Library of Congress* (Boston: G. K. Hall, 1991), 100–101.

81   *New York Herald*, May 14, 1840.

82   Quoted in Goodman, *The Sun and the Moon*, 84.

83   Cornelius Mathews, *The Career of Puffer Hopkins* (1841), quoted in Andie Tucher, *Froth and Scum: Truth, Beauty, Goodness, and the Ax Murder in America's First Mass Medium* (Chapel Hill: University of North Carolina Press, 1994), 160–61.

84   *Memoirs of James Gordon Bennett*, 225; *New York Herald*, May 11, 1834.

85   E. L. Godkin, writing in the *New York Evening Post*, December 30, 1899.

86   *Memoirs of James Gordon Bennett*, 188–89.

87   *New York Herald*, August 31, 1835.

88   Ibid.

89   See announcement of "*The Weekly Herald*," as "printed in French and English" for "sixpence," *New York Herald*, February 20, 1850.

90   *New York Herald*, May 13, 1836.

91   *Memoirs of James Gordon Bennett*, 194, 214; Payne, *History of Journalism*, 262.

92   Hale, *Horace Greeley*, 64; Crouthamel, *Bennett's New York Herald and the Rise of the Popular Press*, 36; Crouthamel, "The Newspaper Revolution in New York, 1830–1860," 98.

93   *New York Herald*, June 1, 1840.

94   Whitman quoted in David S. Reynolds, *Beneath the American Renaissance: The Subversive Imagination in the Age of Emerson and Melville* (New York: Alfred A. Knopf, 1988), 174; anonymous critic in *The North American Review* 102 (April 1866): 402; Marryatt quoted in Lambert A. Wilmer, *Our Press Gang; or, A Complete Exposition of the Corruptions and Crimes of the American Newspapers* (Philadelphia: J. T. Lloyd, 1859), 312.

95   *The Life and Writings of James Gordon Bennett, Editor of the New-York Herald* (New York: Privately and anonymously printed, 1844), 4.

96   A modern analogue may be the Australian-born Rupert Murdoch, whose global press empire includes the politically conservative *New York Post*—ironically the twenty-first-century version of the paper that the liberal William Cullen Bryant once edited.

TWO: NOT LIKE ANY OTHER THUNDER

1   *Cincinnati Gazette* quoted in Harold L. Nelson, ed., *Freedom of the Press from Hamilton to the Warren Court* (Indianapolis: Bobbs-Merrill, 1967), 192.

2   Joseph C. Lovejoy and Owen Lovejoy, *Memoir of the Rev. Elijah P. Lovejoy, Who Was Murdered in Defence of the Liberty of the Press, at Alton, Illinois, Nov. 7, 1837* (New York: John & Taylor, 1838), 277–80.

3   Ibid., 289–91.

4   The best book on the subject is still Paul Simon, *Freedom's Champion: Elijah Lovejoy* (Carbondale: Southern Illinois University Press, 1994).

5   *New York Evening Press*, November 18, 1837; first *New Yorker* quote from Lovejoy and Lovejoy, *Memoir*, 334; second from Russel Nye, *Fettered Freedom: Civil Liberties and the Slavery Controversy* (East Lansing: Michigan State College Press, 1949), 150.

6   Lincoln to "the Editor of the Journal," dated June 13, 1836, published June 18, 1836, in *CW*, 1:48. Lincoln's support may have helped Whig presidential candidate Hugh L. White win New Salem, and by a nearly two-to-one margin, but White lost Illinois—and every other state save for Tennessee and Georgia—to Martin Van Buren.

7   Speech to the Young Men's Lyceum, Springfield, January 27, 1838, *CW*, 1:109, 111.

8   Ibid, *CW*, 1:111, 112, 113.

9   Charles C. Patton, ed., *Glory to God and the Sucker Democracy: A Manuscript Collection of the Letters of Charles H. Lanphier*, 5 vols. (Privately printed, 1973), 1:5.

10   The paper had several names (and a co-publisher) before it adopted the title to which most historians refer to it today: *The Illinois Advocate and State Register, The Illinois State Register and People's Advocate*, and ultimately *The Illinois State Register*.

11   Quoted in Andy Van Meter, *Always My Friend: A History of the State Journal-Register and Springfield* (Springfield, Ill.: The Copley Press, 1981), 91.

12   Joseph Wallace, *Past and Present of the City of Springfield and Sangamon County Illinois* (Chicago: S. J. Clarke Publishing Co., 1904), at http://sangamon.ilgenweb.net/1904/lanphierc .htm.

13   William Lanphier to Charles Henry Lanphier, June 19, 1836, Patton, ed., *Glory to God,* 1.

14   William Walters to William Lanphier, October 28, 1837, ibid.

15   Douglas to Samuel Wolcott, April 16, 1854, in Robert W. Johannsen, ed., *The Letters of*

Stephen A. Douglas (Urbana: University of Illinois Press, 1961), 324; see also Johannsen, *Stephen A. Douglas* (New York: Oxford University Press, 1973), 3–19.

16   Douglas to Julius N. Granger, December 15, 1833, Johannsen, ed., *Letters of Stephen A. Douglas*, 2–3. Following custom, Granger replied by sending Douglas a copy of a newspaper containing one of Granger's political speeches back home (8). For Lincoln's affinity for Major Jack Downing, see Robert B. Rutledge's recollection in Douglas L. Wilson and Rodney O. Davis, eds., *Herndon's Informants: Letters, Interviews, and Statements about Abraham Lincoln* (Urbana: University of Illinois Press, 1998), 427.

17   See Richard J. Jensen, *Illinois: A Bicentennial History* (New York: W. W. Norton, 1975), esp. 41–46.

18   J. S. Buckingham, *America, Historical, Statistic, and Descriptive*, 2 vols. (New York: Harper & Brothers, 1841), 1: 123–25. To be fair, Buckingham acknowledged that the American papers had learned such tricks from the English press.

19   Receipts for notices, September 30, 1842, February 1, 1843, February 15, 1844, originals in the Francis Family Papers, ALPLM.

20   Douglas and others to William Walters, ca. February 18, 1840, Johanssen, ed., *Letters of Stephen A. Douglas*, 74–80; *Illinois State Register*, February 21, 1840.

21   Campaign circular, January 31, 1840, *CW*, 1:202–3; Lincoln to John T. Stuart, March 1, 1840, *CW*, 1:206.

22   Letter "To the Readers of the Old Soldier," like the January 31 circular, signed by Lincoln, Anson G. Henry, Dr. Richard F. Barrett, Edward D. Baker, and Joshua F. Speed, February 28, 1840, *CW*, 1:204–5.

23   "Rebecca Letter," August 27, 1842, *CW*, 1:292.

24   James Gourley, quoted in Wilson and Davis, eds., *Herndon's Informants*, 451. Not long thereafter, Early brandished a chair at an armed neighbor with whom he was also feuding; the cowering victim shot Early to death and Lincoln joined the legal team that successfully defended him from a murder charge. Douglas in turn counseled the prosecution; in Springfield, even murder cases could be political.

25   Lincoln to John T. Stuart, March 1, 1840, *CW*, 1:206; Johannsen, *Stephen A. Douglas*, 80; Van Meter, *Always My Friend*, 82–83.

26   Mark E. Neely, Jr., *The Extra Journal: Rallying the Whigs of Illinois* (Fort Wayne, Ind.: Louis A. Warren Lincoln Library and Museum, 1982), 3.

27   Simeon Francis to Charles Francis, September 6, 1840, Francis to his son and daughter, September 17, 1840, Francis Family Papers, ALPLM.

28   Simeon Francis to his son and daughter, September 17, 1860, and to Charles Francis, April 4, 1840, Francis Family Papers, ALPLM.

29   Roy P. Basler quoted Judge Thomas C. Browne's testimony regarding circulation achievements, February 25, 1840, in *CW*, 1:203n5.

30   *CW*, 1:203.

31   Springfield *Extra Journal*, April 20, 1843. Curator and Lincoln expert James T. Hickey unearthed the only known surviving set of the papers during the 1980s. See Neely, *The Extra Journal*, 3.

32 Springfield *Extra Journal*, May 15, May 30, 1843. The report of an *"Outrage on the Press"* in "Juliet" [*sic*] appeared on July 15, 1843, the last known issue of the *Extra Journal*. According to the report, Democrats, led by politician John Wentworth, had dismantled the printing press of the Whig *Signal* and "secreted" some of its parts in order to stop "publication of the paper until after the election."

33 Paul Angle, ed., *Herndon's Life of Lincoln*, orig. pub. 1930 (Cleveland: World Publishing Co., 1949), 183.

34 Historian Douglas L. Wilson insists the courtship did not resume before this episode occurred, but while the date of the reconciliation remains open to question, Mary later embraced the idea that she and her future husband had conspired in the attacks. See Wilson, *Honor's Voice: The Transformation of Abraham Lincoln* (New York: Alfred A. Knopf, 1998), 265–76.

35 "Letter from the Lost Townships," *Sangamo Journal*, dated August 27, 1842, in *CW*, 1:291–97.

36 *Sangamo Journal*, September 16, 1842, quoted in Richard Lawrence Miller, *Lincoln and His World: Prairie Politician, 1834–1842* (Mechanicsburg, Penn.: Stackpole, 2008), 519; Mary Lincoln to Francis B. Carpenter, December 8, 1865, and to Mary Jane Welles, December 6, 1865, in Justin G. Turner and Linda Levitt Turner, *Mary Todd Lincoln: Her Life and Letters* (New York: Alfred A. Knopf, 1972), 299, 295.

37 Mary Lincoln to Francis B. Carpenter, December 8, 1865, in Justin G. Turner and Linda Levitt Turner, eds., *Mary Todd Lincoln: Her Life and Letters* (New York: Alfred A. Knopf, 1972), 298–99.

38 Shields to Lincoln, and Lincoln to Shields, both September 17, 1842, *CW*, 1:299–300. The entire Lincoln-Shields correspondence ultimately appeared in the *Sangamo Journal*.

39 William Herndon to Jesse Weik, December 24, 1887, quoted in Don E. Fehrenbacher and Virginia Fehrenbacher, eds., *Recollected Words of Abraham Lincoln* (Stanford: Stanford University Press, 1996), 248–49.

40 Mary Lincoln to Mary Jane Welles, December 6, 1865, and to Josiah G. Holland, December 4, 1865, in Turner and Turner, eds., *Mary Todd Lincoln*, 292–93, 296. Holland had revived the long-suppressed story, much to Mary's chagrin, in his recently published biography of the late president.

41 Mary Lincoln to Francis B. Carpenter, December 8, 1865, in ibid., 299; Milton Hay to Thomas Vennum, January 26, 1892, in Louis A. Warren, "Herndon as a Contemporary Townsman Knew Him," *Lincoln Lore*, No. 653 (October 13, 1941).

42 The periodical has no relationship to the modern magazine of the same name.

43 Introductory prospectus quoted in William Harlan Hale, *Horace Greeley: Voice of the People* (New York: Harper & Bros., 1950), 27, 29.

44 J. C. Derby, *Fifty Years Among Authors, Books and Publishers* (New York: G. W. Carleton, 1884), 127. Derby became a noted publisher of books and popular prints.

45 Matthew Goodman, *The Sun and the Moon: The Remarkable True Account of Hoaxers, Showmen, Dueling Journalists, and Lunar Man-Bats in Nineteenth-Century New York* (New York: Basic Books, 2008), 87–88.

46 Edwin Emery, Michael Emery, and Nancy L. Roberts, *The Press and America: An Interpretive History of the Mass Media*, 9th ed. (Boston: Allyn & Bacon, 2000), 132.

47 Greeley autobiographical sketch for Moses A. Cortland, April 14, 1845, Horace Greeley Papers, Library of Congress; Thurlow Weed Barnes, *Memoir of Thurlow Weed*, 2 vols. (Boston: Houghton Mifflin, 1884), 2:283; Glyndon G. Van Deusen, *Thurlow Weed: Wizard of the Lobby* (Boston: Little, Brown, 1947), 97.

48 Harriet A. Weed, ed., *Autobiography of Thurlow Weed*, 2 vols. (Boston: Houghton Mifflin, 1883), 1:466.

49 Quoted in Hale, *Horace Greeley*, 45.

50 Horace Greeley, ms. autobiographical sketch dictated to Moses Cortland, April 14, 1845, Horace Greeley Papers, Library of Congress.

51 Ibid., 49; Weed, ed., *Autobiography of Thurlow Weed*, 1:467.

52 Weed, ed., *Autobiography of Thurlow Weed*, 1:467; John W. Forney, *Anecdotes of Public Men*, 2 vols. (New York: Harper & Bros., 1881), 1:328.

53 Horace Greeley, *Recollections of a Busy Life* . . . (New York: J. B. Ford & Co., 1868), 135.

54 Barnes, *Memoir of Thurlow Weed*, 2:283–84; Hale, *Horace Greeley*, 61.

55 Greeley, *Recollections of a Busy Life*, 139.

56 Ibid., 139–40.

57 McElrath manuscript, December 24, 1887, Horace Greeley Papers, Library of Congress, and quoted in Andie Tucher, *Froth and Scum: Truth, Beauty, Goodness, and the Ax Murder in America's First Mass Medium* (Chapel Hill: University of North Carolina Press, 1994), 130.

58 Greeley, *Recollections of a Busy Life*, 128, 138, 140, 141.

59 Ibid., 154.

60 Prospectus published in the *Log Cabin*, April 10, 1841, reprinted in Willard Grosvenor Bleyer, *Main Currents in the History of American Journalism* (Boston: Houghton Mifflin, 1927), 212–13

61 Greeley, *Recollections of a Busy Life*, 137.

62 Gregory A. Borchard, *Abraham Lincoln and Horace Greeley* (Carbondale: Southern Illinois University Press, 2011), 17; see also Borchard, "From Pink Lemonade to Salt River: Horace Greeley's Utopia and the Death of the Whig Party," *Journalism History* 32 (Spring 2007): 51–59.

63 *New York Tribune*, April 27, 1842; Frederic Hudson, *Journalism in the United States, from 1690 to 1872* (New York: Harper & Brothers, 1873), 524.

64 *New York Herald*, October 28, 1844.

65 *New York Herald*, November 27, 1844.

66 *Hartford Times*, reprinted in *New York Herald*, November 18, 1844.

67 *New York Herald*, February 13, 1845, December 24, 1844.

68 *New York Herald*, February 12, 13, 14, 1845; *New York Tribune*, February 13, 1845.

69 *New York Herald*, February 16, 1845.

70 *New York Tribune*, May 28, 1844.

71 *New York Herald*, December 24, 1844.

72 *New York Herald*, November 27, 1844.

73 *New York Herald*, November 27, December 1, 1844.

74 *New York Herald*, February 20, 1845.

75 James L. Crouthamel, *Bennett's New York Herald and the Rise of the Popular Press* (Syracuse: Syracuse University Press, 1989), 33, 167n51. For attacks by other rivals, see, for example, Frank M. O'Brien, *The Story of the Sun, New York, 1833–1918* (New York: George H. Doran, 1918), 159.

76 The comments, and similar ones, published over a five-month period beginning in April 1841, are quoted in Crouthamel, *Bennett's New York Herald*, 33, 167n51. See also O'Brien, *The Story of the Sun,* 159.

77 For the most recent account of the movement, and Greeley's involvement, see Philip F. Gura, *American Transcendentalism: A History* (New York: Hill & Wang, 2007), esp. 225–26. Greeley sent Fuller to Italy to cover its war for unification, but she died on her voyage home when her ship went down off Fire Island, New York.

78 Horace Greeley, *Essays Designed to Elucidate the Science of Political Economy . . . ,*" quoted in Bernard A. Weisberger, "Horace Greeley: Reformer as Republican," *Civil War History* 23 (March 1977): 11.

79 For the smoking story from his childhood, see Greeley, *Recollections of a Busy Life*, 98–99.

80 Barnes, *Memoir of Thurlow Weed*, 2:287; Greeley, *Recollections of a Busy Life*, 523.

81 See Tyler Anbinder, *Five Points: The 19th-Century New York City Neighborhood That Introduced Tap Dance, Stole Elections, and Became the World's Most Notorious Slum* (New York: Free Press, 2001).

82 Frederick Douglass to Horace Greeley, April 15, 1846, in Philip S. Foner and Yuvall Taylor, eds., *Frederick Douglass: Selected Speeches and Writings* (Chicago: Lawrence Hill, 1999), 27.

83 Ralph Waldo Emerson to Margaret Fuller, March 1, 1842, in Ralph L. Rusk, ed. *Letters of Ralph Waldo Emerson*, 6 vols. (New York: Columbia University Press, 1939), 3:19–20.

84 Ralph Waldo Emerson to Thomas Carlyle, quoted in Hy B. Turner, *When Giants Ruled: The Story of Park Row, New York's Great Newspaper Street* (New York: Fordham University Press, 1999), 43.

85 Horace Greeley to Charles A. Dana, May 13, 1856, Charles A. Dana Papers, Library of Congress.

86 Augustus Maverick, *Henry J. Raymond and the New York Press, for Thirty Years . . .* (Hartford, Conn.: A. S. Hale & Co., 1870), 40.

87 Greeley to C. Chauncey Brown, May 19, 1848, Chauncey Brown Papers, New-York Historical Society.

88 Quoted in Charles J. Rosebault, *When Dana Was the Sun: A Story of Personal Journalism* (New York: R. M. McBride, 1931), 50–51.

89 *New York Tribune*, February 6, 1845.

90 Greeley, *Recollections of a Busy Life*, 142.

91 Brockway, *Fifty Years in Journalism*, 99.

92 Cuyler, "'Uncle Horace.'"

93 Quoted in Van Deusen, *Thurlow Weed*, 56.

94   *New York Courier and Enquirer*, January 27, 1844.

95   Quoted in Rosebault, *When Dana Was the Sun*, 50–51.

96   See *Race Between Bennett and Greeley for the Post Office Stakes*, lithograph, probably by Edward Williams Clay, New York, ca. 1843, reprinted in Bernard F. Reilly, Jr., *American Political Prints, 1766–1876: A Catalog of the Collections in the Library of Congress* (Boston: G. K. Hall, 1991), 196–97.

97   Oliver Carlson, *The Man Who Made News: A Biography of James Gordon Bennetts, 1795–872*, (New York: Duell, Sloan & Pearce, 1942), 213.

98   Greeley, *Recollections of a Busy Life*, 167–68; L. D. Ingersoll, *The Life of Horace Greeley, Founder of the New York Tribune, with Extended Notices of Many of His Contemporary Statesmen and Journalists* (Chicago: Union Publishing Co., 1873), 173.

99   Patton, *Glory to God and the Sucker Democracy*, 1:48.

THREE: THAT ATTRACTIVE RAINBOW

1   Though elected in August 1846, Lincoln did not begin serving his term in Congress until December 1847—in accordance with the slow-moving transition traditions of the day, which remained in effect until ratification of the Twentieth Amendment to the Constitution in 1933.

2   Robert W. Johanssen, *Stephen A. Douglas* (New York: Oxford University Press, 1973), 211; George Fort Milton, *The Eve of Conflict: Stephen A. Douglas and the Needless War* (Boston: Houghton Mifflin, 1934), 34–35.

3   Caption to a print, *Brown's Indian Queen Hotel, Washington City North side of Pennsylvania Avenue . . .*, lithograph by Endicott & Co., ca. 1832, original in the Division of Prints and Photographs, Library of Congress.

4   The Sprigg establishment occupied the plot where the Jefferson Building of the Library of Congress now stands. Lincoln's Whig predecessors, Hardin and Baker, each lived there during their terms, and Baker conceivably recommended it to his successor. Abolitionist Joshua Giddings lived there during Lincoln's residency. See Allen C. Clark, *Abraham Lincoln in the National Capital* (Washington, D.C.: W. F. Roberts, 1925), 3.

5   Theodore Dwight Weld to Angelina Grimké Weld, January 2, 1842, Gilbert Hobbes Barnes and Dwight L. Dumond, eds., *Letters of Theodore Dwight Weld, Angelina Grimké and Sarah Grimké, 1822–1844*, orig. pub. 1934 (Gloucester, Mass.: Peter Smith, 1965), 884.

6   Kenneth J. Winkle, *Lincoln's Citadel: The Civil War in Washington, DC* (New York: W. W. Norton, 2013), 6–7.

7   Charles Dickens, *American Notes: A Journey*, orig. pub. 1842 (New York: Fromm International Publishing, 1985), 116–17, 119–20.

8   Quoted in Johanssen, *Stephen A. Douglas*, 207.

9   Diary of John Quincy Adams (original in the Massachusetts Historical Society, 51 vol.), 44:233, February 14, 1844, online at http://www.masshist.org/jqadiaries/cfm/doc.cfm?id =jqa44_233.

10   Hair "getting up in the world" quoted in Charles Hamilton and Lloyd Ostendorf, *Lincoln in Photographs: An Album of Every Known Pose*, orig. pub. 1963 (rev. ed, Dayton, Ohio:

Morningside Press, 1985), 18; Herbert Mitgang, ed., *Edward Dicey's Spectator of America* (Chicago: Quadrangle, 1971), 91.

11   Mary Lincoln to Francis B. Carpenter, December 8, 1865, in Justin G. Turner and Linda Levitt Turner, *Mary Todd Lincoln: Her Life and Letters* (New York: Alfred A. Knopf, 1972), 298; Mary quoted by Katherine Helm, *The True Story of Mary, Wife of Lincoln . . .* (New York: Harper & Brothers, 1928), 140.

12   Lincoln to Horace Greeley, June 27, 1848, *CW*, 1:494.

13   Quoted in Andrew C. McLaughlin, *Lewis Cass* (American Statesman series, No. 24, Cambridge, Mass.: Riverside Press, 1891), 232.

14   *Baltimore Sun*, April 12, 1847.

15   M. Y. Beach, "A Secret Mission to Mexico," *Scribner's Monthly* 18 (May 1879): 136–40.

16   Michael Emery, Edwin Emery, and Nancy L. Roberts, *The Press and America: An Interpretive History of the Mass Media*, orig. pub. 1954 (9th ed., Boston: Allyn & Bacon, 2000), 115–16.

17   Both quotes from Megan Jenison Griffin, "Jane McManus Storm Cazneau, 1807–1878," *Legacy* 27 (University of Nebraska Press, 2010): 416; *New York Sun*, April 15, 1847; Tom Reilly, "Jane McManus Storm[s]: Letters from the Mexican War, 1847–1848," *Southwestern Historical Quarterly* 85 (July 1981): 35. A veteran foreign correspondent for Greeley's *New-Yorker*, Storm later contributed reviews to the *Tribune* and became a friend of Greeley's wife. At first supportive of Southern expansion, she later opposed secession.

18   George H. Douglas, *The Golden Age of the Newspaper* (Westport, Conn.: Greenwood, 1999), 63–64.

19   Douglas Fermer, *James Gordon Bennett and the New York Herald* (New York: St. Martin's, 1986), 35.

20   Emery, Emery, and Roberts, *The Press and America,* 117.

21   Ben: Perley Poore, "Abraham Lincoln. Reminiscences of an Old Newspaper Correspondent," *Brooklyn Eagle,* September 6, 1885.

22   See, for example, late sessions of August 9 and August 12, 1848, reported in Earl Schenck Miers, ed., *Lincoln Day by Day: A Chronology, 1809–1865*, 3 vols. (Washington, D.C.: Lincoln Sesquicentennial Commission, 1960), 1:318.

23   *Sangamo Journal*, July 2, 1846; *Quincy Whig*, January 27, 1847.

24   "The National Intelligencer and Its Editors," *Atlantic Monthly* 6 (October 1860): 476–77, 486.

25   Mary J. Windle, *Life of Washington, and Here and There* (Philadelphia: J. B. Lippincott, 1859), 150–51.

26   [Josephine Seaton], *William Winston Seaton of the "National Intelligencer." A Biographical Sketch. With Passing Notices of His Associates and Friends* (Boston: James R. Osgood, 1871), 319.

27   Ibid., 271, 273. The English writer recalled "the pleasant hours we spent in your society."

28   Ibid., 289, 299.

29   Culver H. Smith, *The Press, Politics, and Patronage: The American Government's Use of Newspapers, 1789–1865* (Athens: University of Georgia Press, 1977), 169.

30   Quoted in Rufus Rockwell Wilson, *Washington: The Capital City and its Part in the History of the Nation*, 2 vols. (Philadelphia: J. B. Lippincott, 1901), 2:41–42.

31   [Seaton], *William Winston Seaton of the "National Intelligencer,"* 15.

32   William E. Ames, *A History of the National Intelligencer* (Chapel Hill: University of North Carolina Press, 1972), 343–44.

33   Reprinted in the *National Union*, December 7, 1847, quoted in Robert W. Merry, *A Country of Vast Designs: James K. Polk, the Mexican War and the Conquest of the American Continent* (New York: Simon & Schuster, 2009), 404.

34   Quoted in Mark E. Neely, Jr., *The Abraham Lincoln Encyclopedia* (New York: McGraw-Hill, 1982), 209.

35   Speech at Peoria, October 16, 1854, *CW*, 2:252.

36   Typescript of a previously unknown and lost Lincoln document quoted in Mark E. Neely, "Lincoln's Theory of Representation: A Significant New Lincoln Document," *Lincoln Lore*, No. 1683 (May 1978), 2.

37   Resolutions in the U.S. House of Representatives, December 22, 1847, *CW*, 1:420–22.

38   Lincoln to William H. Herndon, January 8, 1848, *CW*, 1:430.

39   *New York Tribune*, May 12, May 13, 1846.

40   Speech in the House of Representatives, January 12, 1848, *CW*, 1:439. The phrase beginning "that he ordered General Taylor" and ending with "to bring on a war," was inserted by Lincoln after the fact for the printing of the speech in the *Congressional Globe*, 30th Congress, 1st Session, New Series, No. 10, 154–56.

41   *Alexandria* (Virginia) *Gazette*, February 8, 1848; *Trenton* (New Jersey) *Star Gazette*, February 14, 1848; *Hudson River Chronicle*, February 15, 1848.

42   *Illinois State Register*, January 14, 1848. The paper attacked Lincoln on January 21, 27, and 28.

43   Charles Lanphier to John A. McClernand, January 16, [1848], McClernand Family Papers, ALPLM, Box 1 (1848).

44   *Illinois State Register*, February 18, March 2, 1848; *Illinois State Journal*, February 10, 1848.

45   Quoted in Johannsen, *Stephen A. Douglas*, 215.

46   Lincoln to William H. Herndon, February 1, 1848, *CW*, 1:447–48.

47   Lincoln to William H. Herndon, February 15, 1848, *CW*, 1:451.

48   Miers, ed., *Lincoln Day by Day*, 1:304.

49   *National Intelligencer*, January 6, 1848.

50   William H. Herndon and Jesse William Weik, *Herndon's Lincoln*, ed. Douglas L. Wilson and Rodney O. Davis, orig. pub. 1889 (Urbana: University of Illinois Press, 2006), 175, 179.

51   See, for example, Albert Beveridge, *Abraham Lincoln: 1809–1858*, 2 vols. (Boston: Houghton Mifflin, 1928), 1:409, 422. The historiography is examined exhaustively in G. S. Boritt, "A Question of Political Suicide: Lincoln's Opposition to the Mexican War," *Journal of the Illinois State Historical Society* 67 (February 1974): 81n5, 83–85.

52   Horace Greeley, *Recollections of a Busy Life* (New York: J. B. Ford, 1868), 211.

53   James Parton, *The Life of Horace Greeley* (Boston: James R. Osgood, 1872), 247.

54   Debate and commentary published in the *New York Herald*, January 25, 1848.

55   *New York Tribune*, January 15, 1848; "Richelieu" described in Harlan Hoyt Horner, *Lincoln and Greeley* (Urbana: University of Illinois Press, 1953), 43.

56   For a compelling look at the politics among Illinois Whigs, see Mark E. Neely, Jr., "Lincoln and the Mexican War: An Argument by Analogy," *Civil War History* 24 (March 1978): 5–24.

57   Lincoln to Benjamin H. James, December 6, 1845, *CW*, 1:352.

58   As he wistfully put it, "I made the declaration that I would not be a candidate again, more from a wish to deal fairly with others, to keep peace among our friends, and to keep the district from going to the enemy, than for any cause personal to myself." See Lincoln to William H. Herndon, January 8, 1848, *CW*, 1:431.

59   Autobiographical sketch prepared for John L. Scripps, ca. June 1860, *CW*, 66–67; the text used here was printed in John Locke Scripps, *Life of Abraham Lincoln*, orig. pub. 1860 (Bloomington: Indiana Universality Press, 1961), 104.

60   Lincoln to William H. Herndon, January 8, 1848, *CW*, 1:431.

61   See Boritt, "A Question of Political Suicide: Lincoln's Opposition to the Mexican War," 79–100.

62   Thomas L. Harris to Charles Lanphier, April 5, 1848, in Charles C. Patton, *Glory to God and the Sucker Democracy: A Manuscript Collection of the Letters of Charles H. Lanphier*, 5 vols. (Privately printed, 1973), 1:57, and full text in Vol. 2 (not paginated); *Illinois State Register*, May 19, 1848.

63   For early experiments in absentee voting for soldiers, see John C. Fortier and Norman J. Ornstein, "Election Reform: The Absentee Ballot and the Secret Ballot—Challenges for Election Reform," *University of Michigan Journal of Law Reform* 36 (Spring 2003): 8. The state of Pennsylvania extended voting opportunities to soldiers as early as the War of 1812, but remained an exception to tradition. The author is grateful to historian Jonathan White for pointing out these early experiments in widening the franchise to men in uniform.

64   The final vote was 7,201 for Harris, 7,095 for Logan.

65   Wilson and Davis, eds., *Herndon's Lincoln*, 179.

66   Lincoln to William Schouler, August 28, 1848, *CW*, 1:518.

67   Harris's version appears in Richard Lawrence Miller, *Lincoln and His World*, 3 vols. (Jefferson, N.C.: McFarland, 2011), 3:204; Francis's version appeared in the *Illinois State Journal*, October 3, 1848.

68   Parton, *Life of Horace Greeley*, 241–42.

69   For thoughtful commentary on what he calls the "ceremony" of newspaper reading, "repeated at daily or half-daily intervals throughout the calendar," see Benedict Anderson, *Imagined Communities: Reflections on the Origin and Spread of Nationalism* (London: Verso, 1983), 35.

70   Quoted in David M. Henkin, *City Reading: Written Words and Public Speeches in Antebellum New York* (New York: Columbia University Press, 1998), 122.

71   Junius Henri Browne, *The Great Metropolis; A Mirror of New York* (Hartford, Conn.: American Publishing Co., 1869), 93–94.

FOUR: A POSITION WE CANNOT MAINTAIN

1   See, for example, Noah Brooks, *Abraham Lincoln: The Nation's Leader in the Great Struggle Through Which Was Maintained the Existence of the United States* (New York: G. P. Putnam's Sons, 1888), 105. Conceding that an "illustrious company of legislators" attended the 30th

Congress, Brooks, who later knew Lincoln, argued that he was immediately "recognized as a man of great ability." If so, he was not so acknowledged in period newspapers.

2   James W. Sheahan, *The Life of Stephen A. Douglas* (New York: Harper & Bros., 1860), 74.

3   Ben: Perley Poore, "Reminiscences of an Old Newspaper Correspondent," *Brooklyn Eagle*, September 6, 1885.

4   *New York Herald*, March 15, 1849.

5   *Intelligencer* editorial reprinted in *Washington Daily Union*, August 3, 1846, quoted (along with the president's veto message) in Robert W. Merry, *A Country of Vast Designs: James K. Polk, the Mexican War and the Conquest of the American Continent* (New York: Simon & Schuster, 2010), 283.

6   Speech in the House of Representatives, *CW*, 1:490.

7   *New York Tribune*, June 22, 1848.

8   *National Intelligencer*, June 22, 1848.

9   Lincoln to William H. Herndon, June 22, 1848, *CW*, 1:491–92. Lincoln was undoubtedly referring to the hometown *Sangamo Journal*, the *Beardstown Gazette,* the (Lacon) *Illinois Gazette*, the (Jacksonville) *Morgan Journal*, and the recently defunct *Hennepin Herald*.

10 J. H. Buckingham, *Illinois as Lincoln Knew It: A Boston Reporter's Record of a Trip in 1847*, ed. Harry E. Pratt., reprinted from *Papers in Illinois History and Transactions for the Year 1937* (Springfield, Ill.: Abraham Lincoln Association, 1938), 13. Observer Buckingham, who further described the "happy" delegates as "uproariously orderly," was the son of the publisher of the *Boston Courier*.

11 *New York Tribune*, July 17, 1847.

12 Elihu B. Washurne, in Allen Thorndike Rice, ed., *Reminiscences of Abraham Lincoln by Distinguished Men of His Time* (New York: North American Publishing Co., 1886), 16.

13 Lincoln to Horace Greeley, June 27, 1848, *CW*, 1:493–94.

14 *New York Tribune*, June 29, 1848.

15 Lincoln to William H. Herndon, July 10, 1848, *CW*, 1:497.

16 Wilson and Davis, eds., *Herndon's Lincoln*, 179.

17 Lincoln called Henry Clay his "beau ideal of a statesman"—or a "great man" (accounts differed) at his first senatorial debate with Stephen Douglas at Ottawa, Illinois, on August 21, 1858; see *CW*, 3:29; Lincoln declared himself for Taylor in a letter to a Taylor committee on February 9, 1848; see *CW*, 1:449.

18 *New York Herald*, February 24, 1848.

19 *New York Herald*, June 10, 1848.

20 Oliver Dyer, *Great Senators of the United States Forty Years Ago (1848 and 1849)* . . . (New York: Robert Bonner's Sons, 1889), 81–83.

21 *New York Herald*, September 25, 1848.

22 *New York Tribune*, September 29, November 6, 1848.

23 Speech in the House of Representatives, July 27, 1848, *CW*, 1:509

24 *New York Herald*, March 31, 1848.

25 *Baltimore Journal*, August 16, 1848.

26 Lincoln to Stephen A. Hurlbut, July 10, 1848, *CW*, 1:498.

27 *National Intelligencer*, quoted in Paul Findley, *A. Lincoln: The Crucible of Congress* (New

York: Crown, 1979), 189; *Baltimore Clipper*, September 2, 1848, cited in Earl Schenck Miers, *Lincoln Day by Day: A Chronology, 1809–1865*, 3 vols. (Washington, D.C.: Lincoln Sesquicentennial Commission, 1960), 1:319.

28   Press reviews quoted in Miers, ed., *Lincoln Day by Day*, 1:320–21.

29   *Boston Daily Atlas*, November 17, 1848.

30   Quoted in Walter Stahr, *Seward: Lincoln's Indispensable Man* (New York: Simon & Schuster, 2012), 110.

31   Frederick Seward, *Autobiography of William H. Seward* . . . (New York: D. Appleton, 1883), 80.

32   Stahr, *Seward: Lincoln's Indispensable Man*, 110–11. The story of this allegedly fateful meeting was first printed by artist Francis B. Carpenter, who collected many Lincoln anecdotes during the six months he worked in the White House in 1864 painting Lincoln, Seward, and other members of the cabinet at the first reading of the Emancipation Proclamation.

33   *Boston Atlas*, September 23, 1848, reported in Robert S. Harper, *Lincoln and the Press* (McGraw-Hill, 1951), 11; *Boston Daily Advertiser*, September 14, 1848, in Herbert Mitgang, ed., *Lincoln as They Saw Him* (New York: Rinehart, 1956), 61, 64.

34   *Boston Daily Atlas*, September 25, 1848.

35   *Illinois State Register*, October 13, 1848.

36   The final vote in Illinois was: Cass, 56,300; Taylor, 53,047; and Van Buren, 15,774. Nationwide, Taylor won 1,360,099 votes to Cass's 1,220,544, winning the electoral votes 163–127.

37   Greeley replaced Congressman David S. Jackson after his opponent, James Monroe, nephew of the former president, contested the election, and the House decided to seat neither.

38   Adam Tuchinsky, *Horace Greeley's New York Tribune: Civil War-Era Socialism and the Crisis of Free Labor* (Ithaca, N.Y.: Cornell University Press, 2009).

39   *New York Tribune*, December 25, 1848.

40   *Congressional Globe*, December 17, 1848, 428.

41   "Greeley's Estimate of Lincoln. An Unpublished Address by Horace Greeley," *The Century Magazine*, 42 (July 1891), 371–382. Greeley's lecture remained undelivered and unpublished during the editor's lifetime. Joel Benton, ed., *Greeley on Lincoln* . . . (New York: The Baker & Taylor Co., 1893), 19–20.

42   Horace Greeley, *Recollections of a Busy Life* (New York: J. B. Ford & Co., 1868), 226.

43   Ibid.

44   Nathan Sargent, quoted in Michael Burlingame, *Abraham Lincoln: A Life*, 2 vols. (Baltimore: Johns Hopkins University Press, 2008), 1:260.

45   Horace Greeley to Margaret Fuller, March (?) 1847, quoted in Gregory Alan Borchard, "The Firm of Greeley, Weed, & Seward: New York Partisanship and the Press, 1840–1860" (Ph.D. diss., University of Florida, 2003), Chapter 7.

46   See Harlan Hoyt Horner, *Lincoln and Greeley*, esp. epiloque, 393–94. Gregory A. Borchard summed up their relationship well in an excellent short book about the two men: see Borchard, *Abraham Lincoln and Horace Greeley* (Carbondale: Southern Illinois University Press, 2011).

47   Lincoln to Gales & Seaton, January 22, 1849, *CW*, 2:24.

48   Merry, *A Country of Vast Designs*, 459–60.

49   Lincoln to Albert G. Hodges, April 4, 1864, *CW*, 7:281; Lincoln to Joshua F. Speed, August 24, 1855, 2:320.

50   Kenneth J. Winkle, *Lincoln's Citadel: The Civil War in Washington, DC* (New York: W. W. Norton, 2013), 32–34.

51   From Lincoln's Peoria Address, October 16, 1854, *CW*, 2:253.

52   Isaac N. Arnold, *The History of Abraham Lincoln and the Overthrow of Slavery* (Chicago: Clarke & Co., 1866), 37.

53   "Greeley's Estimate of Lincoln: An Unpublished Address by Horace Greeley," *Century Illustrated Monthly Magazine* 62 (July 1891): 374.

54   Resolution banning slavery, January 6, 1849, in *CW*, 2:20–22; his recollection of being "abandoned by my former backers" is in Lincoln's letter to James M. McLean, January 11, 1849, ibid., 22.

55   Much has been made of Lincoln's role in the so-called Matson Slave Case in Coles County, Illinois, in which the congressman-elect represented one Robert Matson in his effort to recover his slave Jane Bryant and her four children. The case was not a slavery vs. freedom watershed, but rather a narrow test of whether owners like Matson who took their human property into free states could still consider them "sojourned" there if they stayed permanently. Lincoln took the case principally because Matson's side approached him for representation first, not because he believed in recovering runaways. Nonetheless, his participation—which was successful—has haunted his reputation, particularly among African-American critics. For the full transcript and period reminiscences about the case, see Daniel W. Stowell, ed., *The Papers of Abraham Lincoln: Legal Documents and Cases*, 4 vols. (Charlottesville: University of Virginia Press, 2008), 2:1–43. For a sound recent analysis, see Richard Striner, *An Honest Calling: The Law Practice of Abraham Lincoln* (DeKalb: Northern Illinois University Press, 2006), Chapter 5, "In the Matter of Jane, a Woman of Color," 103–36. Striner notes the tradition requiring lawyers to take up "unjust causes." For sharp criticism of Lincoln's "discreditable" role in the case, see Lerone Bennett, Jr., *Forced into Glory: Abraham Lincoln's White Dream* (Chicago: Johnson, 2000), 278–82.

56   Descriptions of the Intelligencer office from Mary J. Windle, 1857, in Allen C. Clark, "Joseph Gales, Junior, Editor and Mayor," *Records of the Columbia Historical Society* 23 (1920): 128. See also notes for an interview with Lincoln by James Quay Howard, May 1860, reported in Burlingame, *Lincoln*, 293. Seaton later scoffed that he had personally freed "more slaves" at his "own cost" than "all the abolitionists put together . . . including the zealous emancipationist, the editor of the Tribune." See [Josephine Seaton], *William Seaton of the "National Intelligencer"* . . . , 262.

57   *New York Tribune*, September 22, 1849.

58   Prospectus for *The Liberator*, quoted in Wendell Phillips Garrison and Francis Jackson Garrison, *William Lloyd Garrison, 1805–1879: The Story of His Life, Told by His Children*, 2 vols. (New York: The Century Company, 1885–89), 1:224–26.

59   John C. Nerone, *Violence Against the Press: Policing the Public Sphere in U.S. History* (New York: Oxford University Press, 1994), 101–2.

60   Oliver Johnson quoted in *William Lloyd Garrison, 1805–1879: The Story of His Life, Told by His Children*, 1:220.

61   Ibid., 1:221, frontispiece; R. J. M. Blackett, ed., *Thomas Morris Chester: Black Civil War Correspondent—His Dispatches from the Virginia Front*, orig. pub. 1989 (New York: Da Capo, 1991), 5.

62   Frederick Douglass, *Life and Times of Frederick Douglass Written by Himself* (Hartford Conn.: Park Publishing, 1881), 267.

63   Ibid., 320–21, 327.

64   Ibid., 327.

65   Frederick Douglass to Thomas Van Rensselaer, May 18, 1847, in Philip S. Foner and Yuval Taylor, eds., *Frederick Douglass: Selected Speeches and Writings* (Chicago: Lawrence Hill, 1999), 83–84. The *Tribune* at least reprinted Douglass's speech May 13, 1847.

66   The protest was ignited by the seizure of runaway slaves from a ship attempting to flee the District. There was no evidence that the society or its newspaper played a role in the plot.

67   David Grimsted, *American Mobbing, 1828–1861: Toward Civil War* (New York: Oxford University Press, 1998), 267.

68   Rufus Rockwell Wilson, *Washington: The Capital City and Its Part in the History of the Nation*, 2 vols. (Philadephia: J. B. Lippincott, 1901), 2:45; Milton, *The Eve of Conflict*, 38–39.

69   *A Memorial of Horace Greeley* (New York: The Tribune Association, 1873), 258.

70   Greeley, *Recollections of a Busy Life*, 227.

71   Joseph S. Myers, "The Genius of Horace Greeley," *Journalism Series*, No. 6 (Columbus: Ohio State University Press, 1919): 20–21; *Congressional Globe, 30th Congress, 2nd Session*, January 25, 1849, 370; January 23, 1849, 336.

72   Greeley, *Recollections of a Busy Life*, 228.

73   Ibid., 219.

74   Miers, ed., *Lincoln Day by Day*, 1: 321; Fragment on Niagara Falls, ca. late September 1848, in *CW*, 2:10.

75   *New York Tribune*, December 22, 1848. Although the figures remain unclear, Lincoln may have earned more in travel reimbursements during his congressional career than he did in salary. See Clerk's ledger, signed by Lincoln, in the National Archives, reprinted in Findley, *A. Lincoln*, 162.

76   *Congressional Globe, 30th Congress, 2nd Session,* January 11, 1849, 229–30.

77   *New York Tribune*, January 27, 1849.

78   *A Memorial of Horace Greeley*, 257–58; "Greeley's Estimate of Lincoln," 374.

79   *New York Herald*, January 29, 1849.

80   Poore, "Abraham Lincoln."

81   Greeley, *Recollections of a Busy Life*, 223.

82   *New York Tribune,* December 15, 1848.

83   "Greeley's Estimate of Lincoln," 374.

84   Greeley, *Recollections of a Busy Life*, 233.

85   *Congressional Globe*, February 26, 1849.

86   Parton, *Life of Horace Greeley*, 284.

87   Ibid., 286.

88 Reprinted in the *National Union*, June 21, 1849, quoted in Merry, *A Country of Vast Designs* 471–72.

89 Quoted in *Lincoln Day by Day*, 2:15.

90 There are several sources for this Lincoln story. For one, see Edward Dicey, "Washington During The War," *Macmillan's Magazine* 6 (May 1862): 24.

91 William E. Ames, "The National Intelligencer: Washington's Leading Political Newspaper," *Records of the Columbia Historical Society*, Washington, D.C., 66 (1966–1968): 81.

92 Anson G. Henry et al. to Lincoln, April 6, 1849; Josiah M. Lucas to Lincoln, April 12, 1849, all in ALPLC.

93 *New York Tribune*, September 22, 1849.

94 Lincoln to John M. Clayton, September 16, 1849, *CW*, 2:64.

95 Allen Francis to Lincoln, June 12, 1849, ALPLC.

96 John McCauley Palmer, *The Bench and Bar of Illinois, Historical and Reminiscent*, 2 vols. (Chicago: Lewis Publishing, 1899), 2:673.

97 For example, Lincoln outraged Simeon Francis and other local Whigs by promoting his brother-in-law, Dr. William Wallace, for a post as pension agent, even though the editor and others claimed they had "incurred [his] . . . hatred & malice on your account." See Anson G. Henry to Lincoln, June 15, 1849, ALPLC.

98 Stephen Douglas asked Lanphier to examine the poll books that year "with a view to the detection of errors." See Douglas to Lewis A. Ross, October 14, 1839, in Robert W. Johannsen, ed., *The Letters of Stephen A. Douglas* (Urbana: University of Illinois Press, 1961), 73.

99 Stephen Douglas to Charles Lanphier, October 25, 1845, ibid., 119.

100 Ibid., 150–51.

101 Andy Van Meter, *Always My Friend: A History of the State Journal-Register and Springfield* (Springfield, Ill.: The Copley Press, 1981), 115.

102 Statement to Nathaniel Wilcox, quoted in Joseph H. Barrett, *Abraham Lincoln and His Presidency*, 2 vols. (Cincinnati: Robert Clarke, 1904), 1:108.

FIVE: A MEAN BETWEEN TWO EXTREMES

1 Horace Greeley, *Recollections of a Busy Life* (New York: J. B. Ford & Co., 1868), 138–39.

2 Quoted in Henry Luther Stoddard, *Horace Greeley: Printer, Editor, Crusader* (New York: G. P. Putnam's Sons, 1946), 86. Greeley referred to the newspaper debate as "a series of controversial letters between Mr. Henry J. Raymond and myself." See Greeley, *Recollections of a Busy Life*, 151.

3 *New York Times*, June 21, 1869.

4 Augustus Maverick, *Henry J. Raymond and the New York Press, for Thirty Years . . .* (Hartford, Conn.: A. S. Hale & Co., 1870), 17, 19, 20–22, 26–27. Raymond returned to the university three years later to serve as commencement orator. See *University of Vermont. Commencement. August 2, 1843*. Original program in the Henry J. Raymond Papers, New York Public Library.

5 Raymond, "Autobiographical Sketch in Maverick, *Henry J. Raymond*," 362.

6 Henry J. Raymond to Horace Greeley, June 8, 1840, Horace Greeley Papers, New York Public Library.

7   Horace Greeley to Henry J. Raymond, June 20, 1840, George Jones and Henry J. Raymond Papers, New York Public Library. Millerism was a belief in the second coming of Jesus Christ.

8   Maverick, *Henry J. Raymond,* 29, 363 ("Autobiographical Fragment").

9   Ibid., 59–60, 363–64.

10 Raymond, "Autobiographical Sketch," in Maverick, *Henry J. Raymond,* 364.

11 Greeley, *Recollections of a Busy Life,* 138–39.

12 Henry J. Raymond, "Autobiographical Sketch," in Maverick, *Henry J. Raymond,* 361.

13 Raymond, "Autobiographical Sketch," ibid., 364.

14 Ibid., 33–34.

15 Francis Brown, *Raymond of the Times* (New York: W. W. Norton, 1951), 24, 40–41.

16 Maverick, *Henry J. Raymond,* 34–35.

17 Brown, *Raymond of the Times,* 34.

18 James L. Crouthamel, "The Newspaper Revolution in New York, 1830–1860," *New York History* 45 (April 1964): 99; Frederic Hudson, *Journalism in the United States, from 1690 to 1872* (New York: Harper & Brothers, 1873), 360.

19 *New York Courier and Enquirer,* January 27, 1844; reprinted in Maverick, *Henry J. Raymond,* 42.

20 *New York Tribune,* January 28, 1844.

21 Dorothy Dodd, *Henry J. Raymond and the New York Times During Reconstruction* (Chicago: University of Chicago Libraries), 109. For another excellent account of the beginning of the Greeley-Raymond feud, see Gregory Alan Borchard, "The Firm of Greeley, Weed, & Seward: New York Partisanship and the Press, 1840–1860" (Ph.D. diss., University of Florida, 2003).

22 Horace Greeley and H. J. Raymond, *Association Discussed; or, The Socialism of the Tribune Examined. Being a Controversy Between the New York Tribune and the Courier and Enquirer* (New York: Harper & Brothers, 1847), 82–83.

23 *New York Courier and Enquirer,* December 16, 1846. An excellent account of this newspaper debate can be found in Adam Tuchinsky, *Horace Greeley's New York Tribune: Civil War–Era Socialism and the Crisis of Free Labor* (Ithaca, N.Y.: Cornell University Press, 2009), 52–57.

24 Horace Greeley to Henry J. Raymond, April 14, 1853, George Jones and Henry J. Raymond Papers, New York Public Library.

25 Henry J. Raymond, *Reminiscences of Public Life,* autograph manuscript for a memoir in the George Jones and Henry J. Raymond Papers, New York Public Library, 23.

26 Ibid., 24.

27 Ibid., 26.

28 Ibid., 31.

29 Reprinted in *New York Times,* June 21, 1869.

30 John Russell Young, "Men Who Reigned: Bennett, Greeley, Raymond, Prentice, Forney," *Lippincott's Monthly* 5 (February 1893): 192.

31 Typescript version of Raymond reminiscences, George Jones and Henry J. Raymond Papers, New York Public Library, 1.

32 See Culver H. Smith, *The Press, Politics, and Patronage: The American Government's Use of Newspapers, 1789–1875* (Athens: University of Georgia Press, 1977), 109.

33 Raymond, *Reminiscences of Public Life*, 36.

34 Maverick, *Henry J. Raymond*, 87.

35 Elmer Davis, *History of the New York Times, 1851–1921* (New York: New York Times, 1921), 4.

36 This and subsequent quotes from *"New York Daily Times." A New Morning and Evening Daily Newspaper. Edited by Henry J. Raymond. Price One Cent.* Circular, August 30, 1851, copy in the New-York Historical Society.

37 Figures provided in Edwin G. Burrows and Mike Wallace, *Gotham: A History of New York City to 1898* (New York: Oxford University Press, 1999), 677.

38 Lorman A. Ratner and Dwight L. Teeter, Jr., *Fanatics and Fire-Eaters: Newspapers and the Coming of the Civil War* (Urbana: University of Illinois Press, 2003), 9, 12–13, 17.

39 Meyer Berger, *The Story of the New York Times*, 1851–1951 (New York: Simon & Schuster, 1951), 5.

40 Maverick, *Henry J. Raymond*, 92–93.

41 *New York Times*, September 18, 1851.

42 Maverick, *Henry J. Raymond*, 99–100.

43 *New York Times*, September 17, 1851.

44 *New York Times*, September 17, 1852.

45 *New York Times*, October 11, 1851, reprinted in Willard Grosvenor Bleyer, *Main Currents in the History of American Journalism* (Boston: Houghton Mifflin, 1927), 241.

46 *New York Tribune*, February 7, 1849.

47 Horace Greeley to William H. Seward, February 6, 1853, transcript in Horace Greeley Papers, Library of Congress. See also Ralph Ray Fahrney, *Horace Greeley and the Tribune in the Civil War* (Cedar Rapids, Iowa: The Torch Press, 1936), 19.

48 Oliver Carlson, *The Man Who Made News; James Gordon Bennett* (New York: Duell, Sloan & Pearce, 1942), 237–38.

49 Charles F. Wingate, ed., *Views and Interviews in Journalism* (New York: F. B. Patterson, 1875), 156.

50 *New York Sun*, March 13, 1875, reprinted in Bleyer, *Main Currents in the History of American Journalism*, 241; Hudson, *Journalism in the United States*, 621.

51 William H. Herndon and Jesse William Weik, *Herndon's Lincoln: The True Story of a Great Life*, 3 vols. (Chicago: Belford, Clarke & Co., 1889), 2:363.

52 Lincoln to "Editors of the Illinois Journal," June 5, 1850, *CW*, 2:79.

53 Eulogy to Zachary Taylor, July 25, 1850, *CW*, 2:83–90; see esp. 87.

54 Lincoln to John Addison, August 9, 1850, *CW*, 2:91–92.

55 *Illinois Journal*, February 7, 1850, reprinted in Harold Holzer, *Father Abraham: Lincoln and His Sons* (Honesdale, Penn.: Calkins Creek, 2011), 45. Mary Lincoln biographers Ruth Painter Randall, Jean H. Baker, and Catherine Clinton all suggested Mary as the author of "Little Eddie." Not until 2012 did historian Samuel P. Wheeler conclusively identify the real poet; see Wheeler, "Solving a Lincoln Literary Mystery: 'Little Eddie,'" *Journal of the*

Abraham Lincoln Association 33 (Summer 2012): 34–46. Even earlier, historians Wayne C. Temple and Jason Emerson, among others, contended that the Lincolns did not write the verses, basing their argument on the stylistic and rhythmic differences between the "Eddie" poem and Lincoln's known verses in iambic pentameter; arguing further that his parents spelled their late son's name "Eddy," not "Eddie"; and that Mary's agonized mourning make it unlikely she could have collected herself to compose her thoughts so soon after her son's death. See Jason Emerson, "The Poetic Lincoln," *Lincoln Herald* 101 (Spring 1999): 8–9. The author is grateful to Wayne Temple for sharing his knowledge of the poem and its authorship.

56   *CW*, 2:121–32; *New York Tribune*, June 30, 1852.

57   Resolution in behalf of Hungarian Freedom, January 9, 1852, in *CW*, 2:115–16; Maverick, *Henry J. Raymond*, 110–19.

58   David M. Henkin, *City Reading: Written Words and Public Spaces in Antebellum New York* (New York: Columbia University Press, 1998), 127; *New York Times*, December 8, 1851.

59   *New York Tribune*, October 11, 1850.

60   Robert W. Johannsen, *Stephen A. Douglas* (New York: Oxford University Press, 1973), 296–98.

61   Douglas to Charles H. Lanphier, December 30, 1851, in Robert W. Johannsen, ed., *The Letters of Stephen A. Douglas* (Urbana: University of Illinois Press, 1961), 235; 241–43.

62   Douglas to Charles H. Lanphier, August 3, 1860, in ibid., 190.

63   Johannsen, *Stephen A. Douglas*, 300.

64   Ibid., 448–49. A copy of the *Chicago Times* announcement broadside was long in possession of the Martin F. Douglas family in Greensboro, North Carolina.

65   Complicating the race was a third-party bid by New Hampshire's John P. Hale, running under the Free Soil banner.

66   See, for example, Lincoln's speech at the Scott Club, Springfield, August 14 and 26, 1852, in *CW*, 2:150.

67   Horace Greeley to Schuyler Colfax, quoted in Henry Luther Stoddard, *Horace Greeley: Printer, Editor Crusader* (New York: G. P. Putnam's Sons, 1946), 149.

68   *Frederick Douglass' Paper*, February 28, 1852.

69   Maverick, *Henry J. Raymond*, 140–41.

70   Douglas to Charles H. Lanphier, December 2, 1852, in Johannsen, ed., *Letters of Stephen A. Douglas*, 258; Douglas to Franklin Pierce, March [?] and March 4, 1853, in ibid., 261.

71   Douglas to Charles H. Lanphier, November 11, 1853, in ibid., 267.

72   Petition as owners of the Steamboat "Newsboy," by Henry J. Raymond (*Courier and Enquirer*), J. & E. Brooks (*Express*), Grant Hallock (*Journal of Commerce*), Beach Bros. (*Sun*), and James Gordon Bennett (*Herald*), April 9, 1849, James Wright Brown Collection, New-York Historical Society.

73   George E. Prescott, *History, Theory and Practice of the Electric Telegraph* (Boston: Ticknor and Fields, 1860), 385–86; Maury Klein, *Days of Defiance: Sumter, Secession, and the Coming of the Civil War* (New York: Alfred A. Knopf, 1997), 213.

74   Carlson, *The Man Who Made News*, 229.

75   See Isaac R. Pray, *Memoirs of James Gordon Bennett and His Times* (New York: Stringer & Townsend, 1855), 460–88.

76   "Horace Greeley's Manuscript a Source of Much Trouble to Printers Fifty Years Ago: Very Few Could Decipher It—Unable Sometimes to Read It Himself" clipping from an unknown newspaper, May 25, 1951, New-York Historical Society.

77   Ibid.

78   S. W. Jackman, ed., *Acton in America: The American Journal of Sir John Acton, 1853* (Shepherdstown: Patmos, 1979), vii, 12–13.

79   Ford Risley, *Abolition and the Press: The Moral Struggle Against Slavery* (Evanston, Ill.: Northwestern University Press, 2008), 127–28.

80   *New York Times*, June 22, 1853.

81   Carlson, *The Man Who Made News*, 256.

82   *New York Tribune*, January 5, 1854; Stoddard, *Horace Greeley*, 162.

83   Charles A. Dana to James S. Pike, in Pike, *First Blows of the Civil War: The Ten Years of Preliminary Conflict in the United States from 1850 to 1860* (New York: American News Co., 1879), 260–61.

84   Autobiographical sketches, December 20, 1859, June [?], 1860, in *CW*, 3:512; 4:67.

85   *Illinois State Journal*, September 12, 1854, *CW*, 2:229–30.

86   *Illinois State Register*, October 6, 1854, in Herbert Mitgang, ed., *Lincoln as They Saw Him* (New York: Rinehart, 1956), 72–73.

87   Quoted in Lewis Lehrman, *Lincoln at Peoria: The Turning Point* (Mechanicsburg, Penn.: Stackpole, 2008), 65, 67; see also 101, 45.

88   *CW*, 2:255. For an exhaustive and illuminating study of the speech, see Lehrman, *Lincoln at Peoria*.

89   *Quincy Whig*, November 3, 1854, quoted in Lehrman, *Lincoln at Peoria*, 67.

90   *Illinois State Journal*, October 5, 1854. Quoted and explained in Douglas L. Wilson and Rodney O. Davis, eds., *Herndon's Lincoln*, pub. 1889 (Urbana: University of Illinois Press and the Abraham Lincoln Bicentennial Commission, 2006), 227.

91   Original Raymond campaign tickets in the collections of the New York State Museum, Albany. See also *New York Times*, September 20, September 27, September 30, 1854.

92   Horace Greeley to William H. Seward, November 11, 1854, reprinted in Greeley, *Recollections of a Busy Life*, 315–20. The letter remained private until Seward's allies distributed it at the 1860 Republican presidential convention to demonstrate Greeley's bias against the senator's candidacy.

93   Charles E. Payne, *Josiah Bushnell Grinnell* (Iowa City: State Historical Society of Iowa, 1938), 26–27.

94   *Brooklyn Eagle*, undated clipping from John Russell Young scrapbook, John Rusell Young Papers, Library of Congress; Donn Piatt, *Memories of the Men Who Saved the Union* (New York: Belford, Clarke & Co., 1887), 151. Piatt, an interim U.S. chargé d'affaires to Paris during the Buchanan administration, became a Lincoln supporter in 1860, and later wrote for the *Cincinnati Commercial* and other papers.

95   Maverick, *Henry J. Raymond*, 142–45.

96   Lambert A. Wilmer, *Our Press Gang; or, A Complete Exposition of the Corruptions and Crimes of the American Newspapers* (Philadelphia: J. T. Lloyd, 1859), 82, 85.

97   Douglas to Charles H. Lanphier, December 18, 1854; Douglas to James Washington Sheahan, February 6, 1855, in Johannsen, ed., *Letters of Stephen A. Douglas*, 331, 333.

98   Lincoln to Elihu Washburne, February 9, 1855, *CW*, 2:304.

99   *New York Tribune*, February 9, 1855.

SIX: THE PRAIRIES ARE ON FIRE

1   Paul Selby, "George Schneider," *Transactions of the Illinois State Historical Society for the Year 1906* (Springfield: Illinois State Historical Library, 1906), 332–33.

2   Raymond Lohne, "Team of Friends: A New Lincoln Theory and Legacy," *Journal of the Illinois State Historical Society* 101 (Fall/Winter 2008): 36. *Staats Zeitung* is German for *State Newspaper*.

3   Nils William Olsson, "Abraham Lincoln's Swedish Photographer," www.kb.se/document /Aktuellt/…217-222OlssonAbrahamLincoln.pdf.

4   Although most early Lincoln photographic historians long assigned this pose to 1858, more recent scholars convincingly redated it to October 1854, although disagreement remains over which paper Lincoln grasps in the portrait. Stefan Lorant dated the picture to 1858 and claimed it was the *Press and Tribune*, while others have disagreed. See Stefan Lorant, *Lincoln: A Picture Story of His Life* (rev. ed., New York: W. W. Norton, 1969), 72–73. Lloyd Ostendorf, who claimed the photographer was Swedish, reattributed the picture to 1854 based on research by collector Bruce Duncan, see Charles Hamilton and Lloyd Ostendorf, *Lincoln in Photographs: An Album of Every Known Pose*, orig. pub. 1963 (rev. ed., Dayton, Ohio: Morningside, 1985), 18–19. For corroboration see these recent studies: James Mellon, *The Face of Lincoln* (New York: Viking, 1979), 21, 191; and Philip B. Kunhardt III Peter Kunhardt, and Peter Kunhardt, Jr., *Lincoln, Life-Size* (New York: Alfred A. Knopf, 2009), 4–5. See also Lloyd Ostendorf, *Lincoln and His Photographers*, Address at the Annual Meeting of the Lincoln Fellowship of Wisconsin, Historical Bulletin, No. 27 (Madison Lincoln Fellowship, 1972), 3. Other views have been suggested in Matthews Pinsker, "Not Always Such a Whig: Abraham Lincoln's Partisan Alignment in the 1850s," *Journal of the Abraham Lincoln Association* 29 (2009): 27–46; and Ezra M. Prince, ed., "Commemorative of the Convention of May 29, 1856," Transactions of the McLean County Historical Society 3 (1900): 12.

5   Megan McKinney, *The Magnificent Medills: America's Royal Family of Journalism During a Century of Turbulent Splendor* (New York: HarperCollins, 2011), 10; James O'Donnell Bennett, *Joseph Medill: A Brief Biography and an Appreciation*, orig. pub. 1929 (Chicago: Chicago Tribune, 1947), 7.

6   Joseph Medill to Horace Greeley, November 4, 1851, typescript copy in the James Wright Brown manuscript collection, Box 1, Folder G, New-York Historical Society.

7   Bennett, *Joseph Medill*, 9. For evidence supporting the alternative story, see A. N. Cole to "the Editor of the 'Tribune,'" August 1, 1884, in Francis Curtis, *The Republican Party: A History of Its Fifty Years' Existence and a Record of Its Measures and Leaders, 1854–1884* (New

York: G. P. Putnam's Sons, 1904), 210; also Medill obituary, *Chicago Tribune*, March 17, 1899, in Wyatt Rushton, "Joseph Medill and the Chicago Tribune" (Master's thesis, University of Wisconsin, 1916). Others gave credit to coining the name for the new party to Greeley himself. At the very least, Medill hosted an important, all-night planning meeting for disgruntled Democrats, Whigs, and Free Soilers in Chicago around the same time the new party was getting organized in Ripon, Wisconsin.

8   John Tebbel, *An American Dynasty* (Garden City, N.Y.: Doubleday, 1947), 9.

9   The capabilities of Richard Hoe's new, four-cylinder rotary press were described in "The Newspaper Business in Europe and America," *New York Tribune*, October 27, 1849.

10   The recollections of Lincoln's maiden visit to the *Chicago Tribune* come from the *Saturday Evening Post*, August 5, 1899; the remark about Lincoln's feet from Ralph G. Martin, *Cissy: The Extraordinary Life of Eleanor Medill Patterson* (New York: Simon & Schuster, 1979), 12. Both are reprinted in McKinney, *The Magnificent Medills*, 20–21.

11   Recollection by Joseph Wilson Fifter, quoted in Rufus Rockwell Wilson, ed., *Intimate Memories of Lincoln* (Elmira, N.Y.: Primavera, 1945), 154.

12   Andy Van Meter, *Always My Friend: A History of the State Journal Register and Springfield* (Springfield, Ill.: Copley Press, 1981), 155–56. Even crackpots played the opposing Springfield papers against each other. When the inventor of the quickly forgotten "new art of *Tintography*" appealed to Bailhache for an endorsement on the pages of the *Journal*, the politically astute request was accompanied by the warning that such praise had already been procured in the opposition *Democratic Press*. See J. B. Blair to William Bailhache, May 11, 1854, Bailhache Family Papers, ALPLM.

13   Augustus Maverick, *Henry J. Raymond and the New York Press, for Thirty Years . . .* (Hartford, Conn.: A. S. Hale & Co., 1870), 383.

14   Quoted in ibid., 150–51.

15   Douglas to James W. Sheahan, April 9, 1856 in Robert W. Johannsen, ed., *The Letters of Stephen A. Douglas* (Urbana: University of Illinois Press, 1961), 353.

16   Douglas to James W. Sheahan, February 23, 1857, in ibid., 374.

17   *New York Tribune*, April 11, 1856.

18   *New York Tribune*, January 26, 1856.

19   *Chicago Tribune*, January 31, 1856.

20   *New York Times*, May 24, 1856.

21   *Chicago Tribune*, March 31, 1857.

22   *New York Tribune*, March 7, 9, 10, 11, 12, 16, 17, 19, 20, 21, 25, 1857. These excerpts were collected by historian Don E. Fehrenbacher for the chapter "The Judges Are Judged" in his definitive study of the case. See Fehrenbacher, *The Dred Scott Case: Its Significance in American Law and Politics* (New York: Oxford University Press, 1962), 417.

23   *New York Times*, March 9, 1857.

24   *New York Herald*, March 8, 1857; *Richmond Enquirer*, March 10, 1857, quoted in David Goldfield, *America Aflame: How the Civil War Created a Nation* (New York: Bloomsbury, 2011), 140.

25   Address at Springfield, Illinois, June 26, 1857, *CW*, 2:404, 407; *Tribune* commentary in

Mario M. Cuomo and Harold Holzer, eds., *Lincoln on Democracy* (New York: HarperCollins, 1993), 88.

26 Lincoln to Joseph Harding, May 25, 1855, *CW* 2:312; document signed by Lincoln, Ozias Hatch, Jesse Dubois, Lyman Trumbull and others and forwarded to John G. Nicolay, July 3, 1857, *CW* 2:410.

27 Stephen A. Douglas to Charles H. Lanphier and George Walker, December 6, 1857, in Johannsen, ed., *Letters of Stephen A. Douglas,* 405.

28 *New York Tribune,* May 8, 1858.

29 Medill and Douglas quoted in Allen C. Guelzo, *Lincoln and Douglas: The Debates That Defined America* (New York: Simon & Schuster, 2008), 49–50.

30 Lincoln to Lyman Trumbull, December 28, 1857, *CW,* 2:430.

31 Attacks on Greeley in the *New York Herald,* February 3, February 10, March 28, 1858.

32 Ozias M. Hatch and Jesse K. Dubois to Lincoln and Republican State Chairman Norman Judd, March 22, 1858, and Lincoln to Hatch, March 24, 1858, in Roy P. Basler, ed., *The Collected Works of Abraham Lincoln: Supplement, 1832–1865* (Westport, Conn.: Greenwood, 1974), 29–30.

33 William H. Herndon and Jesse W. Weik, *Herndon's Lincoln,* orig. pub. 1889, ed. Douglas L. Wilson and Rodney O. Davis (Urbana: University of Illinois Press, 2006), 240–42.

34 Ibid., 239.

35 Lincoln to Charles L. Wilson, June 1, 1858, *CW,* 2:456–57.

36 Don E. Fehrenbacher, *Prelude to Greatness: Lincoln in the 1850s* (Stanford: Stanford University Press, 1962), 68.

37 Wilson and Davis, eds., *Herndon's Lincoln,* 244–45.

38 Historian Don E. Fehrenbacher was the first scholar to unscramble and explain the printed version of the incomprehensible early paragraphs of the "House Divided" address. See Fehrenbacher, ed., *Lincoln: Speeches, Letters, and Miscellaneous Writings,* 2 vols. (New York: Library of America, 1989), 1:870–71. For the *Journal* version, see *CW,* 2:461–69.

39 Lincoln to "Editors Tribune," June 8, 1858, in Basler, ed., *Collected Works of Abraham Lincoln: Supplement,* 31–32; *Chicago Press and Tribune,* June 11, 1858; David W. Davis to Lincoln (identifying his "Dear Friend" as the author), June 14, 1858, ALPLC; Lincoln to John L. Scripps, June 23, 1858, *CW,* 2:471. For more on the Davis-Lovejoy dispute, see Willard L. King, *Lincoln's Manager: David Davis* (Cambridge: Harvard University Press, 1960), 117–21.

40 Lincoln to John L. Scripps, June 23, 1858, *CW,* 2:471; Horace Greeley, *Recollections of a Busy Life* (New York: J. B. Ford & Co., 1868), 358; Greeley to Joseph Medill (copy in Lincoln's handwriting), July 24, 1858, ALPLC.

41 Lincoln to Joseph Medill, June 25, 1858, *CW,* 2:473–74; David Davis to Lincoln, June 14, 1858, ALPLC; Lincoln to Charles H. Ray, June 27, 1858, ALPLM.

42 David Davis to Lincoln, June 14, 1858, ALPLC.

43 Quoted in Harold Holzer, ed., *The Lincoln-Douglas Debates: The First Complete, Unexpurgated Edition* (New York: HarperCollins, 1990), 3.

44 Ibid., 4.

45 *New York Evening Post,* August 23, September 21, 1858, quoted in Edwin Erle Sparks, ed.,

The Lincoln-Douglas Debates of 1858, Collections of the Illinois State Historical Library 3; Lincoln Series, Vol. 1 (Springfield: Illinois State Historical Library, 1908), 129–30, 319.

46   *New York Tribune*, August 18, 1858.

47   *CW*, 3:146, 16.

48   The story is recounted in Paul M. Angle, *"Here I Have Lived": A History of Lincoln's Springfield., 1832–1865*, orig. pub. 1935 (Chicago and New Salem: Abraham Lincoln Book Shop, 1971), 232.

49   Douglas to Charles H. Lanphier, [August 15, 1858], Lanphier to Douglas, August 26, 1858, in Johannsen, ed., *Letters of Stephen A. Douglas*, 426–27.

50   Joseph Medill to Lincoln, June 23, 1858; Ray, Medill & Co. to Lincoln, June 29, 1858, ALPLC.

51   Charles H. Ray to Lincoln, July [?], 1858, ALPLC.

52   Charles H. Ray to Elihu Washburne, undated [ca. August 1858], Elihu Washburne Papers, Library of Congress.

53   Charles H. Ray to Lincoln, August 27, 1858, ALPLC. Ray proposed that Lincoln avow he would support D.C. emancipation only when a *"Majority* of the people of that District are in favor of ridding themselves of the institution." This, Ray said, would establish his "sincerity of belief in *Real* Popular Sovereignty." Lincoln was already on record in this regard.

54   *New York Tribune*, August 26, 1858.

55   Ibid.

56   Lincoln's opening speech at Ottawa, August 21, 1858, *CW*, 3:14.

57   An examination of the "opposition texts"—that is, the Republican versions of Douglas's speeches and the Democratic record of Lincoln's—suggests that loyal editors indeed worked to polish the raw material from each.

58   *Chicago Journal*, October 9, 1854, quoted in Joseph Logsdon, *Horace White: Nineteenth Century Liberal* (Westport, Conn.: Greenwood, 1971), 21.

59   Holzer, *The Lincoln-Douglas Debates*, 75–77.

60   Quoted in ibid., 88.

61   Ibid., 78.

62   Quoted in Herbert Mitgang, ed., *Lincoln as They Saw Him* (New York: Rinehart, 1956), 110.

63   Ibid., 83–84; *Chicago Press and Tribune*, October 11, 1858.

64   *Chicago Press and Tribune*, August 26, September 6, October 11, 1858.

65   Quoted in Holzer, ed., *The Lincoln-Douglas Debates*, 14.

66   Lincoln to William A. Ross, March 26, 1859, *CW*, 3:373.

67   Quoted in Holzer, *The Lincoln-Douglas Debates*, 15.

68   Sparks, *The Lincoln-Douglas Debates*, 594–95.

69   *New York Tribune*, November 5, 1858.

70   Henry Clay Whitney, *Life on The Circuit with Lincoln* (Boston: Estes and Lauriat, 1892), 457. Lincoln to Horace Greeley, November 8, 1858, *CW*, 3:336.

71   Lincoln to Charles H. Ray, November 20, 1858, *CW*, 3:341–42.

72   Ibid. Lincoln was so eager to commence assembling his scrapbook that he wrote to Henry Clay Whitney ten days later to urge Ray to comply with his request, this time offering to

"pay all charges, and be greatly obliged to boot." See Lincoln to Whitney, November 30, 1858, *CW*, 3:343; Lincoln to Whitney, December 25, 1858, *CW*, 3:347.

73   Holzer, ed. *The Lincoln-Douglas Debates*, 29.

74   Quoted in Fehrenbacher, *Prelude to Greatness*, 96.

75   Speech at Chicago, December 10, 1856, *CW*, 2:385.

76   Lincoln at Ottawa, Illinois, August 21, 1858, *CW*, 3:27.

77   Charles Lanphier to Stephen A. Douglas, January 6, 1859, Lanphier Papers, ALPLM; Douglas to Lanphier January 6, 1859, in Johannsen, ed., *Letters of Stephen A. Douglas*, 433.

78   *New York Herald*, November 10, 1858.

79   Ibid.

80   *New York Tribune*, November 17, 1858.

81   Greeley, *Recollections of a Busy Life*, 357–58.

82   Lanphier quoted in Charles C. Patton, *Glory to God and the Sucker Democracy: A Manuscript Collection of the Letters of Charles H. Lanphier*, 5 vols. (Springfield, Ill.: Privately printed 1973), 1:108; Douglas to Lanphier, January 6, 1858[9], in Johannsen, ed., *Letters of Stephen A. Douglas*, 433; Lincoln to Henry Asbury, November 19, 1858, *CW*, 3:339. Five years to the day after writing to Asbury, Lincoln offered his most unforgettable words on "the cause of civil liberty": the Gettysburg Address.

83   "1858. 17th Year. Prospectus of the Illinois State Journal," supplement in the collection of ALPLM.

84   Lincoln to Gustave P. Koerner, July 25, 1858, *CW*, 2:524. Conversely, Republicans chronically worried that unregistered Irish-Americans were voting illegally for Democrats.

85   Christian Schneider took over the Alton *Freie Presse*, which lasted until the spring of 1859. See Albert J. Beveridge, *Abraham Lincoln, 1809–1858*, 2 vols. (Boston: Houghton Mifflin, 1928), 2:616–27.

86   Canisius originally harbored hopes of printing a Springfield edition of his Alton paper, asking U.S. senator Lyman Trumbull in early 1858 "to give me a recommendation to some influential men in that city as have no acquaintance among the Am[ericans] [t]here." Trumbull may have introduced the editor to Lincoln. See Canisius to Trumbull, January 15, 1858, Lyman Trumbull Papers, Library of Congress.

87   The proposed Massachusetts constitutional amendment withheld voting rights until immigrants were resident for seven years, and naturalized for two.

88   *New York Tribune*, April 25, 1859.

89   *New York Herald*, December 9, 1860.

90   Herndon's speech appeared in the *Illinois State Journal*, May 17, 1859.

91   Lincoln to Theodore Canisius, May 17, 1859, *CW*, 3:380.

92   *Illinois State Journal*, May 18, 1859. Lincoln was not the only prominent Illinois Republican to respond to pressure for denunciations of the Massachusetts referendum. Senator Lyman Trumbull, Congressman Owen Lovejoy, State Chairman Norman Judd, and others also replied. See F. I. Herriott, *The Premises and Significance of Abraham Lincoln's Letter to Theodore Canisius* (Reprinted from *Deutsch-Amerikanische Geschichtsblatter Jahrbuch der Deutsch-Amerikanischenb Historischen Gesellschaft von Illinois*, 15, 1915): 37–45.

93   Canisius even asked for a second round of reprints after determining that initial translations were inaccurate. See his article in *Illinois State Journal*, June 20, 1860.

94   Lincoln's letter to Judd does not survive; we can surmise the gist of his request from Judd's reply; see Norman B. Judd to Lincoln, May 13, 1859, ALPLC.

95   Quoted in Frank Baron, *Abraham Lincoln and the German Immigrants: Turners and Forty-Eighters* (Topeka: Society for German-American Studies for the University of Kansas, 2012), 98. The legal fee story, which came to light in Carl Sandburg's award-winning, but unsourced, Lincoln biography, was never told by Herndon in any of his own writings.

96   The frustrating disappearance of all known copies of the *Staats-Anzeiger* was most recently confirmed in James Cornelius, *From Out of the Top Hat: A Blog from the Abraham Lincoln Presidential Library and Museum* (August 30, 2011), in which the institution's chief historian noted: "Lincoln's ownership of the paper—profits going to Canisius, for his efforts—was secret. Unfortunately, its contents have remained secret, too, since *not a single copy* of it exists today to the knowledge of anyone in the Lincoln field. See http://www.alplm.org/blog/tag/theodore-canisius/.

97   Two co-signed copies of the contract in Lincoln's hand survive, differing slightly in punctuation and capitalization. Canisius's copy—which includes Lincoln's autograph and signed release—is in the John Hay Library at Brown University; presumably Lincoln retained it and gave it at some point to Hay, in whose papers it remained. This copy acknowledges that local banker Jacob Bunn funneled the money for the purchase to Canisius (*CW*, 3:383). Lincoln's copy is in the ALPLM. I am grateful to Lincoln Collection curator James Cornelius for bringing it to my attention and pointing out the small discrepancies. See also Lohne, "Team of Friends: A New Lincoln Theory and Legacy," 36.

98   Contract with Canisius, May [?], 1859, *CW*, 3:383.

99   In fact, the Republican National Convention had yet to meet: it would gather in June and nominate John C. Frémont as its candidate for president.

100 Contract with Canisius, May 1859, *CW*, 3:383.

101 *Illinois State Journal*, June 21, 1860.

102 Lincoln to Frederick W. Koehle, July 11, 1859, *CW*, 3:391. Koehle was a political office-holder: assistant circuit clerk in Lincoln, Illinois. Lincoln's letter mentioned a similar sales pitch to a Mount Pulaski merchant named John Capps.

103 The Democratic newspaper in town ironically speculated earlier that Lincoln had instead helped his friend James Matheny open a conservative paper called the *Springfield American*, established as "a bridge for old whigs to cross to black Republicanism." See *Illinois State Register*, June 26, 1858, and noted in Michael Burlingame, *Abraham Lincoln: A Life*, 2 vols. (Baltimore: Johns Hopkins University Press, 2008), 1:564.

104 *Illinois State Journal*, June 21, 1860.

105 *Illinois State Journal*, November 10, 1860. Lincoln made one reluctant "nonspeech" that August, when he was hoisted to a platform at a massive rally at Springfield. He devoted most of the opportunity to declaring he had "no intention of making a speech" and asking the assemblage to "kindly let me be silent" (*CW*, 4:91).

106 Testimonial, August 14, 1860, *CW*, 4:44–45.

107 Original at the John Hay Library, Providence, Rhode Island.

108   *New York Herald*, December 9, 1860.

109   Gustave P. Koerner to Lincoln, June 13, 1861, ALPLC. Further testifying to the almost obsessive secrecy surrounding Lincoln's investment in the *Staats-Anzeiger*, the ever-loyal Gustave Koerner never mentioned Canisius's name in his exhaustive, nearly 1,500-page memoirs. See Thomas J. McCormack, *Memoirs of Gustave Koerner, 1809–1896: Life Sketches Written at the Suggestion of His Children*, 2 vols. (Cedar Rapids, Iowa: Torch Press, 1909).

110   Lincoln to William H. Seward, June 29, 1861, *CW*, 5:418.

111   Sunderine Temple and Wayne C. Temple, *Abraham Lincoln and Illinois' Fifth Capitol* (2nd ed., Mahomet, Ill.: Mayhaven, 2006), 279. Three weeks after Lincoln's inauguration, the Illinois State legislature passed a joint resolution "allowing the members a bound copy of the Register or Journal." See Charles Lanphier to unidentified correspondent, March 29, 1861, Lanphier Family Papers, ALPLM.

112   Herndon and Weik, *Herndon's Lincoln*, 3:428–29.

113   Simeon Francis to Lincoln, December 26, 1859, ALPLC.

114   Simeon Francis to Lincoln, December 16, 1859, ALPLC.

115   Simeon Francis to Lincoln, October 29, 1859, ALPLC.

116   J. D. Roper (later publisher of the *Journal*), quoted in A. W. Shipton, *Lincoln's Association with the Journal* (Address at an Annual Conference of Copley Press executives, n.d, [10]).

117   Lincoln's so-called Second Lecture on Discoveries and Inventions (more likely part of his first), dated February 11, 1859, *CW*, 3:360, 362; Mark E. Neely, *The Boundaries of American Political Culture in the Civil War Era* (Chapel Hill: University of North Carolina Press, 2005), 5. See also Thomas A. Horrocks's excellent introductory chapter, "Texts, Contexts, and Contests: Politics and Print in the Age of Lincoln," in his *Lincoln's Campaign Biographies* (Carbondale: Southern Illinois University Press, 2014).

118   Horace White to Lincoln, February 2, 1859, ALPLC.

SEVEN: THE PERILOUS POSITION OF THE UNION

1   Junius Henri Browne, *The Great Metropolis: A Mirror of New York . . .* (Hartford, Conn.: American Publishing Co., 1869), 27, 28, 122.

2   Herbert Mitgang, ed., *Edward Dicey's Spectator of America* (Chicago: Quadrangle, 1971), 11.

3   Mark E. Neeley, Jr., *The Boundaries of American Political Culture in the Civil War Era* (Chapel Hill: University of North Carolina Press, 2005), 5.

4   Records can be found in the *New York City Register* (New York: H. Wilson, 1859).

5   Augustus Maverick, *Henry J. Raymond and the New York Press, for Thirty Years . . .* (Hartford, Conn.: A. S. Hale & Co., 1870), 155–56.

6   Ibid., 155–58.

7   "Bennett, Greeley, and Raymond," *The Journalist* 4 (October 2, 1886): 1–2.

8   *Cincinnati Daily Press*, May 14, 1860; Lambert A. Wilmer. *Our Press Gang; or, A Complete Exposition of the Corruptions and Crimes of the American Newspapers* (Philadelphia: J. T. Lloyd, 1859), 75, 82, 311.

9   *Springfield Republican*, quoted in Willard Grosvenor Bleyer, *Main Currents in the History of*

American Journalism (Boston: Houghton Mifflin, 1927), 204. See also George S. Merriam, *Life and Times of Samuel Bowles*, 2 vols. (New York: The Century Co., 1885), 179.

10   *Chicago Daily Journal*, August 16, 1858, quoted in Allen C. Guelzo, *Lincoln and Douglas: The Debates That Defined America* (New York: Simon & Schuster, 2008), 96.

11   Quoted in Maury Klein, *Days of Defiance: Sumter, Secession, and the Coming of the Civil War* (New York: Alfred A. Knopf, 1997), 214.

12   William M. Smith to Lincoln, February 23, 1860, ALPLC.

13   Harold Holzer, ed., *Lincoln's White House Secretary: The Adventurous Life of William O. Stoddard* (Carbondale: Southern Illinois University Press, 2007), 198–99; *Central Illinois Gazette* article reprinted in *Illinois State Journal*, May 12, 1859.

14   Quoted in Earl Schenck Miers, ed., *Lincoln Day by Day: A Chronology, 1809–1865*, 3 vols. (Washington, D.C.: Lincoln Sesquicentennial Commission, 1960), 2:258–59.

15   Preston Bailhache, "Recollections of a Springfield Doctor," *Journal of the Illinois State Historical Society* 47 (Spring 1964): 59, 60.

16   Horace White, *The Life of Lyman Trumbull* (Boston: Houghton Mifflin, 1913), 427.

17   Thomas J. Pickett to Lincoln, April 13, 1859, ALPLC.

18   Lincoln to Thomas J. Pickett, April 16, 1859, *CW*, 3:377.

19   Lincoln to the *Press & Tribune Co.*, June 15, 1859, *CW*, 3:385.

20   H. I. Cleveland, "Becoming the First Republican President," *Saturday Evening Post*, August 5, 1899, 84–85; see also Jeffrey Justin Anderson, "Joseph Medill: How One Man Influenced the Republican Presidential Nomination of 1860" (Master's thesis, Roosevelt University, 2011).

21   Joseph Medill to Lincoln, September 10, 1859, ALPLC.

22   William M. Cornell, *The Life and Public Career of Horace Greeley* (Boston: Lee & Shepard, 1872), 279.

23   Harriet Beecher Stowe, *The Lives and Deeds of Our Self-Made Men* (Hartford, Conn.: Worthington, Dustin & Co., 1872), 294.

24   Wilmer, *Our Press Gang*, 114–15.

25   A. K. McClure, *Recollections of Half a Century* (Salem, Mass.: The Salem Press Co., 1902), 161.

26   See Horace Greeley, *Glimmer of Europe* (New York: Dewitt & Davenport, 1851), and *Hints Toward Reforms: Lectures, Addresses, and Other Writings* (New York: Fowles & Welles, 1853).

27   *New York Herald*, September 17, 1859.

28   Charles H. Ray to Lincoln, October 20 [31], 1859, ALPLC.

29   Charles H. Ray to Elihu Washburne, January 7, 1861, Elihu Washburne Papers, Library of Congress.

30   Summary of remarks at Mechanicsburg, Illinois, November 4, 1859, *CW*, 3:493.

31   Speech at Elwood, Kansas, December 1 [?], 1859, *CW*, 3: 496–97.

32   Speech at Leavenworth, Kansas, December 3, 1859, *CW*, 3:502.

33   *Illinois State Register*, November 12, 1859, quoted in Robert W. Johannsen, *Stephen A. Douglas* (New York: Oxford University Press, 1973), 716.

34   Douglas to Charles H. Lanphier, October 1, 1859, and to Henry J. Raymond, October 24,

1859, in Robert W. Johannsen, ed., *The Letters of Stephen A. Douglas* (Urbana: University of Illinois Press, 1961), 475, 478.

35 *New York Times*, October 19, December 2, 1859.

36 *New York Tribune*, October 19, 1858.

37 *Charleston Mercury*, October 31, November 4, November 28, 1859.

38 *Missouri Democrat*, December 15, 1857, quoted in Lorman A. Ratner and Dwight L. Teeter, Jr., *Fanatics and Fire-Eaters: Newspapers and the Coming of the Civil War* (Urbana: University of Illinois Press, 2003), 77.

39 *Cincinnati Enquirer*, October 19, 1859.

40 *New York Herald*, January 23, 1858, October 18, 1859; Frederic Hudson, *Journalism in the United States, from 1690 to 1872* (New York: Harper & Brothers, 1873), 563. "Interviews with distinguished individuals is now quite a feature in New York journalism," wrote Hudson just fifteen years after the event. "It was commenced by the *New York Herald* in 1859, at the time of the celebrated John Brown raid at Harper's Ferry."

41 *New York Herald*, December 5, 1859.

42 *New York Herald*, June 15, 1859.

43 *New York Herald*, December 5, December 29, 1859.

44 *New York Herald*, quoted in Philip S. Foner and Yuval Taylor, eds., *Frederick Douglass: Selected Speeches and Writings* (Chicago: Lawrence Hill, 1999), 373.

45 *Douglass' Monthly*, November 1859.

46 Stephen A. Douglas, "The Dividing Line Between Federal and Local Authority: Popular Sovereignty in the Territories," *Harper's New Monthly Magazine* 19 (September 1859): 519, 521, 526, 528. See also Harold Holzer, *Lincoln at Cooper Union: The Speech That Made Abraham Lincoln President* (New York: Simon & Schuster, 2004), 35–38.

47 For the interesting assertion that Douglas meant with his article to claim that the rights of community trumped those of equality, see Harry V. Jaffa, *A New Birth of Freedom: Abraham Lincoln and the Coming of the Civil War* (Lanham, Md.: Rowman & Littlefield, 2000), 473–89; Douglas to Harper & Bros., September 14, 1859, in Johannsen, ed., *Letters of Stephen A. Douglas*, 468.

48 Lincoln to James W. Sheahan, January 24, 1860, *CW*, 3:515.

49 Lincoln to Norman Judd, February 9, 1860, *CW*, 3:517.

50 *Chicago Press and Tribune*, February 9, 1860; Norman Judd to Lincoln, February 21, 1860, ALPLC.

51 *New York Tribune*, February 25, 1860.

52 Henry C. Bowen, "Recollections of Abraham Lincoln," in William Hayes Ward, ed., *Abraham Lincoln: Tributes from His Associates* (New York: Thomas Y. Crowell, 1895), 27; Joseph H. Richards, " '57 or Thereabouts: Personal Recollections of a Publisher," *The Independent* 50 (December 8, 1898): 1692.

53 *New York Times*, March 12, 1859. The comment was inspired by reports that Lincoln had become a serious contender for the *vice* presidency.

54 Quoted in Holzer, *Lincoln at Cooper Union*, 104.

55 Quoted in the *New York Times*, February 28, 1860.

56 Francis Fisher Browne, *The Every-day Life of Abraham Lincoln* (New York: N. D. Thompson, 1886), 316.

57 *CW*, 3:538.

58 *CW*, 3:550.

59 *Illinois State Register*, February 22, 1860; *New York Tribune*, February 28, 1860; Joel Benton, ed., *Greeley on Lincoln . . .* (New York: Baker & Taylor, 1893), 24.

60 *New York Times, New York Tribune*, February 28, 1860; *New York Evening Post*, February 28, March 7, 1860.

61 *New York Daily News*, March 1, 1860; *New York Herald*, February 29, 1860.

62 *Chicago Tribune*, February 29, 1860.

63 Lincoln to Mary Lincoln, March 4, 1860, in Roy P. Basler, ed., *Collected Works of Abraham Lincoln, Supplement, 1832–1865* (Westport, Conn.: Greenwood, 1974), 49.

64 Lincoln to James A. Briggs, March 6, 1860, in ibid., 50.

65 *Tribune Tract Number 4: National Politics. Speech of Abraham Lincoln, of Illinois, Delivered at the Cooper Institute, Monday, Feb. 27, 1860.* Original copy in the Gilder Lehrman Collection, New-York Historical Society (GLC-4471).

66 Lincoln to John Pickering, April 6, 1860, *CW*, 4:38–39.

67 Lincoln to Jesse W. Fell with enclosure, December 1, 1859, *CW*, 3:511–12. Politician Fell had previously owned the *Bloomington* (Illinois) *Pantagraph*, which he would reclaim after Lincoln's presidency.

68 Ibid.

69 Greeley, *Recollections of a Busy Life,* 389.

70 *Douglass' Monthly*, June 1860.

71 Bromley quoted in Rufus Rockwell Wilson, ed., *Intimate Memories of Lincoln* (Elmira, N.Y.: Primavera, 1945), 279.

72 Thurlow Weed Barnes, *Memoir of Thurlow Weed*, 2 vols. (Boston: Houghton Mifflin, 1884), 2:268–69.

73 Lucy Lucile Tasher, "The *Missouri Democrat* and the Civil War," *Missouri Historical Review* 31 (July 1937): 402–3

74 *Chicago Press and Tribune*, May 15, 1860.

75 Quoted in Jay Monaghan, *The Man Who Elected Lincoln* (Indianapolis: Bobbs-Merrill, 1956), 169. Medill and Ray were no longer on speaking terms when the former offered this recollection. Others on the scene later recalled that the deal had indeed been struck, but did not mention the Chicago editors as parties to the agreement. Medill in the Ohio delegation quoted in Elmer Gertz, *Joe Medill's War* (Chicago: Abraham Lincoln Book Shop, 1945), 6.

76 Lincoln note in the margins of the *Missouri Democrat*, [May 17, 1860], *CW*, 4:50.

77 William B. Hesseltine, ed., *Three Against Lincoln: Murat Halstead Reports the Caucuses of 1860* (Baton Rouge: Louisiana State University Press, 1960), 142.

78 Wilson ed., *Intimate Memories of Lincoln*, 280.

79 *New York Times*, May 15, 1860; Hesseltine, *Three Against Lincoln*, 146–47.

80 *New York Times*, May 15, 1860.

81 *New York Tribune*, May 18, 1860.

82   Charles H. Ray to Lincoln, May 14, 1860, ALPLC.

83   Hesseltine, *Three Against Lincoln*, 163.

84   Ibid., 171–72, 177; *Cincinnati Daily Commercial*, May 21, 1860.

85   *Cincinnati Daily Commercial*, May 21, 1860, quoted in Herbert Mitgang, ed., *Lincoln as They Saw Him* (Chicago: Rinehart, 1956), 175.

86   For the *Journal* office version, see Charles S. Zane testimony, ca. 1865, in Douglas L. Wilson and Rodney O. Davis, eds., *Herndon's Informants: Letters, Interviews, and Statements About Abraham Lincoln* (Urbana: University of Illinois Press, 1998), 492; "I felt sure" in Henry B. Rankin, *Abraham Lincoln the First American: Personal Recollections of Abraham Lincoln* (New York: G. P. Putnam's Sons, 1916), 189. The *Journal* kept what it called "the chair in which Honest Abe Lincoln was sitting when he heard of his nomination as candidate for the Presidency" until 1886, when the publishers donated it to a Lincoln collection being assembled by S. B. Munson. It was offered for sale on eBay in 2013. See *Illinois State Journal,* January 21, 1865, and *The Lincoln Nomination Chair,* catalogue description, February 2013, www.sethkaller.com/item/625-The-Lincoln-Nomination-Chair.

87   William Schouler to Lincoln, May 21, 1860, ALPLC.

88   Lincoln to A. K. McClure, August 30, 1860, Abraham Lincoln Papers Project, Springfield, Illinois.

89   G. H. Stewart, "Horace Greeley at Lincoln's First Nomination," *The Century Magzine* 41 (November 1890): 157.

EIGHT: I CAN NOT GO INTO THE NEWSPAPERS

1   Mark Delahay to Lincoln, June 8, 1860, ALPLC.

2   *New York Herald*, May 22, 1860.

3   Quoted in Robert S. Harper, *Lincoln and the Press* (New York: McGraw-Hill, 1951), 56.

4   Ibid., 54.

5   *New York Herald*, May 23, May 30, 1860.

6   Quoted in Thurlow Weed Barnes, *Memoir of Thurlow Weed*, 2 vols. (Boston: Houghton Mifflin, 1884), 2:271.

7   Ibid., 274–75; *New York Times*, June 15, June 16, 1860.

8   *New York Tribune*, May 25, 1860. Learning at Auburn that a disappointed Seward was contemplating retirement, Raymond published a sympathetic story in the *Times* describing Seward's home as a paradise, and characterizing their cordial meeting as proof of the senator's manly dignity in defeat. For his part, the New York senator, not quite ready to abandon politics after all, quickly endorsed the Lincoln-Hamlin ticket and scheduled a campaign swing in its behalf.

9   *New York Tribune*, June 14, 1860.

10   Philadelphia journalist John Russell Young kept a scrapbook of undated clippings, from which these comments are extracted. John Russell Young Papers, Library of Congress.

11   *New York Times*, June 15, 1860. Not every paper blamed Greeley for Seward's humiliation. Jane Grey Swisshelm's *St. Cloud* (Minnesota) *Democrat* warned on June 7, 1860, "if this war upon Mr. Greeley, for following his honest convictions, is in any way sanctioned by

Mr. Seward, it shows that we were mistaken in the man; and that his nomination was not fit to be made."

12   Thomas Hicks, in Allen Thorndike Rice, ed., *Reminiscences of Abraham Lincoln by Distinguished Men of His Time* (New York: North American Publishing Co., 1886), 593.

13   *New York Tribune*, October 23, 1860; *New York Tribune*, October 12, 1860.

14   *Douglass' Monthly*, June 1860.

15   Mary J. Windle, *Life in Washington, and Life Here and There* (Philadelphia: J. B. Lippincott & Co., 1859), 66. Windle was an unabashed admirer. "There has been, during the last two years, raised against him a storm of rebuke and misrepresentation," she added to her rosy prognostication about Douglas's political future. ". . . But with the whole storm of unpopularity roaring round him, he sternly pursues his course, breasting the storm, combating the surge."

16   *New York Times*, August 14, 1860; Charles H. Ray to Lincoln, June 27, 1860, ALPLC.

17   William Cullen Bryant to Lincoln, June 16, 1860, ALPLC.

18   *The Rail-Splitter*, June 23, 1860.

19   *New York Tribune*, October 24, 1860. For the Currier & Ives cartoon, *"Taking the Stump": Or Stephen in Search of His Mother*, see [George Buss, ed.], *Out from the Shadow of Lincoln: Stephen A. Douglas* (exhibit catalogue) (Wabash, Ind.: Wabash County Historical Museum, 2010), 15.

20   Robert W. Johannsen, *Stephen A. Douglas* (New York: Oxford University Press (1973), 733.

21   Douglas to Charles H. Lanphier, July 5, 1860, in Robert W. Johannsen, ed., *Letters of Stephen A. Douglas* (Urbana: University of Illinois Press, 1961), 497.

22   Quoted in Johannsen, *Stephen A. Douglas*, 782.

23   *Illinois State Register*, September 1, 1860.

24   For the texts of these bitter complaints, see James W. Sheahan to Charles H. Lanphier, July 28, August 3, 1860, Charles H. Lanphier Papers, ALPLM, reprinted in Charles C. Patton, *Glory to God and the Sucker Democracy: A Manuscript Collection of the Letters of Charles H. Lanphier*, 5 vols. (Privately printed: Frye-Williamson Press, 1973), vol. 5.

25   James W. Sheahan, *The Life of Stephen A. Douglas* (New York: Harper & Brothers, 1860), 527–28.

26   *Chicago Tribune*, May 23, 1860. For Lincoln's role in deleting the phrase, "They shan't do it, d—n 'em," see Herbert Mitgang, ed., *Lincoln as They Saw Him* (New York: Rinehart, 1956), 178.

27   For the second and last Lincoln "autobiography," and notes about its publishing history, see *CW*, 4:60–67.

28   For Bartlett's experience in the campaign biography trade, see Margaret Clapp, *Forgotten First Citizen: John Bigelow* (Boston: Little, Brown, 1947), 104.

29   *Harper's Weekly*, June 9, 1860. See also Louis A. Warren, "Earliest Published Biography Exclusively Lincoln," *Lincoln Lore*, Bulletin of the Lincoln National Life Foundation, No. 668 (January 26, 1942).

30   The author is grateful to Thomas Horrocks for sharing research he amassed for his own study of Lincoln's campaign biographies and biographers: *Lincoln's Campaign Biographies* (Car-

bondale: Southern Illinois University Press, 2014). For Codding, see Ernest James Wessen, "Campaign Lives of Abraham Lincoln 1860: An Annotated Bibliography of the Biographies of Abraham Lincoln Issued During the Campaign Year," *Papers in Illinois History and Transactions for the Year 1937* (Springfield: Illinois State Historical Society, 1938): 198.

31 Lincoln to Samuel Galloway, June 19, 1860, *CW*, 4:79–80.

32 W. D. Howells, *Years of My Youth* (New York: Harper & Bros., 1916), 207.

33 See D. W. Bartlett, *Life and Public Services of Abraham Lincoln . . .* (New York: Derby & Miller, 1860); W. D. Howells, *Life of Abraham Lincoln*, orig. pub. 1860, centennial edition featuring Lincoln's handwritten corrections (Bloomington: Indiana University Press, 1960), comments on Howells's literary career by editor Clyde C. Walton, vii; *The Campaign of 1860* (Albany: Weed, Parsons & Co., 1860).

34 [Horace Greeley]. *A Political Text-Book for 1860: Comprising a Brief View of Presidential Nominations and Elections . . .* (New York: The Tribune Association, 1860), iii-iv; see also advertisement for the book in the *New York Tribune*, September 11, 1860; Gregory Alan Borchard, "The Firm of Greeley, Weed, & Seward: New York Partisanship and the Press, 1840–1860" (Ph.D. diss., University of Florida, 2003), 198–99.

35 J. F. Cleveland, *The Tribune Almanac and Political Register for 1860* (New York: H. Greeley & Co., 1860).

36 John G. Nicolay, *A Short Life of Abraham Lincoln* (New York: The Century Co., 1904), 155. Nicolay reiterated his respect for this material years later when he embarked on his own biography of Lincoln; he acquired the very notes and interviews that law student James Quay Howard had prepared for the disputed William Dean Howells biography in 1860. See James Q. Howard biographical notes in John G. Nicolay Papers, Library of Congress. See also Roy P. Basler, "James Quay Howard's Notes on Lincoln," *Abraham Lincoln Quarterly* 8 (December 1947): 400.

37 "The Hour of Sadness," signed with the pseudonym "Sylva," and the record of Patent No. 9305, in the John G. Nicolay Papers, Library of Congress; lines from Lincoln's "My Childhood Home I See Again," ca. 1846, *CW*, 1:368.

38 Fragment of a letter in the John G. Nicolay Papers, Library of Congress.

39 Helen Nicolay, *Lincoln's Secretary: A Biography of John G. Nicolay* (New York: Longmans, Green & Co., 1949), 30; Louis A. Warren, "John G. Nicolay, 1832–1901," *Lincoln Lore*, No. 718 (January 11, 1943).

40 Nicolay, *Lincoln's Secretary*, 33.

41 Ibid., 34.

42 John Taliaferro, *All the Great Prizes: The Life of John Hay from Lincoln to Roosevelt* (New York: Simon & Schuster, 2013), 33–34.

43 Joseph Medill to Lincoln, June 19, 1860, ALPLC.

44 Joseph Medill to Lincoln, July 5, 1860, ALPLC.

45 *New York Herald*, September 6, September 15, 1860.

46 *New York Herald*, November 6, 1860.

47 Ibid.

48 *New York Herald*, October 2, October 20, 1860.

49 Lincoln to Samuel Haycraft, June 4, 1860, *CW*, 4:69–70, and August 16, 1860, *CW*, 4:97;

New York Herald clipping pasted into Lincoln's letter to George G. Fogg, August 16, 1860, *CW*, 4:96.

50 Lincoln to Samuel Haycraft, August 16, 1860, and to George G. Fogg, August 16, 1860, *CW*, 4:96–97. The glued-in clipping is visible in the original, as reprinted in *Lincoln and the New York Herald: Unpublished Letters of Abraham Lincoln from the Collection of Judd Stewart* (Plainfield, N.J.: Privately printed, 1907), endpapers.

51 George G. Fogg to Lincoln, August 23, 1860, ALPLC; Lincoln to Fogg, August 29, *CW*, 4:102.

52 Samuel Haycraft to Lincoln, n.d., ca. August 23, 1860, ALPLC; Lincoln to Haycraft, [August 23, 1860], *CW*, 4:99.

53 Comments by William Kellogg and a correspondent for the *New York Tribune*, in Michael Burlingame, *Abraham Lincoln: A Life*, 2 vols. (Baltimore: Johns Hopkins University Press, 2008), 2:668.

54 *Easton* [Pennsylvania] *Times*, October 20, 1860; *Daily Omaha Nebraskan*, October 20, 1860; *Boston Herald*, October 31, 1860, all quoted in Melvin Hayes, *Mr. Lincoln Runs for President* (New York: Citadel, 1960), 180–81, 182, 184.

55 Hayes, *Mr. Lincoln Runs for President*, 124.

56 Richard M. Corwine to Lincoln, July 13, 1860; Elliott F. Shepard to Lincoln, October 15, 1860, ALPLC.

57 Quoted in William Harlan Hale, *Horace Greeley: Voice of the People* (New York: Harper & Brothers, 1950), 226.

58 *Belmont* (St. Clairsville, Ohio) *Chronicle*, July 5, 1860.

59 See Harold Holzer, Gabor S. Boritt, and Mark E. Neely, Jr., *The Lincoln Image: Abraham Lincoln and the Popular Print* (New York: Charles Scribner's Sons, 1984), 37.

60 Original in the Prints and Photographs Division, Library of Congress; see also Frank Weitenkampf, *Political Caricature in the United States* (New York: New York Public Library, 1953), 122.

61 Ibid., 39–40.

62 Charles Blondin was a tightrope walker famous at the time for taking a high-wire walk across Niagara Falls, and "Salt River" was an imaginary waterway representing the path to political oblivion.

63 Bernard F. Reilly, Jr., *American Political Prints, 1766–1876: A Catalog of the Collections in the Library of Congress* (Boston: G. K. Hall, 1991), 441, 443.

64 Ibid., 413.

65 *New York Times*, November 7, 1860.

66 Simeon Francis to Lincoln, November 23, 1860, April 16, 1861, ALPLC.

67 *New York Tribune*, November 8, 1860; Gregory A. Borchard, *Abraham Lincoln and Horace Greeley* (Carbondale: Southern Illinois University Press, 2011), 70.

68 Stephen Fiske, "When Lincoln Was Inaugurated," *Ladies' Home Journal* (March 1897), 8.

69 John W. Forney to Lincoln, November 12, 1860, ALPLC.

70 Horace Greeley to Beman Brockway, November 11, November 16, 1860, Horace Greeley Papers, Library of Congress.

71 *New York Herald*, November 9, 1860.

72   Rhett quoted in Lorman A. Ratner and Dwight L. Teeter, Jr., *Fanatics and Fire-Eaters: Newspapers and the Coming of the Civil War* (Urbana: University of Illinois Press, 2003), 22; see also *New York Illustrated News*, February 23, 1861.

73   *Augusta* (Georgia) *Chronicle & Sentinel*, November 8, 1860; *Richmond Enquirer*, November 19, 1860, reprinted in Ford Risley, ed., *The Civil War: Primary Documents on Events from 1860 to 1865* (Westport, Conn: Greenwood, 2004), 31–32.

74   *New York Times*, November 9, 1860; *New York Tribune*, November 10, 1860, and Greeley quoted in David Goldfield, *America Aflame: How the Civil War Created a Nation* (New York: Bloomsbury, 2011), 178.

75   Quoted in Howard Cecil Perkins, ed., *Northern Editorials on Secession*, 2 vols. (Gloucester, Mass.: Peter Smith, 1964), 2:455.

76   *New York Tribune*, November 8, 1860

77   Horace Greeley, *Recollections of a Busy Life* (New York: J. B. Ford & Co., 1868), 398–99.

78   Donald E. Reynolds, *Editors Make War: Southern Newspapers in the Secession Crisis* (Carbondale: Southern Illinois University Press, 2006), 4, 146, 154.

79   M. A. Higginbottom, describing the fate of editor James M. Jones, reprinted in Sally Jenkins and John Stauffer, *The State of Jones: The Small Southern County That Seceded from the Confederacy* (New York: Doubleday, 2009), 78.

80   *New York Tribune*, June 12, 1861.

81   *New York Herald*, December 30, 1860.

82   Reprinted in the *Memphis Daily Appeal*, November 9, 1860.

83   Donn Piatt in Rice, ed., *Reminiscences of Abraham Lincoln by Distinguished Men of His Time*, 480–81.

84   Douglas to the citizens of New Orleans, in Johannsen, ed., *Letters of Stephen A. Douglas*, 499–501.

85   *New York Tribune*, December 21, December 22, 1860; Greeley, *Recollections of a Busy Life*, 396.

86   John G. Nicolay and John Hay, *Abraham Lincoln: A History*, 10 vols. (New York: The Century Company, 1890), 3:253–54, 255, 258.

87   *New York Herald*, December 20, 1860.

88   I am grateful to Daniel Weinberg of the Abraham Lincoln Book Shop in Chicago for inviting me to examine a surviving copy of the broadside, and for explaining the tiny difference that marks the first and second editions: a comma. For the speed with which the *Charleston Mercury* broadside reached the public, see Richard Barksdale Harwell, *Cornerstones of Confederate Collecting* (Charlottesville: University of Virginia Press, 1953) 6, and Swann Auction Galleries Catalogue of Printed and Manuscript Americana, Public Auction Sale 2324, October 10, 2013, No. 112.

89   Joseph H. Gillespie in Rufus Rockwell Wilson, ed., *Intimate Memories of Lincoln* (Elmira, N.Y.: Primavera, 1945), 334.

90   Douglas to Charles H. Lanphier, December 25, 1860, in Johannsen, ed., *Letters of Stephen A. Douglas*, 504.

91   His final letter to Lanphier was written from Ohio on April 22, 1861: "Mrs Douglas & myself leave here for Springfield tonight," in ibid., 510.

NINE: LINCOLN WILL NOT TALK WITH ANYONE

1   Lincoln to Lyman Trumbull, December 10, 1860, *CW*, 4:150.

2   Gibson Peacock (Philadelphia) to Lincoln, January 28, 1861; J. K. Moore, George Gray, William H. Wood, and Jane Grey Swisshelm (Minnesota) to Lincoln, January 1, 22, 23, February 22. 1861; William H. Romeyn (Kingston) to Lincoln, February 27, 1861; Austin Coltin (Rockford) to Lincoln, March 2, 1861; and C. Waggoner (Toledo) to Lincoln, February 13, 1861; David Atwood (Wisconsin) to Lincoln, February 16, 1861 (John Defrees wrote as early as December 15 to endorse Dole), all ALPLM. The author is indebted to Marilyn Mueller for transcribing these newly discovered incoming letters.

3   Henry D. Cooke (Ohio) to Lincoln, February 22, 1861; S. A. Parks (Alton) to Lincoln, February 26, 1861, ALPLC.

4   Theodore Canisius to Lincoln, February 1 [?], 1861, ALPLC.

5   Horace Greeley to Lincoln, February 6, 1861, Henry J. Raymond to Lincoln, February 11, March 1, 1861, ALPLC.

6   Lincoln to Henry J. Raymond, November 30, 1860, *CW*, 4:146.

7   John D. Defrees to Lincoln, December 15, 1860, ALPLC; Lincoln to Defrees, December 18, 1860, *CW*, 4:155.

8   Horace Greeley to Lincoln, December 22, 1860, ALPLC. (Lincoln had apparently written to Greeley the day before, although a copy of his communication has never been located.) Four days later, Greeley wrote to William Herndon, whom the editor had met in New York in 1858 to discuss Lincoln's candidacy for the U.S. Senate, to explain: "I would have liked very much to talk peace and fraternity—begging the Secessionists to look toward a peaceable separation; but our friends will not listen to any thing but fight, so I shall have to let them have their own way. If Mr. L. were [at] once in possession of the White House, this would all do; as it is, I think we mistake in not talking smoothly at least until we are in position to *use* daggers as well as *speak* them." See Greeley to William H. Herndon, December 26, 1860, ALPLC.

9   George Peckham to Mary Campbell, February 28, 1861, collection of Jonathan W. White. The author is indebted to Professor White for this and the other pieces he shared from both his personal collection and his own prodigious research.

10 Lincoln to Thurlow Weed, December 17, 1860, *CW*, 4:154, and to James Watson Webb, December 29, 1860, ibid., 164; William Cullen Bryant to Lincoln, December 25, 1860, ALPLC, and Lincoln to Bryant, December 29, 1860, *CW*, 4:163–164.

11 Lincoln to Nathaniel J. Paschall, November 16, 1860, *CW*, 4:139–40.

12 William C. Smedes to Henry J. Raymond, December 8, 1860; Raymond to Lincoln, December 14, 1860, ALPLC.

13 Lincoln to Henry J. Raymond, December 18, 1960, *CW*, 4:156; Smedes to Lincoln, February 4, 1861, ALPLC.

14 *New York Herald*, December 6, 1860; Leonard Swett to Thurlow Weed, December 10, 1860, in Thurlow Weed Barnes, *Memoir of Thurlow Weed*, 2 vols. (Boston: Houghton Mifflin, 1884), 2:301.

15 Editorial for the *Illinois State Journal*, December 12, 1860, *CW*, 4:150, handwritten copy in ALPLM.

16   *New York Herald*, December 18, 1860.

17   W. Stephen Belko, *The Invincible Duff Green: Whig of the West* (Columbia: University of Missouri Press, 2006), 444.

18   Lincoln to Duff Green and Lincoln to Lyman Trumbull, December 28, 1860, *CW*, 4:162–63.

19   Duff Green to Lincoln, January 7, 1861 ALPLC; *New York Herald*, January 8, 1861, Fletcher M. Green, "Duff Green: Industrial Promoter," *Journal of Southern History* 2 (February 1936): 37.

20   Quoted in Alexandra Villard de Borchgrave and John Cullen, *Villard: The Life and Times of an American Titan* (New York: Doubleday, 2001), 125.

21   Quoted in Henry Villard, *Memoirs of Henry Villard: Journalist and Financier, 1835–1900*, 2 vols. (Boston: Houghton Mifflin, 1904), 1:146; Harold G. Villard and Oswald Garrison Villard, eds., *Lincoln on the Eve of '61: A Journalist's Story by Henry Villard* (New York: Alfred A. Knopf, 1954), 13–14.

22   From the Henry Villard Papers, Houghton Library, Harvard University, typescript of Washington reports, December 8, 1860 (16), January 27, 1861 (66).

23   "Little Raymond" in *New York Herald*, February 9, 1861. For concurrent publication, see *New York Herald*, *New York Times*, February 6, 1861.

24   "Halstead on Henry Villard. When the Dead Millionaire Was a Newspaper Man," *Cincinnati Commercial Tribune*, November 14[, 1900], Henry Villard Papers, Houghton Library, Harvard University.

25   *New York Herald*, December 15, 1860.

26   Margaret Clapp, *Forgotten First Citizen: John Bigelow* (Boston: Little, Brown, 1947), 150.

27   Fredric Hudson, *Journalism in the United States, from 1690 to 1872* (New York: Harper & Brothers, 1873), 553–54; *New York Tribune*, October 3, 1866; *Philadelphia Argus*, comment reprinted in the *Washington Constitution*, February 2, 1861.

28   Jones went on to keep one of the most famous diaries of the war. See J[ohn]. B. Jones, *A Rebel War Clerk's Diary at the Confederate States Capital*, 2 vols. (Philadelphia: J. B. Lippincott & Co., 1866).

29   William O. Stoddard to William H. Herndon, December 27, 1860, ALPLC.

30   Memorandum on appointment of Harrison Fitzhugh, ca. December 15, 1861, *CW*, 5:71; Joseph Medill to "Ray and Scripps," January 6, 1861, Charles H. Ray Papers, Huntington Library, San Marino, California.

31   *New York Herald*, February 6, 1861.

32   Ibid. *New York Tribune*, February 11, 1861.

33   *New York Herald*, February 16, 1861.

34   Horace Greeley to Beman Brockway, November 17, 1860, Horace Greeley Papers, Library of Congress.

35   Horace Greeley to Beman Brockway, November 11, 1860, Horace Greeley Papers, Library of Congress.

36   Barnes, *Memoir of Thurlow Weed*, 2:322.

37   David Davis to Thurlow Weed, February 2, 1861, in ibid., 2:323; Thurlow Weed to Abra-

ham Lincoln and Weed to David Davis, January 28, 1861; David Davis to Lincoln, February 2, 1861, ALPLC; Lincoln to Weed, February 4, 1861, *CW*, 4:185

38   Barnes, *Memoir of Thurlow Weed*, 2:325; *New York Times*, February 4, 1861.

39   *New York Times*, February 5, 1861.

40   *New York Herald*, February 4, February 7, 1861.

41   Horace Greeley to Lincoln, February 6, 1861, ALPLC.

42   Quoted in *New York Times*, July 16, 1861.

43   William H. Bailhache to *McClure's Magazine*, December 16, 1895, Ida M. Tarbell Collection, Allegheny College, Pelletier Library, online at: https://dspace.allegheny.edu/handle/10456/27707.

44   Quoted in Andy Van Meter, *Always My Friend: A History of the State Journal-Register and Springfield* (Springfield, Ill.: The Copley Press, 1981), 196.

45   John G. Nicolay, "Some Incidents in Lincoln's Journey from Springfield to Washington," in Michael Burlingame, ed., *An Oral History of Abraham Lincoln: John G. Nicolay's Interviews and Essays* (Carbondale: Southern Illinois University Press, 1996), 108.

46   Original printed copies survive in the ALPLC. The reading copy Lincoln eventually used at the Capitol was not easy to follow after all: it was filled with handwritten emendations, and several long, handwritten inserts.

47   *New York Herald*, February 10, 1861.

48   *Illinois State Journal*, February 11, February 12, 1861.

49   Jesse W. Weik, *The Real Lincoln: A Portrait* (Boston: Houghton Mifflin, 1922), 311.

50   Michael Burlingame, ed., *Lincoln's Journalist: John Hay's Anonymous Writings for the Press, 1860–1864* (Carbondale: Southern Illinois University Press, 1998), 353n14.

51   Two versions of Lincoln's farewell address are in *CW*, 4:190–91; *New York Herald* and *New York Times* (via the AP), February 12, 1861.

52   *New York Herald*, February 13, February 15, 1861; Villard, *Memoirs of Henry Villard*, 1:152.

53   Burlingame, ed., *Lincoln's Journalist*, 35–36. The author is indebted to New York collectors Robert Hoffman and Joseph Buberger for sharing copies of these dispatches as collected in John Hay's own scrapbook.

54   Ibid., 32; Cleveland *Plain Dealer*, February 14, 1861; Villard and Villard, eds., *Lincoln on the Eve of '61*, 87.

55   Villard, *Memoirs of Henry Villard*, 1:152.

56   *New York Times*, February 20, 1861; *New York Herald*, February 20, 1861.

57   *New York Herald*, February 21, 1861.

58   *Communication from His Honor the Mayor, Fernando Wood, Transmitted to the Common Council of New York* (New York: Edmund Jones & Co., 1861), original copy in the New-York Historical Society; *New York Illustrated News*, January 19, 1861.

59   Lincoln's reply to Mayor Fernando Wood, City Hall, New York, February 20, 1861, *CW*, 4:233.

60   *New York Times*, February 25, 1861; *New York Tribune*, February 25, 1861; *New York Herald*, February 25, February 26, 1861.

61   *Baltimore Sun*, February 25, 1861. The report bore the blistering headline, "The Underground Railroad Journey."

62   *New York Herald*, February 25, 1861.

63   See, for example, *The Flight of Abraham (As Reported by a Modern Daily Paper)*, in *Harper's Weekly*, March 9, 1861.

64   John Swinton, "The New York Daily Papers and Their Editors," *The Independent* 52 (January 25, 1900): part 2:238.

65   Ward Hill Lamon, *Recollections of Abraham Lincoln, 1847–1865*, ed. Dorothy Lamon (Chicago: A. C. McClurg, 1895), 34–35.

66   Lucius E. Chittenden, *Recollections of President Lincoln and his Administration* (New York: Harper & Brothers, 1891), 74.

67   Ben: Perley Poore, "Abraham Lincoln, Reminiscences of an old Newspaper correspondent," *Brooklyn Eagle*, September 6, 1885; *New York Illustrated News*, March 9, 1861. Weeklies like the *Illustrated News* dated their papers a full week in advance—the last day of sale before the next issue appeared—a practice still followed by today's magazines.

68   *Charleston Mercury*, March 7, 1861. Greeley description from Harriet Beecher Stowe, *The Lives and Deeds of Our Self-Made Men* (Hartford, Conn.: Worthington, Dustin & Co., 1872), 294.

69   *Frank Leslie's Budget of Fun*, December 15, 1860, March 1, April 1, 1861; *Vanity Fair*, March 1, 1861. For an excellent discussion of these prints, see Gary L. Bunker, *From Rail-Splitter to Icon: Lincoln's Image in Illustrated Periodicals, 1860–1865* (Kent, Ohio: Kent State University Press, 2001), esp. Chapter 4, "From Springfield to the Battlefield."

70   CW, 4:266, 271; for Douglas, see Harold Holzer, *Lincoln President-Elect: Abraham Lincoln and the Great Secession Winter*, 1860–1861 (New York: Simon & Schuster, 2008), 438–39.

71   *Douglass' Monthly*, April 1861.

72   *New York Times*, March 5, 1861; *New York Tribune*, March 5, 1861.

73   *New York Herald*, March 5, 1861; *Charleston Mercury*, March 6, March 9, 1861.

74   *New York Times*, March 5, 1861

TEN: WANTED: A LEADER

1   *New York Herald*, June 19, 1861.

2   *Louisville Courier*, reprinted in *New York Times*, July 18, 1861.

3   *New York Times*, April 3, 1861.

4   "Some thoughts for the President's consideration," William H. Seward to Lincoln, April 1, 1861, ALPLC; Patrick Sowle, "A Reappraisal of Seward's Memorandum of April 1, 1861, to Lincoln," *Journal of Southern History* 33 (May 1967): 236. The Washington correspondent was John Swain.

5   Lincoln's draft to Seward, April 1, 1861, *CW*, 4:316. This episode is well told in two recent, excellent volumes: Adam Goodheart, *1861: The Civil War Awakening* (New York: Alfred A. Knopf, 2011), 158–59; and Walter Stahr, *Seward: Lincoln's Indispensable Man* (New York: Simon & Schuster, 2012), 270–71.

6   Walt Whitman, *Specimen Days in America* (London: Walter Scott, 1887), 34.

7   Proclamations of April 15, April 19, May 4, 1861, *CW*, 4:331–32, 338–39, 353–54. Still holding out the chance that further secession and civil war could be averted, Lincoln wrote that these would "probably" be the militias' first assignments, though he left unclear whether this ambiguity reflected other demands on their schedules or his own zeal for retaking Sumter and other seized property. Lincoln also called the lame-duck Congress back to Washington for a special session—but not until July 4.

8   *Washington Constitution* quoted in the *Richmond Whig*, April 23, 1861; *States and Union* disloyalty characterized by the *Washington Star*, April 24, 1861.

9   *New York Times*, April 15, 1861.

10 *New York Times*, April 15, April 20, 1861.

11 Horace Greeley, *Recollections of a Busy Life* (New York: J. B. Ford & Co., 1868), 401–3.

12 Horace Greeley to Lincoln, May 19, 1861, ALPLC.

13 *New York Tribune*, April 13, 1861.

14 *New York Herald*, April 27, 1861.

15 *New York Herald*, April 15, 1861; *New York Times*, April 15, 1861. Meanwhile, in the first sign of public anger against pro-peace newspapers, the *Hartford Daily Times* began losing advertising after Sumter "in consequence of its supporting the Southern movement," at least according to the *New York Tribune*, April 16, 1861.

16 Robert Underwood Johnson and Clarence Clough Buel, eds., *Battles and Leaders of the Civil War*, 4 vols. (New York: The Century Co., 1887), 1:85.

17 "The New York Herald," *North American Review* 102 (April 1866): 400.

18 *New York Times*, April 16, 1861; *New York Tribune*, April 16, 1861. An equally hostile crowd numbering several hundred people staged a similar protest against the pro-Democratic *Brooklyn Eagle*, demanding "to have the American flag hoisted from the summit of our establishment." Decrying the "mob dictation," the *Eagle* also obliged, insisting that "arrangements had been made to fling the banner to the breeze this morning, without any prompting of a crowd." See *Brooklyn Eagle*, April 18, 1861.

19 Allan Nevins and Milton Halsey Thomas, eds., *The Diary of George Templeton Strong*, 4 vols. (New York: Macmillan, 1952), 3:187; *New York Tribune*, May 6, 1861.

20 *New York Herald*, April 16, 1861.

21 Ibid.

22 *New York Tribune*, May 15, 1861; Fernando Wood message published in all the city's papers, including the *New York Daily News*, April 16, 1861.

23 *New York Herald*, April 20, 1861.

24 *New York Herald*, April 16, 1861.

25 Robert S. Harper, *Lincoln and the Press* (New York: McGraw-Hill, 1951), 319.

26 Villard reminiscence quoted in Oliver Carlson, *The Man Who Made News: James Gordon Bennett* (New York: Duell, Sloan & Pearce, 1942), 316–17.

27 Technically, the first Union casualty of the Civil War was one of the defenders of Fort Sumter, but he had lost his life after an explosion during the surrender ceremony, not during the Confederate bombardment, The Sixth Massachusetts Volunteer Infantry Regiment followed the same crosstown route Lincoln had been scheduled to employ to change trains in

Baltimore back in February. The mob attack on the Union soldiers suggests that the danger facing the president-elect had been genuine, and his decision to pass through the city wise.

28   *New York Times*, April 25, 1861.

29   Henry J. Raymond, *The Life and Public Services of Abraham Lincoln* . . . (New York: Derby & Miller, 1865), 720.

30   Lincoln to William H. Seward, June 8, 1861, *CW*, 4:397; *New York Times*, April 24, 1861; Francis B. Carpenter, "Anecdotes and Reminiscences," in Raymond, *Life and Public Services of Abraham Lincoln*, 758.

31   *New York Times*, May 25, 1861.

32   See *Remarks of Hon. Stephen A. Douglas in the Senate of the United States, March 6, 1861, on the Resolution of Mr. Dixon to Print the Inaugural Address of President Lincoln*. Undated seven-page pamphlet, Library of Congress.

33   *Illinois State Journal*, April 26, 1861. The speech was also published as a pamphlet.

34   Stephen A. Douglas to Abraham Lincoln, April 29, 1861, ALPLC; Douglas to Charles H. Lanphier, December 25, 1860, in Robert W. Johannsen, ed., *The Letters of Stephen A. Douglas* (Urbana: University of Illinois Press, 1961), 504.

35   Robert Johannsen's beautiful evocation of Douglas's heroic final months is in his *Stephen A. Douglas* (New York: Oxford University Press, 1973), 870–974.

36   *New York Times*, June 4, 1861.

37   Presidential order in John Nicolay's hand, signed by Lincoln, April 11, 1861, *CW*, 4:328; Walter C. Clephane, "Lewis Clephane: A Pioneer Washington Republican," *Records of the [District of] Columbia Historical Society* 21 (1917): 272–74. In 1901, the writer Rufus Rockwell Wilson garbled this history and asserted that it was the *National Republican* that had been "gutted by a mob" on "the night of Lincoln's election." The evidence suggests that while an attack did occur at the newspaper's future headquarters, Clephane did not open the *National Republican* there for more than two weeks; it was still a Wide-Awake clubhouse on Election Day. See Rufus Rockwell Wilson, *Washington: The Capital City and Its Part in the History of the Nation*, 2 vols. (Philadelphia: J. B. Lippincott, 1901), 2:173.

38   John Wein Forney to John G. Nicolay, March 14, 1861, ALPLC.

39   John Russell Young, "Men Who Reigned: Bennett, Greeley, Raymond, Prentice, Forney," *Lippincott's Monthly* 51 (February 1893): 196.

40   See Orville H. Browning to Lincoln, July [?] 1861, ALPLC; Theodore Calvin Pease and James G. Randall, eds., *The Diary of Orville Hickman Browning*, 2 vols. (Springfield: Illinois State Historical Library, 1925), 1:478, 481–82. For an example of Forney's patronage recommendations, see John Wein Forney to Lincoln, August 16, 1861, urging the appointment of a former New York Democrat, John B. Haskin, as an army inspector general; in this case, Lincoln denied the request. For White, see Benjamin P. Thomas and Harold Hyman, *Stanton: The Life and Times of Lincoln's Secretary of War* (New York: Alfred A. Knopf, 1962), 138.

41   *Official Register of the United States . . . 1865 . . .* (Washington, D.C.: U.S. Government Printing Office, 1866),17.

42   Simon Cameron Papers, quoted in Harper, *Lincoln and the Press*, 111.

43   *Philadelphia Pennsylvanian*, January 1, 1861, quoted in Elwyn Burns Robinson, "*The Press*:

Lincoln's Philadelphia Organ," *Pennsylvania Magazine of History and Biography* 65 (April 1941): 158.

44   John W. Forney, *Anecdotes of Public Men*, 2 vols. (New York: Harper & Bros., 1881), 1:167; George Alfred Townsend papers cited in J. Cutler Andrews, *The North Reports the Civil War* (Pittsburgh: University of Pittsburgh Press, 1955), 25.

45   John Wein Forney to Lincoln, August 1, August 6 (with clipping), 1861, ALPLC.

46   For Lincoln's memoranda to Secretary of State William Seward on Webb's appointment offers, May 6 and June 8, 1861, see *CW*, 5:358–59, 397; *New York Herald*, June 25, 1861; see also James Watson Webb to Lincoln, June 8, 1861, ALPLC.

47   See, for example, Lincoln to Hiram Barney, May 13, 1861, regarding "Mr. Greeley's letter introducing" William Ward to Lincoln as a candidate for the New York Customs House, *CW*, 4:367.

48   Quoted in Harper, *Lincoln and the Press*, 111.

49   Presidential message to a Special Session of Congress, July 4, 1861, *CW*, 4:426.

50   Ibid.; Defrees quoted in Roy P. Basler, *A Touchstone for Greatness: Essays, Addresses, and Occasional Pieces About Abraham Lincoln* (Westport, Conn.: Greenwood, 1973), 90; part of the reconstructed quote comes from Frank [Francis] B. Carpenter, "Anecdotes and Reminiscences of President Lincoln," appendix to Raymond, *Life and Public Services of Abraham Lincoln,* 758. Defrees had been ardently recommended for his past by politicians like Senators Henry S. Lane and Thomas Corwin (see Lane to Lincoln, March 6, 1861, Corwin to Lincoln, March 9, 1861), and Indiana governor Oliver P. Morton (Morton to Lincoln, March 14, 1861), all ALPLC. Francis Lieber concluded that Lincoln's literary instincts were right, commenting: "We have to look at other things, just now, than grammar," see Thomas Sergeant Perry, ed., *The Life and Letters of Francis Lieber* (Boston: James R. Osgood, 1882), 317.

51   *CW*, 4:440, 433, 426, 430. In Lincoln's original draft manuscript, he used the term "military power," but, as usual, revised it ingeniously.

52   Ibid., 43.

53   See Mario M. Cuomo and Harold Holzer, eds., *Lincoln on Democracy* (New York: Harper-Collins, 1990), 217.

54   *Douglass' Monthly*, August 1861; Edward Carey, *George William Curtis* (Boston: Houghton Mifflin, 1894), 147.

55   *New York Tribune*, June 26, 1861; Greeley's words published under the headline, "Just Once a Card from Mr. Horace Greeley," *New York Times*, July 26, 1861. See Thurlow Weed Barnes, ed., *Memoir of Thurlow Weed*, 2 vols. (Boston: Houghton Mifflin, 1884), 2:336.

56   *New York Times*, July 24, 1861.

57   William Howard Russell, "Recollections of the Civil War—IV," *North American Review* 166 (May 1898): 621; *New York Times*, March 27, 1898.

58   John Stauffer, "The 'Terrible Reality' of the First Living-Room Wars," ms., July 2011.

59   Quoted in Louis M. Starr, *The Civil War's Bohemian Brigade: Newsmen in Action* (New York: Alfred A. Knopf, 1954), 42; Caroline Chapman, *Russell of the Times: War Despatches and Diaries* (London: Bell & Hyman, 1984), 115.

60   *London Times*, November 29, 1860.

61   Mowbray Morris to J. C. Bancroft Davis, January 25, 1861, in Louis M. Sears, ed., "The London *Times'* American Correspondent in 1861: Unpublished Letters of William H. Russell in the First Year of the Civil War," *The Historical Outlook* 16 (October 1925): 251–52; Morris to Davis, February 22, 1861, quoted in Martin Crawford, ed., *William Howard Russell's Civil War* (Athens: University of Georgia Press, 1992), xxiv.

62   Diary entry, March 25, 1861, in Crawford, ed., *William Howard Russell's Civil War*, 21.

63   *New York Tribune*, May 2, 1861.

64   William Howard Russell, *My Diary North and South*, orig. pub. 1863, ed. Fletcher Pratt (New York: Harper & Bros., 1954), 22–24. For acquaintance with British authors, see Russell, "Recollections of the Civil War," *North American Review* 166 (February 1998): 234.

65   Russell, *My Diary North and South*, 22–23.

66   Ibid, 24.

67   Russell, *My Diary North and South*, 24; Russell, "Recollections of the Civil War," 240, 243–44.

68   Diary entry, November 23, 1861, and letter to Mowbray Morris, March 15, 1862, Crawford, ed., *William Howard Russell's Civil War*, 185, 230.

69   Russell, "Recollections of the Civil War—IV," 629.

70   Chapman, *Russell of the Times*, 122–23.

71   Russell, "Recollections of the Civil War—V," *North American Review* 166 (June 1898): 740, 745.

72   Mowbray Morris to J. C. Bancroft Davis, August 7, 1861, J. C. Bancroft Davis Papers, Library of Congress.

73   Adam Gurowski, *Diary, from March 4, 1861, to November 12, 1862* (Boston: Lee & Shepard, 1862), 79; *New York Herald*, August 27, 1861.

74   *London Times*, August 22, 1861.

75   *New York Tribune*, July 22, 1861.

76   *New York Tribune*, July 23, 1861.

77   William T. Sherman to Ellen Sherman, July 28, 1861, quoted in John F. Marszalek, *Sherman's Other War: The General and the Civil War Press*, orig. pub. 1981 (Kent, Ohio: Kent State University Press, 1999), 65.

78   Edward Dicey, *Six Months in the Federal States,* 2 vols. (London: MacMillan, 1863), 1:35.

79   Crawford, ed., *William Howard Russell's Civil War* (July 28, September 3, September 6, 1861), 96, 118, 122; and Russell to John T. Delane, March 26, 1861, 24. See also *New York Herald*, August 24, 1861.

80   Ben: Perley Poore criticisms in Allen Thorndike Rice, ed., *Reminiscences of Abraham Lincoln by Distinguished Men of His Time* (New York: North American Publishing Co., 1886), 229; William Howard Russell to J. C. Bancroft Davis, June 22, 1861, in Crawford, ed., *William Howard Russell's Civil War*, 74; *Harper's Weekly*, July 20, 1861.

81   Diary entries, July 6, August 26, 1861, and William Howard Russell to John T. Delane, March 26, 1861, in Crawford, ed., *William Howard Russell's Civil War,* 82, 23–24, 111; *New York Tribune*, March 20, 1861

82   Quoted in Chapman, *Russell of the Times*, 128.

83   Crawford, ed., *William Howard Russell's Civil War,* diary entry, December 4, 1861, 196.

84   *New York Times*, July 22, 1861.

85   *New York Times*, July 25, 1861.

86   Harold Holzer and Craig L. Symonds, eds., *The New York Times Complete Civil War* (New York: Black Dog & Leventhal, 2011), 12–13.

87   Richard B. Kielbowicz, "The Telegraph, Censorship, and Politics at the Outset of the Civil War," *Civil War History* 40 (June 1994): 97–98.

88   Scott's notice of July 8, 1861, ordered that "the telegraph will convey no dispatches concerning the operations of the Army not permitted by the Commanding General." See *OR*, Series 3, vol. 1: 324.

89   *New York Times*, July 24, 1861. A *Cincinnati Gazette* reporter similarly tried to report that telegraph censors insisted on his communicating the Bull Run outcome as a federal victory. See Records of the U.S. House of Representatives, 1861–1862, Record Group 233, National Archives.

90   Testimony of Alfred Talcott, Records of the House Judiciary Committee, 37th Congress, 1862 Record Group 233, National Archives, quoted in Michael Hussey, "The Great Censorship Debate," in *Discovering the Civil War* (n.a., Washington, D.C.: Foundation for the National Archives, 2010), 138.

91   *New York Times*, July 22, July 26, 1861, quoted in Starr, *The Civil War's Bohemian Brigade*, 49–50.

92   Chapman, *Russell of the Times*, 128.

93   *The Atlantic* 47 (September 1861), 346.

94   G. F. Williams, "How a Reporter Faced Danger in Disguise," *The Independent* 53 (August 8, 1901): 1860–62; *New York Times*, May 16, 1861.

95   "The Army Correspondent," *Harper's New Monthly Magazine* (October 1863): 627–33; Starr, *The Civil War's Bohemian Brigade*, 232.

96   Franc B. Wilkie, *Pen and Powder* (Boston, Ticknor & Co., 1888). See also Michael E. Banasik, *Missouri in 1861: The Civil War Letters of Franc B. Wilkie* (Iowa City: Press of the Camp Pope Bookshop, 2001), 107–14, 125.

97   James R. Parton, ["The New York Herald,"] *North American Review* 102 (April 1866): 401.

98   Ben: Perley Poore, *Perley's Reminiscences of Sixty Years in the National Metropolis*, 2 vols. (Philadelphia: Hubbard Bros., 1886), 2:126, 127.

99   *Washington Evening Star*, October 16, 1896.

100 James G. Randall, "The Newspaper Problem in Its Bearing Upon Military Secrecy During the Civil War," *The American Historical Review* 23 (January 1918): 307.

101 *New York Herald*, August 14, 1861; total expenditures reported in Andrews, *The North Reports the Civil War*, 21. For cost per telegraphic transmissions, see Brayton Harris, *Blue and Gray in Black and White: Newspapers in the Civil War* (Washington D.C.: Brassey's, 1999), 6.

102 Brayton Harris, *Blue and Gray in Black and White*, 182.

103 *New York Herald*, April 1, 1863.

104 *New York Times*, March 27, 1898.

105 Horace Greeley to Margaret Allen, June 17, 1861, Horace Greeley Papers, Library of Congress.

106 Randall, "The Newspaper Problem," 307.

107 John Wein Forney to John Russell Young, telegram, September 12, 1861, John Russell Young Papers, Library of Congress.

108 Quoted in Chapman, *Russell of the Times*, 115.

109 George Alfred Townsend, *Campaigns of a Non-Combatant* . . . (New York: Blelock & Co., 1866), esp. 49–57; William Swinton, the Twelve *Decisive Battles of the War* (New York: Dick & Fitzgerald, 1867), 5.

110 Quoted in Alexandra Villard de Borchgrave and John Cullen, *Villard: The Life and Times of an American Titan* (New York: Doubleday, 2001), 160–161, 166, 167.

111 L. A. Gobright, *Recollections of Men and Things at Washington During the Third of a Century* (Philadelphia: Claxton, Remsen, & Haffelfinger, 1869), 13. Gobright began his career as a congressional correspondent.

112 Andrews, *The North Reports the Civil War*, 751–59; J. Cutler Andrews, *The South Reports the Civil War* (Princeton: Princeton University Press, 1970), 548–51.

113 Horace Greeley and others to Lincoln, April 18, 1861, ALPLC; Lincoln memorandum, ca. April 8, 1861, *CW*, 4:325.

114 Horace Greeley to Lincoln, July 29, 1861, ALPLC. Greeley also confided his Bull Run–induced insomnia to his friend Beman Brockway; see Greeley to Brockway, August 14, 1861, Horace Greeley Papers, Library of Congress.

115 Secretary of the Navy Gideon Welles, who kept a diary during the Civil War, made no mention of the Greeley letter in his accounts of the period. See Welles, *Diary of Gideon Welles*, ed. John T. Morse, Jr. 3 vols. (Boston: Houghton Mifflin, 1911). Welles's 1861 entries (in Vol. 1) were sketchy. Like his fellow cabinet diarist, Salmon Chase, Welles did not commence his journal in earnest until 1862.

116 John Hay, diary entry, April 30, 1864, in Michael Burlingame and John R. Turner Ettlinger, eds., *Inside Lincoln's White House: The Complete Civil War Diary of John Hay* (Carbondale: Southern Illinois University Press, 1997), 193. Greeley's penmanship described in Albert Gallatin Riddle, *Recollections of War Times: Reminiscences of Men and Events in Washington, 1860–1865* (New York: G. P. Putnam's Sons, 1895), 199.

117 Ruth Painter Randall, *Lincoln's Sons* (Boston: Little, Brown, 1955), 121.

118 For press comments on the contraband issue, see *New York Times*, May 31, 1861 (a "happy fancy"), *New York Herald*, May 24, 1861 (acceptable unless "Greeley & Co." used it to promote "Mexican anarchy and dire confusion").

119 Proclamation published in the *New York Times*, August 31, 1861.

120 Lincoln to John C. Frémont, September 2, 1861, *CW*, 4:506; Frémont to Lincoln, September 8, 1861, ALPLC; Lincoln to Orville H,. Browning, September 22, 1861, *CW*, 4:432.

121 Medill to Salmon P. Chase, September 15, 1861, quoted in Doris Kearns Goodwin, *Team of Rivals: The Political Genius of Abraham Lincoln* (New York: Simon & Schuster, 2005), 394.

122 *Anglo-African*, September 21, 1861, quoted in James M. McPherson, *The Negro's Civil War: How American Negroes Felt and Acted During the War for the Union* (New York: Pantheon, 1965).

123 Horace Greeley to Samuel Wilkeson, September 17, 1862, *Horace Greeley and the Lincoln Administration: An Archive*, Raab Collection catalogue, 2013.

124 *New York Times*, September 8, 1861.

125   Dicey, *Six Months in the Federal States*, 33.

126   Ibid., 25, 33.

ELEVEN: FREEDOM OF THE PRESS STRICKEN DOWN

1   Horace Greeley, *Recollections of a Busy Life* (New York: J. B. Ford & Co., 1868), 405.

2   Ibid., 200; L. E. Chittenden, *Recollections of President Lincoln and His Administration* (New York: Harper & Bros., 1891), 74.

3   Horace Greeley, *The American Conflict: A History of the Great Rebellion in the United States of America, 1860–'65 . . .* , 2 vols., 2nd ed., orig. pub. 1864 (Hartford, Conn.: O. D. Case, 1864), 1:549; see also Greeley, "Greeley's Estimate of Lincoln," ed. Joel Benton, *The Century* 20 (July 1891): 377.

4   Robert R. Raymond, ed., *The Patriotic Speaker: Consisting of Modern Specimens of Modern Eloquence, Together with Poetical Extracts Adapted for Recitation, and Dramatic Pieces for Exhibitions* (New York: A. S. Barnes & Burr, 1864), 92–93.

5   *New York Examiner*, September 5, 1861, in Michael Burlingame, ed., *Dispatches from Lincoln's White House: The Anonymous Civil War Journalism of Presidential Secretary William O. Stoddard* (Lincoln: University of Nebraska Press, 2002), 23.

6   *New York Times*, May 26, 1861.

7   For an example of the *Local News*, see the online newspaper collections of the Library of Congress, *Chronicling America*: http://chrtoniclingamerica.loc.gov/lccn/sn85025008/.

8   Lincoln's Message to Congress, July 4, 1861, *CW*, 4:429

9   Records in the National Archives, Record Group 59 (General Records of the Department of State), Entry 985, Box 1. See also Jonathan W. White, "Unearthing Maryland's Civil War History at the National Archives," *Maryland Historical Magazine* 106 (Fall 2011): 363–68, and White, *Abraham Lincoln and Treason in the Civil War: The Case of John Merryman* (Baton Rouge: Louisiana State University Press, 2011), 45.

10   See Adjutant-General Lorenzo Thomas's report to Col. Justin Dimick, March 10, 1862, *OR*, series 2, vol. 2:786.

11   *New York Times*, August 24, 1861.

12   J[ohn]. B. Jones, *A Rebel War Clerk's Diary at the Confederate States Capital*, 2 vols. (Philadelphia: J. B. Lippincott, 1866), 14.

13   For the *Hagerstown Mail* case, see *OR*, series 2, vol. 2: 298.

14   *New York Times*, July 29, 1861.

15   William F. Swindler, "The Southern Press in Missouri, 1861–1864," *Missouri Historical Review* 35 (April 1941): 398–99.

16   *New York Times*, August 20, 1861.

17   Ulysses S. Grant to William W. Worthington, August 26, 1861, and to Brigadier General Benjamin M. Prentiss, September 3, 1861, in John Y. Simon, ed., *The Papers of Ulysses S. Grant*, 32 vols. to date, now with John F. Marszalek as editor (Carbondale: Southern Illinois University Press, 1967–2012), 2:39–140, 177.

18   *American Annual Cyclopaedia and Register of Important Events of the Year 1861 . . .* (New York: D. Appleton, 1868), 328–29. General John C. Frémont declared martial law in St. Louis County on August 14, 1861.

19   Dennis K. Boman, *Lincoln and Citizens' Rights in Civil War Missouri: Balancing Freedom and Security* (Baton Rouge: Louisiana State University Press, 2011), 48–49.

20   "T—Blank" to Montgomery Blair (forwarded to Lincoln), September 24, 1861, ALPLC.

21   *New York Tribune*, April 12, 1861; Charles Fishback to William H. Seward, September 9, 1861, OR, series 2, vol. 2:806.

22   Case of Charles Morehead, Reuben T. Durrett, and M. W. Barr, OR, series 2, vol. 2: 805–6.

23   George D. Prentice to Lincoln, September 24, 1861 (telegram), ALPLC; Prentice to Lincoln, September 24, 1861 (letter), OR, series 2, vol. 2: 807–8; Lincoln endorsement [September 24, 1861], CW, 4:534.

24   Joseph Holt to Lincoln, September 25, 1861, OR, series 2, vol. 2: 808.

25   OR, series 2, vol. 2: 808–10.

26   W. D. Gallagher to Salmon P. Chase, October 10, 1861; George D. Prentice, Henry Pirtle, Hamilton Pope, Bland Ballard, C. B. Muir, W. F. Bullock, Joseph Dolph, J. Levis, and James Guthrie to Lincoln, n.d. but enclosed with Chase letter, ibid., 810–11; George D. Prentice to Lincoln, November 16, 1861, APLC; Lincoln to William H. Seward, October 4, 1861, CW, 4:549.

27   *New York Ledger*, July 19, 1861, republished in the *Philadelphia Inquirer*, July 21, 1861. For an interpretation of the report as the "screaming" of an "administration mouthpiece"—not really true, since Everett had been an early critic of Lincoln—see Jeffrey Manber and Neil Dahlstrom, *Lincoln's Wrath: Fierce Mobs, Brilliant Scoundrels and a President's Mission to Destroy the Press* (Naperville, Ill.: Sourcebooks, 2005), 132–33.

28   Boman, *Lincoln and Citizens' Rights*, 149; Manber and Dahlstrom, *Lincoln's Wrath*, 329. See also Jonathan W. White, "'Words Become Things': Free Speech in Civil War Pennsylvania," *Pennsylvania Legacies* 8 (May 2008): 18–23; and Ray H. Abrams, "The *Jeffersonian*, Copperhead Newspaper," *Pennsylvania Magazine of History and Biography* 57 (July 1933): 270.

29   *Albany Argus*, August 24, 1861.

30   Robert S. Harper, *Lincoln and the Press* (New York: McGraw-Hill, 1951), 109.

31   Amasa Converse to Lincoln, August 28, 1861, ALPLC; "The Suppression of the Christian Observer," *Philadelphia Inquirer*, August 23, 1861; *Philadelphia Evening Bulletin*, August 22, 1861. The *Christian Observer* moved again, this time to Louisville, Kentucky, where it is still published.

32   *New York Herald*, July 23, 1861.

33   *New York Herald*, July 13, 1861.

34   New York grand jury presentment, *American Annual Cyclopaedia . . . 1861*, 329.

35   *The Confederate States Almanac, and Repository of Useful Knowledge, 1862* [1861] (Vicksburg, Miss.: H. C. Clarke, 1862), n.p.; presentment listed with events, August 1861.

36   Little is known about Gould except that he listed himself in the 1861–1862 New York street directories as a "broker," lived on East Twenty-sixth Street in Manhattan, served with pro-administration men like Francis Lieber on the camp hospital and ambulance corps committee, and chaired several other committees handling arrangements for pro-Union rallies in the summer of 1862. See H. Wilson, *Trow's New York City Directory for the Year Ending May 1, 1862* (New York: John F. Trow, 1862), 152 (he is the only "Charles Gould" in a book that contained

6,995 names under the letter "G" alone—see pp. 3, 5). See also *Reports of the National War Committee of the Citizens of New-York. Report of the Committee Appointed to Examine a Plan to Provide for Greater Efficiency in Ambulance and Camp-Hospital Corps* (n.p., n.d., ca. 1862), pamphlet collection, New-York Historical Society; unsigned printed invitation from the secretary of the committee on arrangements (Gould) to a "War Meeting" on August 27, 1862, in New-York Historical Society broadside collection; *Meeting of Loyal Citizens*, August 11, 1862 (form letter signed by Gould); and *Report of the Proceedings of the National War Committee of the Citizens of New York*, No. 3 (August 1862), broadside collection, New-York Historical Society. Mention of "attacks" by the press in the last-named pamphlet appears on p. 7.

37   Allan Nevins and Milton Halsey Thomas, eds., *The Diary of George Templeton Strong*, 4 vols. (New York: Macmillan, 1952), 3:175.

38   *New York Daily News*, April 15, July 22, 1861, reprinted in *New York Tribune*, July 23, July 25, 1861; *Brooklyn Eagle*, August 3, 1861; J[ohn]. H. Van Evrie, *Negroes and Negro "Slavery:" The first, an inferior race—the latter, it's* [sic] *normal condition* (Baltimore: John D. Toy, 1854?). Van Evrie republished the screed under his own imprint in 1861; see also reports in the *New York Evening Day-Book*, April 6, April 18, 1861, reprinted in Herbert Mitgang, ed., *Lincoln as They Saw Him* (New York: Rinehart, 1956), 255, 261; *New-York Evening Day-Book*, April 15, 1861, in Harper, *Lincoln and the Press*, 121; *New York Times*, August 16, 1861.

39   "Presentment of Secession Journals by the Grand Jury," *New York Times*, August 17, 1861.

40   See Presidential Proclamation of August 16, 1861, *CW*, 4:487–88.

41   Order of the postmaster general, conveyed by Chief Clerk T. P. Trott, and quoted in Edward McPherson, *The Political History of the United States of America During the Great Rebellion . . .* (Washington, D.C.: Philip & Solomons, 1864), 188.

42   George A. Coffey to Lincoln, August 22, 1861, ALPLC. Coffey was U.S. attorney for the Eastern District of Pennsylvania. See also *New York Daily News*, August 27, 1861; *New York Times*, August 24, August 25, August 29, 1861; *Albany Evening Journal* (reporting the hoard as six packages of the *News*), August 27, 1861.

43   *New York Daily News*, August 20, August 23, August 26, 1861.

44   *Annual Cyclopaedia . . . 1861*, 330; *New York Times*, August 27, 1861.

45   *New York Herald*, August 29, 1861.

46   *Philadelphia Evening Bulletin*, April 29, August 20, August 21, August 23, August 24, 1861.

47   *Richmond Daily Dispatch*, September 7, 1861.

48   *New York Times, Tribune*, August 4, November 25, 1861.

49   *New York Herald*, August 26, 1861.

50   Benjamin Wood, *Fort Lafayette; or, Love and Secession. A Novel* (New York: Carleton & Co., 1862). The story focused more on brave soldiers and swooning women than on the Brooklyn prison. The *New York Daily News* returned during the Civil War as an evening paper, but under new ownership.

51   "The Case of William H. Winder," *Boston Courier*, October 30, 1862.

52   William Winder, *Secrets of the American Bastille* (Philadelphia, John Campbell, 1863), 17. Winder's brother, John Henry Winder, was provost marshal of Richmond; their father had been a well-known if controversial American general during the War of 1812.

53   *New York Times,* September 13, September 14, 1861.

54   Durrett to Seward, December 2, 1861, *OR,* series 2, vol. 2: 820.

55   List of "Political Prisoners at Fort Lafayette," *New York Times,* September 24, 1861; *OR,* series 2, vol. 2: 802. McMaster gained his release after taking the oath of allegiance on October 23, 1861.

56   Harper, *Lincoln and the Press,* 124.

57   *OR,* series 2, vol. 2: 771–72. Wall served twenty days; he was released on September 24 after taking the oath of allegiance.

58   Potsdam-based U.S. attorney William A. Dart had complained to Secretary of State Seward that Flanders continued to publish incendiary anti-Union editorials after the Post Office tried banning the paper from the mails. See *OR,* series 2, vol. 2: 938, 941.

59   *New York Times,* September 26, 1861.

60   For a year, Van Evrie continued to seek relief so he could publish freely. See Van Evrie Horton & Co. to William H. Seward, January 23, 1862, ALPLC.

61   *Brooklyn Eagle,* September 7, 1861.

62   *American Annual Cyclopaedia . . . 1861,* 330.

63   Allan Nevins, *The Evening Post: A Century of Journalism* (New York: Boni & Liveright, 1922), 301–2. *Cincinnati Gazette* report quoted in Harper, *Lincoln and the Press,* 224–25.

64   *OR,* series 2, vol. 2: 377.

65   Quoted in *Richmond Daily Dispatch,* August 22, 1861. See also Manber and Dahlstrom, *Lincoln's Wrath,* 119–21. The Manber-Dahlstrom book is generally an overheated, one-sided condemnation of Lincoln's "dictatorial" policies on many fronts; but the writers evidenced careful research even if they reached extreme and generally indefensible conclusions. See also *Bangor Democrat,* April 18, 1861, in Mitgang, ed., *Lincoln as They Saw Him,* 257; New Hampshire account published in the *Brooklyn Eagle,* August 13, 1861; Marcellus Emory letter to the *Brooklyn Eagle,* August 16, 1861.

66   *New York Times,* August 20, 1861; Michael J. Connolly, "Irresistible Outbreaks Against Tories and Traitors: The Suppression of New England Antiwar Sentiment in 1861," in *The Battlefield and Beyond: Essays on the American Civil War,* ed. Clayton E. Jewett (Baton Rouge: Louisiana State University Press, 2012).

67   *New York Times,* August 4, August 27, 1861.

68   See Jeffrey A. Smith, *War and Press Freedom: The Problem of Prerogative Power* (New York: Oxford University Press, 1999), 131.

69   William Howard Russell to John T. Delane, March 26, 1861, in Martin Crawford, ed., *William Howard Russell's Civil War: Private Diary and Letters, 1861–1862* (Athens: University of Georgia Press, 1992), 24.

70   *New York Times,* September 8, 1861; Smith, *War and Press Freedom,* 131.

71   *New York Times,* September 8, 1861.

72   *OR,* series 2, vol. 2, 221, order of February 14, 1862; William H. Seward to Lincoln, April 22, 1861, ALPLC. Seward reported that Cameron's order had been "rescinded, for the present," before the suspensions had "become public." For an example of Interior Department enforcement intervention, see *Albany Evening Journal,* August 26, 1861.

73   Abrams, "*The Jeffersonian,*" 272–75.

74   Swindler, "The Southern in Missouri, 1861–1864," 400.

75   John Wein Forney to Nathaniel Banks, October 14, 1861, copy in John Russell Young Papers, Library of Congress.

76   William T. Sherman, *Memoirs of General W. T. Sherman*, orig. pub. 1885 (New York: Library of America, 1990), 138.

77   Murat Halstead, "Recollections and Letters of General Sherman," *The Independent* 51 (June 15, 1889): 1611–12. This episode is grippingly retold by John F. Marszalek in *Sherman's Other War: The General and the Civil War Press*, orig. pub. 1981 (Kent, Ohio: Kent State University Press, 1999), 37–38.

78   *Cincinnati Commercial*, December 11, 1861. Sherman's wife sent the undated *New York Times* clipping to her brother-in-law, Senator John Sherman, on December 10, 1861. See also Marszalek, *Sherman's Other War*, 78–79.

79   Sherman, *Memoirs*, 234–35.

80   Henry W. Halleck to William T. Sherman, December 18, 1861, in ibid., 234–35.

81   Murat Halstead, "Some Reminiscences of Mr. Villard," *The American Monthly Review of Reviews* 23 (January 1901): 62–63.

82   George B. McClellan, *McClellan's Own Story: The War for the Union . . .* (New York: Charles L. Webster, 1887), 198.

83   George B. McClellan to Simon Cameron, December 9, 1861, in Stephen W. Sears, ed., *The Civil War Papers of George B. McClellan: Selected Correspondence, 1860–1865* (New York: Ticknor & Fields, 1989), 142.

84   Henry J. Raymond to Simon Cameron, December 13, 1861, copy in Henry J. Raymond Papers, New York Public Library.

85   Quintus C. Wilson, "Voluntary Press Censorship during the Civil War," *Journalism Quarterly* 19 (September 1942): 251–61; Michael Hussey, "The Great Censorship Debate," in *Discovering the Civil War* (n.a., Washington: Foundation for the National Archives, 2010), 136. The other papers included the *Cincinnati Gazette*, *Philadelphia Inquirer*, *Boston Journal*, and the *Washington Evening Star*.

86   Testimony by Lawrence Gobright, January 24, 1862, and Adams S. Hill, January 22, 1862, before the House Judiciary Committee, National Archives.

87   George B. McClellan to Chief of Staff Randolph B. Marcy, January 29, 1862, in Sears, ed., *Civil War Papers of George B. McClellan,* 160; Robert E. Lee to Mary Lee, October 7, 1861, in Clifford Dowdey and Louis H. Manarin, eds., *The Wartime Papers of R. E. Lee* (New York: Bramhall House, 1961), 80.

88   For the best account of the *Trent* Affair, see Craig L. Symonds, *Lincoln and His Admirals* (New York: Oxford University Press, 2008), 71–97.

89   *New York Times*, December 8, 1861.

90   A wonderfully vivid account of the crisis, with an emphasis on the ping-ponging debates in London and Washington, can be found in Amanda Foreman, *A World on Fire: Britain's Crucial Role in the American Civil War* (New York: Random House, 2010), esp. 172–98. Duke of Newcastle, the secretary of state for the colonies, quoted on p. 180.

91   Russell to John T. Delane, January 27, 1862, Crawford, ed., *William Howard Russell's Civil War*, 221.

92   *New York Times*, November 25, 1861

93   *Frank Leslie's Illustrated Newspaper*, December 2, 1861.

94   Harriet A. Weed, ed., *Autobiography of Thurlow Weed*, 2 vols. (Boston: Houghton Mifflin, 1883), 2:616.

95   Quoted in Hussey, "The Great Censorship Debate," 136.

96   Adjutant-General Lorenzo Thomas, General Orders No. 10, February 4, 1862, *OR*, series 3, vol. 1: 879.

97   Charles A. Dana, *Recollections of the Civil War with the Leaders at Washington and in the Field in the Sixties* (New York: D. Appleton, 1902), 1–2.

98   *OR* series 2, vol. 2: 787–88. See also Mark E. Neely, Jr., *The Fate of Liberty: Abraham Lincoln and Civil Liberties* (New York: Oxford University Press, 1991), 28. Edwin Stanton to General John Wool, June 30, 1862, National Archives Record Group 197, M473 Reel 79. I am grateful to Walter Stahr for bringing the handwritten order to my attention. See also, "The Arrest of C. C. Fulton," *New York Times*, July 2, 1862.

99   Louis Prang and others, "Petition to Congress to secure the freedom of the Press," dated in endorsement December 24, 1861, and referred to the House Judiciary Committee, National Archives.

100 *The American Cyclopaedia and Register of Important Events of the Year 1862 . . .* (New York: D. Appleton, 1863), 480; Michael Hussey, "The Great Censorship Debate," in *Discovering the Civil War* (Washington, D.C.: Foundation for the National Archives, 2010), 136–38.

101 Testimony by S. P. Hanscom, February 17, 1862, "Allegations of Government Censorship of Telegraphic News Reports During the Civil War." Record of the hearings of the House Judiciary Committee, 1862, original documents in the National Archives, LexisNexis copies of the originals at the Columbia University Library.

102 Testimony by Adams Hill, January 22, 1862, and by D. W. Bartlett, February 19, 1862, ibid.

103 Testimony by Samuel Wilkeson, January 24, 1862, ibid.

104 Testimony by William Mackellar [*sic*], June 17, 1862, ibid.

105 Testimony by Lawrence Gobright, February 5, 1862, ibid.

106 Testimony by Frederick W. Seward, February 19, 1862, ibid.

107 Lincoln's Annual Message to Congress, December 3, 1861, *CW*, 5:53.

108 John W. Forney, *Anecdotes of Public Men*, 2 vols. (New York: Harper & Bros., 1881), 1:366. Forney asserted that Wikoff had first proven his influence with the *Herald* by improving the paper's relationship for a time with former president Buchanan.

109 James Gordon Bennett to Lincoln, October 22, 1862, ALPLC.

110 Diary entry, November 3, 1861, in Crawford, ed., *William Howard Russell's Civil War*, 162; second entry in William Howard Russell, *My Diary North and South*, ed. Fletcher Pratt (New York: Harper & Bros., 1954), 567.

111 Henry Wikoff to Lincoln, December 3, 1861, ALPLC. It is not impossible to imagine that the clever Wikoff wrote this letter after the fact, dating it December 3, to provide him with an alibi should he be accused of purloining the Annual Message in advance.

112 Ben: Perley Poore, *Perley's Reminiscences of Sixty Years in the National Metropolis*, 2 vols. (Philadelphia: Hubbard Bros., 1886), 2:143.

113 Michael Burlingame discovered previously unknown manuscript sources mentioned here

(including an 1864 note from *New York Tribune* assistant editor Sydney Howard Gay), as well as the long-suppressed entry from Orville Browning's original diary (the sanitized edition was edited by Theodore Calvin Pease and published in two volumes in 1927), to reach the conclusion that Mary sold the 1861 Annual Message. Given Mary's gullible reaction to a range of flatterers, it seems entirely plausible that she was indeed responsible for facilitating its leak. Whether or not she actually received a financial payoff cannot be proven. See Burlingame, *Abraham Lincoln: A Life*, 2 vols. (Baltimore: Johns Hopkins University Press, 2008), 2:273–77. Mary Lincoln's biographers have not accepted her complicity. See, for example, Catherine Clinton, *Mrs. Lincoln: A Life* (New York: HarperCollins, 2009), 166–67.

114   Lincoln to James Gordon Bennett, September 28, 1861, *CW,* 4:539.

115   Mary Lincoln to James Gordon Bennett, October 25, 1861, in Justin G. Turner and Linda Levitt Turner, eds., *Mary Todd Lincoln: Her Life and Letters* (New York: Alfred A. Knopf, 1972), 110–11.

116   Anthony Trollope, *North America*, 2 vols. (London: Chapman & Hall, 1862), 2:427.

117   Samuel Wilkeson testimony, January 24, 1862, National Archives.

118   Quoted in Oliver Carlson, *The Man Who Made News: James Gordon Bennett* (New York: Duell, Sloan & Pearce, 1942), 323.

119   Final Report of the House Committee, House Report No. 64, 37th Congress, 2nd Session, National Archives; Record Group 233; see also *Reports of Committees of the House of Representatives* (Washington, D.C.: U.S. Government Printing Office, 1863).

120   *American Annual Cyclopaedia for 1862 . . .* 480–81.

121   *OR,* series 2, 2: 246. See also Benjamin P. Thomas and Harold Hyman, *Stanton: The Life and Times of Lincoln's Secretary of War* (New York: Alfred A. Knopf, 1962), 154–55.

122   Stanton letter and endorsed reply, January 24, 1862, in Edwin M. Stanton Papers, Library of Congress, and *CW*, 5:110.

123   *American Cyclopaedia for 1862*, 480.

124   Ben: Perley Poore recollection in Allen Thorndike Rice, ed,. *Reminiscences of Abraham Lincoln by Distinguished Men of His Time* (New York: North American Publishing, Co., 1886), 227.

TWELVE: SLAVERY MUST GO TO THE WALL

1   William A. Croffut, "Lincoln's Washington: Recollections of a Journalist Who Knew Everybody," *Atlantic Monthly* 145 (January 1930): 56–58. The founder of the organizing entity for the lecture series was none other than Lewis Clephane, editor of the administration's official organ, the *National Republican.* Other speakers were to include Henry Ward Beecher, Wendell Phillips, William Lloyd Garrison, and Ralph Waldo Emerson. See also Croffut, *An American Procession, 1855–1914: A Personal Memoir of Famous Men* (Boston: Little, Brown, 1931), 56–64. Croffut also held an administration patronage post as a Treasury Department stenographer.

2   Ibid., 58.

3   Clipping in the John Hay scrapbook, John Hay Library, Brown University (photocopy in author's collection).

4   James R. Gilmore, "Lincoln: Personal Reminiscences of Him by James R. Gilmore," *New York Times*, October 8, 1898. The new magazine was to be edited by Charles Godfrey Leland.

5   James R. Gilmore [Edmund Kirke], *Among the Pines; or, The South in Secession-time* (New York: Charles T. Evans, 1862).

6   James R. Gilmore [Edmund Kirke], *Personal Recollections of Abraham Lincoln and the Civil War* (Boston: L. C. Page & Co., 1898), 42–46.

7   Ibid.

8   Croffut, "Lincoln's Washington," 63.

9   Joel Benton, ed., *Greeley on Lincoln . . .* (New York: Baker & Taylor Co., 1893), 75.

10 Paraphrased highlights of Greeley's lecture appeared in the *Washington Evening Star* and the *New York Times*, January 4, 1862. For the second part of the quote (no full and reliable transcript survives), see Michael F. Conlin, "The Smithsonian Abolition Lecture Controversy: The Clash of Antislavery Politics with American Science in Wartime Washington," *Civil War History* 46 (December 2000): 305–10.

11 Croffut, "Lincoln's Washington," 59.

12 James E. Pollard, *The Presidents and the Press* (New York: Macmillan, 1947); *New York Herald*, February 5, 1862.

13 Julian quoted in Allen Thorndike Rice, ed., *Reminiscences of Abraham Lincoln by Distinguished Men of His Time* (New York: North American Publishing Co., 1886), 60; Lincoln's remark to Byington in Harry J. Maihafer, *The General and the Journalists: Ulysses S. Grant, Horace Greely, and Charles Dana* (Washington, D.C.: Brassey's, 1998), 129.

14 Russell to Mowbray Morris, March 15, 1862, in Martin Crawford, ed., *William Howard Russell's Civil War: Private Diary and Letters, 1861–1862* (Athens: University of Georgia Press, 1992), 230.

15 Russell to John T. Delane, January 16, 1862, Russell to Mowbray Morris, February 16, in ibid., 218, 224, 229.

16 Mowbray Morris to William Howard Russell, March 15, 1862, in ibid., xlv.

17 William Howard Russell to Mowbray Morris, April 4, 1862, in ibid., 237; Elihu Washburne to Lincoln, June 20, 1861, ALPLC. Russell's letter to Stanton is in Crawford, ed. *William Howard Russell's Civil War*, 235. Amanda Foreman asserted that Russell had written to Lincoln, Seward, Sumner, and "four generals . . . all without success," in *A World on Fire: Britain's Crucial Role in the American Civil War* (New York: Random House, 2010), 235. No letters from Russell survive in the Lincoln Papers at the Library of Congress.

18 Ben: Perley Poore recollection in Rice, ed., *Reminiscences of Abraham Lincoln by Distinguished Men of His Time*, 229.

19 Russell to Charles Sumner, August 31, 1861; "innumerable Senators" quoted in Foreman, *A World on Fire*, 235; William Howard Russell, *My Diary North and South* (Boston: T.O.H.P. Burnham, 1863), 600; Lincoln to Seward, December 19, 1861, *CW*, 5:73.

20 Russell to John T. Delane, December 13, 1861, in Crawford, ed., *William Howard Russell's Civil War*, 204. See also William Howard Russell, *My Diary North and South* (Boston: T.O.H.P. Burnham, 1863).

21 Ward quoted in Allan Nevins, *The War for the Union*, 4 vols. (New York: Charles Scribner & Sons, 1959–1971), 2:3n2.

22 Special Message to Congress, March 6, 1862, *CW*, 5:144–45.

23 Nicolay journal entry, March 9, 1862, in Michael Burlingame, ed., *With Lincoln in the*

White House: Letters, Memoranda, and Other Writings of John G. Nicolay, 1860–1865 (Carbondale: Southern Illinois University Press, 2000), 73.

24 Ibid.

25 Lincoln to Henry J. Raymond, March 9, 1862, *CW*, 5:152–53.

26 Henry Raymond to Lincoln, March 15, 1862, ALPLC.

27 *New York Tribune*, March 8, 1862.

28 Lincoln to Horace Greeley, March 24, 1862, *CW*, 5:169; Greeley to Lincoln, March 24 [?], 1862, ALPLC.

29 Greeley to Lincoln, March 24 [?], 1862, ALPLC.

30 *Douglass' Monthly*, April 1862.

31 Greeley to Lincoln, May 24 [?], 1862, ALPLC.

32 Raymond wrote to the president on New York State Assembly Chamber letterhead in the early days of the session to ask a "personal favor" in behalf of a "personal friend" who hoped to continue in his role as an army surgeon even though he had reached the mandatory retirement age of sixty-two. See Henry J. Raymond to Lincoln, January 16, 1862, ALPLC.

33 George A. Townsend, unpublished scrapbook entry, cited in J. Cutler Andrews, *The North Reports the Civil War* (Pittsburgh: University of Pittsburgh Press, 1955), 208; Townsend, *Rustics in Rebellion: A Yankee Reporter on the Road to Richmond, 1861–65*, orig. pub. 1866 (Chapel Hill: University of North Carolina Press, 1950), 114–15.

34 *New York Times*, May 16, 1862.

35 For McClellan correspondence, see *OR*, series 1, vol. 11, part 3: 194, 214; *New York Times*, June 1, 1862.

36 *Chicago Tribune*, July 14, 1862.

37 *New York Herald*, August 25, 1862.

38 Henry J. Raymond, "Excerpts from the Journal of Henry J. Raymond," *Scribner's Monthly* 18 (January 1880): 419–20. The story also appears in Harold Holzer and Craig L. Symonds, eds., *The New York Times Complete Civil War* (New York: Black Dog & Leventhal, 2010), 13. The author is grateful for the opportunity to have worked with Craig Symonds on the research and writing of this story in our 2010 book.

39 *New York Times*, August 13, 1861.

40 "A Peaceable Man" [Nathaniel Hawthorne], "Chiefly About War-Matters," *Atlantic Monthly* 10 (July 1862): 47, 58. In the suppressed section of his article, Hawthorne described Lincoln's entrance this way: "In lounged a tall, loose-jointed figure, of an exaggerated Yankee port and demeanor, whom, (as being about the homeliest man I ever saw, yet by no means repulsive or disagreeable,) it was impossible not to recognize as Uncle Abe." See *Centenary Edition of the Works of Nathaniel Hawthorne*, ed. Thomas Woodson, Claude M. Simpson, and L. Neal Smith, Vol. 22 (Columbus: Ohio State University Press, 1994): 410–15. Hawthorne had served as consul to both Liverpool and Manchester during the Pierce administration.

41 Quoted in Brenda Wineapple, *Nathaniel Hawthorne: A Life* (New York: Random House, 2004), 350.

42 *Southern Illustrated News*, December 13, 1862; *New York Times*, May 31, 1862.

43 Lloyd Dunlap, "President Lincoln and Editor Greeley," *Abraham Lincoln Quarterly* 5 (June 1948): 108.

44   Horace Greeley to Samuel Wilkeson, April 8, 1862, Rabb Collection archive.

45   Horace Greeley to Lincoln, January 6, 1862[3], ALPLC.

46   See, for examples, James S. Wadsworth to Ward Hill Lamon, May 17, 1862, seeking the release of "three colored men" whom the general claimed were under "military protection," ALPLC.

47   Presidential proclamation, May 19, 1862, *CW*, 5:222–23.

48   *New York Herald,* May 18, 1862; Lincoln to James Gordon Bennett, May 21, 1862, *CW*, 5:225.

49   Bennett's friend Judge Abraham D. Russell felt emboldened to write Lincoln asking that his brother-in-law be retained at the New York Post Office, now under the charge of Greeley ally Theodore Wakeman. Theodore Taylor was indeed spared the ax. See Russell to Lincoln, March 27, 1862; Wakeman to Seward, April 2, 1862, ALPLC.

50   Edwin Wright to Lincoln, May 23, 1862; James W. White to Lincoln, July 7, 1862, ALPLC. White later invited Lincoln to a New York Union rally, but Lincoln politely declined. He did receive White and a small New York delegation at the White House.

51   William Goodell to Lincoln, July 9, 1862 (citing a June 7 *New York Herald* editorial), ALPLC.

52   *New York Tribune*, May 20, 1862.

53   Townsend, *Rustics in Rebellion*, 192.

54   *New York Tribune*, June 24, 1862.

55   *New York Herald*, June 26, 1862.

56   Winfield Scott to Lincoln, June 24, 1862, ALPLC. It was probably no coincidence that when he returned to Washington, Lincoln summoned General Henry Halleck from the West and installed him as administrative general-in-chief.

57   Lincoln's remarks at Jersey City, reported in the *New York Times, New York Herald*, June 26, 1862, in *CW,* 5:284.

58   "Enquirer" to the Editor, *New York Tribune*, July 28, 1862, and to Sydney Gay, August 13, 1862; Gay to Lincoln, July 30, 1862, and Lincoln to Gay, August 1, 1862, in *CW*, 5:353.

59   William O. Stoddard, "The Daily Press of New York," *New York Examiner*, July 31, 1862, in Michael Burlingame, ed. *Dispatches from Lincoln's White House: The Anonymous Civil War Journalism of Presidential Secretary William O. Stoddard* (Lincoln: University of Nebraska Press, 2002), 90.

60   *New York Times*, July 22, 1862; John Hay to Mary Jay (daughter of John Jay), July 20, 1862, in Michael Burlingame, ed., *At Lincoln's Side: John Hay's Civil War Correspondence and Selected Writings* (Carbondale: Southern Illinois University Press, 2000), 23.

61   Lincoln later entitled this draft: "Emancipation Proclamation as first sketched and shown to the Cabinet in July 1862." See *CW*, 5:336–37.

62   F[rancis]. B. Carpenter, *Six Months at the White House with Abraham Lincoln: The Story of a Picture* (New York: Hurd & Houghton, 1866), 21.

63   Ibid.

64   John Niven, ed., *The Salmon P. Chase Papers*, volume 1 (Kent, Ohio: Kent State University Press, 1993), 351.

65   Carpenter, *Six Months at the White House*, 22.

66   *Philadelphia Press*, July 30, 1862, reprinted in Elwyn Burns Robinson, "The *Press*: President Lincoln's Philadelphia Organ," *Pennsylvania Magazine of History and Biography* 65 (1941): 169; Robert Harper, *Lincoln and the Press* (New York: McGraw-Hill, 1951), 175.

67   Lincoln's message is in *CW*, 5:370–75. For a modern interpretation of the meeting and the makeup of the visiting delegation, see Kate Masur, "The African American Delegation to Abraham Lincoln: A Reappraisal," *Civil War History* 56 (June 2010): 117–44, esp. 131.

68   Frederick Douglass, "The Slaveholders' Rebellion," speech at Himrods Corner, New York, July 4, 1862, and "The President and His Speeches," *Douglass' Monthly*, September 1862, in Philip S. Foner and Yuval Taylor, eds., *Frederick Douglass: Selected Speeches and Writings* (Chicago: Lawrence Hill), 506, 511–13. Douglass had also spoken out for immediate emancipation at Boston on February 5.

69   Orville H. Browning to Lincoln, August 11, 1862, ALPLC.

70   "The Prayer of Twenty Millions," *New York Tribune*, August 20, 1862.

71   Conversation with Leonard Swett, March 14, 1878, in Michael Burlingame, ed., *An Oral History of Abraham Lincoln: John G. Nicolay's Interviews and Essays* (Carbondale: Southern Illinois University Press, 1996), 58–59.

72   Lincoln to Horace Greeley, August 22, 1862, *CW*, 5:388–89.

73   "James C. Welling," biographical note in Rice, ed., *Reminiscences of Abraham Lincoln by Distinguished Men of His Time*, 643.

74   [Josephine Seaton], *William Winston Seaton of the 'National Intelligencer': A Biographical Sketch . . .* (Boston: James Osgood, 1871), 360.

75   Ibid., 525–26.

76   James C. Welling, "The Emancipation Proclamation," *The North American Review* 130 (1880): 165.

77   James C. Welling, in Rice, ed., *Reminiscences of Abraham Lincoln by Distinguished Men of His Time*, 523, 540. Welling reflected the administration's view by assailing the Greeley editorial for its "truculence." The clipping from the *National Intelligencer* in the Lincoln Papers is misidentified as "Clipping from Aug. 23, 1862 New York Tribune"—a natural mistake, since of course the original correspondence had been directed at Horace Greeley.

78   *New York Journal of Commerce*, August 27, 1862; Thurlow Weed to Lincoln, August 24, 1862, ALPLC.

79   Joel Benton, ed., *Greeley on Lincoln.* (New York: The Baker & Taylor Co., 1893), 62.

80   *New York Tribune*, September 25, 1862; letter reprinted in James W. Parton, *The Life of Horace Greeley, Editor of "The New-York Tribune," from His Birth to the Present Time* rev. ed., orig. pub. 1872 (Boston: James R. Osgood, 1889), 466–68.

81   Gilmore, *Personal Recollections of Abraham Lincoln*, 81–83.

82   Ibid., 82.

83   Wendell Phillips to "the editor of the New York Tribune," August 20, 1862, speech at the Abingdon Grove, August 1, 1862, in Wendell Phillips, *Speeches, Lectures, and Letters* (Boston: Walker, Wise & Co., 1864), 465, 462; Wendell Phillips to Sydney Howard Gay, September 2, 1862, ALPLC, Sydney Howard Gay Papers, Columbia University.

84   Whitelaw Reid, in James A. Smart, ed., *A Radical View: The "Agate" Dispatches of Whitelaw Reid, 1861–1865*, 2 vols. (Memphis: Memphis State University Press, 1976), 1:215, dispatch of August 24, 1862.

85   Benton, ed., *Greeley on Lincoln*, 84.

86   Ibid., 63.

87   For a discussion of reaction in Missouri, for example, along with a fine discussion of the overall matter of the Greeley letter, see James Oakes, *Freedom National: The Destruction of Slavery in the United States, 1861–1865* (New York: W. W. Norton, 2013), 307–13. See also *New York Tribune*, August 24, 1862.

88   Adam Gurowski, *Diary from March 4, 1861, to November 2, 1862* (Boston: Lee & Shepard, 1862), 259; Ralph Waldo Emerson, journal entry, autumn 1863, in Stephen E. Whicher, ed., *Selections from Ralph Waldo Emerson* (Boston: Houghton Mifflin, 1957), 396. Lincoln had earlier welcomed Emerson to the White House, where the president charmed the distinguished visitor with funny stories.

89   Edgar Cowan to William H. Seward, August 8, 1862, ALPLC.

90   *New York Tribune*, August 22, 1862.

91   The piece predicted, for example, that emancipation would take effect on December 1, 1862, rather than January 1, 1863.

92   *New York Times*, August 24, August 25, 1862.

93   Greeley quoted in Stefan Lorant, *Lincoln: A Picture Story of His Life* (rev. ed., New York: W. W. Norton, 1969), 159.

94   *New York Times*, August 26, 1862.

95   *Chicago Tribune*, August 27, 1862.

96   *New York Times,* August 26, 1862; *New York Evening Post*, September 23, 1862; *New York World*, August 18, 1862.

97   William W. Patton, *President Lincoln and the Chicago Memorial on Emancipation,* paper read to the Maryland Historical Society, December 12, 1887 (Baltimore: Maryland Historical Society, 1888), 13.

98   Lincoln's reply to the Chicago Ministers, *CW*, 5:420.

99   Welling essay in Rice, ed., *Reminiscences of Abraham Lincoln by Distinguished Men of His Time*, 528.

100   *CW*, 5:420–21, 425.

101   Ibid., 419–21.

102   *New York Evening Post*, September 15, 1862.

103   Niven, ed., *The Salmon P. Chase Papers*, 1:393; Gideon Welles, *Diary of Gideon Welles*, ed. John T. Morse, Jr., 3 vols. (Boston: Houghton Mifflin, 1911), 1:143.

104   Even White House insider John Hay fared no better than the Chicago delegation in timing his final predictions on emancipation. Knowing McClellan was heading toward a confrontation with Lee, he, too, prepared a report for the *Missouri Republican*. "Perhaps the time is coming," it prophesied, "when the President, so long forbearing, so long suffering with the South and the border, will give the word long waited for, which will breathe the life that is needed, the fire that seems extinguished, into the breasts of our men at arms." Hay

added a strong defense of Lincoln's recent reticence and mixed messages. The president, he argued, simply believed that any official "utterances would instantly form an issue . . . which would divide and fiercely fight those who were now most strongly united in the defense of the Union. While the contest could be better carried out without an executive pronunciamento, the President thought best to keep silent." Hay's article appeared on September 22—just as Lincoln was issuing precisely the "executive pronunciamento" Hay believed could be avoided. See Michael Burlingame, ed., *Lincoln's Journalist: John Hay's Anonymous Writings for the Press, 1860–1864* (Carbondale: Southern Illinois University Press, 1998), 307–11.

105 *Douglass' Monthly*, October 1862, in Foner and Taylor, ed., *Selected Speeches and Writings*, 518, 520.

106 *Pacific Appeal*, October 4, 1862, quoted in Eric Foner, *The Fiery Trial: Abraham Lincoln and American Slavery* (New York: W. W. Norton, 2010), 245.

107 *Illinois State Journal*, September 25, 1862; Lincoln to Hannibal Hamlin, September 28, 1862, *CW*, 5:444.

108 *New York Herald*, September 27, 1862; L. A. Whitely to James Gordon Bennett, September 24, 1862, quoted in Andrews, *The North Reports the Civil War*, 326; *Chicago Times*, September 24, 1862; *Louisville Journal*, reprinted in the *National Intelligencer*, October 8, 1862; *New York Day-Book*, quoted in Forrest G. Wood, *Black Scare: The Racist Response to Emancipation and Reconstruction* (Berkeley: University of California Press, 1968), 35; *London Times*, October 7, 1862; *New York World*, September 24, 1862; *Richmond Dispatch*, October 2, 1862, quoted in Mitgang, ed., *Lincoln as They Saw Him*, 315. Habeas corpus proclamation, September 24, 1862, in *CW*, 5:436–37.

109 *National Intelligencer*, September 26, 1862.

110 *New York World*, October 23, 1862.

111 Theodore Canisius to Lincoln, October 4, 1862, William H. Seward to Lincoln, October 25, 1862, ALPLC; Lincoln to Seward, October 25, 1862, *CW*, 5:476.

112 *New York Herald*, November 4, November 5, 1862.

113 Lincoln to Carl Schurz, November 10, 1862, *CW*, 5:494.

114 *New York Times*, November 4, November 5, 1862; *New York Times*, November 19, 1862.

115 *New York Tribune*, November 5, November 8, 1862.

116 Henry J. Raymond to Lincoln, November 25, 1862, ALPLC.

117 Lincoln to Henry J. Raymond, December 7, 1862, *CW*, 5:544; Karl Marx, "On Events in North America," *Die Presse* (Vienna), October 12, 1862, translated and reprinted in Saul K. Padower, *Karl Marx on America and the Civil War* (New York: McGraw-Hill, 1971), 221–22.

118 L. A. Gobright, *Recollections of Men and Things at Washington, During the Third of a Century* (Philadelphia: Claxton, Remson & Haffelfinger, 1869), 339.

119 Lawrence Gobright to John G. Nicolay, December 1, 1862, John G. Nicolay Papers, Library of Congress.

120 John Wein Forney to Abraham Lincoln, November 28, 1862, and to John G. Nicolay, December 1, 1862, ALPLC. In another plea, Forney worried that the capital's afternoon paper would get the scoop, writing to Nicolay: "I hear that the Star is resolved to beat the

Chronicle in getting it out." Forney continued to fret on the eve of its release. "We'll see."
See Forney to Nicolay, December 1, 1862.

121   John Wein Forney to John Russell Young, December 11, 1862, John Russell Young Papers,
Library of Congress.

122   Annual Message to Congress, December 1, 1862, *CW*, 5:537.

123   *New York Times*, December 2, 1862; *Weekly Anglo African*, December 1862; the *Herald*
quoted in Nevins, *The War for the Union*, 2:339; *New York Tribune*, December 2, 1862.

124   Gobright, *Recollections of Men and Things at Washington*, 315–18.

125   Schuyler Colfax to Lincoln, December 31, 1862, ALPLC. See also O. J. Hollister, *Life of
Schuyler Colfax* (New York: Funk & Wagnalls, 1886), 30. Greeley had sent a thank-you to
Colfax in 1842.

126   Unsigned memorandum by Lincoln, ca. January 1, 1863, ALPLC; John G. Nicolay to Horace Greeley, and to Henry Raymond, December 31, 1862, in Burlingame, ed., *With Lincoln in the White House*, 98, 225n192. Former journalist John Defrees, the public printer,
wanted only for the president to produce a document "to justify the act in all coming time,"
urging Nicolay to prevent Lincoln from being so "perplexed by 'outsiders' that he will not
give it proper thought." See Defrees to Nicolay, December 17, 1862, ALPLC.

127   John Wein Forney to Lincoln, December 30, 1862, ALPLC.

128   Marchant project and the politically motivated engraving it subsequently inspired are covered in Harold Holzer, Gabor Boritt, and Mark E. Neely, Jr., *The Lincoln Image: Abraham
Lincoln and the Popular Print* (New York: Charles Scribner's Sons, 1984), 102–10.

THIRTEEN: SITTING ON A VOLCANO

1   *New York Times*, January 1, 1863.

2   Ibid.

3   The story is retold in Daniel R. Biddle and Murray Dubin, " 'God Is Settling the Account':
African American Reaction to Lincoln's Emancipation Proclamation," *Pennsylvania Magazine of History and Biography* 137 (January 2013): 75.

4   H. M. Turner, "Reminiscences of the Proclamation of Emancipation," *The A.M.E. Review* 29 (January 1913): 213–14.

5   *Chicago Times*, January 3, 1863; *New York World*, January 5, 1863.

6   *Douglass' Monthly*, January 1863. For a novel discussion of one state's typical journalistic
split over the final proclamation, see Edward Noyes, "Wisconsin's Reaction to Abraham
Lincoln's Emancipation Proclamation with Especial Reference to Editorial Opinion," *Bulletin of the Lincoln Fellowship of Wisconsin*, No. 41 (1986).

7   *New York Times*, February 12, 1862.

8   *New York Times*, January 3, 1863.

9   [Henry Norman Hudson], *A Chaplain's Campaign with Gen. Butler* (New York: Privately
printed for the author, 1865), 14, 16–17.

10   For New Orleans, see *Richmond Daily Dispatch*, May 29, 1862; for the Oregon case, *OR*,
series 1, vol. 50, part 1: 895–97; for the West Coast shutdowns, Thomas C. Hanson, Sr.,
Abraham Lincoln: Press Freedom and War Restraints—How He Suppressed the Los Angeles Star
(Greenville, S.C.: Thomas C. Hanson, Sr., 2004), 48.

11   D[ennis] A. Mahony, *The Prisoner of State* (New York: Carleton, 1863), 138–39.

12   A. W. Spies to William H. Seward, September 24, 1862, and forwarded to Lincoln, ALPLC.

13   Testimony by Benjamin Wood before the House Judiciary Committee, July 11, 1862, transcript in the National Archives.

14   Jonathan W. White, ed., *A Philadelphia Perspective: The Civil War Diary of Sidney George Fisher* (New York: Fordham University Press, 2007), 183.

15   *Philadelphia Evening Journal*, January 20, 1863.

16   Reprinted in the *Philadelphia Evening Bulletin*, January 30, 1863.

17   Arnold Shankman, "Freedom of the Press During the Civil War: The Case of Albert D. Boileau," *Pennsylvania Magazine of History and Biography* 41 (October 1975): 305–9.

18   Quoted in ibid., 309.

19   *Richmond Christian Observer and Presbyterian Witness*, February 12, 1863.

20   George Bergner, *The Legislative Record: Containing the Debates and Proceedings of the Pennsylvania Legislature for the Session of 1863* (Harrisburg, Penn.: "Telegraph" Steam Book and Job Office, 1863), esp. 96–97.

21   *New York Times*, February 3, 1863.

22   *Postmaster General's Authority over Mailable Matter*, House of Representatives, 37th Congress, 3rd Session, Misc. Doc. No. 16, January 20, 1863, 2, 13.

23   William Whiting, *The War Powers of the President, and the Legislative Powers of Congress in Relation to Rebellion, Treason, and Slavery*, 7th ed. (Boston: John L. Shorey, 1863), 59–60; For North Carolina outrages, see William C. Harris, *William Woods Holden, Firebrand of North Carolina Politics* (Baton Rouge: Louisiana State University Press, 1987), 138–140. Governor Zebulon Vance vowed to arrest any newspaper editor who committed "treason." For the governor's correspondence with President Jefferson Davis and others, see Joe A. Mobley, ed., *The Papers of Zebulon Bair Vance*, 2 vols. (Raleigh: Division of Archives and History, 1995), 2:272–279. The author is grateful to historian Joe Mobley for drawing his attention to these incidents.

24   Arthur Charles Cole, *The Era of the Civil War, 1848–1870, Centennial History of Illinois*, Vol. 3 (Springfield: Illinois Centennial Commission, 1919), 303.

25   *Chicago Times* statement of purpose, June 1861, quoted in Justin E. Walsh, *To Print the News and Raise Hell: A Biography of Wilbur F. Storey* (Chapel Hill: University of North Carolina Press, 1968), 3.

26   *Chicago Times*, November 15, 1862.

27   *New York Caucasian*, March 28, 1863, from a copy generously provided by Seth Kaller.

28   See, for example, Major General Charles S. Hamilton to Major General Ulysses S. Grant, February 9, 1863, in John Y. Simon, ed., *The Papers of Ulysses S. Grant*, 32 vols. to date, now with John F. Marszalek as editor (Carbondale: Southern Illinois University Press, 1967–2012), 7:307n.

29   *Congressional Globe*, 37th Congress, 1st Session, 1861, 57–59. For a general view of the question of loyal opposition, see Frank Klement, *The Limits of Dissent*, orig. pub. 1970 (New York: Fordham University Press, 1998).

30   *OR*, series 2, vol. 5: 480.

31   For Hascall's General Orders No. 9 and related history, see Stephen E. Towne, "Killing the

Serpent Speedily: Governor Morton, General Hascall, and the Suppression of the Democratic Press in Indiana, 1863," *Civil War History* 52 (2006): 50–53, 60.

32   For the best biography, see David W. Bulla, *Lincoln's Censor: Milo Hascall and Freedom of the Press in Civil War Indiana* (West Lafayette, Ind.: Purdue University Press, 2008).

33   *The Trial of Hon. Clement Laird Vallandigham, by a Military Commission, and the Proceedings Under His Application for a Writ of Habeas Corpus . . .* (Cincinnati: Rickey & Carroll, 1863), 23.

34   *New York World*, May 6, 1863.

35   Carl M. Becker and Ritchie Thomas, eds., *Hearth and Knapsack: The Ladley Letters, 1857–1880* (Athens: Ohio University Press, 1988), 124, 167.

36   Ex parte Vallandigham, 68 U.S., 243, 244 (1864). For an incisive analysis of the case, see Frank J. Williams, "Civil Liberties in Wartime New York," in Harold Holzer, ed., *Lincoln and New York* (New York: New-York Historical Society and Philip Wilson, 2009), esp. 172–75.

37   *New York Herald*, June 12, 1863.

38   Reed W. Smith, *Samuel Medary and the Crisis: Testing the Limits of Press Freedom* (Columbus: Ohio State University Press, 1995), 109, 130, 137–39. For the case of Captain Benjamin F. Sells, see Jonathan W. White, *Emancipation, the Union Army, and the Reelection of Abraham Lincoln* (Baton Rouge: Louisiana State University Press, 2014), 59.

39   *Albany Atlas & Argus*, May 18, 1863; Erastus Corning to Lincoln, with enclosed resolutions, May 15, 1863, ALPLC.

40   *OR*, series 1, vol. 23, part 2: 381.

41   For a thorough, dramatic overview, see Craig D. Tenney, "To Suppress or Not to Suppress: Abraham Lincoln and the Chicago Times," *Civil War History* 27 (September 1981): 248–59.

42   Union League of Chicago to Lincoln, June 6, 1863, ALPLC.

43   Mark W. Delahay to Lincoln, June 19, 1863, ALPLC.

44   Isaac N. Arnold and Lyman Trumbull to Lincoln, June 3, 1861; resolutions of the Illinois House of Representatives, June 4, 1863; J. Young Scammon and William Kelsey Reed (Chicago Union League) to Lincoln, June 6, 1863; Arnold to Lincoln, June 9, 1863. Even the German Union League, a pro-Lincoln organization, broke with their English-speaking counterparts and condemned the suppression. See German Union League to Isaac N. Arnold, June 5, 1863, all ALPLC.

45   *New York Herald*, June 4, 1863.

46   Lincoln to Edwin M. Stanton, June 4, 1863, *CW*, 6:148; *OR*, series 3, vol. 3: 252.

47   Lincoln to Isaac N. Arnold, May 25, 1864, *CW*, 7:361. It took a sympathetic newspaper summary to stimulate a coda; *New York Times*, June 13, 1863.

48   *New York Times*, June 12, 1863. Another group of Democrats met at the Brooklyn Academy of Music to denounce emancipation, arbitrary arrests, and press suppression. See *New York Times*, June 12, 1863.

49   The editors were identified by name in "The Rights of the Press," clipping sent to Lincoln by Elon Comstock, editor of the *New York Argus*, June 11, 1863, ALPLC.

50   *New York Tribune*, June 9, 1863.

51   *New York Evening Post*, June 9, 1863.

52   Elon Comstock to Lincoln, June 11, 1863.

53   Letter to "Editor of the Chronicle," June 6, 1863, *CW* 6:251–52.

54   Reply to Erastus Corning and others, [June 12], 1863, *CW*, 6:263.

55   Ibid., 6:263, 267, 268–69. Lincoln took special note of the case of one particular New Orleans journalist named Louiallier, pointing out that he had defiantly "published a denunciatory newspaper article . . . Gen. Jackson arrested him. A lawyer . . . procured the U.S. Judge [Dominick] Hall to order a writ of Habeas Corpus to release Mr. Louiallier. Gen. Jackson arrested both the lawyer and the judge."

56   Tribune Co. to John G. Nicolay, June 16, 1863, John Wein Forney to Lincoln, June 14, 1863; Horace Greeley to Nicolay, June 24, 1863, all ALPLC.

57   *New York Herald*, June 16, 1863.

58   *New York World*, June 16, 1863.

59   Erastus Corning and others to Lincoln, July 3, 1863, enclosing a printed copy of their June 30 rejoinder to Lincoln's June 12 letter.

60   See, for example, *President Lincoln's Views. An Important Letter on the Principles Involved in the Vallandigham Case . . .* (Philadelphia: King & Baird, 1863), and *President Lincoln on Vallandigham, The Tribune War Tracts*, No. 5 (New York: The Tribune Co., 1863). The newly established pro-Democratic Society for the Diffusion of Political Knowledge, led by anti-emancipationist Samuel F. B. Morse, published Corning's rejoinder.

61   New York Republican Roscoe Conkling offered the 500,000 circulation number, quoted in Mark E. Neely, Jr., *Lincoln and the Triumph of the Nation* (Chapel Hill: University of North Carolina Press, 2011), 280. See also the King & Baird edition cited in the previous note.

62   Lincoln to Arnold, May 25, 1864, ALPLC.

63   *New York Times*, June 21, 1863.

64   Sidney T. Matthews, "Control of the Baltimore Press During the Civil War," *Maryland Historical Magazine* 36 (June 1941): 159–60. Like many such newspapers that took their names decades earlier, the *Baltimore Republican* was a Democratic paper.

65   *Chicago Times*, July 23, 1863, reprinted in *New York Herald*, July 26, 1863. Under the most bitterly disputed terms of the first Conscription Act, draftees were permitted to identify substitutes who were willing to serve in their place, or "purchase" one for $300. The figure was supposedly set to prevent bidding wars, but impoverished draft-age men in urban areas who seldom earned more than $300 *a year* protested that the system proved that Lincoln had made the conflict into a "rich man's war but a poor man's fight"—and worst of all, many white conscripts complained, to free African Americans.

66   *New York Times*, June 14, 1863.

67   *New York Herald*, June 9, 1863.

68   Jos. C. G. Kennedy to "Pond," July 25, 186, undated clipping in the Lincoln Museum Collection, Fort Wayne, Indiana. Kennedy wrote: "The paper, it is generally known became embarrassed by the entire loss of its large southern circulation, consequent on the rebellion which loss has been followed now by the withdrawal of the official advertisements of the govt Departments, which they have hitherto enjoyed under almost every administration, thus cutting off resources by which they have managed to meet their expenditures."

69   Lincoln to Edwin M. Stanton, July 2, 1863, *CW*, 6:313.

70   *Washington Chronicle*, May 13, 1863; Lincoln to John W. Forney, May 13, 1863, *CW*, 6:214; Lincoln to William Cullen Bryant, May 14, 1863, *CW*, 6:216. For more on the reaction to the death of "Stonewall" Jackson, see Mark E. Neely, Jr., Harold Holzer, and Gabor S. Boritt, *The Confederate Image: Prints of the Lost Cause* (Chapel Hill: University of North Carolina Press, 1987), 109.

71   "Extracts from the Journal of Henry J. Raymond," *Scribner's Magazine* 19 (March 1880), 705.

72   Joseph Hooker to Lincoln, June 26, 1863, ALPLC; Lincoln to Hooker, June 27, 1863, *CW*, 6:297.

73   Grand jury records are in Record Group 21, Records of the Court of the District of Columbia, Entry 45, Case Papers, Appearances, Trials, Judicials, etc., 1831–1863, National Archives. Harding's father, Jesper Harding, had founded the paper in 1829 as a pro–Andrew Jackson organ, later converted it into a Whig paper, and turned it over to his son in 1859.

74   Confederate General Campbell Brown, quoted in Allen C. Guelzo, *Gettysburg: The Last Invasion* (New York: Alfred A. Knopf, 2013), 98.

75   Historian Allen C. Guelzo has convincingly redefined the Gettysburg campaign. See ibid.

76   *OR*, series 1, vol. 36, part 3: 751.

77   James G. Smart, ed., *A Radical View: The "Agate" Dispatches of Whitelaw Reid, 1861–1865*, 2 vols. (Memphis: Memphis State University Press, 1976), 2:68. Lincoln acknowledged his own disappointment in a highly critical July 14 letter to Meade despairing of his failure to follow up his victory, but never sent it. See *CW*, 327–28.

78   Joan Wenner and Andy Waske, "General Meade's Press Warfare," *Pennsylvania Heritage* 36 (Fall 2010): 10.

79   Steven J. Ramold, *Across the Divide: Union Soldiers View the Northern Home Front* (New York: New York University Press, 2013), 25.

80   *New York Times*, July 6, 1863.

81   *Vicksburg Daily Citizen*, July 4, 1863 (wallpaper edition); *Richmond Examiner*, July 8, July 15, 1863.

82   *New York Times*, July 6, 1863.

83   *OR*, series 1, vol. 36, part 3: 670; George Meade, [Jr.], *The Life and Letters of George Gordon Meade Major General United States Army*, ed. George Gordon Meade, 2 vols. (New York: Charles Scribner's Sons, 1913), 2:203. Meade devoted a good part of the appendix to his memoir to recounting several examples he had endured of unfair press criticism. The punishment took place on June 14, 1864.

84   Charles A. Dana, *Recollections of the Civil War . . .* (New York: D. Appleton, 1902), 215–16.

85   William T. Sherman to John Sherman, April 22, 1862, Ellen Sherman to John Sherman, May 7, 1862, William T. Sherman Papers, Library of Congress.

86   William T. Sherman to Lt. Gov. Benjamin Stanton, June 10, 1862, William T. Sherman Papers, Library of Congress.

87   Thomas H. Baker, "Refugee Newspaper: The *Memphis Daily Appeal*, 1862–1865," *The Journal of Southern History* 29 (August 1963): 326.

88   George Sisler, "The Arrest of a Memphis *Daily Appeal* War Correspondent on Charges of Treason," *West Tennessee Historical Society Papers* II (1957): 76–92.

89   See John F. Marszalek, *Sherman's Other War: The General and the Civil War Press*, orig. pub. 1981 (Kent, Ohio: Kent State University Press, 1999), 118–19, 132.

90   Ibid., 135. Another useful summary of the Knox case can be found in John B. Spore, "Sherman and the Press," *Infantry Journal* 63 (October 1948): 28–35.

91   Ramold, *Across the Divide*, 24.

92   Thomas W. Knox to William T. Sherman, *OR*, series 1, vol. 17: 580.

93   *OR*, series 1, vol. 24: 234.

94   Albert D. Richardson, *The Secret Service, the Field, the Dungeon, and the Escape* (Hartford, Conn.: American Publishing Co., 1865), 317; for Richardson's letters to Gay, especially January 3, 1863, Sydney Howard Gay Papers, Columbia University.

95   Richardson, *The Secret Service*, 319–20.

96   Ibid., 320–21.

97   Lincoln's "Whom it may concern" letter, March 20, 1863, *CW*, 6:142–43.

98   Ulysses S. Grant to Thomas W. Knox, *OR*, series 1, vol. 17, part 2: 893.

99   William T. Sherman to Thomas W. Knox, April 7, 1863, *OR*, series 1, vol. 17, part 2, 894–95.

100   Thomas W. Knox, *Camp-Fire and Cotton-Field* . . . (New York: Blelock & Co., 1865), 256, 260.

101   In addition to Richardson, see Junius Henri Browne, *Four Years in Secessia: Adventures Within and Beyond the Union Lines* . . . (Hartford, Conn.: O. D. Case & Co., 1865), esp. Chapters 33–46. An excellent recent book is Peter Carlson, *Junius and Albert's Adventures in the Confederacy: A Civil War Odyssey* (New York: PublicAffairs, 2013).

102   Richardson, *The Secret Service*, 362, 369.

103   See Sydney Howard Gay to Lincoln ("friends are exceedingly anxious for their safety"), May 29, 1863, ALPLC; Lincoln to Colonel William H. Ludlow ("ascertain why they are detained"), June 1, 1863, *CW*, 6:241.

104   Circular, May 20, 1864, *OR*, series 1, vol. 38, part 4: 272.

105   *OR*, series 1, vol. 17, part 2: 895–97; Sherman quoted in *OR*, series 1, vol. 38, part 4: 272.

106   William T. Sherman to the editors of the *Memphis Bulletin*, October 27, October 28, 1863, in Marszalek, *Sherman's Other War*, 171.

107   Lincoln to John M. Schofield, May 27, 1863, *CW*, 6:234.

108   See James O. Broadhead to Lincoln, July 14, 1863, and Henry T. Blow to Lincoln, July 13, 1863, ALPLC.

109   Lincoln to General John M. Schofield, [July 13, 1863] and July 20, 1863, *CW*, 6:326, 338. For Schofield's report to Lincoln, July 14, 1863, see *OR*, series 1, vol. 22, part 2: 373–74.

110   *CW*, 6:326, 234

111   Lincoln to John M. Schofield, October 1, 1863, *CW*, 6:492.

112   Lincoln to Robert T. Lincoln, July 14, 1863, *CW*, 6:327.

113   Joseph Medill to Horace White, March 5, 1863, ALPLC. The letter was officially written to White, but Medill encouraged his reporter to bring it to Lincoln's attention. White evidently did so, for the original was later found in Lincoln's White House files.

114 *New York Daily News*, July 11, 1863. Newspaper and Seymour quotes from Barnet Schecter, *The Devil's Own Work: The Civil War Draft Riots and the Fight to Reconstruct America* (New York: Walker, 2005), 26–27.

115 *New York Herald*, July 9, July 13, 1863.

116 Schecter, *The Devil's Own Work*, 154.

117 Allan Nevins and Milton Halsey Thomas, eds., *The Diary of George Templeton Strong*, 4 vols. (New York: Macmillan, 1952), 3:336, 338, 340.

118 James R. Gilmore [Edmund Kirke], *Personal Recollections of Abraham Lincoln and the Civil War* (Boston: L. C. Page & Co., 1898), 170.

119 Charles T. Congdon, *Reminiscences of a Journalist* (Boston: James R. Osgood, 1880), 250; Schecter, *The Devil's Own Work*, 153–55.

120 Congdon, *Reminiscences of a Journalist*, 249; Gilmore, *Personal Recollections of Abraham Lincoln and the Civil War*, 175–76.

121 Ibid., 249.

122 *New York Tribune*, July 15, 1863; *New York Times*, July 16, 1863.

123 Gilmore, *Personal Recollections of Abraham Lincoln and the Civil War*, 193–95.

124 Royal Cortissoz, *The Life of Whitelaw Reid*, 2 vols. (New York: Charles Scribner's Sons, 1921), 1:113.

125 Schecter, *The Devil's Own Work*, 168.

126 Jerome survived the riots. His daughter Jennie went on to marry an Englishman and give birth to Winston Churchill.

127 *New York Times*, July 14, 1863; Frederic Hudson, *Journalism in the United States, from 1690 to 1872* (New York: Harper & Brothers, 1873), 635.

128 Augustus Maverick, *Henry J. Raymond and the New York Press, for Thirty Years* (Hartford, Conn.: A. S. Hale & Co., 1870), 164–65; *New York Times*, July 15, 1863.

129 *New York Times*, July 14, 1863; *New York Herald*, July 16, 1863; *New York Tribune*, July 16, 1863.

130 *Harper's Weekly*, August 1, 1863.

131 *Harper's Weekly*, July 25, 1863.

132 *Harper's Weekly*, August 1, 1863.

133 Gilmore, *Personal Recollections of Abraham Lincoln and the Civil War*, 199.

134 I was inspired to this conclusion in part by an article about the twenty-first-century trend, as practiced by modern politicians, of bypassing the press and going directly to the people via the Internet. See Frank Bruni, "Who Needs Reporters?," *New York Times* (*Review* section), June 2, 2013.

135 David Wills to Lincoln, November 2, 1863, ALPLC.

136 For the July 7, 1863, impromptu speech, see *CW* 6:319–20; the three New York papers published slightly different versions in their editions of July 8. For the first draft of the final Gettysburg Address, see *CW*, 7:17–18.

137 Noah Brooks, *Washington in Lincoln's Time* (New York: The Century Co., 1895), 285–86.

138 For the August 9, 1863, photographs, see Charles Hamilton and Lloyd Ostendorf, *Lincoln in Photographs; An Album of Every Known Pose* (Norman: University of Oklahoma Press, 1963), 132. For a superb print, see the collection of the Abraham Lincoln Book Shop,

the revered collectors emporium in Chicago. The sitting was arranged not because Lincoln thought he should provide his admirers with a portrait to accompany his upcoming speech at Gettysburg, but because sculptor Sarah Fisher Ames had requested the photographs for use as models in accomplishing her bust portrait of the president. See Harold Holzer, "Seldom Twice Alike: The Changing Faces of Lincoln," in Holzer and Sara Vaughn Gabbard, eds., *1863: Lincoln's Pivotal Year* (Carbondale: Southern Illinois University Press, 2013), 160–65.

139   This and the continued recollections of John Hay are in Michael Burlingame and John R. Turner Ettlinger, eds., *Inside Lincoln's White House: The Complete Civil War Diary of John Hay* (Carbondale: Southern Illinois University Press, 1997), 112–13. For the text of Lincoln's impromptu remarks at Gettysburg on November 18, 1863, see *New York Times*, November 20, 1863, *CW*, 7:16–17.

140   Michael Burlingame, "John Hay Reports on the Events at Gettysburg," *For the People: A Newsletter of the Abraham Lincoln Association* 15 (Fall 2013): 1.

141   Mary D. Russell Young, ed., *Men and Memories: Personal Reminiscences by John Russell Young* (New York: F. Tennyson Neely, 1901), 2.

142   Ward Hill Lamon, *Recollections of Abraham Lincoln, 1847–1865*, ed. Dorothy Lamon (Chicago: A. C. McClurg & Co., 1895), 174. Lamon's reminiscences, edited by his daughter, are often regarded by historians as inauthentic, or at least shaped to make Lamon look especially influential and close to Lincoln.

143   Ibid., 173–74. Gabor Boritt searched Lamon's original manuscript at the Huntington Library in San Marino, California, and discovered that criticism that the president's friend originally made himself were reattributed by his daughter to Lincoln for the published edition See Gabor Boritt, *The Gettysburg Gospel: The Lincoln Speech that Nobody Knows* (New York: Simon & Schuster, 2001), 178, 354n.

144   Joseph Ignatius Gilbert, "Lincoln in 1861; Lincoln in 1863; Lincoln at Washington; the Assassination," *Nineteenth Annual Convention, National Shorthand Reporters' Association, Proceedings of the Annual Meeting* (La Porte, Ind.: Chase & Shepherd, 1971), 134, reprinted in Gilbert, "I Reported the Gettysburg Address," *Chicago Tribune*, November 19, 1978. The author is grateful to AP veteran Richard Pyle for sharing "A Meeting at Gettysburg," his original typescript for a 2010 article on Gilbert. See Pyle, "Dateline Gettysburg," *America's Civil War* (November 2010): 30–37.

145   The Gilbert text is in *CW*, 7:19–20. Young added a memorable phrase at the end. He had heard Lincoln say "this nation under God," and though it is possible he did not find the phrase in the president's manuscript—precisely which manuscript Lincoln read from remains unknown—Gilbert placed it in his dispatch. It was subsequently accepted in all standard printings of the speech—including copies later written out by Lincoln himself.

146   Burlingame, "John Hay Reports on the Events at Gettysburg," 5.

147   Quoted in Harold Holzer, " 'Thrilling Words' or 'Silly Remarks': What the Press Said About the Gettysburg Address," *Lincoln Herald* 90 (Winter 1988): 145.

148   Ibid., 144.

149   Entry in John Hay's diary, November 8, 1863, in Burlingame and Ettlinger, eds., *Inside Lincoln's White House*, 110.

150   Quoted in Boritt, *The Gettysburg Gospel*, 142. For an excellent new account of press reac-

tion to the Gettysburg Address, see Jared Peatman, *The Long Shadow of Lincoln's Gettysburg Address* (Carbondale: Southern Illinois University Press, 2013), Chapter 2, "'The Luckless Sallies of That Poor President Lincoln': Responses to the Gettysburg Address, 1863," 32–71.

151 *Richmond Enquirer*, November 27, 1863, reprinted in Peatman, *The Long Shadow of Lincoln's Gettysburg Address*, 32.

152 See editions of all three papers for November 20 and 21, 1863. Lincoln paraphrase is from the *New York Times*, November 21, 1863, incongruously headlined, "The Gettysburg Celebration."

153 See Ronald Reid, "Newspaper Response to the Gettysburg Addresses," *Quarterly Journal of Speech* 53 (February 1967): 50–53.

154 Noah Brooks, "Personal Reminiscences of Lincoln," *Scribner's Monthly* 15 (February/March 1878): 678; Edward Everett to Lincoln, November 20, 1863, ALPLC.

155 See Boritt, *The Gettysburg Gospel.*

156 Quoted in Lambert A. Wilmer, *Our Press Gang; or, A Completer Exposition of the Corruptions and Crimes of American Newspapers* (Philadelphia: J. T. Lloyd, 1859), 64–65.

157 John Wein Forney to John G. Nicolay, December 8, 1863, ALPLC.

158 Annual Message to Congress, December 8, 1863, *CW*, 7:36–53.

159 *New York Tribune*, December 10, 1863.

160 Nicolay quoted in Mario M. Cuomo and Harold Holzer, *Lincoln on Democracy: His Own Words, with Essays by America's Foremost Historians* (New York: HarperCollins, 1990), 309; *Richmond Examiner* quoted in Mitgang, ed., *Lincoln as They Saw Him*, 364.

161 *CW*, 7: 49–50.

162 *New York World*, December 15, 1864; *Chicago Tribune* December 14, 1864.

FOURTEEN: NO TIME TO READ ANY PAPERS

1 "The American Newspaper Press—The Southern States," *Leisure Hour* 13 (July 30, 1864): 494; Harold Holzer and the New-York Historical Society, *The Civil War in 50 Objects* (New York: Viking, 2013), 195.

2 For paper shortages, see Mary Elizabeth Massey, *Ersatz in the Confederacy: Shortages and Substitutes on the Southern Homefront*, orig. pub. 1952 (Columbia: University of South Carolina Press, 1993), 142; "The American Newspaper Press," 340.

3 Conversely, in 1863, Confederate soldiers at Raleigh sacked the pro-peace *North Carolina Standard*; in retaliation, a crowd of Unionist civilians attacked the office of the local pro-secession paper, the *State Journal*. See *The American Annual Cyclopedia and Register of Important Events of the Year 1863 . . .* (New York: D. Appleton & Co., 1864), 423.

4 *New York Times*, June 28, 1862. In fact, Kentucky and Missouri boasted pro-Union papers throughout the war.

5 William H. Seward to Lincoln, October 20, 1862, ALPLC. Only a few weeks before, *Frank Leslie's* (September 17, 1862) had pointed out the "evils" of straggling after one of its field artists observed "nearly one fourth of a regiment, including officers, dropping off one by one at convenient opportunities."

6   Lincoln to Joseph Hooker, May 27, 1863, *CW*, 6:233.

7   See Lincoln to General John A. Dix, June 6, 1863, *CW*, 6:252.

8   William T. Sherman to William Scott, February 11, 1863, in *Presidential and Other American Manuscripts from the Dr. Robert Small Trust*, Sotheby's catalogue, April 3, 2008, 145; Daniel Butterfield telegram to Lincoln, June 4, 1863, and Lincoln to Butterfield, June 4, 1863, *CW*, 6:247.

9   Herbert Ravenel Sass, *Outspoken: 150 Years of the News & Courier* (Columbia: University of South Carolina Press, 1953), 31–33.

10 *Minutes of the Board of Directors of the Press Association . . .* (Atlanta: Franklin Steam, Publishing House, 1864), preface by R. W. Gibbes, M.D., 5.

11 See Mark E. Neely, Jr., Harold Holzer, and Gabor S. Boritt, *The Confederate Image: Prints of the Lost Cause* (Chapel Hill: University of North Carolina Press, 1987), Chapter 1: "Engravers Wanted."

12 Massey, *Ersatz in the Confederacy*, 142.

13 *Vicksburg Daily Citizen*, July 2, 1863, wallpaper edition, Newspaper Section, Serial and Government Publications Division, Library of Congress; copy in the New-York Historical Society. Fake copies of this famous wallpaper edition abound; it is one of the most frequently forged newspapers of the Civil War era. The story bears eerie resemblance to an account recorded by Union soldier Lorenzo Vanderhoef after occupying the town on campaign near New Creek, West Virginia, in 1864. Vanderhoef recalled: "Finding no soldiers, our troops took down and conveyed to a wagon two secesh Printing Presses, a good share of type, blank paper etc. Some of the boys struck off a few newspapers as the type was already set for next day's issue." See Kenneth R. Martin and Ralph Linwood Snow, eds., *"I Am Now a Soldier!" The Civil War Diaries of Lorenzo Vanderhoef* (Bath, Maine: Patten Free Library, 1990), 50.

14 Original copy in the New-York Historical Society. See also Holzer and the New-York Historical Society, *The Civil War in 50 Objects*, 299–306.

15 Robert McCalmont, ed., *Extracts from Letters Written by Alfred B. McCalmont, 1862–1865: From the Front During the War of the Rebellion* Privately Printed by Robert McCalmont, 1908, 56–57.

16 Helyn W. Tomlinson, ed., *"Dear Friends:" The Civil War Letters and Diary of Charles Edwin Cort* (n.p., 1962), 30–31.

17 Robert W. Daly, ed., *Aboard the U.S.S. Monitor 1862: The Letters of Acting Paymaster William Frederick Keeler* (Annapolis, Md.: United States Naval Institute, 1964), 247.

18 Michael B. Chesson, ed., *J. Franklin Dyer: The Journal of a Civil War Surgeon* (Lincoln: University of Nebraska Press, 2003), 21, 104.

19 Guy C. Taylor to his wife, August 5, 1864, in Kevin Anderson and Patsy Anderson, eds., *Letters from Home to Sarah: The Civil War Letters of Guy C. Taylor, Thirty-seventh Wisconsin Volunteers* (Madison: University of Wisconsin Press, 2012), 84; Thomas P. Lowry, ed., *Swamp Doctor: The Diary of a Union Surgeon in the Virginia and North Carolina Marshes* (Mechanicsburg, Penn.: Stackpole, 2001), 81.

20 Robert E. Bonner, ed., *The Soldier's Pen: Firsthand Impressions of the Civil War* (New York: Hill & Wang, 2006), 19. The letter was written from Petersburg, Virginia.

21   A. Bush to "Mary," in Richard F. Nation and Stephen E. Towne, *Indiana's War: The Civil War in Documents* (Athens: Ohio University Press, 2009), 75.

22   Steven J. Ramold, *Across the Divide: Union Soldiers View the Northern Home Front* (New York: New York University Press, 2013), 23–24.

23   Court-Martial Files, 1864, LL-1359; Jonathan W. White, *Emancipation, the Union Army, and the Reelection of Abraham Lincoln* (Baton Rouge: Louisiana State University Press, 2014), Chapter 2.

24   Jessie Sellers Colton, ed., *The Civil War Journal and Correspondence of Matthias Baldwin Colton* (Philadelphia: Macrae-Smith Co., 1931), 17–18.

25   J. Gregory Acken, ed., *Inside the Army of the Potomac: The Civil War Experience of Captain Francis Adams Donaldson* (Mechanicsburg, Penn.: Stackpole, 1998), 68.

26   James Parton to Benjamin F. Butler, January 4, 1865; Butler to Parton, January 7, 1865; James W. White to Butler, January 5, 1865, in Jessie Ames Marshall, ed., *Private and Official Correspondence of Gen. Benjamin F. Butler During the Period of the Civil War* (Norwood, Mass.: The Plimpton Press, 1917), 5: 467–68, 470. Butler, a careful reader of the press, retained many wartime clippings in his files.

27   *Army and Navy Journal*, debut issue, August 29, 1863; *New York Times*, October 16, 1865.

28   John Chipman Gray and John Codman Ropes, *War Letters, 1862–1865* (Boston: Houghton Mifflin, 1927), 343.

29   See, for example, *Spirit of the Fair*, official newspaper of the 1864 Metropolitan Sanitary Fair in New York, original run in the New-York Historical Society, and the *Albany Canteen*, newspaper of the Albany, New York, Army Relief Association Fair, original run in the New York State Library.

30   McCalmont, *Extracts from Letters Written by Alfred B. McCalmont . . .* , 98.

31   William O. Stoddard, *Inside the White House in War Times* (New York: Charles L. Webster, 1890), 27. For a brilliant summary of Lincoln's evolving relations with the wartime press corps, see Richard Carwardine, "Abraham Lincoln and the Fourth Estate: The White House and the Press During the American Civil War," *American Nineteenth Century History* 7 (March 2006), esp. 8–9.

32   Quoted in James Edward Pollard, *The Presidents and the Press* (New York: Macmillan, 1947), v.

33   Quoted in Francis B. Carpenter, *Six Months at the White House with Abraham Lincoln: The Story of a Picture* (New York: Hurd & Houghton, 1866), 281–82.

34   Stoddard, *Inside the White House*, 27.

35   Ibid., 28.

36   Carpenter, *Six Months at the White House*, 153–54. Carpenter arrived in February 1864.

37   Ibid., 154.

38   Ibid.

39   John G. Nicolay to the editors of the *Chicago Tribune*, June 19, 1863, in Michael Burlingame, ed., *With Lincoln in the White House: Letters, Memoranda, and Other Writings of John G. Nicolay, 1860–1865* (Carbondale: Southern Illinois University Press, 2000), 116.

40   Nicolay to *Chicago Tribune*, June 19, 1863, in ibid., 115–16.

41 Joseph Medill to Lincoln, May 15, 1863, ALPLC.

42 Ida Tarbell interview with Joseph E. Medill, June 25, 1895, excerpted in Don E. Fehrenbacher and Virginia Fehrenbacher, eds., *Recollected Words of Abraham Lincoln* (Stanford: Stanford University Press, 1996), 326. Nearly thirty years after the fact, Medill evidently recalled the meeting as having occurred in 1864, but based on the issue discussed and the date of the angry letter from Medill when confronted with the long line waiting to see Lincoln, it is clear the visit occurred the year before.

43 "I wish Mr. Pickett could have the agency," Lincoln ordered Secretary of War Simon Cameron on March 21, 1861. See *CW*, 4:297.

44 Thomas J. Pickett to John G. Nicolay, March 20, 1863, ALPLC.

45 Thomas J. Pickett to John G. Nicolay, March 30, 1863; Pickett to Lincoln, April 3, 1863; Moline citizens to Edwin M. Stanton, April 8, 1863. Pickett also protested his innocence to Quartermaster General Montgomery Meigs, April 18, 1863, all in ALPLC; Lincoln to Calvin Truesdale, April 20, 1863, *CW*, 6:182.

46 See, for example, William Yates to Lincoln, May 22, 1863, Jesse K. DuBois to Lincoln, May 23, 1863, Jacob Bunn, Shelby Cullom, and Ozias Hatch to Lincoln, May 25, 1863, ALPLC; Lincoln to Dubois and others, May 29, 1863, *CW*, 6:237–38; Edward L. Baker to Lincoln, August 24, 1863, enclosing Bailhache's letter to Baker, August 14, 1863, ALPLC. (Bailhache properly thought it "would be irregular" for him to write Lincoln directly.)

47 Lincoln to Edward L. Baker, June 15, 1863, *CW*, 6:275. The Edwards case is discussed in Mark E. Neely and Harold Holzer, *The Lincoln Family Album* (New York: Doubleday, 1990), 7–8.

48 Edward L. Baker to Lincoln, September 30, 1863; Ada Bailhache to Lincoln, October 8, 1863, ALPLC.

49 Edward Baker to Orville H. Browning, January 27, 1864, ALPLC.

50 Quoted in Michael Burlingame, *Abraham Lincoln: A Life*, 2 vols. (Baltimore: Johns Hopkins University Press, 2008), 2:144.

51 Ward Hill Lamon, *Recollections of Abraham Lincoln, 1847–1865* ed. Dorothy Lamon (Chicago: A. C. McClurg & Co., 1895), 141; Carpenter, *Six Months at the White House*, 156.

52 Michael Burlingame and John R. Turner Ettlinger, eds., *Inside Lincoln's White House: The Complete Civil War Diary of John Hay* (Carbondale: Southern Illinois University Press, 1997), 104 (entry for October 30, 1863). See also Theodore Tilton to Lincoln, October 28, 1863, ALPLC. Tilton took issue with Lincoln's response to a Missouri delegation that asked the president to support immediate, rather than gradual, emancipation in that Border State. The *New York Tribune* (October 1, 1863) reported that Lincoln told his visitors that "their 'set' was a little too fast for his policy." For Lincoln's official reply, see his letter to Charles D. Drake and others, October 5, 1863, *CW*, 6:499–504.

53 Carpenter, *Six Months at the White House*, 230–31.

54 Albert D. Richardson, *The Secret Service, the Field, the Dungeon, and the Escape* (Hartford, Conn.: American Publishing Co., 1865), 326.

55 Stoddard, *Inside the White House*, 134–35.

56 Richardson, *The Secret Service*, 339.

57   Ibid., 323.

58   Lincoln to James C. Conkling, August 27, 1863, *CW*, 6:414.

59   L. A. Gobright, *Recollections of Men and Things at Washington During the Third of a Century* (Philadelphia: Claxton, Remsen, & Haffelfinger, 1869), 337–38; Noah Brooks dispatch of October 29, 1863, in Fehrenbacher and Fehrenbacher, eds., *Recollected Words of Abraham Lincoln*, 45.

60   "I am glad for you to have the relaxation," Lincoln wrote to his faithful if loose-lipped supporter, "though I regret the necessity which compels it." But the president declined to provide Forney with a letter that might show "foreigners that you . . . appreciate me." Replied Lincoln: "I have no European personal acquaintances, or I would gladly give you letters." See John Wein Forney to Lincoln, July 25, 1864; Lincoln to Forney, July 28, 1864, *CW*, 7:468.

61   Lincoln to James C. Conkling, September 3, 1863, *CW*, 6:430; John Wein Forney to Lincoln, September 3, 1863, and Conkling to Lincoln, September 4, 1863, ALPLC.

62   Gobright, *Recollections of Men and Things . . .* , 334, 337–39.

63   Lincoln to James C. Conkling, August 26, 1863, *CW*, 6:410. Addressed as a "letter," the manuscript was more accurately a formal speech crafted to be read aloud in Springfield by a surrogate. For a brilliant interpretation of the speech, see Allen C. Guelzo, "Defending Emancipation: Abraham Lincoln and the Conkling Letter, 1863," *Civil War History* 48 (December 2002): 313–37.

64   *New York Times*, August 27, 1863, *New York Tribune*, September 3, 1863.

65   [George] Forrester Williams, "General Sheridan's Bad Temper," *The Independent* 53 (October 10, 1901): 2400.

66   Henry E. Wing, *When Lincoln Kissed Me: A Story of the Wilderness Campaign* (New York and Cincinnati: Abingdon Press, 1913), 38.

67   Lincoln to the *Cincinnati Gazette*, August 5, 1863, *CW*, 6:366; Richard Smith telegraph to Thomas Eckert, August 5, 1863, ALPLC.

68   Gobright, *Recollections of Men and Things*, 328–29.

69   Ibid., 336–37.

70   Theodore Calvin Pease, *The Diary of Orville Hickman Browning*, 2 vols. (Springfield: Illinois State Historical Library, 1925), 1: 665, diary entry for April 3 describing the meeting of March 26.

71   Lincoln to Albert G. Hodges, April 4, 1864, *CW*, 7:281–82.

72   Lincoln to Albert G. Hodges, April 22, 1864, *CW*, 7:308.

73   *New York Tribune, New York Times, New York Herald*, April 29, 1864. For Lincoln's endorsed copy of the *Tribune* article, see ALPLC.

74   *New York Times*, April 29, 1864.

75   Burlingame and Ettlinger, eds., *Inside Lincoln's White House* 188 (entry for April 24, 1864).

76   Ibid.

77   Carpenter, *Six Months at the White House*, 155.

78   Stoddard, *Inside the White House*, 135.

79   Carpenter, *Six Months at the White House* 167.

80   Allen Thorndike Rice, ed., *Reminiscences of Abraham Lincoln by Distinguished Men of His Time* (New York: North American Publishing Co., 1886), 226.

81   Gobright, *Recollections of Men and Things*, 334–35.

82   Noah Brooks, *The Character and Religion of President Lincoln: A Letter of Noah Brooks* (Champlain, N.Y.: Moorsfield Press, 1919), 9. For a comprehensive analysis of Brooks's career and relationship to Lincoln, see Wayne C. Temple and Justin G. Turner, "Lincoln's 'Castine': Noah Brooks," *Lincoln Herald* 72, 73, 74 (1970).

83   Noah Brooks, *Washington in Lincoln's Time* (New York: The Century Co., 1895), 2.

84   Noah Brooks dispatches in P. J. Staudenraus, ed., *Mr. Lincoln's Washington: Selections from the Writings of Noah Brooks, Civil War Correspondent* (New York: Thomas Yoseloff, 1967), 148–52, 234, 250. It may be instructive that in his dispatches from the front Brooks mistakenly referred to ten-year-old Thomas "Tad" Lincoln as "Tommy," a nickname his parents never used for their son—perhaps a sign that Brooks did not know the family quite as well as he claimed.

85   Noah Brooks, dispatch of May 2, 1863, ibid., 178.

86   Noah Brooks, "Personal Recollections of Abraham Lincoln," *Harper's New Monthly Magazine* 31 (July 1865): 226; Brooks, *Washington in Lincoln's Time*, 200.

87   *CW*, 8:154–55; Noah Brooks, *Abraham Lincoln and the Downfall of American Slavery*, orig. pub. 1888 (New York: G. P. Putnam's Sons, 1894), 411–12. Regarding one aspect of his quirky spelling habits, Lincoln told Brooks that when he was a young man, someone had "persuaded" him that not capitalizing the days of the week was "the proper thing to do," and in later years, "he unconsciously slid into the old trick without noticing it." See Brooks, "Lincoln Reminiscences," *The Magazine of History* 9 (February 1909): 107.

88   John W. Forney to C. S. Pascal, February 4, 1865, John Wein Forney Papers, Library of Congress; *Washington Daily Chronicle*, December 7, 1864. For Lincoln's rejoinder at Alton, October 14, 1858, see *CW*, 3:315.

89   Brooks, *Washington in Lincoln's Time*, 300.

90   Quoted in J. Cutler Andrews, *The North Reports the Civil War* (Pittsburgh: University of Pittsburgh Press, 1955), 55.

91   Ibid.

92   *New York Herald*, September 29, October 8, 1863; Isachar Zacharie to Lincoln, October 22, 1863, ALPLC.

93   See Lincoln to James Hackett, August 17, November 2, 1863, *CW*, 6:392, 559; Hackett to Lincoln, October 22, 1863 and July 1, 1864 ("I have been personally acquainted with Mr. Henry J. Raymond for more than thirty years"), ALPLC; *New York Herald*, September 17, 1863.

94   A. K. McClure, *Lincoln and Men of War-Times: Some Personal Recollections of War and Politics During the Lincoln Administration* (Philadelphia: The Times Publishing Co., 1892), 80–81.

95   See, for example, recommendations for: Charles G. Halpine as a brigadier general (June 1, 1863); former newspaperman Col. T. B. Thorpe for "some position which shall be of value to himself, and where he can be useful to the cause," June 16, 1863; and Abram Wakeman

for the collectorship of the Port of New York, March 10, 1864, copies of all in the George Jones–Henry J. Raymond Papers, New York Public Library.

96   William H. Seward to Lincoln, December 15, 1863, ALPLC.

97   Lincoln to Edwin M. Stanton, May 24, 1864, *CW*, 7:360.

98   Edwin M. Stanton to Lincoln, May 24, 1864, ibid. See also E. A. Paul to Lincoln, May 23, May 25, 1864, and Henry J. Raymond to John G. Nicolay, May 30, 1864, ALPLC. Paul's reports on the Battle of Cedar Creek, as it happened, caused an uproar; critics charged he gave far too much credit to General George Custer, who, according to a *Times* reader, was not even present. See Andrews, *The North Reports the Civil War*, 608–9.

99   Henry J. Raymond to Lincoln, and Lincoln to Raymond, Thurlow Weed, and Edwin Morgan, August 31, 1864, in *CW*, 7:526.

100   Usher and Julian recollections are in Rice, ed., *Reminiscences of Abraham Lincoln by Distinguished Men of His Time*, 60, 87.

101   John G. Nicolay to Horace Greeley, April 25, 1864, in Burlingame, ed., *With Lincoln in the White House*, 138; Greeley to Nicolay, April 26, 1864, Nicolay Papers, Library of Congress, Martha Todd White to Lincoln, December 19, 1863, ALPLC. In truth, there was no love lost between the Lincolns and Martha. The president had barred his half-sister-in-law from the White House when she attempted to visit unannounced; Lincoln even threatened to have her arrested as a spy. The *Tribune's* first and second articles (the second the "correction") were published on March 28 and April 27, 1864, respectively.

102   Rice, ed., *Reminiscences of Abraham Lincoln by Distinguished Men of His Time*, 186–90, 193.

103   Clipping from the John Hay scrapbook, October 14, 1861, John Hay Library, Brown University, reprinted in Michael Burlingame, ed., *Lincoln's Journalist: John Hay's Anonymous Writings for the Press, 1860–1864* (Carbondale: Southern Illinois University Press, 1998), 108.

104   Dispatches of July 31, 1862, December 25, 1862, *New York Express*, in Michael Burlingame, ed., *Dispatches from Lincoln's White House: The Anonymous Civil War Journalism of Presidential Secretary William O. Stoddard* (Lincoln: University of Nebraska Press, 2002), 90, 128.

105   John Russell Young, "Men Who Reigned: Bennett, Greeley, Raymond, Prentice, Forney," *Lippincott's Monthly* 51 (February 1893): 185–86, 188–90.

106   Noah Brooks dispatch of May 28, 1863, in Staudenraus, ed., *Mr. Lincoln's Washington*, 188–89.

107   *Washington National Intelligencer*, June 29, 1842, quoted in Wilhemus Bogart Bryan, *A History of the National Capital from Its Foundation Through the Period of the Adoption of the Organic Act*, 2 vols. (New York: Macmillan, 1914), 2:282.

108   Ibid.

109   Murat Halstead, "Some Reminiscences of Mr. Villard," *The North American Review of Reviews* 23 (January 1901): 62.

110   Henry Villard, *Memoirs of Henry Villard: Journalist and Financier, 1835–1900*, 2 vols. (Boston: Houghton Mifflin, 1904), 1:153–54, 2:267.

111   See H. L. Wayland to Manton Marble, October 13, 1862, and Samuel L. M. Barlow to Marble, June 15, 1868 (Barlow joked that he stepped in to rescue the foundering *World*

because Republicans were unwilling to engage in "hazardous speculation"), both letters in Manton Marble Papers, Library of Congress. See also Mary Cortona Phelan, *Manton Marble of the New York* World (Washington, D.C.: The Catholic University of America Press, 1957), 7–8.

112   *New York World*, September 10, 1862.

113   *New York World*, September 13, 1862.

114   *New York World*, September 24, 1862.

115   *New York World*, May 6, 1863.

116   Samuel Cox to Manton Marble, June 1, 1862, Manton Marble Papers, Library of Congress.

117   *New York World*, May 18, 1864.

118   *New York Tribune*, May 19, 1864. The *Albany Argus* for May 19 assessed the *Herald* print run at "fifty reams."

119   Prime, Stone, Hale, and Hallock, letter to the *New York Times*, published May 19, 1864.

120   Richard Yates to Lincoln, May 18, 1864, ALPLC; Lincoln to Yates, May 18, 1864, *CW*, 7:351.

121   David Homer Bates, *Lincoln in the Telegraph Office: Recollections of the United States Military Telegraph Corps During the Civil War* (New York: The Century Co., 1907), 231–32.

122   Lincoln to Major General John A. Dix, May 18, 1864, *CW*, 7:347–48. Dix had already launched an investigation of his own.

123   Sydney H. Gay and others to Lincoln, May 19, 1864, ALPLC. John Nicolay wrote a personal note to Horace Greeley to shoot down rumors that Salmon Chase had instigated the crackdown.

124   *Boston Commonwealth*, June 6, 1864; Bryant's views reported in the *New York Times*, May 21, 1864.

125   Welles, *Diary of Gideon Welles*, 2:37–38, entry for May 23, 1864.

126   Ibid., 38. For congressional action, see Josiah Grinnell to Lincoln, May 25, 1864 (explaining his watered-down resolution, meant to replace a more condemnatory one introduced by Democratic congressman Samuel "Sunset" Cox, ALPLC. See John G. Nicolay and John Hay, *Abraham Lincoln: A History*, 10 vols. (New York: The Century Co., 1890), 9:47.

127   *New York World*, May 23, 1864.

128   Allan Nevins and Milton Halsey Thomas, eds., *The Diary of George Templeton Strong*, 4 vols. (New York: Macmillan, 1952), 3:451.

129   See Edwards Pierrepont to Edwin M. Stanton, July 3, 1864, ALPLC. This letter from the War Department attorney acting for Dix's defense survives in the Lincoln Papers, indicating that Stanton shared information about the case with the president. For reports of the subsequent hearings, see *New York* Times, July 4, July 10, 1864. For Marble's open letter, see New York World, May 23, 1863. Horatio Seymour letters to District Attorney A. Oakey Hall were published in the *New York Times*, May 25, May 29, 1864. Marble kept the issue alive for years. In 1867 he republished the editorial in pamphlet form with an epigraph from Cicero on the title page: "*Nulla potential supra leges esse debit*" ("There ought to be no power above the laws"). See Manton Marble, *Letter to Abraham Lincoln* (New York: Privately printed, 1867).

130 Thomas F. Carroll, "Freedom of Speech and of the Press During the Civil War," *Virginia Law Review* 9 (May 1923): 527.

131 Henry Ward Beecher to John Defrees, August 2, 1864, ALPLC; Lincoln to Edwin M. Stanton, August 22, 1864, with endorsements by Stanton and Lincoln, August 23, original in ALPLC (also *CW*, 7: 512–13). Defrees agreed with Beecher that "The public good does not require the further punishment of Howard." See Defrees to Lincoln (accompanying Beecher note), September 16, 1864, ALPLC. The three-week delay between Beecher's plea and Howard's pardon does not indicate indecision on Lincoln's part; Defrees was simply away from Washington when the Beecher letter arrived, and did not forward it to the White House until his return.

132 John Defrees to Lincoln, ibid. See also Congressman Moses Odell to Lincoln, September 8, 1864, ALPLC.

133 Joseph Howard, Jr., to Lincoln, September 19, 1864; Lincoln to Edwin M. Stanton, September 20, 1864, *CW*, 8:13.

134 *New York World*, May 23, 1863.

135 For draft, dated May 17, 1864, see *CW*, 7:344.

136 James R. Gilmore to Sydney Howard Gay, May 18, 1864, Sydney Howard Gay Papers, Columbia University.

137 The most authoritative, original, and thoroughly researched article on this subject is Menahem Blondheim, " 'Public Sentiment Is Everything': The Union's Public Communications Strategy and the Bogus Proclamation of 1864," *Journal of American History* 89 (December 2002): 889–92. For Independent Telegraph Company shutdowns in other cities, see Donald E. Markle, ed., *The Telegraph Goes to War: The Personal Diary of David Homer Bates, Lincoln's Telegraph Operator* (Hamilton, N.Y.: Edmonston, 2003), 93.

138 Bates, *Lincoln in the Telegraph Office*, 242. Henry Villard did not mention the humiliating incident in his memoirs.

139 Bates, *Lincoln in the Telegraph Office*, 235–40.

140 Proclamation Calling for 500,000 Volunteers, July 18, 1864, *CW*, 7:448–49.

141 Gilmore, *Personal Recollections*, 146.

142 Charles M. Segal, *Conversations with Lincoln* (New York: G. P. Putnam's Sons, 1961), 320–21.

143 Horace Greeley, *Recollections of a Busy Life* (New York: J. B. Ford & Co., 1868), 409.

144 *New York Tribune*, February 23, 1864.

145 Isaac B. Gara to Simon Cameron, February 20, 1864, ALPLC.

146 Horace Greeley to Salmon P. Chase, September 29, 1863; Chase diary entry, October 2, 1863, both in John Niven, ed., *The Salmon P. Chase Papers*, 2 vols. (Kent, Ohio: Kent State University Press, 1993), 1:459.

147 Quoted in Harlan Hoyt Horner, *Lincoln and Greeley* (Urbana: University of Illinois Press, 1953), 351.

148 Noah Brooks dispatch of June 8, 1864, in Staudenraus, ed., *Mr. Lincoln's Washington*, 335.

149 Carpenter, *Six Months at the White House*, 168.

FIFTEEN: LONG ABRAHAM A LITTLE LONGER

1   William Cullen Bryant to Lincoln, June 25, 1864, June 30, 1864, ALPLC, and Lincoln to Bryant, June 27, 1864, *CW*, 7:410.

2   Lincoln to Thurlow Weed, March 25, 1864, *CW*, 7:268.

3   John G. Nicolay to Lincoln, March 30, 1864, copy in ALPLC.

4   Nicolay met with Weed and other leading Republicans to discuss Customs House patronage on August 30, 1864; see Nicolay to Lincoln of that date, sent by hand via Robert Lincoln, ALPLC. For Raymond endorsement of his candidate for the post, Abram Wakeman, see Henry J. Raymond to Lincoln, March 10, 1864, ALPLC. See also Nicolay to Lincoln, August 29, 1864, ALPLC.

5   Henry J. Raymond to Lincoln, September 11, September 14, 1864, ALPLC.

6   *New York World*, June 20, 1864.

7   Reprinted in Ward Hill Lamon, *Recollections of Abraham Lincoln 1847–1865 by Ward Hill Lamon*, ed. Dorothy Lamon (Chicago: A. C. McClurg, 1895), 143.

8   Unsigned letter to Horace Greeley, April 20, 1864, enclosed in Samuel Wilkeson to John G. Nicolay, September 21, 1864, John G. Nicolay Papers, Library of Congress.

9   Lamon, *Recollections of Abraham Lincoln*, 141.

10 Ibid., 142.

11 "One of Mr. Lincoln's Jokes," *New York World*, September 9, 1864.

12 A. J. Perkins to Ward H. Lamon, September 10, 1864, in *CW*, 7:550; Lincoln quoted in Lamon, *Recollections of Abraham Lincoln*, 144.

13 Handwritten memorandum by Lincoln, signed by Ward Hill Lamon, ca. September 12, 1864, *CW*, 7:549.

14 Lamon, *Recollections of Abraham Lincoln*, 146, 148, 153. Lamon corrected the record only after Lincoln's death.

15 For the lithograph by "CAL," see Bernard F. Reilly, Jr., *American Political Prints, 1766–1876: A Catalog of the Collections in the Library of Congress* (Boston: G. K. Hall, 1991), 536–37.

16 David G. Croly and George Wakeman, *Miscegenation: The Theory of the Blending of the Races, Applied to the American White Man and Negro* (New York: Bromley & Co., 1864), 61, 69. Croly was a former reporter for the *New York Herald*.

17 [James Van Evrie], *Subgenation: The Theory of the Normal Relation of the Races; or, An Answer to "Miscegenation"* (New York: John Bradburn, 1864), 39, 56.

18 *New York Daily News*, April 4, 1864.

19 *New York Freeman's Journal & Catholic Register*, April 30, 1864, quoted in David E. Long, *The Jewel of Liberty: Abraham Lincoln's Re-election and the End of Slavery* (Mechanicsburg, Penn.: Stackpole, 1994), 171.

20 *New York World*, July 12, 1864, September 18, 1864.

21 *New York World*, October 17, 1864.

22 George McClellan to Manton Marble, June 25, 1864, Manton Marble Papers, Library of Congress.

23 *New York World*, October 22, 1864; headlines are from the editions of September 30, October 1, 3, 8, 14, 19, 28, 1864.

24   See for example, the story on Post Office espionage, *New York World*, October 20, 1864, the untitled editorial of October 22, 1864, and "Justifying Mob Law and Outrage," November 2, 1864.

25   For an example of the "Miscegenation Ball" stories, see *New York World* (quoting *New York Tribune*), September 25, 1864.

26   *New York World*, October 3, 1864.

27   Joseph Holt quoted in Richard A. Sauers and Peter Tomasak, *The Fishing Creek Confederacy: A Story of Civil War Draft Resistance* (Columbia: University of Missouri Press, 2013), 23.

28   *New York World*, November 7, 1864.

29   William H. Simpson file, Record Group 21, Records of the U.S. District Court for the District of Maine, August 1864, National Archives, Boston. The author is indebted to Bob Rackmales for uncovering and sharing these documents through Dr. Jonathan White. See also Joseph Williamson, *History of the City of Belfast in the State of Maine from Its First Settlement in 1770 to 1875* (Portland, Maine: Loring, Short, & Harmon, 1877), 355.

30   Gideon Welles, *Diary of Gideon Welles*, ed. John T. Morse, Jr., 3 vols. (Boston: Houghton Mifflin, 1911), 2:109–10. Gilmore's piece was published in the prestigious *Atlantic*.

31   James R. Gilmore, *Personal Recollections of Abraham Lincoln and the Civil War* (Boston: L. C. Page & Co., 1898), 288–89.

32   *The American Annual Cyclopedia and Register of Important Events of the Year 1864 . . .* (New York: D. Appleton & Co., 1869), 393–94. The accounting lists thirty-six incidents, two for the *Columbus Crisis*, plus the closings that occurred after the publication of the bogus presidential proclamation.

33   Isaac N. Arnold to Lincoln, July 2, July 18, 1864, ALPLC; Lincoln to John L. Scripps, July 5, July 20, 1864, *CW*, 7:423–424, 453.

34   See Greeley to W. C. Jewett, January 2, 1863, quoted in James Parton, *The Life of Horace Greeley, Editor of the "New York Tribune" . . .* rev. ed., J. orig. pub. 1872 (Boston: James R. Osgood, 1889), 469.

35   Horace Greeley to Lincoln, July 7, 1864, ALPLC.

36   Shelby M. Cullom, *Fifty Years of Public Service: Personal Recollections* (Chicago: A. C. McClurg, 1911), 101.

37   Chauncey M. Depew, *My Memories of Eighty Years* (New York: Charles Scribner's Sons, 1922), 62.

38   Recollection by Iowa senator James Harlan, quoted in Ida Tarbell, *The Life of Abraham Lincoln*, 4 vols., orig. pub. 1900 (New York: Lincoln History Society, 1907), 3:198.

39   James M. Ashley, *Address at the Fourth Annual Banquet of the Ohio Republican League*, 1891, quoted in Don E. Fehrenbacher and Virginia Fehrenbacher, eds., *Recollected Words of Abraham Lincoln* (Stanford: Stanford University Press, 1996), 182.

40   Horace Greeley to Lincoln, July 10, July 13, 1864, ALPLC; Lincoln to Greeley, two letters of July 15, 1864, *CW*, 7:440–42.

41   Pass for John Hay signed by Lincoln, July 15, 1864, *CW*, 7, 442; Lincoln to Horace Greeley, July 9, 1864, *CW*, 7:435; Michael Burlingame and John T. Turner Ettlinger, eds., *Inside Lincoln's White House: The Complete Civil War Diary of John Hay* (Carbondale: Southern Illinois University Press, 1997), 224—report ca. July 21, 1864.

42   John G. Nicolay and John Hay, *Abraham Lincoln: A History*, 10 vols. (New York: The Century Co., 1890), 9:194; *New York Daily News*, September 22, 1864.

43   Burlingame and Ettlinger, eds., *Inside Lincoln's White House . . . Diary of John Hay*, 226; Francis N. Zabriskie, *Horace Greeley, the Editor* (New York: Funk & Wagnalls, 1890), 249–50.

44   Burlingame and Ettlinger, eds., *Inside Lincoln's White House . . . Diary of John Hay*, 226–27; Welles, *Diary of Gideon Welles*, 2:110–11.

45   Depew, *My Memories of Eighty Years*, 63.

46   Horace Greeley to John Hay, August 4, 1864, Greeley to Lincoln, August 8, 1864, ALPLC; Lincoln to Greeley, August 6, 1864, *CW*, 7:482.

47   Lincoln to Horace Greeley, August 9, 1864, and to Henry Raymond, August 15, 1864, *CW*, 7:489, 494. Excerpt is from Greeley to Lincoln, July 7, 1864, ALPLC.

48   Both comments from the *New York Tribune*, July 26, 1864, in Ralph Ray Fahrney, *Horace Greeley and the Tribune in the Civil War* (Cedar Rapids, Iowa: The Torch Press, 1936), 166.

49   Joseph Medill to John Hay, August 10, 1864, in John Taliaferro, *All the Great Prizes: The Life of John Hay* (New York: Simon & Schuster, 2013), 89. The Clay letter is in *OR*, series 4, vol. 3, 586.

50   Noah Brooks, *Abraham Lincoln and the Downfall of American Slavery*, orig. pub. 1888 (New York: G. P. Putnam's Sons, 1894), 402.

51   William Harlan Hale, *Horace Greeley: Voice of the People* (New York: Harper & Brothers, 1950), 211.

52   Welles, *Diary of Gideon Welles*, 2:112.

53   Chauncey Depew recollection quoted in Allen Thorndike Rice, ed., *Reminiscences of Abraham Lincoln by Distinguished Men of His Time* (New York: North American Publishing Co., 1886), 436.

54   Welles, *Diary of Gideon Welles*, 2:272.

55   Francis B. Carpenter, *Six Months at the White House with Abraham Lincoln: The Story of a Picture* (New York: Hurd & Houghton, 1866), 152. Greeley's new book was the first volume of a comprehensive history of the slavery crisis and the war: see Greeley, *The American Conflict: A History of the Great Rebellion in the United States of America . . .* (Hartford, Conn.: O. D. Case, 1864).

56   Douglass chapter in Rice, ed., *Reminiscences of Abraham Lincoln by Distinguished Men of His Time*, 189; Carpenter, *Six Months at the White House*, 153.

57   Charles D. Robinson to Lincoln, August 16, 1864, ALPLC.

58   Lincoln to Charles D. Robinson, August 17, 1864 (draft), *CW*, 7:500–501.

59   John Wein Forney, *Anecdotes of Public Men*, 2 vols. (New York: Harper & Bros., 1881), 2:180–81.

60   Lincoln to Isaac Schermerhorn, who had invited the president "to attend a Union Mass Meeting at Buffalo," September 12, 1864, *CW*, 8:2; speech to the 148th Ohio Regiment, August 31, 1864, *CW*, 7:528; *New York Tribune*, September 2, 1864.

61   Thomas A. Horrocks, *Lincoln's Campaign Biographies* (Carbondale: Southern Illinois University Press, 2014), 83; Joseph R. Nightingale, "Joseph H. Barrett and John Locke Scripps,

Shapers of Lincoln's Religious Image," *Journal of the Illinois State Historical Society* 92 (Autumn 1999): 262.

62 J. C. Derby to John G. Nicolay, February 24, 1864, John G. Nicolay Papers, Library of Congress.

63 J. C. Derby to John H. Nicolay, March 22, 1864, Henry J. Raymond to Lincoln, April 4, 1864, ALPLC. For Lincoln's message to the workingmen, March 21, 1864, see *CW*, 7:259–60. In an era in which civilians were constantly referred to as "Major" or "Colonel" in recognition of even the most cursory military service, some of Raymond's admirers called him "Governor"—in recognition of his brief service as New York's lieutenant governor.

64 J. C. Derby to John G. Nicolay, April 11, April 19, May 16, 1864. For Lincoln's address at Baltimore, April 18, 1864, see *CW*, 7:301–3.

65 Henry J. Raymond, *History of the Administration of President Lincoln . . .* (New York: Derby & Miller, 1864), 484; "Now Ready . . . Mr. Raymond's History of President Lincoln's Administration," advertising circular in George Jones and Henry J. Raymond Papers, New York Public Library. See also, Louis A. Warren, "Raymond's Lincoln Books," *Lincoln Lore*, No. 848 (July 9, 1945).

66 *New York World*, May 18, 1864.

67 J. C. Derby, *Fifty Years Among Authors, Books, and Publishers* (New York: G. W. Carleton, 1884), 357.

68 See, for example, *The Issues of the Campaign. Speeches of Henry J. Raymond and Gen. J. H. Martindale, Delivered at the Union Meeting in Tweddle Hall, Albany, on the Evening of Wednesday, October 11, 1865*, pamphlet in the George Jones–Henry Raymond Papers, New York Public Library.

69 Practically speaking, the navy secretary also worried that efficient workers might choose to quit rather than tithe, making it harder for the department to maintain its furious pace of shipbuilding. Welles further feared that corrupt party hacks would in any event skim the collections before they reached the national committee. See Welles, *Diary of Gideon Welles*, 2:108, 122–23.

70 Ibid., 2:98, 136–37

71 Ibid., 2:142, 175–76.

72 *New York Tribune*, August 5, 1864; *New York Times*, August 11, 1864.

73 Henry J. Raymond to Lincoln, August 10 and August 22, 1864, ALPLC.

74 Richard M. Corwine to William F. Dole (forwarded "To the President"), August 26, 1864, ALPLC.

75 Thurlow Weed to William H. Seward, August 22, 1864, ALPLC.

76 Blind memorandum, August 23, 1864, *CW*, 7:514; Lincoln to Henry J. Raymond, August 24, 1864, *CW*, 7:517.

77 Frederick Douglass to Lincoln, August 29, 1864, ALPLC; Douglass assessment quoted in Mark E. Neely, Jr., *The Abraham Lincoln Encyclopedia* (New York: McGraw-Hill, 1982), 89; Douglass to Theodore Tilton, October 15, 1864, in Philip S. Foner and Yuval Taylor, eds., *Frederick Douglass: Selected Speeches and Writings* (Chicago: Lawrence Hill, 1999), 572.

78 Nicolay and Hay, *Abraham Lincoln: A History*, 9:221.

79 *New York Times*, September 5, 1864.

80 Theodore Tilton to John G. Nicolay, September 6, 1864, John G. Nicolay Papers, Library of Congress. Nicolay had written Tilton two days earlier: "There is no truth whatever in the report that Mr. Lincoln said he was a 'beaten man.'" See Michael Burlingame, ed., *With Lincoln at the White House: Letters, Memoranda, and Other Writings of John G. Nicolay, 1860–1865* (Carbondale: Southern Illinois University Press, 2000), 158.

81 John F. Marszalek, *Sherman's Other War: The General and the Civil War Press*, orig. pub. 1981 (Kent, Ohio: Kent State University Press, 1999), 186–88; Charles A. Dana, *Recollections of the Civil War with the Leaders at Washington and in the Field in the Sixties* (New York: D. Appleton, 1902), 217.

82 James C. Conkling to Lincoln, September 6, 1864, ALPLC.

83 James T. Lewis to Horace Greeley, Theodore Tilton, and Parke Godwin, September 7, 1864, unendorsed copy in ALPLC.

84 Thurlow Weed to William H. Seward, September 10, 1864, ALPLC.

85 Henry J. Raymond to Lincoln, September 11, 1864, ALPLC.

86 See, for example, Horace Greeley to Lincoln, September 16, 1864 (regarding peace) and September 21, 1864 (regarding a trade permit for "Mr. C. Vanderbilt, junior"), both in ALPLC.

87 Horace Greeley to Lincoln, August 29, 1864, ALPLC. See also Greeley to Lincoln, August 24, 1864.

88 See Montgomery Blair to John G. Nicolay (about Greeley's plan for "distributing the papers . . . gratuitously"), September 13[?], 1864; Horace Greeley to John G. Nicolay (regarding prisoner exchanges), September 19, 1864 ("the McClellanites are making capital on this point"), ALPLC; Nicolay to Greeley, September 15, 1864, in Michael Burlingame, ed., *With Lincoln in the White House*, 159–60; Lucius E. Chittenden to Lincoln, October 6, 1864, ALPLC.

89 *New York World*, September 21, 1864. The author is grateful to Walter Stahr for bringing this report to his attention.

90 *New York Tribune*, September 24, 27, 1864. Greeley launched his sudden barrage of pro-Lincoln editorializing on September 6 by declaring: "Henceforth we must fly the banner of ABRAHAM LINCOLN for the next President," although he later launched another effort to dump Lincoln from the ticket.

91 Max Langenschwartz to George B. McClellan, September 26, 1864, George B. McClellan Papers, Library of Congress.

92 Isaac N. Arnold to Lincoln, August 23, 1864, ALPLC.

93 Lincoln endorsement, June 18, 1864, *CW*, 7:399.

94 *New York Herald*, May 20, 1864.

95 Welles, *Diary*, 2:103.

96 Leonard Swett to William H. Herndon, July 17, 1866, in Douglas L. Wilson and Rodney O. Davis, eds., *Herndon's Informants: Letters, Interviews, and Statements About Abraham Lincoln* (Urbana: University of Illinois Press, 1998), 164. The controversial Todd visitor was Emilie Todd Helm, widow of Confederate general Ben Hardin Helm, who

visited the White House in December 1863 after the death of her husband at the Battle of Chickamauga.

97 Wakeman's affability (also his unreliability), cited by Welles in *Diary of Gideon Welles*, 2:222; Lincoln to Abram Wakeman, July 25, 1864, *CW*, 7:461.

98 James Harlan quoted in Burlingame and Ettlinger, eds., *Inside Lincoln's White House . . . Diary of John Hay*, 299; Horace Greeley to William O. Bartlett, August 30, 1864, Horace Greeley Papers, New York Public Library.

99 Mary Lincoln to Abram Wakeman, September 23 [1864], in Justin G. Turner and Linda Levitt Turner, eds., *Mary Todd Lincoln: Her Life and Letters* (New York: Alfred A. Knopf, 1972), 180–81.

100 William O. Bartlett to James Gordon Bennett, November 4, 1864, in Oliver Carlson, *The Man Who Made News: James Gordon Bennett* (New York: Duell, Sloan & Pearce, 1942), 370.

101 Donald Bruce Johnson, ed., *National Party Platforms*, 2 vols. (rev. ed.; Urbana: University of Illinois Press, 1978), 1:34–35.

102 For the claim that the president's campaign to woo Bennett "brought the *Herald* to Lincoln's support" see, for example, Don C. Seitz, *The James Gordon Bennetts, Father and Son, Proprietors of the New York Herald* (Indianapolis: Bobbs-Merrill, 1928), 191. An excellent historiographical assessment can be found in John J. Turner, Jr., and Michael D'Innocenzo, "The President and the Press: Lincoln, James Gordon Bennett and the Election of 1864," *Lincoln Herald* 76 (Summer 1974): 66.

103 *New York Herald*, September 23, October 6, October 12, 1864; Albert C. Ramsey to George B. McClellan, October 18, 1864, George B. McClellan Papers, Library of Congress.

104 William O. Bartlett to Lincoln, October 20, October 27, 1864, ALPLC.

105 *New York Herald*, October 2, October 22, October 25, October 30, November 4, November 7, 1864.

106 A. K. McClure, *Lincoln and Men of War-Times: Some Personal Recollections of War and Politics During the Lincoln Administration* (Philadelphia: The Times Publishing Co., 1892), 80.

107 *New York Herald*, November 1, 1864.

108 Bartlett told Bennett that Lincoln had described himself as "shut pan, to everybody." See Carlson, *The Man Who Made News*, 370; Welles, *Diary of Gideon Welles*, 2:258.

109 Lincoln to James Gordon Bennett, February 20, 1865, *CW*, 8:308; Bennett to Lincoln, March 6, 1865, ALPLC.

110 Mary Lincoln to Abram Wakeman, March 20, 1865, in Turner and Turner, eds., *Mary Todd Lincoln,* 205.

111 *New York Tribune*, November 9, November 10, 1864.

112 Henry J. Raymond to Lincoln, November 8, 1864, ALPLC; Horace Greeley telegram (lost) quoted in Michael Burlingame, ed., *Lincoln Observed: Civil War Dispatches of Noah Brooks* (Carbondale: Southern Illinois University Press, 1998), "How the President Took the News," dispatch of November 11, 1864, 143–144. See also John Wein Forney, Edward L. Baker, and McKee & Fishback to Lincoln, all November 8, 1864, and Brooks, "Table of Election Returns," undated, probably November 9, 1864, all in ALPLC; Augustus Maverick, *Henry J. Raymond and the New York Press, for Thirty Years* (Hartford, Conn.: A. S. Hale,

Co., 1870), 169. On the matter of forcing out the additional Republican congressional candidate (who only won 8 percent of the vote), see Henry Wilson to Lincoln, October 30, 1864, ALPLC.

113   *New York Times, New York Tribune*, November 10, 1864; *New York Herald*, November 9, 1864.

114   *Harper's Weekly*, November 16, 1864.

115   Response to a victory serenade, November 10, 1864, *CW*, 8: 100–101.

116   Burlingame and Ettlinger, ed., *Inside Lincoln's White House . . . Diary of John Hay*, 243.

117   Stuart Robinson to Lincoln, December 10, 1865, ALPLC.

118   *Rev. Stuart Robinson to President Lincoln*, pamphlet, published in Toronto and dated January 26, 1865. For context, see Preston D. Graham, Jr., *A Kingdom Not of This World: Stuart Robinson's Struggle to Distinguish the Sacred from the Secular During the Civil War* (Macon, Ga.: Mercer University Press, 2002). Although Graham republishes Robinson's letter in its entirety, he inexplicably dates it January 26, 1866 (page 258). For the Indiana reaction to Robinson, see Sean Scott, *A Visitation of God: Northern Civilians Interpret the Civil War* (New York: Oxford University Press, 2010), 162.

119   James C. Welling, "The Emancipation Proclamation," *North American Review* 130 (1880): 182.

120   Henry J. Raymond, *The Life and Public Services of Abraham Lincoln . . .* (New York: Derby & Miller, 1865), 646.

121   Horace Greeley to Lincoln, November 16, 1864; W. N. Bilbo to Lincoln, November 22, 1864, January 26, 1865, ALPLC. History has yet to pass final judgment on the role Bilbo played, if any, in securing House passage of the Thirteenth Amendment resolution. Though still a mystery, Bilbo emerged firmly from the shadows of history as a character in Steven Spielberg's 2012 movie, *Lincoln*.

122   *Congressional Globe*, 38th Congress, 2nd Session, January 5, 12. 1865, 125. Greeley apparently used his time on the floor to confer with Republicans about the latest prospects for peace. An annoyed Congressman Cox retaliated by ordering the *Tribune*'s latest editorial read into the record. The article in part predicted that the country would "regret" any effort to quash armistice talks.

123   Francis Preston Blair, Sr., to Horace Greeley, January 23, January 27, 1865, Horace Greeley Papers, New York Public Library; the former in William Ernst Smith, *The Francis Preston Blair Family in Politics*, 2 vols. (New York: Macmillan, 1933), 2:311.

124   Lincoln to Alexander H. Stephens, John A. Campbell, and Robert M. T. Hunter, January 30, 1865, and Lincoln to Congressman James M. Ashley, January 31, 1865, *CW*, 8:248.

125   Edward L. Baker and Ward Hill Lamon to Lincoln, February 1, 1865, ALPLC.

126   *New York Times*, February 3, 1865; *New York Herald*, February 2, February 3, 1865.

127   Michael Vorenberg, *Final Freedom: The Civil War, the Abolition of Slavery, and the Thirteenth Amendment* (Cambridge: Cambridge University Press, 2001), 202; *New York Tribune*, February 10, 1865. See Horace Greeley on the "Conn. Delegate" to Elihu Washburne, February 6, 1865, Elihu Washburne Papers, Library of Congress.

128   Joseph M. Medill to Lincoln, January 15, 1865, ALPLC; James B. Conroy, *Our One Com-*

mon Country: Abraham Lincoln and the Hampton Roads Peace Conference of 1865 (Guilford, Conn.: Lyons, 2014), 196; *New York Times*, June 26, 1865.

129   Burlingame, *Lincoln Observed,* dispatch for February 12, 1865, 161.

130   *New York Herald*, February 5, 1865; *New York Times*, February 5, February 6, February 11, 1865; *New York Tribune*, February 6, 1865, *New York Daily News* quoted in *New York Tribune*, February 3, 1865; *Richmond Sentinel*, February 7, 1865, quoted in *New York Times*, February 10, 1865.

131   Second inaugural address, March 4, 1865, *CW*, 8:332–33.

132   Rice, ed., *Reminiscences of Abraham Lincoln by Distinguished Men of His Time*, 192.

133   Thurlow Weed to Lincoln, March 4, 1865, ALPLC; Lincoln to Weed, March 15, 1865, *CW*, 8:356.

134   *New York Tribune*, March 5, 1865; *New York Herald*, March 5, March 6, 1865.

135   *New York Times*, March 6, 1865.

136   Henry J. Raymond to Lincoln, March 8, 1865, ALPLC.

137   For Locke's pro-Lincoln editorials during the 1864 campaign, see John M. Harrison, *The Man Who Made Nasby, David Ross Locke* (Chapel Hill: University of North Carolina Press, 1969), 117–18.

138   *New York Herald*, April 4, 1865. For early press reports on Lincoln's planned trip to Richmond, see Richard Wightman Fox, "'A Death Shock to Chivalry and a Mortal Wound to Caste': The Story of Tad and Abraham Lincoln in Richmond," *Journal of the Abraham Lincoln Association* 33 (Summer 2012): 1–19; *New York Herald*, April 3, April 4, 1865.

139   Crook, quoted in Fox, "'A Death Shock to Chivalry,'" 12.

140   Admiral [David D.] Porter, *Incidents and Anecdotes of the Civil War* (New York: D. Appleton, 1885), 297.

141   There are several versions of this exchange, most of the early ones in "Negro" dialect. For this quotation, I have relied on a historian who distilled all the versions before adapting what is regarded as the new standard quote: David Herbert Donald, *Lincoln* (New York: Simon & Schuster, 1995), 576.

142   *New York Herald*, April 9, 1864; *New York Tribune*, April 7, 1865.

143   Reprinted in *The Liberator*, April 28, 1865; see also Thomas Morris Chester, *Black Civil War Correspondent: His Dispatches from the Virginia Front*, ed. R. J. M. Blackett (Baton Rouge: Louisiana State University Press, 1989), 297.

144   Charles C. Coffin, "Late Scenes in Richmond," *Atlantic Monthly* 15 (June 1865): 753–55.

145   Allan Nevins and Milton Halsey Thomas, eds., *The Diary of George Templeton Strong*, 4 vols. (New York: Macmillan, 1952), 3:582.

146   *National Daily Intelligencer*, April 11, 1865.

147   Jonathan Brigham, "Living Lincoln Links" (transcript), in the Brown University Collection, quoted in Fehrenbacher and Fehrenbacher, eds., *Recollected Words of Abraham Lincoln*, 40.

148   *New York World*, April 13, 1865; Noah Brooks, "Personal Reminiscences of Lincoln," *Scribner's Monthly* 15 (February/March 1878): 367; P. J. Staudenraus, ed., *Mr. Lincoln's Washington: The Civil War Dispatches of Noah Brooks, Civil War Correspondent* (New York: Thomas Yoseloff, 1967), 439.

149   L. A. Gobright, *Recollections of Men and Things at Washington, During the Third of a Century* (Philadelphia: Claxton, Remsen & Haffelfinger, 1869), 348–50, 354.

150   Lincoln's Last Public Address, April 11, 1865, *CW*, 8:403; For Booth's reaction, see testimony of Thomas T. Eckert, May 30, 1867, House Judiciary Committee, Impeachment Investigation, 39th Congress, 2d. Session, and 40th Congress, 1st Session (Washington, D.C.: Government Printing Office, 1867), 674.

151   "President Lincoln," undated clipping from the contents of Lincoln's pockets on the night he was assassinated, Alfred Whital Stern Collection, Library of Congress. Other cuttings included "The Disaffection of the Southern Soldiers," "Emancipation in Missouri," "John Bright on the Presidency," "The Message of the Governor of Missouri," "Sherman's Orders for His March," and "The Two Platforms."

152   Gobright, *Recollections of Men and Things at Washington*, 349–50.

153   Nina DePass, ed., *A View from the Inn: The Journal of Anna Marie Resseguie, 1851–1867* (Ridgefield, Conn.: Keeler Tavern Preservation Society, 1993), 116, 251.

154   Caroline Cowles Richards, *Village Life in America, 1852–1872, Including the Period of the American Civil War as Told in the Diary of a School Girl*, orig. pub. 1913 (Gansevoort, N.Y.: Corner House Historical Publications, 1997), 182–83.

155   Jonathan W. White, ed., *A Philadelphia Perspective: The Civil War Diary of Sidney George Fisher* (New York: Fordham University Press, 2007), 251, 253.

156   *New York World*, April 15, 1865.

157   *New York Herald*, April 16, April 17, 1865; *New York Tribune*, April 17, 1865; *New York Times*, April 16, 1865.

EPILOGUE: WE SHALL NOT SEE AGAIN THE LIKE

1   Henry J. Raymond, *The Life and Public Services of Abraham Lincoln, Sixteenth President of the United States* . . . (New York: Derby & Miller, 1865). For publishing figures, see J. C. Derby, *Fifty Years Among Authors, Books, and Publishers* (New York: G. W. Carleton, 1865), 357–58; Mary Lincoln to Francis B. Carpenter, November 15, 1865, in Justin G. Turner and Linda Levitt Turner, *Mary Todd Lincoln: Her Life and Letters* (New York: Alfred A. Knopf, 1972), 284.

2   *Harper's Weekly*, July 3, 1869; John Swinton, *Tribute to the Memory of Henry J. Raymond, Late Editor of the New York Times, New York Times*, June 19, 1869, reprinted as a pamphlet in the George Jones and Henry J. Raymond Papers, New York Public Library; Swinton, "The New York Daily Papers and Their Editors," *The Independent* 52 (Part 2, January 25, 1900): 237.

3   Obituaries quoted in Don C. Seitz, *The James Gordon Bennetts, Father and Son, Proprietors of the New York Herald* (Indianapolis: Bobbs-Merrill, 1928), 210–11. Oddly, the *Herald*'s tribute to its founder was delayed for days; his old competitors published obituaries first—a situation that the senior Bennett would have found intolerable.

4   For the print by C. L. Ludwig, Richmond, see Mark E. Neely, Jr., Harold Holzer, and Gabor S. Boritt, *The Confederate Image: Prints of the Lost Cause* (Chapel Hill: University of North Carolina Press, 1987), 173–74. More typical cartoons of the period more accurately suggested Northern antipathy by suggesting that Davis was a coward who had evaded cap-

ture by Union troops after Appomattox by dressing in women's clothes, or that he should he hanged, hoopskirts and all, from a "sour apple tree." For examples of this genre, see ibid., Chapter 8, "The Belle of Richmond."

5   Horace Greeley to Rebekah K. Whipple, November 13, 1872, quoted in Henry Luther Stoddard, *Horace Greeley: Printer, Editor, Crusader* (New York: G. P. Putnam's Sons, 1946), 320.

6   Theodore Cuyler, "Uncle Horace," *The Temperance Record*, January 25, 1873, 40.

7   Charles C. Parton, *Glory to God and the Sucker Democracy: A Manuscript Collection of the Letters of Charles H. Lanphier*, 5 vols. (Privately printed, Frye-Williamson Press), 1:135.

8   Andy Van Meter, *Always My Friend: A History of the State Journal Register and Springfield* (Springfield: The Copley Press, 1981), 334.

9   Presidential authorization for Charles H. Ray, February 15, 1865, *CW*, 8:299.

10 *Chicago Tribune*, September 25, 1870.

11 Joseph Medill and James W. Sheahan, *Chicago* (New York: Scribner's, 1880).

12 See Harriet A. Weed, ed., *Autobiography of Thurlow Weed*, 2 vols. (Boston: Houghton Mifflin, 1884).

13 *New York World*, May 22, 1876.

14 Mary Cortona Phelan, *Manton Marble of the New York World* (Washington, D.C.: Catholic University of America Press, 1917), Chapter 5: "The Editor in Retirement."

15 *Douglass' Monthly*, August 1863.

16 Oration in Memory of Abraham Lincoln at the unveiling of the Freedmen's Monument in Lincoln Park, Washington, D.C., April 14, 1876, in Philip S. Foner and Yuval Taylor, eds., *Frederick Douglass: Selected Speeches and Writings* (Chicago: Lawrence Hill, 1999), 624. For the phrase from Lincoln's Annual Message to Congress, December 1, 1862, see *CW*, 5:537.

17 For cabinet endorsements, see Benjamin Bannen to Lincoln, and Dillen Luther to Lincoln, both December 7, 1864, ALPLC.

18 L. A. Gobright, *Recollections of Men and Things at Washington, During the Third of the Century* (Philadelphia: Claxton, Remsen, & Haffelfinger, 1869).

19 Noah Brooks, *Washington in Lincoln's Time* (New York: The Century Co., 1895).

20 *New York Times*, December 8, 1885; Theodor Canisius, *Abraham Lincoln. Historiches Charachterbild* (Berlin: Christoph Reiber, 1967).

BIBLIOGRAPHY

NEWSPAPERS

Baltimore Sun
Brooklyn Eagle
Charleston Courier
Chicago Daily Times
Chicago Press and Tribune
Cincinnati Daily Commercial
Cincinnati Gazette
[Frederick] *Douglass' Monthly*
Frank Leslie's Illustrated Newspaper
Freeman's Journal
Harper's Weekly
[Springfield] *Illinois State Journal*
[Springfield] *Illinois State Register*
Journal of Commerce
London Times
New York Courier and Enquirer
New York Daily News
New York Evening Post
New York Herald
New York Illustrated News
New York Independent
New York Journal of Commerce
New York Times
New York Tribune
New York Weekly Caucasian
New York World
Philadelphia Inquirer

Philadelphia News
Prison Times (New-York Historical Society Collection)
Richmond Whig
[Springfield, Illinois] *Sangamo Journal*
Southern Illustrated News
Vicksburg Daily Citizen
Washington Daily Chronicle
Washington Daily Intelligencer
Washington Evening Star

MANUSCRIPT COLLECTIONS

J. C. Bancroft Davis Papers, Library of Congress

James Gordon Bennett Papers, Library of Congress

Chauncey Brown Papers, New-York Historical Society

Charles A. Dana Papers, Library of Congress

Jesse W. Fell Papers, Library of Congress

Francis D. Flanders Papers, New-York Historical Society

John Wein Forney Papers, Library of Congress

Francis Family Papers, Abraham Lincoln Presidential Library and Museum, Springfield, Illinois (ALPLM)

Sydney Howard Gay Papers, Columbia University

Gilder Lehrman Collection, New-York Historical Society

Horace Greeley Papers, Library of Congress

Horace Greeley Papers, New York Public Library

Duff Green Papers, Southern Historical Collection, the Wilson Library, University of North Carolina at Chapel Hill

Herndon-Weik Papers, Library of Congress

George Jones and Henry J. Raymond Papers, New York Public Library

Charles H. Lanphier Papers, ALPLM

Abraham Lincoln Papers (Robert Todd Lincoln Papers), Library of Congress (ALPLC)

Papers of Abraham Lincoln, Springfield, Illinois (ALPLM)

Manton Marble Papers, Library of Congress

George B. McClellan Papers, Library of Congress

McLernand Family Papers, ALPLM

John G. Nicolay Papers, Library of Congress

Charles H. Ray Papers, Huntington Library, San Marino, California

William T. Sherman Papers, Library of Congress

Edwin M. Stanton Papers, Library of Congress

Samuel J. Tilden Papers, New York Public Library, Manuscripts and Archives Division

Lyman Trumbull Papers, Library of Congress

Henry Villard Papers, Houghton Library, Harvard University

Elihu Washburne Papers, Library of Congress

John Russell Young Papers, Library of Congress

PRIMARY SOURCES

The American Cyclopaedia and Register of Important Events of the Year[s], 1861–1864. 4 vols. New York: D. Appleton, 1864–1869.

Andreas, A. T. *History of Chicago: From the Earliest Period to the Present Time*, 3 vols. Chicago: A. T. Andreas, 1884.

Andrews, Sidney. *The South Since the War: As Shown by Fourteen Weeks of Travel and Observation in Georgia and the Carolinas.* Boston: Ticknor & Fields, 1866.

Arnold, Isaac N. *The History of Abraham Lincoln and the Overthrow of Slavery.* Chicago: Clarke & Co., 1866.

Barnes, Thurlow Weed. *Memoir of Thurlow Weed,* (also known as *The Life of Thurlow Weed*) 2 vols. Boston: Houghton Mifflin, 1884.

Barrett, Joseph H. *Abraham Lincoln and His Presidency*, 2 vols. Cincinnati: Robert Clarke Co., 1904.

Basler, Roy P., ed. *The Collected Works of Abraham Lincoln*, 8 vols. New Brunswick, N.J.: Rutgers University Press, 1953–55.

————, ed. *The Collected Works of Abraham Lincoln, Supplement, 1832–1865.* Westport, Conn.: Greenwood, 1974.

Bates, David Homer. *Lincoln in the Telegraph Office: Recollections of the United States Military Telegraph Corps During the Civil War.* New York: The Century Co., 1907.

————. *Diary.* See Markle.

Bates, Edward. *Diary.* See Beale.

Beale, Howard K., ed. *The Diary of Edward Bates, 1859–1866.* Washington, D.C.: U.S. Government Printing Office, 1933.

Belmont, August. *A Few Letters and Speeches of the Late Civil War.* New York: Privately printed, 1870.

Bennett, James Gordon. *Memoirs of James Gordon Bennett and His Times by a Journalist* [Isaac L. Pray]. N.Y.: Stringer & Townsend, 1855.

Benton, Joel. ed. *Greeley on Lincoln with Mr. Greeley's Letters to Charles A. Dana.* New York: The Baker & Taylor Co., 1893.

Bigelow, John. *Recollections of an Active Life,* 2 vols. Vol. 1, 1817–1863. New York: The Baker & Taylor Co., 1909.

Binney, Horace. *The Privilege of the Writ of Habeas Corpus Under the Constitution.* Philadelphia: C. Sherman & Son, 1862.

Blackwell, Sarah Eileen. *A Military Genius: Life of Anna Ella Carroll.* Washington: Judd & Detweiller, 1891.

Brockway, Beman. *Fifty Years in Journalism Embracing Recollections and Personal Experiences with an Autobiography.* Watertown, N.Y.: Daily Times Printing, 1891.

Brooks, Noah. *Abraham Lincoln and the Downfall of American Slavery.* Orig. pub. 1888; New York: G. P. Putnam's Sons, 1894.

———. *The Character and Religion of Abraham Lincoln: A Letter of Noah Brooks, May 10, 1865.* Champlain, N.Y.: Moorsfield Press, 1919.

———. *Washington in Lincoln's Time.* New York: The Century Co., 1895.

Browne, Francis Fisher. *The Every-day Life of Abraham Lincoln.* New York: N. D. Thompson, 1886.

Browne, Junius Henri. *Four Years in Secessia: Adventures Within and Beyond the Union Lines: Embracing a Great Variety of Facts, Incidents, and Romance of the War.* Hartford, Conn.: O. D. Case & Co., 1865.

———. *The Great Metropolis; A Mirror of New York. A Complete History of Metropolitan Life and Society, with Sketches of Prominent Places, Persons and Things in the City, as They Actually Exist.* Hartford, Conn.: American Publishing Co., 1869.

Brownlow, William G. *Sketches of the Pace, Prospects, and Decline of Secession.* Philadelphia: George W. Childs, 1862.

Brummer, Sidney David. *Political History of New York State During the Period of the Civil War.* New York: Columbia University Press, 1911.

Bryan, Wilhemus Bogart. *A History of the National Capital from Its Foundation Through the Period of the Adoption of the Organic Act,* 2 vols. New York: Macmillan, 1914.

Bryant, William Cullen. *Reminiscences of the Evening Post: Extracted from the Evening Post of November 15, 1851, with Additions and Corrections by the Writer.* New York: Wm C. Bryant & Co., 1851.

Buckingham, J. S. *America, Historical, Statistic, and Descriptive,* 2 vols. New York: Harper & Brothers, 1841.

[Butler, Benjamin Franklin] and Jessie Ames Marshall. *Private and Official Correspon-*

dence of Gen. Benjamin F. Butler During the Period of the Civil War, 5 vols. Privately printed, 1917.

Cadwallader, Sylvanus. *Three Years with Grant*, ed. Benjamin P. Thomas, Lincoln: University of Nebraska Press, 1955

Carpenter, F[rancis]. B. *Six Months at the White House with Abraham Lincoln: The Story of a Picture*. New York: Hurd & Houghton, 1866.

Chittenden, Lucius E. *Recollections of President Lincoln and His Administration*. New York: Harper & Brothers, 1891.

Cleveland, J. F. *The Tribune Almanac and Political Register for 1860*. New York: H. Greeley & Co., 1860.

Congdon, Charles T. *Reminiscences of a Journalist*. Boston: James R. Osgood, 1880.

Conway, Moncure Daniel. *Autobiography, Memories and Experiences*, 2 vols. London: Cassell & Co., 1904.

Cornell, William M. *The Life and Public Career of Horace Greeley*. Boston: Lee and Shepard, 1872.

Crawford, Martin, ed. *William Howard Russell's Civil War: Private Diary and Letters, 1861–1862*. Athens: University of Georgia Press, 1992.

Croly, David G., and George Wakeman. *Miscegenation: The Theory of the Blending of the Races, Applied to the American White Man and Negro*. New York: Bromley & Co., 1864.

Cullom, Shelby M. *Fifty Years of Public Service*. Chicago: A. C. McClurg, 1911.

Curtis, Francis. *The Republican Party: A History of Its 50 Years' Existence and a Record of Its Measures and Leaders, 1854–1904*. New York: G. P. Putnam's Sons, 1904.

Dana, Charles A. *Recollections of the Civil War with the Leaders at Washington and in the Field in the Sixties*. New York: D. Appleton, 1902.

Daniel, John M. *The Richmond Examiner During the War*. New York: Privately printed by the author, 1868.

Derby, J. C. *Fifty Years Among Authors, Books, and Publishers*. New York: G. W. Carleton, 1884.

Dicey, Edward. *Six Months in The Federal States*, 2 vols. London: Macmillan and Co., 1863.

Douglass, Frederick. *The Life and Times of Frederick Douglass*. Hartford, Conn.: Park Publishing, 1882.

Dowdey, Clifford, and Louis H. Manarin, eds. *The Wartime Papers of R. E. Lee*. New York: Bramhall House, 1961.

Dyer, Oliver. *Great Senators of the United States Forty Years Ago (1848 and 1849), with Personal Delineations of Calhoun, Benton, Clay, Webster, General Houston, Jefferson*

Davis, and Other Distinguished Statesmen of That Period. New York: Robert Bonner's Sons, 1889.

Emerson, Ralph Waldo. See Whicher.

Fremantle, Arthur. *The Fremantle Diary, Being the Journal of Lt. Col. Fremantle, Coldstream Guards, on His Three Months in the Southern States, April–June 1863.* New York: John Bradburn, 1864.

Garrison, Wendell Phillips, and Francis Jackson Garrison. *William Lloyd Garrison, 1805– 1879: The Story of His Life, Told by His Children,* 4 vols. Boston: Houghton Mifflin, 1885–1889.

Gilmore, James R. [Edmund Kirke]. *Personal Recollections of Abraham Lincoln and the Civil War.* Boston: L. C. Page & Co., 1898.

Gobright, L. A. *Recollections of Men and Things at Washington, During the Third of a Century.* Philadelphia: Claxton, Remsen & Haffelfinger, 1869.

Godwin, Parke. *A Biography of William Cullen Bryant, with Extracts from His Private Correspondence,* 2 vols. New York: D. Appleton, 1883.

Greeley, Horace. *The American Conflict: A History of the Great Rebellion in the United States of America, 1860–'64: Its Causes, Incidents, and Results: Intended to Exhibit Especially Its Moral and Political Phases, with the Drift and Progress of American Opinion Respecting Human Slavery from 1776 to the Close of the War for the Union.* Hartford, Conn.: O. D. Case, 1864.

———. *Glimmer of Europe.* New York: Dewitt & Davenport, 1851.

———. *Hints Toward Reforms: Lectures, Addresses, and Other Writings.* New York: Fowles & Wells, 1853.

———. *An Overland Journey from New York to San Francisco in the Summer of 1859.* New York: C. M. Saxton, Barker & Co., 1860.

———. *Recollections of a Busy Life, Including Reminiscences of American Politics and Politicians . . .* New York: J. B. Ford & Co., 1868.

Greeley, Horace, and John P. Cleveland, *Political Text-Book for 1860: Comprising a Brief View of Presidential Nominations and Elections . . .* New York: The York Tribune Association, 1860.

Greeley, Horace, and H. J. Raymond. *The Socialism of the Tribune Examined, Being a Controversy Between the New York Tribune and the Courier & Enquirer.* New York: Harper & Bros., 1847.

Green, Duff. *Facts and Suggestions, Biographical, Historical, Financial, and Political Addressed to the People of the United States.* New York: C. S. Webster & Co., 1866.

Gurowski, Adam. *Diary, from March 4, 1861, to November 12, 1862.* Boston: Lee & Shepard, 1862.

[Halpine, Charles]. *Boiled Meats at the Funeral: A Collection of Essays, Poems, Speeches, Histories, and Banquette by Private Miles O'Reilly.* New York: Carleton, 1866.

Halstead, Murat. See Hesseltine.

Hamilton, James A. *Reminiscences of James A. Hamilton; or, Men and Events at Home and Abroad During Three Quarters of a Century.* New York: Charles Scribner & Co., 1869.

Herndon, William H., and Jesse William Weik. *Lincoln's Herndon: The True Story of a Great Life.* Chicago: Belford & Clark, 1889.

Hesseltine, William B., ed. *Three Against Lincoln: Murat Halstead Reports the Caucuses of 1860.* Baton Rouge: Louisiana State University Press, 1960.

Hollister, O. J. *Life of Schuyler Colfax.* New York: Funk & Wagnalls, 1886.

Hone, Philip. See Tuckerman.

Hooker, Richard. *The Story of an Independent Newspaper: One Hundred Years of the Spring-field Republican.* New York: Macmillan, 1924.

Howells, W. D. *Years of My Youth.* New York: Harper & Bros., 1916.

Hudson, Frederic. *Journalism in the United States, from 1690 to 1872.* New York: Harper & Brothers, 1873.

[Hudson, Henry Norman]. *A Chaplain's Campaign with General Butler.* New York: Privately printed for the author, 1865.

Ingersoll, L. D. *The Life of Horace Greeley, Founder of the New-York Tribune.* New York: Union Publishing, 1873.

Johnson, Robert Underwood, and Clarence Clough Buel, eds., *Battles and Leaders of the Civil War*, 4 vols. New York: The Century Co., 1887.

Jones, J[ohn]. B. *A Rebel War Clerk's Diary at the Confederate States Capital*, 2 vols. Philadelphia: J. B. Lippincott & Co., 1866.

King, William L. *The Newspaper Press of Charleston, South Carolina . . .* Charleston, S.C.: Edward Perry, 1872.

Knox, Thomas W. *Camp-Fire and Cotton-Field: Southern Adventure in Time of War. Life with the Union Armies, and Residence on a Louisiana Plantation.* New York: Blelock & Co., 1865.

Lamon, Ward Hill. *The Life of Abraham Lincoln, from His Birth to His Inauguration as President.* Boston: James R. Osgood, 1872.

———. *Recollections of Abraham Lincoln, 1847–1865*, ed. Dorothy Lamon. Chicago: A. C. McClurg & Co., 1895.

———. *The Life of Abraham Lincoln as President*, ed. Bob O'Connor. West Conshohocken, Penn.: Montclair, 2010.

Lossing, Benson. *Pictorial History of the Civil War in the United States of America*, 2 vols. Philadelphia: George W. Childs, 1866.

Lovejoy, Joseph C., and Owen Lovejoy, *Memoir of the Rev. Elijah P. Lovejoy, Who Was Murdered in Defence of the Liberty of the Press, at Alton, Illinois, Nov. 7, 1837*. New York: John S. Taylor, 1838.

[Lowell, Robert]. *The Bigelow Papers, Second Series*. Boston: Houghton Mifflin, 1885.

Mahony, D[ennis] A. *The Prisoner of State*. New York: Carleton 1863.

Markle, Donald E., ed. *The Telegraph Goes to War: The Personal Diary of David Homer Bates, Lincoln's Telegraph Operator*. Hamilton, N.Y.: Edmonston, 2003.

Maverick, Augustus. *Henry J. Raymond and the New York Press, for Thirty Years. Progress of American Journalism from 1840 to 1870*. Hartford, Conn.: A. S. Hale & Co., 1870.

McCalmont, Alfred B. *Extracts from Letters Written by Alfred B. McCalmont, 1862–1865: From the Front During the War of the Rebellion*. Privately printed by Robert Mc-Calmont, 1908.

McClellan, George B. *McClellan's Own Story: The War for the Union, the Soldiers Who Fought It, the Civilians Who Directed It, and His Relations to It and Them*. New York: Charles L. Webster, 1887.

McClure, A. K. *Lincoln and Men of War-Times: Some Personal Recollections of War and Politics During the Lincoln Administration*. Philadelphia: The Times Publishing Co., 1892.

———. *Recollections of Half a Century*. Salem, Mass.: The Salem Press Co., 1902.

McPherson, Edward. *The Political History of the United States of America During the Great Rebellion, From November 6, 1860, to July 4, 1864*. Washington and New York: Philip & Solomons and D. Appleton, 1864.

Meade, George [Jr.]. *The Life and Letters of George Gordon Meade, Major General United States Army*, ed. George Gordon Meade, 2 vols. New York: Charles Scribner's Sons, 1913.

Nicolay, John G. *A Short Life of Abraham Lincoln*. New York: The Century Co., 1904.

———, and John Hay. *Abraham Lincoln: A History*, 10 vols. New York: The Century Co., 1890.

Nichols, Thomas Low. *Forty Years of American Life*, 2 vols. London: John Maxwell & Co., 1864.

Niven, John, ed. *The Salmon P. Chase Papers*. Kent, Ohio: Kent State University Press, 1993.

Parton, James. *The Life of Horace Greeley, Editor of "The New-York Tribune" from His Birth to the Present Time*. Boston: James R. Osgood, 1889.

Patton, Charles C. *Glory to God and the Sucker Democracy: A Manuscript Collection of the Letters of Charles H. Lanphier*, 5 vols. Privately printed, Frye-Williamson Press, 1973.

Patton, William. *President Lincoln and the Chicago Memorial of Emancipation, a Prayer Read Before the Maryland Historical Society December 12th, 1887*. Baltimore: Maryland Historical Society, 1888.

Piatt, Donn. *Memories of the Men Who Saved the Union*. New York: Belford, Clarke & Co., 1887.

Pierce, Edward L. See Sumner.

Pike, James S. *First Blows of the Civil War: The Ten Years of Preliminary Conflict in the United States from 1850 to 1860 . . .* New York: American News Co., 1879.

Political Text-Book for 1860: Comprising a Brief View of Presidential Nominations and Elections . . . New York: The Tribune Association, 1860.

Ben: Perley Poore. *Perley's Reminiscences of Sixty Years in the National Metropolis Illustrating the Wit, Humor, Genius, Eccentricities, Jealousies, Ambitions and Intrigues of the Brilliant Statesmen, Ladies, Offices, Diplomats, Lobbyists and other noted Celebrities of the World that gather at the Centre of the Nation Describing imposing Inauguration Ceremonies, Gala Day Festivities, Army Reviews, &c., &c., &c.*, 2 vols. Boston: Hubbard Bros., 1886.

Porter, Admiral [David Dixon]. *Incidents and Anecdotes of the Civil War*. New York: D. Appleton & Co., 1885.

Pratt, Harry E., ed. *Illinois as Lincoln Knew It: A Boston Reporter's Record of a Trip in 1847*. Springfield: Abraham Lincoln Association, 1938.

Prescott, George E. *History, Theory, and Practice of the Electric Telegraph*. Boston: Ticknor & Fields, 1860.

Proceedings at the Unveiling of a Memorial at Chappaqua, N.Y., February 3, 1914. Albany: New York State History[?], 1915.

Raymond, Henry J. *An Address Delivered Before the Citizens of Livingston County, Geneseo, N.Y., July 4, 1854*. New York: Baker, Godwin & Co., 1854.

———. *An Oration Pronounced Before the Young Men of Westchester County, on the Completion of a Monument Erected by Them to the Captors of Major Andre, at Tarrytown, Oct. 7, 1853*. New York: Samuel T. Callahan, 1853.

———. *History of the Administration of President Lincoln: Including His Speeches, Letters, Addresses, Proclamations, and Messages, with a Preliminary Sketch of His Life*. New York: Derby & Miller, 1864.

———. *The Life and Public Services of Abraham Lincoln, Sixteenth President of the United States Together with His State Papers . . .* New York: Derby & Miller, 1865.

Redpath, James. *The Roving Editor; or, Talks with Slaves in the Southern States*. New York: A. B. Burdick, 1859.

Reid, Whitelaw. *Horace Greeley*. New York: Scribner's, 1879.

Rice, Allen Thorndike, ed. *Reminiscences of Abraham Lincoln by Distinguished Men of His Time.* New York: North American Publishing Co., 1886.

Richards, Caroline Cowles. *Village Life in America, 1852–1872, Including the Period of the American Civil War as Told in the Diary of a School-Girl.* Orig. pub. 1913; Gansevoort, N.Y.: Corner House Historical Publications, 1997.

Richardson, Albert D. *The Secret Service, the Field, the Dungeon, and the Escape.* Hartford, Conn.: American Publishing Co., 1865.

Riddle, Albert Gallatin. *Recollections of War Times: Reminiscences of Men and Events in Washington, 1860–1865.* New York: G. P. Putnam's Sons, 1895.

Russell, William Howard. *My Diary North and South.* Boston: T.O.H.P. Burnham, 1863.

[Seaton, Josephine]. *William Winston Seaton of the "National Intelligencer": A Biographical Sketch with Passing Notices of His Associates and Friends.* Boston: James Osgood, 1871.

Seward, Frederick W. *Autobiography of William H. Seward, from 1801 to 1834. With a Memoir of His Life, and Selections from His Letters from 1831 to 1846.* New York: Appleton & Co., 1877.

———. *Seward at Washington as Senator and Secretary of State. A Memoir of His Life, with Selections from His Letters, 1846–1861.* New York: Derby & Miller, 1891.

Sheahan, James W. *The Great Conflagration: Chicago, Its Past, Present, and Future . . .* Chicago: Union Publishing, 1871.

———. *The Life of Stephen A. Douglas.* New York: Harper & Brothers, 1860.

Sherman, William T. *Memoirs of General W. T. Sherman,* 2 vols. Orig. pub. 1885; New York: Library of America, 1990.

Simon, John Y., and John F. Marszalek, eds. *The Papers of Ulysses S. Grant,* 32 vols. to date. Carbondale: Southern Illinois University Press, 1967–2012.

Smart, James G., ed. *A Radical View: The "Agate" Dispatches of Whitelaw Reid, 1861–1865,* 2 vols. Memphis: Memphis State University Press, 1976.

Stegmaier, Mark J., ed. *Henry Adams in the Secession Crisis: Dispatches to* The Boston Daily Advertiser, *December 1860-March 1861.* Baton Rouge: Louisiana State University Press, 2012.

Stevens, John Austin. *The Union Defence Committee of the City of New York: Minutes, Reports, and Correspondence.* New York: Union Defence Committee, 1885.

Stewart, Judd. *Lincoln and the New York Herald: Unpublished Letters of Abraham Lincoln from the Collection of Judd Stewart.* Plainfield, N.J.: Privately printed, 1907.

Stoddard, William O. *Inside the White House in War Times.* New York: Charles L. Webster, 1890.

———. *Lincoln at Work: Sketches from Life.* Boston: United Society of Christian Endeavor, 1900.

Stowe, Harriet Beecher. *The Lives and Deeds of Our Self-Made Men*. Hartford, Conn.: Worthington, Dustin & Co., 1872.

Stowell, Daniel W., ed. *The Papers of Abraham Lincoln: Legal Documents and Cases*, 4 vols. Charlottesville: University of Virginia Press, 2008.

Strong, George Templeton. *The Diary of George Templeton Strong*, ed. Allan Nevins and Milton Halsey Thomas, 4 vols. New York: Macmillan, 1952.

Sumner, Charles. *Memoirs and Letters of Charles Sumner*, ed. Edward L. Pierce, 4 vols. Boston: Roberts Bros., 1874.

Swinton, William. *The Twelve Decisive Battles of the War: A History of the Eastern and Western Campaigns . . .* New York: Dick & Fitzgerald, 1867.

Swisshelm, Jane Grey. *Half a Century*. 3rd ed., Chicago: Jansen, McClurg & Co., 1880.

Townsend, George Alfred. *Campaigns of a Non-Combatant, and His Romaunt During the War*. New York: Belock & Co., 1866.

Trollope, Anthony. *North America*, 2 vols., London: Chapman & Hall, 1862.

Tuckerman, Bayard, ed. *The Diary of Philip Hone, 1828–1851*, 2 vols. New York: Dodd, Mead & Co., 1889.

Turner, Justin G. and Linda Levitt, eds. *Mary Todd Lincoln: Her Life and Letters*. New York: Alfred A. Knopf, 1972.

Vallandigham, *Clement L. The Trial of Hon. Clement L. Vallandigham by a Military Commission: and the Proceedings Under His Application for a Writ of Habeas Corpus in the Circuit Court of the United States for the Southern District of Ohio*. Cincinnati: Rickey & Carroll, 1863.

Van Evrie, J. H., M.D. *White Supremacy and Negro Subordination; or, Negroes a Subordinate Race, and (so-called) Slavery Its Normal Condition*. New York: Van Evrie, Horton, 1870.

Villard, Harold G., and Oswald Garrison Villard, eds. *Lincoln on the Eve of '61: A Journalist's Story by Henry Villard*. New York: Alfred A. Knopf, 1954.

Villard, Henry. *Memoirs of Henry Villard: Journalist and Financier, 1835–1900*, 2 vols. Boston: Houghton Mifflin, 1904.

The War of the Rebellion: A Compilation of the Official Records of the Union and Confederate Armies, 128 vols. Washington, D.C.: U.S. Government Printing Office, 1880–1901.

Ward, William Hayes, ed. *Abraham Lincoln: Tributes from His Associates*. New York: Thomas Y. Crowell, 1895.

Weed, Harriet A. ed. *Autobiography of Thurlow Weed*, 2 vols. Boston: Houghton Mifflin, 1883.

Welles, Gideon. *Diary of Gideon Welles*, ed. John T. Morse, Jr., 3 vols. Boston: Houghton Mifflin, 1911.

Whicher, Stephen E., ed. *Selections from Ralph Waldo Emerson*. Boston: Houghton Mifflin, 1957.

White, Horace. *The Life of Lyman Trumbull*. Boston: Houghton Mifflin, 1913.

White, Jonathan W., ed. *A Philadelphia Perspective: The Civil War Diary of Sidney George Fisher*. New York: Fordham University Press, 2007.

Whiting, William. *The War Powers of the President, and the Legislative Powers of Congress in Relation to Rebellion, Treason, and Slavery*. Boston: John L. Shorey, 1863.

Whitman, Walt. *Specimen Days in America*. London: Walter Scott, 1887.

Wilkie, Franc B. *Pen and Powder*. Boston: Ticknor & Co., 1888.

———. *Personal Reminiscences of 35 Years of Journalism*. Chicago: F. J. Schulte & Co., 1891.

Wilmer, Lambert A. *Our Press Gang; or, A Complete Exposition of the Corruptions and Crimes of the American Newspapers*. Philadelphia: J. T. Lloyd, 1859.

Wilson, Henry. *History of the Rise and Fall of the Slave Power in America*, 3 vols. Boston: Houghton Mifflin, 1877.

Windle, Mary J. *Life in Washington, and Life Here and There*. Philadelphia: J. B. Lippincott, 1859.

Wing, Henry E. *When Lincoln Kissed Me: A Story of the Wilderness Campaign*. New York and Cincinnati: Abingdon Press, 1931.

Wingate, Charles F., ed. *Views and Interviews on Journalism*. New York: F. B. Patterson, 1875.

Winthrop, William. *Military Laws and Precedents*. 2nd ed.; orig. pub. 1880; Washington, D.C.: U.S. Government Printing Office, 1920.

Wood, Benjamin. *Fort Lafayette; or, Love and Secession. A Novel*. New York: Carleton & Co., 1862.

Young, Mary D. Russell, ed. *Men and Memories: Personal Reminiscences by John Russell Young*. New York: F. Tennyson Neely, 1901.

Zabriskie, Francis N. *Horace Greeley, the Editor*. New York: Funk & Wagnalls, 1890.

SECONDARY SOURCES—BOOKS

Abels, Jules. *Man on Fire: John Brown and the Cause of Liberty*. New York: Macmillan, 1971.

Altschuler, Glen C., and Stuart M. Blumin. *Rude Republic: Americans and Their Politics in the Nineteenth Century*. Princeton: Princeton University Press, 2000.

Ames, William E. *A History of the National Intelligencer*. Chapel Hill: University of North Carolina Press, 1972.

Anbinder, Tyler. *Five Points: The 19th-Century New York City Neighborhood That Invented Tap Dance, Stole Elections, and Became the World's Most Notorious Slum.* New York: Free Press, 2001.

Anderson, Benedict. *Imagined Communities: Reflections on the Origin and Spread of Nationalism.* London, Verso, 1983.

Anderson, George McCullough. *The Work of Adalbert Johann Volck* (1828–1912). Baltimore: George McCullough Anderson, 1970.

Andrews, J. Cutler. *The North Reports the Civil War.* Pittsburgh: University of Pittsburgh Press, 1955.

———. *The South Reports the Civil War.* Princeton: Princeton University Press, 1970.

Angle, Paul M. *"Here I Have Lived": A History of Lincoln's Springfield, 1821–1865.* Orig. pub. 1935; Chicago: Abraham Lincoln Book Shop, 1971.

Angle, Paul M., ed. *Annals of the War: Written by the Leading Participants, North and South, Originally Published in the Philadelphia Weekly Times.* Orig. pub. 1888; New York: Morningside, 1988.

Arp, Bill [Charles Henry Smith]. *Bill Arp's Peace Papers: Columns on War and Reconstruction, 1861–1873.* Columbia: University of South Carolina Press, 2009.

Atkins, John Black. *The Life of Sir William Howard Russell*, 2 vols. London: John Murray, 1911.

Balin, Peter, and Paul Shaw. *Blackletter: Type and National Identity.* Princeton: Princeton University Press, 1998.

Beckett, Ian F. W. *The War Correspondents: The American Civil War.* Phoenix Mill, England: Alan Sutton, 1994.

Belko, W. Stephen. *The Invincible Duff Green: Whig of the West.* Columbia: University of Missouri Press, 2006.

Belz, Herman. *Lincoln and the Constitution: The Dictatorship Question Reconsidered.* Seventh Annual R. Gerald McMurtry Lecture. Fort Wayne, Ind.: Louis A. Warren Lincoln Library and Museum, 1984.

Bennett, James O'Donnell. *Joseph Medill: A Brief Biography and an Appreciation.* Orig. pub. 1929; Chicago: Chicago Tribune, 1947.

Berger, Meyer. *The Story of the New York Times, 1851–1951.* New York: Simon & Schuster, 1951.

Biographical Directory of the United States Congress, 1774–2005 . . . Washington, D.C.: U.S. Government Printing Office, 2005.

Bleyer, Willard Grosvenor. *Main Currents in the History of American Journalism.* Boston: Houghton Mifflin, 1927.

Blondheim, Menahem. *Copperhead Gore: Benjamin Wood's Fort Lafayette and Civil War America.* Bloomington: Indiana University Press, 2006.

————. *News over the Wires: The Telegraph and the Flow of Public Information in America, 1844–1897*. Cambridge: Harvard University Press, 1994.

Blumin, Stuart. *The Emergence of the Middle Class: Social Experience in the American City, 1760–1900*. New York: Cambridge University Press, 1989.

Boman, Dennis K. *Lincoln and Citizens' Rights in Civil War Missouri: Balancing Freedom and Security*. Baton Rouge: Louisiana State University Press, 2011.

Bracken, Donagh. *The Words of War: The Civil War Battle Reportage of the New York Times and the Charleston Mercury . . . and What Historians Say Really Happened*. Palisades, N.Y.: History Publishing Co., 2007.

Bradley, William Aspenwall. *William Cullen Bryant*. New York: Macmillan, 1905.

Brantley, Rabun Lee. *Georgia Journalism of the Civil War Period*. Nashville: George Peabody College for Teachers, 1929.

Bray, Robert. *Reading with Lincoln*. Carbondale: Southern Illinois University Press, 2010.

Bridges, Peter. *Donn Piatt: Gadfly of the Gilded Age*. Kent, Ohio: Kent State University Press, 2012.

Brown, Francis. *Raymond of the Times*. New York: W. W. Norton, 1951.

Bulla, David W. *Journalism in the Civil War*. New York: Peter Lang, 2010.

————. *Lincoln's Censor: Milo Hascall and Freedom of the Press in Civil War Indiana*. West Lafayette, Ind.: Purdue University Press, 2008.

Bullard, F. Lauriston. *Famous War Correspondents*. Boston: Little, Brown, 1914.

Bunker, Gary L. *From Rail-Splitter to Icon: Lincoln's Image in Illustrated Periodicals, 1860–1865*. Kent, Ohio: Kent State University Press, 2001.

Burlingame, Michael. *Abraham Lincoln: A Life*, 2 vols. Baltimore: Johns Hopkins University Press, 2008.

Burlingame, Michael, ed. *Abraham Lincoln: The Observations of John G. Nicolay and John Hay*. Carbondale: Southern Illinois University Press, 2007.

————, ed. *At Lincoln's Side: John Hay's Civil War Correspondence and Selected Writings*. Carbondale: Southern Illinois University Press, 2000.

————, ed. *Dispatches from Lincoln's White House: The Anonymous Civil War Journalism of Presidential Secretary William O. Stoddard*. Lincoln: University of Nebraska Press, 2002.

————, ed. *Lincoln Observed: Civil War Dispatches of Noah Brooks*. Carbondale: Southern Illinois University Press, 1998.

————, ed. *Lincoln's Journalist: John Hay's Anonymous Writings for the Press, 1860–1864*. Carbondale: Southern Illinois University Press, 1998.

————, ed. *An Oral History of Abraham Lincoln: John G. Nicolay's Interviews and Essays*. Carbondale: Southern Illinois University Press, 1996.

———, ed. *A Reporter's Lincoln: Walter B. Stevens.* Lincoln: University of Nebraska Press, 1998.

———, ed. *With Lincoln in the White House: Letters, Memoranda, and Other Writings of John G. Nicolay, 1860–1865.* Carbondale: Southern Illinois University Press, 2000.

Burlingame, Michael, and John R. Turner Ettlinger, eds., *Inside Lincoln's White House: The Complete Civil War Diary of John Hay.* Carbondale: Southern Illinois University Press, 1997.

Burrows, Edwin G., and Mike Wallace. *Gotham: A History of New York City to 1898.* New York: Oxford University Press, 1999.

Carlson, Oliver. *The Man Who Made News: James Gordon Bennett.* New York: Duell, Sloan & Pearce, 1942.

Carman, Harry J., and Reinhard H. Luthin. *Lincoln and the Patronage.* New York: Columbia University Press, 1943.

Carnahan, Burrus M. *Lincoln on Trial: Southern Civilians and the Law of War.* Lexington: University Press of Kentucky, 2010.

Castel, Albert. *General Stirling Price and the Civil War in the American West.* Baton Rouge: Louisiana State University Press, 1968.

Chapman, Caroline. *Russell of the Times: War Despatches and Diaries.* London: Bell & Hyman, 1984.

Chester, Thomas Morris. *Black Civil War Correspondent: Thomas Morris Chester—His Dispatches from the Virginia Front,* ed. R. J. M. Blackett. Baton Rouge: Louisiana State University Press, 1989.

Clapp, Margaret. *Forgotten First Citizen: John Bigelow.* Boston: Little, Brown, 1947.

Clark, Allen C. *Abraham Lincoln in the National Capital.* Washington, D.C.: W. F. Roberts, 1925.

Clinton, Catherine. *Mrs. Lincoln: A Life.* New York: HarperCollins, 2009.

Coffin, Charles Carleton. *Eyewitness to Gettysburg: The Story of Gettysburg as Told by the Leading Correspondent of His Day,* ed. John W. Schilt. Shippensburg, Penn.: Burd Street Press, 1997.

Conroy, James B. *Our One Common Country: Abraham Lincoln and the Hampton Roads Peace Conference of 1865.* Guilford, Conn.: Lyons Press, 2014.

Cooper, William J. *We Have the War Upon Us: The Onset of the Civil War, November 1860–April 1861.* New York: Alfred A. Knopf, 2012.

Cooper, William J., Jr., and John McCardell, Jr. *In the Cause of Liberty: How the Civil War Redefined American Ideals.* Baton Rouge: Louisiana State University Press, 2009.

Cortissoz, Royal. *The Life of Whitelaw Reid,* 2 vols. New York: Charles Scribner's Sons, 1921.

Coulter, E. Merton. *William G. Brownlow: Fighting Parson of the Southern Highlands.* Orig. pub. 1937; Knoxville: University of Tennessee Press, 1999.

Crofts, Daniel W. *A Secession Crisis Enigma: William Henry Hurlbert and "The Diary of a Public Man."* Baton Rouge: Louisiana State University Press, 2010.

Crouthamel, James L. *Bennett's New York Herald and the Rise of the Popular Press.* Syracuse: Syracuse University Press, 1989.

Crozier, Emmet. *Yankee Journalists, 1861–1865.* New York: Oxford University Press, 1956.

Curl, Donald W. *Murat Halstead and the Cincinnati Commercial.* Boca Raton: University Press of Florida, 1980.

Curtis, William Eleroy. *The True Abraham Lincoln.* Philadelphia: J. B. Lippincott, 1905.

Davis, Elmer. *History of the New York Times, 1851–1921.* New York: New York Times, 1921.

de Borchgrave, Alexandra Villard, and John Cullen. *Villard: The Life and Times of an American Titan.* New York: Doubleday, 2001.

Dicken-Garcia, Hazel, and Giovanna Dell'Orio. *Hated Ideas and the American Civil War Press.* Spokane, Wash.: Marquette University Press, 2008.

Douglas, George H. *The Golden Age of the Newspaper.* Westport, Conn.: Greenwood, 1999.

Ellis, B. G. *The Moving Appeal: Mr. McLanahan, Mrs. Dill, and the Civil War's Great Newspaper Run.* Macon, Ga.: Mercer University Press, 2003.

Emery, Michael, Edwin Emery, and Nancy L. Roberts. *The Press and America: An Interpretive History of the Mass Media.* Boston: Allyn & Bacon, 2000.

Etulian, Richard. *Lincoln and Oregon Country Politics in the Civil War Era.* Corvallis: University of Oregon Press, 2013.

Fahrney, Ralph Ray. *Horace Greeley and the Tribune in the Civil War.* Cedar Rapids, Iowa: The Torch Press, 1936.

Fehrenbacher, Don E. *The Dred Scott Case: Its Significance in American Law and Politics.* New York: Oxford University Press, 1962.

———. *Prelude to Greatness: Lincoln in the 1850s.* Stanford: Stanford University Press, 1962.

Fehrenbacher, Don E., and Virginia Fehrenbacher, eds. *Recollected Words of Abraham Lincoln.* Stanford: Stanford University Press, 1996.

Fermer, Douglas. *James Gordon Bennett and the New York Herald: A Study of Editorial Opinion in the Civil War Era, 1854–1863.* New York: St. Martin's Press, 1986.

Fergusson, J. *Personal Observations of Men of Intelligence: Notes of a Tour of North America in 1861.* Lambertville, N.J.: True Bill Press, 2009.

Findley, Paul. *A. Lincoln: The Crucible of Congress.* New York: Crown, 1979.

Foreman, Amanda. *A World on Fire: Britain's Crucial Role in the American Civil War.* New York: Random House, 2011.

Forney, John W. *Anecdotes of Public Men,* 2 vols. New York: Harper & Bros., 1881.

Frothingham, Paul Revere. *Edward Everett, Orator and Statesman.* Boston: Houghton Mifflin, 1925.

Fuller, A. James, ed. *The Election of 1860 Reconsidered.* Kent, Ohio: Kent State University Press, 2013.

Gallman, J. Matthew. *Northerners at War: Reflections on the Civil War Home Front.* Lawrence: Kansas State University Press, 2010.

Gertz, Elmer. *Joe Medill's War.* Chicago: Abraham Lincoln Book Shop, 1945.

Gilmore, Michael T. *The War in Words: Slavery, Race, and Free Speech in American Literature.* Chicago: University of Chicago Press, 2010.

Gleason, Timothy E. *The Watchdog Concept: The Press and the Courts in Nineteenth-Century America.* Ames: University of Iowa Press, 1990.

Goldfield, David. *America Aflame: How the Civil War Created a Nation.* New York: Bloomsbury, 2011.

Goodheart, Adam. *1861: The Civil War Awakening.* New York: Alfred A. Knopf, 2011.

Goodman, Matthew. *The Sun and the Moon: The Remarkable True Account of Hoaxers, Showmen, Dueling Journalists, and Lunar Man-Bats in Nineteenth-Century New York.* New York: Basic Books, 2008.

Graham, Preston D., Jr. *A Kingdom Not of This World: Stuart Robinson's Struggle to Distinguish the Sacred from the Secular During the Civil War.* Macon, Ga.: Mercer University Press, 2002.

Greene, Laurence. *America Goes to Press. Headlines of the Past: The History of the United States as Reported in the Newspapers of the Day from the Boston Tea Party to the World War.* Garden City, N.Y.; Garden City Publishing, 1938.

Grimsted, David. *American Mobbing, 1828–1861: Toward Civil War.* New York: Oxford University Press, 1998.

Guelzo, Allen C. *Lincoln and Douglas: The Debates That Defined America.* New York: Simon & Schuster, 2008.

Hale, William Harlan. *Horace Greeley: Voice of the People.* New York: Harper & Brothers, 1950.

Hamilton, Charles, and Lloyd Ostendorf. *Lincoln in Photographs: An Album of Every Known Pose.* Orig. pub. 1963; rev. ed., Dayton, Ohio: Morningside, 1985.

Hanson, Thomas C., Sr., *Abraham Lincoln, Press Freedom and War Restraints: How He*

Suppressed the Los Angeles Star. Greenville, S.C., Privately printed, book on demand, 2005.

Harper, Robert S. *Lincoln and the Press.* New York: McGraw-Hill, 1951.

Harris, Brayton. *Blue and Gray in Black and White: Newspapers in the Civil War.* Washington, D.C.: Brassey's, 1999.

Harwell, Richard Barksdale. *Cornerstones of Confederate Collecting.* Charlottesville: University of Virginia Press, 1953.

Hayes, Melvin L. *Mr. Lincoln Runs for President.* New York: Citadel, 1960.

Henig, Gerald S., and Eric Niderost. *A Nation Transformed: How the Civil War Changed America Forever.* Orig. pub. 2001; Nashville: Cumberland House, 2007.

Henkin, David M. *City Reading: Written Words and Public Spaces in Antebellum New York.* New York: Columbia University Press, 1998.

———. *The Postal Age: The Emergence of Modern Communications in Nineteenth-Century America.* Chicago: University of Chicago Press, 2006.

Herriott, F. I. *The Premises and Significance of Abraham Lincoln's Letter to Theodore Canisius.* Reprinted from *Deutsch-Amerikanische Geschichtsblatter Jahrbuch der Deutsch-Amerikanischen Historischen Gesellschaft von Illinois,* 15 (1915).

Horrocks, Thomas A. *Lincoln's Campaign Biographies.* Carbondale: Southern Illinois University Press, 2014.

Huntzicker, William E. *The Popular Press, 1833–1865.* Westport, Conn.: Greenwood, 1999.

Jackman, S. W., ed. *Acton in America: The American Journal of Sir John Acton, 1853.* Shepherdstown, W. Va.: Patmos, 1979.

Jenkins, Sally, and John Stauffer. *The State of Jones: The Small Southern County That Seceded from the Confederacy.* New York: Doubleday, 2009.

Kielbowitz, Richard. *News in the Mail: The Press, the Post Office, and Public Information, 1700–1860s.* Westpoint, Conn.: Greenwood, 1989.

Kinsley, Philip. *The Chicago Tribune: Its First Hundred Years,* 3 vols. New York: Alfred A. Knopf, 1943.

Klement, Frank L. *The Limits of Dissent.* Orig. pub. 1970; New York: Fordham University Press, 1998.

Krock, Arthur. *The Editorials of Henry Watterson.* Louisville: Louisville Courier-Journal, 1923.

Lathem, Edward Connery. *Chronological Tables of American Newspapers, 1690–1820.* Barre, Mass.: American Antiquarian Society and Barre Publishing, 1972.

Lee, James Melvin. *History of American Journalism.* Boston: Houghton Mifflin, 1917.

Levy, Leonard W., and Harold W. Nelson, *Freedom of the Press: From Hamilton to the Warren Court,* 2 vols. Indianapolis: Bobbs-Merrill, 1967.

Linn, William Alexander. *Horace Greeley: Founder and Editor of the New York Tribune.* New York: D. Appleton, 1903.

Logsdon, Joseph. *Horace White: Nineteenth-century Liberal.* Westport, Conn.: Greenwood, 1971.

Long, David E. *The Jewel of Liberty: Abraham Lincoln's Re-election and the End of Slavery.* Mechanicsburg, Penn.: Stackpole, 1994.

Loughran, Trish. *The Republic in Print: Print Culture in the Age of U.S. Nation Building, 1770–1870.* New York: Columbia University Press, 2007.

Maihafer, Harry J. *The General and The Journalists: Ulysses S. Grant. Horace Greeley, and Charles Dana,* Washington, D.C. Brassey's, 1998.

———. *War of Words: Abraham Lincoln and the Civil War Press.* Washington, D.C.: Brassey's, 2001.

Manber, Jeffrey, and Neil Dahlstrom. *Lincoln's Wrath: Fierce Mobs, Brilliant Scoundrels and a President's Mission to Destroy the Press.* Naperville, Ill.: Sourcebooks, 2005.

Marszalek, John F. *Sherman's Other War: The General and the Civil War Press.* Orig. pub. 1981; Kent, Ohio: Kent State University Press, 1999.

Massey, Mary Elizabeth. *Ersatz in the Confederacy: Shortages and Substitutes on the Southern Homefront.* Orig. pub. 1952; Columbia: University of South Carolina Press, 1993.

Matt, Susan J. *Homesickness: An American History.* New York: Oxford University Press, 2011.

McGinty, Brian. *The Body of John Merryman: Abraham Lincoln and the Suspension of Habeas Corpus.* Cambridge: Harvard University Press, 2011.

McKinney, Megan. *The Magnificent Medills: America's Royal Family of Journalism During a Century of Turbulent Splendor.* New York: HarperCollins, 2011.

McNeely, Patricia G., Debra Reddin van Tuyll, and Henry H. Schulte. *Knights of the Quill: Confederate Correspondents and Their Civil War Reporting.* West Lafayette, Ind.: Purdue University Press, 2010.

McPherson, James M. *Battle Cry of Freedom: The Civil War Era.* New York: Oxford University Press, 1988.

———. *The Negro's Civil War: How American Negroes Felt and Acted During the War for the Union.* New York: Pantheon, 1965.

Meneely, A. Howard. *The War Department, 1861: A Study in Mobilization and Administration.* New York: Columbia University Press, 1928.

Miles, William, ed. *The People's Voice: An Annotated Bibliography of American Presidential Campaign Newspapers, 1828–1984.* Westport, Conn.: Greenwood, 1987.

Milton, George Fort. *Abraham Lincoln and the Fifth Column.* New York: Vanguard, 1942.

————. *Stephen A. Douglas and the Needless War.* Boston: Houghton Mifflin, 1934.

Minear, Larry, Colin Scott, and Thomas G. Weiss. *The News Media, the Civil War, and Humanitarian Action.* Boulder, Col.: Lynne Rienner, 1996.

————, ed. *Lincoln as They Saw Him.* New York: Rinehart, 1956.

————, ed. *Washington in Lincoln's Time by Noah Brooks.* New York: Rinehart, 1958.

Monaghan, Jay. *The Man Who Elected Lincoln. Indianapolis: Bobbs-Merrill, 1956.*

Morris, James McGrath. Pulitzer: A Life in Politics, Print, and Power. New York: Harper-Collins, 2010.

Mott, Frank Luther. *A History of American Magazines,* 2 vols. Vol. 2: 1850–1865. Cambridge: Harvard University Press, 1957.

Mushkat, Jerome. *Fernando Wood: A Political Biography.* Kent, Ohio: Kent State University Press, 1990.

Neely, Mark E., Jr. *The Abraham Lincoln Encyclopedia.* New York: McGraw-Hill, 1982.

————. *The Boundaries of American Political Culture in the Civil War Era.* Chapel Hill: University of North Carolina Press, 2005.

————. *The Fate of Liberty: Abraham Lincoln and Civil Liberties.* New York: Oxford University Press, 1991.

————. *The Union Divided: Party Conflict in the Civil War North.* Cambridge: Harvard University Press, 2002.

Nelson, Harold L. *Freedom of the Press: From Hamilton to the Warren Court.* Indianapolis: Bobbs-Merrill, 1967.

Nerone, John C. *Violence Against the Press: Policing the Public Sphere in U.S. History.* New York: Oxford University Press, 1994.

Nevins, Allan. *The Evening Post: A Century of Journalism.* New York: Boni & Liveright, 1922.

————. *The War for the Union,* 4 vols. New York: Charles Scribner & Sons, 1959–1971.

Nicolay, Helen. *Lincoln's Secretary: A Biography of John G. Nicolay.* New York: Longmans, Green & Co., 1949.

Noyes, Edward. *Wisconsin's Reaction to Abraham Lincoln's Emancipation Proclamation with Especial Reference to Editorial Opinion.* Bulletin of the 42nd Annual Meeting, Lincoln Fellowship of Wisconsin, Historical Bulletin No. 41, 1986.

Oakes, James. *Freedom National: The Destruction of Slavery in the United States, 1861–1865.* New York: W. W. Norton, 2013.

O'Brien, Frank M. *The Story of the New York Sun, 1833–1918.* New York: George H. Doran, 1918.

Paine, Charles. *The Resistant Writer: Rhetoric as Immunity, 1850 to the Present.* Albany: State University of New York Press, 1999.

Patton, Charles C. *Glory to God and the Sucker Democracy: A Manuscript Collection of the Letters of Charles H. Lanphier*, 5 vols. Privately printed, 1973.

Payne, Charles E. *Josiah Bushnell Grinnell.* Des Moines: State Historical Society of Iowa, 1938.

Payne, George Henry. *History of Journalism in the United States.* New York: D. Appleton, 1920.

Peatman, Jared. *The Long Shadow of Lincoln's Gettysburg Address.* Carbondale: Southern Illinois University Press, 2013.

Perkins, Howard Cecil, ed. *Northern Editorials on Secession*, 2 vols. Gloucester, Mass.: Peter Smith, 1964.

Perry, James M. *A Bohemian Brigade: The Civil War Correspondents—Mostly Rough, Sometimes Ready.* New York: John Wiley & Sons, 2000.

Pfau, Michael William. *The Political Style of Conspiracy: Chase, Sumner, and Lincoln.* East Lansing: Michigan State University Press, 2005.

Pisani, Lt.-Col. Camille Ferri. *Prince Napoleon in America, 1861.* Bloomington: Indiana University Press, 1959.

Pollard, James E. *The Presidents and the Press.* New York: Macmillan, 1947.

Potter, David M. *The South and the Sectional Conflict.* Baton Rouge: Louisiana State University Press, 1968.

Pratt, Harry E. *The Personal Finances of Abraham Lincoln.* Springfield, Ill.: Abraham Lincoln Association, 1943.

Putnam, George Haven. *Abraham Lincoln: The People's Leader in the Struggle for National Existence.* New York: G. P. Putnam's Sons, 1909.

Quigley, Paul. *Shifting Grounds: Nationalism and the American South.* New York: Oxford University Press, 2012.

Quitt, Martin H. *Stephen A. Douglas and Antebellum Democracy.* Cambridge: Cambridge University Press, 2012.

Ramold, Steven J. *Across the Divide: Union Soldiers View the Northern Home Front.* New York: New York University Press, 2013.

Randall, J. G. *Constitutional Problems Under Lincoln.* New York: D. Appleton, 1926.

Rankin, David C., ed. *My Passage at the New Orleans Tribune: A Memoir of the Civil War Era by Jean-Charles Houzeau.* Baton Rouge: Louisiana State University Press, 1984.

Ratner, Lorman A., and Dwight L. Teeter, Jr. *Fanatics and Fire-Eaters: Newspapers and the Coming of the Civil War.* Urbana: University of Illinois Press, 2003.

Reilly, Bernard F., Jr. *American Political Prints, 1766–1876: A Catalog of the Collections in the Library of Congress.* Boston: G. K. Hall, 1991.

Reynolds, Donald. *Editors Make War: Southern Newspapers in the Secession Crisis.* Carbondale: Southern Illinois University Press, 2006.

Risley, Ford. *Abolition and the Press: The Moral Struggle Against Slavery.* Evanston, Ill.: Northwestern University Press, 2008.

———. *Civil War Journalism.* Santa Barbara, Calif.: Praeger, 2012.

Risley, Ford, ed. *The Civil War: Primary Documents on Events from 1800 to 1865.* Westport, Conn.: Greenwood, 2004.

Ritchie, Donald A. *American Journalists: Getting the Story Out.* New York: Oxford University Press, 1997.

———. *Press Gallery: Congress and the Washington Correspondents.* Cambridge: Harvard University Press, 1991.

Rosenfeld, Richard. *American Aurora.* New York: St. Martin's, 1977.

Rosewater, Victory. *History of Cooperative Journalism in the United States.* New York: D. Appleton, 1930.

Rushton, Wyatt. *Joseph Medill and the Chicago Tribune.* Madison: University of Wisconsin Press, 1916.

Ryan, Mary P. *Civic Wars: Democracy and Public Life in the American City During the Nineteenth Century.* Berkeley: University of California Press, 1997.

Sachsman, David B., S. Kittrell Rushing, and Roy Morris, Jr. *Words at War: The Civil War and American Journalism.* West Lafayette, Ind.: Purdue University Press, 2008.

Sass, Herbert Ravenal. *Outspoken: 150 Years of the News & Courier.* Columbia: University of South Carolina Press, 1958.

Sauers, Richard A., and Peter Tomask. *The Fishing Creek Conspiracy: A Story of Civil War Draft Resistance.* Columbia: University of Missouri Press, 2013.

Schecter, Barnet. *The Devil's Own Work: The Civil War Draft Riots and the Fight to Reconstruct America.* New York: Walker, 2005.

Schwerzlose, Richard A. *The Nation's Newsbrokers,* 2 vols. Evanston, Ind.: Northwestern University Press, 1989–1990.

Scott, Sean. *A Visitation of God: Northern Civilians Interpret the Civil War.* New York: Oxford University Press, 2010.

Sears, Stephen W. *George B. McClellan: The Young Napoleon.* New York: Ticknor & Fields, 1988.

Sears, Stephen, W., ed. *The Civil War Papers of George B. McClellan: Selected Correspondence, 1860–1865.* New York: Ticknor & Fields, 1989.

Segal, Charles M. *Conversations with Lincoln.* New York: G. P. Putnam's Sons, 1961.

Seitz, Don C. *The James Gordon Bennetts, Father and Son, Proprietors of the New York Herald.* Indianapolis: Bobbs-Merrill, 1928.

Sellers, Charles. *The Market Revolution in Jacksonian America, 1815–1846.* New York: Oxford University Press, 1991.

Shaw, Archer. *The Plain Dealer: One Hundred Years in Cleveland.* New York: Alfred A. Knopf, 1942.

Shipton, A. W. *Lincoln's Association with the Journal.* Pamphlet, n.d.

Sibley, Marilyn McAdams. *Lone Stars and State Gazettes: Texas Newspapers Before the Civil War.* College Station: Texas A&M Press, 1983.

Silbey, Joel H. *The American Political Nation, 1838–1893.* Stanford: Stanford University Press, 1991.

Slotkin, Richard. *The Long Road to Antietam: How the Civil War Became a Revolution.* New York: W. W. Norton, 2011.

Smith, Culver H. *The Press, Politics, and Patronage: The American Government's Use of Newspapers, 1789–1875.* Athens: University of Georgia Press, 1977.

Smith, Jeffrey A. *War and Press Freedom: The Problem of Prerogative Power.* New York: Oxford University Press, 1999.

Smith, Reed W. *Samuel Medary and the Crisis: Testing the Limits of Press Freedom.* Columbus: Ohio State University Press, 1995.

Sprague, Dean. *Freedom Under Lincoln: Federal Power and Personal Liberty Under the Strain of Civil War.* Boston: Houghton Mifflin, 1965.

Stahr, Walter. *Seward: Lincoln's Indispensable Man.* New York: Simon & Schuster, 2012.

Starr, Louis M. *The Civil War's Bohemian Brigade: Newsmen In Action.* New York: Alfred A. Knopf, 1954.

Starr, Paul. *The Creation of the Media: Political Origins of Modern Communications.* New York: Basic Books, 2004.

Stauffer, John, and Zoe Trodd, eds. *The Tribunal: Responses to John Brown and the Harpers Ferry Raid.* Cambridge: Harvard University Press, 2012.

Steiner, Mark E. *An Honest Calling: The Law Practice of Abraham Lincoln.* Dekalb: Northern Illinois University Press, 2006.

Stoddard, Henry Luther. *Horace Greeley: Printer, Editor, Crusader.* New York: G. P. Putnam's Sons, 1946.

Styple, William, ed. *Writing and Fighting the Civil War: Soldier Correspondence to the New York Sunday Mercury.* Kearny, N.J.: Belle Grove, 2000.

Swanson, Stevenson, ed. *Chicago Days: 150 Defining Moments in the Life of a Great City.* New York: McGraw-Hill, 1997.

Tagg, Larry. *The Unpopular Mr. Lincoln: The Story of America's Most Reviled President.* New York: Savas Beattie, 2009.

Tarbell, Ida M. *A Reporter for Lincoln: Henry E. Wing, Soldier and Newspaperman.* Orig. pub. 1926; New York: Macmillan, 1927.

Thomas, Benjamin P. *Lincoln's New Salem.* Orig. pub. 1934; Chicago: Lincoln's New Salem Enterprises, 1973.

Trietsch, James H. *The Printer and the Prince: A Study of the Influence of Horace Greeley Upon Abraham Lincoln as Candidate and President.* New York: Exposition, 1955.

Tucher, Andie. *Froth and Scum: Truth, Beauty, Goodness, and the Ax Murder in America's First Mass Medium.* Chapel Hill: University of North Carolina Press, 1994.

Tuchinsky, Adam. *Horace Greeley's New York Tribune: Civil War–Era Socialism and the Crisis of Free Labor.* Ithaca, N.Y.: Cornell University Press, 2009.

Turner, Hy B. *When Giants Ruled: The Story of Park Row, New York's Great Newspaper Street.* New York: Fordham University Press, 1999.

Van Deusen, Glyndon G. *Thurlow Weed: Wizard of the Lobby.* Boston: Little, Brown, 1947.

Van Meter, Andy. *Always My Friend: A History of the State Journal-Register and Springfield.* Springfield, Ill.: Copley Press, 1981.

Villard, Oswald Garrison. *Fighting Years: Memoirs of a Liberal Editor.* New York: Harcourt Brace, 1939.

Von Drehle, David. *Rise to Greatness: Abraham Lincoln and America's Most Perilous Year.* New York: Henry Holt, 2012.

Vorenberg, Michael. *Final Freedom: The Civil War, the Abolition of Slavery, and the Thirteenth Amendment.* Cambridge: Cambridge University Press, 2001.

Wallace, Joseph. *Past and Present of the City of Springfield and Sangamon County Illinois.* Chicago: S. J. Clarke Publishing Co., 1904.

Walsh, Justin E. *To Print the News and Raise Hell: A Biography of Wilbur F. Storey.* Chapel Hill: University of North Carolina Press, 1968.

Walsh, William S., ed. *Abraham Lincoln and the London Punch.* New York: Moffat, Yard & Co., 1949.

Warshauer, Matthew. *Andrew Jackson and the Politics of Martial Law: Nationalism, Civil Liberties, and Partisanship.* Knoxville: University of Tennessee Press, 1996.

Weissberger, Bernard. *Reporters for the Union.* Boston: Little, Brown, 1953.

Wert, Justin. *Habeas Corpus in America: The Politics of Individual Rhetoric.* Lawrence: University Press of Kansas, 2011.

West, Richard S., Jr. *Gideon Welles: Lincoln's Navy Department.* Indianapolis: Bobbs-Merrill, 1943.

White, Jonathan W. *Abraham Lincoln and Treason in the Civil War: The Trials of John Merryman.* Baton Rouge, Louisiana State University Press, 2011.

Wilson, Douglas L. *Honor's Voice: The Transformation of Abraham Lincoln.* New York: Alfred A. Knopf, 1998.

Wilson, Douglas L., and Rodney O. Davis, eds. *Herndon's Informants: Letters, Interviews, and Statements About Abraham Lincoln.* Urbana: University of Illinois Press, 1998.

Wilson, Rufus Rockwell. *Washington: The Capital City and Its Part in the History of the Nation,* 2 vols. Philadelphia: J. B. Lippincott, 1901.

Wilson, Rufus Rockwell, ed. *Intimate Memories of Lincoln.* Elmira, N.Y.: Primavera Press, 1945.

Wineapple, Brenda. *Ecstatic Nation: Confidence Crisis, and Compromise, 1848–1871.* New York: HarperCollins, 2013.

Winkle, Kenneth J. *The Young Eagle: The Rise of Abraham Lincoln.* Dallas: Taylor Trade, 2001.

Wood, Benjamin. See Blondheim, *Copperhead Gore.*

Wood, Forrest G. *Black Scare: The Racist Response to Emancipation and Reconstruction.* Berkeley: University of California Press, 1968.

Wood, Gordon S. *The Idea of America: Reflections on the Birth of the United States.* New York: Penguin, 2011.

DISSERTATIONS

Anderson, Jeffrey Justin. "Joseph Medill: How One Man Influenced the Republican Presidential Nomination of 1860." Master's thesis, Roosevelt University, 2011.

Borchard, Gregory Alan. "The Firm of Greeley, Weed, & Seward: New York Partisanship and the Press, 1840–1860." Ph.D. diss., University of Florida, 2003.

Phelan, Mary Cortona. *Manton Marble of the New York World.* Washington, D.C.: The Catholic University of America, 1957.

Rushton, Wyatt. "Joseph Medill of the Chicago Tribune." Master's thesis, University of Wisconsin, 1916.

White, Jonathan W. " 'To Aid Their Rebel Friends:' Politics and Treason in the Civil War North." Ph.D. diss., University of Maryland, 2006.

Woodard, David E. "Sectionalism, Politics, and Foreign Policy: Duff Green and Political Expansion, 1825–1865." Ph.D. diss., University of Minnesota, 1996.

JOURNAL ARTICLES

Abrams, Ray H. "The *Jeffersonian,* Copperhead Newspaper." *Pennsylvania Magazine of History and Biography* 57 (July 1933): 260–83.

"The American Newspaper Press." *Leisure Hour* 13 (July 23, July 30, 1864).

Ames, William E. "The National Intelligencer: Washington's Leading Political Newspaper." *Records of the Columbia Historical Society*, Washington, D.C., 66/68 (1966–1968): 71–83.

Andrews, J. Cutler. "The Confederate Press and Public Morale." *The Journal of Southern History* 32 (November 1966): 445–65.

———. "The Press Reports the Battle of Gettysburg." *Pennsylvania History* 31 (April 1964): 176–98.

"Army Correspondence. Its History." *The Nation* 1 (July 20, 27, August 3, 1865).

Baker, Thomas H. "Refugee Newspaper: The *Memphis Daily Appeal*, 1862–1865." *The Journal of Southern History* 29 (August 1963): 325–44.

Basler, Roy P. "James Quay Howard's Notes on Lincoln." *Abraham Lincoln Quarterly* 8 (December 1947).

"Bennett, Greeley, and Raymond." *The Journalist* 4 (October 2, 1886): 1–2.

Biddle, Daniel R., and Murray Dubin. "'God Is Settleing the Account': African American Reaction to Lincoln's Emancipation Proclamation" *Pennsylvania Magazine of History and Biography* 137 (January 2013): 57–78.

Blondheim, Menahem. "'Public Sentiment Is Everything': The Union's Public Communications Strategy and the Bogus Proclamation of 1864." *Journal of American History* 89 (December 2002): 869–99.

Boritt, G. S. "A Question of Political Suicide: Lincoln's Opposition to the Mexican War." *Journal of the Illinois State Historical Society* 67 (February 1974): 79–100.

Boynton, H. V. "The Press and Public Men." *The Century* 42 (October 1891): 853–62.

Brooks, Noah. "Lincoln Reminiscences." *The Magazine of History* 9 (February 1909): 107–8.

———. "Lincoln's Inauguration." *Scribner's Monthly* 18 (August 1879): 584–85.

———. "Personal Recollections of Abraham Lincoln." *Harper's New Monthly Magazine* 31 (July 1865): 222–30.

———. "Personal Reminiscences of Lincoln." *Scribner's Monthly* 15 (February/March 1878): 673–81.

Byars, William Vincent. "A Century of Journalism in Missouri." *Missouri Historical Review* 15 (October 1920): 53–73.

Carey, James W. "Technology and Ideology: The Case of the Telegraph." *Prospects* 8 (1983), reprinted in *Communication as Culture*.

Carpenter, Frank [Francis] B. "Anecdotes and Reminiscences of President Lincoln." Appendix in Henry J. Raymond, *Life and Public Services of Abraham Lincoln* (New York: Derby & Miller, 1865): 725–66.

Carter, L. Edward. "The Revolution in Journalism During the Civil War." *Lincoln Herald* 73 (Winter 1971): 229–41.

Carwardine, Richard. "Abraham Lincoln and the Fourth Estate: The White House and the Press During the Civil War." *American Nineteenth Century History* 7 (March 2006): 1–27.

Childers, Christopher. "Interpreting Popular Sovereignty: A Historiographical Essay." *Civil War History* 57 (March 2011): 48–70.

Clement, Edward H. "19th-Century Boston Journalism." *New England Magazine* 35, 36, 37 (November 1906–September 1907).

Clephane, Walter C. "Lewis Clephane: A Pioneer Washington Republican." *Records of the [District of] Columbia Historical Society* 21 (1917): 263–77.

Conlin, Michael F. "The Smithsonian Abolition Lecture Controversy: The Clash of Antislavery Politics with American Science in Wartime Washington." *Civil War History* 46 (December 2000): 301–3.

Croffut, William A. "Lincoln's Washington: Recollections of a Journalist Who Knew Everybody." *Atlantic Monthly* 145 (January 1930): 55–65.

Crofts, Daniel. "A Fresh Look at the Diary of a Public Man." *Civil War History* 55 (December 2009): 442–68.

Crounse, Lorenzo Livingston. "The Army Correspondent." *Harper's New Monthly Magazine* 27 (October 1883): 627–34.

Crouthamel, James L. "The Newspaper Revolution in New York, 1830–1860." New York History 45 (1964): 91–113.

Dicey, Edward. "Washington During the War," *Macmillan's Magazine* 6 (May 1862): 16–29.

Dunlap, Lloyd A. "President Lincoln and Editor Greeley." *Abraham Lincoln Quarterly* 5 (June 1948): 94–110.

"The Effect of the News in This City." *New York Times*, July 23, 1861.

Ellis, Mrs. L. E. "The Chicago Times During the Civil War." *Illinois State Historical Society Transactions for 1932.* Illinois State Historical Society Publications, No. 39.

Emerson, Jason. "The Poetic Lincoln," *Lincoln Herald* 101 (Spring 1999): 4–12.

Fiske, Stephen Ryder. "Gentlemen of the Press." *Harper's New Monthly Magazine* 26 (February 1863): 361–67.

———. "When Lincoln Was Inaugurated," *Ladies' Home Journal* (March 1897): 7–8.

Fortier, John C., and Norman J. Ornstein. "Election Reform: The Absentee Ballot and the Secret Ballot—Challenges for Election Reform." *University of Michigan Journal of Law Reform* 36 (Spring 2003): 483–516.

Francke, Warren. "Sensationalism and the Development of 19th-Century Reporting: The Broom Sweeps Sensory Details." *Journalism History* 12 (Winter Autumn 1985): 80–85.

Garbade, Kenneth D., and William L. Silber. "Technology, Communications, and the Performance of Financial Markets, 1840–1975." *The Journal of Finance* 33 (1978): 819–32.

George, Joseph, Jr. "Military Trials of Civilians Under the Habeas Corpus Act of 1863." *Lincoln Herald* 98 (Winter 1996): 126–38.

Gilbert, Joseph Ignatius. "I Reported the Gettysburg Address: An Eye-Witness Account by the Man Who Covered Lincoln's Immortal Speech for the Associated Press." *Chicago Tribune*, November 19, 1978.

———. "Lincoln in 1861; Lincoln in 1863; Lincoln at Washington; the Assassination." *Nineteenth Annual Convention, National Shorthand Reporters Association: Proceedings of the Annual Meeting.* La Porte Ind.: Chase & Shepherd 1917): 131–37.

"A Great American Journalist [Murat Halstead]." *American Review of Reviews* 38 (August 1908): 191–92.

Green, Fletcher M. "Duff Green: Industrial Promoter." *Journal of Southern History* 2 (February 1936): 29–42.

Guelzo, Allen C. "Defending Emancipation: Abraham Lincoln and the Conkling Letter, 1863." *Civil War History* 48 (December 2002): 313–37.

Halley, R. A. *A Rebel Newspaper's War Story: Being a Narrative of the War History of the Memphis Appeal.* Reprinted from the *American Historical Magazine* for April 1903.

Halstead, Murat. "Recollections and Letters of General Sherman." *The Independent* 5 (June 15, 1899): 1610–13.

Harwell, Richard Barksdale. "Atlanta Publications of the Civil War." *The Atlanta Historical Bulletin* 6 (July 1941): 165–99.

Hawthorne, Nathaniel [A Peaceable Man]. "Chiefly About War Matters." *Atlantic Monthly* 10 (July 1862): 43–61.

"Henry Villard." *The Nation* 71 (November 15, 1900).

Holzer, Harold. "'Thrilling Words' or 'Silly Remarks': What the Press Said About the Gettysburg Address." *Lincoln Herald* 90 (Winter 1998): 144–45.

Horner, Harlan Hoyt. "Lincoln Replies to Horace Greeley." *Lincoln Herald* 53 (Spring 1951): 2–10.

Huff, Lawrence Adams. "Joseph Addison Turner: Southern Editor During the Civil War." *The Journal of Southern History* 29 (November 1963): 469–85.

Johnson, Albert E. H. "Reminiscences of the Hon. Edwin M. Stanton, Secretary of War." *Records of the Columbia Historical Society* 13 (1910): 69–97.

Jones, John Paul, Jr. "The Confederate Press and the Government." *Americana* 37 (January 1945): 7–27.

Kendall, John S. "The Foreign Language Press of New Orleans." *The Louisiana Historical Quarterly* 12 (July 1929): 363–80.

Kielbowicz, Richard B. "Speeding the News by Postal Express, 1825–1861: The Public Policy of Privileges for the Press." *The Social Science Journal* 22 (January 1975): 49–63.

———. "The Telegraph, Censorship, and Politics at the Outset of the Civil War." *Civil War History* 40 (June 1994): 95–118.

Klement, Frank. "'Brick' Pomeroy: Copperhead and Curmudgeon." *The Wisconsin Magazine of History* 35 (Winter 1951): 106–13, 156–57.

Kyle, Otto R. "Mr. Lincoln Steps Out: The Anti-Nebraska Editors' Convention." *The Abraham Lincoln Quarterly* 5 (March 1948): 25–37.

Littlefield, John H. "Recollections of One Who Studied Law with Lincoln." In William Hayes Ward, ed., *Abraham Lincoln: Tributes from His Associates* (New York: Thomas Y. Crowell, 1895), 200–206.

Lohne, Raymond. "Team of Friends: A New Lincoln Theory and Legacy." *Journal of the Illinois State Historical Society* 101 (Fall/Winter 2008): 285–301.

Malone, Henry T. "Atlanta Journalism During the Confederacy. *The Georgia Historical Quarterly* 37 (September 1953): 210–19.

———. "The Charleston Daily Courier: Standard Bearer of the Confederacy." *Journalism Quarterly* 26 (June 1949): 307–15.

———. "The Weekly Atlanta Intelligencer as a Secessionist Journal." *The Georgia Historical Quarterly* 37 (December 1953): 278–86.

Matthews, Sidney T. "Control of the Baltimore Press During the Civil War." *Maryland Historical Magazine* 36 (June 1941): 150–70.

[Morton, Robert]. "A Reminiscence of the Arrest and Incarceration of Five New York Telegraphers Charged with Conspiracy Against the Government in 1864." *Telegraph Age* (February 1905).

Neely, Mark E., Jr. "Lincoln and the Mexican War: An Argument by Analogy." *Civil War History* 24 (March 1978): 5–24.

Nevins, Allan. "Hiram Barney and Lincoln: Three Unpublished Documents." *The Huntington Library Quarterly* 26 (November 1962), 1–10.

Nightingale, Joseph R. "Joseph H. Barrett and John Locke Scripps, Shapers of Lincoln's Religious Image." *Journal of the Illinois State Historical Society* 92 (Autumn 1999): 238–73.

Nord, David Paul. "Teleology and News: The Religious Roots of American Journalism, 1730–1730." *Journal of American History* 77 (June 1990): 9–38.

O'Laughlin, John Callan. "Lincoln and the Press." *Abraham Lincoln Papers* (1931): 21–45.

Owens, Patricia Ann. "Lincoln and the Springfield Newspapers: The War Years." *Lincoln Herald* 100 (Fall 1998): 129–41.

[Parton, James W.] ["The New York Herald"]. *The North American Review* 102 (April 1866): 373–419.

"The Pen and the Sword." *The United States Magazine* 4 (October 1865): 289–99.

"Pick-Lock Journalism." *New York Tribune*, February 14, 1862.

Poore, Ben: Perley. "Abraham Lincoln, Reminiscences of an Old Newspaper Correspondent." *Brooklyn Eagle*, September 6, 1885.

Poore, Ben: Perley. "Washington News." *Harper's New Monthly Magazine* 26 (January 1874): 361–67.

Pyle, Richard. "Dateline: Gettysburg." *America's Civil War* (November 2010): 30–37.

Randall, James G. "The Newspaper Problem in Its Bearing Upon Military Secrecy During the Civil War." *The American Historical Review* 23 (January 1918): 303–23.

Reid, Ronald F. "Newspaper Response to the Gettysburg Addresses." *Quarterly Journal of Speech* 53 (February 1967): 50–60.

Reilly, Tom. "Jane McManus Storms: Letters from the Mexican War, 1846–1848." *Southwestern Historical Quarterly* 85 (July 1981): 21–44.

Richards, Joseph H. "'57 or Thereabouts: Personal Recollections of a Publisher." *The Independent* 50 (December 8, 1898): 1690–92.

Risley, Ford. "The Confederate Press Association . . ." *Civil War History* 47 (September 2001): 222–39.

Robinson, Elwyn Burns. "The *Press*: President Lincoln's Philadelphia Organ." *Pennsylvania Magazine of History and Biography* 65 (April 1941): 157–70.

———. "The Dynamism of American Journalism from 1787 to 1865." *Pennsylvania Magazine of History and Biography* 61 (October 1937): 435–45.

Russell, William Howard. "Recollections of the Civil War," I–V. *North American Review* 166 (February, March, April, May, June 1898).

Sanger, Donald Bridgman. "The Chicago Times and the Civil War." *Mississippi Valley Historical Review* 17 (March 1931): 557–80.

Sears, Louis M., ed. "The London *Times*' American Correspondent in 1861: Unpublished Letters of William H. Russell in the First Year of the Civil War." *The Historical Outlook* 16 (October 1925): 151–257.

Selby, Paul. "The Editorial Convention of 1856." *Journal of the Illinois State Historical Society* 15 (October 1912): 343–49.

Shankman, Arnold. "Freedom of the Press During the Civil War: The Case of Albert D. Boileau." *Pennsylvania Magazine of History and Biography* 41 (October 1975): 305–15.

Shanks, William Franklin Gore. "How We Get Our News." *Harper's New Monthly Magazine* 34 (January 1867): 511–22.

Sisler, George. "The Arrest of Memphis *Daily Appeal* War Correspondent on Charges of Treason." *West Tennessee Historical Society Papers* 11 (1957): 76–92.

Smalley, George W. "Chapters in Journalism." *Harper's New Monthly Magazine* 89 (August 1894): 426–35.

———. "Notes on Journalism." *Harper's New Monthly Magazine* 97 (July 1898): 213–23.

Smith, Robert Freeman. "John R. Eakin: Confederate Propagandist." *The Arkansas Historical Quarterly* 12 (Winter 1953): 316–26.

Smith, Willard H. "Schuyler Colfax: Whig Editor, 1845–1855." *Indiana Magazine of History* 34 (September 1938): 262–82.

Spore, John B. "Sherman and the Press," Parts 1, 2, and 3. *Infantry Journal* 63 (October 1948: 28–38), (November 1948: 31–35), (December 1948: 30–35).

Storrs, Richard Salter. "The Early Years of the Independent." *The Independent* (December 8, 1898): 1627–36.

Stubbs, Thomas McAlpin. "The Fourth Estate of Sumter South Carolina." *The South Carolina Historical Magazine* 54 (October 1953): 185–200.

Swindler, William F. "The Southern Press in Missouri, 1861–1864." *Missouri Historical Review* 35 (April 1941): 394–400.

Swinton, John. "The New York Daily Papers and Their Editors." *The Independent* 52 (January 18, 1900): part 1: 168–70; (January 25, 1900): part 2: 237–40.

Swinton, William. "Our Historical Writers." *Historical Magazine*, New Series, 6 (November 1859): 295–98.

Tasher, Lucy Lucile. "The *Missouri Democrat* and the Civil War." *Missouri Historical Review* 31 (July 1937): 402–19.

Taylor, Edward L. "Whitelaw Reid in Columbus." *Ohio Archaeological Historical Publications* 18 (1909): 513–19.

Taylor, Maurine Pacenta. "President Lincoln and the Press: An Important Chapter in the History of Presidential-Press Relations." *Lincoln Herald* 84 (Winter 1982): 205–09.

Temple, Wayne C. "Lincoln's 'Castine:' Noah Brooks" (ten-part series for the *Lincoln Herald* 71 (fall 1970): 113–124; (winter 1970): 148–189; 73 (spring 1971): 27–45;

summer 1971): 78–117; (fall 1971): 163–180; (winter 1971): 205–222); 74 (spring 1972): 3–28; (summer 1972): 92–106; (fall 1972): 143–168); (winter 1972): 214–222.

———. "The Linguistic Lincolns: A New Lincoln Letter." *Lincoln Herald* 94 (Fall 1992): 106–12.

Tenney, Craig D. "To Suppress or Not to Suppress: Abraham Lincoln and the Chicago Times." *Civil War History* 27 (September 1981): 248–59.

Towne, Stephen E. "Works of Indiscretion: Violence Against the Democratic Press in Indiana During the Civil War." *Journalism History* 31 (Fall 2005): 138–49.

Trexler, Harrison. "The Davis Administration and the Richmond Press, 1861–1865." *The Journal of Southern History* 16 (May 1950): 177–95.

Turner, John J., Jr., and Michael D'Innocenzo. "The President and the Press: Lincoln, James Gordon Bennett and the Election of 1864." *Lincoln Herald* 76 (Summer 1974): 63–69.

Varon, Elizabeth R. "Tippecanoe and Ladies, Too: White Women and the Party Politics in Antebellum Virginia." *Journal of American History* 82 (September 1995): 494–521.

Villard, Henry. "Recollections of Lincoln." *Atlantic Monthly* 93 (February 1904): 165–74.

Weisberger, Bernard A. "Horace Greeley: Reformer as Republican." *Civil War History* 23 (March 1977): 5–25.

Welles, Gideon. "Administration of Abraham Lincoln [4]. Radical Plottings Against Mr. Lincoln." *The Galaxy* 24 (November 1877): 607–24.

Welling, James C. "The Emancipation Proclamation." *The North American Review* 130 (1880): 163–85.

Wessen, Ernest James. "Campaign Lives of Abraham Lincoln 1860: An Annotated Bibliography of the Biographies of Abraham Lincoln Issued During the Campaign Year." *Papers in Illinois History and Transactions for the Year 1937*. Springfield: Illinois State Historical Society, 1938.

West, Richard. "The Navy and the Press During the Civil War." *U.S. Naval Institute Proceedings*, 63 (January 1937): 33–41.

White, Jonathan W. "The Strangely Insignificant Role of the U.S. Supreme Court During the Civil War." *Journal of the Civil War Era* 3 (June 2013): 211–38.

"Whitelaw Reid." *Scribner's Monthly* 8 (July 23, 1864): 444–51.

Wiley, Bell Irvin. "Camp Newspapers of the Confederacy." *North Carolina Historical Review* 20 (October 1943): 327–35.

Williams, Frank J. "Abraham Lincoln and Civil Liberties in Wartime." *Heritage Lectures*, No. 834 (May 6, 2004).

Williams, G. F. "How a Reporter Faced Danger in Disguise." *The Independent* 53 (April 1866): 1859–64.

Wilson, Quintus C. "Bitter Verbal Battles Between Editors During Civil War Are Recalled." *The Quill* 25 (January 1943): 5, 16.

———. "Confederate Press Association: A Pioneer News Agency." *Journalism Quarterly* 25 (June 1949): 160–66.

———. "Voluntary Press Censorship During the Civil War." *Journalism Quarterly* 19 (September 1942): 252–61.

Winkle, Kenneth J. "The Voters of Lincoln's Springfield and Political Participation in an Antebellum City." *Journal of Social History* 25 (1992): 595–611.

Young, John Russell. "Men Who Reigned: Bennett, Greeley, Raymond, Prentice, Forney." *Lippincott's Monthly* 51 (February 1893): 185–97.

ILLUSTRATION CREDITS

Page 167   *A, B*: Library of Congress; Library of Congress
Page 180   Abraham Lincoln Presidential Library and Museum
Page 190   Abraham Lincoln Presidential Library and Museum
Page 195   Courtesy Thomas Lapsley
Page 199   New-York Historical Society
Page 207   Library of Congress
Page 218   National Portrait Gallery, Smithsonian Institution/Art Resource,
            New York
Page 220   Courtesy Harold Holzer
Page 228   *A, B*: Library of Congress; Library of Congress
Page 229   Chicago History Museum
Page 231   Library of Congress
Page 245   *A, B, C*: Courtesy Harold Holzer; Lincoln National Collection;
            Lincoln National Collection
Page 253   Library of Congress
Page 254   Library of Congress
Page 254   Library of Congress
Page 262   Library of Congress
Page 270   *A, B*: Library of Congress; Library of Congress
Page 273   New-York Historical Society
Page 289   Library of Congress
Page 292   Library of Congress
Page 294   Abraham Lincoln Book Shop
Page 302   *A, B, C*: Library of Congress; Library of Congress; Library of
            Congress
Page 311   Library of Congress
Page 315   Library of Congress
Page 320   Library of Congress
Page 340   Library of Congress
Page 344   *A, B*: Courtesy of Harold Holzer; Courtesy of the Edgar Allan Poe
            Museum, Richmond, Virginia
Page 354   Library of Congress
Page 368   *A, B*: Library of Congress
Page 370   *A, B*: Library of Congress; Picture History
Page 374   Library of Congress
Page 380   *A, B*: Library of Congress; Harold Holzer
Page 389   Lincoln Financial Foundation Collection, Courtesy of Indiana
            State Museum and Historic Sites

Page 396   U.S. Senate Collection
Page 399   Lincoln Financial Foundation Collection held in the Lincoln Library, Allen County Public Library, Fort Wayne, Indiana
Page 425   *A, B*: Library of Congress; Chicago History Museum
Page 427   New-York Historical Society
Page 436   *A, B*: Library of Congress; Print Collection, Miriam and Ira D. Wallach Division of Art, Prints and Photographs, New York Public Library, Astor, Lenox and Tilden Foundations
Page 447   Library of Congress
Page 450   National Archives
Page 453   Gilbert-Molloy-McHenry Archive
Page 463   Library of Congress
Page 472   Library of Congress
Page 480   Courtesy Wayne C. Temple
Page 483   Library of Congress
Page 489   New-York Historical Society
Page 494   Library of Congress
Page 506   Library of Congress
Page 512   Courtesy of the University of Minnesota Libraries
Page 534   Library of Congress
Page 539   Library of Congress
Page 548   Abraham Lincoln Book Shop
Page 552   Library of Congress

INDEX

———————◆———————

Page numbers in *italics* refer to illustrations. Page numbers beginning with 575 refer to end notes.

ABOUT THE AUTHOR

Harold Holzer is the chairman of the Abraham Lincoln Bicentennial Foundation and the Roger Hertog Fellow at the New-York Historical Society. The author, coauthor, or editor of forty-six books on Lincoln and the Civil War, Holzer has also published sixteen monographs, more than five hundred articles in scholarly and popular magazines, and introductions and chapters in another fifty volumes. He lectures throughout the country, appears regularly on national television, and serves on the advisory boards of a number of Lincoln-related institutions, and as vice chairman of the Lincoln Forum.

Holzer has also organized several museum exhibitions, including the award-winning "Lincoln and New York" at the New-York Historical Society. He was historical advisor to Steven Spielberg's film *Lincoln* and wrote the official young readers' companion book.

From 2000 to 2010, Holzer was chairman of the Abraham Lincoln Bicentennial Commission, appointed by President Bill Clinton. In turn, President George W. Bush awarded Holzer the National Humanities Medal in 2008. Holzer's many other awards include a second-place Lincoln Prize for *Lincoln at Cooper Union* and lifetime achievement awards from the Daughters of the American Revolution and Civil War Round Tables and Lincoln Groups in New York, Washington, Chicago, and Cleveland.

In his full-time professional career, Holzer serves as Senor Vice President for Public Affairs at The Metropolitan Museum of Art, where he has worked for twenty-three years. A resident of Rye, New York, Holzer and his wife Edith have two daughters and a grandson.